THE ADMINISTRATION OF THE EAST INDIA COMPANY

THE ADMINISTRATION OF THE EAST INDIA COMPANY

A HISTORY OF INDIAN PROGRESS

JOHN WILLIAM KAYE

GYAN

Published by

Gyan Publishing House
5, Ansari Road
Daryaganj, New Delhi-110002
Phone: 011-47034999, 9811692060
E-mail: books@gyanbooks.com

Distribution Network
gyanbooks.com
India, USA, Canada, UK, Australia, France

ISBN : 978-81-212-9262-7 (PB)
First Published, 1853

2nd Impression 2023

Printed at: Gyan Press, Delhi.

THE ADMINISTRATION OF THE EAST INDIA COMPANY
Author: JOHN WILLIAM KAYE

THE ADMINISTRATION OF THE EAST INDIA COMPANY;

A HISTORY OF INDIAN PROGRESS.

BY JOHN WILLIAM KAYE,

AUTHOR OF "THE HISTORY OF THE WAR IN AFGHANISTAN."

"THERE ARE MANY KINDS OF WAR AND MANY DEGREES OF HEROIC RENOWN, BUT THE HIGHEST PRAISE IS DUE TO THOSE WHO, BY THEIR VICTORIOUS ARMS, HAVE OPENED NEW SCENES FOR THE CIVILISATION OF MANKIND, AND OVERCOME BARBARISM IN SOME IMPORTANT PORTION OF THE WORLD."

RANKE'S "Civil Wars and Monarchy in France."

LONDON:

RICHARD BENTLEY, NEW BURLINGTON STREET.

Publisher in Ordinary to Her Majesty.

MDCCCLIII.

TO THE

CIVIL AND MILITARY SERVICES

OF

THE EAST INDIA COMPANY

THIS VOLUME,

RIFE WITH RECORDS OF THEIR GOOD DEEDS,

IS

RESPECTFULLY INSCRIBED.

London, April 25, 1853.

PREFACE.

I OFFER this volume to the public as a contribution to the general stock of information relating to India and her affairs—information which, in the present juncture, it is very desirable to possess. It contains much that is scattered over a great number of printed books, and much besides that is not to be found in any printed books. It will be seen that it is written almost entirely in a narrative form—that there is little of the disquisitional and controversial in it—and that I have not attempted to elucidate the great question of the future government of India, except by throwing on it such light as is derived from illustrations of the past.

Perhaps, indeed, the volume may best be described as a series of historical illustrations of Indian government, arranged with some regard to completeness and uniformity of design, but not at all pretending to the dignity either of a perfect history of the internal administration of India, or a finished picture of Indian Institutions. The exigencies of time and space have compelled me to pass hastily over the consideration of many matters, of the interest and importance of which I am fully sensible, and in one or two instances I have been necessitated to throw into an Appendix papers illustrative of certain topics of inquiry of which I had intended to treat in the body of the work. The subject of Indian Administration, indeed, is so vast; it branches out into so many different channels; and the materials at my disposal for its illustration have been so ample, that the more I have drawn upon them the further off I have seemed from their exhaustion.

In dealing with a subject of such magnitude, the writer has the choice of two courses which lie before him. He may either so compress his materials into a narrow compass as to divest his fasciculus of facts of all living interest and external grace. Or he may select certain prominent topics of discourse, and illustrate them with that copiousness of detail which, by limiting its range of inquiry, necessarily subtracts from the encyclopædic value of the work, but imparts a vitality to it which I cannot help thinking extends its utility by increasing its attractions. I have followed the latter course. I believe that the reading public is less instructed than it should be on Indian subjects, because it has been less interested than it might have been, if writers had taken more pains to appeal to the common sympathies of mankind. I am not insensible of the value of statistics, and, indeed, I have dealt somewhat largely in them; but it is principally by representing men in action that the writer on Indian affairs must hope to fix the attention of the public.

It is mainly to anticipate any objections which may be raised on the score of omissions, that I make these remarks regarding what may be called the machinery of my work. Of the purpose and tendency of the work itself I have spoken elsewhere; and shall now only add the expression of a hope that, in consideration of what I have done, I shall be forgiven for what I have necessarily left undone in such a volume as this.

London, April, 1853.

CONTENTS.

PART I.

PART II.

CHAPTER I.

THE REVENUES OF INDIA.

CHAPTER II.

THE PERMANENT SETTLEMENT OF BENGAL.

CHAPTER III.

THE LAND REVENUES OF MADRAS.

CHAPTER IV.

SETTLEMENT OF THE NORTH-WESTERN PROVINCES.

CHAPTER V.

PUBLIC WORKS.

PART III.

CHAPTER I.

JUDICIAL SYSTEMS.

CHAPTER II.

THUGGEE.

CHAPTER III.

DAKOITEE.

CHAPTER IV.

JUDICIAL AGENCIES.

PART IV.

CHAPTER I.

THE NON-REGULATION PROVINCES.

CHAPTER II.

THE CIVILISATION OF SAVAGE TRIBES.

CHAPTER III.

HUMAN SACRIFICE.

CHAPTER IV.

SUTTEE.

PAGE

CHAPTER V.

INFANTICIDE.

PART V.

CHAPTER I.

NATIVE EDUCATION.

CHAPTER II.

CHRISTIANITY IN INDIA.

APPENDIX.

THE ADMINISTRATION

OF THE

EAST INDIA COMPANY.

PART I.

CHAPTER I.

The claims of the Governed on the Governing—How they have been discharged—England's Opportunities in India—Impediments to Domestic Improvement—Administrave Difficulties in England and India—Crime and Poverty in the two Countries—Encouragements to Exertion.

WHEN Mr. Barlow, then Secretary to the Indian Government, drew up the elaborate minute, on which the Bengal Regulations of 1793 were based, Sir William Jones, to whom this important document was submitted, struck his pen across the three first words. The correction which he made was a significant one. Barlow had written: "The two principal objects which the Government ought to have in view in all its arrangements, are to insure its political safety, and to render the possession of the country as advantageous as possible to the East India Company and the British Nation." Sir William Jones, I have said, erased the three first words. Instead of "*the two principal* objects," he wrote: "two of the primary objects;" and then he appended this marginal note: "I have presumed to alter the first words. Surely the *principal* object of every Government is the happiness of the governed."* Sixty years have passed away since that significant correction was made, and it is now a moot question, whether the practice of the British Government in India, throughout that time, has been in accordance with the words of Mr. Barlow, or those of Sir William Jones.

Not, however, that Barlow, who may be supposed, in this case, to represent the general body of the Company's servants in India, had overlooked the "happiness of the governed." In the next paragraph he wrote: "It is a source of pleasing reflection to know, that in proportion as we contribute to the happiness of the people and the prosperity of the country, the nearer we approach to the attainment of these objects. If the people are satisfied with our government, we shall be certain that they wish for its continuance; and as the country increases in wealth, the greater will be the advantages which we shall derive from the possession of it." The "happiness of the governed" was to be considered as a means to an end—not as the end itself. But in those early days of Anglo-Indian rule, it was something to think of the people at all. It was no small matter, indeed, to recognise the great truth, that the prosperity of the governing and the governed are mutually dependent upon each other; that, to secure the former, we must, at all events, promote the latter. The servants of the Company had been for nearly two centuries regarding the natives of India only as so many dark-faced and dark-souled Gentiles, whom it was their mission to over-reach in

* *MS. Records.*—I have copied this from the original note in Sir W. Jones's handwriting. The draft, which contains the autograph corrections of Lord Cornwallis, as well as the marginal notes of Sir W. Jones, is thus endorsed by Sir George Barlow: "This is the minute which led to the formation of the constitution of the government of our possessions in India, in 1793. It was drawn up by me, and contained my suggestions to Lord Cornwallis. The notes in the margin are by Sir W. Jones, for whose opinion it was submitted. The corrections in the body are those made by Lord Cornwallis." I need not say that the document is an extremely interesting one. I purpose to make larger references to it in another work.

business, and to overcome in war. But out of these hucksters and spoliators had now arisen a race of embryo statesmen with dawning perceptions of the duties and responsibilities of governments and the rightful claims of the people. Barlow, who sate at the feet of Cornwallis, was far in advance of his predecessors—far in advance of the great mass of his cotemporaries. There may be expressions in his suggestive minute to jar upon the sensitive chords of modern philanthropy; but we must read it, not with the eyes of meridian enlightenment, but with the hazy vision of men just awakening, as it were, from dreams of conquest, and only then ceasing to look upon the inhabitants of India as a race of men to be defrauded and subdued.

"A spirit of industry," continued Barlow, "has been implanted in man, that in seeking his own good he may contribute to the public prosperity. The husbandman and manufacturer will toil incessantly, if they are permitted to reap the profit of their labours." But a question arose in practice, and one which has not yet received any very satisfactory solution, as to the extent to which, regard being had to the prosperity of the State, the people might be suffered to "reap the profit of their labours." If the question had been satisfactorily solved, that would have been achieved by Indian administrators, which, as far as the range of my own knowledge extends, has yet been achieved by no administrators under Heaven. This, humanly speaking, indeed, is the greatest problem in the world. It is nothing, therefore, to say, that in India the rights of labour have not been determined—that its claims have not been acknowledged—in a manner to give entire satisfaction to every benevolent mind. Under the most favourable circumstances, we can only arrive at something of an approximation.

And what ought now properly to be considered is, not whether India has been governed by its European conquerors after any imagined model of abstract perfection, but whether, all circumstances duly considered, all obstacles and hindrances fairly weighed, as much has been done, within a certain time, and with certain appliances and means at our disposal, as reasonable men might rightfully expect.

All government is, more or less, an experiment. In India, it is, especially, an experiment; and it is one on a gigantic scale. We have been compelled to experimentalise upon a foreign people not easy to understand—upon a people whose character and institutions are not only extremely dissimilar to our own, but so fenced in with exclusiveness, so bristling with all kinds of discouragements and denials, that it is difficult, above all things, to acquire that comprehensive knowledge of their feelings and opinions which alone can enable us to adapt our legislation to their moral and physical requirements. It is the great evil of English legislation, that it is based upon an imperfect knowledge of the wants and wishes of the people. But an English legislator may converse with whomsoever he will, on any subject, in his own language. He may walk into the poor man's cottage, and ascertain for himself what are the poor man's wants. He has something in common with the poorest. He was born on the same soil—he speaks the same tongue—he prays to the same God. The two classes, to a certain extent, may be severed by imperfect sympathies; but there is *some* bond of sympathy to unite them. They are not utterly strangers and aliens to each other. They do not regard each other as infidels and blasphemers. They cross the threshold of the same temple together, and they may eat, without contamination, from the same dish. There is a vast difference, I repeat, between St.

James' and St. Giles'. The aristocrat of Belgravia but imperfectly comprehends the feelings of the inhabitants of the clanging rookeries. The great territorial lord has little in common with the wretched labourer who poaches by night on his overgrown estate. And hence the blunders of English legislation. But these privileged classes cannot help knowing more about the natural history of their own countrymen, however wide the distinction of rank, than the privileged classes of British India—the English conquerors—know about the dark-faced inhabitants of the country which they have subdued.

It is little more than sixty years since we began to govern India at all. Lord Cornwallis is the first Indian ruler who can be properly regarded as an administrator. Up to the time of his arrival, the English in India had been engaged in a great struggle for existence. Clive conquered the richest province of Hindostan. Hastings reduced it to something like order. But it was not until Cornwallis carried to India the large-minded liberality of a benevolent English statesman, that our administrative efforts took shape and consistency, and the entire internal management of the country under our rule was regulated by a code of written laws,* intended to confer upon the natives of India the benefits of as much European wisdom and benevolence as was compatible with a due regard for the character of native institutions. During those sixty years, India has never enjoyed any protracted season of rest. We have continually been engaged in wars and contentions, which have resulted in the extension of our empire, until it has reached the confines of the Afghan dominions; and many who

* Barlow, in the minute of which I have spoken above, always used the word "laws;" but Cornwallis invariably erased it, and substituted the word "regulations."

would fain have been peaceful administrators, have been conquerors in spite of themselves. During the sixty years of which I speak, we have been building up our present enormous empire. When, therefore, we come to consider the time at our disposal, and the opportunities at our command, with reference to the ameliorative measures which have emanated from the British Government, we must not take account of the result, as though we had been for sixty years in possession of our present territory, and those sixty years had been years of settled tranquillity; but as though we had all that time to do with an empire inchoate and imperfect, calling for measures—in the first instance, of defence, then of aggression—which have left neither leisure to consider, nor money to provide the means of domestic improvement.

For let us only just glance at the history of India during the last century—at the reigns of our different chief Governors, from Clive to Dalhousie, and see how they have been consecutively engaged, with but two exceptions, in great and engulphing wars. Think of the wars in Madras and Bengal—the Rohilla wars—the Mysore wars—the Mahratta wars—the Java war—the Pindarree war—the Burmese war—the Afghan war—the Sindh war—the Sikh war—with all kinds of minor wars occupying smaller space in the great history of Indian conquest. Of all our Governors-General, either reared in India, or despatched thither from our English bureaux, Shore and Bentinck alone contrived to surround themselves with an atmosphere of peace during the entire period of their administration. And yet all these warriors and statesmen, who were continually pouring their battalions into the field, were not all of them men, "out of measure addicted to fighting"—men of large ambition, greedy of conquest, unmindful of the blessings of peace and the claim of an industrial people. Cornwallis—Minto—Amherst—Auckland—Hardinge—Dalhousie—were all by nature peace-Governors. Neither Hastings—commoner nor peer—can be justly accused of unscrupulous aggressiveness. And yet, somehow or other, all these rulers have been arrested in their career of internal improvement, or utterly prevented from giving a thought to it, by the necessity of concentrating their efforts on great schemes of military organisation, for the subjection of enemies who have threatened the security of our frontier, and compelled us to possess ourselves of new territory to enable us to retain possession of the old.

It is not for me now to consider in detail, whether this or that war "might have been avoided." The more thoughtful reader of Indian history will, perhaps, arrive at the general conclusion, that although some of our wars with our immediate neighbours might have been delayed, few, if any, could have been avoided.* It is enough for my present purpose, that the English in India, though not fairly chargeable with that lust of conquest which is often said to have marked our whole career in the East, have been, for a century, engaged in an almost continued struggle, which has paralysed the humane efforts of men, the desire of whose hearts has ever turned towards the domestic improvement of the country. If it had been possible for us to have held possession of a single province—say the rich province of Bengal—never to have gone beyond its limits—never to have been disturbed by fears of invasion—never to have been engaged in warlike operations, offensive or defensive—we might, perad-

* I say "with our immediate neighbours," for where we have crossed the frontier to attack another country, separated from us by an extensive tract of intervening territory, this necessity is not to be pleaded.

venture, have established a model empire on the banks of the Hooghly. An overflowing treasury, at the command of an enlightened statesman, never arrested by any threatenings from without, in his quiet career of beneficence, never, indeed, looking beyond the limits of his own narrow territory, might, in the course of a century, have enabled us to build up an Eastern principality, so compact in itself, and complete in all its internal arrangements, as to leave little or nothing for the philanthropist to desire. But Providence has not willed that *such* should be our Eastern Empire. If one of the little handful of European officers, who, a century ago, in gaiters and perukes, followed the fortunes of Lawrence in the Carnatic, were now to stand again on Indian soil, and in one of our North-Western cantonments, to spread out before him a map of our Eastern Empire as now established, he would be overwhelmed with astonishment and incredulity. He would declare, that not one of his contemporaries, in the wildest flight of imagination, ever contemplated the possibility of the erection of such an empire as we have now built up in the East. But, in these times, it is equally difficult to imagine the existence of such an empire—limited, unexpansive, compact—as the Anglo-Indian of 1750, regarded as the extreme result of our conquests in the East. Grown wise by experience, we now declare that it is in accordance with a law of nature, universal and immutable, that our empire should have so expanded. Be this as it may, the history of India has been hitherto a history of expansion—of acquisition; and it is only by so considering the fact, that we can rightly estimate the much or the little which the British conquerors of the Indian world have done to promote the happiness of the people who inhabit it.

Many great political problems are yet unsolved—many great social evils are yet unremedied. Much, doubtless, has yet to be done before the voice of complaint can be authoritatively called upon, in the name of reason, to be still. Unqualified commendation in such a case would be as unreasonable as unqualified censure—not because it is unqualified commendation of the Indian Government, but because it is unqualified commendation of a terrestrial government, and, therefore, of one prone to all sorts of short-comings, and liable to all kinds of error. If there were nothing more to be complained of there would be nothing more to be done. Now, in India, it must be acknowledged that there is much to be done. But in England, also, there is much to be done. The Government of England has been, and is, a Government of Progress. We are astonished at the evils which our fathers permitted, and our sons will be astonished at those which we in our turn are permitting. And yet generations of Englishmen have boasted, and will boast, of the blessings of the British Constitution. We have not to consider whether this or that Government has attained perfection, but whether it is making reasonable efforts to approximate to it; we have not to consider whether the mass of the people are positively happy under any particular Government, but whether they are happier than they were fifty or twenty years ago under that Government. Progressive improvement is all that we have a right to expect, or a vocation to consider.

The history of Civilisation is the obituary of Error. We are continually burying defunct fallacies, and making Suttees of huge practical mistakes. I am not an old man. I have seen little more than half of the years allotted to humanity, and yet I have lived in times which, compared with the present, were years of barbarism and darkness. I have witnessed the cremation of social and political evils, the existence of which, in such recent times, my children will scarcely credit. When I was a boy, the green slopes of Old Sarum were my habitual play-ground. There was a little inn on the white chalk-road which sent two members to Parliament, whilst Manchester and Birmingham sent none. A Roman Catholic could not sit in our Legislative Assemblies, or in our Municipal Corporations, or lead a regiment or command a ship. Slaves were held as property by English gentlemen in the colonies, and bought and sold like sheep. A man might be transported for seven years for knocking down a partridge or a hare. Such was the general effects of the game-laws, that it was said of them that "for every ten pheasants fluttering in a wood, one English peasant was rotting in gaol."* The Court of Chancery, with its agonising delays and its desolating voracity, made playthings of human life and human reason, and wrote its fearful annals on the walls of the lunatic's cell and the grave of the suicide. The state of our prisons was so detestable, that a young and modest girl thrown into gaol for some trifling offence, or perhaps wrongfully accused, came out an abandoned criminal. The gibbet was in such repute, that a man might be hanged for stealing a yard of silk from a shop-counter, for destroying a tree, or breaking down the embankment of a river. And it was no uncommon thing for men to be lured on to the gallows by a detective police, who made it their business to associate in flash houses with thieves and prostitutes, and incite them to the commission of crimes which it should have been their duty to prevent.

* Sydney Smith.

These are a few of the social and political evils which I have lived to see abolished by the intervention of a humane legislature. Perhaps I may be spared to see many more great changes; for many more great changes are needed, and this is an age of progressive amelioration. But although I see clearly around me many things which I know cannot be right, and I hope earnestly that some day they may be remedied, I know how difficult it is to devise a fit remedial application, and how the best efforts of benevolent statesmen may be baffled by the magnitude and obstinacy of the disease. There are clamorous social evils crying out for redress almost under the walls of the Palace at Westminster. From the windows of the committee-rooms of that great costly senate-house, our legislators may look out upon hundreds of miserable dwellings, overcrowded with squalid and hungry tenants, whose sufferings far surpass any endured by the inhabitants of a village in Bengal. It is not long since it was stated in Parliament by a nobleman, who has made the misery and the crime of the London poor his peculiar study, that "there were 30,000 naked, filthy, deserted, roaming, lawless children, who formed the seed-plot of 19-20ths of the crime which desolates the metropolis;" and again repeated at a public meeting, "that ninety-nine cases of crime out of every hundred were the result of want of honest occupation." I have no wish to dwell upon these things. I would only say that it becomes us, before we indignantly expatiate upon the sufferings of the people of India, to think of the suffering at our own doors; and to consider whether we have yet contrived, with all our Ministerial Cabinets, our Legislative Assemblies, our great corporate bodies, and our gigantic press, to furnish anything like a remedy for this the greatest of social evils—the physical necessity of crime. The most enthusiastic advocate of the Government of the East India Company would not claim for it the merit of abolishing poverty and wretchedness, and annihilating crime; but the people of India are not driven to crime by want of honest occupation. It is easy to conceive what would be said on the subject if they were.

I would say something, too, regarding material wants. A well-informed practical man, writing in 1822, says, "The fertile plains of [ ], [ ], and [ ], are separated from each other by a deserted country, hitherto nearly an impassable barrier. This large district comprehends upwards of 900 square miles; in many places it is very populous. As might be expected under such circumstances, the people are turbulent, and their houses, being inaccessible for want of roads, it is not surprising that during the disturbances of 1821-22, this district was the asylum for smugglers and robbers, and that stolen cattle were drawn into it as to a safe and impenetrable retreat." The blank spaces which I have left at the commencement of this extract the reader will, doubtless, feel disposed to fill with the names of some Indian cities or districts. But the fertile plains, separated from each other by a deserted country, the populous places rendered inaccessible, and the people turbulent and lawless by want of roads, are not in any part of the mighty Indian peninsula, but in a little island upon the other side of the Irish Channel. The places whose names I have omitted are Limerick, Cork, and Kerry.* "Notwithstanding," adds the writer, "its present desolate state,

* The extract is taken from a report by Mr. Griffith, quoted in Mr. Porter's admirable work on the "Progress of the Nation." I grieve to think that during the passage of this volume through the press, this esteemed writer and valuable public servant has paid the ordinary penalty of a life of unceasing intellectual labour, and that his career of usefulness is at an end.

this country contains within itself the seeds of future improvement and industry."

It would be easy to multiply instances of tracts of country in Ireland, containing within themselves the seeds of improvement and industry, which, even at the present time, are little better than howling wildernesses. But I have no wish to enlarge upon the failures of our domestic administration. I merely desire to express my conviction that such failures, though deeply to be lamented, furnish no proof of the general incompetency of the Government which has unwillingly permitted them; I would not argue that because Ireland has been and is misgoverned—that, because there are large tracts of desolate country, and thousands of inhabitants in an extreme state of physical and moral destitution, the repeal of the Union is an event to be desired as an act of justice to the Irish people. I would give the British Government credit for the best intentions—I would believe that it has laboured, and not laboured in vain, for the benefit of the people, though it has left much to be done for their amelioration before we can congratulate ourselves on the general result. I willingly believe that it is no easy thing to govern Ireland, although it is a small island within a few hours' journey, by land and sea, from the senate-house of Great Britain, and contains less than eight millions of souls, all speaking the same language, and worshipping the same God.

But believing as I do that it is no easy thing to govern Ireland—no easy thing to govern England—no easy thing in one island or the other, to abolish human misery and eradicate human crime, I would wish it also to be believed that the Government of India, a country whose area it is difficult to compute, and whose population it is difficult to number, whose people present almost as many varieties of character and language as the entire continent of Europe, and the whole of which are utterly dissimilar to our own, may be also difficult to govern.

I would wish it to be believed that in the government of such a country some credit is due for what is done well, and some allowance to be made both for what is done amiss and what is not done at all. I am afraid that too many amongst us are prone to make a severe reckoning of the errors and short-comings, and of the good deeds and successful results to take no sort of account.

It is because I believe that, under the Government of the East India Company much has been done for the benefit of the people of India of which little is known in this country, or if known, purposely ignored, that I now desire to throw together, in an historical form, some information, derived from a variety of sources, relative to the administrative results of British connexion with the East. In a word, I desire to show what we have done for India, and what we have attempted to do. The review may not at all points present matter for congratulation, for our efforts in India, as elsewhere, have not always been crowned with success. But I believe that, viewed in a calm, candid, judicial spirit, without passion and without prejudice, the aggregate result reflects no little honor on the Company and their servants, and may be honestly applauded by men jealous of the interests of mankind.

And assuming that there is much yet to be done—that much has been left undone which ought to have been done—that those to whom the administration of India is entrusted, require at times to be roused and stimulated by the consideration that there is a great tribunal at home—the tribunal of the British public, which takes cognizance of all their doings—I cannot help thinking that the great object of securing the zealous activity of our Indian administrators is best to be attained by recording and commending their good deeds, than by an indiscriminate condemnation of what are presumed to be their bad. I doubt, indeed, whether the effect of all the vague general censure which is lavished upon British administration in the East, has not a tendency rather to cramp and repress than to foster and develop the beneficence of our exiled countrymen who constitute the executive Government of our Indian Empire. But I am certain, on the other hand, that nothing is more likely to develop all their best feelings, and stimulate all their energies and activities, than the knowledge that their exertions are not overlooked by their brethren at home—that their good deeds are duly reported to the British public, and by the British public read with interest, and commented on with applause. If there be full warrant for the belief that the British public will not be left in profound ignorance of all the good that is done in our far-off Indian possessions, nothing is so animating, so invigorating as the reflection, "What will be thought of this at home?" But if the only response that can be given to the stirring question is "Nothing"—if a general conviction is left to impress itself on the minds of Englishmen in India, that, let them do what they may, and suffer what they may for the people, scorning delight and living laborious days, still one general sentence of condemnation will be passed on our Indian administration—still ignorance and malevolence will be obstreperous in their denunciations—it is easy to conceive how all warmth may be chilled, and all activity paralysed; how in time they may be made to conform to the erring judgment. People are very prone to become what the world believes them to be.

Influenced by such considerations as these—rooted in the faith that I shall best subserve the interests of

India and her teeming millions of inhabitants, by encouraging the zealous and stimulating the active, than by writing what can only dishearten and repress, I purpose, in the following chapters, to show what our countrymen have done, and what they have attempted to do, for the better government of India, and the amelioration of the condition of the people—as evidenced in the development of the industrial resources of the country, the purification of justice, the civilisation of savage tribes, the suppression of unholy rites and cruel abominations, and the general diffusion of enlightenment and truth. It will be my privilege, in the course of this attempt, to record some incidents of our Indian rule, little known beyond the area that has been the scene of them, but which are not to be chronicled without the strongest emotions of national pride. And if ever such chronicle of good deeds done by English gentlemen, under the fiery skies of the East, isolated from their kind, far removed from all the ordinary incentives to exertion, amidst dangers and difficulties more than sufficient to repel the brave and deter the resolute, should stimulate one other Indian exile to go and do likewise, I shall not have written in vain, and I shall not be without my reward.

CHAPTER II.

India under the Moguls—The Arab and Tartar Conquests—The House of Toghlak—Feroz Shah—The first Indian Canal—The House of Timour—The Emperor Akbar—His internal Administration—Shah Jehan—Public Works—Decline of the Mogul Empire—Comparison of Mogul and British Rule—Their General Effects on the Happiness of the People.

I DO not know that it is of much real importance to inquire whether the people of India would have been more or less happy and prosperous if they had been left to the government of their old Mahomedan conquerors and rulers. The inquiry must, at best, be unsatisfactory and inconclusive. But, from the days of Burke to the days of Ellenborough, the insatiable benevolence, the magnificent philanthropy, of these Mussulman despots has been so often vaunted, either as a reproach or an encouragement to us, that I cannot persuade myself to pass on without devoting a few pages to the subject.

The rulers whom we supplanted were, like ourselves, aliens and usurpers. We found the Hindoos a conquered people, and, little by little, we substituted one yoke for another. The tide of conquest had hitherto set in from the inland northern counties. It was rolled back by a power whose approaches commenced from the southern sea-board. From the Oxus and the Jaxartes, from the borders of the Aral lake, and from the snowy mountains, had come the overwhelming desolating stream of northern conquest. The Greeks and Arabs, who had preceded the Tartar hordes, scarcely passed the limits of the country which modern history knows as Hindostan. British arms have now again extended the Indian Empire to the banks of the Indus, and our legions have encamped themselves, permanently and securely, upon the seat of the old Macedonian conquests. But of neither Greeks nor Arabs can it be said that they conquered India. A race of men, in whom the shepherd and the soldier were strangely blended, streamed from the countries watered by the Oxus and Jaxartes, and established themselves in Afghanistan; looking down from which, as from a platform of observation, upon India, they sighed for its legendary treasures, and meditated the invasion of the coveted land.

How at the dawn of the present millenium, before the Norman William, on the southern coast of England, had stricken down the last of the Saxon kings, Mahmoud of Ghuznee, the son of a Toorkhee slave, crossed the waters of the Jumna, and with a multitudinous army, appeared before the stately walls of Canoorj—how he attacked, plundered, and destroyed Muttra; and how he returned to Ghuznee laden with glittering spoil, and attended by a train of five thousand captives;—how, at another time, crossing the great desert, he poured his battalions into Goozrat, and made the walls of the far-famed idol-temple echo with the cry of *Allah Akhbar*—how he desecrated that beloved Pagan shrine and carried off its hoarded wealth; and how, on its backward march to Afghanistan, his army perished miserably on the burning sands;—are great historical events, not less interesting for their remoteness, at which it is scarcely necessary to glance. For although Mahmoud entered India—fought and conquered—he never there established an empire. He coveted the fabulous treasures which, it was believed, were hidden in its gorgeous palaces and rich idol-shrines; and his lust was satisfied with the gold and jewels, which he bore away from this romantic land. But he was a spoliator, rather than a conqueror; and his victories left upon India little more than the impress of transient calamities.

It was by a prince of less note in the page of history—by Shahab-oo-deen, of the house of Ghor, that India was first really conquered. It is hard to say why the life of one who reduced to subjection almost the entire country from Ajmere to Bengal, and left at his death the conquered provinces under his own officers, or under tributary princes, should stand out with so little individual distinctness from the great level of the Mahomedan chronicles. Little, however, is popularly recorded of his personal history and character. On his death, about the time when the great Charter of English privileges was signed at Runnymede, India became an independent Mahomedan kingdom, under the rule of the conqueror's favorite slave; and the dynasty of the Slave-Kings was commenced. Then the Empire of Delhi was established. Hindostan was nominally subject to one sovereign, the extent of whose real influence was mainly dependent on the energy of his personal character, and the vigor with which he held his satraps in control.* Much of his time was consumed in efforts to suppress the rising power of his provincial governors; and those governors, instead of concerning themselves about the welfare of the people, were continually striving to advance what they believed to be their own. Some splendid architectural remains, conspicuous among which is the *Kootab Minar* of Delhi, still bear pleasing testimony to the

* "All Hindostan, except some insulated portions, now acknowledged the government of Delhi; but the obedience of the different portions was in different degrees, from entire subjection to very imperfect dependence; and in this state, with various fluctuations, it remained till the end of the Mogul Empire. In a succession of strong reigns, the subject country would greatly exceed the rest, and the princes who retained the internal government of their territories would be quite submissive and obedient in general politics; but two or three weak rulers would again throw all into confusion; new princes would start up, and old ones would become unruly, until the next vigorous monarch had almost to begin the conquest anew."—[*Elphinstone.*]

magnificent tastes of the Slave-Kings; but, as peaceful administrators, and guardians of the public weal, they can lay little claim to the approbation of posterity. Indeed, the judgment is not over harsh which would pronounce them, for the most part, either unscrupulous tyrants or indolent debauchees. Nor were the Ghilji successors of a higher class. Their efforts at internal administration often took the shape of arbitrary interference of the most irritating kind, and they most incensed the people when they interfered most in their domestic affairs.

Of the succeeding dynasty—the house of Toghlak—one of the greatest monarchs was a madman.* His successor—Feroz Shah—left behind him, perhaps, the brightest name of all the early Mahomedan princes. Considering the age in which he lived, and the circumstances by which he was surrounded, he was really an enlightened prince. Greatly in advance of his predecessors, he initiated many important public works; and though the accounts of them which have come down to us are somewhat vague and general, and perhaps fairly open to some suspicion of their accuracy, it is not to be doubted that he did much to promote the prosperity and to advance the civilisation of the country which he governed.† By Feroz Shah was constructed, in the middle of the fourteenth century, the first Indian

* Mahmoud Toghlak.

† "His reign, though not brilliant in other respects, was distinguished for the enlightened spirit of his regulations, and the extent and utility of his public works. He limited the number of capital punishments, and put a stop to the use of torture and the practice of mutilation, which last prohibition was the more meritorious, as it was at variance with the Mahomedan law. He abolished a great number of vexatious taxes and fees, put an end to all fluctuating and precarious imposts, and fixed the revenues in such a manner as to leave as little as possible to the collectors, and to give precision and publicity to the demands of the state. . . . The following list is given of his public works, for the maintenance of which, lands were assigned:—50 dams across rivers, to promote navigation; 40 mosques; 30 colleges; 100 caravanserais; 30 reservoirs for irrigation; 100 hospitals; 100 public baths; 150 bridges; besides many other edifices for pleasure or ornament." Elphinstone, from whom this account is taken, adds—"The round numbers, as well as the amount of some of the items, suggest doubts of the accuracy of the list; but the works of Feroz which still remain, afford sufficient evidence of the magnitude of his undertakings."

canal. The water seems to have been drawn from the Chetang *nullah*, at the foot of the lower range of Himalayahs west of the Jumna, and the line extended thence to Hissar, where were the favourite hunting-grounds of the emperor. Whatever may have been the purposes for which it was constructed—and I see no reason to question that it was designed for the irrigation of the country, and the benefit of the people—it was but a little time in full fertilising operation. Not very long after the death of Feroz Shah, it seems to have been dried up; and it is believed that it never drew a permanent flow of water, until, two hundred years afterwards, the Emperor Akbar issued an order for its restoration.*

In 1389, full of years and trouble, Feroz Shah was gathered to his fathers. It was during the reign of his grandson, only a few years later, that India was laid prostrate by that stupendous calamity, the invasion of Tamerlane. Girt with the strange legend of miraculous conception, the lame shepherd-prince, with a frame of iron, and a heart of stone, came with a mighty Tartar army, bristling with pikes and javelins, from the country beyond the Oxus, and over-ran the provinces of Hindostan. Lust of conquest—nothing else—brought him to Delhi. He had no wrongs to redress—no insults to wipe away. But he had conquered the countries of Central Asia lying nearer to his home. Persia, Georgia, Mesopotamia, Syria, had fallen before his arms. He had captured Herat—thus made himself master of Khorassan—and thence crossing the Punjab, moved

* Elphinstone says that it was disused, "perhaps, since the death of Feroz" (in 1389); but it seems, from the following passage in a curious document discovered in Khytul, by Lieutenant S. A. Abbott, to have been in operation at a later date. The document is an edict of the Emperor Akbar, relative to the restoration of the canal. "The Chetang Nuddi, by which Feroz Shah Badshah, two hundred and ten years ago, brought water from the nullahs and drains in the vicinity of Sudhourah, at the foot of the hills, to Hansi and Hissar, and by which, for four or five months of the year, water was there available, has in the course of time, and from numerous obstacles, become so choked, that it is scarcely discernible," &c. &c.—[*Calcutta Review.*]

down with irresistible force on the beautiful capital of the Indian Empire. No language can exaggerate the horrors of that invasion—horrors which have rendered the name of "Timour the Tartar" familiar to every school-boy in Western Europe, as the type of an insatiable tyrant and a scourge of the human race.

It is certain, indeed, that these Mahomedan conquests were achieved at an enormous cost of human life—that the misery which the conquerors diffused in their desolating careers, makes by comparison the victorious progress of British arms in the East a mild and merciful migration. The Arabs and the Tartars were equally remorseless. Each in turn murdered and pillaged with as little pity and compunction as the others. In the first, the spirit of proselytism was the strongest. They went forth as children of the Prophet, and fought and conquered in his name. A genuine religious enthusiasm stirred the hearts of those early Mahomedan invaders. But the Tartar hordes were little better than lukewarm neophytes. They over-ran a new country; they made its treasures their own; but they rather merged themselves into the general population, and took shape from the surrounding mass, than stamped their own conformation upon it. It was in no spirit of toleration and forbearance, however, that they spared the idols of the Hindoos.* Their enthusiasm found vent through other channels than those of religious zeal. They murdered the idolaters, and plundered their temples, only because they delighted in cruelty, and were greedy of spoil.†

* This is only metaphorically and spiritually true. Literally and substantially, it is incorrect. The Mahomedan conquerors often did *not* spare the Hindoo idols; but their iconoclasm was very different from that of the Spanish conquerors of South America. The latter, when they struck down the idols of the Mexicans, struck at the false gods which the images represented. When the former broke the graven deities of the Hindoos into pieces, they did so to see what they contained.

† The history of the Mahomedan dynasties in India is full of lamentable instances of the cruelty and rapacity of the early conquerors. Take, as illustrative of Arab cruelty, the following from Elphinstone's account

Tamerlane was proclaimed Emperor of Delhi, but he soon withdrew his army from India, leaving anarchy

of Casim's conquest of Sindh:—"Casim at first contented himself with circumcising all the Brahmins; but incensed at their rejection of this sort of conversion, he ordered all above the age of seventeen to be put to death, and all under it, with the women, to be reduced to slavery." And again, from the same writer—"The women and children were first sacrificed in flames of their own kindling; the men bathed, and with other ceremonies took leave of each other and the world; the gates were then thrown open, the Rajputs rushed out sword in hand, and, throwing themselves on the weapons of their enemies, perished to a man. Those of the garrison who did not share in this act of desperation, gained little by their prudence: the city was carried by assault, and all the men in arms were slaughtered in the storm. Their families were reduced to bondage." Speaking more generally of the character of Arab conquests, he says: "On the first invasion, each city was called on, as the army approached, to embrace the Mahomedan religion or to pay tribute. In case of refusal, the city was attacked, and if it did not capitulate, all the fighting-men were put to death, and their families were sold for slaves. Four cities held out to this extremity; and in two of them the number of soldiers who refused quarter is estimated at 6000 each."

Take the following from the record of the career of Mahmoud of Ghuznee:—"During a halt of twenty days, the city (Muttra) was given up to plunder, the idols were broken, and the temples profaned. The excesses of the troops led to a fire in the city, and the effects of this conflagration were added to its other calamities. . . . This expedition was attended with some circumstances more than usually tragical. At Mahawan, near Muttra, the Rajah had submitted, and had been favorably received; when a quarrel accidentally breaking out between the soldiers of the two parties, the Hindoos were massacred and driven into the river, and the Rajah, conceiving himself betrayed, destroyed his wife and children, and then made away with himself. At Munj, after a desperate resistance, part of the Rajput garrison rushed out through the breaches of the enemy, whilst the rest dashed themselves to pieces from the works, or burned themselves, with their wives and children, in the houses; so that not one of the whole body survived." In Persia, Mahmoud seems to have been even more remorseless than in India. "He invaded Irak, and, ungenerously, if not perfidiously, seized the person of the prince who had trusted himself in the camp before Rei. He then took possession of the whole territory, and having been opposed at Ispahan and Cazvin, he punished their resistance by putting to death some thousands of the inhabitants of each city." "Perhaps, however," says Elphinstone, "the most odious trait of his religious wars is given incidentally by a Mahomedan author, quoted in Price, who states, that such was the multitude of captives brought from India, that a purchaser could not be found for a slave at four shillings and sevenpence a head."

Again:—"Shahab-u-din was more sanguinary than Mahmoud. When he took Ajmir, he put some thousands of the inhabitants, who opposed him, to the sword, reserving the rest for slavery." But it is in the history of such conquerors as Genghis Khan and Tamerlane that the horrors of these Mahomedan inroads are most clearly revealed. I can afford space only for one more example, taken from Elphinstone's account of the latter. "He (Tamerlane) then proceeded to Batner, and massacred the country people who had taken refuge under the walls. The place afterwards surrendered on terms; but, by one of those mistakes which so constantly accompanied Tamerlane's capitulations, the town was burned, and all the inhabitants put to the sword. He then marched to Samana, where he joined his main body, having slaughtered the inhabitants of every place he passed. From Samana the towns were deserted, and consequently there were no more general massacres. Many prisoners were, however, taken; and on reaching Delhi, Tamerlane put to death all of them above fifteen years of age (to the number, according to the exaggerated accounts of the Mussulman historians, of 100,000). . . . Delhi surrendered under a solemn promise of protection, and Tamerlane was publicly proclaimed Emperor of India.

and desolation behind him. The great cities were depopulated. The country was without a government. The empire had been gradually falling to pieces since the early years of the reign of Mahomed Toghlak, and when now, after the withdrawal of Tamerlane, an attempt was made to re-establish imperial power in Hindostan, it was found that the sceptre of the new dynasty was waved over only a remnant of the extensive kingdom which had owned the sovereignty of the princes of Delhi. Everywhere independent monarchies had risen up, and it was not until a descendant of Tamerlane—known to the present generation by one of the pleasantest autobiographies ever written by sovereign or subject, a memoir as instructive as Xenophon's, and as amusing as Pepys',—came from the countries which had poured forth the teeming multitudes with which his great ancestor had conquered India, followed in his footsteps, and re-conquered Delhi, that any attempt was made to consolidate these distracted provinces. Baber found the empire broken up into a number of small principalities. Rebellion after rebellion in distant provinces had shorn the throne of Delhi of its strength, and reduced it almost to a pageant. In some of the principalities there was a sort of nominal dependence, in others there was not even that. But the successor of Tamerlane, having established himself in the imperial city, had no thought of halting there, or of returning to his royal home. He had not come merely as a conqueror and a spoliator. He had

What follows is so constant a concomitant of Tamerlane's promises of protection, that we are at a loss whether to ascribe it to systematic perfidy, or to the habitual ferocity and insubordination of the troops. On this occasion, the most credible accounts attribute *the commencement* to the latter cause. Plunder and violence brought on resistance; 'this led to a general massacre; some streets were rendered impassable by heaps of dead; and the gates being forced, the whole Mogul army gained admittance, and a scene of horror ensued, easier to be imagined than described.' — *Brigg's Ferishta.*" We fear that the insatiable cruelty of the Mahomedan conquerors stands recorded upon more undeniable authority than the insatiable benevolence of the Mahomedan rulers.

come to establish a great empire on the banks of the Hindoo rivers; and he realised, in the fulness of time, the pregnant dreams of his imaginative boyhood.

Baber was sixth in descent from Tamerlane. A space of time, exceeding a century and a quarter, intervened between the invasion of the latter and the accession of the former prince.* And again, after the death of Baber, was the succession interrupted by the revolt of a noble of the house of Ghor, who wrested the sceptre from the hand of the descendant of Tamerlane, and established himself on the throne of Delhi. Shir Shah reigned only nine years; but his reign was a lustrous one. No prince had, up to this time, done so much for the improvement of the conquered country. He devoted himself, when not actually in the field, to the better ordering of the civil administration, and the construction of great public works. He improved both the fiscal and judicial systems of the empire. And the native annalists head the list of great works which he accomplished, with an account of a broad road, which in those days it took four months to traverse, stretching from Bengal to the banks of the Indus at Rhotas, along which noble rows of trees, and wells of good water at short intervals, shaded and refreshed the traveller; and caravanserais, at every stage, supplied with food for the poor, and attendants, alike for Mahomedan and Hindoo, invited the weary and the hungry to enter.†

* India, during that interval (from 1399 to 1526), was governed by the Sayuds and the house of Lodi. It was a period of great intestine commotion, and little appears to have been done for the improvement of the country.

† It is not, however, to be supposed that he was the first monarch who gave his attention to these things. "The roads," says Elphinstone, "may have been improved by Shir Shah; but Ibn Batuta, 200 years before his time, found the highways shaded by trees, with resting-houses and wells at regular intervals along a great part of the coast of Malabar, then under the Hindus; and in an inscription lately discovered, which there is every reason to think is of the third century *before* Christ, there is an especial order by the king for digging wells and planting trees along the public highways." Ibn Batuta, however, makes no mention of the existence of any such works as these in Northern India, where the greater part

The revolts which interrupted the reigns of Shir Shah's successors paved the way for the restoration of the house of Timour. About the middle of the sixteenth century, the expelled son of Baber recovered a portion of his lost dominions; but only survived by a few months his return to the capital after sixteen years of ignominious exile. An accident deprived him suddenly of life; and history would, in all probability, set down against him that he had done nothing to earn the gratitude of posterity, if he had not forgotten the greatest monarch who ever sat on the throne of Hindostan.

Akbar was thirteen years old when he began to reign. Our English Mary was then lighting up the fires of Smithfield in honor of the Pope of Rome. The Portuguese had rounded the Cape of Storms, and established themselves in Southern and Western India; but the British merchant had not yet begun to freight his argosies with the rich silks and fine muslins of the Indian world. India itself was then broken up into many principalities. The empire of the young king, on his accession, extended little beyond the government of the Punjab and the country about Delhi and Agra. A series of revolutions had destroyed, not only the integrity of the empire itself, but the regularity of civil administration and the continuance of social order and prosperity. But the young king, as he entered on

of his time was spent, but says, on the other hand, that the highways were infested by robbers. According to this traveller, the South was in a more advanced state of civilisation, for he says that theft was unknown in Malabar. "Should anything fall from a tree, none except its proper owner would attempt to touch it." This was supposed to be the result of the extreme severity of the laws. The account of the great Malabar road, alluded to by Elphinstone, is worth quoting. "We next came into the country of Malabar, which is the country of black pepper. Its length is a journey of two months, along the shore from Sindabur to Kanlam. The whole of the way by land lies under the shade of trees, and at the distance of every half mile there is a house made of wood, in which there are chambers fitted up for the reception of comers and goers, whether they be Moslems or infidels. To each of these there is a well, out of which they drink, and over each is an infidel appointed to give drink."—[*The Travels of Ibn Batuta, translated from the Arabic, by the Rev. Samuel Lee.*]

manhood, soon began to perceive the true character of the work which then lay before him. He determined to restore the integrity of the old empire of Hindostan, and to place its internal administration upon a secure and permanent basis. Year by year he extended his conquests, until the rich country of Bengal lay at his feet, and Cashmere became a province of the empire. He again reduced to subjection his hereditary kingdom beyond the Indus, and then, turning his eyes towards the southern countries, meditated the conquest of the Deccan. He was, indeed, continually engaged in war, up to the time of his death; but in spite of these external distractions, he found time to fix his thoughts, as his heart was ever fixed, upon schemes of domestic improvement. He was at once a conqueror and an administrator. He had no delight in conquest. He fought when it was necessary to fight—and he fought with courage and vigor seldom surpassed. But he was happiest when engaged in the work of civil administration; and history delights to contemplate him rather as a philanthropic statesman, whose internal policy has placed him in the first rank of the great kings of all ages and all countries, than as a warrior whose victories have secured him the applause of more vulgar and unreflecting minds.

I wish briefly and fairly to state what the Emperor Akbar did for the improvement of the country and the people of Hindostan. He improved the system of land-assessment, or rather he improved upon the improvements instituted by Shir Shah. He adopted an uniform and improved system of land-measurement, and computed the average value of the land, by dividing it into three classes, according to the productiveness of each. This computation being made, one-third of the average produce was fixed as the amount of tax to be paid to the state. But as this was ordinarily to be paid in money, it was necessary to ascertain the value of the produce, and this was done upon an average of the nineteen preceding years, according to local circumstances; and if the estimate was conceived to be too high, the tax-payer was privileged to pay the assessment in kind. These settlements were at first made annually, but afterwards were fixed for a period of ten years. The regulations for the collection of the revenue enforced by Akbar, were well calculated to prevent fraud and oppression, and, on the whole, they worked well for the benefit of the people; but it has been said of them, and with truth, that "they contained no principle of progressive improvement, and held out no hopes to the rural population, by opening paths by which it might spread into other occupations, or rise by individual exertions within its own."*

The judicial regulations of Akbar were liberal and humane. Justice, on the whole, was fairly administered. All unnecessary severity—all cruel personal punishments, as torture and mutilation, were prohibited, except in peculiar cases, and capital punishments were considerably restricted. The police appears to have been well organised, and subject to specific instructions, involving perhaps a little more interference than it was expedient to entrust to such hands, but, on the whole, not ill suited to the temper of the people and the character of the government. His enactments were, on the whole, of a humanising tendency. He prohibited those trials by ordeal, of which it is difficult to say whether they are more cruel or more absurd; he suppressed the barbarous custom of condemning to slavery prisoners taken in war; and he authoritatively forbade the burning of Hindoo widows, except with their own free and uninfluenced consent. He even interfered in person to suppress the

* *Elphinstone.*

horrid rite, when he believed that an unwilling victim was about to proceed to the funeral-pile. It is recorded in the Akbar-Nameh, that when the Rajah of Joudpore was about to force his son's widow into this horrible self-immolation, the Emperor mounted his horse, rode to the scene of the intended sacrifice, and prevented its consummation.*

That something of the historical lustre which surrounds the name of the Emperor Akbar was derived rather from the personal character of the man than from the great things that he accomplished, is, I think, not to be denied. His actual performances, when they come to be computed, fall short of his reputation. But his merits are to be judged not so much by the standard of what he did, as of what he did with the opportunities allowed to him, and under the circumstances by which he was surrounded. Akbar built up the Mogul Empire, and had little leisure allowed him to perfect its internal economy. He was

* No mention is made, by the historians of his reign, of Akbar's efforts to extend the system of canal irrigation initiated by Feroz Shah. But from the edict discovered by Lieut. Abbott some information may be gleaned. It is thus epitomised by the writer already quoted, in the *Calcutta Review:* "The indications given of his canal system are faint and feeble, and may be condensed into few words. A superintendent of canals was nominated, under the title of Mir-ab (chief of the waters), with absolute authority throughout his jurisdiction. In his hands were vested the charge of the works, the distribution of the water, in short, all executive revenue and police details connected with the canal. The works would appear to have been constructed by forced labor, since all local officers are enjoined to furnish laborers, &c., without delay. To those, however, who complied with this requisition, water is promised during the season of cultivation, and for the entire year. How this water was distributed is but faintly indicated. The Mir-ab was to determine the number of cuts necessary for each pengunnah, and in a spirit of equal justice, he is directed to be careful that all parties, rich or poor, strong or weak, share alike. From other sources of information, it is supposed that the amount of water-rent was rated according to the time the heads of the cuts, probably of fixed dimensions, remained open. While the necessities of the Zemindars were thus ministered to, the comfort of travellers was not forgotten; and it is directed, 'that on both sides of the canal, down to Hissar, trees of every description, both for shade and blossom, be planted, so as to make it like the canal under the tree in Paradise, and that the sweet flavor of the rare fruits may reach the mouth of every one, and that from these luxuries a voice may go forth to travellers calling them to rest in the cities, where their every want will be supplied.'"

so much in the stirrup, that the wonder is his portfolio sent forth what it did. But he was a man of a large and plastic mind, and so readily adapted himself to external circumstances, that the transitions from the camp to the council-chamber but rarely disquieted and unhinged him.

The successor of this great and wise king was a monarch of a very different stamp. Jehanguire inherited the vast possessions of his father, but none of his father's greatness of soul. There was no element of greatness in his character. He was, indeed, a very little man. Inconstant and self-indulgent, easily pleased with trifles so that there was some stamp of novelty upon them, he lived a careless, sensual life; now excited by wine, now stupified by opium, oblivious of the responsibilities of his station, and regardless of the welfare of his people. But he made great progresses to Cashmere, and the way was made pleasant for him. His public works were such only as benefited himself. Around the elegant licentiousness of the voluptuous monarch the genius of the poet may throw a halo of romance, but all that the historian can say of him is, that he was a marvellously poor creature and a singularly bad king. It is true that there was one not unlike him, who wrote letters from " our palace of Westminster," beseeching him to cherish and support our English traders, by the continuance of his favorable assistance and protection; but I am not sure that the character of Jehanguire will gain much by the admission that he was not, either as a monarch or a man, worse than our first James.

The most interesting personage to be met with in all the annals of Mahomedan India is, doubtless, the Emperor Akbar; but it was during the reign of his grandson, Shah Jehan, that the Mogul Empire reached its highest state of prosperity.* Old travellers, who found their way from Europe to the Empire of the Great Mogul, speak with rapture of the paternal government of Shah Jehan, and of the grandeur of the cities which dotted his vast empire. It was the good fortune of this prince to reap the benefit of his predecessor's conquests. He was not free from the distractions of war, but the wars in which he was engaged were for the most part carried on beyond the limits of his own dominions, so that they were not torn and desolated by the fierce conquests which, both before and after his reign, had rent and convulsed the provinces of Hindostan. If great public works were ever executed in India under the sway of the Moguls, it was whilst Shah Jehan ruled over the country from the Peacock throne of Delhi.

Shah Jehan was the cotemporary of our first Charles. Like that prince, he reigned for more than thirty years, and was then violently deposed. The Company of English merchants, who, under the sanction of his predecessor, had established factories at Surat and on the coast of Coromandel and Malabar, were struggling for a precarious existence against their powerful rivals, the Dutch. It would be difficult to exaggerate the idea which in those days was entertained by our countrymen of the power, wealth, and grandeur of the Great Mogul. Far above all kings and emperors, in the imaginations of men, ranked this mighty Eastern potentate; and two centuries later, the name of the Great Mogul capped, with its traditionary magnificence, those of all the potentates of the earth, in the nursery-sports of English children. Nor did the conception owe much to the prodigality of the imagina-

* "Khafi Khan, the best historian of those times, gives his opinion, that although Akbar was pre-eminent as a conqueror and lawgiver, yet, for the order and arrangement of his territory and finances, and the good administration of every department of the state, no prince ever reigned in India that could be compared to Shah Jehan."—[*Elphinstone.*]

tion. The prince who covered acres of land with carpets of silk and gold, who reared above them stately pavilions glittering with diamonds and pearls, whose elephants and horses were lustrous with trappings of jewels and gold, whose crimson tents stretched out over long miles of level country, and whose throne the practised eyes of European lapidaries valued at six millions of English money, might well be regarded as the most magnificent sovereign of the earth. But magnificence is not benevolence. It must be admitted that the most lavish of our English viceroys has never been more than partially *sultanised.** Our splendor is at best but tinsel and tawdriness beside the lustrous magnificence of the Mogul Courts. We have never attempted to compete with them in this direction. Let credit be allowed them for their royal progresses —their stately palaces—their gorgeous tombs. The genius of our country does not display itself in demonstrations of this kind. But we have far greater wonders to show—far grander spectacles to exhibit. When we have got millions to spend, we do not lock them up in peacock-thrones.

Did these royal progresses benefit the people? I am very certain that they did not. The approach, indeed, of the Mogul camp was something like the dreaded descent of a great flight of locusts. The inhabitants of the country through which the Emperor progressed shrunk from the contact of the royal traveller. The honor may have been great, but the injury was greater. Even if the personal character of the monarch himself was such as to cause him to desire the full indemnity of the people, his influence was not sufficient to secure it. If his benevolence dictated

* Sir James Mackintosh spoke of Lord Wellesley as a "*sultanised* Governor-General." Lord Wellesley had as good an idea of vice-regal pomp as any man who ever went out to India, but at best he was only a very little "Great Mogul."

payment to the uttermost *pice* of every one who supplied the royal camp, it may not uncharitably be doubted whether his satraps were equally scrupulous and equally honest. My impression is that the people paid heavily for the honor of these royal visits. There is one legend, at least, which favors the idea that the coming of the Great Mogul was looked upon almost with as much horror as English people anticipate the approach of the cholera in these days. The Emperor had constructed a sort of regal hunting-box, at a place called, in his honor, Badshah-mehal. The waters of the Doab canal ran past it, and supplied its sporting fountains and its marble baths. Thither went Shah Jehan, with his courtiers and his servants, his wives and his concubines. Brief, however, was their rustication. From this pleasant retreat the Court, as tradition asserts, was soon scared away in fluttering confusion. At the foot of the hills, that disfiguring disease so well known among Alpine residents, the *goitre*, happened to be very common. There were some clever people in the neighbourhood of Badshah-mehal, who turned it to good account. Assembling a number of women so afflicted, they sent them into the Zenana with supplies. At the sight of the unseemly facial appendages with which these poor women were decorated, the ladies of the Court, filled with horror and pity, eagerly asked what had produced such cruel deformities. Well instructed beforehand, the women answered, that the air and water of the place had caused these ailments—that no one ever escaped the affliction who resided long in these parts—and that the ladies would soon discover this unhappy truth for themselves. Such alarming intelligence as this burst like a loaded shell among the inmates of the Zenana. They soon appealed to the Emperor. Would he leave them in such a pestiferous country, to be so afflicted and disfigured? Their entreaties are said to have prevailed. He sent them away from Badshah-mehal, spent a week or two in the surrounding forests, enjoying the pleasures of the chase, and then followed the ladies into a part of the country more favorable to the retention of their charms.* He never made his appearance in so dangerous a locality again.

Whether, after this mischance, the waters of the canal continued to flow in the direction of the regal hunting-box, does not very clearly appear. The ground upon which we here tread is rough with controversial asperities. They who, desiring to produce strong contrasts unfavorable to the British-Indian Government, greatly extol and exaggerate the beneficence of the Mogul Emperors, are ever pointing to the remains of the great aqueducts and reservoirs, which the traveller in India stumbles upon and pauses over; whilst another party, perhaps, with equal want of candor, declares that the Mogul princes were nothing better than selfish tyrants, and that all the roads which were made, all the trees that were planted, all the wells that were dug, all the caravanserais that were erected, and all the canals that were excavated by them, owed their origin to nothing more ennobling than a desire to render their journeys more agreeable and their residences more habitable to their Imperial Majesties themselves. In all probability, the truth is to be found midway between these two extremes. To a certain extent, both parties are right. The Mogul Emperors may not have been wholly unmindful of the interests of their subjects. They were never unmindful of their own. Fortunately for the former, the claims of the two were not wholly antagonistic. If

* I have borrowed this story from the article on "Canals of Irrigation in the North-West Provinces," in the *Calcutta Review*, No. XXIII. I have never met with it elsewhere; and it is probable that the ingenious and experienced writer derived it from local tradition.

the Emperor had shut himself up in a single palace, it is possible that the fine causeways and the noble aqueducts, over the remains of which we now shed our archæological tears, would not exist to agitate the sources of our regret. But as the Great Mogul was, by nature, of the peripatetic class—as he delighted in change of scene and change of residence—it was necessary that there should be roads over which to move the material mass of his leviathan camp, and it was desirable that the sultriness of his regal halting-places should be mitigated by baths and fountains, supplied with a constant flow of the refreshing element. The roads were made, and they benefited the people. The canals were dug, and they benefited the people. But when the Emperor ordered the construction of a road, or the excavation of a canal, and determined the direction which either should take, it may be doubted whether the line that was taken was always that which most promoted the internal traffic or the agricultural irrigation of the country. The personal convenience of the Emperor himself was of more account than the happiness and prosperity of the people. But the happiness and prosperity of the people were not wholly forgotten. The Mogul Emperors somewhat reversed the sentiment contained in Barlow's initiatory minute on the Regulations of 1793.* "It is a source of pleasing reflection," they thought, "to know that in proportion as we contribute to the happiness of ourselves and the prosperity of the Court, the nearer we approach to these objects"—*i. e.,* the welfare of the people. The "principal object" of the Mogul Government was certainly not the happiness of the governed.

That Shah Jehan did much which in effect promoted the prosperity of the country, is not to be denied. He was aided by the greatest executive officer

* See *ante*, page 2.

who ever served a Mogul prince. Ali Murdan Khan, an architect and engineer, who would have been conspicuous in any age in any country, was at the Emperor's right hand. The Delhi canal was his work.* The Eastern Jumna, or Doab canal, is also said to be his work. The former appears to have been more or less in operation up to the year 1753. The efficacy of the latter was more short-lived. Indeed, it has been questioned whether it very long survived the panic of the Court ladies at the sight of the disfigured throats of the poor women who entered the Zenana with their

* I give the following account of the direction it took, and the countries it traversed, from an article, already quoted in the *Calcutta Review*, by the best historiographer of our Indian canals:

"Ali Murdan Khan's first line parted from Feroze's canal at a place called Madlonda, and pursuing a southerly course to Korana, it there entered an extensive natural hollow, the head of a great drainage line, and following that, in a highly embanked channel, as far as Gohana, it turned thence to the south-east by Intoula, and, nearly on the existing line, entered Delhi. On the first opening of the new canal, it was found that the embankments near Gohana were inadequate. The water, entering the great hollow there, found no efficient line of escape: it gradually rose over, and ultimately burst, the banks, and committing fearful devastation, destroyed the town of Lalpur, the extensive ruins of which are still to be seen in a hollow near Rohtuk. The inefficiency of the line having been thus fatally demonstrated, an entirely new channel was excavated from Rehr to Intoula, traversing the anticlinal ridge, or natural water-shed of the country, until it reached the vicinity of Bowana. Between this point and the city of Delhi, very low land intervenes; and to carry the canal successfully across this hollow much caution and skill were required. To give command over the supply, an escape or outlet was constructed at the upper extremity of the line of embankment, by opening which the surface-level of the canal could be greatly reduced. Over the lowest part of the hollow the canal was carried by a masonry aqueduct, beneath which the drainage-water of the country found escape. Clearing the low land, the canal wound for some distance along the base of the Aravulli hills, and, at a favorable point, boldly crossed this ridge by a channel cut through the solid rock, no less than sixty feet deep at the crest. It then flowed through the city in a masonry bed, throwing off to the right and left innumerable minor streams, by which the residences of the nobles, and the various divisions of the city, were abundantly supplied. Throughout the great halls, and courts, and private apartments of the imperial palace, the plentiful stream was carried in numerous channels, both above ground and below, supplying the graceful fountains, filling the marble baths, watering the rich fruits and flowers of the adjoining gardens, and adorning, throughout its entire extent, that truly regal abode in a manner worthy of the magnificent taste of its great architect.

"The success of Ali Murdan Khan's labors was complete. The immense number of old water-courses along the whole line of the Delhi canal show to how great an extent the agriculture of the country benefited by its existence. Traditions of incredible amounts of revenue having been realised from villages on its banks still linger among the people there; and a proverbialism, current at Delhi, intimates that the clear returns from the canal were sufficient for the maintenance of 12,000 horsemen. The permanent establishment, maintained for purposes of police and repair, consisted of numerous bildárs (diggers), 1000 armed peons, and 500 horse, stationed, under their officers, at points three or four miles apart."

supplies. But if the *goitre* had not destroyed it, there were engineering difficulties of too formidable a character to be surmounted even by Ali Murdan Khan; and though an attempt was made long afterwards to re-open it, it seems wholly to have failed.*

The reign of Shah Jehan may be regarded as the golden age of Mogul rule. Soon after his deposition, it was evident that the seeds of decay had been sown in that vast empire. Aurungzebe was a prince of greater energy of character; but it was not permitted to him to enjoy the blessings of repose, and to turn its opportunities to the advantage of the people. His reign was a long and troublous one. He lived in an atmosphere of strife. And what were the effects of these civil wars may be gathered from the letters of our own people. Industry was paralysed; trade was at a standstill. People buried their money in the ground: "It does not a little trouble us," wrote one of the Company's chief servants, "to pay nine per cent. interest for what money we shall be forced to take up for your account towards providing of goods for the next year, and at that rate little to be had, every one rather burying

* The following account of the Eastern Jumna, or Doab canal, is from the same source as the preceding note:

"In common with the Delhi branch, the construction of this canal is ordinarily attributed to Ali Murdan Khan. Its head was established immediately under the sub-Himalayan, or Sowalik hills; possession having been taken of an old bed of the river, bearing at this day the name of the 'Budha Jumna.' Passing by the hunting-palace of Shah Jehan, called Badshah-mehal, it entered the bed of the Raipur-nala, and, carried thence in an excavated channel across the Intunwala and Nowgong mountain torrents, it was thrown into a low ravine near the town of Behut, which it followed until it reached the head of the Muskurra river, near the village of Kulsia. Entering there upon the high land, the canal was carried past Saharunpur, Rampur, Jellalabad, Shamli, and other large towns, until it descended again into the valley of the Jumna, and, passing another imperial palace at Ranup, fell into the river nearly opposite the city of Delhi. . . . .

"The great difficulties at the head of the canal were doubtless beyond the skill of the Mogul engineers: and, as there are no signs of irrigation in the southern part, and no masonry works of any kind, it may be concluded that, after the first opening, which is said to have been followed by great injuries to the towns of Behut and Saharunpur, the attempt to maintain the supply was abandoned.

"About 1780, Zabita Khan, Rohilla, is said to have re-opened the channel, and to have brought a stream of water, through the bed of the Kirsunni river, to the site of the great city projected by him in the neighbourhood of Jellalabad, Thana Bhown, and Lohari, in the district of Muzuffernuggur. But his canal could have been open only for a few months; and with the first rain-floods, it was doubtless seen that the difficulties were too formidable to be overcome."

their money than adventuring to trust it out in this time of war."* And with good reason, too, was the treasure buried deep in the ground, for another of the old Company's servants writes, about the same time, that "upon any occasion of war the king will either have the purses, or else purse and head."† Nothing was more dangerous, in those days, than to be the possessor of a little available coin. The Mogul princes opened their loans at the edge of the scimetar.

In the eyes of the general body of Mahomedans, Aurungzebe stands upon a higher pinnacle of reputation than any one of his predecessors. He was the most magnificent of potentates, and the most arbitrary of despots. He was every inch a king, according to the Mussulman standard of consummate royalty. No man was more prodigal of money, or more prodigal of life. The gorgeousness of his Court, and the unscrupulousness of his acts, reached a height that had not been attained during the reign of his predecessors. By this time European intercourse with the countries of the East had greatly increased; and we have, therefore, more vivid and more faithful pictures of the splendor of Aurungzebe's Court, and more detailed accounts of the general state of the empire during his reign, than the Mahomedan historians have handed down to us. And it must be acknowledged that no traveller, before or since, has dazzled the world with such a glitter of words, signifying gorgeous realities, as the pleasant French physician‡ who accompanied the royal camp from Delhi to Cashmere, and has told us in rapturous language, of the stately spectacle of Rowshera Begum, on her Pegue elephant, "glittering with gold and azure, followed by five or six other elephants almost as stately as her own," and "a troop of Tartarian and

* *Nathaniel Wyche to the Company, Feb.* 14, 1658-59. *India House Records.*

† *Henry Revington and others to the Company,* 1659. *India House Records.*

‡ Bernier.

Cashmerian maids of honor around her person, all fantastically dressed."

But the only question to be considered is, what effect had all this upon the happiness of the people? It is certain that regal magnificence is no test of national prosperity. The wealth which was lavished upon all the sumptuous palaces and the panoramic camps of these restless Emperors, must have been primarily extracted from the people. How the imperial coffers were filled it is not difficult to conjecture. Some of the early Mogul conquerors enriched themselves by a series of stupendous burglaries. If we could trace the career of any particular emerald or ruby from the days of Mahmoud of Ghuznee to those of Shah Jehan, there are few who would not rather think of the costly jewel in the blaze of the peacock's tail, than in the deep obscurity of the bowels of a hideous idol. But we have no means, amidst so many broken dynastic chains, of establishing any imperial succession of this kind; and we might fairly assume, even if we had no positive evidence to rest upon, that, directly or indirectly, the people paid the price of all the gorgeous magnificence which rendered the Court of the Great Mogul a type of regal splendor throughout the whole of the civilised world. It is stated that the progresses of Shah Jehan had no perceptible effect upon his coffers—that all his vast undertakings, indeed, were managed with so much economy that he left an overflowing treasury, and a jewel-house groaning with wealth.* We may gather from this significant fact some idea of what it was that caused the people to regard with unmingled horror the approach of the Mogul Court. It would be curious to ascertain what was the amount of

* *Elphinstone.* Bernier computes the amount at something under 6,000,000*l.* of our money, Khafi Khan at 24,000,000*l.*, "and," says the historian, in a note, "he is not likely to exaggerate, for he makes Shah Jehan's revenue 23,000,000*l.*, whilst it is generally reckoned to have been 32,000,000*l.*"

forced labor extracted from the people, and to what extent they were paid for their supplies. It is easy to "manage vast undertakings with economy," if little or nothing is to be paid for work or materials. And I hardly think that with such data before us—as costly expeditions undertaken at little cost, and the popular dread of the Emperor's approach—it is very unfair to assume that the rights of the people inhabiting the country through which the despot dragged the cumbrous length of his gorgeous camp, were very slenderly regarded either by the sovereign himself, or the officers who attended his Court.*

That the Mogul Emperors left behind them some magnificent works, rests not merely on the authority of the Mahomedan historians. There are many picturesque evidences of the fact still patent to the senses of all who journey through the provinces of Hindostan. But only a small portion of these works ever conferred any substantial benefit on the people, and a still smaller portion were intended, primarily, to promote their happiness. If they did, it was more by accident than by design. Many of the works of which traces are still to be seen, were in active operation for any one's benefit but for an extremely short space of time. Many of them had served their purpose when a particular king ceased to migrate in a particular direction. There is nothing more remarkable, indeed, in this florid picture of Mahomedan beneficence, than the fact that there is nothing of a *sustained* character about it. The beneficence of the Mogul Emperors was personal and accidental. It was never the growth of any fixed principle inherent in the Government, and, as such, handed down from one representative of monarchical power to another; but was dependent entirely on individual character, which was often only

* It is evident from Akbar's Canal Act, quoted *ante*, page 29, that canals, in his time, were excavated by forced labor.

another name for individual caprice. Fortunately, these individual changes were then of occurrence unusually rare in Mahomedan countries. The epoch of which I am now writing extended over a period of about a century and a half, and embraced only four reigns. Akbar ascended the throne in 1556, and Aurungzebe was carried to the tomb in 1707. The evil, therefore, of that capricious exercise of power, of those frequent mutations in the system of government, which are inseparable from all despotisms, was not experienced to that extent which is entailed upon a people when they have not merely to contend against the caprices of an individual, but against the caprices of a series of capricious individuals. I confess that I have little faith in the happiness of the people under such a despotism as that of the Great Moguls.*

Neither life nor property was secure under their rule. The Mahomedan conquerors took what they wanted, and executed whom they would. If a merchant possessed gold or jewels, he was careful to hide his wealth. If an artisan was more than commonly ingenious in his craft,

* I am speaking here of the flower of the Mogul princes. It is almost superfluous to allude to the cruelties of the earlier Mahomedan rulers. Ibn Batuta says that owing to the tyranny of the Emperor, Delhi, when he entered it, was almost a desert. "The greatest city in the world had the fewest inhabitants." The particular instances of the prince's cruelty which are given, are too numerous for citation—one or two instances will suffice: "One of the Emirs of Fargana came to pay him a temporary visit. The Emperor received him very kindly, and bestowed on him some rich presents. After this the Emir had a wish to return, but was afraid the Emperor would not allow him to do so; he began, therefore, to think of flight. Upon this, a whisperer gave intimation of his design, and the Emir was put to death; the whole of his wealth was then given to the informer. For this is the custom, that when any one gives private intimation of the designs of another, and his information turns out to be true, the person so informed of is put to death, and his property is given to the informer." Again: "Upon a certain day, when I myself was present, some men were brought out who had been *accused* of having attempted the life of the Vizier. They were ordered accordingly to be thrown to the elephants, which had been taught to cut their victims to pieces. Their hoofs were cased with sharp iron instruments, and the extremities of these were like knives. On such occasions the elephant-driver rode upon them; and when a man was thrown to them, they would wrap their trunk about him and toss him up, then take him with the teeth and throw him between their fore feet upon the breast. If the order was to cut him to pieces, the elephant would do so with his irons, and then throws the piece among the assembled multitude; but if the order was to leave him, he would be left lying before the Emperor, until the skin should be taken off and stuffed with hay, and the flesh given to the dogs."

he concealed the extent of his skill. It was dangerous to be rich. It was dangerous to be clever. It was dangerous in any way to be a marked man. If the sovereign was accessible to his subjects, so was the executioner. Justice was administered with such extraordinary promptitude, that offenders were hurried into the presence of their Maker almost before they knew that they had committed any offence. Nor was the personal clemency of the sovereign himself any defence against such gross abuse of arbitrary power. He had no means of communicating his own mild nature to the provincial viceroys and governors who ruled over remote parts of his empire, or even to the ministers of his own immediate cabinet.* His delegated authority was often cruelly abused. Old travellers tell of barbarous acts committed even in the presence of European gentlemen, at the recital of which humanity shudders, and credulity is well-nigh staggered.† There is hardly a native of India in

* Behram, Akbar's prime minister, was a great man, and, on the whole, not a bad one. But it is recorded of him, that "he took advantage of Akbar's absence on a hawking-party, to put to death Tardi Beg, the former governor of Delhi, without even the ceremony of taking the king's orders on so solemn an occasion. One day, while Akbar was amusing himself with an elephant-fight, one of these animals ran off the field pursued by its antagonist, and followed by a promiscuous crowd of spectators; it rushed through the tents of Behram, some of which were thrown down; thus exposing the minister himself to danger, whilst it threw all around him into the utmost confusion and alarm. Irritated by this seeming affront, and, perhaps, suspecting a design against his life, Behram ordered the elephant-driver to be put to death. . . . . . . A nobleman, of consequence enough to oppose Behram, was put to death on some slight charge by that minister. The king's own tutor, Pir Mahomed Khan, narrowly escaped the same fate, and was banished on pretence of a pilgrimage to Mecca." If men of rank were treated to this wild justice, it is little likely that the commonalty escaped.

† Take, for example, the following from the travels of John Mandelslo, written in 1640. The governor of Ahmedabad had invited the principal directors of the English and Dutch trades to an entertainment, of which, as usual, displays of the dancing-girls were among the chief features. One party having danced themselves out, another was sent for; but they refused to come, for a reason which need not be given, and were then forcibly dragged into the presence of the governor. He listened to their excuse, "laughed at it, but immediately commanded out a party of his guard, and ordered their heads to be struck off. They begged their lives with horrid cries and lamentations; but he would be obeyed, and caused the execution to be done in the room before all the company—not one of the lords then present daring to make the least intercession for those wretches, who were eight in number. The strangers were startled at the horror of the spectacle, and inhumanity of the action, which the governor taking notice of, fell a laughing, and asked them what they were so much startled at."

the present day, who does not hug to himself the precious thought that there is no longer any power in the state that can order, under the influence of a gust of passion, or a spasm of caprice, even the meanest laborer to be trampled to death by elephants, or disembowelled with a sharp knife. The poorest Cooley is entitled to all the solemn formalities of a judicial trial, and the punishment of death, by whomsoever administered, and on whomsoever inflicted, without the express decree of the law, is a murder for which the highest functionary in the Company's territories is as much accountable as a sweeper would be for the assassination of the Governor-General in Durbar.

It must be admitted that the later Mogul Emperors were not intolerant—that they seldom or never gave way to the littleness of religious persecution. It would seem that the earlier Tartar monarchs filled all the chief offices of the state with strangers and aliens, and that the Hindoos were almost wholly set aside. But the princes of whom I am now writing were more tolerant and more liberal. The claims of the Hindoos were not disregarded. Men were appointed to offices of high trust and emolument, without reference to the religion which they professed, or the country from which they drew their origin.

It is not easy to arrive at a clear conception of the general condition of the great mass of the people during the reign of the Mogul princes. Materials are greatly wanting. Early travellers and historians tell us much of the Court—little or nothing of the people. Ibn Batuta, the Arab traveller, whom Mahomed Toghlak made Judge of Delhi, tells us nothing of the condition of the inhabitants of Northern India, but leaves us to infer that the country was considerably over-run with robbers and wild beasts. Of the country on the coast of Malabar, however, he gives a flourishing account. "In all this space," he says, "of two months' journey, there is not a span free from cultivation. For everybody has here a garden, and his house is placed in the middle of it, and round the whole of this there is a fence of wood, up to which the ground of each inhabitant comes." The Italian travellers, who visited India about the same time, speak with rapture ot the flourishing state of Guzerat and Cambay; and describe the populous towns, the rich orchards, and the beautiful gardens which everywhere decorated the banks of the Ganges, and indicated the prosperity of the people. But the knowledge possessed by these travellers was superficial in the extreme; what they saw they but imperfectly comprehended, and of what they heard they had but scanty means of estimating the truth. One fact was always related to them, and always carefully set down in their tablets. In every city that they passed were stored up immense heaps of jewels and gold. That there were, in those days, vast accumulations of this kind of unproductive capital is not to be doubted. But the many profited little by the hoarded wealth of the few. The indications of national prosperity were, I believe, local and accidental; and I have no faith in the general result. The wealth of India may have been great, but it did not circulate. It is now diffused over a larger space —is more reproductive. That, to some extent, these once stored-up treasures have, by a gradual process of extraction, been drained out of the country, is not to be denied. But the residue is of more service to the people than the gross amount secretly garnered up in the most affluent days of the old Mahomedan kings.*

Of this gorgeous display of imperial wealth our own

* A very experienced and intelligent friend, to whom this work is indebted for some of its most valuable details, writes, with reference to this and the passage at p. 24: "The question here suggested is a very curious one, and one regarding which I once had a talk with James Skinner. Even so late as in the days of his youth, the exhibition of wealth at the great gatherings of native chiefs, Mahrattas, and others, was dazzling—what has become of it? Has it, I asked — has it not spread among the people, and so raised the general level, though the eminences may have been lowered? Skinner would not admit this—at least, not to the extent I desired—and maintained, with the Shroffs and Bunneahs, that we drain the land."—[*MS. Notes.*]

countrymen spoke in the same exalted strains, but they contrasted it with the general poverty of the people. "Touching the wealth of the king," wrote one of the oldest of the Company's servants, in the reign of Jehanguire, "though I cannot be otherwise persuaded than that it is very great, yet I cannot believe it to amount to that exceeding height that Captain Hawkins hath very fabulously written of it; but howsoever, it is certainly marvellously great; and this he raiseth two principal ways, by the rent of his lands, and by the goods of his noble subjects, for almost the whole estate of all the greater persons of his kingdom returneth to him after their decease. The main sum of his wealth consisteth partly in ready money in his coffers, whereof he is said to possess wonderful store; for there is still an importation of all sorts of money into his country, but never an exportation; and partly in rich stones, pearls, and jewels, wherewith he is reported to be better furnished than any prince on the face of the earth." And the same writer adds, that though some of the courtiers are very wealthy, "the plebeian sort is so poor, that the greatest part of them go naked in their whole bodies, saving about their [middle] which they cover with a linen coverture;"* a state of beatitude in respect of which they, in no degree, differ from the people of the present day.

Of the dangerous state of the public ways at this time, a clear conception may be gained from the statements of the same writer. "On my passage from Surat," he says, "over a large tract of country as far as Agra, I was subject to a world of dangers on the way, it being well known that no country more dangerous to travel is in the whole world than this, by reason of many thousands of blood-sucking villains, that for so much as one of their

* *Joseph Salbank to the Company, Nov.* 22, 1617. *India House Records.*

brass pieces of money that countervaileth the third part of a penny sterling will cut a man's throat, which doth appear by the example of one of our poor countrymen, travelling about a year past betwixt Surat and Agra, over certain woody and desolate parts of the country, was so often assaulted by thieves on the way, whereof some stripped him of all his little money about him; yet when charitable people did offer him money to buy him victuals, he would take none of them, knowing he should quickly be deprived of it, besides the fear of his life, but contented himself only with such poor food as people presented to him." "Howbeit," adds the writer, in a spirit of grateful veneration, "I for my part passed through all those hellish weapons that these cannibal villains used to kill men withal, securely enough, through the tender mercies of my gracious God."* This does not bring out in very favorable colors the internal administration of the Moguls.

Some stress has been laid upon the amount of revenue raised under the Mahomedan dynasties ; but I do not regard this as any real test of the prosperity of the country. Ibn Batuta says that the revenue raised from the district of Dowlatabad, in "taxes and fines," amounted to seventeen crores of rupees, or seventeen millions of our money. What the extent of country subject to the lieutenantcy of Dowlatabad may have been, is only to be vaguely gathered from the assertion that "it extends through a distance of three months," *i. e.*, a three months' journey. During the reigns of the later Mogul Emperors, from Akbar to Aurungzebe, the revenue seems to have averaged from twenty-six to twenty millions of our money. During these reigns, varying according to the personal character of the monarch, a considerable amount was realised from the questionable sources of fines and pre-

* *Joseph Salbank to the Company, November,* 1617. *India House Records.*

sents. Besides these, there was little else than the land-tax to recruit the royal treasury.* It would seem that in Akbar's reign, Upper India yielded more, and Lower India less, than at the present period. A comparison of the wealth of the different districts will be in some respects to our advantage; in others, to our disadvantage. But, on the whole, rightly estimated, the balance is not against us.†

There have necessarily been great changes, and of those changes advantage has been taken by writers eager to elevate the Mahomedan rule at the expense of that of the British Government in India. Doubtless, some once-prosperous places exhibit now no sign of prosperity—doubtless, there is nothing but waste and ruin visible in spots which were once smiling with cultivation, or stately with the evidences of mercantile wealth. But look at the state of England at the present time. If a traveller were

* It should be borne in mind that, under the government of the Mahomedan princes, the productiveness of the soil was more uncertain and accidental than under our own. The disturbed state of the country often caused large breadths of land to remain fallow for some years, and when they were again brought under cultivation, the yield was necessarily great.

† A very able writer in the *Calcutta Review* (Article, *The Life and Times of Akbar*) has given some interesting details of the relative amounts of revenue raised from different districts in Akbar's time and in our own:—"We will take at random the revenue of different zillahs in various parts of the kingdom, and the balance-sheet will be struck in our favor. Chittagong or Chatgaon, in Abul Fazl's scheme, paid three lakhs a year. Now, though over-run with jungle, and burdened with an extraordinary revenue and judicial establishment, it yields almost six. Purnea gave barely two: it now yields above twelve. Tirhut gave hardly five lakhs, and it now produces fourteen: Budaon shows us a balance of nine lakhs, and it gave eight in the time of Akbar: Allahabad presents a score of twenty-two with us, in opposition to seven with the Mogul. We have selected the above almost at a venture, and on the other hand it would be unfair not to mention several districts where the balance seems in favor of the old scheme. These, it may be augured, are mostly in Upper India, nor were the mighty resources of Bengal ever brought into full play by the Mahomedan sovereign or by the ablest of his viceroys. Kemaon, under the great financier of Akbar, paid in ten lakhs at least, and it is now set down as giving only two. Bahar showed twenty-one lakhs, and its actual land-revenue is probably about the same, and Agra, which is now thought rich at fifteen, is set down as giving the almost incredible return of fifty-one lakhs of rupees. [This, however, may be explained away. In the Subah were probably comprehended several smaller *Sircars* or zillahs, as Muttra, Furrukabad, Etawah, &c.] But our present great strength lies in the revenues of Bengal and Behar. Here we surpass the best days of the Mussulmans, and to this alone we trust for a *corps de reserve* when war or the expenses of a province unable to pay itself have drained the coffers of the state."

now to undertake a journey into the interior by road, he would stumble upon many signs of what, with equal candour and truth, might be declared to be evidences of the decadence of Great Britain. He would pass through many once-flourishing country towns, now in a state of visible desertion and prostration. He would enter once-magnificent caravanserais (posting-houses and hotels), on the spacious court-yards of which the grass is now growing. If the windows are not broken, and the house and the stables empty, the probability is that the traveller will find the many-roomed edifice inhabited by the ancient landlord, now a needy farmer, and the parish curate, who finds there permanent accommodation at a lower rent than is demanded by any other inhabitant of the place. The little town, which once was in a continual state of bustle and excitement, is now like a city of the silent. Little children play securely in the streets, unscared by the clanging hoofs of post-horses, or the smacking of post-boys' whips. But, for all this, England is not in a state of decay. The tide of traffic and the course of our pleasure-progresses run in a different direction. But if old towns are falling into decay, new ones are springing up. As it is in England, so is it in India. It would be as reasonable to declare that the prosperity of Great Britain is declining, because there are evidences of decay along the Great North Road, as to comment upon the decrepitude of the Indian Empire, because about the grand imperial highway from Delhi to Cashmere there are indications of a state of bygone road-side grandeur, in the shape of ruined caravanserais and wells. The similitude is not a perfect one, but its imperfections are decidedly to the disadvantage of my argument. The change is, in the one case, from a state of things in accordance with the interests of the people, to another state of things, under altered circumstances, advantageous to the interests of the people. In the other case, the change is from a state of things advantageous to the Emperor and his immediate followers, to a state of things advantageous to the general mass of the people. The evidences of decline which we see around us in India, are evidences, in reality, of little more than the decline of the paramount power of imperial selfishness. We need not much concern ourselves about such a decadence as this.

I have touched upon the subject of the relative amount of revenue raised under the Mogul dynasties and under the British-Indian Government. But of far more importance and interest than the question of the amount of revenue raised, is the question of the manner of its expenditure. I doubt whether the revenue actually collected under the most prosperous Mogul Government ever exceeded that now raised by our own. I am certain that, whatever the amount may have been, it was less beneficially expended. Now it is paid into what is emphatically called the *public* treasury. It is held in trust, and expended for the benefit of the people. But in the old times, much of the money collected from the people by legitimate, and much besides that was extorted from them by illegitimate means, was poured into the coffers of the Emperor and his dependents. Save in rare exceptional cases, there was a lavish waste of money on the costly accompaniments of a licentious Court—on dancing-girls and fighting animals, and pleasure-progresses and great panoramic camps. The contributions of the people were not sown, as it were, in the national soil, to spring up speedily again multiplied into a rich harvest. That which was taken from the husbandman did not return to him, but went, perhaps, to decorate the tail of a jewelled peacock, or to beautify the costly mosaic on the tomb of a Mussulman dame. It is very true that the English in India have erected no Taj-Mehals. If a Governor-General were to attempt to spend a tithe of the hundreds of thousands of pounds which the Taj is said to have cost, on the tomb of a defunct wife, he would be recalled long before the work could be completed, and impeached soon after his recall.

I have no wish to blacken the character of the Mahomedan Emperors. I am anxious to give them credit for all that they have done. But I am almost ashamed of myself for having spent so much time in showing—what is so patent to the unaided comprehension of all who have not contented themselves with ignorance or abandoned themselves to prejudice—the manifest inferiority, in the scale of benevolence and beneficence, of even the best of these Mahomedan despots, as rulers of Hindostan, to the most indolent and selfish of our own Governors-General. It is enough, indeed, to write that they were despots. Under such a despotism, the people could not have been prosperous or happy. There was no security for life or property. The luxurious selfishness of the Emperors depressed and enfeebled the people. It could not be otherwise. The country, indeed, is still prostrated by that great curse of Mogul tyranny. It has never recovered from the corrupting influences of the slavish fear which that great domination engendered. India owes the confirmed debasement of her morals, no less than her mosques and cenotaphs, to the Moguls. It may be that a conquered people are always, more or less, a false people—that it is not in the nature of men to be truthful with the yoke on their necks. But the form of government observed, and the character of the religion professed by the conquerors, must always regulate the degree to which political prostration is accompanied by moral debasement. Falsehood is the child of fear. And who can estimate the tremendous amount of falsehood against which the English legislator has now to contend?—falsehood which baffles the wisdom of the enlightened, and sets at nought the best efforts of the humane. The state of things which existed under the rule of the Mogul despots was too surely calculated to corrupt both Mahomedans and Hindoos—to perpetuate among both classes the selfishness and faithlessness which years of milder rule and more ennobling example have yet scarcely even begun to eradicate.

We found the people of India abject, degraded, false to the very core. Mussulman domination had called into full activity all the bad qualities which Hindooism has in itself a fatal tendency to generate. To the esoteric vices inseparable from such a religion were added the exoteric vices born of circumstances, injurious to any people, but to such a people fatal in the extreme. The faithlessness, if not engendered, aggravated, and perpetuated by Mussulman despotism, is now the grand stumbling-block of British legislation. There is hardly an hour of his official existence in which it does not present itself in the path of the Christian functionary, to impede his advance and embarrass his movements. It is as patent to him as the Taj-Mehal, or the Kootab-Minar; and, go where he will, it is sure to stare him in the face.

It has not been my object in this chapter to draw any regular comparison between the general features of Mahomedan rule and those of our own dominion in the East. There is one point of difference, which will readily present itself to the mind of even the most inexperienced reader. It will at once occur to him, that the Mussulman conqueror, though differing in religion, and to a certain extent in manners, from the Hindoo, was still a member of the same great Oriental family, and exhibited, in his ordinary intercourse with the inhabitants of the conquered land, as many points of resemblance as of difference, and even in the latter very often assimilated his own customs to those of the country of his adoption. He sat on the ground; he ate his dinner with his fingers; he covered his head and uncovered his feet in-doors; he secluded his women, and if he did not bring with him the same amount of regard for ceremonial observances, and the same rigid ideas on the subject of the cleanliness and uncleanliness of external things, he was very soon impregnated with them. The Mahomedan conqueror rapidly became Hindooised. He fused himself into the general mass of the people. He was not a Tartar, or an Afghan, but a Mahomedan Indian. India was his country; he was not merely in it, but of it. He, or his father, or some more remote ancestor, had emigrated thither, and had forgotten the country he had left behind. But between the English conqueror and his Hindoo subject there is an impassable gulf. There is nothing in common between them. The British gentlemen, who fill all the principal offices of the state, are not Christian Indians, but Christian Englishmen. They have brought their own costume and their own customs with them, and they keep them on the banks of the Ganges as they would on the banks of the Thames. They live alone—utterly separated from the mass of the people—and are surrounded with a prestige of superior wisdom and superior strength; but still, in many respects, an astonishment and a reproach in the eyes of our benighted brethren.

It is within the scope of this inquiry only to consider the very obvious difference of which I speak in relation to the happiness and prosperity of the people. And, on this point, it needs not that much should be said. The more you know of a man's circumstances—the more clearly you understand his character, and are acquainted with his feelings and opinions—the more familiar you are with his domestic habits, and the more unrestrained is your intercourse with him—the more good you may do him, if you will. But the greater, at the same time, is the injury which these advantages enable you to inflict upon him. Doubtless the orientalism of our Mahomedan predecessors might have wrought mightily for the benefit of the people of India, but it may be fairly doubted that it did. It was used rather as an engine of oppression than of protection. It manifested itself rather in arbitrary interference than in kindly concernment. It was insolent and magisterial, rather than tender and paternal in its demonstrations. If the familiarity of the Mahomedans with the language, the usages, the feelings, and opinions of the people of India had been associated with our own earnest and sustained desire to turn these advantages to account, great, doubtless, would have been the gain. But it was the study of the Mahomedans to turn them only to their own account, and they were rarely used as anything else than as instruments of extortion and oppression.

Apart from these considerations, it is probable that the points of resemblance between the conquerors and the conquered rendered the yoke more irritating and oppressive. The greater the difference between the master and the servant, the less intolerable is the state of servitude. But not merely upon this account is the latter less restless beneath it. It is certain that under the Mahomedan Governments the people were continually breaking out into revolt. Under the British Government internal rebellion is a thing almost unknown. I believe that this is in no small measure attributable to the approximation in the one case, and the divergence in the other, of which I have been speaking. When the difference between the master and the servant is slight, the latter is little able to understand why the relationship should exist, and little willing to suffer its continued existence. He does not recognise either the physical or the moral superiority which should place one in subjection to the other. And, therefore, he is restless under the yoke, and endeavors to cast it off. But when the master comes from a distance —from some far-off fabulous country—when he speaks another language, has another complexion, wears another dress, and comes with all the environments of wealth, and wisdom, and physical power, great alike in activity and endurance—the servant recognises the necessity of submission; his self-love is less wounded, he is more patient under the yoke. Now, if the yoke is to be borne at all, it cannot be borne too patiently. Every effort to cast it off increases the cost of the subjugation.

I have one more argument to notice in this chapter, which has swollen to a length which I did not contemplate at its commencement. It is said that if the people of India were happier under our rule than under that of their Asiatic conquerors, they would emigrate largely into the British provinces from those states, as Oude and Hyderabad, which are still under Asiatic domination. And it has been urged by a very high authority that this circumstance is to be attributed to the fact that, although under British rule there is more security and more tranquillity, our monopoly of all the chief offices of the state more than counterbalances these advantages, and deters men from seeking our protection. But it appears to me that we need not look further than the known character of the people of India for the cause of their immoveability and quiescence. The natives of India are not a migratory people. They are not an enterprising people. Apathy is one thing; content is another. Of the misgovernment of the Oude and Hyderabad provinces I need not speak in this place. It is argued that this misgovernment is submitted to, because the natives under native rule may rise to offices of dignity and emolument. But how little, after all, does this affect the happiness of the great mass of the people. It is small consolation to the husbandman whose crops are destroyed, or to the artisan whose house is burnt to the ground, that there is no law against his sitting as a judge, or commanding a regiment of horse. It is of far more importance to him that they who command regiments of horse should protect instead of oppressing, and that they who sit as judges should conscientiously administer justice to the people. It appears to me that the view taken of this matter by the Court of Directors of the East India Company is pre-eminently sound. "Facilities of official intercourse," they wrote in an admirable letter to the Supreme Government of India, enunciating their opinions respecting the interpretation of the Charter Act of 1834, "can little affect the bulk of the people under any government, and least under a good government. It is not by holding out incentives to official ambition, but by repressing crime, by securing and guarding property, by creating confidence, by ensuring to industry the fruit of its labors, by protecting men in the undisturbed enjoyment of their rights, and in the unfettered exercise of their faculties, that government best ministers to the public wealth and happiness. In effect, the free access to office is chiefly valuable when it is a part of general freedom."*

But it is time that this inquiry should cease. The paper upon which I have written these last pages has rested upon a folio "Blue Book," containing a return "of all public works which have been completed in India by the East India Company within the last ten years; including embankments, canals, and works of irrigation, roads and bridges, buildings, factories, docks, and all other public works."—"Also, a similar return of all public works now in progress in India (with the addition of any proposed railways), showing in each case the object of the work, the date of its commencement, and (where terminated) its termination, the amount of expense incurred, the amount estimated for completion, and the probable time of completion, of all

* *The Court of Directors to the Governor-General of India in Council, December* 10, 1834. *MS. Records.*

unfinished works; with such statements or documents as may be deemed necessary to explain or illustrate the above returns."—(Ordered by the House of Commons to be printed, August 1, 1851.) I shall have occasion to refer to this, in less general terms, in a subsequent portion of this work. In the mean while, there it is, as a solid argument in itself, against which little can be said by those who vaunt the superior beneficence of the Mahomedan Emperors, and discourse upon the short-comings of our British rule in the East. It may not be all that I could desire; but, even as it is, could Akbar and his famous minister, Abul Fazul, have brought out such a "Blue Book" as this?

Note.—Illustrative of what I have remarked, at page 39, on the subject of forced labor employed in the construction of the great public works of the native princes of India, I find a passage in Mr. Robertson's very interesting work, "Political Incidents of the First Burmese War," which I should have quoted in the right place had the volume been in existence when I was writing on the subject. Speaking of the remains of a great wall in Arracan, Mr. Robertson says: "It is always to be borne in mind, in drawing conclusions from the great doings of ancient rulers, of whom no other record remains, that the power unscrupulously exercised by the monarchs of those early days, at least in Asia and Africa, of compelling the whole mass of their subjects to devote their labors to the accomplishment of any favorite design, rendered it possible for a very feeble state to leave very bulky vestiges to excite the admiration and curiosity of succeeding generations. What ancient Egypt suffered that the Pyramids might rise no one can tell; and who thinks now of the 30,000 men, women, and children, said to have perished, since this century commenced, to accelerate the excavation of the canal connecting the Nile with Alexandria?" It was observed, too, by Lord Aberdeen, in the House of Lords, with reference to the "humiliating" fact of the "great works of the Mogul Emperors," that we "might as well draw an inference from the Pyramids of Egypt, and conclude that their builders were superior to us in moral qualifications." — [*Parliamentary Proceedings, March* 11, 1853.]

CHAPTER III.

Our European Predecessors—The Portuguese in India—The Dutch—Discouragements at the Outset—Progress of Empire—Our First Administrative Efforts—The Conquest of Bengal—Efforts of Clive and Hastings—The Regulating Act—Cornwallis and the Regulations—Subsequent Administrative Advances.

THERE is no need that, in pursuing the history of Indian Administration, I should treat in detail of the measures of our European predecessors on the great field of Eastern adventure. They were traders; they were conquerors; they were spoliators; they were proselytisers. But they were not administrators.

I would only speak of them in so far as their doings influenced the rise and progress of our own power in the East. On the last day of the sixteenth century the London East India Company became a substantial fact. The Portuguese had preceded us on the great pathways of the Eastern seas, and had even claimed a sort of exclusive right to the traffic of the far Indies. They had led the way to the great discoveries, by which other countries were eager to profit, and looked upon our merchant-ships as piratical interlopers. They had navigated and traded; they had fought and conquered; they had intrigued and proselytised, before the traders of London had met at Alderman Goddard's house or Founders' Hall, and taken measures to equip certain vessels of their own "upon a pure mercantile bottom." The commercial enterprise of the substantial Flemings, too, had been roused into activity before our own, and they sent out their heavy vessels to the spice-islands before we had done more than talk about it. When, therefore, we fairly started as adventurers in the Eastern seas, we had rivals to cope with, whose antagonism cannot be estimated by those who would measure it in accordance with the relative powers of the three nations in the middle of the present century.

The progress of the Portuguese on the Continent of India had been rapid and dazzling. But the seeds of decay had been planted deep in the constitution of the Indo-Lusitanian power from its birth. Encouraged by the first successes of their countrymen, all kinds of adventurers, bound by no laws, and restrained by no scruples, flooded into the country, and made a deluge of licentiousness wherever they went. Soldiers swaggered, and priests crept about the seaports. Forts and churches rose up at their bidding. Strong in numbers, with all the muniments and equipments of war by sea and by land, they had no need to crouch to the native princes and humbly solicit their protection. Insolence and violence were the characteristics of the "braggard Portugals," and for a little while they carried everything before them.

It is not easy to arrive at a just conception of the extent of Portuguese immigration in the sixteenth and seventeenth centuries. Some, at least, of the statements illustrative of this subject should be received with extreme caution. It is related, for example, that when the Moguls attacked Hooghly, where the Portuguese were garrisoned, in 1632, ten thousand of the latter fell in the course of the siege. Such statements as these may be safely discarded. The stamp of exaggeration is too plainly upon them to suffer us to hesitate about their rejection. But when every allowance is made for these over-charged traditions, it still remains to be accredited that Portugal poured her thousands into India in the sixteenth and seventeenth centuries, and that a large proportion of them were desperate and unscrupulous adventurers, who loved neither God nor Man.

The evil influence of the Portuguese was, in those early days, recited as the main hindrance to our advancement in the East. But it only kept us in check for a time to contribute to our ultimate greatness. At first, it would seem that the native powers, already alarmed and irritated by the fortifying of the Portuguese, had done their best to restrain a like evil habit in the new tribe of Feringhees; but they began, after a while, to understand that the countrymen of Hawkins and Roe could fight as well by sea and land as the descendants of Albuquerque; and it was conjectured that we might expel the lawless intruders, who had plundered their towns, massacred their people, and broken their idols without remorse. These things were in our favor. And whatever reproaches we may rightfully heap on the iniquitous career of the Lusitanian conquerors, this much at least must be conceded to them, that they were the first to breast the heady torrent of Mussulman usurpation in Hindostan, and to destroy the prestige of the invincibility of the Mogul. It was no light thing to bring the skill and enterprise of western civilisation face to face with the embodiment of that great Mahomedan power, which, streaming from its wild home in Central Asia, had overrun so many countries, and absorbed so many principalities. It was no light thing to drive a thorn into the flesh which had swollen so proudly under the influence of years of unbroken prosperity, and to raise festering anxieties and misgivings where before had been only security and triumph.

It is clear to me that the errors of the Portuguese wrought mightily to our advantage. Not that we voluntarily profited by them in the way of example, but that we were compelled to avoid the excesses into which they had hurried themselves, and those very excesses tended to facilitate our gradual progress. We have established ourselves in India, because our progress has been gradual. Whilst we were slowly advancing step by step, the Portuguese Empire in India was rapidly falling to pieces. We need not look to any foreign sources for the cause of its decline and fall. The enmity of the Dutch may have precipitated the event, but sooner or later it must have fallen to pieces by the innate force of its own corruption.

Outwardly these Flemish adventurers, who were so eager to grapple with the Portuguese, were our allies. But they were false friends, and, as such, more dangerous than open enemies. Our own seamen and factors had from the first been suspicious of the designs of these "honest Dutch," and had written one to another, from our insular establishments, warning them that they were "our enemies to the utter ruin of our trade, so far as their power will give them leave."* And this was very soon apparent. They obstructed us, and dictated to us. They compelled us to do what we did not wish, and prevented us from doing what we did. They committed excesses, and we paid the penalty of them in vicarious forfeitures and imprisonments. They wronged us, and lorded it over us; and we were perpetually seeking redress at home and abroad, but never succeeded even in obtaining an instalment of tardy justice. According to all human calculations at this time, the Dutch were about to establish a great empire in India, and the English were about to be driven ignominiously into new fields of enterprise in another quarter of the globe. All that the Company could do at this time was to maintain a gasping existence against the threatened danger of total destruction. But the very obstructions which

* *Letter of George Ball, from Macassar, to Bantam. India House Records.*

seemed to menace the life of the Company were the elements of its permanent success.

For these very discouragements, which beset the Company at the commencement of their career, averted envy and compelled caution, and were therefore their protection and support. If India had really embraced within its limits the "*arva beata divites et insulas*," which the imaginations of our countrymen pictured to them so luxuriantly at the dawn of the seventeenth century—if the traffic had been as profitable, if the fields of adventure had been as alluring in reality as in expectation—if the young men of good family who went out in our early fleets had met with brave entertainment from the native princes, and had sent home dazzling accounts of their marvellous success, there would soon have been an end of the Company. A little cluster of London merchants could never have kept in their own hands the privilege of exclusive trade with the far Indies, if it had not been that this privilege appeared to be little worth contesting. The Company were opposed abroad and vilified at home. Their dividends were unexpectedly low. Their shares were at a discount. Their factors wrote home that English goods "would not vent among the Gentiles;" and the Lord Ambassador, whom King James sent out to the Mogul, protested that "the country was mistaken." This embassy seemed for a time to raise the dignity of Indian adventure, and to give an impetus to the ignorant ambition of the unprofitable classes at home. But they soon discovered the error they had committed, and returned home to report that there was no hopeful entertainment for them in the kingdom of the Great Mogul. The war in the Low Countries gave better prospect of employment to our younger sons. And so, in this the seeming hopelessness of Indian enterprise, lay strong and deep all our hope. If the Company's monopoly had not been preserved we should have established no Indian Empire.

Not that the Company ever thought of empire. The London merchants, who looked anxiously for the return of their rich argosies, when the Stuarts sat in Whitehall, and the Moguls ruled the empire of Hindostan from the Peacock throne of Delhi, were no more than adventurous traders. They were never stirred by dreams of conquest, or perplexed by projects of government. Their wildest speculations were bounded by the vision of a few factories within sight of the white surf of the southern and western coasts, or washed by the dark waters of the Ganges. They were settlers only by sufferance of the native princes, of whom they stood in continual awe; and it would have seemed as impossible to them to reduce the "Great Mogul" to a pensioner and a suppliant, as to float the continent of Hindostan into the British Channel, and annex it materially to the British Isles.

In all their counsels at home—in all their instructions to their servants abroad—the trader was everywhere dominant. It was their policy to retain the slightest possible hold of the soil—to encumber themselves with as little as possible that they could not carry off at a moment's notice. They hated the thought of an increase of "dead stock." The multiplication of factories was odious to them; and a fort was an abomination. They looked only for a brisk trade and a good dividend. And although for "neglecting to establish fortified factories"* they were nearly losing their monopoly altogether, they reprehended their servants abroad for thinking of territorial acquisition and military defence. Indeed, so little did it seem to them that there was any chance of ever fighting with the natives of India, that, during the war of succession at the end of Shah Jehan's reign, they exported ordnance and ordnance-stores "on a pure mercantile bottom," calculating that there would be a demand

* This was one of the grounds assigned for the grant of the charter to Courten's Association.

for such articles of merchandise, and that the royal princes would pay highly for goods which they could turn to such profitable account. But the disposal of events was far beyond the reach of that little handful of London merchants. All things were working quietly, but powerfully, when least they thought it, towards the establishment of that great empire of the Merchant Princes which now stretches from Peshawur to Pegu.

Eager as the Company were, and earnestly as they tried, to limit the number of their factories, the number continued to increase. Expansion seemed to be the natural law which governed our position in the East. From the Bombay coast, where the Company's factors first settled themselves, they made their way by land to Agra, then rounded Cape Cormorin, settled themselves on the coast of Madras, and soon stretched up the Bay of Bengal, to establish themselves in that rich province.* This was not the result either of commercial cupidity or territorial ambition. Naturally disposed towards slow and cautious movement, the Company were hurried onward by an irresistible power, which made them, in spite of themselves, Merchant Princes and great territorial Lords. Wonderful, indeed, was the manner in which the road was cleared for the advance of the Company. Everything was falling to pieces and decaying around them. The Mogul power was crumbling at their feet. The Portuguese Empire was rotting away, devoured by worms and maggots—a filthy mass of corruption. Nothing had any vitality and progressiveness in it, except that little body of London merchants, which seemed beyond the reach of human accident to damage or to repress. Heavy blows and great discouragements gave them only new courage and

* It was not, however, considered a rich province in the early days of British adventure. Our factors looked askance at it. "Bengalla," they wrote, "is a hot country—the most of the people very poor Gentiles." — [*MS. Records of the East India Company.*]

new strength. He whose ways are not our ways wrought for them deliverance out of peril—power out of weakness—victory out of defeat. There is no more instructive lesson in all history than this. The great structure of our Indian Empire has been reared as no human intellect would have designed, and no human hands would have fashioned it. It has been reared for us as for a chosen people, and mighty is the responsibility which a trust so imposed upon us entails. The more we consider all the circumstances of the Rise and Progress of the British power in the East, the more palpable and obstinate appears the scepticism which would attribute so stupendous and mysterious a movement to anything but the special interference of an almighty Providence for a purpose commensurate with the grandeur of the design.

It is not the object of this work to trace the triumphs of British arms and the extension of our territorial dominion. I have here to do only with matters of internal administration, and I assume the possession by the reader of a general knowledge of the salient events of Anglo-Indian history, from the day on which Captain Best wrote to the Company, "we have settled in Surat," to the time when Lord Dalhousie announced the annexation of Pegu.* We traded; we conquered; we governed. It was long before this matter of government came very palpably before us. At first, all that we had to do was to govern ourselves, and this we did in a very loose manner—rather according to laws of power and impulses of passion, than to principles of justice and reason. At the outset of our career the Company's factors were under the immediate orders of their own chiefs—Surat being the seat of the central authority—but the "General," or commander of the Fleet, seems to

* We had a factory of old in Pegu—but it was soon abandoned. Our traders used to report that the country was full of rubies.

have had a controlling power. The factors complained that he regulated their promotion,* and that the captains of his ships sat in their councils and interfered with their affairs.† As the British population of Surat consisted, in no small measure, of the people of the Fleet, perhaps this fusion of the two authorities was not altogether unreasonable or inexpedient. The consultations were often held on board the ships in the Roads; and the chief of the factory signed his name after that of the principal naval officer.

The laws under which our people lived at this time were necessarily two-sided. In regard to all our transactions with the native inhabitants of the place, we were subject to the judicial tribunals of the country. On the first establishment of our factory at Surat, Captain Best, in his treaty with the Viceroy, had stipulated that "in all questions, wrongs and injuries that shall be offered to us and to our nation, we do receive from the judges and those that be in authority speedy justice, according to the quality of our complaints and wrongs done us, and that by delays we be not put off or wearied by time or charge."‡ But our people had no great liking for these native courts, and when it could be done without manifest danger, took the law into their own hands. Among themselves justice was administered in criminal cases by virtue of a King's commission under the Great Seal, which empowered the Commissioners to punish and

* Joseph Salbank, one of the oldest of our factors, wrote home to the Company in 1617, complaining "that your proud Captain Keeling, towards whom I have ever carried myself very genteelly, or rather more humbly than I ought to have done, should offer me that indignity as to place me under punies and younglings to whom, for my years' sake, I might be esteemed grandfather—yea, this he did, though he never saw them to whom he gave precedence above me."—[*MS. India House Records.*]

† "Whereby the way your worships may be pleased to take notice, that it may be a thing of ill consequence, when you make commanders of ships to be of your Council of India, though to be consulted without by your President and Council in some things, especially such as concerns sea-affairs, hath been their continual practice, and is also very necessary."—[*F. G. Merry to the Company, January*, 1649. *MS. India House Records.*]

‡ *MS. India House Records.*

execute offenders by martial law.* In civil cases the will of the President or Chief of the Factory seems to have been absolute.

As our factories increased in number, there became a divided authority and control. The establishments on the western coast and in the interior of the peninsula were subordinate to Surat, whilst those on the Coromandel coast were off-shoots from, and subject to, the factory at Bantam. But the Company's servants in India recommended a system of greater centralisation. "We are told," they wrote, "to declare our opinions that your affairs, like those of other nations which are far greater, would be best managed if they were submitted under one government, which you might place at your pleasure either at Bantam or here (Surat), as you shall find to stand with your most conveniency."† It could hardly be questioned whether the central authority could be fixed more expediently at Surat or Bantam. The importance of our insular establishments had been great, when it was doubtful whether we should be able to

* And this power was exercised too. I find among the Surat consultations, as far back as February, 1616, the following record of criminal proceedings:

"Consultations held on board the ship *Charles*, dated Swally Road, Feb. 28, 1616. Present, Captain H. Pepwell, Chief Commander of the fleet, &c.

"Whereas Gregory Lellington had on Sunday, the 16th of February last past, in or near the town of Surat in the dominions of the Mogul, killed Henry Barton, Englishman, and belonging to the company of the good ship the *James*, then riding in or near the Road of Swally, it was concluded by the council aforesaid, that the said Lellington should be called to answer for the said murder; which being effected, the King's Majesty's Commission, under the Great Seal, in point of authority and power to punish and execute by martial law, where need required, was read publicly before the prisoner, and that done it was laid to his charge as followeth." [Here follow the crimes with which he was charged.] "Wherefore the said Gregory Lellington being convicted by his own confession, it was generally resolved on, that as well in respect of the offence itself as for example and prevention of others in the like, that he should suffer pains of death whereof he received judgment by the mouth of the Chief Commander, which was (according to his own desire), that he should the next day be conveyed ashore, and by the musketeers of the guard be shot to death—and so the Lord have mercy upon his soul.—Signed Henry Pepwell (Chief Commander of the fleet) — Thomas Kerridge, *Chief of the Factory*, &c."—[*MS. India House Records.*] I have given this at length, as the earliest account of our judicial proceedings in India with which I am acquainted.

† *William Tremlen and others to the Company*, *Jan.* 4, 1638. *MS. India House Records.*

establish a trade with the continent of India, but it had continued gradually to decline as our factories took root on the great Indian peninsula, and we had become more willing to leave the island trade to the Dutch. Surat was therefore erected into a presidency. As time advanced, the control of the naval authorities was shaken off; and the President at Surat became the chief representative of the Company in the East.

The power which this officer possessed was great; and it was often fearfully abused. Everything depended upon the personal character of the man; and the Company were not always fortunate in their representatives.* But great local changes were now impending. In 1653 the settlement of Madras, or, as it was now officially known, of Fort St. George, was erected into a presidency. In 1668 the island of Bombay, which had formed a portion of the dowry of the Infanta on her marriage to our second Charles, was granted to the Company, and placed under the government of the Company's servants. It soon began to rise into importance. But at this time Bengal, which has now dwarfed the other Indian presidencies, held the lowest place in the scale, and was subordinate to the Presidency of Madras. It was not until the year 1715 that it was created an independent presidency, under the name of the Presidency of Fort William.† Our first efforts at improved administration were made upon the western coast.

On the first grant of Bombay to the Company, a Governor was appointed, with a Council, from among the members of which a Deputy-Governor was to be selected by the chiefs. But this Council was held subordinate to

* It appears to me that as time advanced, the character of the chiefs, or presidents, rather deteriorated than improved. The earliest were among the best—Mr. Thomas Kerridge, for example, the first chief of Surat, seems to have been a man of great integrity and ability.

† In 1699 the villages of Chuttanuttee (or Calcutta) and Govindpore were granted to the Company. Sir Charles Eyre was sent out as chief agent in Bengal, with instructions to build a fort, which, in honor of the reigning monarch, was called Fort William.

the Presidents and Council of Surat, and in the following year an effort was made by the Court of Directors to place upon some better and more substantial footing the general administrative agency of their several settlements. It was then determined that the central authority should consist of a President at Surat, with a Council of eight members, five of whom were to reside permanently at the Presidency.* In this year, 1669-70, two Courts of Judicature were established at Bombay. The lower Court was presided over by one of the Company's civil officers; and the other, which was a Court of Appeal, was composed of the Deputy-Governor and members of Council.† The Deputy-Governor and three military officers were to constitute a Court for the administration of martial law. The Court of Directors took this matter of the legal tribunals into their serious consideration at this time; and were anxious, whenever it was possible, that trial by jury should be the practice in force. At the same time they recommended the establishment of a mint. But they were extremely jealous of the growth of military influence at their settlements, and turned their soldiers into civilians and their civilians into soldiers at discretion; that the pure military element might not anywhere assert itself in dangerous predominance.‡

There was another advantage, too, in this. It appeared to the Company that indifferent book-keepers and accountants might make very decent soldiers; and that if their civilians were trained to arms, an occasional hard bargain might be got rid of by the gift of a military commission. Three-quarters of a century afterwards the force of this reasoning met with the most remarkable

* *Bruce.*
The writer adds: "This plan merits particular notice, from being the first example of a regular constitution, with chiefs, in the Company's foreign dependencies."

† In 1672-73 the President and Council recommended the establishment of a police force at Bombay.

‡ Mr. Bruce relates that one Captain Shacton, who was sent to Bombay in command of troops, was made a factor forthwith, "that he might combine his military with his civil duties."

illustration to be found in the history of the world. There was a young man at Madras, who had gone out as a writer on the establishment, but who made no great progress with accounts, and exhibited no very warm passion for the ledger. But he had been described, when a boy, as one "out of measure addicted to fighting," and no sooner were our settlements on the coast threatened by the enmity of our French rivals than he pushed aside the ledger, accepted a military commission—and laid, broad and deep, the foundation of our British Empire in the East.

The only recognised substantive service at the close of the seventeenth century, was what is now known as the Civil Service; and that the Court of Directors were eager, in those early days, to organise after a fashion of their own—a fashion, which was preserved unchanged long after the English had become the lords-paramount of the Indian world. The gradations of Writers, Factors, Merchants, and Senior Merchants were then established, and the names of the Company's servants enrolled in a regular seniority list.* They passed, however, from one presidency to another; and, it sometimes happened, that when any emergency arose—when the Company's servants were at strife among themselves, or the trade of any particular agency was embarrassed—that the Directors sent out one of their own body, or a relative of one of their chief members, to bring matters to a favorable adjustment. It appears, too, to have been

* The following are the service regulations as contained in the Court's letters:—"For the advancement of our apprentices we direct that, after they have served the first five years, they shall have 10*l.* per annum for the last two years; and having served those two years, to be entertained one year longer as writers, and have writers' salary; and having served that year, to enter into the degree of factors, which otherwise would have been ten years. And knowing that a distinction of titles is, in many respects, necessary, we do order that when the apprentices have served their times, they be styled *writers;* and when the writers have served their times, they be styled *factors;* and factors, having served their times, to be styled *merchants;* and merchants having served their times, to be styled *senior merchants.*"

very much the custom, even in those early days when the mercantile affairs of the Company were in a bad way—when trade was slack and money was scarce, or when their dead stock was consuming their revenue, to send out instructions to reduce the pay of their servants, and so to save a few hundreds a year.* This was not the way to obtain good service, and to keep the Factors and Merchants from trading on their own accounts at a greater loss to the Company than would have been entailed upon them if they had doubled, instead of reduced, the salaries of their servants.

It is in the records of the year 1679-80 that I trace, for the first time, anything like a scheme of general administration, embracing the whole question of Inland Revenue. In that year instructions were sent out to the Local Government to make Bombay discharge its own civil and military expenses. A duty was to be levied on the houses in the island; and the land was to be surveyed and assessed — or rather let out on lease. There was a dim idea, too, even in those days, of the development of the resources of the country by means of artificial works, and a system of drainage was recommended, by which the low marshy grounds of the Bombay island might be rendered fit for cultivation.

In 1681-82, Bengal was established as a distinct agency, with instructions to communicate immediately with the Court of Directors. This arrangement, however, did not last long. The chief Agent, who had been sent out directly by the Court, mismanaged affairs and misconducted himself; and Bengal was accordingly brought back again to its old subordination to Madras. About

* For example, in 1678-79, orders went out to reduce the pay of the President of Surat to 300*l.* a year, and to change his title to that of *Agent.* The senior member of Council was to have 80*l.* per annum; and the Deputy-Governor of Bombay 120*l.* The entire expenses of Bombay, civil and military, were limited to 7000*l.* a year. The result of these measures was a rebellion, headed by the chief military officer, which well-nigh lost Bombay to the Company altogether.

the same time Bombay was constituted an independent settlement, and in 1685-86 it was erected into the chief seat of the British power in the East Indies, whilst Surat, with a subordinate Agent and Council, was reduced to a Factory. In April, 1686, a new charter was granted to the Company, confirming all their former privileges, and further empowering them to erect courts of judicature, to exercise martial law, and coin money at a mint of their own. The establishment of a mint had long before been recommended to the Company by their servants abroad; and it had been much considered and discussed, but had never before taken practical shape. It was now, however, actually to pass into a fact by the express permission of the Crown. The Company regarded it simply as an instrument of trade, but their servants, five-and-twenty years before, had been looking at the matter of a Tankshall in the Deccan, in connexion with the question of war.*

In 1687, Bombay, in imitation of the more ambitious style of the Portuguese and the Dutch, was elevated to the dignity of a Regency, and the Governor was created General-in-Chief of all our Indian settlements. This was a matter, however, merely of outward titles and dignities. It is of more importance to record, that at this time Madras was formed into a corporation, with a Mayor

* The factors at Rajapore—Henry Revington and others—wrote, in 1659, during the war of succession, recommending the Company to take advantage of the weakness engendered by this internecine strife, to coin money and make war on the Mogul. "For your worships may please to know," they said, "that all these artificial mines of money which were made in time of peace, are now exhausted through a civil war; and what better time than now to make them sensible of the benefit they have for many years received from you, and likewise of the injuries, oppressions, and wrongs, that you have received from them, which would be a good time to call them to account for, when your worships shall think fit to call the Persian to account for his (and both together must be, if ever you call the latter to account)? Will it not be necessary to have a Tankshall in the Deccan, and a coin that will be current to carry on a trade here, as large as you please, during your war with India, which will continue no longer than you please? . . . Then judge if you would not make the Tankshall cry as mournful to the King of India's ears as the liver, the fountain of blood, should complain in a natural body, and then what conditions you may bring him to, is easy to foretel."—[*MS. India House Records.*]

and Aldermen on the English model. But the charter of incorporation came not from the King himself, under the Great Seal, but under the seal of the Company. Already had it been seen, in the case of legal no less than of military officers bearing commissions direct from the Crown, that, in the words of the Court, "the wind of extraordinary honor in their heads made them haughty and overbearing." The Company, jealous of such interference, argued against the use of the Great Seal, and maintained their ground with such good effect, that they carried the point in Council, and the Charter, under their own seal, was duly engrossed, and sent out to Madras.*

I set these things down in a fragmentary insequential manner, because there is nothing of a sustained character —no evidences of any comprehensive design—in these early efforts of the Company at civil administration. But it was about the period which I have now reached that they began to think seriously of their position in India—not merely as traders, but as representatives of a great nation. The power of the Mogul had sensibly diminished as their own power had increased. They had become more conscious of their strength, and had begun to weary of subservience to the native princes. Indeed, it had become apparent that these proud Mussulmans were no such formidable enemies after all. The enemies whom they most dreaded at this time were much nearer at home. A rival Company was starting up. The seas were bristling with interlopers. The Company's own servants were conniving at the piratical trade. The mer-

* "The corporation of Madras, under this charter, were to consist of a mayor and ten aldermen (three to be Company's servants and seven to be natives), who were to be justices of the peace, and to wear thin silk scarlet gowns, and of one hundred and twenty burgesses, to wear black silk gowns; a town clerk and a recorder were to be appointed, and all the subordinate officers were to be elected by the mayor and aldermen, subject to the approbation of the president. A sword and mace were to be carried before the mayor, and a silver one before the judge-advocate. A record was to be kept of their proceedings, and regularly transmitted to the Court."—[*Bruce's Annals of the East India Company.*]

cantile prosperity of the old corporation was threatened, and with their increased establishments and accumulated dead stock they were naturally alarmed by the thought of the loss of their commercial profits. Thus situated, they turned their thoughts with increased anxiety to the matter of revenue, the importance of which had been greatly enhanced by the jeopardy of the trade. "The increase of our revenue," they wrote out to Bombay, "is the subject of our care as much as our trade; 'tis that must make us a nation in India—without that we are but as a great number of interlopers, united by his Majesty's Royal Charter, fit only to trade where nobody of power thinks it their interest to prevent us—and upon this account it is that the wise Dutch, in all their general advices which we have seen, write ten paragraphs concerning their government, their civil and military policy, warfare, and the increase of their revenue, for one paragraph they write concerning trade."* The drift of this is not that the Company had become ambitious, but that the trade had become precarious. It appeared to be a necessity to think of revenue, if they were to maintain their position at all. But the national phase of the question would not have forced itself upon them with this urgency if there had been more hopefulness in the aspects of their commercial life.

Indeed, all this talk about the wise Dutch, their military establishments and their warfare, seems to have been little more than a spasmodic outbreak of bitterness incited by the evil circumstances of the trade, for instead of increasing their armaments, we find the Company at this time reducing them. They were wise enough,

* Mr. Mill, quoting this passage, says: "It thus appears at how early a period, when trade and sovereignty were blended, the trade, as was abundantly natural, but no less unfortunate, became an object of contempt, and from an object of contempt by necessary consequence an object of neglect." But, it appears to me, that it had become not an object of contempt, or an object of neglect, but an object of uncertainty. If the trade had not been in jeopardy, these paragraphs would never have been written.

however, to look after their revenue and exert themselves to improve the internal condition of their settlements—they kept a steady eye on the municipal institutions of Madras—approved of the erection of a new Town-hall, "recommended that a Post-office and an Insurance-office should be established, and repeated their instructions to offer encouragement to artists who were eminent for ornamenting cloths, to settle at the Fort."* To accomplish these objects, the "revenue was to be increased." But the Company's servants do not appear to have been very successful in this department, and circumstances were greatly against them, for we are told that, at this time, the revenue of Bombay had fallen down to less than a third of its previous amount. External enemies and internal disputes had embarrassed their fiscal proceedings; and the Company's debt continued to increase.

Those were cloudy days for the Company at the end of the seventeenth century. They had made their way, for a hundred years, against all kinds of impediments and obstructions, foreign and domestic, and now a greater peril than any stared them obtrusively in the face. The interlopers, under shelter of a needy Government, glad to sell any privileges or patents for which they could obtain purchasers, were consolidated into a chartered company, which was intended to supplant the centenarian association which had planted its settlements along the whole coast of the Indian peninsula. But the old Company did not lose heart. Allowed by their constitution three years of grace, they determined to make the best use of their time, and to battle it out manfully with the intruders, still hopeful of driving them from the field.† In the discreditable contest which then

* *Bruce's Annals.*

† They wrote out to their servants in India that "two East India Companies in England could no more subsist than two kings at the same time regnant in the two kingdoms—that now a civil battle was to be fought between the old and new Company, and that two

ensued, all thought of the improvement of the internal administration of our settlements was swallowed up. The two Companies obstructed each other; injured each other; maligned each other. And the character of the nation suffered in the eyes of the princes and people of India. But the old Company had wisely predicted that such a contest could not last long, although they did not foresee the manner in which it would be brought to a close. I need not add that a compromise was effected; that the two Companies, sinking their animosities and making arrangements about their stocks, were consolidated into one; and that in the year 1702 the "United Company of Merchants trading to the East India" was prospectively incorporated under the Great Seal.*

The evil that this unseemly strife had engendered "lived after it." The violence of the Companies' servants in India did not easily subside. Whilst the affairs of the two associations were being wound up, preparatory to their practical incorporation as one joint stock, all sorts of outrages were committed. There was no law, there was no decency. The revenue fell off. The administration was at a stand-still. They were evil days for the dignity of Indian adventure. But when, in 1709, the United Company were fairly in operation, a brighter day began to dawn. The trade of the Company revived; their administrative affairs recovered something of order and regularity. At all events, there was no open scandal of a very notorious kind. Of government, as we under-

or three years must end this war, as the old or the new must give way—that being veterans, if their servants abroad would do their duty, they did not doubt of the victory — that if the world laughed at the pains the two Companies took to ruin each other, they could not help it, as they were on good ground and had a charter—that when the three years expired, still they had revenues and possessions, and had a share in the new Company's stock, to the amount of 315,000*l.*, and were therefore entitled to trade annually to that amount."—[*The Court of Directors to the Council of Bengal, August* 26, 1698. *Bruce's Annals.*]

* The union was not completed until 1709. The intervening years were devoted to the winding up of the concerns of the two Companies, under a committee of management at home, composed of equal numbers of members belonging to the two associations.

stand it, in these days there was little. We did not get much beyond temporary shifts and expedients. There was no system; no uniformity. During the first quarter of the eighteenth century there was a Court of Justice at Bombay, and one at Madras, known as the Mayor's Court; but in Bengal there was none. The records of these courts contain some curious illustrations of the morals and manners of the early settlers, and of the natives, Portuguese and Indian, who clustered round them at the presidencies. The people in whose cases they adjudicated were for the most part the public or private servants of the settlers themselves, or people connected with the shipping in the ports. The Court carried on all kinds of business. It was at once a civil, a criminal, a military, and a prerogative court. It proceeded with remarkable promptitude and despatch, from the proving of a will to the trial of a murderer; from the settlement of a dispute regarding the sale of a slave-girl to the punishment of a drunken trooper or an extortionate witch. Flogging was the usual remedy prescribed. It was one of general application, and fell with the greatest impartiality on all offenders, old and young, male and female alike.*

But it was not on the southern or western coasts, but on the banks of the Hooghly, on those low lands of which our first settlers spoke contemptuously as of a hot country inhabited by very poor Gentiles, that in the early part of the eighteenth century there was made the greatest administrative progress. In the year 1715, as I have said, the English settlements in Bengal were erected into an independent Presidency; and some ten years afterwards a Mayor's Court was established in Calcutta, which had become the chief place of our trade in that part of the world. But we

* *MS. India House Records of the Mayor's Court of Madras and Court of Justice of Bombay.*

had become by this time Zemindars, or landed-proprietors, under the Soubahdar of Bengal, and, in this capacity, with the consent of the native Government, we had erected a criminal court, a civil court, and a revenue court in the neighbourhood of Calcutta, for the management of our affairs with the people located upon our estates. The CUTCHERRY, indeed, was fast becoming an English institution. The Company's servants were rising into administrative importance as heaven-born judges and territorial financiers. They constituted themselves tribunals for the trial of their own causes; they had power without responsibility, and dealt in judgments without law. They had liberty to fine, to imprison, to sentence to labor on the roads, but they could not hang the subjects of the Mogul. The lash, however, took the place of the gibbet, and malefactors were whipped into another world by the manual skill of the native flagellants.

From this time, up to the eventful day when Robert Clive, in the heavy turban and loose trousers of a Mogul, escaped from Madras to Pondicherry, and turned his back for ever on the drudgery of the desk, no very noticeable events, bearing upon the progress of English government in India, present themselves for specific mention. But great events were now hurrying the English into an open manifestation of national power, and their territorial possessions, from obscure farms, were fast swelling into rich principalities. Clive and his little army appeared before Fort William, and the power of the Soubahdar of Bengal was broken by a handful of English strangers. The French, who had been contending with us for the European mastery of the southern coast of India, had taught us how to discipline the natives of the country, and we had learnt that these hireling troops would be true to the hand that gave them their salt. The first great battle ever fought by the English in India placed Bengal at our feet. In a little while, the Dewannee, or administration of the provinces of Bengal, Behar, and Orissa, with all their wealth, was placed at our disposal by a power no longer able to stem the irresistible tide of European domination; and territorial revenue now began to take a substantial place in the considerations of the East India Company, and to attract the delicate regards of the Crown.

But although, in 1765, the revenues of these provinces became our own, motives of policy, natural but short-sighted, impelled Clive to leave the actual administration in the hands of the old native functionaries to be carried on in the name of the Soubahdar. It seemed expedient that we should be content with the unambitious part of gorging ourselves upon the revenues of the Dewannee, and leaving all the responsibility, and all the danger of its internal management and its external defence, in the hands of the native power. "The first point in politics which I offer to your consideration," he wrote to the Select Committee in 1767, "is the form of government. We are sensible that since the acquisition of the Dewannee, the power formerly belonging to the Soubah of these provinces is totally, in fact, vested in the East India Company. Nothing remains to him but the name and shadow of authority. This name, however, this shadow, it is indispensably necessary that we should venerate. Under the sanction of a Soubah, every encroachment that may be attempted by foreign powers can effectually be crushed, without any apparent interposition of our own authority, and all real grievances complained of by them can, through the same channel, be examined into and redressed. Be it, therefore, always remembered that there is a Soubah; and that though the revenues belong to the Company, the territorial jurisdiction must still rest in the chiefs of the country, acting under him, and thus presiding in conjunction. To appoint the Company's servants to the offices of collectors, or, indeed, to do any act by any exertion of the English power, which can equally be done by the nabob at our instance, would be throwing off the mask, would be declaring the Company Soubah of the Province. Foreign nations would immediately take umbrage, and complaints preferred to the British Court might be attended with very embarrassing consequences."* It seemed, indeed, inconvenient at this time to do anything but swallow the emoluments of power; its risks and responsibilities were to be studiously ignored. We were to remember whenever there was an emergency, that there was a Soubahdar.

But the mask had its pains and penalties, too; it did not sit easily upon us, and it was now soon to be discarded. Old Mr. Holwell, who had escaped the destroying horrors of the Black Hole, to write pleasant "tracts" in England, which now, after the lapse of nearly a century, are still to be read with interest, had protested strongly against this "ringing changes on Soubahs," from the first. "Let us boldly dare," he exclaimed, "to be Soubahs ourselves." "We have nibbled at these provinces," he added, "for eight years, and notwithstanding an immense acquisition—an immense acquisition of territory and revenue—what benefit has resulted from our successes, to the Company? Shall we then go on nibbling and nibbling at the bait, until the trap falls and crushes us?" He wrote this, and much more, in the same strain, in

* Clive had been appointed in 1764 President and Governor in Bengal, with a Select Committee of four gentlemen. They were empowered to act upon their own authority, independently of the existing Council. The Council endeavoured to resist their authority; but Clive beat down all opposition.

1765, just as Clive was receiving the Dewannee from the Soubahdar and the Emperor; but we still continued "to ring changes on Soubahs," and to nibble at the administration of the country. The collection of the revenue, and the administration of justice, were at first left uncontrolledly in the hands of the native officers. It was found that, in every respect but the promotion of their own interests, they were utterly inefficient. It would be difficult, indeed, to exaggerate the vices of such a system. Natives and Europeans alike took advantage of it. There was no responsibility and no control. The strong preyed upon the weak—and the weak had none to look up to for protection. Misgovernment brought its wonted bitter fruit, and the revenue soon began to decline. So, in 1769, European supervisors were appointed as a check to the native functionaries. The most elaborate instructions were issued to them. It is hard to say what they were not expected to do;—but still the double government continued to work grievously. And there were those who thought that the supervisors only made confusion worse confounded and corruption more corrupt.*

After all due abatement made for the rhetorical exaggerations of florid writers and speakers, it is not to be denied that our administrative agency was at this time exceedingly vicious and corrupt. The temptation to excess was very great, and the power of resistance was of the slenderest order. The Company's servants in Bengal did very much what they liked, and grew rich on unhallowed gains without compunc-

* Mr. Verelst says that it was impossible at that time for the Company to have taken the management of the Dewannee into its own hands, for that the number of civil servants was barely adequate to the due performance of the commercial business; they were quite ignorant of the genius of the people, and totally unfit for the work of administration.—[*View of the English Government in Bengal*, p. 62.]

tion or remorse. It was not to be supposed in those days, it is not to be supposed in these, that men would leave their homes, to rot like sheep, among strangers, in a destroying climate, without some adequate reward. The Company's service, in all its open recognised conditions, presented nothing that could be regarded as a moderate compensation for all the pains and penalties of Eastern exile. The pay was so miserably small that the whole of it would not cover the house-rent of a civilian, and the young writer was sometimes obliged to go to bed soon after the early day-close of the tropics, because he could not afford to supply himself with the luxury of a candle or a supper.* Yet in those days large fortunes were made—how, has often been told before. The evil was one which necessarily increased with the progress of the administration, for the more determined the administrative character of the Company's servants, the more important it was to divest them of the prestige of dishonesty and rapacity, and to withdraw them from the practice of such crimes. Nothing could be more clear than this to the soldier-statesman Clive, who declared that the Company's servants should cease altogether to touch the profits of trade, and never handle native money. On his return to India in 1765, he had taken the resolution, to use his own words, "to cleanse the Augæan stable;" and it is hard to say how much the purity of the civil service at the present time is assignable to the efforts of the President and the Select Committee.

But it was not until some time after the final departure of Clive that the principle for which he contended became the rule of the Company, and the administrative business of our empire in the East was performed by men receiving fixed salaries, proportionate to the respectability of their position and the

* *Forbes' Oriental Memoirs.*

services which they rendered to the State. There was a season of shifts and expedients—of devices and experiments—during which the character of the Company's service continued to improve, because there was more rigorous supervision, but did not reach a high standard of integrity or efficiency. Affairs, indeed, at this time were in a transition state. The Company, unaccustomed to their new character of great territorial lords and incipient administrators, seemed to stagger under the responsibility which had been thrust upon them, and to wonder what would come next. They were eager to confine their territorial possessions to Bengal, and fearful of expansion on the side of Madras.* Great questions of government were new to them. They were suddenly called upon to administer the affairs, not any longer of a few factories, but of an empire of the internal concerns of which, except in their commercial relations, they had the most limited knowledge, and could hardly in reason be expected to have more. In this conjuncture, they did the best thing that could be done, though it grievously miscarried in the issue. They sent out a Commission, consisting of three gentlemen† of high character and extensive experience, with large powers of superintendence and control over all the Company's settlements, with instructions to inquire into and remedy all abuses, and to dismiss without scruple any of the Company's servants convicted of incapacity or corruption. What they would have done it is impossible to say. They sailed for Bengal in 1769, and nothing was ever heard of them again.

* Even Clive shrunk from the idea of a further extension of dominion. "My resolution was, and my hopes will always be," he wrote in 1765, "to confine our assistance, our conquests, and our possessions to Bengal, Behar, and Orissa. To go further is, in my opinion, a scheme so extravagantly ambitious and absurd, that no governor and council in their senses can ever adopt it, unless the whole scheme of the Company's interest be first entirely new-modelled."

† Messrs. Vansittart, Scrafton, and Forde.

No noticeable changes in the internal administration of Bengal took place under the governments of Mr. Verelst and Mr. Cartier; but in 1772 there succeeded to the chief seat at the Presidency a man destined, in the fulness of time, to take the very highest place among our Indian statesmen. Warren Hastings, one of the civil servants of the Company, was appointed President of Bengal. The double government had by this time fulfilled its mission. It had introduced an incredible amount of disorder and corruption into the state, and of poverty and wretchedness among the people; it had embarrassed our finances and soiled our character, and was now to be openly recognised as a failure.* On the 11th of May, 1772, it was proclaimed that the Company had determined to "stand forth publicly in the character of Dewan;" and the whole fiscal administration of the country now passed avowedly into our hands.

This was the greatest step in the progress of Anglo-Indian administration ever made by the Company—the greatest administrative revolution, perhaps, to which Bengal had ever been subjected. But although the Directors at home clearly enunciated the evils of the old double government, and ordered that a new system should be introduced directly in the name of the Company, they did not instruct their servants in India what the nature of the new government was to be. They

* The appointment of the supervisors, intended to remedy some of the defects of the system, wrought more harm than good. The Court of Directors, who seem to have been at this time considerably in advance of their servants, wrote to Mr. Hastings, in 1773, "We wish that we could refute the observation that almost every attempt made by us and our administration at your Presidency, for the reforming of abuses, has rather increased them, and added to the miseries of the country we are anxious to protect and cherish. The truth of this observation appears fully in the late appointment of supervisors and chiefs, instructed as they were to give relief to the industrious tenants, to improve and enlarge our investments, to destroy monopolies, and to retrench expenses, the end has by no means been answerable to the institution. Are not the tenants more than ever oppressed and wretched? Are our investments improved? Have not the raw silk and cocoons been raised upon us 50 per cent. in price? We can hardly say what has not been made a monopoly. And as to the expenses of your Presidency, they are at length settled to a degree we are no longer able to support."—[*Minutes of Evidence on Hastings' Trial, quoted in Mill's History.*]

left to their own servants the great work of sketching out the system and filling in the details; and fortunate was it that, at that time, the administration was in the ablest hands to which it had ever been entrusted.

In subsequent chapters on the Revenue and Judicial systems of India, some account will be given of the changes introduced on the first standing forth of the Company as Dewan. For a few days there seems to have been an administrative hiatus. We had not yet come very clearly to understand the duties and responsibilities of government, or to take those clear constitutional views of the relations subsisting between the rulers and the ruled, and the necessity of a precise definition of authority, which are now inseparable from even the crudest ideas of Indian administration. The working of one machine was stopped, before another was ready to be set in motion. It is instructive to contemplate a state of things, which in these days could have no existence, and mark what progress we have made since we first stood forth as Dewan.

But the new Regulations were hot upon the anvil, and Hastings soon began to set the administrative machinery again at work. I will only here state that he wisely determined not to wield the besom of destruction at the outset in too fierce and uncompromising a manner. He knew that the first step towards the reform of the administration of Bengal was the acquisition of information relating to the institutions of the country. He knew that the most experienced servants of the Company were groping in the dark, amidst errors and delusions, and that to base a system, of the highest abstract excellence, on such errors and delusions, unsuited to the character and the usages of the people, would be to inflict greater injury upon them than had resulted from the double government which had ground them down to the dust. All that he did was of a probationary, experimental character. He was the first to come face to face with the inhabitants of the country as their immediate ruler and protector, and he was the first to acquire extensive information relating to the people who bowed to his rule and looked up to him for protection.

But other great changes were now impending. By this time the British Parliament and the British public had begun to bestir themselves about Indian affairs. There have been ever since that important year, 1772, periodical spasms of intense interest in the details of Indian administration, which come and go like the cramp or the colic, and are very formidable whilst they last, but do not seem to have any abiding effect upon the constitution which they assail. The year 1772 was the first spasm-year—but it was a great one. It opened with an Indian paragraph in the King's Speech, and closed with a report from a Select Committee of Secrecy which had been intermediately appointed. India was not so large a subject in those days as in these. The following year produced the Regulating Act.

I shall speak of this more fully in the next chapter. I have only now to do with its effects on the constitution of the Indian Government. And those effects were prodigious. A Governor and Council, consisting of four members, was to be appointed to Bengal, with supreme authority over all the presidencies of India; and a Supreme Court of Judicature was to be established in Calcutta, with civil, criminal, and ecclesiastical jurisdiction over all persons except the Governor-General and the Councillors. The appointment of the Councillors, as of the Judges, was to be vested in the Crown. One member of the Indian service, Mr. Barwell, was selected, and three strangers—General Clavering, Colonel Monson, and Mr. Philip Francis—were sent out to Bengal. The Government of this new body was declared by Act of Parliament to commence on the 1st of August, 1774, but the Councillors did not reach Calcutta before the 19th of October. On the day following the old Government was formally dissolved, and the Governor-General and Council entered upon their administrative duties.

By the Act of 1773 (13th Geo. III., cap. 63) the Presidency of Fort William, or Bengal, was erected into the seat of the chief power in India; and the Presidencies of Madras and Bombay were rendered subordinate to it. The Bengal Council was to consist of a Governor-General and four members, one of whom was Commander-in-chief. The salaries of these officers were fixed at 25,000*l.* for the Governor-General, and 10,000*l.* for each member or Council—a tarif which has existed without alteration up to the present time.* The Governor-General had a casting vote in Council, but no power to act independently of his colleagues. There was a general authority vested in them "from time to time to make and issue such rules, ordinances, and regulations, for the good order and civil government of the settlement of Fort William, and other factories and places subordinate or to be subordinate thereto, as shall be deemed just and reasonable—such rules, ordinances, and regulations not being repugnant to the laws of the realm." They were empowered also to act as Justices of the Peace, and to hold quarter sessions four times a year within the settlement of Fort William. Such were the powers of the Governor-General and Council under the Regulating Act. For any offence against this Act, or for any "crimes, misdemeanors, or offences committed by them against any of his Majesty's subjects, or any of the inhabitants of India within their respective jurisdictions, they were

* It is said that Lord Clive recommended that the councillors should each have an additional 5000*l.* a year for table-money.

rendered amenable to the Court of King's Bench, and liable, on conviction, to "such fine or corporal punishment as the said Court shall think fit to inflict."

Thus, for the first time, was the administrative character of the Company's government fixed and determined by Act of Parliament. Up to this period there had been nothing more than a general recognition of the Company's right to "have the ordering, rule, and government of all their forts, factories, and plantations;" and to "appoint governors and officers for the said forts, factories, and plantations."* But the system of government and the powers of the governors had been left entirely to the discretion of the Company to define and limit. The administration of these distant settlements had been matter of little concernment to the Crown; but now that the Company had become great territorial lords, and the possessors of a large territorial revenue, it became necessary for the Parliament of Great Britain to fix and regulate the administrative agencies and authorities to be established in the British possessions in the East, and to exercise, through the ministers of the Crown, a direct control over the Directors of the Company themselves. The administration of the East India Company had now become a great recognised fact.

The Act of 1773 continued in force up to the year 1781, throughout the whole of which time Warren Hastings presided over the Supreme Council of India. It was, in spite of the intestine strife which so embarrassed the administrative efforts of the Governor-General, a period of progressive improvement. The Company's servants had everything to learn as administrators,

* See the charter granted by William III. to the English Company, and subsequently confirmed to the United Company. A subsequent Act was passed, 11 and 12 William III., cap. 12, "to punish governors of plantations in this kingdom for crimes by them committed in the plantations." It was of general application to governors, &c., of any colony beyond the sea.

and those great lessons were not to be learnt in a day. But considering the strangeness of the duties which then devolved upon them—the magnitude of the labor imposed and the extreme difficulty of acquiring a competent knowledge of the language, the institutions, the usages, and the character of the people, in all their multiform social aspects, a people whom before they had only known in the one relation of trader, the wonder is not that they advanced so little towards good government, but that they advanced so much. During this great experimental period of British rule there was gradually springing up a race of trained administrators, around whom the old commercial traditions did not cling—who had not graduated in chicanery, or grown grey in fraud and corruption, and who brought to their work not only a sounder intelligence but purer moral perceptions, and a higher sense of what they owed to the people of the soil. When, therefore, in 1786, it seemed to the authorities at home expedient to appoint to the chief seat in the council of India, not one of the Company's own servants, but an English nobleman of good parts, unsullied character, and extensive influence, the Governor-General so selected from the aristocracy of Great Britain, found himself on his arrival surrounded by a class of men with little resemblance to the old denizens of the Augæan stable which, twenty years before, Clive had so courageously ventured to cleanse. The Shores and the Barlows were at his elbow—men whose talents attracted admiration, and whose integrity commanded respect.

Under the rule of Lord Cornwallis the progress made in the internal administration was great and striking. He gathered up the scattered fragments of government which he found, and reduced them to one comprehensive system. He gave substance and permanency to what had before been light and transient. He laid the foundation of the present Indian constitution — not hastily and unadvisedly, as has been often said, but after much profound thought and earnest consideration, with the advice and instruction of some of the ablest and most experienced of the Company's servants. A peculiar merit of the system which he introduced was that, broadly enunciating the principles of the Government, it created a code of written laws or regulations, to which publicity was to be given; it made legislation thenceforth proceed in the presence of the people; it taught the Company's servants, clearly and distinctly, the laws or regulations which they were to administer, and opened the Indian statute-book to every man in the country who had the will and the power to peruse it. But its leading feature was the recognition of the great constitutional truth that the legislative, the executive, and the judicial powers of the State ought to be in separate hands. It is true that no despotic Government ever submits to the fetters imposed by this great protective principle. But in no other way was Cornwallis's system an arbitrary setting aside of existing usages, in disregard of native prejudices and predilections; it recognised those usages, it respected those prejudices and predilections, and was most honestly and humanely devised for the protection of the people.

Of the changes which, during this great administration, were introduced in the Revenue and Judicial systems, I shall speak in detail when I come specially to consider these important subjects. But this would seem to be the right place in which to speak of the legislative powers and functions of the Indian Government, as they existed at that time. It has been seen that the Charter of 1773 gave the Governor-General and Council authority to frame from time to time rules, ordinances, and regulations for the good order and civil government of the Company's settlements. There was something rather vague and indeterminate in this; but the Company's servants thought that they discerned in it the indication of general legislative power, and Barlow, who drew up the minute containing the first rough draft of the new constitution, freely used the word "laws," instead of "regulations," in all parts of the document.

Clearly setting forth the principles by which the Government were actuated, and establishing such a system of checks as would leave it "for the Government only in its collective capacity to have the power to commit oppression." It proposed that every law thenceforth to be passed by Government should be printed and published, so that if it be unwise it may stand in evidence against the framers of it, and then went on to say—"It may be urged that these ideas of justice are incompatible with our political situation—that as the people become rich they will feel their power, and combine to subvert our Government. But there appears to me to be no ground for such a supposition, for although we hope to render our subjects the happiest people in India, I should by no means propose to admit the natives to any participation in the legislative power."

The draft of this famous minute was submitted by the Governor-General to Sir William Jones, Sir Robert Chambers, and others, and was by them diligently examined. Their verdict was all in its favor. "I return," wrote Sir William Jones to Mr. Barlow, "Lord Cornwallis's incomparable minute, with which I have been so charmed, that I have read it attentively five or six times, and I have scribbled a few marginal notes without reserve. The plan is so perfect that I could suggest no material addition to it."* "In obedience to your lordship's commands," wrote Sir R. Chambers to Lord Cornwallis, "I have perused with attention the judicious and elaborate minute which I received therewith."† But there were one or two points contained in the document which startled the English lawyers, and made them hesitate before they could express their entire approval of all the contents of Barlow's minute. Against the Regulation which made British residents in the Mofussil amenable to the local courts, they respectfully protested. "I recommend," wrote Jones, "a serious re-consideration of the article concerning British subjects residing in the provinces." And Chambers recorded at some length an opinion differing in no great measure from that of his brother judge.‡ But that which seemed most to stagger the English lawyers was the assumption, indicated in the minute, of legislative power by the Indian Government—power of which the Judges of the Supreme Court denied their possession. "Many passages in this excellent minute," wrote Sir William Jones, "seem to imply a general *legislative* power in the Government, but I

* *MS. Records.*—Sir W. Jones to Mr. Barlow. "Gardens—December 2, 1792."

† *MS. Records.*—Sir R. Chambers to Lord Cornwallis, Feb. 4, 1793. A still stronger opinion was afterwards expressed by Mr. (subsequently Sir) W. Burroughs.

"They (the Regulations)," wrote the Advocate-General, "are worthy of every praise which can be bestowed upon them, and would do credit to any legislator of ancient or modern times. I am, I do assure you, sincere in thinking that they are as likely to prolong our empire in Asia, as they are certain of promoting the prosperity and happiness of the millions which inhabit it. Should we ever, as probably we must, be driven from our present power in the East, they will remain a monument of our justice and true glory, and may continue to the people for whom they have been framed many blessings which under them they now enjoy."—[*Mr. Burroughs to Mr. Barlow.—MS. Correspondence.*]

‡ The proposed Regulation called upon Europeans desiring to settle in the provinces to sign a bond making them amenable in civil cases to the local courts. Jones doubted the legality of such a process, and argued that the validity of such a bond would not be recognised in any court of justice; but Chambers on the whole "inclined to the opinion that such a bond, if enforced in a proper manner and on a proper occasion, might be supported in an English court of justice." But he contended that it would be expedient to confine the condition "to actions for small sums, such as a native manufacturer or mechanic living at a great distance from Calcutta, would find it difficult to sue for in the Supreme Court."—[*Marginal Notes of Sir W. Jones, and MS. Correspondence of Sir R. Chambers.*]

have searched in vain for the statute by which such a power is given. The *rules and orders* of Courts may, indeed, be called laws of those Courts; but I should think *rules and orders*, or *regulations*, a clearer and better expression than *laws*." And again: "These and many similar phrases in the minute seem to assert a greater power of legislation than (I believe) the executive Government has been entrusted with."* Chambers wrote a long letter on this especial subject to the Governor-General, urging that the 9th article of the proposed Regulations seemed to "take for granted a general legislative power, and supposes that laws affecting property and private rights may be passed by the English Government in this country, just as they are by the King and Parliament of Great Britain;" and setting forth, after a full statement of the argument, that "the conclusion which may be reasonably inferred from all these particulars is, that the King and Parliament having taken into their hands the legislation of this conquered country, no subordinate legislature can exist here, but such as is derived from Act of Parliament, or such as, either expressly or by fair implication, is recognised and allowed by Parliament." "And," continued this excellent man, and upright judge, "it will, I believe, be found on examination, that there is no general legislative power here which can be so derived, or which has been so recognised."†

Nor did the English lawyer stop here. He laid it down as his opinion that even the British Parliament

* *Marginal Notes of Sir W. Jones to rough draft of Minute. MS.*—It is curious to observe the different views taken of this particular subject by the most eminent Company's servants. Mr. J. H. Harrington, to whom the Minute had been submitted, wrote: "Even the substitution of the term Laws for Regulations, though it be but a verbal amendment, will, I am persuaded, tend to substantial advantages. There is an habitual association of ideas attached to the term *Law*, which involuntarily influences a more serious and deliberate attention as to a solemn act of the legislature, which is not so much excited by the less appropriate and more familiar term *Regulation*."—[*MS. Records.*] The lawyers, however, could not tolerate what they thought an abuse of the sacred word; and Lord Cornwallis erased it.

† *MS. Correspondence.*

could not righteously interfere with the existing laws of Mahomedans and Hindoos. "By the Parliament," he wrote, "they certainly may *legally* be altered, for what is enacted by the supreme legislative power must, *ex vi termini*, be legal. But it may be doubted whether even the Parliament, after all that has been done and declared, can consistently with prudence, mercy, and natural equity, overturn the established doctrines of the Hindoos, or the Mahomedans, on any of the subjects before enumerated, or on any other points which either of those two classes of people consider as fundamental principles of their respective religion. More especially when it is remembered that their native princes, whether Mussulmans or Idolaters, though they might sometimes infringe those laws which they believed to be divine, never claimed or pretended to have any right to abrogate or alter them."* But it was this very overturning of the established doctrines of the Hindoos and the Mahomedans, which the authors of the new constitution declared was ever furthest from their thoughts. The arguments, however, against the use of the word "laws" seem to have prevailed, for Cornwallis erased it and substituted *Rules* or *Regulations.*

Many years afterwards Barlow, in his green old age, looking back through a vista of half a century upon those early days, when at the elbow of Lord Cornwallis he sketched the Regulations, which have since been the basis of our Anglo-Indian code, wrote, in the clear delicate penmanship of his youth, these retrospective notes:

"Great misunderstandings have prevailed with regard to the new constitution for the civil government of the British possessions in India, established by the Marquis Cornwallis in 1793, and completed by his successor, Marquis Wellesley. The change did not consist in alterations in the ancient customs and usages of the

* *MS. Correspondence.*

country, affecting the rights of persons and property. It related chiefly to the giving security to those rights, by affording to our native subjects the means of obtaining redress against any infringement of them, either by the Government itself, its officers, or individuals of any character of description.

"Every Government in the world, from the most free to the most despotic, consists of the same elements. In each of these, there must necessarily be a power to make laws, a power to administer these laws, and a power to conduct what is termed the executive branch of public affairs. The difference between the two descriptions of government consists chiefly in the union or separation of these powers in the same or different hands. In the despotic Government, all authority—the making of laws, the administration of them, and all the duties of the executive branch, are lodged in the same hands. In a free Government these powers are lodged in different hands, so as to ensure the enactment of good laws and the just administration of them, and to provide for the due conduct of the executive duties. The despotic Government may be compared to the natural world in a state of chaos—the well-regulated Government to the natural world with all the elements assigned to their proper purposes. In this distinction consists the difference between an Asiatic or Turkish Pashalick and British form of Government, and each is known by its different effects on the lives, properties, and persons of the people.

"Lord Cornwallis made no innovations on the ancient laws and customs of the people. On the contrary, the main object of the constitution which he established was to secure to them the enjoyment of those laws and customs with such improvement as times and circumstances might suggest. When he arrived in the country the Government was, in fact, a pure despotism, with no other check but that which resulted from the character of those by whom the Government was administered. The Governor-General not only was the sole power for making all laws, but he exercised the power of administering the laws in the last resort, and also all the functions of the executive authority. The abuses to which such a system of government is liable from corruption, negligence, and want of information, are too well known to require being particularised. It is, in fact, from the want of a proper distribution of these authorities in different hands that all abuses in government principally proceed.

"His lordship's first step was to make it a fundamental law (see Regulations XLIII, 1793), that all laws framed by the Government should be printed and published in the form prescribed by that Regulation, and that the Courts of Judicature should be guided by the laws so printed and published, and no other. It had before been the practice to carry on the affairs of the Government, and those of individuals, by a correspondence by letter with all the subordinate officers."*

In this Barlow repeated what he had often emphatically insisted upon at the time. It was his wont to declare that improvement was one thing—innovation another; and that he had only improved upon the laws of the Moguls.†

Lord Cornwallis governed India with enlarged powers. The "Regulating Act" had invested the Governor-General with no power independent of his Council; and Pitt's India Bill, which passed into law in 1784, though it had given to the Court of Directors the power of nominating and recalling the Governor-General‡ and Councillors, had introduced no further change into the constitution of the supreme Govern-

* *MS. Memoranda.*

† "By improvement," he wrote, "I understand the gradual correction of defects in the existing Laws or Regulations, and the providing by new regulations for cases which have never before occurred. The new is thus in a manner the offspring of the old, always arising out of it, and preserving a close relation; but innovation proceeds in a different way. It sets out with rejecting all connexion with the past, and adopts principles and measures that can never assimilate with it." — [*November* 26, 1795.] And in the same letter he says: "The Regulations of 1793-4-5 are filled with injunctions for the observance of the Hindoo and Mahomedan law in all matters to which they have invariably been applied, and contain all the specific rules affecting private rights and property, about which alone the people can be immediately interested, that have passed during the last twenty years, with alterations and amendments to render them better fitted to the intended purpose. The distribution of the three powers (which constitutes one of the essential differences between the present and past arrangements) is calculated to ensure to our subjects what they never enjoyed before, the full benefit of all laws and regulations; and from the mode in which it operates renders the introduction of any principles or measures, which would afford ground for the objections urged by the favorers of the Mogul system, next to impracticable."—[*MS. Correspondence.*]

‡ The recall clause in Pitt's India Bill runs thus—"And be it further enacted, that it shall and may be lawful to and for the King's Majesty, his heirs and successors, by any writing or instrument under his or their sign manual, countersigned by the Secretary of State, or for the Court of Directors of the United Company, for the time being, by writing under their hands, to remove or recall the present, or any future Governor-General," &c.—[*Act* 24 *George III., chap.* 25.]

ment than that of the reduction of the number of Councillors from four to three, on the occurrence of the first vacancy. But two years afterwards, a Bill was introduced to "explain and amend certain provisions" of this Act. It enacted that no person (except the Governors or Commanders-in-Chief) should be appointed to the supreme or subordinate Councils who had not "been twelve years at the least, in the whole, resident in India, in the civil line of the Company's service;" and it empowered the Governor-General and minor Governors in extraordinary cases to act without the concurrence of the Council, inasmuch as that such power would tend greatly to the strength and security of the British possessions in India, and give energy, vigor, and despatch to the measures and proceedings of the executive Government." This was in effect a public recognition of the utter failure of the system under which Francis* and his colleagues had been sent out to India to "regulate," by their ignorance and impetuosity, the proceedings of a really capable Governor-General, who had graduated in the Indian service; and though the restraint of Council has since the passing of this Act been sometimes a little too loosely regarded, the new provision was a salutary one. Under this Act (26th George III., chap. 16) it was decreed that all acts of the supreme or minor Councils should be "expressed to be made" by the Governor-General, or by the Governor or President "*in Council*"—a nomenclature, expressive of the supremacy of the Governor, which has been maintained to the present day.†

It was under this Act that Lord Cornwallis governed our Indian possessions. In 1793 a new Charter Act

* Francis, who had been by this time returned to Parliament, endeavoured to introduce a Bill of his own, intended to upset that which Dundas had framed —but he was unsuccessful.

† A subsequent Act of the same year (1786) decreed or explained that the Court of Directors should have the power of appointing their Governors and Councillors without the approbation of the Crown.—[*26th George III., chap.* 25.] This was subsequently confirmed by the Charter Act of 1793.—[*33rd George III., chap.* 52.]

was passed, continuing the Company's privileges for twenty years; and in this the powers and responsibilities of the Governor-General and minor Governors were more clearly defined. It was then provided that they should have no power to act without the concurrence of their Councils in matters of purely civil government—that is, in the words of the Act, in any matter which shall come under their consideration "in their judicial capacity"—"or to make, repeal, or suspend any general rule, order, or regulation, for the good order and civil government of the United Company's settlements, or to impose of his own authority any tax or duty within the said respective Governments or Presidencies."* By this Act the Governor-General was empowered, during his absence from the Presidency, to appoint one of the members of his Council Vice-President, and Deputy-Governor of Bengal, with authority coincidental with that exercised, in Council, by the Governor of one of the minor Presidencies.

Those minor Presidencies, under the Act of 1773, had been left very much in the same constitutional state as they were prior to the passing of the Bill. They were at this time three in number—"the Presidencies of Madras, Bombay, and Bencoolen;" their chief officer was designated President; the number of their Councillors was arbitrary, not limited by Act of Parliament; and they were directed and required to pay due obedience to the Governor-General and Council, who had the power of suspending them from office. But the Act of 1784 had decreed that "the Government of the several Presidencies and settlements of Fort St. George and Bombay shall, after the commencement of this Act, consist of a Governor or President, and

* *Act* 33*rd George III.*, *chap.* 52, *clause* 51.—By clause 55 of this Act, the Court of Directors are empowered, with the approbation of the Board of Commissioners, "to suspend all or any of the powers hereby given to the Governor-General to act upon his own sole authority."

three Councillors only"—of whom the Commander-in-Chief was to be one. And this is the constitution of the minor Governments as established in the present day. At the same time it was enacted that the Governor-General and Council of Fort William should have "power and authority to superintend, control, and direct the several Presidencies and Governments in all such points as relate to any transactions with the country powers, or to war or peace, or to the application of the revenues or forces of such Presidencies and settlements in time of war;"* and that this subordination to the supreme Government might be complete, another change was introduced, which compelled the minor Governments to obey the orders of the supreme authority, notwithstanding any doubts that they might entertain of such instructions coming within the limits assigned by the wording of the statute. By the subsequent Charter Acts of 1793, this subjection to the chief Presidency was confirmed; and the Act of 1833 more distinctly and minutely defined it. The general authority of the supreme Government is declared in one clause†—and in another it is expressly enacted that "no Governor or Governor in Council shall have the power of making or suspending any regulations or laws in any case whatever, unless in cases of urgent necessity (the burden of the proof whereof shall be on such Governor or Governor in Council), and then only until the decision of the Governor-General in Council shall be signified thereon; and provided also that no Governor or Governors in Council shall have the power of creating any new office or granting any salary, gratuity, or allowance, without the previous sanction of the Governor-General of India in Council."‡

The Governments of the minor Presidencies had be-

* *Act* 24 *Geo. III., chap.* 25, *clause* 31.

† *Act* 3 *and* 4 *Will. IV., chap.* 85, *clause* 65.

‡ *Act* 3 *and* 4 *Will. IV., chap.* 85, *clause* 59.

fore this possessed the power of framing laws or regulations for themselves, but this clause of the Charter Act of 1833 deprived them wholly of this power, and rendered their humiliation complete. The passing of this Act is one of the most important events in the whole history of Indian administration. The commercial privileges of the Company were no longer recognised, and the new Bill related, therefore, entirely to matters of government. Under the Acts existing previous to this date, it has been seen that there were three Governments, each similarly constituted, with a Governor (or Governor-General) and three Councillors, of whom the Commander-in-Chief was one. The new Act left the minor Governments with their old constitutions,* but remodelled the supreme Government, and erected two other subordinate Governments—the Governments of Agra and Bengal.

Under this Act the Supreme Council of India was to consist, and does now consist, of a Governor-General, appointed by the Court of Directors with the approbation of the Crown, and four ordinary members of Council, three of whom were to be servants of the Company, civil or military, of ten years' service, appointed by the Court of Directors, and the fourth, a member not of the Company's service, to be appointed by the Court with the approbation of his Majesty, and "not to be entitled to sit or vote in Council, except in meetings thereof for making laws and regulations."† The Commander-in-Chief might also be, and always has been, an extraordinary member of this Council—that is, he has always drawn the salary, and sometimes he has taken his seat. The effect of the new law was to constitute the Supreme Council of two members of

* The Act, however, conferred on the Court of Directors authority, with the consent of the Board, to reduce or to abolish the Councils of the minor Governments.

† Known as the legislative member of Council, and selected always from the legal profession at home.

the Bengal civil service—one member of the Indian army, and a member of the legal profession from home. Sometimes the Governor-General presided over it—sometimes the Commander-in-Chief bestowed himself upon it; but these functionaries were more frequently at a frontier station superintending an unhappy war, or refreshing mind and body under the bracing influence of the cool breezes of the northern hills.

Under this Act I have said two new Governments were erected, that is, the old Presidency of Fort William in Bengal was "divided into two distinct Presidencies, one of such Presidencies in which shall be included Fort William, to be styled the Presidency of Fort William, in Bengal, and the other of such Presidencies to be styled the Presidency of Agra." The administration of the Lower Provinces of the Bengal Presidency was entrusted to what is called the Bengal Government, and its precise limits were to be defined by the Court of Directors. The Governor-General was to be *ex-officio* Governor of Bengal, with power to appoint one of his Councillors to act for him, in the capacity of Deputy-Governor, with three members of Council. The Presidency of Agra was to consist of the Upper Provinces of the old Bengal Presidency; and its affairs were to be administered by a Governor and Council of three.* The Court of Directors, however, had the power of determining, with the sanction of the Board, whether there should or should not be Councils in the subordinate Presidencies;† and the original design of the Bengal and Agra Governments was revised. It was deemed expedient that these new Presidencies should have no separate armies—no separate civil establishments; and therefore it was conceived that Councils were unnecessary. By a subse-

* *Clause* 56, *Act* 3 *and* 4 *Will. IV., chap.* 85.

† *Clause* 57, *Act* 3 *and* 4 *Will. IV., chap.* 85.

quent Act,* "to authorise the Court of Directors of the East India Company to suspend the execution of the provisions of the Act of 1833, so far as they relate to the creation of the Government of Agra, the Governor-General was empowered to appoint any member of the Company's service, of ten years' standing, Lieutenant-Governor of the North-Western Provinces of India. And such has been the system pursued up to the present time. The two Governments of Bengal and the North-Western Provinces administer, without a Council, but with a separate Secretariat, the civil affairs, and have the general domestic superintendence of, all that tract of country, which previously constituted, and in respect of military arrangements does still constitute, the Presidency of Bengal. But they have no military or political authority, and no financial control except in subordination to the supreme Government. In fact, the system is one of extreme centralisation, and the Governor of Bombay or Madras, or the Governor of Bengal, being also Governor-General of India, cannot lawfully entertain an additional Cooley, on a salary of seven shillings a month, without the recorded assent of the Governor-General in Council.

But that which most of all imparted a distinctive character to the new Act, was the earnestness with which it addressed itself to the great matter of Indian legislation. It recognised the necessity of constructing a comprehensive code of laws for the protection and restraint of our Anglo-Indian subjects, of all colors and all creeds;† it vested, as I have shown, the sole

* 5 *and* 6 *Will. IV., chap.* 25.

† "It is expedient that, subject to such special arrangements as local circumstances may require, a general system of judicial establishments and police, to which all persons whatsoever, as well Europeans as natives, may be subject, should be established in the said territories at an early period, and that such laws as may be applicable in common to all classes of the inhabitants of the said territories, due regard being had to the rights, feelings, and peculiar usages of the people, should be enacted, and that all laws and customs having the force of law within the same territories should be ascertained and consolidated, and as occasion may require amended."—[*Preamble to clause* 53, 3 *and* 4 *of William IV., chapter* 85.]

power of legislating for all parts of India in the Supreme Council, and it not only imparted to that Council a distinctive legislative character and a presumed legislative efficiency such as it had never known before, but it afforded, by the establishment of a body of Law Commissioners, certain external legislative aids which were calculated to contribute largely to the success of its codifications.

This Law Commission, of which the legislative member of Council was generally President,* was to consist of not more than five members, selected by the Court of Directors with the approbation of the Board of Control. It was to be their care "fully to inquire into the jurisdiction, powers, and rules of the existing courts of justice and police establishments, and all existing forms of judicial procedure, and into the nature and operation of all laws, whether civil or military, written or customary, prevailing and in force in any part of our territories;" and "from time to time to make reports, in which they shall fully set forth the result of their said inquiries, and shall from time to time suggest such alterations as may in their opinion be beneficially made in the said courts of justice and police establishments, forms of judicial procedure and laws, due regard being had to the distinction of castes, difference of religion, and the manners and opinions prevailing among different races and in different parts of the said territories." In a word, it was their duty to supply the materials of legislation; and considering the extent of the country, and the diversity of its inhabitants, it would be difficult to over-rate the magnitude of the task.

Excellent as was the intention, and apparently sound in theory as was this provision of the Legislature, there

* This was a matter, I believe, of private arrangement. It is not "so nominated in the bond." The Commission was principally composed of the Company's civil servants; and dwindled down at last to one member.

were many grave reasons to doubt, if not to despair, of its practical success. And some of the ablest members of the Court of Directors looked upon the experiment as one from which it would be expedient to abstain. They questioned the wisdom of this centralisation of the legislative power; and contemplating the many varieties of our Indian subjects—of a people with different languages, different creeds, different social institutions, different social usages, different tempers, and different intelligences they could not bring themselves to think that an uniform code of laws, applicable to all these varieties of mankind, could be framed by any number of men with the head of a Bentham or a Romilly, and the heart of a Wilberforce or a Howard. But, as a body, the Court of Directors, bowing to the behests of the Legislature, accepted the scheme, for better or worse, and wrote out to the Supreme Council, exhorting them to do their best to give it beneficial effect. Nothing could be more liberal than the spirit of their instructions. They exhorted the Legislative Council to legislate for the people; and urged them to spare no pains to obtain for themselves the aid of all the wisdom and experience of the country, to whomsoever it might belong, as the basis of their legislative enactments.*

* The following extracts from this letter will indicate the tenor of their instructions:—"We shall say no more of the necessity of deliberation among yourselves. Another point not less important, is to provide that in the work of legislation you shall, as far as may be practicable, avail yourselves of external aid. Persons who are not members of your body may afford you valuable assistance, either by suggesting laws that are required, or by pointing out what is improvable or objectionable, in the drafts or projects of laws under consideration. With respect to the suggestion of new laws, the Act, by clause 66, expressly requires you to take into consideration the drafts or projects of laws, or regulations, which any of the subordinate Governments may propose to you; but on this point we shall afterwards have occasion to observe more particularly. The Act also, we need not say, contemplates constant communications from the Law Commissioners, which communications are intended to furnish the grounds or the materials for legislation. Useful intimations may also be derived from the Public Boards, from the Judges of the Supreme Court, from all persons, whether native or European, invested with a judicial character, or holding official stations of eminence; from all colleges and other constituted bodies, perhaps from the native heads of

It is possible that this scheme of uniform codification would soon be forgotten—buried in that "Limbo of Vanity," where all decayed errors and rotten fallacies are stowed away—but for one circumstance connected with it. It will be remembered by future generations, wherever the English language is spoken or understood, that the great historian of England, whose captivating pages charm the young and fascinate the old with equal power, was sent out to India, in the year 1834, to take his place in the Council to which sixty years before another great writer had imparted an evil reputation. That Macaulay was for some years an Indian legislator will be held in popular remembrance long after the duties of the legislative member of the Supreme Council of India, and the labors of the Law Commissioners, have ceased to be matters known to any but the laborious student of remote Indian chronologies, who perhaps, in those days when the "New Zealander stands on the ruined arch of London Bridge," and the Anglo-Saxon races of America and Australia are contending for the empires of India, China, and Japan, or are amicably partitioning these vast territories among them, more as missionaries than as conquerors, may be writing, after the manner of Gibbon, a history of the "Decline and Fall of the British Empire in the East."*

I would speak tenderly of the labors of the Commission. Some able English lawyers, and some of the ablest of the Company's servants, have been connected with it. They carried to their work as much zeal and

villages, or even private individuals of personal weight and influence. We do not mean that these parties should by law be entitled to call on the Legislature to discuss such suggestions, or to come to any decision respecting them. No such right belongs to those who petition the Houses of Parliament in this country. We mean only that their suggestions should be received, and should even be invited."—[*The Court of Directors to the Supreme Council of India, December* 18, 1834. *MS. Records.*]

* It was, I believe, for some time a question whether Robert Grant or Macaulay should be the first legislative member of Council.

industry, as ability and experience. Such men as Amos and Cameron, Macleod, Eliott, and Millett, were not likely to address themselves carelessly to their new duties, or to toil on without profitable results. They have at least brought together an immense mass of serviceable information—the raw materials of legislation; and what they have done will go far to lighten, as indeed it has already lightened, the labors of those whose duty it is to send out the fabric, full fashioned, from the legislative loom. The mistake that was made, was made by the British Legislature. It prescribed duties, the adequate performance of which, according to the intent signified in the Act of Parliament, was simply an impossibility. The Law Commission were expected to prepare a comprehensive code of laws—to suit men of all denominations living in the territories of the East India Company—Englishmen, Eurasians, Portuguese, Armenians, Parsees, and every variety of Mahomedan and Hindoo. But it was felt after a time that the work entrusted to the Commissioners could not be performed in all the integrity and completeness of the original design. People looked impatiently for results before results were forthcoming. The Court of Directors had written out to the supreme Government, that with respect to this matter of codification "no time should be lost by delay—none should be worse than lost by precipitation." Doubtless, there was some precipitation at the outset; and afterwards there were apparent delays, the result of an earnest desire on the part of the Commissioners to sift all subjects of inquiry to the bottom. The Commissioners did their duty, but it was only in the nature of things that the Commission should have disappointed public expectation, and left the design of the Legislature unfulfilled. It was suffered therefore, little by little, to die a natural death; and it must be acknowledged that it has left behind it only an impression that it was a failure, as costly as it was complete.*

I think that this condemnation is far too sweeping. It is not to be denied that the Act of 1833, under

* I may advantageously give here the substance of the evidence given before the Lords' Committee in 1852, by Mr. C. Hay Cameron, lately legislative member of the Supreme Council of India, and President of the Law Commission, relative to the performances of that body. "Practically, the functions of the Law Commission have ceased. Some years ago the Government discontinued filling up the vacancies as to the now legal members of the Commission, and its existence would have been entirely terminated, but for doubts which began to be entertained whether it was competent for the Government to dispense with its maintenance as directed by the Act. But it not being considered necessary to incur the expense of paid Commissioners, certain members were requested to act as Commissioners without additional salary, simply that the Act might be complied with, and that the only remaining paid Commissioner might be enabled to complete and submit to Government some reports on which he was engaged. Mr. Cameron stated, that when the Law Commission was nearly extinct (consisting only of two members, himself and another), it proceeded, by reference from the Governor-General in Council, to examine the criticisms upon Mr. Macaulay's Penal Code, made by all the judges of the Supreme Court and the judges of the Company's Sudder Courts, which criticisms, it is said, had accumulated to an unmanageable bulk. Upon these the Law Commission reported, recommending that the code, as revised by that Commission, should be passed into law. Permission for the Commissioners to travel into various districts, for the purpose of instituting inquiries into slavery and other subjects, was sought, but not obtained. Plans were proposed for a Model Criminal Court for the trial of offences not of the gravest character; as well as for a Model Civil Court and a plan of civil procedure, under which the administration of law and equity was to be united, and the whole case brought under the cognisance of one judge, while small-cause judicature was not to be committed to inferior judges, but all causes, whatever their amount, were to be cognisable in the same Courts. In regard to appeals, the scheme of the Law Commission was to have a general Court of Appeal in each Presidency, consisting of the judges of the Supreme Courts and the judges of the Sudder Courts, which should receive appeals both in civil and criminal cases, and from all the Courts in the country. The Mahomedan law was to be codified, the Hindoo law was to be codified, and a third civil code, the *lex loci* was to be applicable to all but Mahomedans or Hindoos. This was much wanted, as, beyond the jurisdiction of the Supreme Courts, there is difficulty in knowing how to deal with foreigners. The course of the Company's Courts is to inquire what is the law of the country of every man that comes before them. If a Frenchman, they consult French authorities; if a Portuguese, Portuguese authorities; and so with regard to all foreign nations. The condition of the Armenians, who consider themselves a separate nation, is also peculiar, and the position of the East India or half-caste population seems unsettled. Then in cases between persons of different nations, as when one party is a Frenchman and the other not, increased difficulty arises. There was also to be a single penal code, the Mahomedan law, in this respect, being swept away, and that substituted applying to all classes of persons without exception, but varying the penalties according to the diversities of birth, class, and circumstances. The Courts of first instance all over the country were to administer the three codes of civil law, and the new code of criminal law. Subsequently, the Law Commission proposed a Small Cause Court, with jurisdiction extending to 1000 rupees, but it was not adopted. Certain parts of the *lex loci* code, which protected converts from Mahomedanism or Hindooism from loss of ancestral or other property which they previously incurred, have since become law."

which the legislative member of council was appointed, and the Law Commission established, found the laws of India in a very confused and anomalous state, and that now, after twenty years, it still leaves much anomaly and confusion behind it. But there is little room to doubt that, since the passing of that Act, there has been a great improvement in the character of Indian legislation. The labors of the Law Commission may not have resulted in any very large number of substantial acts, but they have had a sensible effect upon the working of the legislative forge; and much of what the Commissioners have done has been infused into the Acts which, from time to time, have passed the Legislative Council.* And I am certain that all future Indian legislators will derive extensive benefit from the materials which they have amassed. Nor must it be forgotten, when speaking of the general progress of legislation, that since the establishment of the Legislative Council, the people of India, Europeans and natives, have had a larger share in the manipulation of the law. A draft of every new Act is now published; the community are thus invited to comment on its provisions, and often the result of these commentaries is discernible in the modification, or even the withdrawal, of the proposed law, when it has been found to be obnoxious to the people.

Looking now to general results, it would appear that this system of extreme concentration of power in the hands of the supreme Government has imperfectly fulfilled the intentions of the Legislature. It has

* With regard to the criminal code, Mr. Prinsep, no great admirer of the Law Commission, but a great authority, said in his evidence before the House of Commons, in 1851, "A code of criminal laws has been prepared, but has not been passed. It is, no doubt, frequently referred to, and extracts are made from it in any cases of importance that arise where a law is required for the purpose; and several of its chapters have so been incorporated, I believe, into the laws that have been passed from time to time."

borne, indeed, the accustomed fruits of centralisation.* It has dispirited and enervated the local governments. It has thrown upon the central authority an accumulated burden, under which it has not made much progress in the work of provincial improvement. I speak especially with reference to the governments of Madras and Bombay. The Bengal and Agra governments are immediately under the eye of the Governor-General. He passes from one to the other, traverses the whole tract of country from Peshawur to Pegu, and has a kindly paternal interest in the welfare of all those provinces, which, in spite of the divided administration, still integrally constitute the one great Presidency of Bengal. The vast progress, therefore, which has been made, under the government of the North-Western Provinces, can hardly be admitted as an argument in favor of this excessive centralisation. We must look for arguments on the southern and western coasts; and I fear that we shall not gather, from the apparent results, any very satisfactory proofs that the tendency of the system is to kindle much administrative zeal, or to develop much internal improvement.

* I think that Mr. Helps has so fairly stated the advantages and disadvantages of centralisation in the following passage, that I am tempted to quote it. It is written with especial reference to a "free Government," but it equally applies to such a Government as that of India:—"How much depends upon the happy admixture of local and central authority. If there be too much local power, how much time will elapse before the results of collected wisdom and the experience of the shrewdest men in public affairs will be carried into the local administration . . . . how completely the imperial ideas are likely to be sacrificed to petty privileges and near-sighted interests. On the other hand, if the central power prevails too much, the minds and energies of the small communities dependent on it are weakened by disuse; at the centre itself too much influence falls into the hands of faction, so that sullenness becomes the arbitress of national affairs; and, moreover, there is danger of everything being sacrificed to any one idea or fancy prevailing at the seat of Government.—[*Friends in Council, Book II.*]

CHAPTER IV.

Establishment of the East India Company—Early Management of its Affairs—Becomes a Joint-Stock Company—Its successive Charters—Progress of the Interlopers—The English Company—Union of the two Companies—Territorial Rights—The Regulating Act—Pitt's India Bill—The Charter Acts of 1793, 1813, and 1833—Present State of the Company.

HAVING rudely traced in the preceding chapter the progress of British administration in India up to the present time, I proceed to give some account of the Home Government—of the authorities and agencies which direct the movements of the foreign Governments, and to which the whole body of Indian administrators are responsible—the Authorities and Agencies which are now known as the Court of Directors of the East India Company and the Board of Control, but which for more than a century and three-quarters were all included in the former.

The bells which rang out the year 1600 rang in the first East India Company. It was incorporated, by a charter from Queen Elizabeth, under the name of "the Governor and Company of Merchants of London trading into the East Indies." It was a very small beginning. A few English traders—ironmongers, clothiers, and other substantial people of that kind—headed by the Lord Mayor, subscribed 30,000*l.*,* and, as soon as they obtained their charter, began to or-

* The precise amount was 30,133*l.*,—subscribed by 101 different parties. The highest subscription was 3000*l.*, set down opposite to the name of Messrs. Corkain and Co.—[*India House Records.*]

ganise their system of management, and to adopt measures for the equipment of their fleets. First seventeen—then twenty-four—directors, or, as they were called, "committees," were chosen, and from among them a Governor was elected—the first being Sir Thomas Smith, Alderman of London—to serve for a single year. The Company in the first instance had not even the dignity of a Joint-Stock. The adventures were promoted by private subscription, and the profits divided in the proportions of the sums subscribed by individual shareholders.

The business of the Committees at this time consisted mainly in the equipment of their ships, the purchase of goods likely to have a ready "vent" among the Indians, and the supply of bullion wherewith to procure the rich produce of the Eastern world. Occasionally, at long intervals, came in a letter from the commander, or "general" of one of their expeditions, setting forth the doubts which perplexed his mind, and the difficulties which beset his career—how their efforts, in one quarter, to establish a factory had proved fruitless, and that there was "no way but to remove and go;" how, in another direction, "the bloodthirsty Turks" had come down upon them, "murdered their distrustless naked men, and seized their goods;" how the Portugals had obstructed their trade until they had turned round and "checked their insufferable saucy insolence by taking one of their bragging frigates;" how the drunken Flemings had hindered them less openly in another place, and how our own people had been drinking with the said Flemings, and trusting them over-much; how their goods would not vent among the Gentiles; how the Gentiles, in their dealings, contrived to overreach them, and how they were compelled to submit to heavy losses, or else to carry back their damaged goods.* The

* *India House Records. MS.*

record of these things still survives in quaint homely English, and in spite of some obscurities of style and penmanship, render the Indian correspondence of the beginning of the seventeenth century as patent to the historian as the effusions of "our Governor-General in Council" at the beginning of last month.

There were other anxieties than these to disturb the Committees in the infancy of the Company's existence—anxieties generated by popular complaints at the very doors of their council-chamber. The trade went on briskly enough in one department of commerce, but very flatly in another. It was nearly all buying—little or no selling. English produce did not "vent" among the Gentiles. It was necessary, therefore, to export large quantities of bullion. This was nearly proving fatal to the Company at the very outset of their career.* There arose a cry in London that the India Company was draining the country of its wealth. Men spoke loudly against the system in places of public resort, and wrote wordy pamphlets against it. It is curious, now that the English traders have well-nigh absorbed the whole of India, whilst the prescient exclusiveness of Japan has preserved its integrity inviolate, to read that, two centuries and a half ago, the Company were seriously meditating the abandonment of their trade with the former country, and confining their efforts to the establishment of commercial intercourse with the latter.

For nearly a century this London Company continued nominally to enjoy the exclusive privilege of trading with all parts of Asia, Africa, and America, beyond the Cape of Good Hope eastward of the Straits of Magellan. During that century eight successive charters were granted by different monarchs to the London Com-

* "The Honorable Company, as they wrote to us, make doubt of continuing their East India Trade, being daily murmured at and scandalised for shipping away so much money yearly for India, Bantam, &c., and their large and hopeful intimations now lately given them of the Japan trade."

pany.* The second of these charters, granted under the reign of the first James, conferred upon them exclusive privileges in perpetuity—or at least as long as they could be continued without prejudice to the interests of the nation. Under this second charter, in the year 1612, the Company became, by a resolution of its members, a joint-stock; money was no longer subscribed arbitrarily for the promotion of a particular adventure, but was thrown into a general fund, to be managed according to the discretion of the Governor and the Committees. In 1617-18 there were nearly a thousand proprietors of India Stock, who in that year had subscribed 1,600,000*l.* towards a new fund. There was hopeful assurance in this. But increase of trade did not bring increase of profit; and in 1626-27 they had a debt of 200,000*l.*, and their shares were selling at a discount of 20 per cent.

The charter of 1609 continued in force for more than half a century. But those were not days when kingly faith stood on a very lofty eminence. The needy Stuarts and their profligate courtiers made what they could out of the Indian trade, and many were the injuries inflicted upon the Corporation by the hands of the denizens of Whitehall. Just at the close of the first James's reign that dissolute "Steenie," the Duke of Buckingham, in his capacity of Lord High Admiral, extorted 10,000*l.* from the Company, as a douceur, to obtain his sanction to the despatch of a fleet. Some years afterwards, Charles, in one of those pecuniary straits which always drove all sense of justice out of him, bought up all the Company's pepper on credit, sold it for cash, and never paid for it after all.

These, however, were mere temporary, accidental hindrances. A heavier blow was aimed at the Com-

* That is, under date December 31, 1600; May 31, 1609; April 3, 1661; October 5, 1677; August 9, 1683; April 12, 1686; October 7, 1693; and April 13, 1698.

pany, when back-stairs influence induced the needy Stuart to strike at the monopoly which had been granted by his predecessors, and to issue a license authorising a private association to embark on those fields of commercial enterprise which had hitherto been deemed, in their relations to English trade, the exclusive domains of the Company.

It has been observed, in the preceding chapter, with no love of paradox, that the enmity of the Portuguese, and the treachery of the Dutch, were long the defences of the London Company. If any further proof of this be needed, it may be found in the fact that, when the English and Portuguese patched up a sort of covenant, which promised to shield the former against the outrages of their unscrupulous rivals, and gave them, moreover, access to their ports, competitors for a share of the Indian trade rose up in London, and haunted the back lobbies of Whitehall. The Indian trade was now likely to become more profitable, and less dangerous. So it seemed to the gentlemen of London that a share of it was worth grasping. They had left the Company to breast the storm alone; but now that there was a glimpse of fine weather and smooth seas, the West-end people began to sound the depths of Charles's fidelity, and to bait their hooks with the promise of a share of the contemplated spoil. A convenient gentleman of the bed-chamber, named Endymion Porter, acted as the go-between. Sir William Courten and others obtained a license for a new Association, and the King received a share in the venture.

For this violation of the charter, granted to the London Company, it was necessary to find an excuse. It was alleged, therefore, and duly set forth in the preamble to the grant, that "the East India Company had neglected to establish fortified factories, or seats of trade to which the King's subjects could resort with safety—

that they had consulted their own interests only, without any regard to the King's revenue—and, in general, that they had broken the conditions upon which their charter and exclusive privileges had been granted to them."

It has always been the fate of the Company to be subjected to charges of the most opposite and inconsistent character. One day they are charged with doing too little—another, with doing too much. The "Lord Ambassador," whom King James had sent out to the Court of the Mogul, had recommended the Company to establish as few factories as possible, and not to fortify them at all; and now, in a public document, presumedly expressing the sentiments of the King, the Company were charged with the offence of "neglecting to establish fortified factories." The Company, indeed, were in no hurry to fortify. Sir Thomas Roe had told them that the Portuguese had "never made advantage of the Indies since they defended them;" and that "the Dutch, who had sought plantations by the sword," had found that "their dead pays consumed all their gain." Profiting by these cogent hints, the Company had never forgotten that their position in India was that of traders, and not of princes. Territorial acquisition and military defence formed no part of their policy. And as it was at the outset of their career, so has it been from generation to generation. It is nothing to say that no such empire as the British Empire in the East has ever been built up by the exercise of so little deliberate aggression, but that nothing even remotely resembling it is to be found in the history of the world.

But although the sun of royal favor brought Courten's Association into life, that great chartered party of Interlopers achieved no very brilliant success. They endeavoured to carry everything before them—*more Lusitanorum*—by a series of rapid *coups de main.*

But the aggressive hostility of the Dutch, who treated them as pirates, cramped their energies, and contracted their efforts. They encountered many difficulties, and were assailed by many disasters. But more than all the malice of their enemies, did their own unscrupulous conduct hasten their undoing; and when an arrangement was made by which they were swamped into the legitimate body of the London Company, they were nearly at their last gasp. A failure such as this had a natural tendency to discourage private adventure in the Indian seas. Domestic dissensions, too, which filled men's minds, and evoked their bodily activities, shut out all thought of foreign speculation; and when new homes beyond the seas were dreamt of by men weary of intestine strife and oppression, their imaginations turned to the gentle clime and the green savannahs of the western world, where, with their wives and little ones around them, they might live and pray in quietude and peace.

The civil wars did not promote the Company's trade,* but their tendency was to keep down competition, and so far they benefited the Company. But when the King's head had been brought to the block, and the

* Mr. Bruce, a staunch Royalist, says, under the year 1644-45, that the King of Persia refused the usual *firman* to the Company because our agents did not take off the wonted quantity of silk. "It is a memorable proof," he adds, "of the effects of the political distractions in England at this period, that the agent was compelled to explain to the King of Persia the reason of this change to be, the distracted state of the Government in England, in which the rigid and austere manners of the Republicans had rendered silks (an article of former luxury) less an article in demand than under the polished manners of a Court—a melancholy example of the effect of political anarchy on commercial prosperity." It is not very clear from this whether, in Mr. Bruce's estimation, the "political anarchy" of the times, or the "austere manners of the Republicans," had this disastrous effect upon the commercial prosperity of the country. The passage is not very logical as it stands. It would seem, however, that Mr. Bruce intended to build up an argument in favor of absolutism, for he goes on to say, "If the convulsed and austere manners of England thus struck at the prosperity of the Company's trade in Persia, it is a remarkable contrast to find, at the same juncture, that the settled, though absolute Government of Turkey, was favorable to the introduction of the Company's trade; because, under such a Government, articles of foreign import found a ready sale for the luxuries of the great, whilst this luxury facilitated the exports of Turkish produce."

monarchy for a time suspended, it was natural that the general vindication of liberty should embrace liberty of trade, and that the Company's monopoly should be in danger. During the first years of the Commonwealth, however, the war with the Dutch kept this experiment in abeyance, and it was not until the peace had been completed that the Company found that their exclusive privileges were again threatened. It was not even then that their charter was endangered by a general demand for license to trade with the continent and islands of India, but that some of the members of their own proprietary body urged their right to be emancipated from the trammels of the Joint-Stock, and under the name of Merchant-Adventurers, set forth their grounds for desiring to substitute for the existing system "a free regulated trade." An eager controversy then ensued; argumentative petitions from both sides were laid at the feet of the Protector, and for a time it seemed that the chances of the contending parties were pretty equally balanced. Certainly, as we regard with the eyes of modern enlightenment the arguments which were thus paraded by the two disputants, the Merchant-Adventurers have the best of the controversy. But the Free-trade arguments of 1813-33, which are here foreshadowed, do not apply with equal force to the great commercial question raised in 1654-55. The reasoning of the Company in favor of the United Joint-Stock was not unsound in its application to the existing state of things, and when the question at issue was referred in 1656 to a committee of the Council of State, that body, after hearing evidence, delivered a private opinion in favor of the Joint-Stock, but left it to the Council to pronounce an authoritative decision.* The Council

* Mr. Mill says: "These contending pretensions were referred to a committee of the Council of State, and they, without coming to a decision, remitted the subject to the Protector and Council, as too difficult and important for the judgment of any inferior tribunal." There is here discernible something of the *suppressio veri.* The historian ought to have stated that the

declared in favor of the "United Joint-Stock, exclusive of all others," and Cromwell ratified the decision.

But in the mean while—*pendente lite*—the Merchant-Adventurers had subscribed 46,000*l*., fitted out a fleet of three ships, appointed a committee of management, and obtained a commission from Cromwell to trade with the East Indies. Courten's Association had been broken up, but it had left a trail of piratical spawn behind it. The troubles of the Company and their servants had been great ever since the evil "Khutput" of Mr. Endymion Porter had covered the Indian seas with these reckless corsairs, and now a new tribe of chartered Interlopers were pouring in, seemingly with a fair chance of superseding the Company altogether. But the decision of the Council of State brought the Merchant-Adventurers back to their old allegiance; they fused themselves again into the general Joint-Stock, and the only interlopers left on the seas were pirates without charter or commission.

But the days of the Commonwealth, adverse, doubtless, to corporations and monopolies, were numbered. The people of England, though erring and straying, for a little space, from their monarchical ways, like lost sheep, were eager to return to their old allegiance to a royal master; and the Restoration was at hand. They were willing to try another of the false Stuarts, and Charles the Second was proclaimed.

To the Company this seemed a propitious event. It was natural that the restored monarch should have looked with a benignant eye on all kinds of legitimacies, real or supposed—upon all vested interests and corporate privileges, and especially those which had

committee reported that they had heard evidence on both sides, and that their private opinion was, that the trade ought to be conducted on an United Joint-Stock, but that, as the subject was one of so much difficulty and importance, they deemed it expedient to refer it, with the papers, to the Council of State, for their formal decision. This is duly stated in "Bruce's Annals," to which Mill refers in the margin.

been violated by the sacrilegious hand of the lawless Protectorate. The opportunity was a good one—not to be neglected by the Company; and they sought renewed protection from the Crown. They sought for such a recognition and confirmation of their privileges as would secure them against all intrusion, chartered or unchartered; and they obtained for themselves a new charter, which promised at least all that they desired.

It promised them "for ever, hereafter," "the whole entire and only trade and traffic to and from the East Indies." It established them as a body politic and corporate in perpetual succession. It gave them the power to change and alter whatever might be for the common interest and weal of the Company; to hold general courts, to make by-laws, and to establish a constituency, each adventurer voting according to his stock. It gave them full control over all their plantations, forts, factories, and colonies in the East Indies. It empowered them to make peace and war with any prince or people not being Christians, to build fortifications, and to send out soldiers and military stores. It further gave them the power to seize and ship off to England all unlicensed persons invading the Company's privileges; in fact, it conferred upon the Company a strict monopoly with very large powers; and it acknowledged what in the time of the new King's sainted father had been authoritatively denied, that the Company had for a long series of years been enjoying the liberties and exercising the privileges granted to them by Elizabeth and James "for the honor and profit of the nation."*

This was the Company's third charter. It continued without alteration or infringement until October, 1677.

* Letters patent from King Charles to the East India Company, April 3, 1661, in what, by a pleasant constitutional fiction, was called "the thirteenth year of his reign."

It had been granted, as I have said, under letters patent from the second Charles; but about this time the legality of such charters began to be questioned, and people openly declared that nothing but an Act of Parliament could legalise the monopoly which the Company sought to enjoy. It was urged, moreover, that they had forfeited their privileges, by divers acts of omission and commission; but the popular clamor seems to have had little effect either on the fortunes of the Company, or the favor of the King; for letters patent were again issued, under date October 5, 1667, confirming to the Company "all rights, liberties, and franchises" granted by former charters. It gave them also the further power of establishing mints in any of the Company's settlements, and to issue money of any kind, so long as it was not called by the name of the current coin in other parts of his Majesty's dominions.

In 1683, the Company received their fifth charter from the Crown.* The "Interlopers" had, by this time, risen to a height of daring which the Company's powers were insufficient to repress. They applied, therefore, for additional powers to seize on the ships and the merchandise of these lawless intruders, to try them, as pirates, by martial law, and to execute them upon conviction. The charter was granted. It empowered them to seize the ships and goods of Interlopers, within the limits of their exclusive trade—to hold forts, factories, and plantations—to make war—to

* Mr. Wissett, in his "Compendium of East Indian Affairs, collected and arranged for the use of the Court of Directors," says, under this year (1683): "The Company's trade having been materially injured by the proceedings of the Interlopers, Charles II. granted the Company a new charter (the fifth in his reign)," &c., &c. It is fortunate that there is much more trustworthy information than this in Mr. Wissett's volume. The Charter of 1683 was the fifth charter granted to the Company since its first establishment in the reign of Queen Elizabeth. There were three charters granted by Charles II., the last of which was little more than an act for the suppression of the Interlopers. There were besides these the grants of the Islands of Bombay and St. Helena; but they are not properly to be described as charters.

muster forces—to execute martial law—to erect Courts of Judicature, and to appoint Judges thereof, who were "to determine according to equity and good conscience and the Laws and Customs of Merchants." But this charter was not sufficient; and three years afterwards another was granted to the Company, giving them further power "to make war on such Indian princes as may hurt the Company," if satisfaction for injuries should not be obtained in a peaceable way, and authorising to use their ships in a martial manner, to appoint Admirals, Vice-Admirals, Rear-Admirals, Captains, &c., who may raise and muster seamen and soldiers on board their ships. All the wrongs which the Company had sustained at the hands of the native princes were attributed to the Interlopers, who were recited to have instigated the Mogul's people to make war upon the lawful traders.

These charters granted by the Stuarts related almost entirely to the foreign management of the Company's affairs, but the next, which was conferred on them in 1693 (3rd and 4th of William and Mary, chapter 15), related to their domestic arrangements. Various rules and orders for the Company's observance were prescribed by the Crown. Every subscriber to the Joint-Stock was to be a member of the Company. A proprietor of 1000*l.* stock was to have one vote in the General Court. No proprietor was to hold more than 10,000*l.*, or to have more than ten votes. Each Director or Committee-man was to be possessed of 1000*l.* stock, and the Governor and Deputy-Governor of the Company were to possess 4000*l.* stock. The Governor (and in his absence the Deputy-Governor) was to have a casting vote in all Courts. And the Company were to be required to export to India goods "the growth and produce of England," every year, of the minimum value of 100,000*l.*

But these regulations were not altogether pleasing to the Company, so they besought the King to modify them. Letters patent were accordingly issued, on the 13th of April, 1698 (this was the eighth charter), by which the qualification of voters, in General Courts, was materially altered. The possession of 500*l.* stock was to confer one vote—1000*l.* was to give two votes—3000*l.* four votes—4000*l.* five votes—a much lower qualification than exists at the present time—and it became necessary for a Director to possess 2000*l.* stock at the lowest.

This was the last charter granted to the old London Company, which, for the space of nearly a century, amidst all sorts of difficulties and discouragements, had maintained itself, with singular courage and constancy; but whose existence was now threatened by the promise of a charter to a new Company, made up, in no small measure, of the Interlopers whom the old corporation had resisted and assailed with so much vigorous severity, and against whom, it has been seen, the principal provisions of more than one of their recent charters had been directed. The London Company were at the mercy of the King. In 1793 they had subjected themselves, by the non-fulfilment of their engagement to pay a 5 per cent. duty on their capital stock, to the entire loss of their charter; and though it had been confirmed to them by an act of grace, a condition had been attached to its renewal, that the Company's privileges should be terminable at any time, after three years' notice. The King wanted money. The Government, indeed, of that period was in a chronic state of financial embarrassment; and some instructive chapters of English history might be written from existing materials, in the shape of the correspondence of those whose chief business it was to provide money for the requirements of the State and the exigencies of the Court. It is no strange thing, therefore, that now the temptation offered by the project of a new India Company, willing to bid high for its commercial privileges, should have been unresisted by the King. The new Company offered to lend 2,000,000*l*., at 8 per cent. interest, to the Government—and the old Company's charter was terminable upon three years' notice. The time seemed now to have arrived, therefore, for the suppression of the London Company, and the elevation of the new English Company upon the ruins of its venerable predecessor.

Brief mention has been made in the preceding chapter of the struggle which then ensued. The reader is acquainted with the result. The United Company of Merchants trading to the East Indies then entered on an existence which endured for a century and a quarter. The charter of 1698, under letters patent of William III., granted to the English Company, and subsequently transferred to the "United Company," supplies some of the materials of the present constitution of the Courts of Directors and Proprietors.* Twenty-four Directors were to be chosen, between the 25th of March and the 25th of April, every year, by the members of the Company—or, as they are now denominated, Proprietors of East India Stock. The qualification for the Direction was the possession of 2000*l*. Every proprietor of 500*l*. stock was entitled to one vote, and no proprietor had more than one. The Directors were chosen only for one year. Thirteen were sufficient to constitute a Court. It was incumbent upon them to convene a General Court of Proprietors four times in the year, and these Courts were empowered to make by-laws, for the better regulation of the Company.

* The charter decreed that the Company should "for ever hereafter freely trade unto and from the East Indies, &c."

The Directors of the United Company, as it has been shown, were, at first, elected every year. Every week, on proceeding to discuss the business before them, they appointed a new chairman. In 1714, this practice passed into desuetude. A resolution was adopted, to the effect that a chairman and a deputy-chairman should be elected annually, and sit throughout the entire year. And on the 14th of April, being the first Court-day after the election of Directors, Chairs were appointed by ballot. This arrangement has remained unchanged up to the present time. The chairman and deputy-chairman are elected every year; but the general body of Directors are no longer subject to annual election. In 1773, an Act was passed (13th of George III., chapter 63) for the better management of the Affairs of the East India Company, which contained some important provisions affecting the constitution both of the Court of Directors and the Court of Proprietors. It was enacted that, at the next general election, instead of twenty-four Directors being chosen for one year, six should be elected for one year; six for two years; six for three years; and six for four; and that at the expiration of every year, six new Directors, and no more, should be chosen. The effect of this provision has been to constitute a body of thirty Directors, of whom six, forming a sort of non-effective list, go out every year by rotation. For although it is competent upon the proprietors, at such annual elections, to choose six new members, the power is never exercised. The Court of Directors, as thus established by the Act of 1773,* the well-known "Regulating Act," of which some mention has been made in the preceding chapter, has survived to the present day.

* The Act recited the reason of the change—viz., that the annual election of Directors "had not answered the good purposes intended thereby, but on the contrary, by limiting the duration of their office to so short a time, evidently tended to weaken the authority of the Court of Directors, and to produce instability in the councils and measures of the said Company."

The last eighty years have seen no change in its constitution.

By the same Act, the qualification of proprietors underwent a revision, which has seen no subsequent change. The possession of 500*l.* stock had qualified a proprietor to vote; but this system, as the Act recited, had "been productive of much inconvenience," as tending "to promote the mischievous practice of making collusive transfers," and was, therefore, to be amended. No member was to be thenceforth qualified to vote, unless the proprietor of 1000*l.* stock. Two votes were conferred by the possession of 3000*l.* stock; three votes by 6000*l.*; and four votes by 10,000*l.* These, as I have said, are the qualifications in force at the present time.

At this time, the East India Company continued to enjoy the privilege of exclusive traffic with the East Indies, under the charter of 1698, which conferred these privileges upon them in perpetuity—or for as much as perpetuity is worth in letters patent. But, in 1781, when Indian affairs were pressing impetuously upon the attention of the Legislature, an Act (21st of George III., chapter 65) was passed, confirming these privileges for a fixed period of ten years, at the end of which the Company were entitled to three years' notice of an intention to resume them.

Up to this date, it has been seen that the Home Government of India was vested entirely in the East India Company. The control which Parliament had hitherto sought to establish was a control over the Indian Governments. They had sent out from England new men—men without Indian antecedents, and unconnected with Indian interests—to regulate the proceedings of the local administration, by a fusion of the English or Parliamentary element into the authorities and agencies in operation at the seat of the

Supreme Government. But the experiment was a failure. The control was at once too great and too little—too great in evil, too little in good. It clogged the wheels of Government; it threw the affairs of the administration into confusion; and really regulated nothing except the continual supply of internal strife. It was evident that this was not the kind of check to be advantageously interposed between India and bad government. So Parliament began seriously to think of some new scheme for the better ordering—not so much of our Indian possessions, as of the Government to which the welfare of those Indian possessions was entrusted.

The idea of the Board of Control took shape slowly and gradually in the minds of our English legislators. In this year, however, the small end of the wedge was introduced by Parliament. In the Charter Act of 1781 a clause was inserted which gave one of the Secretaries of State a controlling authority over the Company's affairs. It was enacted "that the Court of Directors should deliver to the Lords of the Treasury copies of all letters and orders relating to the Revenues of the Company, and to one of his Majesty's Secretaries of State copies of all letters and orders relating to the civil and military government and affairs of the Company, or of their servants in India; and that the Court should be bound by such instructions as they might receive from his Majesty, through one of the Secretaries of State, so far as related to the conduct and transactions of the Company and their servants with the country powers in India, as well to the levying war as to making peace."*

The following year was a year of inquiry. A Select Committee of the House of Commons was appointed to

* *Auber's Analysis of the Constitution of the East India Company.—Collection of Charters and Statutes relating to the East India Company*, 1817.

investigate the subject of Indian administration, and to consider how the British possessions in the East could be governed with most advantage to Great Britain and to the native population. And in the succeeding year (1783) leave was given to bring in a bill, by which the Company's affairs were vested in the hands of Commissioners, for the better government of our Indian possessions.

I should like to dwell upon the events that ensued, but I can only speak of the actual results. Charles James Fox was then one of the chiefs of the British Administration. The Bill which was then introduced is known in history as Fox's India Bill.* It was very adverse to the Company. It proceeded on the assumption that they had betrayed their trust—mismanaged their affairs—oppressed the natives of the country, and brought themselves to the verge of bankruptcy. It proposed to place the entire territorial government of India, for four years, in the hands of seven Directors, to be nominated by Parliament, whilst its commercial affairs were to be left in the hands of nine "Assistant Directors," elected by the Proprietors, but acting under the instruction of the Directors nominated in the Act, and removable by them. It entirely degraded the Directors of the Company to the character and condition of mercantile clerks. The humiliating proposal threw the Company into a ferment of indignation. The Court of Directors appealed against it. The Court of Proprietors appealed against it. Pitt, with the old head on the young shoulders, then only a youth of five-and-twenty, earnestly and eloquently denounced it. He declared that the promoters of the Bill were "proceeding to the protection of the oppressed abroad by an act

* Originally there were two Bills, one relating to domestic, the other to foreign administration—one for vesting the government of India in the hands of Commissioners or Parliamentary Directors, and the other for the revision of the local authorities, and the better government generally of the country. The two bills were subsequently merged into one.

of unparalleled oppression at home." But the House of Commons were with the Minister; and on the 8th of December his Bill was carried by a majority of two to one.

But the Company in the hour of their need had one friend; and that friend lived in a palace, and his likeness was stamped on the coin of the realm. The India Bill was obnoxious in the extreme to George; he conceived it to be an unconstitutional and dangerous movement, and it was soon noised abroad how the King had declared that no friend of his would support so oppressive a measure. The Bill was carried up to the Lords, and thrown out on the second reading. The Ministry was dissolved. The country, now about to subside into a chronic state of Pittism, received the youngest of her statesmen as the chief of her councils. Early in the following year, 1784, the new Minister moved for leave to bring in a Bill for the better government and management of the affairs of the East India Company. But the new Minister and the old Parliament could not carry on the business of the country together. Pitt was outvoted in his attempt to bring in an Indian Bill, and Parliament was dissolved. The new Parliament brought with them a new temper; and the young Minister carried them with him. On the 6th of July, 1784, he introduced his India Bill. It did not seek to destroy the East India Company, but to control them. It neither stripped them of their commercial privileges, nor divested them of their territorial rights. It left the constitution of the Court of Directors untouched, but decreed that a Board of Commissioners, composed of six Privy Councillors, of whom one of the Secretaries of State and the Chancellor of the Exchequer were to be members, should be appointed by the Crown, with authority to scrutinise and to control the proceedings of the Company. They were to have access to all the Company's papers. Drafts of all despatches to be sent out to India were to be submitted for their inspection and revision. They were empowered to call upon the Court of Directors to prepare despatches on any subject, and on their failure within fourteen days, to do the required work themselves. The Directors were at the same time required to nominate from among the members of their own body a Committee of Secrecy, not exceeding three in number; and it was enacted, that if the Board of Commissioners should be of opinion "that the subject-matter of any of their deliberations concerning the levying of war, or making of peace, or treating or negotiating with any of the native princes or states in India, should require secrecy, instructions should be sent to the said Secret Committee, who should thereupon, without disclosing the same, transmit their orders and despatches." Thus was the constitution of the Secret Committee established. Two years afterwards, it was enacted that the members of the Secret Committee should be sworn, and the words of the oath were prescribed.*

The famous Bill embodying these provisions—(Act 24th George III., chapter 25)—was carried triumphantly through both Houses, and the *imperium in imperio* was established. These provisions remain substantially in force up to the present time; but the personal composition of the Board of Commissioners has been materially changed. By the Charter Act of 1793† (33rd George III. cap. 52), which confirmed the Company in their privileges for twenty years, the

* *Act 26th Geo. III., cap.* 16.

† I may mention here, that this Act of 1793 contains the important clauses prohibitory of war-making—"Forasmuch as to pursue schemes of conquest and extension of dominion in India are measures repugnant to the wish, the honor, and the policy of this nation; be it further enacted, that it shall not be lawful for the Governor-General in Council, without the express commands and authority of the Court of Directors, or of the Secret Committee, by the authority of the Board of Commissioners for the affairs of India (except where hostilities have actually been commenced, &c., &c.), either to declare war, or commence hostilities, &c."

Board was made to consist of certain members of the Privy Council (of whom the two principal Secretaries of State and the Chancellor of the Exchequer were to be three) and two other members. The first named in the letters patent constituting the Board, was to be its President. The Commissioners were authorised to appoint secretaries, and enjoined to "enter their proceedings in proper books." Under this Act the Secret Committee was constituted, as under the Act of 1784, with the further power of receiving, as well as forwarding, certain despatches in the Secret Department.

Such is the constitution of the Home Government, as it is represented by Acts of Parliament. But how, in its infancy, the conjoint authorities worked together, and to what extent the Board of Commissioners was a really living operative power, is nowhere represented. Something, however, of the secret history of the working of the Board may be gathered from the following extract of a letter, written by Mr. Beaufoy, one of its first secretaries, in 1795:

"Having mentioned that the Revenue despatch of the 30th of April, 1794, was written by myself, you may, perhaps, be desirous of knowing in what manner the correspondence to India is conducted. In general, the business of preparing all despatches, those in the commercial department excepted, is assigned by the Directors to Mr. Johnson, a gentleman of very considerable talents, and of great experience in their service. Two assistants are allowed him, whose principal duty, when a letter is to be answered, consists in examining the consultations of Government, together with the proceedings of the subordinate Boards, and in marking all such passages as furnish in detail the information which that letter professes to convey. These passages are afterwards extracted by the numerous writers at the India House, and enable Mr. Johnson to form his own opinion on the facts related and the sentiments expressed, in the letter to which he replies.

"The process is laborious, but, on the whole, is the easiest and the best. As soon as the Directors have read and approved the intended despatch, their secretary sends it to the office of the Commissioners for India affairs, and care is taken that the private copy for my own use shall be accompanied by the volume of extracts (often amounting to many thousand pages) on the authority of which the despatch was formed. If doubts arise upon any point as to the fairness of the extract, recourse is had to the original record; but no instance in my time of intentional omission has ever yet occurred. The labor of reading these extracts falls, of course, upon the secretary, but this is the lightest of his employments; for as Mr. Dundas is seldom present at the Board, and afterwards requires at very uncertain times, and often at the shortest notice, complete information on such points in the despatch as engage his particular attention, it becomes necessary to form a written abridgment of these bulky materials. This the custom of writing short-hand enables me to do.

"Before the Act of 1793, the Board of Commissioners for India affairs was little more than nominal, except as the term applies to the principal Commissioner; for as the papers, which required their signature, were usually sent in circulation, they seldom were convened, and I, who had been invited to the office, as to a situation in which my services were particularly wanted, was surprised to find that it not only had been a sinecure in the hands of my predecessors, but that no active duties (the labor of writing reports on points of extensive discussion excepted) appeared to belong to the appointment.

"Fortunately, however, the Act of 1793 relieved me from the embarrassment by declaring that the sentiments of the Board of Commissioners for India affairs, upon any proposed despatch transmitted to them by the Directors, shall be certified under the hand of their chief Secretary by order of the Board. The consequence of the Regulation is, that no public despatch can be transmitted to India without a previous meeting of the Commissioners; that information is expected from the secretary on all the principal points of every such letter; and that his office has become efficient and important."*

The Charter Act of 1813 introduced no material change into the constitution of the India Board. The alterations were merely those of detail management; but the Act of 1833 determined that in addition to the principal Secretaries of State and the Chancellor of the

* *MS. Correspondence.*

Exchequer, the Lord President of the Council, the Lord Privy Seal, and the First Lord of the Treasury, should be *ex-officio* Commissioners, and that such other Commissioners as the Crown might please to appoint should also be members of the Board—the first named being its President. The Act of 1793 had specified that there should be two Commissioners—not of the Privy Council; and these two junior Commissioners had received salaries, but had attended the meetings of the Board or not, according to their conscience or convenience. Under the Act of 1833, no junior salaried member has been appointed. But an alteration has been introduced into the constitution of the Secretariat; for instead of a chief secretary and an assistant secretary, as in Mr. Beaufoy's time, two joint secretaries are appointed—"each of the said secretaries to have the same powers, rights, and privileges, as by any Act or Acts, now in force, are vested in the chief secretary of the Commissioners for the affairs of India." The President and the Secretaries are the paid working members of the Board. All the rest is a mere fiction.

In fact, the Board of Commissioners for the affairs of India is now one man—a fourth Secretary of State. He may, or may not, have any knowledge of India, acquired from actual experience or the study of books; but his power to control the proceedings of the Court of Directors is absolute and complete. He has constitutionally, in respect of all matters of internal administration, only a controlling power; that is, he is empowered to correct the despatches of the Court on all subjects that come under their consideration. But this unlimited power of correction is in effect co-extensive with the power of initiation, and it would be easy to name cases in which despatches, relating to matters of internal administration, have lost under the hands of the Minister all traces of their original significance, and have been made to convey sentiments the very opposite to those entertained by the members of the Court.

In respect of all transactions with foreign powers—all matters bearing upon questions of Peace and War—the President of the Board of Control has authority to originate such measures as he and his colleagues in the Ministry may consider expedient. In such cases, he acts, presumedly, in concert with the Secret Committee of the Court of Directors—a body composed of the Chairman, Deputy-Chairman, and the Senior Member of the Court. The Secret Committee sign the despatches which emanate from the Board—but they have no power to withhold or to alter them. They have not even the power to record their dissents. In fact, the functions of the Committee are only those which, to use the words of a distinguished member of the Court,* who deplored the mystery and the mockery of a system which obscures responsibility and deludes public opinion, could as well be performed "by a Secretary or a seal."†

It should ever, therefore, be uppermost in the minds of those who, considering the constitution of the Indian Government, and its effects upon the happiness of the people, would judge rightly of the responsibility of its different Agencies and Authorities, that the whole

* The late Mr. Tucker.

† How little, until very recently, the real constitution of the Indian Government had become known even to intelligent men, living immediately under it, may be gathered from an anecdote told by Lord Hardinge, in his evidence before the House of Commons (1852). After stating that the constitution of the Secret Committee was "a mystery not understood by the public," he went on to illustrate his position. "I recollect," he said, "an instance, in which an officer of very high position and ability in India, had written a letter to the President of the Board of Control, in which he had, in somewhat indignant terms, complained of the Secret Committee: the letter which had come out to him being signed by the Chairman and Deputy Chairman: this officer felt amazed, and wrote his letter to the President of the Board of Control. When I heard of it, I wrote to him: 'I hope you have not sent the letter, for, though the order was signed by the Chairman and Deputy-Chairman, it in fact came from the President of the Board of Control,' with whom this officer was on friendly terms. This officer did not understand the mystery of the President of the Board of Control being in fact the Secret Committee; it is, however, a convenient arrangement."

foreign policy of the East India Company is regulated by the Board of Control—that in the solution of the most vital questions—questions of peace and war—affecting the finances of the country, and, therefore, the means of internal improvement, the Court of Directors have no more power than the Mayor and Aldermen of any Corporation Town. The happiness of the people of India is dependent less upon the will of a deliberative body of four-and-twenty English gentlemen, a large majority of whom have studied India under an Indian sky—who are experienced in the languages and the usages of the people, and to whom the system of administration in all its details is as familiar as household words—who have, as a body, no connexion with Party, no dependence on the fate of ministries, whose official lives do not hang upon an adverse vote, and who can, therefore, pursue from year's end to year's end a consistent course of administrative conduct—than upon the caprice of a single man, who may be gone to-morrow, who may preside over the India Board and govern India for a fortnight, and then be suddenly deposed by some gust of Parliamentary uncertainty, by the mistaken tactics of an inexperienced Party leader, or the neglect of an inefficient "Whipper-in."

The Acts of 1813 and 1833 affected, in a very important manner, the character of the Board of Control, and rendered its controlling powers more absolute and entire. The authority of the Board had not extended to the trade of the Company. But now the Company were about to be deprived of their trade, and so of nearly all their remaining independence. The "United Company of Merchants trading to the East Indies" were fast ceasing to be a Merchant Company at all. Ever since the British flag had first waved over the Soubahdarry of Bengal, it had been said that a trading Company and a fighting Company were antagonistic one with the other, and that in course of time the greater would swallow up the less.* But it took nearly half a century of increasing empire to absorb even the first moiety of the Company's trading privileges. And then, I fear it must be said of them, that they had lived their time. At all events, they had outlived the patience and forbearance of the people. The temper of the age was growing less and less attuned to the conservation of exclusive rights and corporate monopolies; and now, in 1813, the gigantic preserve, the legal boundaries of which had been maintained for more than two centuries, was about to be thrown open to the incursions of all the vulgar traders of the land. I do not know what I might have thought of the matter had I been alive at that time. I have great respect for the Company's trade. I believe that, under Providence, to the preservation of the Company's monopoly we owe our Empire in the East. But long before 1813, it had fulfilled its mission; and I can not look back upon its extinction with regret.

For this much at least is certain—that when the Company began to think less of trade, they began to think more of government. Under the Charter Act of 1813, which deprived them of the monopoly of the Indian trade, their administrative efficiency considerably increased. But it was under the Act of 1833, which left them without the compromise of the China monopoly—which deprived them of the last remnant of their trading privileges, and took from them even the name of a Merchant Company, that greater progress

* Old Zephaniah Holwell wrote, in 1765, "A trading and a fighting company is a two-headed monster in nature that cannot exist long, as the expense and inexperience of the latter must exceed, confound, and destroy every profit or advantage gained by the former—new *temporary* victories stimulate and push us on to grasp at new acquisitions of territory; these call for a large increase of military force to defend them, and thus we shall go on grasping and expending, until we cram our hands so full that they become cramped and numbed, and we shall be obliged to quit and relinquish even that part, which we might have held fast, if bounds had been set to our progress, which, upon the present system, we now see is utterly impossible, therefore a total change in our politics becomes indispensably necessary."

has been made towards good government, than throughout all the long years—the long centuries—when trade was uppermost in their thoughts. I believe that the Directors of the East India Company, since they ceased to be the managers of a leviathan mercantile firm, have taken more serious and enlarged views of their duties and responsibilities as guardians of a country inhabited by a hundred millions of fellow-men. I believe that there has been more wisdom in their councils—more nobility in their aims—more beneficence in their measures. They have now become a purely administrative body; and it is impossible for any one, tracing, step by step, as I have done, the growth of that close connexion which now exists between them and the people of India, not to mark a progressive enlargement in the scope of their views, and a progressive improvement in the character of their measures. There have been more good things done for India—there has been more earnest, serious, enlightened legislation for the benefit of the people, under the Act of 1833, than during the previous two centuries and a quarter of British connexion with the East. And yet never has a benevolent Government, recognising the great truth that Peace is the mother of Improvement, ever been confronted, in its career of internal amelioration, by so many impediments to success.

That Act was a most important one in other respects than in the total abolition of the Company's commercial privileges. Of some of its provisions I have already spoken. Indeed, the changes which it introduced affected principally the local Governments. I speak of it here mainly because I date from it the dawn of a brighter era—because I believe that under that Act the administrative machinery of the Home Government, divested of all commercial clogs and incumbrances, began to perform its appointed functions as it had never performed them before. It would have been difficult for any Government, invested, by an Act of the supreme Legislature, with new powers and responsibilities, to have taken a more enlarged statesman-like view of its position, or to have recorded its sentiments in a more humane and enlightened spirit, than did the East India Company in this great conjuncture. Reviewing the whole question of Indian Government, as affected by the provisions of the new Act, they wrote out to the supreme Government of India a comprehensive letter,* in which they earnestly exhorted the local authorities to give, in all respects, the most liberal interpretation to its enactments, and to make it the instrument of conferring the greatest possible benefit upon the people under their rule. It can never, with truth, be said that they had not a due sense of the mighty responsibility entailed upon them as the rulers of a hundred millions of their fellow-creatures, when it is seen how reverently they bethought themselves of their own obligations, and how earnestly they exhorted the Indian Government to the due performance of theirs. Speaking of their extended powers of legislation, they wrote in December, 1834:

" In contemplating the extent of legislative power " thus conferred immediately on our supreme Govern- " ment, and in the second instance on ourselves, in " considering that on the use of this power the differ- " ence between the worst and the best of Governments " mainly depends—in reflecting how many millions of " men may, by the manner in which it shall in the " present instance be exercised, be rendered happy or " miserable—in adverting to the countless variety of " interests to be studied and of difficulties to be over- " come, in the execution of this mighty trust, we own

* I have already quoted this letter with reference to the subject of legislation in the preceding chapter.

"that we feel oppressed by the weight of responsibility "under which we are conjointly laid. Whatever "means or efforts can be employed on the occasion— "whatever can be effected by free and active discussion, "or by profound and conscientious deliberation—what-"ever aids can be derived from extrinsic counsel or "intelligence, all at the utmost will be barely com-"mensurate with the magnitude of the sphere to be "occupied and of the service to be performed. We "feel confident that to this undertaking your best "thoughts and care will be immediately and persever-"ingly applied; and we invite the full, the constant, "and the early communication of your sentiments in "relation to it. On our part, we can venture to affirm "that no endeavour shall be wanting in promoting your "views and perfecting your plans. Others, also, who "are in a situation, by advice or exertion, to assist in "the work, will contribute to it, we hope, to the extent "of their power. And we trust that by the blessing of "Divine Providence on our united labors, the just and "beneficent intentions of this country, in delegating "to our hands the legislative as well as the executive "administration of the mightiest, the most important, "and the most interesting of its transmarine posses-"sions, will be happily accomplished."

Since this admirable letter was written,* the general principles which it enunciated have been repeatedly illustrated, from time to time, in the correspondence of the Court of Directors; and I believe that nothing would so much redound to their honor—nothing would so clearly exhibit the progressive improvement in the administrative earnestness and efficiency of the East

* Mr. Tucker was chairman at this time, and his is, therefore, the first name appended. It breathes much of his spirit. I believe that the original draft was written by Mr. James Mill, the historian of India, then at the head of the Examiner's Department in the India House, and that Mr. Robert Grant was concerned in its revision.

India Company, as a selection from their own despatches. Shackled by debt—embarrassed by exhausting and distracting wars, of which they have been not the authors, but the victims*—they have not been able to give full effect to those measures of internal amelioration which demand the material support of an overflowing treasury. But I do not see any reason to suppose that, under such circumstances, any other administrative body would have done more; and, if it can be shown by a recital of what they have done, that the progress of good government, all obstacles and impediments fairly weighed and considered, has been relatively commensurate with that in our own country, I think that it would be more just and more reasonable to commend them for their good deeds than to censure them for their omissions. The good deeds are assuredly theirs. The omissions may be the growth of Circumstance.

* In a note at page 128, it is stated that the Charter Act of 1793 contains the clause prohibitory of war-making. I should have written "repeats," for the clause is contained in the Act of 1784. It is based upon certain Resolutions of the House of Commons (April 9, 1782), commencing, "That the order of the Court of Directors of the East India Company, which have conveyed to their servants abroad a prohibitory condemnation of all schemes of conquest and enlargement of dominion, by prescribing certain rules and boundaries for the operation of their military force, and enjoining a strict adherence to a system of defence, upon the principle of the treaty of Illihabad, were founded no less in wisdom and policy than in justice and moderation," &c., &c.

PART II.

CHAPTER I.

The Revenue System of the East India Company—English and Indian Systems of Taxation—The Land Revenue—The Salt-tax—The Opium Revenue—The Customs—The Abkarree—State of the East India Company's Finances—Evils of War-making.

It has been seen how, in time, with sore reluctance the merchants of London trading to the East Indies came to be great territorial lords. It has been seen, in brief outline, how they came to establish revenue and judicial systems, and to turn their ledger-keepers and investment-makers into tax-collectors and judges. From that time the welfare of millions of Hindoos and Mahomedans became dependent upon the wisdom and integrity of a little handful of European strangers.

The Revenue and Judicial Systems of the East India Company are two extensive and important subjects. I cannot hope, in a such a work as this, to do more than render an unsatisfactory account of them. In giving precedence to the former, I only follow, wisely or unwisely, the prevailing custom. I think it is too much a characteristic of modern Indian administration to exalt the Revenue branch of the public service at the expense of the Judicial. And I believe that this opinion is shared by many of our ablest Indian administrators.

The Revenue System maintained by the English conquerors in India differs but little in its main features from that which was before enforced by the Moguls. The people of India being, for the most part, a people wanting little and consuming little, the taxes were necessarily few and comprehensive. They were fitted to a state of society simple and primitive, and were little affected by the mutations of time or the advances of civilisation. It was, doubtless, an uncomfortable necessity that presented itself to us, but it *was* necessary to raise revenue for purposes of government. And it was necessary that in so doing we should subtract from the scanty means of subsistence enjoyed by the great mass of the people. It was, doubtless, a painful and deplorable fact; but benevolence could suggest no remedy for the evil—wisdom could find no substitute for the thing so grievously deplored.

Taxation, in all countries, at best, is bad. It is difficult to hit upon a good tax—a tax that is not open to some very grave objection. It may be admitted, therefore, that all the taxes which feed the treasury of the Anglo-Indian Empire, are inherently bad; that something reasonably is to be said against them; that solid arguments may be adduced in demonstration of the fact that they are loaded with pernicious results. I do not know any tax of general application in this country of which the same may not truthfully be said. But there is this difference between the fiscal histories of the two countries—that whereas in England we are continually throwing out new expedients and fashioning new modes of taxation, in India we go on from generation to generation without introducing any substantial changes. In England, every new Chancellor of the Exchequer has some new financial scheme to propound. The taxation of the country is the battle-field of party. We are continually being taxed or untaxed in one direction or another. It seems sufficiently easy and reasonable, if one scheme of taxation is not found to answer, to try another. The Finance Minister of the day stakes his reputation and his place upon some pet project of his own which is publicly enunciated in Parliament, and in the course of twenty-four hours disseminated by the press throughout all the remote places of the empire. If the project be unpopular, it is abandoned. The scheme falls to the ground, and perhaps the Minister falls with it. There is a little excitement for a few weeks, but the popular indignation is soon appeased, and the triumph is not that of the people over the Government, as the representative of constitutional authority, but over Government as the representative of a party. Constitutional authority is not weakened by these miscarriages. A new phalanx of administrators take their place on the Government benches, and a new experiment is made. The people of England have no horror of change. Indeed, they do not think that justice is done them if financial novelties of one kind or another are not from time to time presented to the country. They must have something for their money, even though it be a change for the worse.

But nothing of this is applicable to India. In every single respect the case is precisely the reverse. The people of India will bear a great deal so long as they are used to it. They are very intolerant of change. They do not understand it. They are timid and suspicious. Benevolence and wisdom may go hand and hand in our measures, but the people are not easily persuaded that what we are doing is for their good.

There is for them no Parliament and no Press. They have the vaguest possible idea of the intentions of their rulers. They do not think—they do not inquire—but with child-like haste and impetuosity resent the innovations which are intended to confer benefits upon them. Fiscal changes are especially dangerous. We cannot experimentalise without peril on such a people. We may relieve them of old burdens, and impose lighter ones upon them; but the probability is, that the open disaffection of the ignorant masses would compel us to abandon our benevolent projects, with a loss of dignity and an injury to the *prestige* of our authority not easily to be computed. The failure in such a case is not the failure of a party or the failure of a man, but the failure of the paramount governing power in its abstract constitutional integrity.

It is necessary, to a right understanding of the subject of Indian taxation, that these considerations should have reasonable weight. If the Government could be administered without money, or if money could be raised without taxation—one or both of which beatitudes some writers would seem to consider attainable—we might leave the land unassessed, the salt untaxed, and cease to cultivate the poppy. But we must assume in this case not only the necessity of taxation, but the necessity of maintaining such taxes as will embrace in their network the largest possible area of population. In such a country, and with such a people, there is little choice left to the financier. Where the millions live almost entirely on the produce of their rice-fields, with only a rag about their middle, and a few brass pots for their household goods, there is no very extensive field for the display of financial ingenuity. There are fifty different ways in which the English tax-gatherer may get at the poor man. But in India the approaches to the mud hut of the laborer are few;

and the tax-gatherer must advance by them or keep away altogether. He has been going for a long time along the same beaten roads. The people have learnt to look for him in certain directions, and even if better paths to their domiciles could be found, they would resent his approach by them. A tax on cultivation is not a good thing—a tax on salt is not a good thing. But the people cultivate the lands, and they eat salt; it would be difficult to find a substitute for these imposts, and if a substitute were found, it is probable that the people would reject it.

The taxes of which I have spoken—the Land-tax and the Salt-tax—are those which most immediately affect the bulk of the people, and they are those which yield the largest revenue.* Next in importance are the Customs, the Opium sales, and the Abkarree, or tax on spirituous liquors. Besides these, there are the Post-office, the Stamp-duties, the Mint, the Tobacco-monopoly, and other smaller sources of income entered in the Government returns.

Of the entire revenue of our Indian possessions the Land-tax yields considerably more than half. It is raised in different ways, and from different classes of men, but in all cases it is in effect a rent paid to Government for the use of the land. On the disputed question of the rightful ownership of the soil I do not intend to enter. A vast amount of learning has been brought to bear upon its elucidation, but it has been left in all its original obscurity, and I cannot hope to throw light upon it. It is sufficient that when the East India Company, as stewards of the Crown, became, by right of conquest or cession, the disposers first of one tract of country, then of another, they

* In saying this, I include also the duty on imported salt, which is entered in the Government returns under the head of Customs.

began to lease it out to different tenants, upon no uniform system, but according to local circumstances and personal convictions. Upon the different modes of land assessment, which we have recognised in practice, I shall presently come to speak in detail. I would here only generally set down that there are three principal systems now in force, besides other modes, of limited extent and partial application, which do not belong either to one system or another. These three principal systems are known as the Zemindarry, or great landlord system, the chief seat of which is in the lower provinces of Bengal; the Ryotwar, or petty cultivator system, which is enthroned in certain parts of Madras; and a mixed system, which aims at a less partial recognition of rights, and is neither as permanent as the one nor as fluctuating as the other—a system which is principally represented by the "Settlement of the North-Western Provinces."

The Zemindarry settlement of Bengal is a fixed assessment, made with a certain class of landholders, whom the Government of 1793 recognised, rightly or wrongly, as the legitimate owners of the soil. The amount payable to Government on each estate is fixed in perpetuity. The productiveness of the land may increase a hundred per cent., but still the Zemindar carries the same amount of revenue to the office of the collector. He may lease it out as he pleases, in large or in small holdings; may make what amount of money he can, directly or indirectly, from the immediate cultivators—but so long as he pays the fixed amount of assessment punctually to the Company, he and his descendants remain, at this fixed rate, continually in possession. The chief seat of this Permanent Settlement is the lower part of what is known as the Bengal presidency—embracing the provinces of Bengal,

Behar, Orissa, and Benares. There are also some tracts of land settled in perpetuity in some parts of the Madras and Bombay presidencies.

The Ryotwar system recognises the proprietary right of the sovereign to the lordship of the soil, and brings him into immediate communication with the actual cultivator. No intermediate agency is employed. The Government let the land to the cultivator* generally on an annual lease. The amount of rent is increased or diminished each year according to the ascertained value of the holding. The assessor fixes the amount to be paid, and the Ryot takes it or not, as suits his convenience.

The third system, now in force, in the North-Western Provinces of India, is neither that of a permanent settlement nor of a fluctuating annual assessment. It is a system of long settlements, or leases—settlements made for twenty or thirty years, with different descriptions of tenants. The village communities have been recognised wherever they existed in a perfect state, and each village, whether the proprietary right was claimed by an individual or by a community, was made the limit of a separate settlement.

Such, described in a few words, are the principal arrangements entered into with different classes of native tenants, for the supply of the territorial revenue of India. The amount levied varies considerably, but on the aggregate the assessment cannot be said to be heavy. In the North-Western Provinces, of which detailed statistics have been supplied by Government, it is set down at 1 rupee 12 annas, or 3s. 6d. the acre. This average refers to the land actually under cultivation; and, perhaps, does not differ greatly from the general average of the whole country.

* In some parts of Bombay there are Ryotwar settlements made for thirty years.

The next source of Revenue which I have set down is Salt. The article is one of universal consumption, and contributes to the Revenue in three different ways. Firstly, there are the profits on the home-manufacture, which is retained in the hands of Government. Secondly, there is the inland duty, levied in that part of the country where the manufacture is not restricted; and thirdly, there is the Customs duty on imported salt. The salt manufactured by Government, principally at the mouths of the Ganges, is sold for between three and four rupees the maund (or 82lbs.). The prices, generally "wholesale on account of Government, are fixed with reference to the principle that they shall not fall short of the cost of production, plus the duty on imported salt." The tax, whatever form it may take, may be estimated at about 2½ rupees, or 5s. for the 82lbs., being less than a penny a pound. It is calculated that each consumer pays on an average about 12 annas, or 1s. 6d. a year, to the Treasury on account of the article.*

The next item of Revenue is the Customs duties, regarding which little need be said in this place. The amount is principally derived from import duties, of which the duty on imported salt constitutes a considerable portion. With this exception, there is no local peculiarity worthy of especial mention.

The next source of income, however, is one of a peculiar and exceptional character. It is known as the Opium-monopoly.† The Government reserves to itself the right of cultivating the poppy, or rather the right of purchasing, at fixed rates, the produce of such cultivation. Opium is manufactured under the auspices of the Company's servants, and sold by auction to traders, who export it for the consumption of the Chinese. It is, to a very limited extent, a tax

* See Appendix A. † See Appendix B.

upon our own subjects, and the objections which may be raised against it have little bearing upon the question of the happiness of the people of India. Humanity cannot allege against it that we sell opium, as we sell salt, at a high price, but that we sell it at all. The two "monopolies," to use the current word, are in almost every respect the very reverse of each other.

It only remains that I should bestow particular notice upon one other source of Revenue. The Abkarry, or spirit-tax. It is, in fact, a tax levied upon spirit-licenses. Government farms out a particular district to the highest bidder, who under certain restrictions sells the privilege of spirit-vending, at a profitable rate, to a number of small dealers.

I would now proceed to give some account of the productiveness of these several taxes. The gross receipts from the Land-assessment of the several presidencies now amounts to about fourteen millions and a quarter of our money. It is thus derived, according to the latest detailed statements yet published :*

	Rupees.
Bengal	3,56,25,000
North-Western Provinces	4,97,50,000
Madras	3,52,89,200
Bombay	2,21,65,480
Total	14,28,29,680

The estimated receipts under the head of CUSTOMS for the same financial year amount to nearly two millions sterling, in the following divisions:

	Rupees.
Bengal	1,02,73,500
North-Western Provinces	52,22,000
Madras	11,36,460
Bombay	31,13,600
Total	1,97,45,560

Both in Bengal and the North-Western Provinces the principal item in the Customs receipts is the duty

* *Finance Letter of the Court of Directors to the Governor-General of India in Council, June 3, 1852. Appendix to Commons' Report on Indian Territories.*

on salt. In the former alone, it amounts to more than 61 lakhs of rupees.

This it will be understood is the duty on imported salt. The gross receipts from the sale of the SALT manufactured by Government, amounts to nearly a million and three-quarters of English money. It is thus derived:

	Rupees.
Bengal	1,02,89,300
Madras	46,76,120
Bombay	22,79,560
Total	1,72,44,980

But from this is to be deducted for "advances and charges" 48,31,139 rupees, leaving a balance of 1,24,13,841 rupees, or a million and a quarter.

The last estimate of the amount realisable for the OPIUM sales — that for the year 1851-52 — is between three and four millions sterling; thus divided between Bengal and Bombay:

	Rupees.
Bengal	2,99,71,184
Bombay	72,70,600
Total	3,72,41,784

From this, however, a deduction of something more than a million sterling is to be made for "advances and charges," and the net-receipts are thus reduced to a sum little exceeding two millions and a half of our money, or 2,68,78,184 rupees.*

Thus it will be seen that these four principal items of Revenue yield, in round numbers, twenty millions of money:

	Millions.
Land	14¼
Customs	2
Salt	1¼
Opium	2½
Total	20

* In calculating the Indian Revenue, I carry to account only the net-receipts of salt and opium, because under the gross receipts are calculated actual money advances, which when recovered cannot properly be called Revenue.

There then remain six millions to be accounted for. Of these the SAYER and ABKARREE yield one million; thus:

	Rupees.
Bengal	31,52,100
North-Western Provinces . .	29,50,000
Madras	33,44,430
Bombay	10,23,310
Total	1,04,69,840

Then come the following various items of receipt:

	Rupees.
Stamps	46,37,490
Post Office	20,44,170
Marine	18,00,000
Subsidies from Native Princes .	65,10,181
Tobacco monopoly	6,04,980
Calcutta—Mint (net receipts) .	1,14,162
Total	1,57,10,983

To these net receipts, now swollen by these last additions to more than twenty-two millions and a half, are to be added the revenues of Lahore, Sindh, the Eastern Settlements, and the territories acquired from the Burmese, Arracan, and the Tenasserim Provinces:

	Rupees.
Lahore	1,30,00,000
Sindh	28,00,000
Eastern Settlements	13,00,000
Burmese Territory	20,00,000
Total	1,91,00,000

This amount added to the preceding, raises the net receipts to about twenty-four millions and a half,* which according to the last published accounts may be set down, in round numbers, as the correct amount.

Having thus briefly given an account, in a rough general manner, of the Revenues of India, I proceed to make some statements relative to the expenditure of the country. The principal heads under which this expenditure may be ranged, are Revenue Charges, Judicial Charges, Customs Charges, Marine Charges,

* Or twenty-six millions with the addition of the million and a half, which I have subtracted for advances, &c., when calculating the receipts for the salt and opium.

Military Charges, Home Charges, and interest on the Company's Debt.

The REVENUE CHARGES, according to the estimate for the financial year 1850-51, amount to two millions sterling. The distribution, in the several presidencies is this:

	Rupees.
Bengal	40,37,376
North-Western Provinces . .	75,85,000
Madras	55,16,230
Bombay	28,74,460
Total	2,00,13,066

In these charges are included the expenditure on account of the revenue surveys; of canal irrigation in the North-Western Provinces, and on the repair of tanks in the Madras Presidency. The first item is estimated at an amount somewhat exceeding 8 lakhs of rupees (80,000*l.*); the second at 30 lakhs of rupees (300,000*l.*); and the last, at 9 lakhs (90,000*l.*)—thus reducing the cost of actual revenue collection to a million and a half of English money.

The JUDICIAL CHARGES are estimated at a sum equal to about two millions sterling:

	Rupees.
Bengal	74,98,732
North-Western Provinces . .	59,88,000
Madras	34,74,155
Bombay	26,21,717
Total	1,95,82,604

The CUSTOMS CHARGES do not much exceed 200,000*l.*

	Rupees.
Bengal	5,17,759
North-Western Provinces . .	8,80,000
Madras	2,14,010
Bombay	4,15,970
Total	20,27,739

It will be gathered from these statements that the purely civil charges of the Indian Government do not exceed four millions and a quarter annually—less than one-sixth of the Indian revenue.

The MARINE CHARGES—belonging both to the War and the Peace department—including, as they do, the expenses of the Indian navy, the pilot establishment, harbor duties, lighthouses, &c., are estimated at less than half a million :

	Rupees.
Bengal	19,41,200
Madras	1,36,613
Bombay	26,35,660
Total	47,13,473

To this amount is to be added, however, the cost of Europe stores and coals, supplied to the Marine department and the Indian navy, amounting to upwards of nine lakhs of rupees, and raising the entire amount of Marine expenditure for the last estimated year to 56,32,853 rupees.

Thus we see that the ordinary expenses of the Civil establishments, including the Marine, do not amount to five millions of money:

	Rupees.
Revenue charges, including Canals, Tanks, and Surveys	2,00,13,066
Judicial charges	1,95,82,604
Customs charges	20,27,739
Marine charges	56,32,853
Total	4,72,56,262

The ordinary MILITARY charges exceed *ten* millions a year:

	Rupees.
Bengal	5,57,57,700
Madras	2,72,60,540
Bombay	1,79,37,800
Total	10,09,56,040

This is exclusive of the cost of Europe stores sent out from England, and charged to the Home accounts. Under the head of military expenditure, also, are to be accounted the "extraordinary military charges," including the cost of "additional commissariat supplies, extra allowances to the troops, donation batta, compensation for loss of baggage, &c., &c." In the last twelve years, the aggregate amount of these extraordinary military charges (a deduction being made for extraordinary military receipts) has reached a sum of seven millions, making an average of nearly sixty lakhs, or 600,000*l.* a year.

These heavy military charges could not be met without increasing the Indian debt. The treasury being exhausted, the Government were compelled to borrow money where they could. I shall speak of this presently more in detail. In this place, it is sufficient to mention that the interest on the debt charged in the Bengal accounts, reaches nearly to two millions and a quarter sterling—that is, in Indian currency:

	Rupees.
	2,22,38,918
To which is to be added the Interest on the Home Bond Debt	47,45,685
Total	2,69,84,603

Thus far I have accounted for about eighteen millions sterling:

	Rupees.
Civil charges (including Revenue, Judicial, Customs, and Marine)	4,72,56,262
Ordinary Military charges	10,09,56,040
Extraordinary Military charges, on an average of 12 years	58,81,372
Interest on Debt	2,69,84,603
Total	18,10,78,277

The next considerable items of expenditure are those which are comprehended under the head of General Charges, and which include the stipends and allowances made to the native princes and chiefs who have suffered by the assertion of our supremacy, the expenditure upon public works, upon education, upon the ecclesiastical establishments, and other component parts of the great administrative machine. These general charges amounted, according to estimate, in the year under review, to nearly four millions and a half:

	Rupees.
Bengal	1,28,52,640
North-Western Provinces . .	72,44,000
Madras	93,18,008
Bombay	1,54,37,440
Total	4,48,52,088

The charges, as we have seen, have now reached the amount of twenty-two and a half millions. To these are to be added the Home charges, amounting to two millions and a half more, raising the total charges to twenty-five millions, and leaving a deficit of half a million.*

These statements are extracted from the last general review of the Company's finances, taken by the Court of Directors. But they are intended here rather to convey a general idea of the revenues of India, and the charges incurred in the government of the country, than to determine the financial results of a particular year with any degree of precision. Indeed, nothing is more difficult than to secure, in any such statement, an amount of accuracy that will satisfy all financiers. The accounts are made up, by different authorities so differently, that the inquirer is often staggered by the discrepancies which look him in the face, and bewilder the understanding. As a general rule, it may, I think, be laid down that the Indian financiers make out a more favorable balance-sheet for the Company than those who make their calculations in Leadenhall-street. I have shown, for example, that the estimated *deficit* for the year 1850-51, according to the Company's last general financial letter, was about half a million of money. But since the body of this chapter was written, the Government of India have announced in their Finance Letter of December 16, 1852, that the actual ultimate result in 1850-51 was a surplus of half a million.† Estimates are generally more favorable than actual results. But here we see that the actual results of the Indian Government are better by a million

* The amount of deficit, according to estimate in the Home calculations for 1850-51 (the last year in the Company's Finance Letter of June last), is 678,709*l.* Wishing to make the balance-sheet as clear as possible to the general reader, I have dealt principally with round numbers.

† Or 50,85,107 rupees.

of money than the estimates of the Court of Directors.

The estimate of the last financial year 1852-53, is almost equally favorable. The surplus is again set down at half a million. I give the statement as contained in the Finance Letter of the Indian Government. It will be understood that it represents the gross revenues of the country.

Sketch Estimates of the Revenues and Charges of India, for 1852-53.

The results are as follow:

	Revenues.	Charges.
	Rupees.	Rupees.
Bengal	11,44,71,845	12,93,81,137
North-Western Provinces, including Punjab and Trans-Indus Territory	7,66,51,000	3,18,25,300
Madras	5,26,22,820	4,97,68,660
Bombay	4,85,36,860	5,22,00,164
	29,22,82,525	26,31,75,261

	Rupees.
Probable Indian Surplus	2,91,07,264
Home Charges Estimated	2,41,57,854
Estimated Ultimate Surplus in 1852-53	49,49,410

The Debt estimated to be increased in 1852-53 aggregates	8,35,96,021
Ditto to be paid off in ditto	8,64,24,364
Net amount to be paid off	28,28,343

The Cash Balances on 30th April, 1851, amounted to	12,98,21,744
On 30th April, 1852	14,85,88,750
On 30th April, 1853, they are estimated at	15,23,96,044

These results are regarded as in every respect most highly satisfactory, and indicative of a very favorable condition of the finances of India. It is hoped that the improvement now gradually developing itself in the resources of India, may not only prove to be permanent, but progressive hereafter, as general tranquillity is restored to the country,

(Signed) DALHOUSIE.
F. CURRIE.
J. LOWIS.

December 16, 1852.

These assurances are most cheering at a time when people had begun almost to fear that the deficit had become chronic.

It is easy to trace the causes of this continued deficit. In the financial year 1835-36 the Indian revenues yielded a surplus of nearly a million and a half. In the following year, the surplus was a million and a quarter; in the next, three-quarters of a million. In the next year (1838-39) the surplus had altogether disappeared, and the awkward word "deficit" appeared in the accounts. Then came the Afghan war. A British army was pushed across the Indus; and the deficit for the year 1839-40 reached the alarming amount of more than two millions sterling. From this time to the year 1848-49 there has been an average deficiency of a million and a half a year.

How these extraordinary expenses swelled the Indian debt may easily be seen. In 1836, the debt amounted to less than thirty millions; in 1850, it had nearly reached forty-seven millions. The debt had been reduced in the former year by the application to that purpose of a portion of the Company's commercial assets, realised on the cessation of their commercial privileges. At the outset of the war in Afghanistan there was an abundance of money flushing the public Treasury. There was the happy surplus of three good years to indent upon. It was not, therefore, until the beginning of the year 1841, that the financial embarrassments of the Indian Government gathered so oppressively around them, that they could only look for extrication to the opening of a new loan. Then they began to borrow money at five per cent. interest; and as affairs beyond the frontier grew worse and worse, and a new war was undertaken to repair the disasters of the old, it was not until the commencement of 1843 that the subscription was closed. During that interval five millions of money had been received into the Treasury of India. The debt then in 1843 amounted to thirty-six millions sterling. A new four per cent. loan was then opened; but money came in slowly at this rate of interest, and from February, 1843, to October, 1846, only two millions and a half were attracted to the hands of the Government financiers. By this time the Sikh war had commenced, and more money was required. It was necessary, therefore, to stimulate the cupidity of the money-holders by the offer of a higher rate of interest. The five per cent. loan was therefore re-opened in October, 1846, and from that time to April, 1851, during a portion of which the second Sikh war was in full operation, eight millions and a half were subscribed. The debt had then been swollen by these additions to nearly forty-seven millions. The increase of interest, since 1839, payable on this debt, is ninety lakhs of rupees, or nearly a million sterling per annum.*

But the full extent of the evil is not here adequately represented. But for these exhausting wars we should have had a continued surplus, and been able to reduce the original debt. The cost of our military operations far exceeded the amount subscribed to the loan. The aggregate excess of ordinary military charges from the year 1838-39 to 1850-51 amounts to more than twenty millions and a half; and the excess of extraordinary military charges to upwards of seven millions. The

	Rupees.
* Interest on debt in 1839-40	1,31,99,549
Ditto in 1850-51	2,22,38,918

Company's financiers, indeed, estimate the cost of these wars at thirty millions. "We have already," they write, "explained the grounds on which we have come to the conclusion that 30 *crores* had been expended in increased military charges since 1838-39, and we have now shown that 5¾ *crores* more have been paid for interest on the money borrowed in India."* And when these wars, beyond our north-western frontier, commenced, the country was only beginning to recover from the exhausting effects of another great war beyond our south eastern boundary. The Burmese war in 1824-26 cost fifteen millions of money.

Having briefly shown the present state of the Indian Revenue, I must say something about its antecedents. Under the administration of Lord Cornwallis in 1792-93, the Indian Revenue amounted to *eight* millions of English money. Under Lord Wellesley's administration in 1804-05, it had risen to nearly *fourteen* millions. At the close of Lord Minto's period of government in 1813-14, it was set down at *seventeen* millions. Under his successor, Lord Hastings, in 1821-22, it exceeded *twenty-one* millions.† And now, at the present time, the gross Revenue is estimated at twenty-nine millions.

But with all this increase of territory, and increase of Revenue, we are poorer than we were. In the year 1792-93, when our gross Revenue was only eight millions, we had a surplus of a million and a half. In 1804-05, the drainings of the Mahratta war had brought about a deficit of more than two millions and a half. During Lord Minto's peaceful reign, our financial position continued steadily to improve, and at the close of it, there was a surplus of a million and

* *Company's Finance Letter*, June 3, 1852.

† *Tucker's Review of the Financial Situation of the East India Company in* 1824.

a half. In the course of Lord Hastings' long administration, there were two bad years; but at the close of it, in 1821-22, there was again a surplus of more than a million and a half.* In 1835-36, at the close of Lord William Bentinck's administration, the disturbance in the Exchequer occasioned by the Burmese war had been allayed, and there was again a surplus of a million and a half; but in 1839-40 the Afghan war having been commenced, there was a deficit of two millions.† Since that time the deficit, with some slight fluctuations, has diminished; and it has now been seen that the Indian financiers are gratifying us by the unaccustomed exhibition of a surplus.

These facts are worthy to be held in remembrance, briefly indicating as they do the effect of all our great Indian wars upon the finances of the country. But although in India we would seem to live in a chronic state of warfare, there is nothing discouraging in them. They are, as it were, the accidents of our position — external hindrances and encumbrances — but there is real vitality within. All our principal sources of revenue have been continually increasing. In 1834-35 the Land-assessment, Sayer, and Abkarree, &c., yielded *thirteen* millions gross revenue; in 1850-51 they yielded nearly *seventeen* millions. In 1834-35 the Customs yielded a million and a half; in 1850-51 they yielded more than a million and a half,‡ although in the interval the transit-duties had been abolished in all the three presidencies. The Bengal Customs receipts, principally owing to the large importations of salt, have increased nearly a hundred per cent. since 1842-43. In 1834-35 the Salt revenue yielded *two* millions; in 1849-50 *two and a half* millions; in 1850-51 *two* millions, besides 610,000*l.* derived from

* *Tucker's Review.*

† *India House Returns.*

‡ The increase is 41,000*l.*, upon the years mentioned.

the duty on imported salt. In 1834-35 the Opium revenue reached only to a million and a quarter; in 1850-51 it exceeded three millions and a half.* In 1834-35 the Stamp-duties produced 350,000*l.*; in 1850-51 they had risen to 443,000*l.* In fact, every branch of the Revenue has considerably increased.

Lord Hastings, in 1822, declared that he saw no reason why in time of peace the Revenues of India should not yield an annual surplus of four millions. Mr. Tucker, one of the ablest financiers who has ever addressed himself to the illustration of Indian affairs, wrote, in 1826, that a surplus of two millions might be fairly looked for, but that from this sum must be deducted a million and a half for Home charges. I see no reason why, after a few years of peace, we should not have a clear surplus of a million.

This subject of Indian finance is not an attractive one, and I do not wish to dwell wearisomely upon it. But it is absolutely necessary to the right understanding of our position in India that the financial status of the Company should be clearly ascertained. What I wish to be gathered from these statements is this—that the welfare of the people of India mainly depends upon the preservation of peace. The finances of India have continually been in an embarrassed condition, because the Company have continually been, in spite of themselves, engaged in great and engulphing wars. The policy which they have avowed and honestly endeavoured to maintain has been pacific to the very core. But they have seldom been permitted to see the disturbance of their Exchequer more than readjusted before they have been again called upon to find money to prosecute a new war. Under these repeated pressures they have been compelled from time to time to borrow

* Some may say that this is a bad rather than a good sign, inasmuch as that this source of income is precarious.

money at a high rate of interest, and by so doing have created a permanent embarrassment which has kept them, and still keeps them, poor. So circumstanced, so impoverished, they cannot be generous—they can barely afford to be just. They are compelled to take a financial view of almost every question that is presented to them. They are compelled to repress humane instincts and kindly impulses—to narrow enlarged schemes of policy, and to give themselves up to petty shifts and temporary expedients. They are condemned on the one hand for exacting so much from the Revenue-payers, though they exact barely enough to keep themselves from bankruptcy. And they are condemned, on the other, for not spending more of the Revenue which it is said to be shameful to collect. Indeed, as far as I understood it, the whole drift of the popular clamor which in some quarters is raised against the existing Government of India, is that they ought to have less money, and ought to spend more.

There are many things in the Government of India which I would fain see amended—there are many things to be done, and many things to be left undone before any man of enlarged views and humane desire can look on with complacency and content. But it were well that it should be clearly understood how, at the bottom of all our misdoings and our short-comings, is this miserable want of money. With an overflowing treasury impure taxes might be remitted, and great public works might be completed. The interest alone of the increased debt, which has accumulated since 1839, would have sufficed for the construction of some great material work, which at the same time would have increased our revenue and benefited millions of people, or for the extensive diffusion among them of the blessings of intellectual enlightenment and practical education.

The past history of India is a history of revenue wasted, and domestic improvement obstructed by War. But I see no reason why we should not be hopeful of the future. Already, as I have shown, is there a marked improvement in the financial returns; and there is every reason to believe that the Company will soon be enabled to reduce their outstanding obligations. The reduction of the debt will release year by year, for purposes of national improvement, sums of money hitherto disappearing, under the name of "interest," without a sign. The good or bad government of India is mainly a question of money, and, therefore, a question of War or Peace.

I have shown in this chapter what the Revenues of India are—what the moneyed resources of the Indian Government. I purpose now to write more in detail of these revenues and resources, and especially of the great tax, which, in different parts of India, under different systems, is levied upon the Land. I have briefly stated what these systems are. I am anxious now to show how they took shape under our rule, and what have been their effects upon the happiness of the people.

CHAPTER II.

First Possession of the Dewanee—Primal Efforts at Revenue Collection—Instructions to the Supervisors—Quinquennial Settlements—Hastings, Francis, and Shore—Arrival of Lord Cornwallis—The Decennial Settlement—The Permanent Zemindaree Settlement—Its Results.

THE land-revenue of India is a very large subject. A man of more than ordinary intelligence may confess, without discredit, that after thirty years' study he but imperfectly comprehends it, in all its bearings and relations. I know very few men who have attained to anything beyond this imperfect comprehension. It is a subject on which volumes might be written without exhausting it, and on which volumes, indeed, have been written, only to leave it as obscure as before. As for myself, I purpose only in this volume to give a very slight account of the systems of land-assessment introduced into different parts of India under the British Government, and the influence which they seem to have had upon the happiness of the people.

It was in the year 1765 that this great question of land-revenue first opened out before us. Up to this time the English in India had been buyers and sellers of produce—compelled at last to buy and sell under the protection of ships of war and battalions of Sepoys, but still no more than traders, trading with military escorts at their backs. With the taxation of the people for purposes of government we had had little to do; for we had owned no territory, and lorded it over no subjects.

But in 1765 the reigning prince conferred on the East India Company a grant in perpetuity of the provinces of Bengal, Behar, and Orissa; and the whole civil and military government of this fine tract of country fell under our sovereign control. The country became our own, and with it the revenue. So the matter of taxation from that time became one in which we were vitally concerned.

But it appeared at this time, no less to Clive and his associates in the local Government than to the Directors at home, that it would not be expedient to interfere, hastily and ignorantly, in the collection of the revenue. The Company's servants at this time were dead hands at investments; but they knew nothing of landed tenures. How could they be expected to know anything of them? They had other things to do than to study either the patriarchalities of the Hindoos, the oligarchisms of the Mussulman supplanters, or the bastardising effects of Mahratta intrusion. The philosophy of the question of right-in-the-soil was quite out of their reach, and its practicalities were equally beyond them. It was enough that somehow or other the revenue had been collected by the native officers of the Newab, from whom we received the territory, and it was thought expedient that the collection should remain, for a while at least, in their hands.

But it was soon found that these native officers required vigilant supervision and active control. So, in 1769, supervisors were appointed from among the covenanted servants of the Company to every district or province in the new territory.* What these European officers were

* "Agreed unanimously, that in every province or district, a gentleman in the service be appointed, with or without assistance, in proportion to the extent of the district, whose office or department is to be subordinate to the Resident of the Durbar, and managed as is expressly set forth and defined in the following letter of instructions," &c.—[*Proceedings of the President and Select Committee, Aug.* 16, 1769.]

now instructed to do was no slight thing, considering that they had had little or no training for business of this description. They were ordered to collect and to report information regarding "the form of the ancient constitution of the province compared with the present;" to give "an account of its possessors or rulers, the order of their succession, the revolutions in their families, and their connexions; the peculiar customs and privileges which they or their people have established and enjoyed; and, in short, every transaction which can serve to trace their origin and progress, or has produced any material change in the affairs of the province." They were to report on the state, produce, and capacity of the lands; on "the amount of revenues, the cesses, or arbitrary taxes, and all demands whatsoever which are made on the Ryots, either by Government, Zemindar, or collector, with the manner of collecting them; and the gradual rise of every new impost." These might have been considered duties sufficiently onerous for men not much accustomed to the work of drawing up elaborate reports of this kind. But their studies were not to be limited to the nature of landed tenures and the system of territorial assessment. They were instructed also to report on the best means of regulating the commerce of the country, with especial reference to the development of its internal resources, and the best means of removing all internal obstructions, in the shape of unauthorised exactions between the producer and the market, foreign or domestic. And having dismissed the great agricultural and commercial questions, they were required to report on the judicial system, or no system, of the ceded country. I do not know whether any of the reports so elicited are extant; but the paper of instructions is a very curious and important one, for they are the first which assume a real administrative character, and in them the foundation of the Indian civil service seems to be laid, broad and deep, to future generations.

But I have spoken of this more generally in another place. My immediate concern now is with the land-revenue. And, in connexion with the question of assessment and collection, under British administration, this paper of instructions to the supervisors of 1769 is very interesting and suggestive. It clearly sets forth the difficulties with which we had to contend at the outset, and shows that the revenue administration, which we found in force on first assuming the Government of Bengal, was vicious and corrupt in the extreme. In fact, we had then, as we still have, to surmount the great stumbling-block of native corruption. "It will require the greatest care," so ran the paper of instructions, "to enable you to form a general and particular 'hustabood,' or rent-roll, of the districts; you may perhaps find what is called a 'hustabood' in the suddur or principal cutcherry, but this, instead of satisfying must stimulate your curiosity; for the contents of it are merely adapted to the private interests of the Zemindars (or landholders), filled with representations designedly disguised to ignore with their offers and accounts to Government, loosely, unfaithfully, and partially formed in every instance. In fact, they can supply you with little more than a progressive history of the present dismemberments, and only suggest to you the degree of oppression which the multiplication of collectors and changes has, on that account, from time to time brought on the Ryots" (or cultivators of the soil). Nothing, indeed, is more certain than that when first we began to dabble in revenue matters, we found that, whatever may have been the system of land-assessment in force, it was bearing only the bitter fruits of extortion and oppression. Every man tried in his turn to pay as little to, and exact as much from, his neighbour as fraud and falsehood could compass. The revenue-collector over-reached the landholders, and the landholders over-reached the cultivators. Cruelty and chicanery had full sway.

All this was plain enough. But the Indian revenue system, or systems, so varied and unstable, were not very readibly intelligible to our merchants and factors. This much, however, was clear—that, although the cultivation of the soil was the main source of revenue, the cultivators were one class of people, and the revenue-payers were another. The Company's servants may have heard something of village communities, which had once, perhaps, existed in the very districts over which they had obtained a delegated sovereignty, and were still flourishing inviolate in other parts of the country; but they found that the actual payment of the revenue to the collecting officers of Government was in the hands of a few responsible parties, known as "Zemindars," or landholders, who looked to the actual cultivators for the means of meeting the Government demands.* The titles of these landholders were often extremely doubtful. In many cases they had been fraudulently obtained. In all it seemed that the landowners were a class who had very little claim upon the sympathy and forbearance of the governing body, whether native or foreign. The good old rule, the simple plan was theirs, to take what they could from the cultivators, and to keep all that they could from Government. Often this was best accomplished by means of collusion between the payers and the collectors of the revenue. The strong tyrannised over the weak, and authority was on the side of the former.

This was a state of things not to be upheld; and it is pleasant to see, that in the very first revenue-paper of

* I do not mean to say that the Zemindarry system was exclusively, but that it was principally, in operation throughout the Dewanee.

any importance emanating from the British-Indian Government, on record, the claims of the cultivators to our sympathy and protection were distinctly enunciated. "The Ryot," it said, "should be impressed in the most forcible and convincing manner, that the tendency of your measures is to his ease and relief; that every opposition to them is riveting his own chains, and confirming his servitude and dependence on his oppressors; that our object is not increase of rents, or the accumulation of demands, but solely by fixing such as are legal, explaining and abolishing such as are fraudulent and unauthorised, not only to redress his present grievances, but to secure him from all further invasions of his property." And the supervisors were, in conclusion, earnestly exhorted to do everything that could conduce "to the improvement of the lands, the content of the Ryot, the extension and relief of trade, the increase and encouragement of any useful manufacture or production of the soil, and the general benefit and happiness of the province in every consideration and point of view."*

But enlightened as were the instructions thus issued to the supervisors, the supervision was wholly inadequate to the requirements of the case. The double Government, as I have shown, did not work well.† It was altogether a sham, and an imposture. It was soon to be demolished at a blow; and on the 11th of May, 1772, a proclamation was issued, setting forth that the Honorable the Court of Directors had been pleased to divest the Nabob Mahomed Reza Khan of his station of Naib Dewan, and had determined to stand forth publicly themselves in the character of Dewan. Three days afterwards certain "regulations for the settlement and collection of the revenue" were passed; and from that time the collection of the revenue became one of the most

* **Proceedings of the President and Select Committee, 16th August, 1769.—[*Colebrooke's Digest—Supplement.*]**

† See *ante*, page 83.

important duties of the civil servants of the Company, and the European "collector" started into life.*

The management of the revenue having now passed into our own hands, a new system of landed tenures was to be introduced. The Court of Directors had instructed the local Government not to introduce any very violent changes into the existing system—not suddenly "to deprive the Zemindars, &c., of their ancient privileges and immunities." What those ancient privileges and immunities were was not very clearly understood. Indeed, it had puzzled the servants of the Company from the first to satisfy themselves regarding the rightful ownership of the land. There it was, so many square miles of noble country, yielding all sorts of produce, and a revenue of two millions; but, in whom the rightful ownership of all these broad *beegahs* were vested, we knew no more than we did of the landed proprietorship of the moon. Whether we have yet arrived at any very satisfactory solution of the great question, may yet admit of a doubt; but in those early days, even the information, on which the profound discussions of the present enlightened period are based, was wanting to our English officials. Whatever they did in those days could be regarded only as an experiment. The first experiment was not a successful one. The land was let to the highest bidder, for a fixed term of five years. The country was at this time in an impoverished condition, for there had been a mighty famine in the land, and the farmers not sufficiently considering the results of this great calamity, and eager to obtain the benefits of the five years' proprietorship, were too liberal in their offers, and they failed. A large number of defaulters appeared.† The machinery of

* One of the regulations was, that "as the Company have determined to stand forth as Dewan, the servants employed in the management of the collections shall be henceforth styled "collectors," instead of the present appellation of "supervisors."

† The remissions, on the five years' leases, amounted to more than 118 lakhs, and the balances, mostly, irrecoverable

collection, too, was not found to work as well as had been anticipated. The European collectors were inexperienced in business of this kind; and it was found necessary to replace them by a staff of native revenue-officers, known as *aumils*, to be controlled by a permanent Committee of Revenue, meeting daily at the Presidency, and by occasional Commissioners, selected from the Company's covenanted servants, and "deputed to visit such of the districts as may require a local investigation." At the same time, other subsidiary regulations were passed tending to facilitate the collections by a new distribution of the collectorates, and a better system of subordination to central control.

The settlement had been made for five years, commencing on the 10th of April, 1772. As the period of its expiration approached, the future arrangements for the management of the land-revenue became a subject of warm discussion in the Council-chamber. It was a period of sharp intestine strife. The Governor-General, in those days, had no absolute power. He had merely a vote in council, like his colleagues, and was not seldom out-voted. It is not to be denied that, on all questions of internal administration, Hastings knew more than all the other counsellors together. But Francis was in hot and heady opposition. He was a man of energy and ability, with an uncommon opinion of his own importance, a weak judgment, and a bad heart. On the great question of landed tenures in India, he knew little or nothing. What could a clerk fresh from the War-office be expected to know on such a subject? But he knew how to avail himself of other men's experience, and John Shore was at his elbow. In the unhappy dissensions which then agitated the settlement, Shore had taken part against the Governor-General, and was not

at the end of the time, had reached the still larger figure of 129 lakhs—in all, nearly two millions and a half of our money.

unwilling to supply his enemies with information which might be turned to profitable account. He was one of the best authorities on questions of revenue in the country, and he wrote with fluency and precision. Francis' revenue minutes were mainly the work of Shore. The counsellor seasoned them when necessary with the due amount of acrimony, and then served them up as his own. When Shore fell sick, Francis, it is said, was silent, and Hastings smiled grimly at the ludicrous discomfiture of his foe.

There were two points to which Hastings had especially directed his attention, two objects which he was eager to carry out in furtherance of his plans for an improved system of revenue collection. He desired to get together the largest possible amount of information on the subject of landed tenures, and the actual capabilities of the lands, before committing himself to a settlement with any class of men, or fixing the rates of assessment for any protracted period of time.* And he was anxious, in any future arrangement, fairly to recognise and protect the claims of the actual cultivators of the soil.† The Ryots under the existing system, not having their contracts with the landholders clearly defined, were subject to all kinds of arbitrary exactions. "It is the Zemindar's interest," wrote Hastings, in his minute of November 1, 1776, "to exact the greatest rent he can

* "In whatever manner it may be hereafter determined to form the new settlement of the provinces after the expiration of the present leases, it will be equally necessary to be previously furnished with the accurate states of the real value of the lands, as the grounds on which it is constructed."—[*Minute of Mr. Hastings' Revenue Consultations, Nov. 1, 1776.—Colebrooke's Digest.*]

† "Many other points of inquiry will also be useful, to secure to the Ryots the perpetual and undisturbed possession of their lands, and to guard them against arbitrary exactions. This is not to be done by proclamations or edicts, nor by indulgences to the Zemindars and farmers. The former will not be obeyed, unless enforced by regulations so framed as to produce their own effect without requiring the hand of Government to interpose its support; and the latter, though it may feel the luxury of the Zemindars, or the rapacity of the farmers, will prove no relief to the cultivator, whose welfare ought to be the immediate and primary care of Government."—[*Ibid.*]

from the Ryots; and it is as much against his interest to fix the deeds by which the Ryots hold their lands and pay their rents, to certain bounds and defences against his own authority. The foundation of such a work must be laid by Government itself; all that I would propose is to collect materials for it." Nothing could have been more reasonable than this; but the office which he proposed to establish for the collection of this information was to be under his immediate control, and this was in itself sufficient to secure the opposition of the imported counsellors to any measure, wise and beneficent in itself, though signed by a Prophet, and sealed by an Angel of light.*

But the ink with which this important minute was written was hardly dry, before Colonel Monson fell a victim to the climate of Bengal. Hastings was now Governor, indeed. Barwell was by his side, to preserve the balance of numbers, and the Governor-General had the casting vote. The proposed office was therefore established. Three experienced covenanted servants of the Company, Anderson, Croftes, and Bogle, were appointed to superintend it, and a bevy of native officers were sent into the country, "for the sole and express purpose of collecting such accounts and information as have reference to the business of the office."

The establishment was formed at the end of 1776. In the April of the following year the old leases expired; but the expected instructions from the Court of Directors relative to the new settlement had not, at that time, arrived. When they came at last, in July, it was found that they extended no further than to a temporary arrangement for the collection of the current revenue.

* Francis fell upon the plan, in detail, opposing it with a string of frivolous objections. Clavering denounced it in sweeping language as an attempt to wrest from the Council the ordering, management, and government of the territorial acquisitions.

The lands were to be let for a year on the best terms procurable from the Zemindars, or others, the preference being given to the Zemindars; if on the terms of the old contract so much the better, if not, at any rent "judged adequate to their real worth."* An important change was introduced at this time into the mode of obtaining security for the payment of the Government dues. The security was henceforth to consist in the right of selling the estates of defaulting holders, for the realisation of the arrears. "In case of their falling in arrears," said the terms of the settlement, "they shall be liable to be dispossessed, and their Zemindarees, or portions of them, shall be sold to make up the deficiency."† Here we have the germ of the Sale law, which has since been productive of such mighty results.

The same plan of annual settlements was adopted for the three following years. It was a season merely of experiment and preparation. The system was declaredly instituted "for the temporary purpose of introducing another more permanent mode by an easy and gradual change, by which the effects of too sudden an innovation might be evaded."‡ It was now determined to place the revenue administration of the provinces upon a more permanent footing. So, at the commencement of 1781, certain "regulations," relating to the machinery of collection, were proposed in the Supreme Council. By these regulations the provisional councils were abolished, and a metropolitan Board of Revenue was appointed. The Board was to consist of four members, all experienced revenue-officers, Anderson, Shore, Charters, and Croftes.

* They were let eventually, on an average of the collections of the three preceding years. It was not to be doubted that the assessment, under the quinquennial settlement, had been too high. Indeed, at the end of it there was scarcely an estate paying the amount agreed upon in the original lease.

† *Plan of Settlement, in Revenue Consultations, July* 16, 1777.

‡ *Introduction to Resolutions for the Revenue Administration, &c., &c., February* 20, 1781.

It was left to them to propose a new plan for the settlement of the revenue. In little more than a month after their appointment they made their report.* "The two principal objects," it stated, "for consideration are, the amount of the settlement, and the form of it." "The amount of the assessment," it continued, "must depend on the capacity of the different districts. In some, the assessment will be found already too great; others again, and the greatest part, will admit of an increase." The country had by this time recovered from the effects of the great famine of 1770; and the natural fertility of the soil had begun to proclaim itself. The four experimental years of annual assessment had sufficed to restore the balance which had been disturbed by the great drought. And the measures, of which I have spoken, seem to have brought together a sufficiency of accurate information to enable the Board to fix the amounts of assessment, without any very signal violation of justice in subordinate cases. Having thus sufficient materials for the ascertainment of the proper amount of settlement, they proceeded "to consider the mode of it." "The mode," they said, "which appears to the Committee the most convenient and secure for the Government, and the best for the Ryots and country, is, in general, to leave the lands with the Zemindars, making the settlement with them." The preference was, as in former instances, to be given to the Zemindars, and only in the event of their unwillingness, or disability, were the contracts to be concluded with others. "The considerations," it was added, "which ought to preclude the Zemindars, are their gross mismanagement, oppression, or incapacity." The leases were to be for one year, renewable by all who had punctually paid their rents. The proposed plan was adopted by the supreme Government, with some slight modification not affecting the principles upon which it was based,

* March 29, 1781.

and it was duly carried into effect, and remained in force, but with no very brilliant results, until the arrival of Lord Cornwallis. The Zemindars proved to be no better paymasters than the Adventurers under the settlement of 1772; the revenue fell off, and the home Government were alarmed and discouraged by the unfavorable out-turn of events.

That full success did not crown our initial efforts in the department of Land-Revenue, must be truthfully admitted. But the work was altogether new to the Company's servants at this time, and they may be forgiven if they only carried to it the amount of experience which, in the ordinary course of events, had gathered round such barren antecedents. It would seem, however, that they addressed themselves to their new labors with a sincere desire to respect the rights both of the Zemindar and the Ryot, and to develop the industrial energies of the country. What their efforts seemed to want at this time, was a sustained and systematic character; and this was now to be imparted to them, and in such a manner as to excite a controversy which sixty years of continued discussion have not sufficed to allay.

Lord Cornwallis arrived in India in the autumn of 1786. Mr. Shore, then appointed—in no small measure through the instrumentality of Warren Hastings—a member of the Supreme Council,* sailed from England in the same vessel with the new Governor-General, and soon cemented a close friendship with him. Hitherto India had been governed by men who had entered the country in early youth, and risen to high place, through all the gradations of service, military or civil. Cornwallis was an English nobleman, who had commanded armies in America, and sat in English Parliaments, but who

* Shore had originally been a partisan of Francis, but he lived to repent of this, to acknowledge that he had been mistaken in the man, and to cement a close friendship with Hastings.

knew little or nothing of India, the nature of its institutions, and the character of its people. But he was neither a hasty, nor a self-willed man. Equally willing to obey the instructions of his superiors and to profit by the advice of his inferiors, he formed no visionary projects of his own. He did not rush into authoritative execution of ill-digested measures, in defiance of the remonstrances of the experienced men by whom he was surrounded. Judged by the remarks which have been passed upon his civil administration by very opposite writers, he would appear to have been a presumptuous and self-opinionated man; but he was the very reverse of this. He adopted a measure only when it was his deliberate conviction that the balance of evidence was in its favor, and that it was his duty to carry it into effect.

As far as all predilections or prejudices for or against any particular system of revenue administration are concerned, it may be safely said, that when Cornwallis quitted England, his mind was a blank. It is not to his discredit to affirm, that he knew nothing about the land-revenue of Bengal and Behar. But the best revenue-officer in India was his fellow-passenger on board the *Swallow;* and it may be presumed that, from his conversation with Shore, he derived at least some general ideas of a subject of such pressing importance. His first lessons in Indian revenue were, doubtless, learnt during his passage to Bengal. But specific instructions had been sent to him by the Court of Directors, and he was not a man to toss them aside with haughty unconcern.

The Court of Directors had regarded with disapprobation the recent proceedings of the Indian Government in the Revenue department. They had seen that the measures adopted had not been successful; that the annual settlement had left the contractors, whether Zemindars or farmers, heavily in arrears, and that whilst the Government had been great losers by the system, it had benefited no class of the community. They therefore laid down as a fixed principle, for the future guidance of their executive, that a moderate permanent assessment would be more beneficial, both to the State and to the people, than a heavy fluctuating one. "A moderate assessment, regularly and punctually collected," they wrote, "unites the considerations of our interests with the happiness of the natives, and security of the landholders, more rationally than any imperfect collection of an exaggerated *jumma* (assessment), to be enforced with severity and vexation." The amount of the assessment was to be determined by the experience of the four preceding years, but not to be fixed without reference to the home Government; and, although it was intended by the Directors that the assessment so determined should be fixed in perpetuity, it was deemed expedient, at this time, for special reasons, to introduce it by a settlement instituted, in the first instance, for ten years. They expressly declared their intentions, that the contract should be made with the Zemindar—that "the humane intention of the Legislature towards the native landholder should be strictly fulfilled."

Such was the tenor of the instructions written to the Governor-General in Council, in April, 1786. Neither the Zemindaree settlement, simply as such, nor the *perpetual* Zemindaree settlement, was the growth of his own imagination. He found that the idea had taken root in Leadenhall-street, and when he arrived in India he found that some of the most intelligent and experienced revenue-officers in the country were in favor of the latter—nearly all in favor of the former. All men seemed to have made up their minds that the claims of the Zemindars, as proprietors of the soil, should be amply recognised; and many were of opinion that no effectual settlement—a settlement advantageous to the State, to the landholder, and to the actual cultivator—could be completed without embracing a permanency of tenure. But so little disposed was Lord Cornwallis to complete such a settlement "at once," that he hesitated even to enter upon the decennial settlement recommended by the Court as an initial measure. He did not think that the information before the Government warranted such a measure; and he began his career as a civil administrator with a recurrence to the system of annual leases. And whilst these annual leases were in operation, no effort to increase the store of available information was spared by the Governor-General and his colleagues. All the most experienced revenue-officers were encouraged to give their opinions, and other sources of information were resorted to without stint.

A vast body of information was thus collected—"information" declared in the celebrated "Fifth Report" to be "too voluminous to lay before the House." Foremost amongst those who advocated a perpetual settlement to be made with the Zemindars, was Mr. Thomas Law,* Collector of Behar, and afterwards a member of the Council of Revenue. He had the strongest possible faith in the virtue of a permanent Zemindarree settlement, and he did not hesitate to lay his plans before the Government, through the ordinary channel of the Board of Revenue, with an overwhelming array of argument in their support. Vigorously contrasting, in a series ot juxta-posed paragraphs, the farming and the permanent system, he made out a strong case in favor of the latter. "Every year (under the permanent system)," he wrote, "increases confidence by length of possession. Every man will lay out money in permanent structures, as such works enhance the value of his estate, and promise future benefit. If a scarcity happens, the landholders will forego demands, and encourage cultivation to preserve

* Mr. Law was a brother of the late, and uncle of the present Lord Ellenborough.

their tenants, who become a part of their necessary property. The increasing independence will raise a class of native gentlemen proprietors, who will gradually have established themselves in good houses, with the various comforts of life." In short, he wrote, after a long array of detailed blessings, "The mocurrery (permanent) system founds on a permanent basis the future security, prosperity, and happiness of the natives, and ensures stability. A long and painful observation," he added, "of the evils of the farming system, which have dwindled great families into the commonalty, diminished rich cultivation, and exhausted the country; and a subsequent war, which has not only drained the resources of public credit, but the hoards of individuals, have induced me to reflect upon the subject."*

Nor was it only the expression of speculative opinions which Mr. Law forwarded to Government. He declared that already, in the districts of which he had the fiscal management, the expectation of the permanent settlement had produced the happiest results. He declared that these results were developing themselves in an increase of general confidence, and a corresponding increase of revenue. Men of ancient family, who had been ruined by our assumption of the Dewanee, who had mortgaged all their available property, and were pining under the aggravating contrast of their present penury with their past splendor, now began again to breathe an atmosphere of hope.† Other classes of the community, de-

* *Mr. Law to the President and Members of the Revenue Board, Oct.* 4, 1778.

† "I cannot refrain," said Mr. Law, in a letter to the Board of Revenue, "from communicating the pathetic expressions of the descendant of a great family. 'Our fathers,' said he, 'for adhering to the Company's arms, obtained pensions and jagheers; and they fondly imagined they had benefited their posterity, by introducing a mild administration in lieu of feudal anarchy; they foresaw not that offices of state and command of troops would naturally be excluded from us by conquerors. Under adventuring farmers they could not submit to extortion and insult, or expose themselves to caprice for temporary tenures. Look, sir, into our houses; our widowed mothers, reduced to penury, in vain call upon us who have mortgaged almost every valuable in their support; our sisters pine in celibacy for want of portions, and men of property equal to their rank; when we look forward, future misery adds

pressed and impoverished by our previous operations, were, he represented, eager for the introduction of the permanent system, which was to restore them to their lost property. The bankers were petitioning for it. Under the old system, they said, they had no security for the recovery of their advances to the agriculturists, but that if the permanent system were introduced, they "would be greatly encouraged, and could confidently advance loans of money to the under-renters and Ryots," and "by this means," they added, "two advantages are apparent; first, the Ryots will daily exert themselves in improving the cultivation, and will become more capable and responsible, while the bankers will have an eye to the produce; and secondly, if any mocurreydar (permanent landholder) should happen to die, the accounts may be kept open with his successor, and the debts will be recovered without any risk whatever." All these things were duly pressed upon the Revenue Board by Mr. Law, until at last, overwhelmed by the formidable array of facts and arguments poured forth by the worthy collector of Behar, the President of the Board (Mr. Shore) requested him to afford certain specific information required at the time, "without reverting to the comparative advantages of the plan over any other system, *as I see no reason to doubt them*."*

But although Thomas Law was of all the servants of the Company at this time the stoutest advocate of the permanent system, he was by no means the only one.

poignancy to present want, and the retrospect of past splendor aggravates all. But we have now a hope upon the mocurrery (permanent) plan, that some may be favored with grants, and those who have jewels or plate remaining from the wrecks of their family may purchase villages and at length settle, by degrees to become affluent—our gratitude daily increasing to the British Government, who at once grant us places of tranquillity, and secure us from invasion, thus making the superior policy and discipline which subdued us the sources of our happiness.' The look, the manner of the speaker," added Mr. Law, "cannot be conveyed; much, therefore, is lost; yet I trust that even this faint participation will be grateful to sensibility and reason."—[*Mr. Law to the Board of Revenue, Nov. 26, 1788.*]

* *Mr. Shore to Mr. Law, Jan.* 23, 1789.

Among others, Mr. Brook, collector of Shahabad, came forward, with his unsought testimony, earnest and emphatic, in support of the proposed measure. "My earnest desire," he wrote to the Board of Revenue, "to see so beneficial a measure as a permanent quit-rent carried into execution, has induced me to trouble you with this public expression of my sentiments of Mr. Law's benevolent plan—a plan which, with a few subsidiary emendations, will ensure the relief of anxious millions, diffuse universal satisfaction through every subordination of landholders, and extend the fame of our justice through the remotest kingdoms of the East."

Of all the information which flowed in from the provincial revenue-officers, John Shore was the recipient. He was in immediate communication with the Governor-General, as member of the Supreme Council and chief of the Revenue Board, and to him had been entrusted the work of preparing the details of the new settlement. He labored at it, in his own words, "like a galley-slave." And in the summer of 1789 he was enabled to report that the arduous task which had been assigned to him, was complete. A masterly minute, dated the 18th of June, recorded his views on the subject of the proprietary rights of the Zemindars, and took a comprehensive survey of the whole civil administration of the Company's territories in Bengal. The plan now to be carried into effect was a decennial Zemindarree settlement. This had been suggested to the Governor-General, on his departure from England, three years before. But the measure had, as has been seen, been delayed for want of sufficient information to enable the Government to give it detailed effect. During the interval, information had been diligently sought and carefully collected. The home authorities had rebuked Hastings nearly ten years before for hesitating to mature a system of land-revenue on the ground of insufficient information. And now the ablest revenue-officer in the country reported that the subject was exhausted, and that it was useless further to discuss a matter which had been removed beyond the regions of doubt. From all quarters came assurances that the interests of the country could only be promoted by a Zemindarree settlement. A remarkable unanimity prevailed, upon this point, among all the civil servants of the Company; and the opinion which was so generally expressed in India was shared by the Directors at home.

I have never been able to understand how, in the knowledge of such simple facts as these, it could ever be asserted that the Zemindarree settlement was an idea hastily conceived by Lord Cornwallis—the aristocratic plan of an aristocratic statesman*—an ignorant *Englishism*, in short, utterly unsuited to the country in which it was designed to make it strike root. The measure, whether good or bad, was not one of aristocratic conception, English importation, or precipitate execution. It was emphatically the work of the Company's civil servants—members of the middle classes, who had come out to India in their boyhood—and they had been incubating it for a quarter of a century. It had nothing whatever to do with the personal character of Lord Cornwallis. If Mr. Macpherson, who had been a ship's husband, had remained at the head of the Government, the settlement would still have been completed with the aristocratic Zemindars.

The terms of the decennial settlement were announced at the close of 1789; and it was then notified to the proprietors, with whom the settlement had been made, that at the expiration of the ten years the assessment would be continued, and "remain unalterable for

* Mr. Mill says: "Full of the aristocratical ideas of modern Europe, the aristocratical person now at the head of the Government avowed his intention of establishing an aristocracy upon the European model."

ever," provided that such continuance should meet with the approbation of the Court of Directors. It is contended that this was a mistake. Shore, who had been the framer of the Zemindarree settlement, protested against its hasty perpetuation. He did not urge that it might not be rendered permanent; but that such a measure would be premature under the circumstances then existing. Law, on the other hand, had from the first declared in favor of its permanency, arguing that, under a perpetual settlement, every year increased the interest of the holder in the prosperity of his estate, whereas, under an arrangement for a term of years, as every year brought him nearer to the close of it, and therefore nearer to a chance of being dispossessed, his interest naturally declined, and his efforts diminished. Cornwallis recognised the force of this argument. But other motives than these impelled him to recommend the perpetuation of the settlement. He would have yielded to Shore's weighty reasoning, but he feared that such a concession would be fatal to the entire project. If he or his colleague could have continued to watch the operation of the settlement during the ten years of probation, and been supreme at their close, he would have been contented to give a merely experimental character to the new settlement. But he had no guarantee that the prejudices of his successor might not reverse the entire scheme. He was thoroughly in earnest about it himself. He believed that a great boon had been conferred on the people of Bengal, and that every year would see an increase in the prosperity of the country and the happiness of the people. Anxious to secure to them what he regarded as so mighty a blessing, he recommended to the Court of Directors that the settlement should be fixed beyond the reach of reversal. And it was so fixed.

But if, in the month of September, 1789, Cornwallis hastily announced his intention, with the permission of the Court of Directors, to render the settlement irreversible, that permission was not hastily accorded. It was not until September, 1792, three years after the first promulgation of the terms of the decennial settlement, with the conditional promise of its perpetual continuance, that the Court of Directors completed their reply to the reference of the Governor-General. The answer, when it came, was one of concurrence and approbation. It had been drawn up, after long consideration and much discussion, and was mainly, I believe, the work of the King's Ministers—Pitt and Dundas, aided by Mr. Charles Grant.

In the spring of the following year these instructions reached Bengal, and on the 22nd of March a proclamation was issued, setting forth that "the Marquis Cornwallis, Knight of the most Noble Order of the Garter, Governor-General in Council, now notifies to all Zemindars, independent Talookdars, and other actual proprietors of land in the provinces of Bengal, Behar, and Orissa, that he has been empowered by the Honorable Court of Directors for the affairs of the East India Company, to declare the jumma, which has been or may be assessed upon their lands under the regulations above mentioned, fixed for ever. The Governor-General in Council accordingly declares to the Zemindars, independent Talookdars, and other actual proprietors of land, with or on behalf of whom a settlement has been completed, that at the expiration of the term of the settlement, no alteration will be made in the assessment which they have respectively engaged to pay, but that they and their heirs and lawful successors will be allowed to hold their estates at such assessment for ever."

* I gather this from a letter written by Mr. Beaufoy, secretary to the Board of Control, to Sir G. Barlow. "The revenue letter of the last year," he writes, "was considered as the sequel of that which confirmed the decennial settlement, and which was written (principally, I believe, by Mr. Pitt) on the plan of a report, prepared by the secretary, from the original records." And he adds in a marginal note: "Particular parts of the letter are said to have been written by Mr. Dundas, and some by Mr. C. Grant."—[*MS. Correspondence.*]

Such is the history of the permanent Zemindarree settlement. It passed into law nearly seven years after Lord Cornwallis descended from the quarter-deck of the *Swallow*. It was sanctioned by the Court of Directors and the Board of Control after at least two years of consideration. It was approved, as a Zemindarree settlement, by all the first revenue-officers in the country, and as a permanent settlement by many of them. It was based upon information acquired during twenty-eight years of diligent inquiry. And yet it has been said that Lord Cornwallis, an aristocratic personage, saturated with aristocratic English ideas, hastily and unadvisedly completed in perpetuity a settlement with the wrong people.

I come now to speak of the results of this Bengal settlement. It is a large subject fearfully overloaded with controversy, and it is my desire in this work rather to state facts than to deliver opinions. No measure that ever emanated from the Anglo-Indian Government has been so warmly extolled on the one side, and so fiercely assailed on the other. Clouds of witnesses to be gathered from among the ablest revenue-officers of the Company, may be cited on either side of the controversy; and there is nothing in history to which a one-sided writer, not unwilling to make foul use of the materials within his reach, may so easily color according to the complexion of his own mind. Thus it has been asserted that the utter failure of the experiment was palpable within ten years of its initiation. But it was in the cold weather of 1801-1802 that Sir John (then Captain) Malcolm, who, in the capacity of Private Secretary, was in attendance upon Lord Wellesley, then travelling through Bengal, wrote to Mr. Barlow: "We have, since you left us, passed through one of the finest and most highly cultivated tracts of country in the world. What adds to my pleasure in contemplating these scenes, is to hear every man I ask tell how jungles have been cleared, and waste lands brought under cultivation. I cannot but envy your feelings on this subject. I confess, before I travelled through these provinces, I was not perfectly reconciled to your system. I have now observed its effects, and must ever think it one of the most wise and benevolent plans that ever was conceived by a Government to render its subjects rich and comfortable. We can only hope that a sense of gratitude will be the primary feeling in the breasts of those who benefit by this admirable system, and that they will repay the State for the care it takes of their interests by a firm and lasting attachment."*

It was one of the main objects of the Permanent Settlement to give the landholder such a beneficial interest in the improvements of the land as would induce him to venture upon this reclamation of the jungle. The theory was excellent, and so, up to a certain point, was the result. But there were errors of detail which threatened to vitiate the broad and beneficent principle. The Government reserved to itself the right of selling the estates of defaulting Zemindars for arrears of revenue, and it is not to be doubted that, in the first instance, whilst the authority of the Zemindar over the Ryot was insufficient to enable him to obtain his dues, the power of the State over him was exercised in too summary a manner. The period of grace allowed to the landholders was too brief. The revenue-officers were empowered at any time in the course of the year to bring the lands of defaulting Zemindars to auction if the monthly instalment were not paid. And under the operation of this law a large number of estates were put up to sale. Some of the oldest and most respectable families in Bengal were, it is said, to be found in the list of defaulters. It seemed,

* *MS. Correspondence, quoted by me in the Calcutta Review.*

indeed, that the old aristocracy of the country was about to be speedily extinguished.*

The grievance was a palpable one, and Government was not unwilling to redress it. Accordingly, in 1799, a regulation† was passed, decreeing that sales of land for arrears of revenue should not take place until the end of each year. As the Zemindar was invested, at the same time, with the power of summary distraint over the goods of the defaulting Ryot, he was thus enabled to realise his own dues before he was called upon to give strict account to the Government; and it was the opinion of the larger number of experienced revenue-officers that he was now sufficiently protected. The Zemindars had alleged that the dilatory payments, or the actual non-payments of the cultivators, had been the occasion of their default; but under the new regulation they could not any longer put forward this extenuating plea. The whole question was sifted by Government. A series of interrogatories were circulated among the collectors, and their collective answers exhibit the result of the Zemindarree settlement during the first ten years of its operation. Among the most important questions submitted to the revenue-officers was this: "Are the existing regulations calculated to enable Zemindars to obtain payments from the Ryots without affording them ready means of oppression?"‡ Several collectors stated in reply, without qualification, that the regulations answered every purpose—

* I give this as the received version of the story; but it is my belief that "the old aristocracy" had nearly disappeared before 1793.

† Act VII., 1799.

‡ A few of these answers may be briefly given. Mr. Ricketts of Tirhoot replies, that "the regulations are well adapted for the purposes intended." Mr. Elphinstone of Sarun says: "The regulations are perfectly well calculated for the purposes intended." Mr. Cowell of Bírbhúm makes answer, that "the existing regulations are most favorable for realising the rents from the under-farmers and Ryots, and in general are acknowledged to be so by the Zemindars, and other description of landholders." Mr. Smith of Dinagepore curtly answers: "I conceive that they are." Mr. Wright of Rungpore says: "The regulations which have been issued for the benefit of the landholders have answered the purposes intended."

that the Zemindars had the power of obtaining punctual payment of his rents, and had not the power of oppressing the Ryots. Several stated that the Zemindar had the power of obtaining his rents, but that the system did tend to the oppression of the Ryots. A few stated, on the other hand, that the Regulations enabled the Ryot to cheat the Zemindar; and Sir Henry Strachey stated outright that there was not a Zemindar left in Bengal.

Now, the truth appears to have been this. Immaculate Ryots do not grow in Bengal any more than immaculate Zemindars. As there was tyranny on the one hand, there was fraud on the other. But the balance of wrong-doing must have been greatly on the side of the Zemindar. The ignorant husbandman was no match for the landed proprietor—still less was he a match for the middle-man or agent. Cunning he may have been—dishonest he may have been; but he was weak and cowardly too, and had little heart to systematise fraud, and to fight it out boldly with his superiors. He paid his rents when he could. He generally paid them, indeed, when there was no attempt to overreach him;

Mr. Seton of Kishnaghur replies: "The powers vested by the regulations in the Zemindars, and other proprietors and farmers, holding lands immediately of Government, are fully adequate to enable them to collect their rents from their under-farmers and Ryots." Mr. Le Gros of Mymensing answers in almost the same words: "The existing regulations are perfectly well calculated for enabling Zemindars and other proprietors of land, and farmers of land holding their farms immediately of Government, to realise their rents from their under-farmers and Ryots." Mr. Hayes of Múrshedabad emphatically declares that the "Zemindars, and other descriptions of landholders, are unanimous in acknowledging that the existing regulations, for enabling them to realise their rents from the under-farmers and Ryots, are well calculated for the purposes intended;" and the Collector of Midnapore commences a long able minute with the words: "I am of opinion that, since the Regulation VII. of 1799 has been generally known and enforced in the Mofussil, the Zemindars have been very well able to realise their rents." "Lands," says Mr. Grant, collector of Midnapore, "being now exempted from sale for the recovery of arrears of revenue till the end of the year, it appears to me much less necessary to expedite the sale of distrained property than it was before Regulation VII. of 1799 was issued, when they were liable to be sold every month. . . . I have frequently had occasion to state to the Board that, as far as my experience goes, I have found that the common Ryots, or the lowest tenants, who are the cultivators of the soil, pay their revenues with great punctuality. . . . They are much more apt to submit tamely to exaction, than to hazard a contest with a Zemindar; and they pay a kist or two in advance much oftener than they fall in arrear."

but when he fell into arrears, and the war began, he did all that he could, in his weakness, with fraud and lying and the collusion of his friends, to outwit his antagonist. He got the start, when he could, of his enemy, carried off all his moveables to a neighbour's house, cut his standing crops in the night time, concealed them by the connivance of his friends, and met the distraining party with no worldly goods in his possession, but the rag about his middle, and a few earthenware pots in his house. The Zemindars certainly did complain that in this way the weapon of distraint became a *telum imbelle* in their hands; that they had great difficulty in obtaining the assistance of the police—that, if a small party went to distrain, they were beaten; and that, if a large party went, the expense was so heavy, that it was better not to distrain at all; and that, as to suing the defaulter in our law courts, the process was so tedious, and the cost of maintaining the defendant in prison so onerous, that they seldom gained anything but a heavy loss by the proceeding.

Such was the plaint of the Zemindars. I do not doubt that such things happened. But the power of the Zemindar to oppress the Ryot must have been far greater than that of the Ryot to outwit the Zemindar. The husbandman was generally better disposed to submit to imposition than to battle it out with the proprietor, or the agent, who was sure to be a greater tyrant than his master. The Ryot had not much to lose, it is true; and it is argued that the constitutional indolence of the native character made him look upon mere loss of liberty as no evil, and that he was content to exist in gaol at the expense of his oppressor. But indolent and debased as he may have been, he was not utterly hardened and reckless. He could not meet with indifference a calamity that severed all family ties, and left wife and children at the mercy of the spoiler, and exposed to all the accidents of life. He had, too, whatever he may have thought of the immunities of gaol-life, a horror of the police—a horror of the long journey to the justice-seat—and of a thousand vaguely apprehended evils, to which even the natural litigiousness of his character could not fortify him to look forward with complacency. The balance, indeed, was greatly against him, and he had sense enough to know it. He seldom invited a contest, which he knew must end in his ruin. It was better, he thought, to compromise with fate, and bear the lesser evil of the two. So he acceded in patience to the extortionate demands made upon him, when he could; when he could not, the Regulations took their course. And how destructive that course was, may be gathered from the evidence of Mr. Rees, the collector of Purneah, who speaks of "repeated instances of families, nay whole villages, reduced to penury and distress by their (the middle-men's and agents') oppressive use of that power of distraint, which is vested in them with equal authority as in the actual proprietor of the soil." It was not till ten years afterwards that the Zemindar was prohibited from seizing even the agricultural implements and farm cattle of the Ryot: it was not till ten years afterwards that he was compelled to give due notice of his intention to distrain before coming down, with one fell swoop, upon all the property of his debtor.*

If, then, the large estates, under the Permanent Settlement, continued to fall to pieces, and the wealthy Zemindars were still stripped of their lands, it would hardly appear that the cause of this decadence of the old aristocracy is to be found in the fact that "Government had given to themselves the benefit of summary process with regard to the Zemindars, but had left the Zemindars to the tedious progress through all the technical forms of the courts in extracting payment from the

* *Author in the Calcutta Review.*

Ryots."* Nor was it that the assessment itself was excessive. Under able and economical management the estates yielded readily the required revenue. But the management, in most instances, was neither able nor economical. The Zemindars were often indolent and extravagant; they mismanaged their estates, left them to the superintendence of underlings; and were fatally given to ruinous litigation. These causes combined to stimulate the Sale Act into unhealthy excited action; and many of the families (old or new) whom we found in possession of the land, were doubtless brought to ruin by them.† Property has undergone a great revolution, since the Regulations of 1793 brought the Zemindars of Bengal directly into the hands of the English collector. Mr. Law was of opinion that the Permanent Settlement would "raise a class of native gentlemen proprietors, who would establish themselves in good houses, with the various comforts of life;"‡ and it certainly did raise a class of native proprietors—of mushroom gentlemen—who built up their prosperity upon the ruins of others more unfortunate or improvident than themselves.

The Bengal officials admitted this—but they doubted whether the change was to be greatly deplored. I think that they treated the matter of this great revolution in a very cool and off-hand manner, and I by no means share in the satisfaction expressed by some of them at the

* *Mill's History of India.*

† A very able writer on Indian affairs, speaking of the revolution of property in India, states the causes very truthfully and forcibly, in the following passage: "A minute inquiry into the causes which had transferred landed property from the older families to the traders and merchants, who owe their rise to the Company, might in a very few instances certainly prove that the transfer had been occasioned by causes beyond the control of the proprietor; by famine, by drought, by inundation, by the over-assessment of a zealous revenue-officer, by the absence or the delay of an adequate remedy to hastiness. But, in a far greater number of instances, the change of circumstances would be owing to the culpable indifference, or the reckless extortion of the landlords; to the rack-rent of evil advisers or agents; to a spirit of litigation which is unrivalled in the forensic annals of Europe, and to a forgetfulness of the memorable aphorism that the immutable laws of Providence have decreed vexation to violence, and poverty to rapine."—[*Letters on the Government of India.—Morning Chronicle, March,* 1853.]

‡ See *ante*, page 178.

thought that the extinction of the large Zemindarries; however much to be regretted as affecting the individual proprietor, would probably be beneficial to the country at large, from the estate falling into the possession of more able and economic management. But I am inclined to believe that the evils of this revolution have been considerably over-stated. Indeed, it is remarkable that the Permanent Settlement is charged with two offences of an antagonistic and wholly irreconcileable character. It is said, on the one hand, that the settlement was completed with men who had no title to the privileges it accorded to them; and on the other, that it has stripped the ancient gentry of Bengal of privileges inherited from remote ancestral generations. One of these may be the rule; the other, the exception. They cannot both be the rule.

It is not, however, to be denied, even by those who recognise nothing but evil in the Regulations of 1793, that the cruel operation of the Sale Law is rather an accident of the Past than of the Present.* In spite of the publicity given to the new Regulations, the Zemindars were at first but imperfectly acquainted with them. They had been accustomed to personal coercion, but not to the sale of their lands; and they may, in the first instance, have believed that the threat would not be car-

* Mr. Campbell, one of the most strenuous as he is one of the ablest opponents of the Permanent Settlement, makes candid admission of this. "The general view," he says, "of the present working of the Permanent Settlement, shown by the last reports, proves that the Bengalees now understanding our system, and the bad estates having fallen to Government, the revenue is realised with considerable punctuality. A good many sales for arrears still take place, but they are principally of small estates. Some, probably, are permitted to go to the hammer by those wishing to dispose of them, and to give a good title to the purchasers. Remissions are occasionally made on the ground of natural calamities, but they are small in amount. The regularly settled estates of 1848-49 bore a rent of 3,45,98,603 rupees, of which upwards of 90 per cent. was realised within the year, along with 87 per cent. of the last year's balance, showing that the greater portion of the 10 per cent. current balance is the portion due at the end of the year, and collected in the next year. A little more than 1 per cent. was remitted or transferred to defaulters' register. . . Of the total demand on account of land-revenue, the whole is eventually realised within 1 to 1½ per cent."—[*Campbell's Modern India*, 1852]

ried into effect. It was often the interest of the agent to keep the Zemindar himself in ignorance of the danger which threatened his estate, and he awoke perhaps, from the false security in which he had been lulled, only to find himself stripped of his lands, and his agent, under cover of some man of straw, in actual possession of a large portion of the dismembered estate. But when the proceedings of the collector's office became better understood, and the larger and more unmanageable estates fell to pieces, the operation of the Sale Law lost all its severity. The assessment, originally light, has become lighter by the improvement of the land, and the cases of default are few. The unrealised balance every year does not exceed one and a half per cent. on the entire revenue of the land under assessment.

But there are still more important considerations than the transfer of these proprietary rights. It is time that I should say something of the effect of the measure on the general happiness of the people. When, in 1802, Malcolm wrote that the visible results of the settlement were of the most satisfactory description, he only wrote what now, fifty years afterwards, every traveller through Bengal would cheerfully endorse. The aspect of the country, under the operation of the Perpetual Settlement, seems to give the lie to the assertion that the people are ground down and depressed. There is hardly a rood of land not under cultivation. The jungle has entirely disappeared. "A man," says a recent writer, "may go for miles in any direction, east and north of the metropolis, and see plains succeeding to plains, where there is not one *bigah* of unproductive soil, and where many thousands of *bigahs* give their return of two crops in the year, without irrigation, and without that careful labor which seems indispensable, in the Upper Provinces, to successful agriculture. More new bazaars will be found to have been established within the last thirty years than old bazaars to have decayed. The circulation of money in the interior of such districts is very considerable. The number of men who derive competence and consequence from the soil, is large. Is it fair to say that all these results are independent of the Perpetual Settlement?"*

It would seem then, that if the old aristocracy have been ruined, the country has not been ruined with them. The provinces under the Perpetual Settlement are the most thriving provinces in India. It is a great thing I know that they have enjoyed, under British rule, nearly a century of unbroken peace. Nature, doubtless, too, has done much for them. Their natural fertility is great. They are independent of artificial irrigation. But it is only since the Permanent Settlement was introduced that the country has been exempted from the curse of periodical famine; and some of the ablest men who have ever given themselves to the study of Indian affairs, foremost among whom were Edmonstone and Tucker,† have

* *Calcutta Review.*

† Sir Henry Russell says in his published Letters:

"In one of my last conversations on the subject with Mr. Edmonstone, to whose guidance and instruction I owe anything that I may have learned in India, and whom I have looked up to all my life with reverence and affection, he ascribed the present exemption of Bengal from those periodical famines, to which it was formerly subject, and by which other tracts are occasionally visited, to the influence of the permanent system. In this I cannot concur, without depreciating the value of good government, uniform protection, and shelter behind a wide and secure boundary. Unquestionably many able men, besides Mr. Edmonstone, have been from the first, and still are, the advocates of the *Zemindarry* system. The fact is, that we all of us lean to the doctrine of the school we have been brought up in. Independently of the force of habit, we cannot easily bring ourselves to think that that, which we have spent our lives in learning, is of no substance or effect. The advocates of this system have all been brought up in Bengal, where they have seen no other in action. Among the eminent authorities on this subject, Mr. Hodgson is the only one I remember, who, having made himself conversant with both systems, gives the preference to that of Bengal. With this single exception, as far as I am aware, the whole of those, who have witnessed the working of the two, are in favor of the native machinery of the *Ryotwar* system."

The testimony of Mr. Tucker may be added: "I never," he wrote to a brother Director, "can be persuaded that the Regulations of 1793 were not framed on sound and just principles—but no person will contend that the Permanent Settlement was not concluded with undue haste, and upon defective materials; but if the measure had not been prosecuted at the time, it would probably never have been undertaken, and the country and the people would have remained in the wretched condition to which they had been reduced under short and corrupt settlements. If this great measure had no other merit, I would say that (under Providence) the

declared their opinion that it mainly is to the settlement that this exemption (under Providence) is to be attributed. This in itself is no small thing. It is no small thing to know that the peasantry of Bengal are never starving. "As to the poverty and misery of the actual Ryot," says the writer I have quoted above—one of the ablest men now in India—"so much insisted on by several writers at the present day, we deny that matters are as bad as represented. What strikes the eye most in any village, or set of villages, in a Bengal district, is the exuberant fertility of the soil, the sluttish plenty surrounding the Grihasta's (cultivator's) abode, the rich foliage, the fruit and timber-trees, and the palpable evidence against anything like penury. Did any man ever go through a Bengallee village and find himself assailed by the cry of want or famine? Was he ever told that the Ryot and his family did not know where to turn for a meal; that they had no shade to shelter them, no tank to bathe in, no employment for their active limbs? That villages are not neatly laid out like a model village in an English county, that things seem to go on, year by year, in the same slovenly fashion, that there are no local improvements, and no advances in civilisation, is all very true. But considering the wretched condition of some of the Irish peasantry, or even the Scotch, and the misery experienced by hundreds in the purlieus of our great cities at home, compared with the condition of the Ryots, who know neither cold nor hunger, it is high time that the outcry about the extreme unhappiness of the Bengal Ryot should cease."

I quote this, instead of putting forward the same truths on my own authority, because it was written in Bengal, only a few months ago, by one whose opinions are supported by the evidence of his own senses, and

absence of that frightful scourge, famine, with which the country had been periodically visited, is mainly to be attributed to it."—[*MS. Correspondence.*]

who speaks of what he sees around him. I know that the Bengal Ryot lives in an enviable state of *sans-culotteism.* I know that he enjoys the inestimable privilege of living with only a rag about his middle—

O fortunati agricolæ! sua si bona norint!

I know that the abode in which he dwells is one of very primitive construction. I know that he does not drink beer, or eat beef, or read the newspaper by a sea-coal fire.* I know that he does not trouble himself much about Government paper, or other public securities, and that he lives from hand to mouth, in a rude, simple manner, well content if he can feed himself and the other inmates of his clay-built cottage. But all that I gather from my knowledge of these facts is, that Bengal is very much unlike England, and that what is a hardship in England is not a hardship in Bengal.

The peasantry of Bengal are unquestionably poor. I do not know any peasantry who are rich. "Riches," however, is, after all, only a comparative term, and the question is whether, according to their wants and requirements, the peasantry of Bengal are poorer than the peasantry of any other part of the world. I do not think that they are. Doubtless, there are some evils inherent in the system under which they live. In some parts of the Lower Provinces there is a system of underletting which is very injurious to the cultivator. There is a middle-man, or more than one middle-man, between him and the Zemindars, and a profit must be made by

* This may appear to be trifling, but I can assure the most solemn of my readers that it is not. It is a fact that many people who have never visited India look upon the condition of the Bengal peasantry with English eyes, and bring all their ideas of English poverty and destitution to bear upon the subject. Thus it is related that Sir Elijah Impey, on his first arrival off Calcutta, told "brother Hyde" to look at the nakedness of the people, and assured him that it would not be long before the beneficial action of the Crown Courts would clothe them all in shoes and stockings. This is an old story in India—but it may not be equally well known in England. I may add to it, that Lord George Bentinck was reported by the London papers to have alluded, in a famous speech on the Sugar Question, to the necessity of the hundred millions of the people of India having to go without *sugar in their tea.*

each. But is this peculiar to Bengal—is it peculiar to India?* It is the commonest thing possible in England. A tradesman in a country village, or a little townlet, will take a lease of a stack of cottages, each with a little garden behind it. He will let these cottages severally, without the gardens—realise from his tenants collectively much more than the entire rent of the estate—then throw all the gardens into one and let them, at a high rent, to some well-to-do person whose grounds are contiguous to them, and who is anxious to increase his domain. In this manner the middle-man will, perhaps, double the rent that he pays to the actual landlord; and all at the expense of the peasants who are compelled to submit to his terms. In the towns, too, this system of under-letting is carried to a still more abominable extent. Think what are the profits derived by the middle-man from a London lodging-house, and what those lodging-houses are. The tenants pay from 200 to 400 per cent. above the actual value of the accommodation as estimated by the real owner of the house, which is parcelled out among a number of families, or let to a promiscuous crowd of nightly occupants reeking with fever and filth.

There is nothing in any part of India, except in famine times—and famine times have ceased in Bengal—to indicate the misery and degradation of which these London lodging-houses are the visible signs. I am speaking now of them, however, only in connexion with the subject of middle-men, simply as respects the matter of rent. It

* Mr. Shore (Lord Teignmouth), in his famous minute of June 18, 1789, thus described the intermediate agency: "The Ryots who cultivate the soil pay their rent to a Mundel (head Ryot) or Gomastah (agent), of which each village has one or more, according to its extent. 2nd. The Mundel pays his rent to a renter of two or three villages. 3rd. The renter pays to the farmer of a division comprehending many villages. 4th. The farmer of a division pays to the farmer of a Pergunnah. 5th. The farmer of a Pergunnah pays to the Zemindar. And 6th. The Zemindar carries his rent to the office of the Government." This classification, in all its details, only applies to the very large estates, but with more or less modification it may be said to represent the general system.

may be said that with the Indian cultivator rent means something more than house accommodation. The land which is let to him by the middle-man is the arena of his industry—the source of his subsistence—in fact, that the middle-man stands between him and the very well-spring of life. But this, too, is the commonest thing possible in England. We have heard a great deal lately about the "sweating system," and other vile systems, which intercept and diminish the rightful earnings of the working-man, and enrich the intermediate agent. These are great evils. It were well that we should think about them sometimes, when we are volubly discoursing of the sufferings endured by the unhappy Bengal Ryot. It were well that we should think, too, whether we may not lay them at the door of Free-trade, or the Income-tax, or the new Police, or the Great Exhibition, as reasonably as we may attribute the poverty and misery of the Bengal Ryot to the Permanent Zemindarry Settlement.

Again, it is unquestionable that the Ryot suffers much under the burden of that great calamity, debt. He borrows money at an exorbitant rate of interest, and the "Mahajun," who lends it to him, compels him to purchase everything he requires from people in whom the usurer is interested, and in whose gains he participates. But is not this a system again well understood in England? It little matters in what manner this payment of interest diminishes the daily comforts of the poor man—whether it reduces the profits of his own little cultivation or the wages paid to him as the cultivator of other men's lands. There is nothing from which our own people suffer more than from this slavery of debt. I do not believe that the Ryots in any part of India suffer as much from the avarice of the Mahajuns as our own workmen have suffered, and do suffer, from the "truck" and the "tally" systems, and other schemes by which advantage is taken of the improvidence of the poor. Our tradesmen prey as greedily upon the peasantry who once get on their books, and intercept their earnings with as ruinous a gripe, as the most wily Mahajun in Jessore.

It may be alleged that the Ryot is driven into debt by the exactions of the Zemindar, and that the great inherent vice of the Permanent Settlement is, that whilst the amount leviable from the landed proprietor is definitely and permanently fixed, there is no definition of the claim to be made by him upon the under-tenant. It has been said, indeed, that "in the permanently settled districts of Bengal, nothing is settled, and little is known, except the Government assessment."* And there is no doubt that this is the great blot of the Permanent Settlement. The Zemindars, except in a few special cases, exact from the Ryots as much as they can be made to pay; and there is no doubt that what is left to the actual cultivator, after all these exactions, is little more than suffices to keep the souls and bodies of the peasantry together. Hastings, it has been seen, was especially anxious to "secure to the Ryots the perpetual and undisturbed possession of their lands, and to guard them against arbitrary exactions,"† and he maintained that it was the duty of Government "to fix the deeds by which they hold their lands and pay their rents, to certain bounds and defences against the authority of the Zemindar." But the ablest revenue-officers in the country admitted that it was difficult, if not impossible, to reduce such a fixation to anything like system; and the attempt was abandoned in despair. It was decreed, indeed, that the Ryot had no rights, and he was left to fight it out with the Zemindar. The result is, that the assessment levied upon the actual cultivator is extremely variable, but that it seldom falls far short of the amount which, with extreme diffi-

* *Report of the Calcutta Finance Committee, July* 12, 1830.

† See *ante*, pp. 155, 156.

culty, he can contrive to pay.* He is, in fact, left with what is sufficient only to supply the bare necessities of life. But there is nothing in this peculiar to the state of the rural population of Bengal. "In every country," says Sismondi, "the share assigned to the laborer is most frequently only just what is sufficient to support his existence." Existence is easily supported in Bengal; and I believe that, in proportion to his wants, the peasant is as well supplied in that flourishing province as in any part of the world.

It is readily admitted that, if the advantages derivable from the increased productiveness of the settled districts could have been shared between the Zemindar and the Ryot, instead of passing entirely into the exchequer of the former, the arrangement would have afforded greater matter for congratulation. Under the existing system, the increased value of the land directly benefits neither the Government nor the people. But the men, who stand between the Government and the people, are greatly the gainers by it. The residuary produce is theirs. The effect has been to raise up a body of moderate capitalists, whose existence is decidedly advantageous to the State;† and, though I fear much cannot be said in favor of their enlightenment and liberality—of their practical recognition of the duties and responsibilities which property entails, it may be hoped that they will learn in time the great truth that, by serving others,

* "The standard," said Mr. Shore, "was so indeterminate, that the Ryots neither knew what they had to pay, nor could the officers of Government, without the most difficult investigation, ascertain whether the Ryots had been imposed on, or not;" and again the same authority declared, that "of all subjects relating to the Revenue, this, though the most important, was, at the same time, the most difficult to explain," and that "he distrusted his own knowledge, and still more his ability, to render it intelligible."

† Mr. Tucker, in his very able "Review of the Financial Situation of the East India Company in 1824," says: "There are persons who, witnessing the flourishing condition of the Bengal provinces, and knowing that the rents and income of the Zemindars have, in many instances, been immoderately increased, seem disposed to impute to Lord Cornwallis an improvident sacrifice of the public revenue. The inference is as gratuitous as the imputation is unjust. The prosperity of the country and the growing opulence of the Zemindars are the happy effects of the Permanent Settlement."

they serve themselves—that nothing contributes so largely to the wealth of the landlord as the prosperity of his tenantry, and that nothing so surely hastens his ruin as grinding the faces of the poor.

I cannot afford to pursue the subject further in this place. Indeed, I had intended to confine myself entirely to the record of events; and having briefly given the history of the incubation of the Permanent Settlement, to speak of its present results only so far as they are exemplified by ascertained facts. What I have shown, or proposed to show, is this:

1. That the Revenue System, which we found in operation on the assumption of the Dewanee, was not conducive to the happiness of the people.

2. That our initial experiments of brief leases and fluctuating assessments were advantageous neither to the Government nor to the people.

3. That all the ablest revenue-officers in the country were in favor of a Zemindaree Settlement, and that the Court of Directors held the same opinion.

4. That these officers had been for a great number of years collecting information whereupon to base this settlement—and that the Court of Directors were of opinion that sufficient information had been collected.

5. That Lord Cornwallis came out to India instructed to complete this settlement—that he was not, in any way, the author or originator of it—and that he sought for further information before carrying it into effect.

6. That three years after his arrival in India he promulgated the terms of the settlement—a decennial Zemindaree settlement—with an intimation, that with the consent of the Court of Directors, it would be rendered a permanent one.

7. That three years after this promulgation the Court of Directors and the King's Ministers consented to the perpetuation of the settlement; and that nearly seven

years after his arrival in India Lord Cornwallis made the Permanent Zemindaree Settlement of Bengal the law of the land.

8. That the first effect of the regulations was to bring, under the operation of the Sale Law, a large number of estates to the hammer, and greatly to impoverish several influential Zemindars.

9. That a new Act—Act VII. of 1799, which relaxed the extreme strictness of the Sale Law, and gave the Zemindar increased power over the defaulting Ryot, greatly improved the condition of the former, and diminished the number of sales.

10. That by successive enactments the relations of the Zemindar and Ryot were further improved; and that at the present time the quantity of land sold for arrears of revenue is very small in proportion to the area under assessment.

11. That the assessment is in itself a moderate assessment, and does not press severely upon the industrial energies of the people.

12. That from the very first the provinces have prospered under the Permanent Settlement—that large tracts of waste land have been reclaimed—that capital has accumulated—and that the country has been exempted from the periodical famines which had so grievously afflicted them before.

Lastly, that the peasantry of Bengal, in so far as their happiness is affected by the Revenue Regulations, cannot be said to be more miserable than the peasantry of any other part of the world.

CHAPTER III.

Our First Territory in Madras—The Northern Circars—Old Revenue System—The Committee of Circuit Permanent Assessment—The Baramahl—Read and Munro—The Ceded Districts—The Ryotwar System—Village Settlements—Their Discontinuance—Return to the Ryotwar System—Its Results.

WHILST in the latter years of the last century the servants of the Company in Bengal were endeavoring to frame a system of land-revenue advantageous alike to the Government and the people, a similar experiment was being carried on under the Presidency of Madras. We had possessed ourselves of territory in that part of the Mogul Empire at about the same period that first saw us assuming, on the banks of the Hooghly, the new dignity of territorial lords. A portion of the country known as the "Northern Circars"* was granted to the British by the Mogul, at the request of Lord Clive, in 1765. This is the country which lies on the northern extremity of the present Madras Presidency between the seaboard and the Orissan hills.

On our first acquisition of these territories the Company's servants did very much what they were doing in Bengal. They knew nothing about landed tenures and

* The Northern Circars formed part of the ancient kingdom of Ooria and Telinga. The territory which passed into our hands, and which consisted of Chicacole, Rajahmundry, Ellore, and Condapelly, had been granted by Salabut Jung to the French East India Company; but on the capture of Masulapatam by the British in 1759, they reverted to the government of the Nizam. They were made over to us in 1765, and in 1788 Guntoor, upon which we had a *post obit*, was added to our possessions.

revenue settlements. They could carry the revenue to account, when it was collected; but they did not know how to collect it. So they let the native administration take its course—they entered into engagements with one or two large capitalists, for the payment of a certain amount of annual revenue or rent, and left them to collect it from farmers and under-tenants and others, and did not much concern themselves about the manner of its collection.

This arrangement, however, was but of brief continuance. In 1769, the native administration was abolished, and the management of the Circars was placed in the hands of the Company's servants—of certain provincial chiefs and councils, who had no administrative knowledge or experience of any kind, and could not talk the native languages with more fluency or correctness than a cadet in the first year of his inexperience, or a Chief Justice at the end of his career. But the condition of affairs before their interference had been so irredeemably bad, that they could not introduce greater disorder into the administration, or greater misery among the people. There were two kinds of landed tenures then recognised. There were Zemindarry lands—lands held by certain chiefs as their hereditary estates, paying tribute to the Government of the day; and there were "Havelly" lands, or "portions of territory not in the hands of Zemindars, but in those of the Government, and in which it was, therefore, optional to adopt any system of management for collecting the land-revenue from the Ryots."* The land was for the most part leased out to speculators, grasping Dubashes and others, who had as little regard for the welfare of the cultivators as the worst of the Zemindars. On both descriptions of lands the Ryots were defrauded and oppressed. The Zemindars, or contrac-

* *Fifth Report.*

tors sub-rented the lands. The middle-man had to make his profits, and so it happened that little more than a fifth or sixth of the produce could be retained by the actual cultivator.

On the Circars passing into our hands, the Company's servants were glad to make any arrangement which would save them the necessity of a detailed management of unfamiliar business, so they allowed the Zemindars and large renters to appropriate the revenues on condition of their paying certain stipulated amounts to Government. The provincial chiefs, ignorant of the language, and inexperienced as revenue-collectors, were obliged to conduct all inquiries through their native underlings, or rather to leave them to do all the business for themselves. Little or no progress was made towards good government, and, probably, none for some time would have been made, but that the state of affairs in the Northern Circars fixed the attention of the home authorities; and in those days the Court of Directors greatly surpassed their Indian servants in enlightenment and benevolence. They were eager to see a better system of administration introduced into their Madras territories, and they ordered that a Special Commission, or, as it was denominated, a Committee of Circuit—to be composed of certain members of the Madras Council—should proceed into the districts and institute rigid inquiries into their general condition, with a view to the definition of the rights and the protection of the interests of all classes. The instructions of the Court of Directors were conceived in a liberal and enlightened spirit, and clearly and emphatically expressed. But the Committee of Circuit was a failure. The Provincial Courts thwarted its operations. The Zemindars would render the Commissioners no assistance, but rather endeavoured to throw dust in their eyes. They could not speak the native languages, and all their information reached them through the lying medium of men who were interested in concealing or distorting the truth.

So it happened that though the Committee of Circuit continued its operations from year's end to year's end, no fixed system was introduced. Annual leases were granted in the first instance—then settlements for three or five years. The "Havelly" lands were let, in most cases, on the system of Village Settlements, but they were very imperfectly made. And altogether the humane intentions of the Home Government were most inadequately fulfilled. But the tendency of all our administrative efforts at this time was towards gradual improvement. In 1786, a Board of Revenue, after the Bengal fashion, was established at Madras; but it was in continual collision with the Provincial Councils, which obstructed the working of its machinery, whilst they did no good by themselves. So Lord Hobart, who was then Governor of Madras, abolished the Provincial Councils, and appointed collectors in their stead. But the collectors, like the other functionaries of whom I have spoken, had small acquaintance with the native languages, and were compelled to leave the minutiæ of revenue detail to their Dewans and Dubashes, and other native underlings, who throve upon the ignorance of their masters.

But the Permanent Zemindaree Settlement had been by this time introduced into Bengal; and it had many advocates in high places both at home and abroad. The Madras Board of Revenue had been studying the minutes of Shore and Cornwallis; and the Court of Directors had written out, that "being thoroughly sensible of the propriety and expediency of the late revenue and judicial regulations established in Bengal, they directed the Madras Government to consider the expediency of adopting similar plans for the Northern

Circars, including the Jaghire and the Ceded Districts." This was written in 1795, but at this time the Board were hardly prepared to recommend the perpetuation of the settlement; they required time for the collection of further information; and it was not until 1799 that they reported to the Supreme Government that they were possessed of materials for a permanent Zemindarry settlement. Lord Wellesley, who had by this time succeeded to the Governor-Generalship of India, earnestly supported the plan of his predecessor, and recommended its extension to Madras. The Court of Directors supported the recommendation, and early in 1801 wrote to the Government of Madras that "they had determined to concur in the instructions of the Governor-General for proceeding at once to the permanent assessment of the lands on the coast." A special Commission was accordingly appointed to carry out these instructions, and between the years 1802 and 1804 the northern districts of Madras were permanently assessed.*

Thus were the principles of the Permanent Zemindarry Settlement applied to that tract of country, under the Madras Presidency, which first passed into our hands. The country, too, around Madras, known as "the Jagheer," which had been obtained from the Newab of Arcot, partly in 1750, and partly in 1763, in return for services rendered to that state, was at the same time subjected to the same process.† But whilst all these measures for the settlement of the ancient territories of

* The manner of the assessment, in respect of the division of estates, is thus indicated in the Fifth Report. "The lands already in the hands of Zemindars were confirmed to them in perpetuity on the prescribed conditions. The assessment on each Zemindarry necessarily varied according to the local extent. In some it considerably exceeded a lakh of star pagodas; in others it was under 1000 star pagodas. The Havelly lands having been parcelled out into estates of a convenient size, yielding from 1000 to 5000 star pagodas annual rent, but in some instances more, were sold at public auction, subject to the terms of the Permanent Zemindarry tenure." A pagoda is about 3½ rupees, or 7 shillings.

† "The Permanent Settlement of the Jaghire took place in 1802, the lands having been divided into sixty-one estates, bearing an assessment of from 2000 to 5000 star pagodas, and sold to individuals in the same manner as the 'Havellys' of the Northern Circars.

the Company at Fort St. George were in progress, we were adding new territories to that Presidency, and the question of land-assessment came up again for discussion and decision, in connexion with new countries ceded to us far down in the Southern Peninsula. In 1792, the first war with Tippoo placed a considerable tract of country, which had before owned the Sultan of Mysore for its master, in the hands of the Company. A treaty was signed, which delivered over to the British the Baramahl (or Salem) and the provinces of Dindighal and Malabar. The second war with Tippoo, which overthrew the only power in Southern India which dared to resist or molest us, added to our territories Canara and Soondah; and in 1801 all the possessions of the Newab of Arcot in the Carnatic were made over to us by that prince. We had now new problems of revenue to solve, new districts to settle.

The Court of Directors, when unfolding their opinions regarding the application of the permanent system to the Madras territories, had pointed out the peculiarities of our new acquisitions in the Carnatic, and had suggested that, as they were not so far advanced in civilisation as the Bengal provinces, they might not be ripe for the reception of the benefits and blessings intended for them—that indeed "any attempt to introduce a regular system of order or just sentiments respecting the value of permanent rights, would be idle and nugatory till their minds were to a certain extent prepared to feel the importance of these benefits." The success which had attended our efforts to establish a fixed system in the Northern Circars had not been sufficient to encourage us to extend the experiment to the new lands obtained by cession and conquest in the Southern Peninsula. We

The date on which the land-tax, payable by the Zemindars to Government, was calculated and determined, were the actual state of the resources and certain accounts of the produce and gross collections in preceding year."—[*Fifth Report.*]

found, too, that a different description of landed tenures had existed under the native governments; and we had always endeavoured to assimilate our system of revenue collection to that which had presumedly obtained before our assumption of the fiscal management of the country. Moreover, on the cession of these tracts of Tippoo's old country, the duty of settling the ceded districts had been entrusted to a class of men very different from those who had carried out the settlement of Bengal and the Northern Circars. It was entrusted—not to the Company's civil servants, but to a little band of soldiers, who brought to this new work more zeal than knowledge, more honesty than experience, and who, whatever may be the opinion entertained of the result of their labors—whether it be determined that they carried out "a system which ensures, at the same time, the just dues of the Government and the just rights, not of a new-made Zemindar, but of an industrious peasantry,"* or one which has "resulted in the impoverishment of the country, the people, and the Government itself"†—still deserve all honor for the benevolence of their intentions, the singleness of their aims, and the unwearying perseverance with which they prosecuted their labors.

At the head of the Commission first appointed in 1792 was Captain Read, an officer who had been for some time employed on the staff of the Madras army, and who had exhibited great aptitude for business as well as an intimate acquaintance with the language and manners of the people.‡ With him were associated three junior

* *Calcutta Review*, vol. xvii. Article: "The Land Revenue of Madras"—a very valuable and interesting paper, compiled principally from manuscript records. I am indebted to it for many of the details contained in this chapter.

† *H. St.G. Tucker.*

‡ The following is Munro's account of the man at whose feet he sat as a revenue student: "Read is no ordinary character. He might, in Mysore, have amassed as much money as he chose, and by fair means too; but he was so far from taking advantage of his situation for this purpose, that he even gave up his bazaar and many other perquisites of his military command, and received nothing but his prize-money and commission, which altogether, I believe, amounted to about 6000*l*. Whatever I might have done, had I been left to myself, I could get no pickings under such a master, whose conduct is invariably regulated by private honor and the

officers, Macleod, Graham, and Munro—a name which has become inextricably associated with all our ideas of the land-revenue of Madras. "Our only system," said Munro, "is plain hard labor." "We have only to guard the Ryots from oppression, and they will create the revenue for us." But in these days, when so much has been written about different systems of Land-revenue, the working of all of which involves no inconsiderable amount of "plain hard labor," it is necessary to adopt a more specific style of description. The system is that which is now (under fuller development) known as the "Ryotwar system." It recognised the Government as proprietor of the soil, and undertook to determine the rights of every man who paid a single rupee to the Sircar. It was a settlement to be made directly with the Ryots themselves; and its object was to protect the interests of the actual cultivators of the soil.

It was, however, in the first instance only an experiment. What Read and his associates did, at this time, was not to determine a system, or to settle the future mode of assessment, but to collect information and to ascertain rights, with a view to ulterior measures. How they proceeded has been detailed by Munro himself. "Captain Read," he wrote in 1794, "in order to be en-"abled to turn his attention to general arrangements, "has divided the ceded countries, among his assistants,

public interest. These, and unwearied zeal in whatever he undertakes, constitute the great features of his character. The enthusiasm in the pursuit of national objects, which seizes others by fits and starts, is in him constant and uniform. These qualities, joined to an intimate knowledge of the language and manners of the people, and a happy talent for the investigation of everything connected with revenue, eminently qualify him for the station which he now fills with so much credit to himself and benefit to the people."—[*Gleig's Life of Sir Thomas Munro.*] The writer in the *Calcutta Review*, quoted above, says: "If any further testimony were necessary to the indefatigable zeal and pure unaffected philanthropy of this excellent man, the whole of the public records and the traditions of the district afford it in ample abundance; and there is something peculiarly interesting in comparing in these local records, the speculative views, the imperfect sentences, and even the imperfect spelling of this pioneer in Indian Revenue, with the clear and decisive views, the transparent style, and the strong practical decision of the pupil then rising into fame."

"into three divisions.* These are again subdivided "into 'Tehsildarrees,' few of which are under ten or "above thirty thousand pagodas.† The Tehsildars, "who have charge of them, are mere receivers of "the Revenue, for they cannot either raise or lower "the rent of a single individual. They are not per-"mitted to give any decision, unless on matters of the "most trifling nature—to refer all disputes respecting "property to a Court of Arbitration, to order the "members of such Courts to assemble, to receive the "kists (instalments) from the head farmers of the "villages, and the accounts from the village ac-"countants, and to transmit them to the collector of "the division, is the whole of their duty. Every "Tehsildarree is farmed out in villages to the 'gours,' "or head farmers, who, having the management of "the details of cultivation, may be considered as "renters of the country, though they are in fact "answerable only for the amount of their own par-"ticular lands, for the whole inhabitants are jointly "answerable for the Revenue of the village, which is "seldom less than ten pagodas, or more than one "thousand. Every man, who pays a single rupee to "Government, has the rent of his land fixed by the "division collector, for which he has a roll, signed by "him, specifying the nature and quantity of it, and the "periods of payment. As the gour can demand no "more than the stipulated rent, he can, of course, "gain nothing by the Ryots, and as every man enjoys "the profits of his own lands, it is for these reasons "that the whole are made jointly responsible for the "deficiency."‡

Such, as described by Munro, were some of the main features of the system as our Government found it,§

* Munro, Macleod, and Graham.

† That is to say, the amount of the revenue raised from each was seldom under 10, or above 30,000 pagodas.

‡ *Captain Munro to Captain Allen, June* 8, 1794.—*Gleig's Life of Munro.*

§ "Hyder's system of finance was much the same as under all other native

and as it was now to be experimentally continued. But the young officer clearly saw that there was a vital defect in it, which it was incumbent on the new Government to remedy. "The exertions of industry," he wrote, "have always been restrained by the demands of Government keeping pace with their profits, and often outrunning them."* It was in obviation of this very evil that the Bengal administrators had introduced the Permanent System into the Soubahdarry; and Munro gave his evidence, indirectly but emphatically, in favor of that system, when he wrote: "The ceded countries have, however, many natural "advantages, and are capable of great improvements. "The first step for the attainment of this object must "be the settlement of the lease at a moderate rent, for "all attempts to better their situation will be in vain "as long as the land-tax is not only high, but arbi-"trary." It would have been well if, a few years afterwards, this truth had been held more distinctly in remembrance.

This, indeed, was the principle that Read enunciated, and on which he desired that the settlement should be based. "Correspondent with my original design," he wrote, "you will find my grand objects are these: The securing the Revenue its dues, to the industrious their fair advantages, and to all the inhabitants every accommodation consistent with good policy." There was obviously at that time some leaning in his mind towards the Permanent System so much favored in

governments; he rented the country in large districts to Aumildars, who were pretty regular in their payments, because the terms were favorable; but, besides collecting the public revenues, they amassed large sums for themselves . . . Tippoo began his reign with changing every civil and military arrangement of his father, and he changed his almost every year, and always on these occasions framed new codes of Regulations to send to different provinces. His last was much the same as we have now in the Ceded Provinces."—[*Capt. Munro to Capt. Allen, June* 8, 1794.—*Gleig's Life of Munro.*]

* "The tanks are few," he added, "and having been neglected ever since Hyder made himself master of Mysore, are in so ruinous a condition, that it will require a considerable sum to save the present produce of the land beneath them from being lost altogether."—[*Ibid.*]

high places, both in India and in England; but he was a man much given to speculation, and he was little disposed to pronounce a decisive judgment in emphatic support of one kind of assessment or another. He called upon his assistants to expound their views, and they all responded to the call. Munro sent in a lengthy and elaborate paper, which has never yet been given to the world, reviewing the whole question of Ryotwaree Settlement, and pronouncing a strong opinion in its favor. The plan—he wrote in conclusion, summing up the practical suggestion, each one of which is powerfully elaborated in the body of the letter—"The plan," he wrote, "which it appears to "me would be best calculated to secure to the people "the fruits of their industry, and to Government a "permanent Revenue, is comprised under the following "heads:—1. A reduction of 15 per cent. to be made "on the lease settlement. 2. The country to be "rented immediately of Government by small farms "as at present, every one receiving just as much land "as he demands. 3. Settlements to be annual; that "is to say, every man to be permitted to give up or "take whatever land he pleases every year. 4. Every "man to have a part, or the whole of his lands on "lease who wishes it: and in order to encourage the "application for leases, all lands held under annual "tenures to be taken from the occupants and given to "such other farmers as may demand them in lease, or "their paying to Government, as purchase-money, one "year's rent for any particular field, or one half "year's for the whole farm. 5. Villages and districts "to be responsible for all individual failures. 6. All "lands included in the lease should remain invariably "at the rent then fixed after the proposed reduction of "15 per cent. 7. All lands, not included in the lease, "should be rented at the average of the village to "which they belong. 8. Lands included in the lease, "being given up and allowed to lay waste, for any "number of years, should, when again occupied, pay, "the very first year, the full rent as before. 9. All "castes, whether natives or aliens, to pay the same "rent for the land. 10. No additional rent ever to be "demanded for improvements—the farmer, who by "digging a well, or building a tank, converts dry land "into garden or rice-fields, to pay no more than the "original rent of the ground. 11. No reduction of "the established rent ever to be allowed, except "where the cochineal plant, mulberry, &c., are culti-"vated."*

This was the plan conceived by Munro, when an assistant to Colonel Read, in the Baramahl—but although, in those days as now, there was a good deal of lengthy writing, there was no lack of working too; and the materials for the settlement were being collected apace. "The Baramahl has now been completely surveyed, and the rents of it fixed," wrote Munro, in September, 1798. "They are on an average nearly what they were under Tippoo. The inhabitants paid the same then as now; but the deficiency of his receipts arose from the peculations of a host of revenue-officers. The rent here, as I believe, in every other part of India, is too high."† The rent was certainly too high in Madras, for Colonel Read ascertained and reported, that whilst in Bengal the rent paid to Government amounted to forty-seven pagodas the square mile, in Madras it was not less than *seventy*. "The increase to the public revenues," wrote Graham to his chief, "has been obtained in consequence of Government having added thereto that portion of the

* *MS. Records, quoted in the Calcutta Review.* It is to be regretted that the author of this able and interesting paper has not, in all instances, given the dates of the original documents which he quotes.

† *Gleig's Life of Sir Thomas Munro.*

produce which is the life of future exertions in husbandry, and, as a compensation for a variety of disasters peculiar to the country, ought undoubtedly to go to the former. Upon this view of the subject, although it may be deemed unusual official language, yet I hesitate not to regret every pagoda that has been thus added to the jumma, because I am sensible of its evil tendency, and because I have ever been taught to believe that the affairs of Government flourish in proportion to the prosperity of its servants."* The assessment, too, varied greatly in the different divisions. The average assessment per acre was, on the dry lands, in the Southern Division, two rupees; in the Centre, one and a half; and in the Northern, one. On the wet lands, it was in the Southern Division, eleven; in the Centre, six and a half; and in the Northern, five and a half rupees.† The average rent may be set down at little more than three shillings an acre on the common soils; and the average contribution of each farmer was about seventy shillings a year.‡

Whilst the revenue settlement of the lands ceded to the British, after the war of 1792, was still in an experimental state, the field of investigation was greatly enlarged by the results of the second war with Tippoo. Our possessions in Southern India were extended by the conquest of Mysore in 1799. Read and Munro both joined the grand army. After the fall of Seringapatam, the former resigned his office, as chief collector of the Baramahl; and Munro, who ought to have succeeded him, was sent to settle the revenue of

* *Records, quoted in Calcutta Review.*

† *Calcutta Review.*

‡ "The average rent of cultivated land in this country is not more than three shillings an acre. Waste lands pay nothing. . . . . The average rent of the whole body of farmers is not more than ten pagodas each. . . . . This extreme poverty is the principal cause of the lowness of the rent, and not any fault of the soil; for at least three-fourths of the lands in cultivation are capable of producing cotton, sugar, and indigo; but though the Ryots have little money, I imagine that they suffer less real distress than the peasantry of Europe."—[*Munro to his Father, May, 1796.—Gleig's Life.*]

Canara. The appointment was unwelcome—the duties were irksome to him—but he was soon removed to another and more extended sphere of action. In 1800, the country, which on the partition of Tippoo's domains had been made over to the Nizam, was ceded by him to the British; and on the districts passing into our hands, Munro was made chief collector, or superintendent, with a staff of civil assistants to conduct the detail duties under his eye.*

It was during the seven years that followed the cession of these districts that Munro perfected himself in the service, in which he had graduated under Read. And whatever may be thought of the theories which he advocated, all men will admit that, in practice, he was the model of an Indian administrator. He was one of the first who, in that part of the country, carried to the work of revenue-settlement a thorough acquaintance with the language and manners of the people. He was, in the happy language of Mr. Webbe, an *undubashed* officer—one who moved about familiarly among the rude villagers without an interpreter at his elbow, and who not only knew and understood all classes, but had a heart to sympathise with them. They looked up to him with veneration; called him their father; and whatever might be their condition, knew that he would respect their rights. From year's end to year's end he toiled on unremittingly, scorning delight and living laborious days, but, in the weariness and waste of a life of continued labor and isolation, in an unhealthy climate, preserved in all his early freshness and warmth, by the good home

* That excellent man, Mr. Webbe, the chief secretary of Madras, of whom Wellington said that he was one of the ablest men he ever knew, wrote to Munro, "The assistants may be Mr. Cochrane, Clive's head-assistant, who is master of Persian and Hindostanee; Mr. Thackeray, who has received the reward for the Gentoo language; Mr. Stodart, who has been for a long time assistant to one of our northern collectors; and some other *undubashed* Persian if I can find him."

feeling which was perpetually bubbling up within him. His strong natural sagacity was remarkable. He read character at a glance. But he had more valuable qualities even than these. It was the conscientiousness of the man which raised him to high station. No man—not even the great captain, who was the friend and correspondent of "dear Munro," and who wrote him pleasant letters about his first victory at Assye—had a stronger sense of the paramount claims of duty. The character and career of such a man should be held in affectionate remembrance by every young soldier in the Indian army. There is not one of them whose unaided talent, industry, and integrity, may not raise him to the same high eminence as was attained by the young Scot, who began his career without a pagoda in his pocket, a blanket to cover him at night, or a pillow whereon to lay his head. His schoolfellows said of him that, as a boy, he carried everything before him, by "his coolness, his courage, and his unequalled endurance." The same characteristics, in the moral, no less than in the physical signification of the words, made the fortune of the man. And there is not a cadet who joins in the general salute, on the examination day at Addiscombe, for whom the due exercise of the same high qualities may not win the same high reward.

For seven years Munro labored diligently and unceasingly in the Ceded Districts. He has given us, in his own clear, forcible words, an account of the labors of a collector, and of the general system of collection in the Ryotwaree country, which sparkles up, fresh and bright, amidst a somewhat dreary waste of "Revenue Selections," and makes the whole process of assessment intelligible to the dullest understanding. "The collector," he wrote, "sets out on his circuit in "September or October, when the early crops begin to be "reaped, and the late ones to be down. On arriving in a "district he assembles all the Ryots of the four or five "nearest villages. The first business is, to learn how "far the cultivation of the present year is more or less "than that of the last. This is soon done, by the help "of the Tehsildars' and Curnums' accounts, compared "with the reports of the Potails and Ryots. Where "there is a decrease it is commonly owing to deaths, "emigrations, or loss of cattle. Where there is an "increase, it is usually derived from new settlers, or "additional lands being occupied by the old ones. In "the case of decrease, the rent of the lands thrown up "is deducted from the settlement of last year; in that "of increase, the rent of the land newly occupied is "added; and in both cases the rent of the remaining "lands remains the same as before. The rent of the "land newly occupied is determined by the accounts "of what it was in former times; or, if such accounts "cannot be procured, by the opinions of the most in-"telligent Ryots: but the full rent of waste land is "not exacted until it has been in cultivation from two "to seven years. The number of years, and the gra-"dational rise in each year, depend upon the nature "of the land and the custom of the village. They are "known to all parties; and all doubts are removed by "their being detailed in a proclamation, or cowle "namah, under the collector's seal, circulated to every "village.

"If the cultivation is the same as last year's, and "no failures occur among the Ryots, the rents remain "unaltered. If the crops are bad, and it appears that "some of the poor Ryots must have a remission, the "loss, or a part of it, is assessed upon the lands of the "rest, where it can be done without causing any ma-"terial inconvenience. This assessment never exceeds "ten or twelve per cent., and is much oftener relin-

"quished than carried into effect. In cases where it "can be easily borne, it is frequently agreed to with- "out difficulty; and if opposition is made, it is gene- "rally soon got over, by the mediation of the Ryots "of the neighbouring villages present. These discuss "the point in question with the Ryots of the objecting "village, tell them that it is the custom of the coun- "try, use such other arguments as may be applicable "to the subject, and never fail in persuading them to "accede to the demand, unless it is really too high, in "which event it is lowered.

"Wherever individuals or villages object to their "rent, it is always the most expeditious and satisfac- "tory way of settling the dispute, to refer it to the "Ryots of other villages, who do more on such occa- "sions in half an hour than a collector and his cut- "cherry in a whole year."

All this, however, was merely experimental. The question of the eventual settlement of these districts remained still in abeyance. But experience had strengthened Munro's convictions; and the plan which he had recommended, as the disciple of Read, in the Baramahl, was now, with some modifications, more authoritatively enunciated by the chief collector of the Ceded Districts. Writing, in August, 1807, to the Board of Revenue, Munro thus particularised the terms of his proposed Ryotwaree Settlement—"The "following articles contain the principles on which "the settlement should be formed:—1st. The settle- "ment should be Ryotwaree. 2nd. The amount of "the settlement shall increase and decrease annually, "according to the extent of the land in cultivation. "3rd. A reduction of 25 per cent. on all land shall "be made in the survey rate of assessment. 4th. An "additional reduction in the assessment of 8 per cent., "or 33 per cent. in all, shall be allowed on all lands

" watered by wells, or by water raised by machinery " from rivers and nullahs, provided the cultivators " keep the wells or embankments (dirroas) in repair " at their own expense. A similar reduction shall " be allowed on the lands watered by small tanks, " wherever the cultivators agree to bear the expense " of repairs. 5th. Every Ryot shall be at liberty, at " the end of every year, either to throw up a part " of his land, or to occupy more, according to his " circumstances; but whether he throw up or occupy, " shall not be permitted to select, but shall take or " reject proportional shares of the good and bad toge-" ther. 6th. Every Ryot, as long as he pays the rent " of his land, shall be considered as the complete " owner of the soil, and shall be at liberty to let it to " a tenant, without any hesitation as to rent, and to " sell it as he pleases. 7th. No remission shall be " made, on ordinary occasions, for bad crops or other " accidents. Should failures occur, which cannot be " made good from the property or land of the de-" faulters, the village in which they happen shall be " liable for them, to the extent of 10 per cent. addi-" tional on the rent of the remaining Ryots, but no " further. 8th. All unoccupied land shall remain in " the hands of Government, and the rent of whatever " part of it may be hereafter cultivated, shall be added " to the public revenue. 9th. All taxes on houses, " shops, and professions, all duties, licences, &c., shall " belong exclusively to Government. The Ryot on " whose land houses or shops may be built, shall not " be entitled to receive a higher rent from them than " the equivalent of the survey rent of the ground " which they occupy. 10th. The repairs of all tanks, " which are not rendered private property by an extra " remission, or *duswundum enam*, shall be made at the " expense of Government. 11th. Tuckavy (advances)

" shall be gradually discontinued. 12th. Potails, Curnums, and all other village servants, shall remain as " heretofore, under the collector. 13th. Private creditors, who may distrain the property of Ryots, shall " discharge the rent which may be due from such Ryots " to Government, and shall give security for it before " they begin the distraint."

But this Ryotwaree system, to which Munro clung with the tenacity of a man of strong convictions, was doomed to see many remarkable vicissitudes before it achieved an ultimate triumph. In the first instance, he who had graduated as a revenue-officer in the Barahmal, and there first propounded his scheme of assessment, was condemned to see that tract of country given up to the Permanent Zemindarry system. Imperative orders were forwarded from the higher authorities to carry out the Bengal plan of perpetual assessment. In the years 1803-4-5 these lands were divided into Zemindarries, or allotments, of different sizes, and sold upon terms fixed in accordance with the original settlement. "The extent of the available resources of each Zemindaree was shown from the original surveys, under the heads of cultivated, fallow, and cultivable lands."* But these surveys had been somewhat loosely conducted. There was an entire want of uniformity in them, except in one particular—that all the lands were more or less over-assessed. Upon the introduction of the Permanent Zemindarry system this became miserably apparent. The new settlement, of course, was a failure—not because the system was bad in itself, but because it was applied to districts not prepared for its reception. It failed, indeed, because the early Ryotwaree men had greatly over-assessed the lands, and no system could have borne up against such an exorbitant valuation.

* *Calcutta Review.*

In 1807, Munro returned to England. Whatever may be thought of Ryotwaree or Zemindaree settlement, it is certain that during his long residence in the Ceded Districts he conferred substantial advantages on the people. It was said of him by the head of the Madras Government, that "under his administration the inhabitants, from disunited hordes of lawless freebooters, had become as far advanced in civilisation, submission to the laws, and obedience to the magistrates, as any of the subjects under the Madras Government; that every one seemed satisfied with his situation, and that the regret of the people was universal on the department of the principal collector."* He had been thinking of Cleveland, who had "established the Company's Raj in the hearts of the hill-people of Bhaugulpore"†—whose name, after the lapse of half a century, is still held in affectionate remembrance by the people of that country, and to whom even now the Court of Directors often refer, with approbation, in encouragement of others of their servants whom they desire "to do likewise."‡

Of the general results of Munro's Ryotwaree settlement two or three years after his departure from India, the Committee of the House of Commons, in their Fifth Report, expressed a most favorable opinion.§ But he had scarcely turned his back upon

* *Minute of President of Fort St. George, Oct.* 26, 1807.

† Writing from Canara of the distrust of the villagers, he said: "Perseverance on my part, however, brought over some deserters, and by talking to them as your friend Cleveland would probably have done, they brought over more, and I am now getting on as well as I can expect."—[*Munro to Cockburn.—Gleig's Life.*]

‡ See letters of the Court, quoted in subsequent chapters, on the Civilisation of the Bheels and the Hill Tribes of Orissa—Part IV.

§ "It appears to the Committee, from the examinations which they have made into the effects of the Ryotwar principle of settlement, throughout the modern possessions of the Company under the Madras Presidency, that it has greatly improved the situation of the cultivator by limiting the bounds of the public assessment and adjusting the actual demand on each person according to his ability to satisfy it.........So favorable a change in their condition has necessarily excited a confidence among the Ryots in the equity and justice of the Company's government," &c., &c.—[*Fifth Report of the House of Commons* 1810.]

Madras, when instructions were received by the Government of that presidency, which compelled them to abandon the principle for which Munro had contended. The system of individual responsibility, which brought each separate cultivator into immediate communication with Government, was now to be given up; and the old system of joint responsibility, or the assessment of villages, was, under certain modified rules, to be restored.

This was a system of leases granted, for a certain number of years,* to the chief cultivator of each village, who was to farm the revenue, or wherever it was practicable to the whole body of the Ryots collectively. "It differed from the Ryotwar chiefly in the assessment being fixed on the entire aggregate lands of the village, not on each distinct and separate field; in its being concluded with all the Ryots collectively, not with each individually; and in its giving up to the Ryots not only the revenue to be derived from the arable lands, but that also to be obtained by after exertion from the waste also. In fact, in leaving, in consideration of a contract to pay a given sum as public revenue, the entire internal administration of affairs to the village community."†

"The object in view," continue the same high authorities, "was to adapt the revenue administration to the ancient institutions and ancient usages of the country, to which the Hindoos are proverbially attached; to suit the system to the people, and not to tempt to bend the people to the system." And there were practically many advantages in such an arrangement, not the least of which was that stated by Mr. Place, that "no difficulty occurs in fixing the value of all the lands together of one village, but it would be

* First for three, then for ten years.

† *Minute of Madras Board of Revenue, January 5, 1818.—Madras Revenue Selections.*

nearly impossible to assign to every small allotment its portion so exactly, and with such due regard to fertility of soil, and other circumstances, that some should not benefit and others suffer." At all events, it did not to the same degree, if at all, place the people bound hand and feet at the mercy of unscrupulous Tehsildars.

I cannot afford to dwell, as I could wish, upon the discussions which arose respecting the advantages and disadvantages of this village system. I am greatly disposed to think that the Madras Board of Revenue, who contended strongly in its favor, had the best of the argument. But they had not the best of the struggle which then ensued. The higher authorities were against them. Munro's visit to England had probably not been without its effect upon the opinions of the Court of Directors and the Board of Control; and towards the close of 1817 instructions were received at Madras for the abolition of the village system, and the confirmation in all practicable cases of the plan of Ryotwar Settlement, with individual holders. It was alleged that the village system had been tried and had failed. The highest revenue authorities declared that it had not been subjected to a fair trial, and that it had not failed. They alleged, too, that the home authorities had decided hastily on insufficient evidence. "The judgment," they wrote, "which has been pronounced in England against the village system, is founded on a very partial and unfavorable view of its results; for it does not appear that the authorities at home had, at the time when that judgment was passed, any information before them respecting any other portion of it than its commencement, the triennial settlement."* And they urged that the result

* *Minute of Madras Board of Revenue, January* 5, 1818.

of that settlement was no test of the success or failure of the system, inasmuch as that the lands had been subjected to an over-assessment, "founded upon the fallacious data of the Ryotwar collections." "In fact, it was nearly everywhere," they said, "a mere rack-rent."

But the Ryotwar system was in favor at home, and orders were sent out for its reintroduction, in all possible cases, under certain modifications prescribed by the Court. At this period, the different districts of the Madras Presidency were subject to three different systems. In Ganjam, Vizigapatam, Rajahmundry, Masulapatam, Guntoor, Salem, Chingleput, the Cuddalore district, and the Western, Southern, and Chittoor Pollams, the Permanent Zemindarry system prevailed. In Malabar, Canara, Coimbatore, Madura, and Dindigul, the Ryotwar system was in force. Into the Ceded Districts, Nellore, the two divisions of Arcot, Palnaud, Trichinopoly, Tinivelly, and Tanjore, the village system had been introduced. For a quarter of a century now under the Madras Government a series of experiments in land-revenue had been going on. One system had been displaced to make way for another; each had been tried in turn, and it was alleged that in turn each system had failed. They had all failed, more or less, because the lands had been over-assessed. They had none of them been fairly tried under a light assessment.

But there were evils peculiar to the old Ryotwar system, which its own advocates acknowledged, and which now, from the new modified system, were to be erased. Indeed, under the force of circumstance and the mutations of time, they had pretty well erased themselves. The introduction, in 1802, to the Madras Presidency, of the Cornwallis regulations, which "engrafted on the Indian codes the principles of British justice," rendered the arbitrary and illegal acts* which were perpetrated for the enforcement of the Ryotwar system no longer practicable. "The new Regulations," it was well said, "declared revenue to be subordinate to justice, while the Ryotwar system had rendered justice entirely subordinate to revenue." "The new laws," it was added, "by their general principles, and not by any specific enactment, took from the native revenue-officers the power to 'punish and confine,' which they had exercised to coerce the Ryot to cultivate, and annually to take from him all that he was able to pay."† Under the improved

* What these arbitrary and illegal acts were, may be gathered from the following, which the Madras Board declare to be "no exaggerated description:"—"Ignorant of the true resources of the newly-acquired countries as of the precise nature of their landed tenures, we find a small band of foreign conquerors no sooner obtaining possession of a vast extent of territory, peopled by various nations, differing from each other in language, customs, and habits, than they attempt what would be deemed a herculean task, or rather a visionary project, even in the most civilised countries of Europe, of which every statistical information is possessed, and of which the Government are one with the people—viz., to fix a land-rent, not on each province, district, or country, not on each estate or farm, but on every separate field within their dominions. In pursuit of this supposed improvement, we find them unintentionally dissolving the ancient ties, "the ancient usages" which united the republic of each Hindoo village, and by a kind of agrarian law, newly assessing and parcelling out the lands which from time immemorial had belonged to the village community collectively, not only among the individual members of the privileged order (the Meerassidars and Cadeems), but even among their inferior tenantry (the Pyacarries); we observe them ignorantly denying, and by their denial abolishing private property in the land; resuming what belonged to a public body (the Grama manium), and conferring in lieu of it a stipend in money on one individual; professing to limit their demand on each field, but in fact, by establishing for such limit an unattainable maximum, assessing the Ryot at discretion; and, like the Mussulman Government which preceded them, binding the Ryot by force to the plough, compelling him to till land acknowledged to be over-assessed, dragging him back to it if he absconded, deferring their demand upon him until his crop came to maturity, then taking from him all that could be obtained, and leaving to him nothing but his bullocks and his seed grain—nay, perhaps obliged to supply him even with these in order to renew his melancholy task of cultivating, not for himself, but for them."

† *Madras Board of Revenue.*—And how this was done may be gathered from the continuation of the passage describing the good effects of the Cornwallis Regulations:—"The Tehsildar was stripped of the *ketticole* or hand torture, the stone placed on the head under a burning sun, the stocks, and other of his former insignia of office, by the display and occasional use of which he had been enabled to saddle the Ryots with the rents of such lands as he deemed proper. The lictor deprived of his fasces was no longer terrible to the people." This is a worthy illustration of the progress of British justice. We wonder now how anything of the kind could ever have existed.

Ryotwar system this mighty oppression was now to be formally repudiated and renounced. All compulsion or restraint on the free labor of the Ryot was to cease under the new system, and the native revenue-officers were to be especially warned against the assumption and exercise of improper power. Freedom of labor was declared by the Court of Directors to be the basis of the new settlement, and the Madras Board of Revenue enforced upon the collectors the paramount duty of restraining their native underlings, and protecting the liberties of the people. Under the new system, too, proprietary rights were to be recognised, which had not been recognised before; and, above all, the heavy assessment, which had pressed so severely on the industrial energies of the Ryots, was to be considerably reduced. The orders of Government were "to fix such a rate of assessment" as was calculated to "give encouragement to agricultural industry, and thereby promote the general prosperity of the country."

All the necessary preliminaries having been gone through—the village leases having expired—many of the new Zemindarries, or "Mootahs,"* having lapsed, or been bought in, the improved Ryotwar system was declared to be established in Madras; and Munro himself, who had been appointed to the chief place in the Government, took his seat just in time to give the finishing stroke to the act of final restoration. In the spring of 1820, the Ryotwar system was formally enthroned at Madras.

It would appear, on an impartial review of all the circumstances I have here briefly recited, that many of the defects of the original Ryotwar system, as founded at the close of the last century by Colonel

* That is, the allotments into which the Baramahl lands were divided, on the introduction of the Permanent Settlement.—See *ante*, page 220.

Read, and since developed and maintained by Sir Thomas Munro, have been to a great extent remedied or removed under the system which is now in force. The old system was generally better than that which we found on assuming the government of the ceded districts. Read and his assistants may have made many mistakes, and the subordinate revenue-officers, doubtless, committed many excesses. But, compared with the oppression to which the people had been subjected under the Mysore princes, the defective administration which resulted from our infant experiments must have sat lightly on the people. That these experiments, though carried on in good faith, and with the most benevolent intentions, by very honest and very able men, were extremely faulty in principle and unsuccessful in result, is not to be denied. It was wholly impossible, not merely for a little knot of soldiers, fresh from their military duties, but for thrice the number of experienced revenue-officers — the "crack collectors" of the present day—to have adequately superintended the assessment of the immense number of small holdings into which each village was parcelled. Every field was to be assessed; and these multiplied assessments were necessarily left to the "Tehsildars," or native revenue-officers—an extremely corrupt and licentious set of men, who plundered the people without stint, and oppressed them without remorse. The assessments made, under the circumstances, were extremely unequal; but excessiveness was their general character. These excessive assessments were the curse of the country. They brought everything to ruin. First one system was tried—then another. But over-assessment brought them all to the ground. It has never been said, that under the Permanent Zemindarry settlement, Bengal is over-assessed.

Such would seem to have been the causes of the failure of all our initial efforts during the first quarter of a century of experiment. But it is only just that we should separate what may be called accidental circumstances of this kind from the inherent defects of the system. Over-assessment, it may be said, is one thing—the Ryotwar system is another. But I am not sure that it may not be fairly answered, that although over-assessment is not an inherent defect of the system, it is the result of one of its defects. If the land is not fairly assessed, it is pretty certain to be over-assessed. There is little fear of the valuation falling short of the mark. Now, the principal feature of the Ryotwar system is the multiplication of holdings; and the greater the number of rights to be adjusted, the greater the chance of their not being fairly adjusted. In this point of view, the over-assessment, from which so much evil arose, was a result of the system. But it was so far accidental, that it was remediable. It was not necessarily inseparable from the system. It might be eradicated by an equitable revision. The assessments may be rendered less burdensome, and it is to be hoped that the people will soon reap the benefit of the change.

The grievance of enforced tenancy—of the compulsory occupation of undesired lands—under which the Ryots were for some time compelled to suffer, was a pure abomination. The practice was never openly recognised, and it is to be hoped that the European officers were never cognisant of it. It arose out of a state of things peculiar to the Ryotwar settlement; for the great division of responsibilities—the minute parcelling of the territory—necessarily caused a run upon the good lands, and exposed Government to the risk of having all the indifferent soil thrown upon their hands. When it was resolved that this cruel, most outrageous system should be openly suppressed, the chief revenue authorities, though eager for its suppression, could not help admitting this practical evil, and acknowledging that the result of the reform would be injurious to our finances. But they declared that it was thenceforth "to be clearly understood that the revenue is to continue, as at present, subordinate to justice." It needed that nothing more should be said to give the death-blow to every argument in favor of the old Ryotwar settlement, than that it could not exist cotemporaneously with an improved system of justice.

Another inherent defect in the system of annual settlements was, that it gave the tenant no proprietary interest in his improvements—that under such an arrangement every man, who by his own industry or enterprise had increased the productiveness of the soil under his cultivation, was liable at the end of the year to pay the penalty of his exertions in the increased assessment of his lands. But an evil, at once so unjust to the cultivator, and so disadvantageous to the great Government landlord, was not likely to be perpetuated by administrators who, as time advanced, took progressively more sound and more liberal views alike of their interests and their duties. I believe that under the modified Ryotwar system of 1820, some efforts have been made to remedy this evil, and to give the cultivator a proper interest in his improvements. In 1834, a series of questions was proposed by Lord William Bentinck to some of the principal revenue-officers of Madras, relative to the working of the Ryotwar system. Among these questions was the following: "If a Ryot improves a field that has always been in his occupancy, by making a well, or by other extraordinary application of capital, is his assessment increased, and if increased, is the increase either not immediately taken, or so moderate as to give him an ample return for his expenditure?" To this question the principal collector of Coimbatore replied: "If a Ryot makes a well on his 'punjah' land that has always been in his occupancy, in order to convert it into garden land, he receives a cowle or lease, on favorable terms, to give him ample return for his expenditure; this cowle extends to a period of five years; punjah rent is paid for the first two years; half garden rent for the third year; three-quarters rent for the fourth; and in the fifth year he pays a full garden rent, being about quadruple of the original rent of the punjah field, of whatever class it may be." So it would seem from this, that if a man improved his holding so as to convert it from a field into a garden, his rent was quadrupled at the end of five years. This was the practice in Coimbatore. But the principal collector of Salem, in answer to the same question, said: "In the Salem district no increase of assessment follows improvement effected at the expense of the cultivator."* I believe it may be generally stated, that although the cultivator has more interest in the improvement of his lands than he had under the old Ryotwar settlement, it would be far better if he had still more.

In reply to a question, put by Lord William Bentinck, relative to the amount of land not under cultivation, the Salem collector replied that in his district one half of the culturable land was uncultivated.† The reply of the Coimbatore collector was much more favorable. He repeated that there was about 22 per

* *Replies to the Governor-General.—Lord William Bentinck's queries respecting the Ryotwar system of Revenue Administration in the Presidency of Fort St. George, by the principal Collectors of Coimbatore and Salem.*—These papers were printed for official use; but I do not know whether they have ever been published.

† The writer in the *Calcutta Review* already quoted, whose statistics principally relate to the Salem district, says that some of the best lands there are lying waste, on account of over-assessment. No one will venture to take lands the cultivation of which must be unproductive of profit, if not productive of loss.

cent. of waste land in his district. These local variations may sometimes be accounted for by a reference to the state of the country when it first passed under our rule, but they are commonly regulated by the amount of the assessment. And looking at the general state of the districts under the Ryotwar settlement, it would seem not to have been favorable to the progress of cultivation. In 1821, Munro acknowledged that there was no means of bringing more land under cultivation, and so increasing the revenue, except by reducing the assessment. And twenty years afterwards Lord Elphinstone enunciated the same truth. But although in all parts of the Bengal Presidency under the Zemindarry and Village Settlements cultivation has greatly increased, the most recent authorities on the subject of the Ryotwar settlements admit that we are "still collecting the revenue inherited from the most oppressive of native governments."*

Still, in spite of the over-assessment, the revenue is collected with considerable punctuality. The unrealised amounts are not large, though much larger than they were. "The Ryotwar system," wrote the Salem collector, in 1834, "having now been in operation here for many years, and the Ryots being aware of the exact sum they have each to pay, and of the time in which it must be paid, are in general pretty regular in their instalments." This authority gives a tabular statement of ten years, from which it appears that the net-settlement in the first was 1,690,240 rupees, and in the last 1,410,624 rupees, but that whereas the per-centage of irrecoverable balance in the first year was 7 annas, 6 pie (or less than $\frac{1}{2}$) per cent., in the last it was 2 rupees, 3 annas (or 2 $\frac{3}{16}$) per cent. In Coimbatore we have a similar account of

* *Calcutta Review, June*, 1852.

diminished receipts and increased balances. The net-revenue had diminished in the last ten years; and the per-centage of the balance has risen from 2 annas, 6 pie (or about $\frac{1}{7}$) per cent., to 2 rupees, 10 annas (or more than $2\frac{1}{2}$) per cent. To what extent this may be attributable to the increased forbearance of the revenue-officers, I do not know; but it would be just to take it into reasonable account. The legitimate means of coercion are principally distraint and attachment. But sometimes the native revenue-officers resorted to illegitimate means of extracting blood from a stone. The heads of the villages, too, are said to have "occasional recourse privately to various unauthorised modes of stimulating the tardy payer; such as confining, placing him in the sun, obliging him to stand on one leg, or to sit with his head confined between his knees, till the constrained position becomes painful." But all such violent modes of coercion are merely the remains of native barbarism—relics of old customs favored by the mild Hindoo under the native governments. The European functionary has ever set his face steadfastly against them, and has not been slow to punish, on conviction, such cruelties as these. Even imprisonment is seldom or never resorted to in these days. "No defaulters have been confined in gaol of late years," said the collector of Coimbatore in 1834; "in cases of mere default this measure is not deemed essential."

Looking impartially at all these things, I think it must be admitted that, although the Ryotwar settlement was undertaken, not hastily or heedlessly, but after due consideration, and with a sincere desire to benefit the people, the results do not indicate the success of the experiment. But unsuccessful experiments are no uncommon things in the history of human administrations. There is nothing more remarkable, as there is nothing more mortifying than the fact, that many of the best efforts which have been made for the advancement of the happiness of mankind have resulted only in the extension and perpetuation of human suffering. It would be easy to multiply instances illustrative of this. But I conceive it to be one of those admitted facts which need only to be asserted.*

I turn now to another great revenue experiment, the results of which, as far as they have yet been ascertained, are only cheering evidences of the forethought and wisdom which have designed and fashioned it—I turn to that great experiment known as the settlement of the North-Western Provinces.†

* "It is mortifying to the pride of human wisdom to consider how much evil has resulted from the best and least exceptionable of its boasted institutions—and how those establishments which have been most carefully devised for the repression of guilt or the relief of misery, have become themselves the fruitful and pestilent sources both of guilt and misery in a frightful and disgusting degree. Laws, without which society could not exist, become, by their very multiplication and refinement, a snare and a burden to those they were intended to protect, and let in upon us the hateful and most intolerable plagues of pettifogging chicanery and legal persecution. Institutions for the relief and prevention of poverty have the effect of multiplying it tenfold—hospitals for the cure of diseases become centres of infection. The very police which is necessary to make our cities habitable, give birth to the odious vermin of informers, thief-catchers, and suborners of treachery—and our prisons, which are meant chiefly to reform the guilty and secure the suspected, are converted into schools of the most atrocious corruption, and dens of the most inhuman torture."—[*Lord Jeffery.*]

† I regret very much that in writing this chapter, I had not the assistance of Mr. Dykes' interesting volume, "Salem—an Indian Collectorate," which appeared about the same time as the first edition of this work. It may be studied with very great advantage by all who would make themselves acquainted with the working of the Madras revenue-system.

CHAPTER IV.

The Settlement of the North-West Provinces—First Acquisition of the Country—Primal Measures of our Revenue-Officers—Their Insufficiency—Injustice to the Old Proprietors—Frauds of Native Officials—Government Measures—Commissioners Appointed—Partial Remedies—Further Enactments—Mr. R. Bird—The New Settlement—Its Agents—Its Character—Its Results.

When the armies of Lake and Wellesley broke the Mahratta power on the banks of the Jumna and the plains of Berar, and the north-western provinces of Hindostan became subject to the white men, who ruled in the Carnatic, the Deccan, and Bengal, and had established themselves in the priestly city of Benares, the settlement of the revenue of the ceded and conquered districts became a matter of primal concernment. Somehow or other the thing was to be done; and it was to be done quickly. The country was conquered, and now it was to be forced to give up its treasures to the conqueror. Those treasures were no longer to be found in a state of glittering condensation, hidden in the bowels of grotesque idols, in gorgeous Pagan fanes, or buried in the palaces of prostrate princes. The wealth of our new possessions was spread over a vast surface. It was to be found only in the soil; and being so found, there arose a question regarding the mode of acquisition and appropriation—a question not quite so easy as that presented for the solution of Mahmoud of Ghuznee, when the treasures of the conquered country dazzled the eyes and stirred the heart of the invader.

The territory first ceded was a portion of the great

province of Oude. Lord Wellesley was Governor-General of India. His two brothers, Arthur and Henry Wellesley, had followed the fortunes of their vice-regal relative, and were now within reach of his directing hand. The soldier was laying broad and deep the foundation of his military renown. But provision had to be made for the civilian. Mr. Henry Wellesley was in a more equivocal position than the major-general, who was about to lead a division of the British army against the Mahrattas of Berar. He was not a Company's servant. He had not graduated as an Indian administrator. He was simply what in the case of common men would be called an adventurer—a hanger-on. Lord Wellesley now made him lieutenant-governor of the ceded districts in Oude.*

It would be difficult to conceive a more onerous and more delicate duty than that which was entrusted to him. It was his to superintend the entire administration, fiscal and judicial, of a new and extensive tract of country, inhabited by a race of people officially declared to be "unaccustomed to any regular system of order or law, and habituated to commit the utmost excesses of violence and oppression." It demanded a thorough knowledge of the country and the people, but that which was not possessed at all by Mr. Wellesley, was possessed to some small extent by his coadjutors. A board of commissioners was associated with him; and under them were set to work the required array of judges, and magistrates, and collectors, with their Regulations in their hands. The misrule, which preceded our assumption of dominion, and the disorder which we found in every department, were so vast, that it would have been a miracle if any great amount of success had attended

* I do not wish to convey the impression that this was merely a job, for there may have been sound policy, at that time, in placing the brother of the Governor-General at the head of the provisional administration of the new provinces. Such an arrangement may have given something of character and dignity to the new movement not to be derived from any other personal source.

our initial operations. A triennial settlement was undertaken, mainly with the landholders, on the expiration of the current financial year; and a Permanent Settlement was promised, after two more experiments similar to the first, of three and four years' duration.

But soon to these ceded Oude districts were added those which we had gained, by right of conquest, from the Mahratta chieftains—a large and noble tract of country between the Jumna and the Ganges. The Bengal Regulations, already applied to the Oude districts, were now to be presented to our newly-acquired North-Western Provinces. There was, after the current year, to be a three years' settlement, and then a four years' settlement, and then a settlement in perpetuity. So strongly impressed was Lord Wellesley with a conviction of the advantages of the Permanent System, and so eager was he to promise those advantages to the North-Western Zemindars, that he omitted in the Regulations, which he promulgated to make the permanency of the settlement, conditional on the confirmation of the Court of Directors.* The omission was subsequently repaired by his successor. A new Regulation announced to the landholders that the permanency of the settlement was to depend upon the will of the authorities at home.

The system of land-revenue which obtained at this time was based upon the old establishment of village communities. These institutions existed but in an imperfect, fragmentary state; and when the officers of the British Government began hastily and loosely to establish some intelligible system of revenue collection, or at all events to make out clearly the parties to whom the State were to look for the apportioned amount of revenue, they groped about painfully in the dark. All sorts of claimants arose, with titles good, bad, and in-

* In 1803 and 1805. The provisional Government was dissolved at the beginning of the former year. Mr. Wellesley settled his accounts and returned to England.

different, and flocked to the Collector's Court at the chief station, urging their proprietary rights. Embarrassed by these conflicting claims, the Collector placed himself in the hands of the "Canoongo," or native Notary, and decided according to his dictum upon the claims that were laid before him. There was little or no inquiry, and the decision was wrong. The amount of revenue had then to be fixed; and here again the authority of the village functionary was generally followed, and the valuation was generally wrong.

The difficulty of the task was very great, and it would have been strange if our first efforts had been more successful. One thing alone was certain at this time—that the amount of information possessed by the revenue-officers in the Ceded and Conquered Provinces was not sufficient to enable the Government, with any hope of doing justice to its subjects, to introduce a permanent system of assessment in that country. When, therefore, under the government of Lord Minto, who had taken up the revenue opinions with the high office held by Cornwallis and Wellesley, and had notified to the Zemindars and other proprietors (by Regulation X., 1807) that the assessment under the existing settlement would remain fixed for ever, if the arrangement should receive the sanction of the Court of Directors, a Special Commission was deputed to the Ceded and Conquered Country to give effect to this declaration, it is not strange that they should have hesitated to commit the State irrevocably to a measure which its executive officers were not prepared to recommend, and the country was not prepared to receive. A settlement, fixed in perpetuity at that time, could only be based upon error, the results of which would be laden with injury to the State and injustice to the people.

The Commissioners of whom I speak were Mr. H.

St.George Tucker and Mr. R. W. Cox. Setting out on a tour of inquiry early in the cold season of 1807, they visited all the different collectorates, and diligently sought the opinions of all the different collectors. They had the strongest possible faith in the principles of the Permanent System, but the further they proceeded the more obvious it became, that such a measure as the declaration of a perpetual assessment would then be premature and dangerous.*

The collectors were nearly all of this opinion. They recommended short settlements, further inquiries, and detailed surveys. It was clear to them, and it was clear to the Commissioners, that the Ceded and Conquered Provinces did not at all resemble Bengal. "When we reflect," wrote the latter, "that the miseries of famine have perhaps been averted in Bengal by the lamented patriot who gave the Permanent Settlement to that country, we feel the utmost repugnance at the idea of opposing its extension to our new possessions. But Bengal is different in many particulars. The land is more easily cultivated, and is fertilised by a periodical inundation; water is easily procured; wells, reservoirs, and aqueducts are unnecessary; and a large capital is seldom required for agricultural purposes. The inferior landholders, and even the peasantry, can carry on the cultivation of their lands without those aids which must be furnished to secure

* Mr. Tucker, in after years, often spoke of this Commission; and I am enabled, therefore, clearly to state, on his own authority, the course which he pursued at this time, and the opinions which he entertained. "I was appointed in 1807," he wrote, "to carry into execution a measure which successive administrations had considered to be essential to the prosperity of the country. Although concurring most unreservedly in the opinion that it was wise and salutary, and that it contained a vital principle which must in due season work out all the good anticipated, I ventured to counsel delay, upon the ground that we were not at the moment in a state of preparation to consummate so great an undertaking; but it never occurred to my mind that the principle of the measure was to be abandoned, or that the landholders who had received from us the most solemn pledge given in the most authentic form, were to be denied for ever the promised benefit, and that in the end they were to be cast aside as a mere incumbrance upon the earth. That pledge can never be effaced, although it remains unfulfilled." —[*MS. Records.*]

the prosperity of the Western Provinces. But, above all, we were in every respect better prepared in Bengal to undertake a measure, which, at a future period, we shall gladly see extended to the rest of our possessions."*

The reluctance of the Commissioners, though not altogether acceptable in Calcutta,† found favor in Leadenhall-street. The Court of Directors approved of these recommendations, and wrote out earnest letters to Bengal, cautioning the local Government against committing them to any system of unalterable assessment. "Before undertaking so arduous a task as that of irrevocably settling in perpetuity the lands of a province, and fixing the demand of Government upon those lands in perpetuity, we have always considered a patient and laborious scrutiny of individual rights, a careful investigation of local peculiarities, together with a minute and detailed survey of the extent, cultivation, and productive powers of the territory, as indispensable. . . . Supposing that in Bengal our expectations had been realised to their full extent, it would not follow that a plan of settlement which had succeeded in a country, of which we had been from twenty or thirty years in possession, was equally applicable to provinces which have lately devolved under authority."‡ And a few months later they wrote still more decidedly on the subject—"The object of this present despatch is to caution you in the most pointed manner against pledging us to the extension of the Bengal fixed assessment to our newly-acquired territo-

* *Report of Messrs. Cox and Tucker, April 13th,* 1808—*Revenue Selections.*—This elaborate and very able report was written by Mr. Tucker. It is not only full of valuable information, but it contains the expression of sound statesmanlike views on many questions of general policy.

† Mr. Colebrooke recorded a long minute on the subject, in which he said —"There is room for regret that the gentlemen to whom the execution of the measure was committed should have put into deliberation not the best means for carrying it into effect, but the expediency of the measure itself which they were selected to execute."

‡ *Court's Letter to Bengal, February* 1, 1811.

ries. We are aware of your resolution not to declare any settlement permanent till it has obtained our sanction and approbation. It is not, however, without anxiety that we have learned from your late despatches that a triennial lease has been concluded in the Upper Provinces, which expires, we believe, in the course of April, 1812, whereby the assessment in the third year of the lease has been declared by you to be permanent, provided that we shall confirm the terms of settlement, because this arrangement may have exerted an expectation on the part of the natives which we are not by any means prepared to satisfy."*

Thus was the question of the permanent assessment of the Ceded and Conquered Provinces settled, at all events for a time.† In the mean while short leases were granted, from three to five years, to proprietors, or pseudo-proprietors of different kinds, to Zemindars, to independent Talookdars, and other claimants; but even during those short periods it was often necessary to re-adjust the amount of assessment. All this created much discontent. Many, unjustly deprived of their proprietary rights, clamored for redress, and were told to appeal to the civil courts. This, in effect, was a mockery and a delusion. The perplexity was only increased. The errors of the revenue were often perpetuated by the judicial department; and the suitor involved in new embarrassments more painful than the old. "Decrees," it is said, "were constantly passed so irreconcileable with truth and justice, that it was absolutely impossible to execute them."

The mode of collecting the revenue tended equally to the perpetuation of injustice. The collectors en-

* *Court's Letter, Nov.* 27, 1811.

† The question was from time to time revived at the India House, and some very able members of the Court, including Mr. Edmonstone and Mr. Tucker, advocated the introduction of the Permanent Settlement into the North-West Provinces; but the majority of the Court did not entertain the project.

deavoured to guard against default by placing watchmen over the standing crops. If, in spite of this precaution, there was a deficiency of revenue, the property of the registered landholder was distrained, and he himself thrown into prison. Then the estate was put up to sale, and perhaps purchased, at a nominal sum, by some astute native official—often a stranger from the lower provinces.* But as these large estates, although standing on the Government records in the name of some one recognised proprietor, were in reality often held in coparcenery among a number of sharers, of whom Government had no knowledge, it happened often that the default of a few caused the punishment of many. All were immersed in one indiscriminate ruin. The hereditary cultivators were deprived, hastily and absolutely, of their rights, and compelled to sue for leases under some fortunate, perhaps fraudulent, purchaser, whom they hated and despised.

The processes by which the old landholders were defrauded of their proprietary rights varied, more or less, according to circumstances and to character, but they all belonged to one common family, and had many features of general resemblance. Many personal sketches might be given in illustration of the trickery practised upon unsuspecting proprietors by astute native officials. One, however, will suffice for the purpose; it is a striking one; and I give it almost in the words in which the story was related to me. During the prevalence of the hot winds of 1818, a zealous and intelligent civil officer in the judicial department was abroad in his district, on duty. He was fixing the position of a line of police-stations for the protection of the highways, when he came upon a sequestered village, near the banks of the

* Nearly one-half of the Cawnpore and Allahabad districts passed into the hands of native officials.

Jumna, and halting upon one of those artificial mounds which in that part of the country mark the sites of ancient villages, was quietly enjoying the noble sunset and the fine prospect around him. Whilst thus engaged, an old and respectable-looking Hindoo crawled out of a neighbouring hut, and approached him. The European official and the native villager soon fell into conversation. There was something in the language of the latter which fixed the attention and excited the interest of the English gentleman, and after a while he asked the native who he was. "Who I *am*, do you ask?" answered the man. "I *am* the owner of that hut which you have just seen me leave. Who I was, would you know? I *was* the chief of all that your eye can take in from this height."*

The English gentleman asked how this had happened. "Oh!" said the old man, "in the usual manner, by a *neelam*" (auction). And when the sahib pushed his inquiries further, told his story nearly in these words:—"When your rule was first established in these parts, I had never seen an European, and naturally sought for some native authority through whom to make my approaches towards the personage of this new race, who was henceforth to be the ruler of my native province.

"I was advised to apply to a certain Nusser Ali, then the Dewan, and reported to possess great influence with the European collector. To him, accordingly, I repaired. His story was, that the collector was like a tiger, and that I ought, for my own safety, to shun his fearful presence. To enable me to pay my revenue without incurring this risk, he advised me to send every instalment as it became due to him, and promised that he would pay the amount faithfully to the collector.

* Whether the Hindostanee word was *malik*, *zemindar*, or what other, my informant does not remember; but the meaning conveyed was, that he had been the chief landed proprietor in that part of the country.

"In an evil hour I took his advice, and sent my money regularly to Nusser Ali. And so things went on very well for a year or two, when suddenly I was alarmed by the announcement that a stranger had appeared on my domain, and was enjoining all the cultivators to pay their several dues to him. I sought the stranger out, and asked him how he came to exercise such authority within the limits of my estate. 'Oh!' said he, 'I have bought this estate at auction; and it is mine.' I had never heard the world (*neelam*) before, and I hardly knew what it meant. But I hastened to Cawnpore, and there discovered that the Dewan, to whom I had paid the Government dues, had kept back the amount remitted, so as to throw the estate into arrears; he had then obtained an order for its sale, which, possessed of early information, he had easily managed to prevent, and had finally got it purchased for himself, under a fictitious name.

"The fictitious name stood on the records until the Dewan retired from official life, when his own name was inserted as purchaser by private sale from the man of straw, and thenceforth the estate was openly held as his own."

This is one of many instances which might be cited in illustration of the evils attending our first hasty efforts to "settle" the revenue of the North-Western Provinces. But perhaps the largest amount of injustice inflicted upon the landed proprietors at this time arose out of a confusion of terms. Many a man found that he had lost his old territorial rights simply because the new English rulers had described him by a certain word, the dire import of which he himself by no means clearly understood. The revenue-contractors under the first settlement were set down in the Government records, with few exceptions, as *Moostajirs*, or Farmers. There was another column, headed with the word *Malik*, signifying Proprietor, which was generally a blank in the original books. The contractor little knew the relative importance of the two words—little dreamt that, in the course of a few years, the ominous title under which he was registered would prove fatal to his claims to the continued occupancy of the land. But when the period for which he had first contracted was at an end, he found how "the letter killeth." The astute native functionaries, who had followed the British revenue-officers from the Lower Provinces, hit the blot in a moment. They saw how they could turn it to account, and devised a scheme whereby a large portion of the land was swept into their own possession. When the original lease granted to the recorded "Moostajirs" was at an end, the native functionaries reported that the first contractors were only farmers —that they had no proprietary rights at all—but that certain other men, whose names they mentioned (principally Mussulman names), were the legitimate proprietors, and ought to be so entered in the Government books. The collectors placed too much confidence in these specious stories, and the names of some men of straw—some relatives or dependents of the native officials—crept into the columns of the register, headed with the word *Malik*. The man of straw made way in due time for the real Jacob. And such was the wholesale work of these supplanters, that one man (a Dewan, or chief native functionary under the collector) contrived to possess himself of ninety large villages, "whilst another had become sole proprietor of the whole pergunnah, or subdivision, which at first constituted his official jurisdiction as *Tuhseeldar*."* No wonder that it was said, with asto-

* *Mr. Robertson's "Remarks."*

nishment, by the people of the Upper Provinces—"Yours is a strange rule. You flog a man for stealing a brass pot, and reward him for stealing a pergunnah!"*

Thus were all the estates in the country passing away, one by one, from the hands of the ancient proprietors, who stood, bewildered, confused, dismayed, scarcely knowing by what strange juggle they were suddenly, but almost imperceptibly, deprived of their rights. Many, as their descendants related, died of a broken heart. Others, less capable of silent endurance—high-caste and high-spirited Rajpoots—stung by this authoritative injustice, took the law into their own hands, and boldly asserted their rights—the rights of centuries of possession—in the teeth of the upstart claimant who had been yesterday installed by the fall of the Government hammer, or the juggle of a fraudulent Dewan. Acts of open violence—even midnight murders—were committed under a sense of this intolerable wrong. The eyes of Government were then opened. It had become clear that something must be done.

It must not be supposed, however, that the civil servants of the Company were wholly ignorant of, or indifferent to, the wrongs which were thus pressing upon the very existence of the old proprietors. The eyes, at least of some of them, were opened to this monstrous injustice, and strenuous efforts were made to redress the grievances which stared them so obtrusively in the face. Foremost among these may be mentioned the names of Mr. Henry Newnham and Mr. Thomas Campbell Robertson. In 1813, Mr. Newnham took charge of the collectorate of Cawnpore. He examined into many of these

* There were three settlements made during our first ten years' possession of the North-Western Provinces (from 1803 to 1813). In the first book, the column headed *Malik* (Proprietor) was almost entirely a blank. In the second, the name of Mahomed Roostum, or some other equally real newly-discovered proprietor, was inserted; and in the third, that of Nusser Ali, ex-Dewan, or some other of the same class, was registered as purchaser from the said fictitious Mahomed Roostum.

cases of fraudulent transfer of property, and reported upon them to the Revenue Board at Furruckabad. The Board, however, had no power to interfere, and the sufferers were referred, for their remedy, to the civil courts. Many suits were then instituted, but the *word*, again, was more potential than the fact. Our judges read the unhappy word "Moostajir," and could not possess themselves of the idea that a Moostajir could be anything but a temporary leaseholder, in the English sense of the term, and so either the case was dismissed, or the plaintiff was nonsuited.

Matters were in this state when, in the early part of 1817, Mr. Robertson assumed the office of Judge at Cawnpore. He had heard little or nothing of the peculiar cases of which I am now writing, and took up the first on the file without any idea of its especial importance. He saw at once the hideous injustice of ousting a man in actual possession, solely on the strength of the word under which his name had been entered in the Government books, and he called for proof of the title under which the supplanting Meer Roostum, who had crept in so insidiously as "Malik," held the litigated estate. No proof, of course, was forthcoming; so the English judge ignored his claims, and decided in favor of the original "Moostajir," who was shown at the same time to have been, from time immemorial, the head man of the village, and as such, the legitimate contractor. When this decision was pronounced, an excited buzz ran through the court-house, and the excitement was caught up by the natives outside the walls. The triumph of the village landholders was great; but unfortunately it was short-lived. The case was referred to the Court of Appeal at Bareilly, and the court cancelled the decision. It was held that any man's title was better than that of the unfortunate contractor who had once been registered as a Moostajir.

Fortunately, Mr. Robertson was not a man to be checked, when on the right path, by such obstructions as this. The court continued to reverse his decisions; but on a special appeal to the Sudder Court of Calcutta, of which Mr. Courtenay Smith was a member, there was some inclination in that highest quarter to side with the Cawnpore judge. The process, however, was too dilatory for Mr. Robertson's eager sense of justice, and he took the irregular course of translating some of the awards of the Court of Appeal, and forwarding them with a letter to Government. This mode of procedure, though unusual, was not unsuccessful. In 1821, a Regulation was passed recognising the injustice which, under cover of the Sale Law, had been done to "poor and ignorant men," and appointing a Commission to inquire into all the transfers of property which had taken place during the first eight or ten years of our government of the North-Western Provinces, and the general state of the landed tenures.

Little permanent benefit resulted from this. The machinery was not suited to the purpose. It was too stately and formal. An immense quantity of work was thrown upon it; some inquiries were instituted; some unjust decisions were reversed, and many compromises were effected. A partial remedy was applied to individual cases; but the root of the evil was not touched. Indeed, these judicial tribunals were not suited to such a purpose as the adjustment of territorial claims.* They who had thought most on the subject were of opinion that the required settlement was best to be effected by revenue-officers, moving among the people, conversing freely with them, and altogether extricating themselves from the formal incumbrances of official state.

* The first commissioners appointed were Mr. W. W. Bird and Mr. H. G. Christian, and as long as the special powers, so created, were in the hands of such men, the regulation worked advantageously; but when they were conferred on all the commissioners of revenue, without regard to their especial fitness, the consequences were most pernicious.

Foremost among these was Mr. Holt Mackenzie, a man of large and liberal views, and of a thoughtful nature, who told the collectors to shoulder their guns, to go out among the people, and bring back information with their game. Views of this kind led to the framing of a regulation—very famous in the history of Indian Land-Revenue—known as Regulation VII. of 1822, which was, doubtless, an advance upon anything that had been before promulgated, but which was not without inherent defects. It was stuffed too full of requirements. It imposed upon a limited agency almost unlimited duties. It emanated from one, indeed, who had not graduated in the revenue department, and who had over-estimated the amount of detail work which our revenue-officers could adequately perform. The principle was sound—the proposed system was excellent—but for want of sufficient means to carry it into effect, it was one of difficult accomplishment. So it happened that the work of revision went on so slowly, that when ten years had elapsed from the time of its initiation, it was calculated that it would take sixty more years to render the work complete.

From all that I have written up to this point the reader will gain no very clear conception of what is the nature of the revenue settlement existing in the North-Western Provinces of India. Up to this point, indeed, there is little but confusion and obscurity in my pages, as there was little but confusion and obscurity in the revenue administration of that part of the country. We found that a great variety of tenures had been recognised by the native governments, prior to the cession of the provinces; and we took what we found without considering whether we were adopting indigenous institutions, or merely the corrupt growth of usurpation and abuse. We were not answerable for the fruits of disorganisation and misrule, which came ripe to our hands; nor could we obviate the necessary evils of that worst of all transition-states —the transition of a people from one government to another. It would have been strange if, at such a time, there had not been a scramble; it would have been strange if some impostors had not stepped in, if just rights had not been temporarily obscured and fraudulent claims erroneously recognised. Our British administrators, in this epoch, knew just as much as they could reasonably be expected to know. They had a clear conception of a Zemindar, and some idea of a Ryot. All the proclamations and regulations issued at this time, were addressed to "Zemindars, independent Talookdars, and other proprietors." Doubtless, there were such personages in the Ceded and Conquered Countries, but the "other proprietors" included a far more important class. The collectors, who were pushed up damp from Bengal, knew little or nothing of the village communities, which, from remote generations, had flourished in Upper India. But from year to year, as time advanced, knowledge dawned more clearly upon them. The darkness began to disappear. Our revenue-officers saw with greater and greater distinctness facts instead of fictions before them. They had peopled the provinces in the first instance with the latter, carrying their own preconceived notions of landed tenures and agricultural systems to a country which knew little or nothing of the things which their new rulers had stereotyped in their minds. But in time, the ancient institutions which had been shrouded from them, or which they only saw in a glass darkly, they now saw face to face; and with this knowledge came the conviction of the burden of wrong which our ignorance must have brought upon the land.

The settlement of the North-Western Provinces is

now officially described as a "Putteedaree" Settlement*—that is, a settlement made with the "Putteedars," or sharers of estates. But in our earlier revenue transactions in the Upper India little or no account was taken of such people as "Putteedars."† They were the proprietors of the several allotments of estates held under the old village system—that system which our administrators in the early part of the present century trod down so remorselessly in their chase of Zemindars and Talookdars, and other great individual proprietors or contractors of the same class. We had, indeed, contrived almost to crush these village communities, and had committed the great cardinal error of governing the people after any other fashion than their own. But with a progressive increase of knowledge came a progressive improvement in the administration of our new provinces, and we began more and more to shape our system in accordance with the institutions and usages of the people. It would be easy to trace through the Regulations of the first quarter of the present century growing indications of this expansion of knowledge—of this ever-increasing desire to lessen the gulf between the rulers and the ruled, and to adapt our forms of government to the real requirements of the country. But it was long before so difficult a subject—one so intricate in itself,

* Land-Revenue definitions are no easy things to write, so I gladly borrow a description of the Putteedaree Settlement from the "Statistical Papers relating to India," recently prepared at the India House:—"Under the Putteedaree tenure the same estate is parcelled out into allotments, and thenceforward the shares in the net profits are commuted for equivalent portions of land. Each proprietor or shareholder undertakes the agricultural management of his separate allotment, paying through the representative of the proprietary body (the lumkerdar, or, perhaps, the head man of the village) such instalment of the Government revenue as may have been agreed to among themselves, in distributing the aggregate assessment. In the event of individual default, a joint responsibility attaches to the whole proprietary body; but any proceedings instituted by the Government for the realisation of the deficiency, would be directed, in the first instance, against the defaulting allotment. The characteristic of the Putteedaree tenure is cultivation in severalty with joint responsibility."

† The first Regulation which I can find, manifesting anything like an acquaintance with the Putteedaree system, is Regulation IX. of 1811.

and to the eye of a foreigner rendered doubly indistinct and mysterious by the social exclusiveness of the people—was fully mastered, in all its bearings. The more we learnt, the more clear it became that we had committed a grievous mistake in overlooking the village communities, and the more eager we became to make atonement for the evil we had done.

The new Regulation, of which I have spoken, was a prodigious advance upon all its predecessors. It indicated a larger knowledge and a purer benevolence. It pledged the Government to ascertain, and when ascertained to recognise, the territorial rights of all classes. It was its object "to introduce a general and scientific survey of the country, to mark carefully and to record the boundaries of every village, to register the separate possessions, rights, privileges, and responsibilities of those communities who hold their lands in severalty, and of the several interests of those who hold land in common."*

The sum payable to Government by every individual shareholder was to be recorded; but every individual shareholder was not to have immediate transactions with Government. The payments of the shareholders were to be made collectively, by the head man of the village, or other representative; and a joint responsibility was recognised. "It was intended," says Mr. Campbell, "to combine the advantages of the Ryotwar system with that of village leases."† It

* *Raikes' "Notes on the North-Western Provinces of India."*—A very interesting work, which all should consult who desire further information regarding the history of this great settlement, and the nature of landed tenures in the North-West. A clearer conception of the village communities is to be derived from it, than from any other work with which I am acquainted.

† *Modern India*, page 323.—"The most common tenure of all in the North-West," says Mr. Campbell, "is that where a village belongs not to a single individual, but to a single family. In this case the great proportion of the land is cultivated by tenants; and the sharers have not their shares separately divided off—the tenants are the tenants of all in common. The proprietors generally live in the village, and their own cultivation is taken into account at lower rates. The whole collections are brought together, the revenue paid, and the surplus divided among the proprietors, according to the fractional share possessed by each. When there are many proprietors, one or two are chosen representatives and managers."

afforded ample protection to individuals without clogging the wheels of the administrative machinery with a mass of individual contracts.

Such, briefly stated, was the intent of the new system of revenue administration which was to be introduced into the North-Western Provinces of India. But the great reform, as I have said, did not proceed apace, for want of an efficient agency to reduce it to energetic practice. Ten years passed away, and the progress towards a thorough revision of the settlement was painfully small. It was plain, therefore, that the machinery must be improved.

Lord William Bentinck was at this time Governor-General of India, and he was on a tour through the Upper Provinces. He saw at once that it was necessary to do something to give more effective operation to the provision of the famous Regulation VII. of 1822. Halting at Allahabad, where a Board of Revenue for the North-Western Provinces had been recently established, he took counsel with all the best authorities on the spot, and the result was another famous regulation, known as Regulation IX. of 1833, under which the present settlement has been prosecuted, with so much vigor, to its completion. It embraced all the objects of the previous regulation, with other collateral aims, and it greatly improved the machinery of revision, and enlarged the personal agency to be employed. Special settlement officers were to be appointed, not burdened with other duties; civilians, with all their time and all their energies to bestow upon the great work that opened out before them.

The objects which it was now proposed to embrace were these:

1. The revision of the assessment.

2. The better division of the instalments of revenue payable to Government.

3. The demarcation of the exterior boundaries of estates and villages.

4. The correction of the system of accounts at the Tehsildar's offices, and the arrangement of their records.

5. The formation of a fund for the construction of roads.

6. The establishment of a provision for the support of the village police.

7. The resumption of all hidden rent-free tenures brought to light by the surveys.

8. The recasting or retention of the large tenures.

9. The demarcation of the component portions of every village; the recording of the several rights comprised therein, and providing for their maintenance; and the registering of all rights which may spring up hereafter.

The tract of country subject to these operations equalled in extent the whole of England and of Scotland. It stretched from Goruckpore on the south-east, to Hissar on the north-west, across a line of 700 miles, for the most part along the valleys of the Ganges and the Jumna.* In

* The North-West Provinces contain, by the last and most accurate returns, 71,985 square statute miles, with a population of 23,199,668 souls. The land-revenue, demanded from them in 1846-7, amounted to rupees 4,05,29,921; in addition to which they paid in the same year a nett sum of rupees, 16,60,901 (including collections due for former years), on account of Abkarí, and of rupees 12,33,903 for stamps. The customs duties, levied on the frontier during the same period (by far the greater part of which must be considered a tax upon these provinces), amounted to about rupees 26,00,000; thus making up, with other minor sources of income, a total revenue of more than five crores of rupees. The whole territory is divided into thirty-two districts, which are classed in six divisions. The whole of these have come under survey; but there has, of course, been no general revision of the revenue in those parts of the Benares division, of which the Government demand was permanently fixed in the year 1795. The revenue has there remained unaltered, except in cases where an estate had always been farmed, and the demand had therefore never been determined in perpetuity; or where the permanent demand had broken down, and required reduction. . . . . .

In extent of territory, therefore, the provinces which, with the above partial exceptions, have come under settlement, are about equal to England and Scotland, without Wales. In point of population, they about equal Italy, including Sicily and Sardinia; while the gross revenue, realised from them, exceeds by one-half that of the kingdom of Belgium. Following the line of the Ganges and Jumna, the extreme distance, from Goruckpore on the south-east, to Hissar on the north-

this country was embraced a large variety of soils and climates, and numerous races of people, differing from each other in language and character and in the institutions which they favored and developed. Between the country to the east of the Ganges, and that which lies westward of the Jumna, the difference is peculiarly striking. On one side noble forests and mango-groves, fields rich with an abundant harvest, sparkling streams and pools of water vary and refresh the landscape, whilst on the other there is little more than a dull uniformity of arid plain. Between these two extremes lies the Doab, the country between the two rivers. Here there are signs of a more advanced civilisation—of a fuller development of industrial energy and skill. Here are the large towns and the more important villages, and here the labor of man has striven to compensate for the deficiencies of nature, and to make the soil yield abundant produce without the aid of the heavenly nourishment, which is seldom wanting in the country to the west. Mainly upon artificial irrigation is the country dependent for the security of the crops. Within the boundaries of the North-West Provinces there are soils of all kinds, from wet clays to light sands, adapted to the growth of various descriptions of produce—of sugar, of wheat, of rice, of cotton—and as many varieties of cultivators as there are soils under cultivation—Rajpoots and Brahmins, Jats and Goojurs, with different manners, different characters, and different descriptions of landed tenures, different methods of measurement and modes of assessment, different distributions of property, different laws of inheritance.

west, is nearly 700 miles. In this wide expanse of country, much diversity of race, language, and character, is naturally met with among the occupants of the soil. The Rajpût of Azimghur, the Brahmin of Cawnpore, the Ahír of the ravines of the Jumna, the Gujur of Meerut, and the Jât of Delhi, have all peculiarities which distinguish them, not only from other tribes, but also from men of the same tribe in other places.—[*Calcutta Review*, No. xxiv. Article: "The Settlement of the North-Western Provinces."]

There were, of course, generic resemblances establishing a certain unity of descent; but the varieties were so distinct as to render it necessary that nothing should be done without a close study of the local peculiarities which distinguish the different members of the great family.*

* The writer of the Settlement article in the *Calcutta Review*, above quoted, gives the most graphic picture of the general outward characteristics of the North-West Provinces with which I am acquainted.

"The North-West Provinces," he writes, "are situated almost entirely in the valleys of the Ganges and Jumna; the principal part of them lying between those rivers. There is little variety in the flat alluvial soil to attract the admiration of a passing traveller, accustomed to the interchange of hill and dale in other countries. Nevertheless, if he leaves the high road, and penetrates into the more secluded parts of the country, he will acknowledge that, even here, the hand, 'which makes all nature beauty to his eye,' has not been wanting. If he visits the districts to the east of the Ganges, which border on the Sub-Himalayan hills, he will find much of the luxuriance of tropical vegetation, together with a brisk air and healthy climate in the winter months, such as few tropical regions can boast. There he will see the groves, of which Virgil had heard,

'Quos gerit India lucos;
———— ubi aëra vincere summum
Arboris haud ullæ jactu potuere sagittæ.'

The tiger and the elephant still dwell in the remains of the primæval forests, and magnificent mango topes cover large tracts not yet required for the plough. There the fields are rich with abundant harvests, produced with slight labor, and subject to a few uncertainties. The little hamlets, with their low thatched roofs, stand closely together, but do not yet contain a population adequate to the full occupation of the land. Patches of bush and grass jungle are thus interspersed with the cultivation, and relieve its uniformity; nor have the palm and bamboo, the banian and the peepul, yet been proscribed as intruders. Streams and pools abound on every side, and assist in varying the landscape.

"If the traveller now crosses into the Duáb, he will perceive a considerable change. There is no longer the same moisture in the soil or climate, nor the same spontaneous fertility. The industry of man has succeeded to the profusion of nature. He now meets with more towns of note from their size or antiquity. The villages are larger, and stand further apart; while their flat roofs, and the height to which, in the course of ages, they have risen above the plain, give them an imposing appearance from a distance. The walls, with which they are often enclosed; the mud fort, perhaps, at the foot of which they are built; the distance which the people have to go to their daily labor; all point to those former troubled times, when a defenceless cottage in the open fields was a most insecure habitation. Yet the face of the country is by no means bare or unpleasing so long as the crops are on the ground. These are raised with greater toil than in the more humid districts, but are generally plentiful, except in seasons of peculiar drought. Wheat, sugar, and rice, are less extensively raised; but cotton, as a valuable article of produce, in some degree supplies their place. The trees, which love the water side, have disappeared, but many remain; and some of these, as the mhowa, the tamarind, and the jamun, still attain a noble size. It is not till the visitor reaches the arid plains to the west of the Jumna, from Etawah to Hissar, on the extreme verge of the British territory, that vegetation really languishes. There the red sandstone hills rise through the hitherto level surface. Except in those favored spots where wells can be formed, or down the line of the Delhi Canal, the husbandman trusts almost entirely to seasonable rains. The hardy babúl and ferash alone break the line of the horizon, and everything betokens the nearer approach to the deserts of Marwar and Bikanir.

"In common with most parts of

It was a great work, assuredly, which now had to be done, and it required all the energies of a great man to carry it out. It was not to be done by one man—not by a score of men—but it was necessary that over the extensive agency now to be employed should be cast the equal light of one directing mind. There was fortunately a man at hand fitted for the work, and eager to accomplish it. Mr. Robert Mertins Bird was a member of the chief Board of Revenue at Allahabad. He had been reared in the judicial department; but during a connexion of some twenty years with the law courts he had brooded over the great question of Indian revenue, and had, perhaps, as large a knowledge of the subject as

Southern and Central Asia, the fertility of the soil in this part of India depends mainly upon artificial irrigation. When the means for this are available, not only will a sandy soil yield a good crop, but the nature of the soil itself is often gradually improved. Vegetable matter accumulates in the course of years from the remains of former harvests, and from the manure, which it is worth the while of the cultivator to expend upon the land. If, on the other hand, water be wanting, the produce is always uncertain; the cultivation is less cared for; and the usually light soil drifts about with the fierce winds of May and June, till pure silex alone is left in it, or till the barren under stratum of kunkur, or of red indurated clay, appears. The lands nearest the villages are naturally those which receive most attention, and are worked up to the greatest productiveness. These lands often bear two crops in the year, and pay rents of ten rupees, or more, the acre. Their extent varies according to the populousness and prosperity of the village, and to the classes who inhabit it, but seldom exceeds six or eight per cent. of the total area of the estate. Next to these come the second-rate lands, varying up to twelve per cent. of the whole; while the great bulk of the area is thrown into the third or lowest class. This threefold division, with the additional distinction of irrigated and non-irrigated, is prevalent under different names in most parts of the country. Other local peculiarities are of course everywhere to be found. In the vicinity of the rivers it is necessary to distinguish between the low *khadir* land on the borders of the stream, and the *baugur* land on the level of the high bank. In other places the gentle undulations of the surface cause a succession of clayey hollows and sandy ridges, each of which has its peculiar products and capabilities. Even in level tracts, there is often much difference in the stiffness and strength of the soil, according as the sand, which forms its principal basis, is mixed with more productive ingredients. Some local soils are noted for their suitability to peculiar articles, as a certain wet clay in the eastern parts of Goruckpur for sugar, and the black soil of Bundelcund for the Al root. The quantity of saline matter in the earth and water is another point, deeply affecting the value of the land. Where the water is brackish, the agriculturist is much restricted in his choice of crops; many refusing to grow at all under such circumstances, and others requiring an abundant supply of rain-water to counteract the quality of that drawn from the wells. Where much soda is present in the soil, large plains are found entirely destitute of vegetation from this cause, nor has any remedy yet been discovered for the sterility thus produced."—[*Calcutta Review*, No. xxiv.]

any man in the country who had been trained in that branch of the service. The measures which he was now summoned to carry out "had been many years previously planned and elaborated by him, as measures of a purely judicial character when he was holding a judicial office, and had no prospect of ever being connected with the revenue department. His experience in the discharge of his functions as a judicial officer led to the conviction in his mind that the existing tribunals were insufficient for the ascertainment of rights or their protection, and that the combined effect of the revenue and judicial systems would be injurious and oppressive, unless those systems could be made to bear a more exact relation to the institutions and habits of the people."* The opinions thus formed in the judicial department had taken further shape and consistency, when, as Commissioner of Goruckpore, in 1829, he had first been directly concerned in the revenue management of the country; and when, on his subsequent elevation to the Revenue Board, the chief control of the settlement operations passed into his hands, he brought to the work a combination of rare qualities almost without a parallel in the entire range of a service bright with the names of distinguished men. All men do not concur in his opinions, for he pushed them too far, but all acknowledge his merits. All acknowledge that he had a large grasp of mind, great energy of character and honesty of purpose, catholic sympathies, and a warm heart. They who served under him regard him reverently and affectionately, as with the faith of a disciple and the love of a son, and seldom mention his name without an inward genuflexion. He selected his own agents, and he selected them well. And when he had made his choice, he did not withhold his confidence.

* Despatch of the Court of Directors, August 13, 1851 (a very valuable document). See also Mr. Bird's Report.

He was a man of too genial a temperament and too kindly a nature to wrap closely around him a cloak of official reserve. He kept up a familiar intercourse with his subordinates, encouraged and upheld them. It was not to be expected that among so large a number of agents there should not have been some who disappointed him. It is said that he was not very tolerant of carelessness, or very patient of dulness, but examples of these irritating qualities were few; it fell to the lot of Robert Bird to commend far more frequently than to censure; and whilst he made few enemies he drew around him many friends.

The duty of revising the settlement of the North-Western Provinces was entrusted to a number of young civilians, who went out into the country, pitched their tents in the neighbourhood of the villages, summoned the villagers around them, and instituted their inquiries into the state of the different tenures. The Court of Directors of the East India Company, last year, reviewing the whole question of revenue settlement in the North-West Provinces, declared that the review had left on their minds an impression "of the high honor reflected on the civil service by the zeal, industry, ability, and good feeling of the several officers employed, necessarily with differences of degree, but with so little room for exception, that it would be invidious to particularise where there is such ample ground for general satisfaction." And the praise thus bestowed was not undeserved. Doubtless there *were* "differences of degree." Some men carried to the work of revision a larger zeal and a clearer understanding than others. And two different pictures of a settlement officer might be drawn by those who are expert in such limnings.* Hence it is that we read on one side of "the

* There is so much vitality in the annexed sketch of the life of a settlement officer, that I cannot refrain from quoting it:—"To all who have been experimentally acquainted with the work of settlement, it is associated with the remembrance of severe exertion, but at the same time of great and

fair-haired Saxon youth opposing his well-trained intellect to the new difficulties which crowd around him,"

varied enjoyment. We look back, as through the vista of many years, and see the white camp rising in the long aisles of the ancient mango tope. We see the fair-haired Saxon youth opposing his well-trained intellect to the new difficulties that crowd upon him. We see him exerting daily, and with no vain or fruitless result, all his faculties of observation, of research, of penetration, of judgment. It is a strange sight—a wonderful proof of the power of intellectual and moral education—to watch the respect and confidence evinced by grey-headed men towards that beardless youth. We see him, in the early morning mist, stretching at an inspiring gallop over the dewy fields. Not unmindful is he of the hare, which scuds away from his horse's feet; of the call of the partridge from the brake; or of the wild-fowl on the marsh. The well-earned holiday will arrive, when he will be able to follow these, or perhaps nobler game; but at present he has other work on hand. He is on his way to some distant point, where measurements are to be tested, doubts resolved, or objections investigated. This done, he returns to his solitary breakfast, cheered by the companionship of a book, or perhaps by letters from a far-distant land — doubly welcome under such circumstances. The forenoon is spent in receiving reports from the native officers employed under him; in directing their operations; in examining, comparing, analysing, and arranging the various information which comes in from all quarters. As the day advances, the wide-spread shade begins to be peopled with living figures. Group after group of villagers arrive in their best and whitest dresses; and a hum of voices succeeds to the stillness, before only broken by the cooing of the dove, and the scream of the parroquet. The carpet is then spread in the open air; the chair is set; litigants and spectators take their seats on the ground in orderly ranks; silence is proclaimed, and the rural court is opened. As case after case is brought forward, the very demeanor of the parties, and of the crowds around, seems to point out on which side justice lies. No need here of *ex parte* decisions, or claims lost through default. All are free to come and go, with little trouble, and at no expense. No need of lengthened pleadings. A few simple questions bring out the matter of the suit, and the grounds on which it rests. No need of lists of witnesses. Scores of witnesses are ready on the spot, alike unsummoned and untutored. No need of the Koran, or Ganges water. The love of truth is strong, even in an Indian breast, when preserved from counteracting influences; still more so, then, when the sanction of public opinion assists and protects the rightful cause. In such a court Abraham sat, when arbitrating among his simple-minded herdsmen. In such a court was justice everywhere administered in the childhood of the human race; before wealth increased, and with wealth complicated interests, and law became a science requiring a life's study to understand.

" Strange must that man's character be, and dull his sympathies, who, in the midst of occupations like these, does not find his heart accompanying and lightening his labors. He sees the people in their fairest light; he witnesses their ceaseless industry, their contented poverty, their few and simple pleasures, their plain sense of justice, their general faithfulness to their engagements. He finds them, as a nation, sober, chaste, frugal, and gifted with much of that untaught politeness in which the rustic classes of colder climes are so often deficient. For months together he uses no language, enjoys no society, but theirs. To these causes of attachment is added that powerful tie which unites us to those whom we have labored long to benefit. The knowledge and feelings, thus acquired under the greenwood tree, will not be forgotten in after days, when the dark side of the picture will alone be presented to his view; when he has to deal with roused passions and selfish desires, uncontrolled by a true Faith; when his intercourse with the people is confined to the prisoner at the bar, or to the vakils of a grasping plaintiff, and of a fraudulent (perhaps because oppressed) defendant." — [*Calcutta Review.*]

and see him compared with the patriarch "Abraham arbitrating among his simple herdsmen," and "administering justice in the childhood of the human race;" and on the other we are told of ignorant upstarts, slenderly acquainted with the native languages, and not at all acquainted with native feelings, laying down the law, according to the most approved principles of generalisation, and committing errors of the most irritating kind with an incredible amount of assurance and conceit. It is very possible that examples of both kinds might be found; but, taking them as a whole, the settlement officers went about their work zealously and conscientiously, and carried to it a remarkable amount of serviceable intelligence. Perhaps they sometimes acted in disregard of judicial principles, and were impatient of restraints imposed by laws of evidence and rules of judicial practice. Perhaps they did not always make sufficient allowance for the differences of race and the provincialisms of locality; perhaps they did not always understand the precise character of the various tenures upon which they adjudicated. And so it happened that the people sometimes shrugged their shoulders and went away surprised and disappointed, perhaps angry, at the decisions which cost the English gentlemen so little trouble, but which were to them such matters of life and death concernment.* But, as a whole, the new settlement compared with the old was as light to darkness. The people gained mightily by it. There was an admi-

* One illustration of the manner in which fixed rules were often set aside, and local circumstances disregarded, may be given in this place. It is a standing rule that in districts bordering upon the hills, no man having possessions in the plains, but habitually residing in the hill country, shall be impleaded on account of such possessions during that season of the year when the deadly malaria renders it perilous to traverse the intervening *terai*. A young deputy-collector, however, having a resumption-suit before him, in which the defendant was one of this class of dwellers on the hills, took it up and decided it *ex parte* during this very season of the malaria, when the party had every right to believe that he was for the time secure against any such proceedings.

rable system of checks. If sometimes the settlement officers went wrong, there were the Commissioners to rectify their errors; above them there was the Sudder Board; and supreme over all was the Lieutenant-Governor of the North-Western Provinces.

It was not to be expected that all these authorities should entertain similar opinions and convictions. The most important portion of the settlement work was accomplished when Mr. Robertson (of whose proceedings as Judge of Cawnpore I have already spoken) was Lieutenant-Governor of the North-Western Provinces. This gentleman—one of the ablest and most distinguished civil servants of the Company—was not one of the new school of revenue-officers. He had seen in Bengal, perhaps, a little too much of the off-hand manner in which landed tenures of old standing were dealt with by young civilians, and he was rather suspicious of the operations of the clever but inexperienced youngsters to whom this important work was entrusted. He thought that they were too fond of generalising, that they started with certain fixed principles which they believed to be of universal application;* that their predilections, for example, in favor of the village communities often led them into error; that in their eagerness to create an extensive subdivision of property they committed many acts of injustice; and that their resumption operations were frequently harsh and ill-advised. "The settlement officer," he declared, "swept up without inquiry every patch of unregistered land; even those under ten *beegahs*, exempted by a subsequent order, which did not come out until five-sixths of the tenures had been resumed;" and added,

* The Sudder Board disclaimed all sympathy with these generalising views, and declared that they were eager to discourage them. Upon this the Lieutenant-Governor expressed his satisfaction at finding "the sentiments of the Board so directly opposed to what he imagined that he had occasionally detected in the writings of their subordinates."

that "in one district—that of Furruckabad—the obligations of a treaty and the direct orders of Government were but lightly dealt with, and in all a total disregard was evinced for the acts even of such men as Warren Hastings and Lord Lake." And this opinion was afterwards confirmed by the Court of Directors, who declared that it was always their desire that the resumption measures should be carried out with great lenity and forbearance. "In many instances," they added, "it has been so. In others, the results have been attended with much hardship. But the solicitude of the several Lieutenant-Governors has been carefully directed to remedying the evil in question, by money provisions of more or less duration. We think this is the best method of disposing of such cases. It provides for the incumbents and their families, and secures the ultimate rights of Government."

Still, when we come to consider the aggregate results of the settlement, how much food is there for hearty congratulation. "The first settlement," it has been said, and truly said, "ruined the persons for whose benefit it was devised. The last settlement saved millions of much-enduring men from ruin and misery." The expediency of the measure, too, was as clear as its justice. The revenue progressively increased under it, and the sales for default of payment diminished with equal steadiness. In the course of six years* the amount of property sold on this account had decreased by more than five-sixths.† The lightness of the assessment, which is computed to average less than a third of the gross produce, has tended to increase alike the prosperity of the people and the State. Over-assessment was found in practice to be as injurious to the one as to the other.

* From 1842-43 to 1847-48, inclusive.

† That is, from 259,686 rupees to 40,616 rs.

The principle, in spite of occasional deviations, was one of moderation; and the Court of Directors, reviewing the proceedings of the settlement officers, lost no opportunity of declaring in favor of moderate assessments. Where the result showed that a district had been over-assessed, they recommended a revision of the settlement.

The happy effects, indeed, of this light assessment are visible upon the face of the country. There is no lack of cheering evidence of good government. The indications of the advancing prosperity of these fine provinces are, such as he who runs may read, across the whole length and breadth of the land. A mild and equable rule, giving security to person and to property, repressing the violent and the lawless, encouraging the peaceful and the industrious, has borne its accustomed fruit. Many illustrations of this might be readily adduced; but none more satisfactory than the following, written in 1852:

"I have just marched," writes a distinguished British functionary, "to this place along the strip of country reaching from the Sutlej to the Jumna by Hansi and Hissar. You must remember that country when it was inhabited by a wild and lawless set of people, whom no one could manage. Native chiefs would not take the lands at a gift. Our own troops were frequently repulsed by the communities of Rangurs, and Bhuttees, and others, who lived in large fortified villages and subsisted by plunder. Now the country is thickly inhabited and well cultivated, and the most peaceful that could possibly be. This year the 'Khurreef' crops have failed entirely, and very little 'Rubbee' had been sown. Yet the revenue had been paid up without a balance, and had occasioned no perceptible distress. This is the effect of firm rule and a light assessment. Mr. R. Bird (all honor to his name!) insisted, at the late settlement, on a considerable reduction of the assessment. The consequence is, that land which before was worthless now bears a high value, and a people who were before lawless now yield implicit obedience to the laws. It is a cheap Government of which the strength consists in low taxation." *

The secondary advantages sought to be obtained by the settlement were not all so clearly established. The division of the revenue payments into four instalments, falling due after full time has been allowed for the sale of the produce, was unquestionably a boon to the cultivators. But the creation of the road-fund met with considerable opposition; and the establishment of a paid village police was still more generally unpopular. The people were slow to appreciate the advantages of good roads, and were very unwilling to pay for them. But they came in time to be satisfied with the arrangement, and, perhaps, to understand that the trifling *per-centage* devoted to this purpose was in reality not an addition to the assessment, but a deduction from it. The advantages, however, of the salaried village police dawned more slowly on their comprehension; and writing in August, 1851, the Court of Directors could say nothing more than that they were "disposed to hope that, with careful supervision, it may be found satisfactory to the people."†

Of the resumption of the rent-free tenures I have already spoken. There are one or two other points of considerable importance which require to be mentioned. The tendency of the settlement operations was towards

* *MS. Correspondence.*

† Mr. Robertson had always been opposed to this measure. He expressed a strong opinion to the effect that such a functionary as a paid watchman could never be acceptable to the people, even if it entailed no additional charge upon them. Such an official, he said, would be likely to lord it over the Brahmin and Rajpoot on his own domain. "There is in this," he observed, "an inversion of the social order of the country such as must cause heart-burnings and mortifications in that class of our subjects whose affections it is most our interest to conciliate. An abatement in the number of thefts and burglaries is but a sorry compensation for such a consequence, or for the no less pernicious result of the Zemindar taking advantage of the presence of a paid police-officer to exonerate himself from all responsibility for what occurs."

the disruption of the large estates. There was a class of large landed proprietors, known as Talookdars—the territorial aristocracy of the country. The settlement officers seem to have treated these men as usurpers and monopolists, and to have sought every opportunity of reducing their tenures. It was not denied that such reduction was, on the whole, desirable, inasmuch as that these large tenures interfered with the rights of the village proprietors. But the reduction was undertaken in too precipitate and arbitrary a manner; and the Court of Directors acknowledged that it had caused great practical embarrassment to Government, against whom numerous suits were instituted in the civil courts by the ousted Talookdars, and many decided in their favor.*

Another point of great importance was this. I have shown that, under the original imperfect settlement which succeeded our first occupation of the country, much injustice was done, and much confusion created, by the indiscriminate sale of lands held in coparcenery by several sharers, for the shortcomings of one or more defaulting partner. The new law accorded the privilege —for so it was esteemed—of separate responsibility.† The shares of each member of the community were

* The writer in the *Calcutta Review* questions the justice of these decisions. The cases were generally tried —"always in the first instance, and frequently also in appeal—by the uncovenanted judges;" and the result, he says, "has not been satisfactory." The tendency, it is added, of the lower courts, "has been to look only at the records of past settlements, though these were confessedly imperfect or erroneous; and finding the plaintiff therein mentioned as Zemindar, to consider him as being the sole and exclusive proprietor. This feeling, on the part of the inferior courts, together with the expense and delay of a civil suit, felt of course most by the poorer party, have caused many of the decisions to be adverse to those passed at the settlement, and it has not been always possible to have these proceedings set right on appeal."

† That is to say, whenever the privilege was claimed. But the right was only partially exercised. "There are great differences in the extent to which separate responsibility prevails. In some districts it is universal; in some the instances are numerous; in some few; in others none."—[*Report of the Court of Directors.*] Mr. Thomason (September, 1848) wrote: "In practice, it is customary to attempt to realise first from the individual, then to offer his property to any coparcener who will pay up the arrears, and if no one accepts the offer, then to hold the entire body jointly responsible for the balance."

distinctly parcelled out and recorded, and each separate defaulter suffered for his own particular default by the sale of his individual share. But as this might have a tendency to introduce strangers into the coparceneries, and destroy the integrity of the village communities, the right of pre-emption was given to the other shareholders; so that, to a certain extent, the remedy lay in their own hands. The provision, indeed, would have been an excellent one, but that it was set aside by the custom of granting fictitious mortgages, "against which," says the Court, "there appears to be no remedy but a valuation on fixed principles, at which the right of pre-emption shall be given to the community." And some of the best authorities—as Lord Metcalfe, Mr. Robertson, and Mr. Thomason—were of opinion that the system of joint responsibility on the whole is advantageous to the village communities.* No alteration of the existing law is proposed; but every effort is made by the Government of the North-Western Provinces to induce them to adopt voluntarily the system of joint responsibility; and in this view the Court fully concurs.

Viewed as a whole, it is difficult not to regard the settlement of the North-Western Provinces as a great work. It is not free from errors of design and execution. Its originators do not claim for it the credit of being a perfect conception carried out to perfection in all its parts. The truth is, that every large scheme with the stamp of *thorough* upon it involves more or less error of detail. No one will ever achieve anything great who is haunted by the fear of exceptional cases and small mistakes. Mr. Bird was, at least, in earnest. His disciples were in earnest. They did not falter; they did not hesitate. They went intrepidly to their work, with a firm faith in the excellence of the design, and an honest

* The question is very fairly argued by Mr. Thomason, in his Minute of 25th September, 1848.

intention to carry it out worthily and well. And in spite of errors—errors not many and large in proportion to the magnitude of the undertaking—resulting from original defects or inefficient agency, they may, without any large amount of self-glorification, look back on what they have done, and proudly compare the present state of the agricultural population with what it was before their labors commenced.

The North-Western Provinces of India have now been, for half a century, under British rule. The great experiment of Indian government has there been pushed forward with remarkable energy and uncommon success. In no part of India are the signs of progress so great and so cheering. There is a freshness, a vigor, a healthy robust youth, as it were, apparent everywhere in the administration of these provinces. The physical improvement of the country, and the moral improvement of the people, are advancing, under our eyes, with a rapidity which would fill the bygone generation of Indian administrators with as much astonishment as the ancient race of soldiers would experience at the sight of the magnificent dimensions of our Indian Empire. I do not believe that there is in the world a more conscientious and more laborious class of

* The collateral advantages derived from the settlement are thus summed up by its historian in the *Calcutta Review*:—"The revision of the settlement has made us better acquainted with the people, whom we have been called upon to govern, than we might otherwise have been in centuries. It has given us an insight into their condition, feelings, desires, and wants. It has thrown a flood of light on all the relations of the people with the State. It has furnished the Government with means, never before possessed, for encouraging industry and protecting private rights; while it has accustomed our subjects themselves to familiar intercourse with their rulers, and has inspired them with confidence in our moderation, and reliance on our justice. It has done more to prevent affrays, and to lead to the peaceable adjustment of disputes regarding real property, than all the terrors of the penal law could ever have effected. While in progress, the settlement afforded the best school for fitting men to fill other offices of every description; and, even now, the necessity of maintaining its arrangements, and acting up to its provisions, supplies a training of nearly equal efficacy. Those who, after such a training, are called to preside in a civil court, are enabled by the settlement arrangements and records to decide confidently, where they must before have groped hopelessly in the dark. A measure, which has been followed by such results, besides its more immediate object of equalising taxation, must deserve the attention of all who take any interest in the welfare of India."

civil functionaries than those who, under one of the best men and ablest administrators who have ever devoted their lives to the service of the people of India, are now bearing the burden and heat of the day, in serious toilsome efforts to make the yoke of foreign conquest sit lightly on the native subjects of the British Crown. Earnestness and energy are contagious; and in the North-Western Provinces of India the heavy-paced are soon roused into activity—the phlegmatic into tingling life. What Thomason and his associates have done for Upper India can only be fairly appreciated by those who know what was the state of the Ceded and Conquered Provinces of India fifty, or even twenty, years ago. It is not easy to represent the true character of these great achievements to those who, in Westminster or Belgravia, sit in judgment upon British rule in the East, and decide that our administrators have done nothing, because they do not know what they have done. But the servants of the East India Company may find abundant consolation in the fact that the happiness of the people of the East is not to be gauged by the knowledge of the people of the West.

There is one characteristic of the present Government of the North-Western Provinces of which I would further speak in this place, though perhaps it might more fitly be introduced into another chapter. There is a communicativeness about the system, which is a peculiar feature of the administrative progress now making in India. The representatives of the paramount power have there shaken off their secrecy and reserve. They no longer live with a cordon of official exclusiveness around them; they no longer move about with sealed lips and veiled faces. The doors of their palanquins are thrown back; the sides of their tents are drawn up; and the people are invited to come freely to them. The Lieutenant-Governor, who is continually moving about from one district to another and watching the results of the great measures with which he is so honorably associated, is one of the most accessible of men; and his subordinates emulate the courtesy and openness of his demeanor. But it is not so much of this personal diffusiveness of which I would speak, as of the great efforts which are being made, principally through the agency of the press, to render the people familiar with the acts and principles of Government—to help them thoroughly to understand the manner in which we are endeavoring to administer their affairs. "Compendious treatises," says Mr. Raikes, "embracing not only the rules of revenue process, but also the principles of revenue science, have been drawn up. Translations of these have been distributed right and left. The more intelligent of the people are being thus fast led to co-operate with their rulers, whose principles are better understood and appreciated. All candidates for Government employ find the necessity of mastering the existing revenue code. The consequence is, that numbers of books in the language of the country, some of considerable merit, are issuing from the press at Agra, Delhi, and elsewhere, explanatory of the laws affecting landed tenures and of the principles of agriculture and rural economy. The collectors of revenue have been encouraged to disseminate memorials of useful knowledge, suited to the capacity of the rising generation, among the students at the village schools. Such books, for which, also, the people have to thank the Government of the North-Western Provinces, will, we trust, supersede the trash which has hitherto been taught at these schools."

Let these efforts be weighed, and let it be remembered that in 1811 an old Indian Chief Justice—Sir John Anstruther—asked, tauntingly, in the House of Commons, with reference to the freedom of the Indian press, "whether it was intended to illuminate the people of India?"—"Was this exactly desirable?" he continued. "Would it be very expedient to inform them of the peculiar tenure by which the British Government hold their power?" There was nothing startling, at the time when they were asked, in such questions as these—but we look at them now as we would at a thumb-screw, or any other relic of a barbarous age. The principle of modern Indian Government is thoroughly to illuminate the people, and to render them as familiar as they can possibly be with all the tenures by which they are connected with their foreign rulers. It is not concealed that this enlightenment may have the effect of breaking all these tenures; but when the people of India are ripe for self-government, England will have fulfilled her mission, as a ruler, in the East; and she must be prepared to abide the result.

I cannot conclude this chapter without remarking that the instructions sent by the Court of Directors to their servants in India, and the opinions expressed regarding the settlement operations, have been uniformly conceived in a liberal and enlightened spirit. It has been their leading desire so to carry out the work, with leniency and moderation, and with a due regard to the feelings of the people, as to render it a blessing to them and their successors. I can trace no signs of covetousness and rapacity in their recommendations; but rather a sincere desire to allow the cultivators to till the fields mainly for their own benefit, and to reap the reward of their own ameliorative efforts. The settlements, as I have said, were made some for twenty and some for thirty years. One of the principal arguments in favor of the permanent settlement is, that it holds out the strongest inducement to landholders to improve their estates. There is not an Englishman who does not shrink from expending money on property, whether house or land, of which he holds but a brief lease. He increases the value of the estate, and in return his landlord raises his rent. The Court of Directors have already begun to consider "whether an agriculturist on the renewal of a settlement shall be allowed the full benefit of his improvements, or whether the Government shall be held entitled to a share of the additional value which his capital and industry, aided by other circumstances, have added to the land." And they have expressed their opinion, that "the only satisfactory principle upon which all future renewals of settlements can be made, will be that reference must be had to the value of the land at the time, a liberal consideration being given for the improvements attributable only to the efforts of the tenant himself, and especially with regard to such as are of a comparatively recent date, and with regard to which he has reaped the advantage only for a short period under the old settlement."

Indeed, the unvarying tenor of the Court's instructions to their servants in India is to impress upon them the duty of fixing light assessments, and passing only such Regulations as will encourage agricultural improvement, and raise the condition of the cultivators of the soil. It is their earnest effort to stimulate production by light assessments ; and so far from their fiscal measures being conceived in an extortionate spirit, or having a tendency in execution to restrict the cultivation of such staples as cotton and sugar, they have consistently impressed upon their servants the duty of encouraging such production, by keeping down the assessment of the lands so cultivated to an equitable valuation. "Our object," they wrote some years ago, "is to prevent the land from being assessed in such a manner as to impose a tax upon those commodities—it being contrary to our intention that such commodities should be taxed. The land bearing a particular product should never be so assessed as to give an artificial value to such product—in other words, raise its price by force of taxation—which the imposing a higher assessment on land, whenever it is made to bear that particular product, obviously does." And when it was suggested by one of their chief servants in India that such liberal measures would occasion a considerable loss of revenue, they replied, with happy irony: "We are aware that when a tax is abolished the revenues which it yielded ceases to be received." They scouted, indeed, this narrow view of a great question, and trusted rather to the general results of a liberal policy than to such individual details.

Of the general results of the administration of the Indian land-revenue by the British Government, it is almost unnecessary to write, as they will be gathered from the details of these last three chapters. As far back as 1815, the Marquis of Hastings recorded an elaborate minute, the result of a tour through Upper India, on the Revenue Administration of the Presidency of Fort William, which takes, in one section, a condensed view of the general advantages of our system. He sums them up thus in a few paragraphs:

The advantages of our system over those of former Governments may be summed up in a few words. The former systems left entirely at the discretion of the Aumils the lives and properties of all the population of their several jurisdictions. There was only an appeal to the immediate sovereign of the state, and he was generally inaccessible.

From the moment of the establishment of our Government, the lives of all were secured under the shield of the law; and the substitution of the practice of contracting only for the realisation of a fixed assessment, instead of contracting for the revenue of a given district, to be raised at the discretion and the cost of the contractor, secured their properties also, except against minor abuse and covert villany. The annihilation of the contract system in all its branches has now, in some degree, given protection against those evils.

Instead of the population being subjected to the arbitrary exactions of every Aumil, and of every farmer he might choose to impose, an uniform and universal system has been introduced, under which every one may know his rights, and be secure of having them respected. The system is certainly not yet sufficiently perfect for its ministerial officers to know of themselves the exact amount of revenue which is demandable from all; but that is only because they cannot ascertain the actual amount of produce, the requisite information being suppressed from interested motives. All that is wanting, however, to give perfection on this point, is a fixed criterion, from which the amount of produce may be known or fairly estimated, so that settlements may be formed on uniform principles and data, known to be correct, instead of only believed to be so, as at present.

It is this very desideratum which the new settlement has so beneficially supplied.

It were worth while to quote further:

The advantage to the country is, however, best judged of by its effects. There is, at present, little or no emigration of the agricultural class; indeed, it is found that proprietors, before driven into exile, or into the search of other means of livelihood, such as military service, daily return to reclaim the lands they had been obliged to abandon, in the certainty that they must now have ceased to be unprofitable.

The wages of agricultural labor are much higher than they used to be, which is solely attributable to the increased demand for labor of this description. The more valuable articles of produce are also cultivated with much more spirit; and the most astonishing efforts are daily made to conquer natural defects of soil, as well as to preclude the evils of casual calamity of season.

There can be no doubt, indeed, that the produce and the profits of agriculture have been increased in a very surprising degree, since the country fell under our administration. The comparative prosperity of the several cities may form a good criterion of this; and the rapidity with which they are increasing, both in size and population, is scarcely credible.

The abolition of those arbitrary sayer imposts which each Zemindar conceived himself entitled to levy on all goods that entered his domain, has now left open to every proprietor a free market for all his produce, to which it may be carried, without the fear of violence or exaction in the transport.

The beneficial system on which the customs and town-duties are now collected here, at the same time, left the rates of that market free from the operation of any local circumstances, and solely regulated by the broad commercial interests of the whole of India. In consequence of these facilities, commercial capital and enterprise have been turned towards the land, and an activity has been infused, of which every class begins to feel the benefits.

The display of wealth is no longer avoided as dangerous; but perhaps the most direct and positive advantage to the landed interest which has resulted from our occupation of the country is, the discontinuance of the arbitrary practice of quartering troops on districts, from which they were to be provided gratis, in addition to the public dues of Government, as well as the requisition of free gifts of several descriptions, besides the obligation gratuitously to furnish supplies, laborers, artificers, and carriage of every sort, whenever circumstances might bring a man in power or a body of troops to the neighbourhood of a village. The occasions for demands of this description were unlimited, and payment never was offered, nor could it be asked with safety. . . . .

The above advantages are amongst those which have particularly attended our revenue-administration, and are in addition to those incalculable benefits resulting from the comparative total absence of external or internal violence, induced by the strength of our political Government and the authority of the law.

More than thirty-five years have passed since these passages were written; and the prosperous condition of the North-Western Provinces is now as much in advance of what it was under the administration of Lord Hastings, as, at that time, it excelled the old state under the Mahrattas. The abolition of the Transit-duties, and the new Settlement, have ripened and perfected the blessings which Hastings saw only immature and undeveloped; and there are others, of which he had but a dim conception, now spreading themselves over the land, under the saving influence of a great remedial agent, of whose power he was not wholly unconscious, though it was left to his successor to give it free scope and permanent expression.*

* I feel that in this chapter I ought to have made more particular mention of the operations of the Revenue Survey. I must refer the reader to a brief paper in the Appendix (D), and to the excellent work of Captains R. Smith and Thuillier, of the Artillery.

CHAPTER V.

Famines in Upper India—Importance of Irrigation—Early Mahomedan Works—Our first Canal Efforts—The Western Jumna Canal—The Eastern Jumna Canal—The great Ganges Canal—The Baree Doab Canal—The Great Trunk Road—Other Public Works—Their Cost—General Financial Results.

THE chapter which I have just written on the Revenue Settlement of the North-Western Provinces is a testimony, however imperfect its execution, to the industry and ability of the men employed on this great work. But there was one thing which might at any time mar the results of all this industry and ability. If the heavens should deny to the country their wonted tribute of rain, the Settlement, though it might mitigate the evils of a famine, could not wholly prevent it.

Over a large portion of these fine provinces all the staple products of the land are at the mercy of the seasons. The effects of a drought are more terrible than language can describe. Upper India has been visited by periodical famines, the terrors of which all the wisdom and all the resources of the best and strongest Government have not even mitigated. The famine of 1837-1838 is still fresh in the recollection of many European gentlemen, who saw then what they will remember to their dying day, and yet were powerless to alleviate the suffering which gathered around them. Parents sold their children for a few shillings, and were glad not merely to fill themselves with "the husks that the swine did it eat," but to dispute with the ravenous crows for the filthy refuse of the grain which had already fed the horses of the troops on the line of march.

There could be nothing more worthy of a humane Government than the prevention, as far as human wisdom can prevent these providential calamities, of such a gigantic evil as this. There was but one manner of meeting it, and this was by an extensive system of canal irrigation. The Mogul Emperors had in their uncertain, spasmodic way, addressed themselves from time to time to the consideration of this great prophylactic measure. The extreme value of water in such a country is dwelt upon, by many incidental references, in the oldest writings extant. Kings and Sages combined to punish the waste of the precious element, and to reward the profitable disposal of it. In the code of Menu the breaker of a dam is sentenced to long immersion under water, and in the Institutes of Timour it is ordained that "whosoever undertakes the cultivation of waste lands, or builds an aqueduct, or makes a canal, or plants a grove, or restores to culture a deserted district, nothing shall be taken from him in the first year; in the second year what the subject voluntarily tenders; and in the third year the Government dues according to regulation." But the word which is here translated "canal," has but a limited signification, and by no means represents those great works which some of the later Mahomedan Emperors designed and executed, and which the British-Indian Government is now carrying out on a scale far beyond the speculations of the most large-minded of the Mogul princes.

It has been said that "God meant rivers to feed

canals."* Upper India abounds in canal-food. The numerous rivers which flow from their mountain homes on the great Himalaya range supply volumes of water, of which commerce has little need; whilst thirsty agriculture would not suffer a single foot to escape. The conversion of this water to agricultural purposes is now the main object of the great engineering operations, which for many years, with some temporary interruptions, have been progressing in the Ceded and Conquered Provinces of Hindostan.

Soon after these territories passed into our hands the subject of canal irrigation attracted the attention of some of the most earnest of our British officers. The remains of the old Mahomedan works seemed to look us encouragingly in the face.† But those were days when our ideas of internal administration were somewhat crude, and the development of the resources

* "To no country in the world, perhaps, does the emphatic declaration of the famous Brindley, that 'God meant rivers to feed canals,' apply more emphatically than to those fertile and populous plains which stretch away southward from the Himalayas in irregular forms between the 70th and 34th parallels of longitude, and the 34th and 24th of latitude, and are traversed by the numerous rivers which flow from the great range. These rivers, in the upper portion of their courses, are commercially useless; agriculturally they are, or with a little skill might be, made invaluable."—[*Calcutta Review*, vol. vi. Article: "Canals of Irrigation in the North-Western Provinces."]—This excellent treatise—a very mine of information relating to Indian canals, has been so often publicly attributed to Lieutenant Baird Smith of the Bengal Engineers, the accomplished author of the work on "Italian Irrigation," that I believe I am guilty of no impropriety in naming him as my chief authority for the statements in this chapter.

† In connexion with these old Mahomedan works there is a curious circumstance, very interesting to geologists: "When describing the excavations of Feroze, Ferishta mentions incidentally that the workpeople employed upon them found near the lower hills quantities of 'giants' bones.' For nearly two centuries and a half this seemingly fabulous statement passed unnoticed. To minds familiar with discoveries in fossil geology the old chronicle had, however, a faint gleam of significance; and, guided by its feeble light, English officers of the canal department re-examined the localities indicated, and found, associated with others of different dimensions, not 'giants' bones,' but bones most gigantic, from which, in course of time, they were able to add to the system of nature many new and strange animals before unheard of. Pursuing their labors at remote stations in Upper India, drawing their materials for comparison from the forests and rivers around them, denied many of the facilities for research which happier local positions would have afforded, they yet won for themselves European fame, and rewards ranked among the highest which the courts of science in their own land had it in their power to bestow."—[*Calcutta Review.*]

of the country was little studied by its rulers. Mr. Mercer is said to have offered to open, at his own expense, the old Delhi Canal, which lay before him a lifeless excavation, if he were suffered to receive the proceeds for twenty years. The offer did not meet with acceptance, and it was not until 1810 that, under the administration of Lord Minto, any steps were taken to inquire into the state of the old canals, and the expediency of restoring them to efficiency. A Committee of Survey was then appointed to report on the lines, both east and west of Jumna. But nothing came of the effort. The higher scientific authorities, as the Chief Engineer and the Surveyor-General, when called upon for their opinions, poured over the survey report such a flood of contradictory learning, and seemed to take such antagonistic views of the great question, that the Government, sorely perplexed and bewildered, and utterly unable to derive wisdom from the multitude of councillors, seem to have abandoned the worthy project in despair.

But under the subsequent administration of Lord Hastings, the vast importance of these works was recognised. A beginning was made. And from that time up to the present period, the work has progressed with more or less constancy and vigor, according to the state of the public finances, and the temper of the local Government. It has met, from time to time, with temporary hindrances and obstructions. It has fallen on evil days under one ruler, and basked in vice-regal sunshine under another. But it has gone on through evil report and good report, and there is satisfaction in the aggregate result.

I must speak of these measures and their results more in detail. The line of the Western Jumna, or Delhi Canal, was first surveyed by Lieutenant Blaine, of the Engineers, an officer of rare promise, which he barely lived to fulfil. He had been directed to report on the practicability of re-opening the canal, and on the expenses that would attend the operation, before the breaking out of the Nepaul war. The engineer was called to the field, and for a time the work was suspended; but Lord Hastings, in his famous minute of September 21, 1815, the result of his tour to the Upper Provinces, dwelt emphatically upon the advantages that would attend its completion. "To the canal on "the opposite side of the Jumna," he wrote, "generally "known by the name of the Delhi, or Ali Murdan's "Canal, it is necessary for me to call your attention. "Measures were, I believe, taken, and were already in "a train of execution, with a view to ascertain the ex-"pense and practicability of re-opening it; and though "these measures were interrupted for a time only by "the military operations incident to the Goorkha war, "which required the services of Lieutenant Blaine in "the field, I presume your Honorable Board will be "disposed to resume them, now that the more impor-"tant calls for the services of the engineer officers have "ceased.

"I will only say," he adds, "that my own inspection "has fully convinced me of the facility and the policy of "immediately restoring this noble work. Setting aside "the consideration of its certain effect, in bringing into "cultivation vast tracts of country now deserted, and "thereby augmenting importantly the landed revenue "of the Honorable Company, the dues to be collected "for the distribution of the water from it would make "a most lucrative return. This is held so sure, that "individuals (for propositions were made to me) would "now undertake the business, were it fitting that the "credit of a work so dignified, so popular, and so bene-"ficial, should fall to the share of any but the Govern-"ment. Were a lakh of rupees to be laid out yearly for "three years on this object (and I believe I specify "much more than would be actually required for perfecting the canal), it would be money laid out more "profitably for the Company than it could in any "other mode of application."

The work was sanctioned. Lieutenant Blaine commenced operations. But his efforts were very limited at the outset. There was altogether a want of faith in the success of the experiment. The work seemed only to proceed by sufferance. All sorts of shifts and expedients were resorted to that money might be economised. "Earthen bunds were used for carrying the canal across the beds of the intersecting mountain streams. Few if any bridges were considered necessary, the canal being fordable throughout; and natural channels were invariably taken possession of in spite of their defective levels and tortuous courses." But whatever could be done, with such scanty means and in face of such difficulties, Blaine's skill and energy accomplished. He lived to see the canal re-enter Delhi, after a suspension of half a century; but not further to extend the good work of which he was the pioneer. He was succeeded by Captain Tickle, of the Bengal Engineers, and subsequently by Colonel John Colvin, of the same corps—whose name is still held in affectionate remembrance by the people, for whom, bringing all his professional skill to bear upon the labor of love, he toiled with so much energy and such hearty goodwill. In 1823 he was appointed to the general superintendence of the works of irrigation in the Delhi territory, and from that time they continued to advance to maturity with the steadiness which commands permanent success. There were many engineering difficulties to be overcome, but they were overcome by our resolute engineers; and there were financial difficulties —the growth of a false economy, which neither science nor enthusiasm could easily overleap. But, in spite of all hindrances and impediments, the Western Jumna Canal was brought into effective operation throughout the country it was intended to fertilise, and is now conferring incalculable benefits upon its agricultural population.

The canal extends from the foot of the Hills to Delhi and to Hissar. Its total length is 425 miles. It is spanned by 159 masonry bridges, 54 of woodwork, and one suspension-bridge; and there are nearly 700 irrigation outlets from the main channel.

Of some of the results of the Irrigation system I would now speak. It would appear, from statistical tables prepared by the Government of the North-Western Provinces, that the extent of irrigated land in different districts, within the influence of the Western Jumna Canal, varies from one-half to one-tenth of the entire area. In this computation the total area of the irrigating villages is taken into account. But it is not to be inferred that the whole extent of these lands is actually watered by the canal. It is estimated that from one-half to one-third is the average of land brought under immediate irrigation—those irrigating villages, which are fewer in proportion to the entire area, using the water most freely. Thus the district of Paniput, one-half of which is covered by irrigating villages, seems only to bring a third of the area of those villages actually under irrigation, whilst Hissar, which only shows one-tenth of its entire area to consist of irrigated villages, actually waters one-half of the area of these lands. "The best watered of all," it is said, "in proportion to its irrigable area, is the once sterile district of Hissar, the chief towns of which were found, in 1807, to be literally without an inhabitant. The canal here has almost called into being an active, contented, and prosperous peasantry."*

* *Baird Smith, in the Calcutta Review.*

The progressive extent to which the people have availed themselves of this artificial water-supply may now be shown by a reference to tables of receipts on account of water-rents. A small rent-charge, ranging between one shilling and ten shillings an acre, according to the nature of the ground and the value of the produce, is made for the water supplied; and, in the course of twenty-seven years, from 1820-21 to 1846-47, the amount received has not much fallen short of 355,000*l.* The annual receipts have progressively increased. In 1820-21 the amount received on account of irrigation was about 1450*l.*; in 1846-47 it was 26,250*l.* The last returns before me show for one half year in 1851 a water-rent of 13,341*l.*; or 26,681*l.* on the entire year.

"The exceedingly unsettled state," it is said, "of the agricultural population, the constant fluctuations of the summary settlement of the Government land-revenue, and the novelty in many localities of continual irrigation, were the chief causes of this slow progress. The permanent settlement of the land-revenue gave a great impetus to the extension of canal irrigation; and 1837-38, the year of the great famine, fatal as it was to districts not protected by canals, exhibits a remarkable increase—a fact pregnant with meaning."

It is calculated that in that grievous famine-year the gross value of the crops grown on land irrigated from the Western Jumna Canal, the greater part of which land would have been totally unproductive without the use of canal-water, amounted to a million and a half of English money. Of this sum about one-tenth, or 150,000*l.*, was paid to Government, as land and water rent, whilst the remainder "supported in comfort, during a period of devastating famine, the inhabitants of nearly 500 villages."

But the water-rents, paid on account of irrigation, do not constitute the sole profits of the canal. Some revenue is raised from the rents paid by the proprietors of flour-mills* in the neighbourhood of Kurnaul, Delhi, and Hissar. Between the years 1822-23 and 1846-47, the sum derived from this source exceeded 31,400*l.* In the first of these years the receipts amounted to only 302*l.*; in the last they had risen to nearly 1500*l.*; and in 1850 had exceeded that amount. There are also smaller sums receivable from certain pastoral villages, which depend entirely upon the canal for the means of watering their cattle; and others paid, in the shape of transit-duties, principally upon timbers floated down by the canal.

The Eastern Jumna Canal is a work of inferior proportions. The entire length of it is estimated at 155 miles. It runs for the most part along a beautiful country between the Ganges and the Jumna. "Most beautiful in all parts it truly is," says the canal-historian, "with its broad road smooth as an English lawn, its double rows of trees drooping over the stream, its long graceful sweeps, its rich bordering of the most luxuriant crops, its neat station-houses, and the peculiar care with which all its works are maintained. It is certainly one of the most interesting and attractive of Indian sights. The gem of the whole is the southern division, where, for nearly sixty miles, the visitor passes through a country which is the garden of the North-West, and finds constant cause to admire the beautiful, although limited scenes, which every turn of the canal brings before him."†

* The following account of these mills is taken from the authority already quoted. It affords an apt illustration of the unprogressiveness of the natives of India: "These mills consist of substantial buildings of masonry, located near the large towns of Kurnaul, Delhi, and Hissar. The machinery is of the most primitive kind, being a small vertical wheel, with oblique horizontal spokes, slightly hollowed, on which the water impinges. Although these machines do not economise more than thirty per cent. of the effective power of the water, and are liable to be interfered with during the rainy season by back water, yet they are so much preferred by the native community to any more complicated arrangement, that every attempt to supersede them by machinery of European form has signally failed."

† *Baird Smith.*

Towards the close of the year 1809, the Board of Commissioners called the attention of Government to the canal, "generally known as Zabita Khan's, from an attempt which he made to re-establish it, and which, previous to its being suffered to fall into decay, must have fertilised in its windings an extent of country of not much less than 200 miles."* The senior Commissioner had visited the head of the canal, and taken counsel with the chief engineer, who had reported favorably upon the expediency of restoring the great work. "On the important advantages," said the Commissioners, "which may be expected to result from the measure, if feasible, there can be no difference of opinion. Several Pergunnahs, now almost entirely desolate, will be rapidly restored to cultivation, and plenty will soon be diffused over a part of the country where wild animals now usurp the dominion over mankind."† The recommendations of the Commissioners were not without effect. Captain Tod, of the 25th Native Infantry, was ordered to survey the line of canal, and to report upon the feasibility and the cost of its restoration. He sent in a rough estimate of the probable expenditure, which was set down at a lakh and a half or two lakhs of rupees. But either the same cause which had deferred the restoration of the Western Jumna Canal, or unwillingness on the part of Government to incur the estimated expenditure, postponed also this experiment, and for some years nothing was done.

But in 1822 the line was surveyed by Lieutenant Debude, of the Engineers, and active operations were

* *Report of the Board of Commissioners, October* 7, 1809—*quoted in Lord Moira's Minute, September* 21, 1815. *Revenue Selections.*—It is doubtful, however, whether in Zabita Khan's time the canal was long in operation. "About 1780," says the canal-historian in the *Calcutta Review*, already quoted, "Zabita Khan Rohilla is said to have re-opened the channel, and to have brought a stream of water through the bed of the Kursunni river to the site of the great city projected by him. . . . But his canal could have been open only for a few months; and with the first rain-floods it was, doubtless, seen that the difficulties were too formidable to overcome."

† *Ibid.*

commenced. On his removal to other duties, he was succeeded by Colonel Robert Smith, under whose superintendence it was prosecuted to the completion of the original design in 1830. But much still remained to be done. There were serious defects in the execution of the plan, which threatened the destruction of many of the works almost as soon as the canal was opened;* and Captain Cautley was appointed to rectify those errors. The professional skill of this eminent engineer overcame every difficulty. He carried out many great improvements, and recommended others, which, on his removal to the higher appointment of chief superintendent of canals in the North-Western Provinces, were carried into effect by Lieutenant Baird Smith, who succeeded him in charge of the eastern line of works, and has since won for himself so high a reputation.

Deducing from statistical tables the same results as in the case of the Western Jumna Canal, it would seem that the proportion of irrigated to unirrigated lands ranges from a fourth to a ninth of the entire area in different districts; and that of these lands from a third to a fifth is actually watered by the canal. There has been the same progressive increase in the consumption of water, and, therefore, a progressively increasing revenue. The gross amount derived from water-rent between the years 1830-31 and 1846-47, inclusive, is 109,500*l*. In the first year of the series the amount realised was only 600*l*. In the last it was 10,770*l*. In 1837-38, the great famine year, the rents were more than doubled. They rose

* "On the 3rd of January, 1830, the canal was opened for the first time, and by the 20th of the same month nearly every bridge north of Seharunpore, and south of Surrowli, was in imminent peril of total destruction. Rapids established themselves at different points on the steep slopes between the bridges, and working back, as such rapids invariably do, they exposed the foundations, and in course of time would have completely undermined the works."—[*Calcutta Review*.]

at once from 4400*l.* to 9100*l.* In that calamitous year it is estimated that the value of the crops grown on irrigated land, "the greater part of which land would have been totally unproductive but for the canal-water," fell very little short of 500,000*l.*; of this a tithe, or 50,000*l.*, went into the Government treasury, and the remainder was bestowed upon the people by the agency of the canal. Of the other sources of revenue from the water-supply, it may be stated, that the mills have furnished to the amount of about 8300*l.* within the years above mentioned; that the cattle-supplies have yielded only about 190*l.*; the transit-duties 450*l.*; and the plantations about 2200*l.**

To combine in one view the financial results of these canal operations, and to exhibit the progressive demand that has been made upon the Government water-supply, the following facts, gathered from more detailed tables, may be stated:

WESTERN JUMNA CANAL.

	£
Gross receipts from 1821 to 1846-47	420,000
Gross expenditure	353,000

EASTERN JUMNA CANAL.

	£
Gross receipts from 1830 to 1846-47	125,000
Gross expenditure	198,000

WESTERN JUMNA CANAL.

	£
Income in 1821-22	2,700
Income in 1846-47	30,000

* "In addition to the plantations of forest trees, grafted mango gardens have lately been established with the view of introducing a superior fruit into the country adjoining the canal. Of these gardens five are in existence, containing about 300 trees each, and being from three to five acres in extent. The result of their establishment has been very satisfactory; and, although only one of the number has yet arrived at maturity, they have proved very successful—the demand for grafts and fruit being much in excess of the means of supply. The native community, for whom they were chiefly intended, have shown their appreciation by purchasing a large number of grafts; and there is every probability that the intention of Government in sanctioning the project will be fully realised."—[*Calcutta Review.*]

EASTERN JUMNA CANAL.

	£
Income in 1830-31	800
Income in 1846-47	12,000

In both cases the highest amount is to be found opposite the last year of the series, and with slight deviations only the increase has been regularly progressive. The surplus revenue derived from the two canals amounted in the year 1846-47 to 15,000*l*.

I come now to speak of the great Ganges Canal—a work still in progress of execution, which, when complete, will scarcely bow to a rival in any part of the world. It is one of comparatively recent conception, for it took birth only since the passing of the last charter. The originator of this great design was Colonel Colvin, who did so much to bring to perfection the Western Jumna Canal. It seems to have taken shape in his mind about the year 1836, at which period he held the office of Superintendent-General of Canals. But although he met with little encouragement at the time, he had full faith in the success of the experiment—he believed that the waters of the great river might be made to contribute abundantly to the wants of the thirsty soil of the Doab, to fertilise the land, and to enrich the people. The subject, though replete with interest alike to the philanthropist and the man of science, was then, and might still have continued to be, one only of speculation and discourse. But the winter of 1837-38 witnessed a grievous famine in Upper India. The whole staff of bread was broken. The heavens had not yielded their rain in due season, and the earth had not yielded her increase. The calamity came suddenly upon the people, and in this mortal extremity their rulers could do little for them. But it set such men as Colvin and Cautley thinking over the great project of the Ganges Canal, and it prepared Lord Auckland—a man of a humane nature, and, when left to himself, of sound discretion in quiet times—to give it favorable acceptance. The Governor-General sanctioned a full practical inquiry. Major Cautley was entrusted to examine the country through which the proposed canal would pass, and to send in a report on the subject. His first report was completed in May, 1840. It fully established the practicability of the great design.

It was now left to the Government to determine the scale upon which they would give effect to the project —the nature and the extent of the works of which they would sanction the execution. The times were not propitious. The war in Afghanistan, and the miserable encumbrance of the Douranee Empire, which only British money could sustain, was causing a chronic derangement of our Indian finances. But the Court of Directors saw clearly the immense benefits which such an extensive system of irrigation would confer upon the people of Upper India, and they worthily determined to sanction the proposed undertaking on such a scale as would secure an adequate water-supply to the whole of the country lying between the Ganges, the Hindun, and the Jumna.

But ordinary prudence dictated that so great a work should be cautiously approached—that the fullest examination should precede the final setting of the seal of authority upon this costly undertaking—so a Committee, composed of three of the ablest engineer officers in the country, Frederick Abbott, Baker, and Cautley, was appointed to ascertain and to report upon the best method of giving effect to the liberal views of the Court. In February, 1842, they submitted their report. In February, 1842, Lord Ellenborough arrived in India.

Lord Ellenborough went out to India to emulate the magnificent philanthropy of the Mahomedan Emperors. He returned to England to speak of the humiliation he had experienced on witnessing the great works of those native rulers, and contrasting them with our own. But one of his first measures, as Governor-General of India, was the suspension of the great undertaking of the Ganges Canal, which his predecessor had sanctioned. A vigorous prosecution of the work had been ordered. Lord Ellenborough arrested its progress.

There may have been State measures for this with which I am not acquainted. I think that public writers are too hasty in condemning measures with the secret history of which they have but imperfect acquaintance. Lord Ellenborough may have arrested the progress of the great Ganges Canal, because the political crisis which had arisen seemed to render it imperative upon him to devote every rupee in the public treasury to equipment of the armies which were retiring from Afghanistan—or he may have required for more warlike uses all the engineer officers at his command—or he may have had good reason to apprehend that the projected work, if it rescued the people from famine, would destroy them by disease—or he may have believed that navigation was more important than irrigation, and that in this case they were antagonistic objects. He may have been moved by one, or all, of these considerations. All I would say is, that no one knows so well as a Governor-General the difficulties with which, in such cases, Government have to contend, and that no one should be so slow to condemn the omissions which paramount circumstances may have enforced.

A season of dreary stagnation ensued, and when again there were symptoms of revival, the activity which was manifested was almost worse than the quiescence; Lord Ellenborough turned his thoughts towards the Ganges Canal, and directed that it should be primarily a canal of navigation. The projectors of the great enterprise stood aghast at this decision. Irrigation was the great object of the contemplated works, and now it was proposed that only the surplus water, after securing the navigation of the canal, should be devoted to its original purpose. The Colvins and the Cautleys—the Abbotts and the Bakers—who knew well what were the real wants of that part of the country, had regarded the great question not in its commercial, but in its agricultural bearings. They remembered the great famine of 1838; and they were eager to prevent the recurrence of its horrors. It was not for this that Cautley had been bringing all his science to bear upon the survey of the line.* But a new Governor-General soon came to preside over the Councils of India; and the whole question was reconsidered. Another difficulty had started up in the way of the great project, and had come to arrest the progress of the work. It was suggested that the canal would have a fatal effect upon the climate of the surrounding district—that the miasma which it would en-

* The Court of Directors entirely concurred in the views of the engineer officers, and wrote out to the supreme Government, clearly enunciating their views in favor of irrigation:—"Major Cautley's original plan was for a canal of irrigation, adapted, as far as could be done consistently with its efficiency in that respect, for navigation also; in 1844, the Government determined that the canal should be constructed with a view to navigation in the first instance, and that irrigation should be made a secondary object. We altogether disapprove of this project; and we are satisfied that its employment as a navigable canal should in any case be made altogether subordinate to its use as a means of irrigation; the advantage of possessing a good line of water communication through the centre of the Doab is undoubted, more especially if the navigation of the Ganges above Cawnpore should be rendered impracticable from the abstraction of its water. On the other hand, the efficiency of the canal for purposes of irrigation may possibly be impaired by specially adapting it to purposes of navigation; the expense of its construction will certainly be very much increased; the injury occasioned to the banks by the passing of boats will probably add to the costs of the annual repairs; and it must not be left out of view, that the canal, as a means of transit, may be hereafter superseded by the construction of a railway. These considerations must be borne in mind in determining on the expediency of adapting the Canal to purposes of navigation; and we would desire you to consider whether the sum which would be saved out of its cost by making it a canal of irrigation exclusively, might not be better applied in improving the ordinary means of communication through that tract of country, either by clearing the rivers of existing obstructions, by improving the roads, and eventually to the construction of a railway."—[*Court of Directors to the Governor-General, July* 7, 1847.]

gender would be destructive to the health of the people; and that, therefore, it would be prudent to pause until the medical question had been fully examined. So a Committee, of which Major Baker and Dr. Dempster were the chief members, was appointed, and, after a temporary interruption, caused by the Sikh invasion and the military operations which followed, they formally reported the result of their labors.

The report was satisfactory, and so were the results. Lord Hardinge fully recognised the merits of the scheme. He clearly saw the engineering practicability of the work in such hands as those to which it had been entrusted; and he saw, too, the immense effect which it would have in promoting the prosperity of the country and the happiness of the people. He gave it, therefore, his entire sanction and approval. Men and money were freely forthcoming. The Court of Directors readily consented to the expenditure of more than a million of money upon the prosecution of this gigantic enterprise.* And the work was pushed forward with becoming vigor. It is now in rapid progress towards completion. One-half of the money granted has been expended, and if the predictions of 1851 be verified, the present year will see the admission of water to the main lines.

The great Ganges Canal is the most magnificent work ever undertaken in India—one of the most magnificent works in the world. It traverses with its several branches more than 800 miles. The reader will do well to place the map of India before him and trace the course of this gigantic work. He must start from Hurdwar,† which he will find by following the

* The first revised estimates were a million and a quarter—but they were subsequently raised to a million and a half.

† "At about $2\frac{1}{4}$ miles north of Hurdwar, a branch leaves the right bank of the river Ganges, and, flowing past the sacred ghats, and under the picturesque buildings of the town, follows a course, generally parallel to that of the parent stream, which it rejoins at a point 30 or 40 miles to the southward.

30th degree of latitude till it intersects the 78th of longitude; and from Hurdwar he must proceed south-east in a slightly circular direction to Alighur. This distance is 180 miles. Here the canal follows two different lines—one towards the Ganges at Cawnpore, a distance of 170 miles—the other towards the Jumna at Humeerpore, which may be computed at about the same amount.* These are the main lines; but, having traced them, the reader must go back to the great trunk which he followed from Hurdwar to Alighur, and between these points three lesser canals branch off—one to Futtehghur, on the Ganges, a distance of 170 miles—another stretching to Bolundshahur, a distance of 60 miles; and a third to Coel, the length of which is estimated at 50 miles. The total length is officially computed to be 810 miles—thus:

	Miles.
Hurdwar to Alighur	180
Alighur to Cawnpore	170
Alighur to Humeerpore	180
Branch to Futtehghur	170
Ditto to Bolundshahur	60
Ditto to Coel	50
	810

As the work is still only a work in progress, no complete account of it can yet be given; but from the many interesting details before me, one or two may be selected in illustration of its nature and extent. "The grand, indeed the only, obstacles to the construction of

"Possession has been taken of the upper portion of this branch for the head of the canal; and through it the supply of 6750 cubic feet per second will be brought to Myapúr, a point about 1¾ miles south of Hurdwar, where the artificial channel commences.

"The first masonry works are constructed at Myapúr. They consist—1st, of a dam across the branch of the Ganges, having 38 openings of 10 feet each, fitted with gates or sluices and flank overfalls, by which a clear water-way of 517 feet is secured for the passage of floods from the Ganges during the rainy season; and 2nd, of a regulating bridge across the canal bed, having 200 feet of water-way in 10 openings of 20 feet each, fitted with all the machinery necessary for regulating the admission of water into the canal. The dam and bridge are connected by a long line of masonry revetement; and, on the opposite bank, the similar line of revetement with bathing ghats, &c., complete the works at the head of the artificial channel."—[*Calcutta Review.*]

* In the India House Statistics it is set down at 180 miles. I see that some other writers say 165 miles.

the canal," says Captain Baird Smith, "are met with on the first twenty miles from the head, or between Hurdwar and Roorkhi. These difficulties arise from the course of the canal intersecting at right angles the whole of the drainage of the Sub-Himalayas, of which the western valley of the Ganges is the receptacle.

"This drainage, independently of numerous minor channels, which are unimportant, is collected into three great lines, being the valleys of the Puthri, the Ruthmu, and Solani rivers, draining respectively about six, eleven, and eight miles in length of the hill country. The Puthri drainage, being divided among a number of minor channels, is not difficult to control; but the Ruthmu and Solani are impediments of the highest class.

"The artificial channel of the canal leaves Myapur with a transverse section, having a constant width at bottom of 140 feet, and a variable width at top, dependent on the depth of excavation, but which may be stated generally to be about 200 feet. The depth of water provided for is 10 feet, and the slope of the bed about 18 inches per mile. After pursuing its course for about 6½ miles, and crossing several lines of drainage, which are disposed of either by dams, or inlets and outlets, the canal is lowered into the valley of the Puthri river by means of the Bahadurabad Falls, which consists of two descents in masonry of 8 feet each, exactly similar to, although on a very much larger scale than, those of the Eastern Jumna Canal. These will be very massive works; and when the canal is opened, and its huge volume of water is poured over them, the sight will be a most striking one. Even with the small supply of the Eastern Jumna Canal, the turmoil at the base of the Belka Falls, which are 15 feet in height, is most formidable to behold. What then will it be, when ten times the quantity of water is thrown over falls 16 feet?"

Engineering difficulties are of one kind; financial difficulties are of another. Where there is a sufficiency of skill the magnitude of the work is nothing, if the labor and materials can be supplied. The great trunk line of the Ganges Canal has to be brought across the Solani river. "The river itself," says the same high authority, "is crossed by a masonry aqueduct, which will be not merely the largest work of the kind in India, but one of the most remarkable for its dimensions in the world. The total length of the Solani aqueduct is 920 feet. Its clear water-way is 750 feet, in 15 arches of 50 feet span each. The breadth of each arch is 192 feet. Its thickness is 5 feet; its form is that of a segment of a circle, with a rise of 8 feet. The piers rest upon blocks of masonry, sunk 20 feet deep in the bed of the river, and being cubes of 20 feet side, pierced with 4 wells each, and undersunk in the manner practised by natives of India in constructing their wells. These foundations, throughout the whole structure, are secured by every device that knowledge or experience could suggest; and the quantity of masonry sunk beneath the surface will be scarcely less than that visible above it. The piers are 10 feet thick at the springing of the arches, and 12½ feet in height. The total height of the structure above the valley of the river will be 38 feet. It will not, therefore, be an imposing work, when viewed from below, in consequence of this deficiency of elevation; but when viewed from above, and when its immense breadth is observed, with its line of masonry channel, which, when completed both north and south of the river, will be nearly 3 miles in length, the effect must be most striking.

"The water-way of the canal is formed in two separate channels, each 85 feet in width. The side walls are 8 feet thick, and 12 deep, the expected depth of water being 10 feet. Various buildings are provided at the flanks of the aqueduct, and many minor arrangements are made, which it would be wearisome to describe here. A continuation of the earthen aqueduct, about $\frac{3}{4}$ of a mile in length, connects the masonry work with the high bank at Roorkhi, and brings the canal to the termination of the difficult portion of its course. Such details convey but a very imperfect idea of the work. They are, however, the only substitutes for plans, or other graphic representations; and it may be hoped that they are intelligible enough to give some conception of the magnitude of the structures.

"It will perhaps give additional clearness to what has now been stated, if some details of the amount of labor, and the quantity of materials, which will be required to complete the work within six years, are exhibited; and with this view the following calculations made by Major Baker, late director of the canal, are given:

Calculation of means required to complete the Solani Aqueduct in six years.

"For 8,749,524 cubic feet of masonry in aqueducts and revetements will be required:

Bricks (L. 12" × B. 6" × D. $2\frac{1}{2}$) . . .	69,996,192
Surkhi (1,924,894 cubic feet) . . .	13,474,258
Total of Bricks . . .	83,470,450
Lime	962,447 cubic feet.

Or say eighty-four millions of bricks, and one million cubic feet of lime.

"The work people required in preparing and using the materials are as follow:

	Brickmakers.	Laborers.
In Brickmaking (inclusive of wood cutting) . .	141,666	3,143,333
	Masons.	
In building Masonry and laying Floors	306,233	781,946
In pounding Surkhi		641,632
In undersinking the foundation Blocks		311,040
In earthwork of Aqueduct (exclusive of draught cattle)		1,972,750

"The total labor required is therefore—

Brickmakers	141,666
Masons	306,233
Laborers	6,850,701

"The brickmaking, to be completed in five years, allowing 190 days each year (deducting Sundays and rainy seasons), would require per diem 149 brick-moulders and 3309 laborers. The remaining work, to be completed in six years, allowing 250 working days per annum, would require per diem 204 masons for five years, and for the sixth year 2471 laborers. The work-shops will require 50 smiths, and 80 to 100 carpenters per diem. An establishment of about 1000 bullocks (exclusive of contract carriage) will be required for the earth waggons, and other purposes."

This will be something to leave behind us, in those future days when we shall no longer sit at the receipt of custom among Mussulmans and Hindoos, and our Empire in India is a dream of the past.* It will be something to leave behind us; and it will be something, too, that it should be said that every laborer employed on this gigantic work received his wages on the appointed day, and that for every beast of burden the lawful hire was duly paid.†

* "Five centuries," says Baird Smith, "were not sufficient to obliterate the canals of Feroze, and these, as compared to the works of the British Government, were limited in extent, temporary in construction, and feeble in their powers of resistance to the destroying hand of time."

† A passage in a little book by Sir Digby Neave ("Three Days in Connemara") has attracted my attention whilst this sheet is passing through the press. Writing primarily on the subject of Irish famines, and the measures which have been taken, in case of their recurrence, to mitigate their severity, the tourist alludes to Indian famines, and what has been done to prevent them, and comments on the money-wages paid for the people's work.

"The country," he says, "is being opened up, for the civilising process is now begun, coupled, as I trust it will be, with a boon never before extended to India under any dynasty—a blessing, I really believe it may be fairly termed a Christian one, a lever which has never been applied except in the Christian era to the elevation of the masses—money-wages.

"We have been slow enough in marking our career with great works of utility; thank God these modern triumphs of civilisation, which are striking through the jungles, will be unspotted with blood. They will not be made as the tanks, the pyramids, and, in our days, as the Mahmoody Canal, with men's, women's, and children's lives, and a villanous calculation of the powers of human endurance, but by a fair day's wages for a fair day's work. Then will the Christian be had in honor among the heathen, and his creed in reverence among the nations.

"'Le physique influe sur la morale,

Of the estimated agricultural results of this great enterprise it is time to speak. I continue to quote the same authority, because I know the evidence to be the best:

"The first point to determine is the extent to which the Doab will be irrigated by the canal and its branches; and fortunately, by means of the invaluable statistical tables prepared by the Agra Government, this can be done with a degree of accuracy not before attainable. The districts to which the influence of the Ganges Canal and its branches will extend, together with details of their assessed areas, are given below. From the areas of Saharunpur, Muzuffernuggur, and Meerut, we have deducted the portions already provided with means of irrigation from the Eastern Jumna Canal. We have taken from the tables only the cultivated and culturable areas, because it is for these alone that irrigation has to be provided.

	Cultivated area in acres.	Culturable area in acres.
1. Saharunpur	501,606	392,508
2. Muzuffernuggur	505,830	236,216
3. Meerut	972,213	476,427
4. Bolundshahur	657,071	359,713
5. Alighur	901,405	129,710
6. Muttra	676,323	106,129
7. Furruckabad	652,075	305,095
8. Mynpuri	613,338	182,000
9. Etawah	477,901	139,850
10. Cawnpore	781,173	163,565
11. Futtehpur	518,812	123,985
12. Allahabad	997,508	231,597
Totals	8,255,255	2,846,795

"The total area, cultivated and culturable, of the above twelve districts, is therefore 11,102,048 acres.

"Now, supposing that the full supply of the canal, being 6750 cubic feet per second, is rendered available for irrigation, as ultimately we have no doubt it will be, we know, from experience on the canals of the

et la morale sur le physique.' I do not recite the remark for the truism it contains, but to call attention to the just order in which this reciprocating action is placed, as the imperious demands of the 'physique' must take precedence of the requirements of the 'morale.'"

Jumna, that each cubic foot of this discharge is sufficient for the irrigation during the year of 218 acres. The total area which would be actually watered during the year would consequently amount to 6750+218= 1,471,500 acres, or, for facility of calculation, say 1,500,000 acres.

"Assuming, as a standard of comparison for the whole of the Doab, the best irrigated districts on the Eastern Jumna Canal, namely, the western portion of Meerut, we find, by reference to the statistical tables, that irrigating villages actually water one-third of their total areas. Consequently the supply of the Ganges Canal would furnish abundant irrigation for an area of 1,500,000×3=4,500,000 acres.

"In districts benefiting by canal irrigation, it is found that for such localities as, from position, difficulties of level, or other causes, cannot be provided with water, irrigation from wells is extensively employed. From data given in the Special Committee's report, it would appear that, in the best irrigated district on the Western Jumna Canal, the proportion of canal to well irrigation is as five to one; assuming this for the Doab, we should have an area, irrigated from wells, amounting to 900,000 acres.

"The total area for which irrigation would be provided would accordingly amount to 5,400,000 acres. But the whole irrigable area of the Doab is, as formerly shown, 11,102,048 acres. This tract of country would therefore be irrigated to the extent of very nearly one-half its surface—a proportion equal to that of the best district west, and nearly double that of the best district east, of the Jumna. In making this comparison, it should not be overlooked that the best districts on existing canals have been selected as standards for the whole Doab—a measure which tends to give a more limited range to the influence of the Ganges Canal than would have been the case had inferior tracts been selected. But we are anxious to avoid all appearance of exaggeration in estimating the benefits to be anticipated from this great work, and, as a rule, will select such data as give minimum results, believing these to be abundantly convincing."

Having shown the actual amount of the land to be brought under irrigation, it remains only to exhibit its value, and to indicate the increased produce which the canal system will secure to the producer.

Calculation of the gross value of crops which will be secured from injury in famine seasons by the grand Ganges Canal.

		Rupees.
	KHURIF CROPS.	
250,000	acres of Sugar and Indigo, at Rs. 80 per acre .	2,00,00,000
125,000	„ of Cotton, at Rs. 48 per acre	60,00,000
375,000	„ of Rice and Sundries, at Rs. 38½ per acre .	1,44,37,500
	RUBBI CROPS.	
750,000	„ of Wheat, Barley, &c., at Rs. 48 per acre .	3,60,00,000
1,500,000	Total . . .	7,64,37,500

"Of this sum (upwards of 7½ millions sterling per annum) about one-tenth will return to Government in the form of land and water-rent, while the remainder will be the property of the agricultural community. It is needless to dwell on the importance of placing property, equal to between one-fifth and one-sixth of the value of the agricultural produce of the entire Presidency of Agra, beyond the influence of the seasons, and of insuring to the cultivators, under all circumstances, a certain return for their labor. The influence of the canal on the improvement of the Doab must necessarily be immense. This great tract will become the garden of the North-Western Provinces; and we shall hear no more of those devastating famines, which have hitherto swept across it, bringing physical wretchedness and moral degradation in their train.

"In addition to the certainty of returns, the actual

produce of irrigated land exceeds materially that of land unirrigated. From data collected during the progress of the Revenue Survey, it appears that the excess on irrigated over unirrigated land may be taken for the Rubbi, or cold weather crops, as being about 550lbs. per acre for wheat, and about 730lbs. for barley. Assuming the average of these for the general excess, we have the following estimate of the increase of produce due to the existence of the canal: 750,000 acres under Rubbi crops will amount,

at 640lbs. per acre, to . . . . . 480,000,000lbs.

The value of this increase, allowing the market rate to be one maund, or 80lbs. per rupee, would amount to rupees 60,00,000, or 600,000*l*. per annum.

"We have not data sufficient to enable us to estimate in detail the increase on the Khurif crops; but considering that this season, including as it does sugar, indigo, and cotton, is by far the most profitable to the cultivator, and that irrigation exercises an equally beneficial effect upon it, as upon the produce of the Rubbi, we may with great safety conclude that the increase during the Khurif will be at least equal to that during the Rubbi. Hence the total increase of the value of the produce would amount to 1,200,000*l*. per annum, a sum nearly equal to the total capital invested in the canal."*

Leaving the line of the Ganges, let us now cross the Sutlej and see what is doing in the Punjab to fertilise the thirsty land. The development of the resources of the country by means of improved methods of irrigation and channels of communication, was from the very first one of the leading ideas in Lawrence's mind. He was continually pressing upon the su-

* It may be mentioned here that the writer very clearly demonstrates that the great Ganges Canal, after paying for repairs and increased establishment, will yield an annual surplus of 350,000*l*.—more than twenty per cent. on the capital invested.

preme Government the expediency of devoting large sums of public money to the construction of roads and canals, and urging that such an expenditure would soon return itself tenfold, in increased revenue, to the treasury of the State. "If the Punjab," such was the language of the Lahore Board, "is to be made to pay its expenses; if we can hope to keep up efficient military and civil establishments, while taxing the people less than they have been taxed by previous rulers (and unless we can do so we assuredly cannot expect to win their good will); if we wish to feed the thousands of human beings whom the change of rule must necessarily throw out of employment, we cannot more readily do so than by cutting new canals, and improving the beds of the old ones."*

To no one could an earnest appeal of this kind have been addressed with greater certainty of eliciting an echo responsive to every word than from Lord Dalhousie. "Since I first addressed the Court of Directors on this subject," he wrote in a minute dated December 6, 1850, "I have personally visited the several districts of the Manjhir, as well as the southern portion of the Baree Doab, near Mooltan, and the lower portion of the Sindh Saugur Doab, and of the Trans-Indus province. Everywhere I found evidence of the wonderful effect produced by irrigation, wherever the means could be obtained; everywhere I found lands of vast extent, fertile properties now lying comparatively waste, but wanting only water to convert them into plains of the richest cultivation; and everywhere I found among the people the keenest anxiety to be supplied with that by which alone they could be enabled to turn their labor to good account. It is impossible to exaggerate the political importance of holding out to the people of this Doab an early prospect of the

* *Secretary of Lahore Board to Secretary of supreme Government, Nov. 29, 1850. MS. Records.*

formation of canals throughout its length and breadth, whilst the statements which have recently been, and which now are, submitted to the Court, appear to afford satisfactory proof that the revenue of the new province will fairly warrant this large expenditure, and that the undertaking itself will be richly profitable to the treasury of the State."*

As freely and as earnestly as the Governor-General responded to the Lahore Board, the Court of Directors responded to the Governor-General. "We have already," they wrote, "in our despatch of the 5th December, 1849, shown the importance which we attach to the extension and improvement of public works in the Punjab, and concurring entirely in the views taken by the Governor-General of the advantages, social, political, and financial, likely to result from the construction of the canal in question, we readily give our cordial assent to the undertaking, in the full confidence that the utmost care will be exercised in selecting officers competent in every respect for designing and carrying into execution, with efficiency and a due regard to economy, a work involving so large an expenditure of the public money."†

The great work here recommended is known as the Baree Doab Canal. The projected line stretches from the Ravee river, some miles below the fort of Shalipoor, across the Baree Doab, west of the town of Butteeala, and falls again into the Ravee sixty miles above Mooltan. The entire length of the canal, with its several branches, will be 450 miles.‡ It will be available for navigation

* *MS. Records.*

† *Court of Directors to Governor-General, April* 25, 1851.

‡ The course of the canal, with its branches, is thus described by Colonel Napier, of the Engineers, under whose superintendence the work is proceeding: "The Baree Doab Canal will leave the Ravee some miles below the fort of Shalipoor, and following the highest land between the Ravee and the Beeas, will throw off a large branch at the village of Tibbree, eight miles below Deena-nuggur. This branch will supply two channels terminating in the Sutlej —the one at Sobraon, the other at Kussoor. The main channel passes west of the town of Butteeala, nearly parallel with which it again throws off a branch, which will water the country

as well as irrigation. Its estimated cost is 500,000*l.*; and it is calculated that it may be completed within five years from the date of its commencement.

Of the immediate productiveness of such a work—apart from the after-results of increased cultivation—there seems to be little doubt. An equitable water-rate would yield, after deducting all expenses of establishment and repairs, 24 per cent. annually on the outlay. "Supposing," says Colonel Napier, "that 2500 cubic feet of water will be available for irrigation, and adopting Colonel Cautley's data for the Ganges Canal, that one cubic foot of water per second will irrigate 350 beegahs, or 218¾ English acres, 2500 cubic feet of water, at the rate of 1 rupee per Punjab beegah, or R. 2 6 10 per acre, will yield a return of

	Rupees.
Water Rent	13,27,311
Water Mills	40,000
Transit-duties and sale of canal produce	30,000
	13,97,311
Deduct annual expense of establishment and repairs .	1,90,000
Balance	12,07,000"

or 24 per cent. upon the outlay. But I have written too much already on the advantages of canal irrigation, to render it necessary for me to say, in this place, that the direct money return for the sale of the water is but a small element in the financial consideration of the question, and has no bearing upon the moral aspects of the case.*

I have shown what are the grand material results already realised or anticipated, on the securest data, of the system of canal irrigation, which the British Government is now carrying out so vigorously in Upper India. How it will change the whole face of the

in the neighbourhood of Lahore, and will fall into the Ravee about thirty miles below that city. The main line continues its course down the centre of the high land, and falls into the Ravee sixty miles above Mooltan."—[*Memorandum by Colonel Napier. MS. Records.*]

* See for further details of the Baree Doab Canal, Appendix E.

country, and what will be the magnificent effect, when the entire scheme, including that of the proposed Sutlej Canal,* is perfected in all its parts, I leave it to the imagination of the reader to conjecture. I have heard a man, advanced in years, who had retired to this country after years of honorable service, declare that the completion of the great Ganges Canal would take him back to India on a pleasure tour.

Of the moral results of these great reproductive works I need not particularly speak, for they are those which ever attend increased security and prosperity, the accumulation of capital, and the diffusion of wealth. To fertilise the land is to civilise the people. It is impossible to conceive anything that will have a greater effect upon the civilisation of the inhabitants of Upper India than the great remedial measure which guards them collectively against all the barbarising and demoralising effects of famine, and secures to every man individually his daily bread.†

* See Appendix E.

† Before quitting this attractive subject of canal irrigation, I may mention that Captain Baird Smith, during his recent furlough to Europe, visited Italy, and inspected the great canal works of Lombardy and Piedmont, and afterwards, with a similar scientific object, the United States of America, at the expense of the East India Company. He has now returned to India, and has been appointed, I believe, to superintend the execution of the great Ganges Canal. The results of the Italian tour have been given in a very important work on Italian irrigation, in which the writer thus comprehensively states his impression of the relative merits of the Italian and Indian works:—"As regards the works themselves, whether reference is had to their designs or modes of execution, I do not think that the Italians are inferior to ourselves; and in regard to the manner in which the efficiency of the work is maintained, I must frankly say decidedly inferior." There is another passage in his work which I am tempted to quote; for the lesson it conveys is an important one:—"I have thought it right to say these few words on the comparative dimensions of Italian and Anglo-Indian canals, because I found that nothing whatever was known of the latter among the intelligent engineers of Lombardy and Piedmont. Nor do I wonder at this, for in England there is nearly equal ignorance; and I cannot refrain from saying that I think the Government of India does itself the most grievous injustice by taking no measures whatever to convey to the public authentic information regarding these great works, which with equal advantage to its subjects and itself, it has been occupied in developing vigorously during the last thirty years. The impressions of the character of the British Government in India, among intelligent foreigners, I found to be of a very unsatisfactory kind, and it was gratifying neither national nor my personal feelings, to have to rectify the idea that we had done little or nothing to improve the condition of the people. As men's

I have devoted so much space to these great works of irrigation in the North-Western Provinces of India, that I cannot afford to write much in detail of the lesser public works which everywhere dot the country. A list of these works occupies a folio volume. Some of them, of course, are of limited extent; but they indicate the continued, quiet, beneficial action of an enlightened Government, eager in small things as in great, to contribute to the happiness of the people. I am necessarily obliged, in such a work as this, to pass over very much that might be adduced in illustration of the great subject of Indian Progress, for my space and my time are both restricted, and even at a period of unusual excitement, the patience of the public, in respect of matters of Indian administration, has no very extensive limits. Much might be said of the irrigation system of Southern India, differing as it does greatly from that of the North; but still most beneficially affecting the productiveness of the soil and the prosperity of the country. The works known as the "Cauvery Annicut"—works intended to secure, by embankments, the waters of the Cauvery river in the Southern Peninsula for purposes of irrigation, are approaching towards completion. Similar works for the Godavery and Kistnah rivers, in the northern parts of the Madras Presidency, have been sanctioned, and are in progress of execution. In 1849, an expenditure of 91,000*l.* was sanctioned for the former work; and in 1850, 150,000*l.* for the latter.*

minds in Northern India were thoroughly familiar with the nature and influences of works of irrigation, I found that, even the imperfect accounts that I was able to give of what the English in India had already effected in this department, were productive of good. The constant commentary on the information given was, however, 'Why are no accounts of such works communicated to the world?' And I earnestly hope it may yet be considered desirable that a worthy record of them should be made."

* With reference to the Kistnah Annicut, the Court observe in their letter of January 8, 1851: "The pro-

Whilst these great works of Irrigation were in progress, the improvement of the means of internal land-communication, in all parts of the country, was engaging the attention of the Indian Government, and evoking the energies of their executive officers. And steadily and effectually has the good work been prosecuted. Foremost among recent achievements is the great Trunk Road. It stretches from Calcutta to Delhi, and thence to Lahore and Peshawur. Its total length is estimated at 1423 miles, and is thus divided:

	Miles.
Calcutta to Delhi	887
Delhi to Kurnaul	78
Kurnaul to Loodhianah	124
Loodhianah to Ferozepore	74
Ferozepore to Lahore	50
Lahore to Peshawur	210
Total	1,423

This fine road was commenced soon after the Act, under which India is now governed, came into operation. It has been completed as far as Kurnaul, a distance of 960 miles, and is now being pushed forward with vigor. It is a metalled or macadamised road, "smooth as a bowling-green," and has hitherto cost about 1000*l.* per mile. It is estimated that the cost of keeping

ject has been submitted to the examination of those whose scientific acquirements, general experience, and local knowledge render them the most competent to form an opinion as to its merits, and has received the strongest recommendation from those authorities under whose consideration it has passed. We have carefully examined the papers submitted to us, and have satisfied ourselves that every possible means have been adopted to obtain the fullest assurance of the practicability of the proposed undertaking, and that the greatest care has been taken to prevent future disappointment in respect to the estimates, both of costs and returns. Under these circumstances, and concurring fully in the observation of Sir Henry Pottinger, that independently of the undoubted benefit which must in due time accrue to the State by a great increase of revenue, it is 'a positive duty which the British Government owes to the inhabitants of the districts which the Annicut is meant to fertilise, to adopt a measure which, under God's blessing, will for ever avert the horrors of famine under which they have before so deplorably suffered,' we readily give our cordial sanction to the undertaking, and trust that matters will be so arranged, that the establishment employed on the Godavery Annicut may not be broken up and dispersed, but may be made fully available for the works on the Kistnah."

the entire line in repair will not fall short of 50,000*l.* per annum.

Of the amount of traffic on this road, some idea may be gathered from the following statement, derived from statistical tables published by the Government of the North-Western Provinces. "During the year 1846-47, a party of five individuals, with one overseer, were stationed at the two principal bridges. The men relieved each other night and day. The following figures may convey some idea of the importance of this great artery in the body politic, of the traffic which annually passes along this great channel of communication ; and of the advantages which might be anticipated from a railway. During the year 1846-47, there passed along the road at the Paudu-bridge, as transport—

			Maunds.
Hackeries	Laden. 48,489	weight of goods at 20 maunds each,	969,780
	Unladen. 14,417		
Camels	Laden. 9,782	" " at 6 maunds each,	58,692
	Unladen. 3,766		
Bullocks and Buffaloes.	Laden. 16,261	" " at 4 maunds each	65,044
	Unladen. 13,212		
		Total weight of Goods ...	1,093,516

Besides these, there passed travelling,—

Foot Passengers ...	565,347	... Sheep and Goats...	21,738	... Buggies	617
Coolies and Banghis	7,883	... Elephants	287	... Behlis ...	9,950
		... Horses and Ponies	40,304	... Palkis ...	1,798
Total	573,230		62,329		12,365*

Of the measures which have been taken to give security to the traveller along this great public way, something may be said in this place. A very recent writer—a gentleman of high character and elevated

* *Statistics of Cawnpore, quoted in Calcutta Review.*

official position—speaking immediately with reference to the state of the country about Cawnpore, which does not unfairly represent the general condition of the Upper Provinces of India, says:—

"Since the year 1848, numerous measures have been adopted for the comfort and protection of travellers. Besides the halting-grounds for troops, serais have been erected at convenient intervals, and provision depôts have been established by Government, which stations its own contractors there, and compels them to conform to rules framed for the prevention of extortion or exorbitance. So that the traveller finds board and lodging, and accommodation for man and beast, at road-side inns provided by the State. For the protection of the road, there are fixed, at intervals of not less than two miles, either guard-houses with two watchmen each, or police-stations of greater or smaller calibre, according as the locality may require. Taking the number of the watchmen, and of the regular police employed upon the road, into consideration, there cannot be much less, upon an average, than one officer, of one kind or other, to every half mile of road."*

* *Calcutta Review.* Article: "Statistics of Cawnpore." I may add in confirmation of the above statement, the following by another writer, who speaks of his part of the country:

"The arrangements for watching the Grand Trunk Road in the district with which we happen to be best acquainted, are as follow: Every two miles along the road there is a police-station, with three policemen. These men are drafted from the body of the district police, are well armed, and wear a becoming uniform. The hours of their respective night-watches are fixed, and each man, on joining a road police-station, has a written notice given him, specifying the precise duties of his office From 10 p.m. to 4 a.m. two of the three night guards patrol the roads. Horse patrols are stationed at convenient distances, and to keep them on the alert, a written and verbal parole is sent from the magistrates court to each end of his district. The written parole is returned by the district post, so that the authorities have proof that once, at all events, each night, the horsemen patrol their portion of the road. To keep all up to this work, along the forty miles of road, three mounted jemadars are stationed, who send in written reports every morning of the exact spot where they passed each horse or foot patrol during the night. In the district to which we allude, in addition to the forty miles of Grand Trunk Road, there is, at least, an equal length of Branch Trunk Road leading towards Agra, which is watched and patrolled in the same manner. During the past year, no one single case of highway robbery has taken place; and though the traffic has been great, the amount of property stolen at night from travellers at halting-places, so far

Let these statements be compared with what I have shown to be the security of the highways in the time of the Emperor Jehanguire, and let us strike the balance with an honest hand.*

Two other trunk roads, of lesser proportions, but still of very considerable extent, have also been commenced and carried some way towards completion. The Bombay and Agra Trunk Road was commenced in 1840, under the government of Lord Auckland. Its total extent is 734 miles. The expense of construction has amounted to 243,676*l.*—about 330*l.* per mile. It is not metalled, except in parts.† The cost of repair is calculated at about 5000*l.* per annum. The formation of the Calcutta and Bombay mail road was sanctioned by the home Government in 1840. A portion of the distance—that is, from Bombay to Ahmednuggur—158 miles, had been previously completed. The remaining distance from Ahmednuggur to Calcutta is upwards of 1000 miles. The estimated expense is about half a million.‡

as can be ascertained, does not exceed 1200 rupees (900 of which are the value of a bale of silk cut off a cart under the nose of a sleepy watchman). When it is considered that in this district there are no restraints put upon travellers as to where they shall halt, and that parties of wearied merchants are spending the night all along the road under the canopy of heaven; when the following table of traffic, too, is taken into account, it will be acknowledged that due care is taken to protect the commerce of the country. Of loaded carts (of one to eight bullocks each) there were 28,168 drawn by 99,714 bullocks. The beasts of burden, camels, bullocks, horses, &c., carrying loads, amounted to 34,820. This is the account of what passed on the Grand Trunk Road alone, in the year 1851. Above, *i.e.*, to the west of the point where the Agra Branch Road meets the Grand Trunk Road, from and to Agra along the branch road, an almost equal amount of traffic passed. Now, allowing that each bullock and beast of burden drew or carried on an average property worth ten rupees, the losses of merchants by theft, in the two roads, cannot be set down at more than two pie per hundred rupees, and by robbery *nil.* And as no single instance of cattle theft occurred during the year on the road, either of loaded or not loaded cattle, the ten pie per hundred rupees, or fourpence per hundred pounds sterling." — [*Raikes' North-Western Provinces.*]

* See *ante*, pages 45, 46.

† Whether the highly metalled roads are acceptable to the people, is somewhat doubtful—admirable as, in many respects they are, and greatly as they contribute to the furtherance of improved means of communication. We must not, at all events, look at the subject with our English eyes, for the natives of India seldom shoe their cattle, and they complain that the metalled roads wear out the hoofs of their beasts. They are often to be seen travelling by the sides of the trunk roads — anywhere rather than on them.

‡ *India House Statistics.*

Of the cross-roads which intersect all parts of the country, it would be impossible to give any detailed account. These roads are made and repaired by means of funds raised, in some places from the tolls on public ferries, in others, from a rate of one per cent. paid by the landholders on the Government Revenue, and which in reality is a remission to that amount.* One local example will illustrate both the extent of these roads, and the manner of their management. "The district," says a recent writer on the Statistics of Cawnpore, "is intersected in every direction by unmetalled road, passable for nine months in the year. These roads are repaired every year after the rains. Exclusive of the trunk road (which is under the superintendence of an engineer officer), the aggregate length of road under charge of the committee amounts to 500 miles. The members of the committee are composed partly of European and partly of native gentlemen."

I have spoken of what has been done in the Punjab for the irrigation of the country by means of the Baree-Doab Canal. I may add here that smaller canals of irrigation have been opened out, or old ones have been repaired. Good roads, too, are starting up everywhere. In less than two years the great trunk road—one of the finest in the world—will be extended to Peshawur, and so link the capital of British India with the frontier of Afghanistan. Cross-roads are being made in every direction. Already eight hundred miles of new road have been laid down in the Lahore district alone. At every stage along the new main roads serais have been constructed, and police posts established at an interval of every two or three miles. Thousands of trees have been planted by our English administrators; and soon, from one end of the country to the other, the reproach of want of verdure will be wiped away.

* See preceding chapter, page 264.

The state of the roads in the Madras Presidency would seem to vary according to local circumstances. An expenditure of four lakhs of rupees a year upon the trunk roads has been authorised by the Court of Directors; but it does not seem that progress has been made commensurate with this liberality. Some of the district reports represent the roads in the interior to be in a state of decay, whilst others show that internal communication has been greatly facilitated by their excellent condition. From Salem, for example, the reports are very favorable. "The roads in this district," it is said, "are kept in repair without expense to Government. It is worthy of remark, that in 1847, there were no less than 400 miles of road traversed by carriages without obstruction at all seasons, besides branch roads, which only require some bridges to place them in equally good condition. The amount expended by Government from 1821 to 1840, was large, but the results were also very great. In 1848, the number of carts employed by the community exceeded that of the previous year by eighty, which is attributed to extended trade from the improved state of the roads."* A more recent writer, who brings down the statistics of this district to the beginning of 1852, shows that the improvement has been progressively increasing. "Next to freedom of commerce," he says, "we would place the facility of locomotion, the state of public roads; and on this subject we can speak with unmixed satisfaction. From one end of the district to the other, from north to south, and from east to west, excellent roads, bordered by flourishing avenues, do honor to the zeal and perseverance of several collectors, who have successively turned their attention to this subject; and, above all, the late Mr. John Orr. The whole extent of roads within the district, which has been completed,

* *Official Returns—Report on Public Works,* 1851.

planted, guarded by ditches, and with few exceptions marked by mile-stones, amounts to 726 miles. They are traversed, night and day, by hundreds of country carts, without let or hindrance, and may be traversed by any English traveller in his own carriage."* From Tanjore, too, it is reported that "considerable improvement has recently been effected throughout the province in the formation and opening out of roads, and the bridging of streams. The public have been greatly benefited by the completion of the repairs sanctioned in 1847 for the lines between the towns of Tanjore and Tivady, Tanjore and Combaconum, and the chain of communication is thus rendered perfect."†

One more illustration of the progress that has been made, in some parts of the Madras Presidency, may here be advantageously adduced. It is stated that the number of bridges built in the Salem district amounts to eighty-four. In connexion with this fact, a curious circumstance is stated by a local writer. "When the district was first handed over to our Government, an application was made to Colonel Read, by the officer commanding, for bricklayers to assist in building the officers' bungalows. Colonel Read's answer is on record, and states that no such person as a bricklayer existed in the district. In the last two seasons a bridge has been built over the river Cauvery of twenty-six arches, each of sixty feet span, chiefly by bricklayers and artificers of the Salem district."‡

Under the Bombay Presidency considerable progress has been made, especially in the improvement of internal communication. Something had been done before the Act under which India is now governed

* *Calcutta Review, June,* 1852. *Article: "Land Revenue of Madras."*

† *Return from the Presidency of Fort St. George.—Report on East India Public Works, August* 1, 1851.

‡ *Calcutta Review.*

passed into law. The administration of Sir John Malcolm saw the construction of the Bhore Ghât road, which opened the communications along a line of country upon which even military stores had been previously carried on the backs of bullocks, or on coolies' heads. There has been for some years an excellent road from Bombay to Poonah, and another from Bombay to Thannah, now soon to be superseded by the railway. Under the administration of Sir George Clerk, the Phonda Ghât road from Vizier-droog to Kolapore and Belgaum has thrown open the Southern Mahratta country. The road from Bombay to Sattarah has been greatly improved; and within the latter newly-acquired country there has been a large outlay on the public thoroughfares. Considerable progress has been made in the execution of the Thull Ghât road under Major Peat of the Engineers;* and a good road from Sholapore to Nassick commenced in a season of famine, with the object of supplying work to the starving people, has conferred substantial benefits on that part of the country. Of the lesser lines of communication I cannot afford to speak. I believe, too, that the only extensive irrigation works under the Bombay Presidency† are those in Kandeish, where the "bundarahs," by means of which the country was formerly watered, have been restored. In Bombay, as elsewhere, the want of money has been severely felt; and I am not sure that more would not have been done, if there had been less of centralisation in our system.

I have confined myself almost entirely, in this chapter, to the subject of roads and canals. Of the

* This is part of the line between Bombay and Agra, a continuation of the Thama road.

† The principal irrigation of the country is effected by means of wells and tanks. The revenue-officers are empowered to supply the agriculturists with money for the improvement of these works.

construction of railways and their effects on the prosperity of the country it is too early a day to speak in detail. In each of the three Presidencies of India the construction of a line of railway has been sanctioned by the home Government, and commenced under the auspices of a private company. The East India Company have guaranteed the payment of interest on the subscribed capital to the extent of from 4½ to 5 per cent.* The Electric Telegraph has also been introduced into India. A line of wires between Calcutta and Kedgeree, near the mouth of the Hooghly, now flashes the message from the ship to the counting-house. The success of this experiment, conducted by a member of that service to which science in various branches is so much indebted—the medical service of the East India Company—convinced the Court of Directors of the practicability of a vast extension of the system, and, under the superintendence of Dr. W. O'Shaughnessy, an entire line of telegraphic communication, extending to 3150 miles, and connecting Calcutta, Madras, Bombay, Agra, Simlah, and Lahore, is now speedily to be established. The estimated cost is 35*l.* per mile, or 110,250*l.* for the entire distance.†

The amount, according to the official returns, expended on "Public Works in India, comprising Roads, Bridges, Embankments, Canals, Tanks, and Wells," is shown to be, on the average of the last fifteen years, about 300,000*l.* a year.‡ But averages of this kind, as I have said, are not worth much; and it is my object to show not the average, but the progressive expenditure on these works. In 1837-38, the first year of the series, the total expenditure was little above seven-

* That is, in Bengal, 5 per cent. on the first million; 4½ on the second. In Madras, 4½. In Bombay, 5 per cent.

† To this, and other scientific operations, as the Trigonometrical Survey, &c., I may, perhaps, allude in another place.

‡ In exact figures, 299,732*l.*

teen lakhs of rupees (170,000*l.*); in 1851-52, the estimated expenditure was nearly seventy lakhs of rupees (700,000*l.*)* Of this latter sum, nearly fifty lakhs of rupees (500,000*l.*) are debited to the expenditure of the North-Western Provinces, including the Punjab, and are appropriated mainly to the great works of irrigation, of which I have given this hasty account. In these estimates of expenditure no account is taken of the salaries or allowances of the civil and military servants employed in the superintendence of the construction and repair of the works. Neither is any credit given for the cost of convict labor, which, for the five years between 1833 and 1838, is estimated at 156,000*l.* It is to be borne in mind, also, that, in Bengal, the Zemindars are under an obligation to repair the roads and embankments of rivers in their several estates, and as these disbursements are in reality met by proportionate remissions of revenue, the payments are in fact made by Government. They are estimated at not less than 100,000*l.* a year.

Therefore, although the total amount of the expenditure on public works, set down in figured statements, amounts to no more than four millions and a half† during the last fifteen years, this amount does not fairly represent the cost of their construction and repair. It is to be remembered, too, that these statements only relate to Roads, Bridges, Embankments, Canals, and Wells, and that "all buildings, civil or military, except so far as they are connected with such works, as bridges or roads, are excluded."‡

The estimated expenditure on Canals, Roads, &c., for the year 1850-51, has been shown to be 700,000*l.*—precisely quadruple the amount expended on similar

* That is, in 1837-38, 17,35,913 rupees; and in 1851-52, 69,35,290 rupees.

† 4,49,59,921 rupees.

‡ *India House Statistics.*

works in 1837-38. But even this amount inadequately represents the annual expenditure at the present time. "There can be no doubt," we are told, on official authority, "that the disbursements in the two or three years following 1850-51, will be greatly in excess of the expenditure of that year, inasmuch as in addition to the ordinary outlay they must include the larger proportion of the sum of two millions sterling, which has been specially sanctioned for the construction of the Ganges and Punjab canals, the former of which is fast approaching to completion."*

On the whole, it would appear from these statements that there has been a progressive tendency, on the part of the Indian Government, both in its local and its home relations, to promote great works of public utility. That the amount of money expended on such works is miserably small in comparison with the immense sums lavished on unproductive wars, is a fact which cannot be too deeply deplored. But there is no single truth which ought to stand out so prominently from every picture of Indian Progress as this—that the exhausting wars, which have swallowed up the resources of India, have obstructed and limited this progress; and that roads have not been made, canals have not been dug, bridges have not been built, in the number and to the extent which the interests of the country demanded, and the benevolence of its rulers desired, solely because the money, which was necessary to the construction of such works, has been abstracted from the public treasury to meet the expenditure incurred by the ruinous wars in which we have been

* *India House Statistics.*—It is stated by the same authority, that "In 1847 sanction was given for an annual expenditure of 40,000*l.* for a system of trunk roads in Madras. No great progress appears to have been made by the local Government in this work; but as a system of railroads is now about to be established in India, it appears most desirable to determine the direction in which these lines shall traverse the country, before incurring any great outlay on ordinary roads, which for the most part must be altered in their directions so as to become subsidiary to the great arteries of communication."

engaged. It is a truth to be wept over by every friend of humanity, that, within the last fifteen years, whilst some five millions of money have been spent on great national works, tending to the development of the resources of the country, and the promotion of the happiness of the people, thirty millions have been spent on War. And, in every consideration by Parliament or Press, by communities or individuals, of the good or bad government of our Indian possessions, this should be the foremost fact of all. It is right that, when account is taken of what has been done, and what has been left undone by the rulers of our Indian possessions, we should measure not only the progress that has been made, but what, judging by actual results under the most unfavorable circumstances, would have been made, if, throughout the last fifteen years of which I have been speaking, Peace had smiled down upon the land. It is right that, in every investigation of the working of the administrative machinery of what is called the East India Company, an inquiry into the causes of the melancholy retardation of domestic improvement should be prominently instituted; and that the responsibility of all this lamentable waste of public money, which, properly expended, might have conferred incalculable benefits on millions of our fellow-subjects, should be traced to its legitimate source.

PART III.

CHAPTER I.

The first Judicial Tribunals—The Mayor's Courts—Efforts of Warren Hastings—The Supreme Court of Calcutta—Cornwallis and the Regulations—The Provincial Courts—Reforms of Lord William Bentinck—Increase of Native Agency—Present State of the Company's Courts.

I WOULD proceed now to speak of the administrative efforts which have been made by the British Government in India for the protection of life and property, and the suppression of crime; and to inquire into the effect which these efforts have had upon the general happiness of the people.

In the early chapters of this work it has been briefly shown in what manner the first settlers provided for the occurrence of those mischances of lawlessness which are inseparable from all conditions of society,* and, most of all, from such a condition of society as obtained amongst us when we first planted our factories in the East. Collisions, whether civil or criminal, with the natives of the country, subjected our people to the decisions of the native tribunals; and when we fell out among ourselves, in matters affecting property or person, our disputes, if of the former character, were settled by the President, or if of the latter, a Court was held, under

* See *ante*, pages 65, 66.

the King's Commission, probably on board one of the vessels in the roads, and the offender was dealt with as its members, consisting of the chief naval and mercantile functionaries, might determine and decree.

As time advanced, and the number of British subjects on the eastern shores steadily increased, and with the increase necessarily arose more complicated relations both with the natives of the country and among ourselves, it became necessary to establish in our settlements judicial tribunals with more defined powers. The Charter of 1661 empowered the Company to appoint Governors and other officers in their several factories, and decreed that "such Governor and his Council may exercise civil and criminal jurisdiction in the said factories, &c., according to the laws of England;" "and if the offence," continued the Letters Patent, "shall be committed in a place where it cannot be tried, the offender may be sent to such other plantation or fort, where there is a Governor and Council to try him, that justice may be done." A further clause set forth, that "the King's subjects, employed by the Company in the limits aforesaid, shall suffer such punishment for offences there committed as the Company's President and Council shall think fit and the quality of the offences require, and in case of appeal the offender shall be sent home for punishment. And for the better discovery of offenders, all persons may be examined on oath before the Company's President and Council, touching the same." In the grant of the island of Bombay, in 1669, the Court of Proprietors, or the Governor and Committees of the East India Company, were authorised "to make and publish, under the Company's seal, laws and constitutions for the good government of the island and its inhabitants, and to impose punishments and penalties extending to the taking away of life or member, when the quality of the offence shall require it; so that the punishment and the penalties are consonant to reason, and not repugnant to, but as near as may be agreeable to, the laws of England, and subject to the provisos and restrictions contained in the Charter." The proviso was that the offender did not appeal; but as every man sentenced to death was pretty certain to appeal, it would not seem that these Courts had any great power over the life of an offender, so long as they respected the letter of the Charter.

It was, probably, this restriction which rendered the Courts, so established, ineffective for the restraint of crime. At all events, in 1726, the Court of Directors laid at the foot of the throne a representation that "there was great want at Madras, Fort William, and Bombay, of a proper and competent power and authority for the more speedy and effectual administering of justice in civil causes, and for the trying and punishing of capital and other criminal offences and misdemeanors." That they had good reason for this plaint is not to be doubted. The records which still remain of the proceedings of the Courts of Justice anterior to this period, exhibit some curious instances of the manner in which men sat in judgment in their own cases, and put their names to sentences against prisoners whom they themselves had really prosecuted. Strange charges were made, and stranger punishments decreed—but they are to be judged, not by a reference to the state of our judicial administration, either in England or in India at the present time, but to what it was, even in Great Britain, at the close of the seventeenth and the commencement of the eighteenth century. Such an entry, as the following, has a strange appearance in these days, but, a century and a quarter ago, there may have been nothing startling in it. It is taken from the records of the Court of Justice at Bombay:

"July 5, 1724, a woman named Bastook, accused of diabolical practices, having been before whipped for the like, it appearing to proceed from her ignorance, which leads her sometimes to mingle rice and other foolish ceremonies, which she thinks effectual to cure sick persons, ordered she receive eleven lashes at the church-door, and afterwards she and all persons that are found guilty of the like, do such penance in the church as customary."*

So ignorance was to be whipped, and to stand in a sheet at the church-door. But as not very long before the same ignorance was burnt at the stake in England, there was nothing, at that time, very noticeable in such a sentence.

Certainly the plaint of the East India Company at this time was not without just cause. But the remedy, which was sought to be applied, was scarcely a shade better than the disease. Justice gained little by the establishment of the Mayor's Courts. The Letters Patent of September, 1726, which established these tribunals, really did but little to advance the interests of substantive justice.† These Courts were to consist of a Mayor

* *MS. Records.*—This Court took cognisance also of military offences, and sentenced insolent troopers to be flogged. Take the following specimen, which I have extracted from the records of the Court:

"*Court of Justice at Bombay, the Worshipful John Hope, Chief Justice.*—*April* 15*th*, 1724.—Mr. Braddyll, having been much insulted by a trooper last Monday night, when he was walking out with his lady, having been almost rid over, and Mr. Braddyll calling to him bidding him take care and keep off, he returned in answer, 'God d—n you; if I had a pistol I would shoot you through the head for a farthing.' Mr. Braddyll answering, 'Would you so?' he again returned, 'Yes, I would—you are a rogue and a rascal.' On inquiry being made who was down on duty that time of night, one Matthew Bogle was fixed upon, who denies it; but the corporal of the first guard declaring that it was him and no other, and the officer of the guard confirming of the same, and two witnesses to the insult, besides Mr. Braddyll, viz., Captain Montague and Ensign Mainwaring, both at the time in the same place with Mr. Braddyll, the Court considering the circumstances, the voice agreeing (no other trooper at that time being at the fort), the corporal's confirmation, the words plainly proved, and nothing to the contrary but a plain denial, the Court condemned him to receive thirty-nine lashes in the public bazaar, and to be sent on board one of the Company's vessels, there to serve during the Governor's pleasure, without pay."—(Mr. Braddyll himself was one of the Court which tried him and signed the sentence.)

† The Mayor's Court of Madras had existed before this, but with less defined judicial constitution, and less extended powers. "They have a mayor and aldermen," says an old writer, at the commencement of the eighteenth century, "who exercise the same authority as in corporations in England. Quarrels, small debts, and other business of the meaner sort, are decided by them at a Court of six Aldermen, held twice a week in the Town Hall. Black merchants commonly apply to this Court, but Europeans usually seek favor of the Governor. When any are not satisfied with the Mayor's Justice, they may appeal to a higher court, where for much money they have little law, with a great deal of formality. Here a judge allowed by the Company presides, who, on the report of a jury, gives a final decree of European male-

and nine Aldermen, seven of whom, with the Mayor, were to be British subjects. They were, in fact, composed of the Company's mercantile servants—men of the slenderest legal attainments, and the slightest judicial training. They undertook all kinds of business, civil, criminal, and prerogative—but were, to a certain extent, controlled by the executive Governments, which were constituted Courts of Appeal. The President and Council and the members of the Mayor's Courts were thus often brought into collision; and between the two, I fear that neither law nor justice was treated with much respect.

I have little doubt that the excesses committed by these early Courts have been considerably exaggerated by writers, who, not belonging to the privileged class of Company's servants, looked askance at their doings, and magnified their misdeeds. But making every allowance for these exaggerations, it would still appear that justice was administered in a very arbitrary manner, and that law was held of little account. It was a story very current in those days that as the Company's Courts had power only to inflict capital punishment for piracy, the widest possible interpretation was given to the word, and men were hanged as pirates who had committed some offence that had no sort of likeness to it.* The laws

factors; they hang none but pirates, though, formerly here, have been men put to death for other crimes, whence I am apt to think that the Governors had then great powers."—[*Account of the Trade in India, by Charles Lockyer*, 1711.] The same writer adds: "Lawyers are plenty, and as knowing as can be expected from broken linendrapers and other crack'd tradesmen who seek their fortunes here by their wits."

* "A private trader," said one writer, "if he has the misfortune to incur the displeasure of the Governor, is soon found guilty of piracy." Speaking of the Mayor's Court of Madras, he says, "In matters of consequence, a few pagodas, well placed, could turn the scales of Justice, the cause generally going according to the favored inclination of the Governor." Another writer, the well-known Captain Hamilton, who was an interloper, says: "If any private trader is injured by the tricks of a Governor, and can find no redress, if the injured person is so bold as to talk of *lex talionis*, he is infallibly declared a pirate." The captain gives one or two instances of the extensive application of the word. "They have no martial law," he says, "at Fort St. George, so they cannot inflict the pain of death any other way than by whipping or starving, only for piracy they can hang, and some have been so fond of that privilege, that Mr. Yale hanged his groom (Cross) for

against piracy were wound up to a state of extreme stringency, and the Company's servants, maddened by the insolence and audacity of the interlopers, doubtless abused the power which was vested in them by those laws, and committed many grievous excesess.

But such as they were, these Mayor's Courts existed for half a century. As time wore on, the evil of a defective administration of justice became more painfully apparent. So long as these tribunals took cognisance only of cases, civil or criminal, in which the hangers-on of the Factories were concerned—such as deserters from the shipping, small traders of Portuguese or Eurasian stock, native dubashes, speaking the English language, and others who lived upon the English connexion—the evil consequences of an ineffective judicial system and an imperfect judicial agency were comparatively limited. But when our territorial dominion was extended—when on the banks of the Hooghly we became occupants of land which we called our own, and the natives of India submitted themselves to our authority and protection, it became obvious that we required something more than the power of administering justice according to the laws of England, and that the whole question of judicial administration demanded our most serious thoughts. The natives of India knew nothing of English law, and if they had known anything of it, would have seen at a glance how utterly inapplicable it was to the social condition of either Mahomedans or Hindoos. We had a very sanguinary code in those times. There were many offences, which to English eyes in the present day have a strange effect with the word "capital" prefixed to them. The enormity of these crimes no native of India could possibly be made to understand. And yet the people of Bengal, in and around Calcutta, were brought within the

riding two or three days' journey off to take the air"—probably for horse stealing, which Mr. Yale, perhaps, regarded as an act of land-piracy. It should be mentioned, that these cases refer to a period anterior to 1726.

network of these laws, and were sometimes made to feel their terrible significance. The powers of the Courts were extended by law; our judges made other extensions for themselves; and the natives of India were hanged for the commission of acts which they believed to be justifiable, if not commendable, in the eyes both of God and man. One example of this will suffice. It is given on the authority of Mr. Verelst:

"In the year 1762 a native detected one of his women in an act of infidelity. Throughout the East women are wholly subject to the will of their masters, and every husband is the avenger of his own wrongs. The man, therefore, satisfied of her guilt, proceeded to punishment by cutting off her nose. He was arraigned at the Calcutta Sessions. He confessed the fact, but urged that he had done nothing to offend the laws and customs in which he had been educated—that the woman was his property, and that by such customs he had a right to set a mark upon her for her infamy—that he had never heard of the laws by which they tried him, but desired to put one question to the Bench—Did they believe that if he had known the punishment to be death, he would ever have committed what they now called a crime? The man, notwithstanding this defence, was condemned and hanged—for if the Court possess jurisdiction, they must proceed according to the English laws."

This state of things could not be long endured. The people cowered beneath this new terror—a terror doubly terrible, because they could not discern the shape thereof. It might meet them, at any time, in strange places—come upon them unawares, and destroy them suddenly in their sleep, ere they had time to understand the unexpected danger that was coiling around them. In this extremity they presented, in March, 1765, a petition to the President and Council of Fort William, setting forth "the general consternation, astonishment, and even panic with which the natives at all parts, under the dominion of the English, are seized by this example of Radachurn Mettre. They find themselves subject to the pains and penalties of laws to which they are utter strangers, and are liable, through ignorance, unwillingly to incur them; as they are no ways interested in those laws, they cannot tell when they transgress them, many things being, it seems, capital by the English laws, which are only fineable by the laws of your petitioners' forefathers, subject to which they have hitherto been bred, lived, and been governed, and that till very lately under the British flag." The hand of the English lawyer was plainly discernible beneath the transparent covering of this petition,* as beneath other petitions of much more recent date; but it really represented the feelings of the more intelligent native inhabitants of Calcutta and the surrounding country. At all events, there was abundant reason on their side, which there is not always in native petitions. It is characteristic of the people of Bengal, that as soon as they began to obtain some little insight into the powers of the Mayor's Court, and to understand the class of offences which the Court was competent to punish with extreme severity, they began to avail themselves of the existence of those powers as an instrument of oppression among themselves, and to set forth charges one against another of such a character as would bring them most perilously under the heavy hand of the English law.

But a time was now approaching when the necessity of looking more seriously at the whole question of internal administration, could no longer be withstood. The Dewanee passed into our hands; and although we did not at once stand forth as administrators, it became our duty to keep a watchful eye upon the system, which

* The petition was primarily for the remission of the sentence passed on Radachurn Mettre for forgery. The petitioners are made to say: "And further your petitioners are advised that the said indictment was very erroneous and naught, and that the said prisoner could not have been arraigned thereon had he been versed in the laws to make his exception thereto—Lord Chief Justice Hales saying, that 'there is great exactness required in indictments where life is at stake.'"

was to be maintained under the double Government, and to endeavour to give it more beneficial effect. The Mayor's Courts had yet some years of life remaining; but the evils of which I have spoken diminished under a growing conviction, on the part of the chief servants of the Company, that English law was wholly inapplicable to the usages of native society. We began now, more and more, to look into the practice of the Native Courts, and to endeavour to understand the laws which their own magistrates administered. A great and solemn duty was now spreading itself out before us—the duty of infusing the principles of English justice into the administration of the Mahomedan law—of regulating and purifying the dispensation of that law, and improving existing institutions, rather than demolishing them. During the years intervening between the grant of the Dewanee, and our open assumption of the duties of Dewan, the Company's servants had acquired some knowledge and experience, which might be turned to profitable account. But they were not then competent to take into their own hands the entire management of the Courts of Justice. The experiment at that early period would have been a dangerous one, and Hastings knew too well the character and the attainments of his associates to incur so formidable a risk.

When, therefore, by the public announcement that the Company had determined to stand forth in the character of Dewan, the whole responsibility of the civil administration of the country was thrown upon the President and Council, Hastings, though he was prepared to turn his supervisors into collectors of revenue, was not prepared to deliver into their hands the administration of criminal justice. He established in each district two Courts of Judicature—a civil and a criminal court.* Over the former the European collector of

* Known as the "Dewanee Adawlut" and "Fouzdaree Adawlut."

each district was to preside, on the part of the Company, attended by the provincial native Dewan, who with his officers was to be appointed by the President and Council. Over the others the old Mogul judicial officers were to preside, with two Moulavees, or Mahomedan doctors, to expound the law. The Company's European servants had no immediate connexion with the business of these criminal courts. But the collector was ordered to exercise a sort of general superintendence over their procedure—"so as to see that all necessary evidences are summoned and examined; that due weight is allowed to their testimony, and that the decision passed is fair and impartial, according to the proofs exhibited in the course of the trial."*

At the same time were established two superior courts, which were to sit at the chief seat of Government—the one known as the Sudder Dewanee Adawlut, and the other as the Sudder Nizamut Adawlut. The first of these, or chief civil court, was to be presided over by the President and two members of Council; the latter by a Mahomedan judge, or "chief officer of justice," appointed by the Nazim, and attended by a sufficient staff of Mahomedan law officers. Over the general procedure of this court the same control was to be exercised by the President and Council as was vested in the collectors over the provincial criminal courts.

These Sudder Courts were Courts of Appeal from the different civil and criminal tribunals in the provinces. Their precise powers and duties were clearly defined; whilst, at the same time, many subsidiary regulations for the furtherance of justice were laid down and publicly announced. They exhibit on the whole a sincere desire to secure equal justice to the

* *General Regulations for the Administration of Justice, August 15, 1772.—Colebrooke's Digest, Supplementary volume.*

people—to protect the rights of all men without encouraging the litigiousness which is so formidable an ingredient in the native character.* As the first essay towards the establishment of a judicial system for our new territories, these Regulations of 1772 are very creditable to our infant administrators. And it must not be omitted in any statement of the benefits they conferred on the people, that the oppressive exactions, under the head of fines and fees, which had fed the revenue and paid the law officers, under Mogul management, were abolished, "conformably to the wise and humane instructions of our honorable masters, who, from the same spirit of equity have renounced the right, hitherto exercised by the country Government and authorised by the Mahomedan law, to a commission on the amount of all debts, and on the value of all property recovered by the decrees of the Courts—a practice repugnant to every principle of justice."†

Such were the Regulations in force throughout the Presidency of Bengal when the "Regulating Act" was passed. The thirteenth clause of this Act recited, that "whereas his late Majesty George II., by Letters Patent, dated January 8, of the 26th year of his reign,

* Thus, on the one hand, it was ordered—"That as nothing is more conducive to the prosperity of any country than a free and easy access to justice and redress, the collectors shall at all times be ready to receive the petitions of the injured; and further to prevent their being debarred this access, from motives of interest, partiality, or resentment, in the officers or servants of the Cutcherry, that a box shall be placed at the door of the Cutcherry, in which the complainants may lodge their petitions at any time or hour they please. That the collector shall himself keep the key of the box, and each court-day have such urgees as he may find in it read immediately in his presence by the Arzbeggy of the court." And on the other it was decreed—"That as the litigiousness and perseverance of the natives of this country, in their suits and complaints, is often productive, not only of inconvenience and vexation to their adversaries, but also of endless expense and actual oppression, it is to be observed, as a standing rule, that complaints of so old a date as twelve years shall not be actionable; and further, should they be found guilty of flying from the one court to the other, in order to prevent and protract the court of justice, the party so transgressing shall be nonsuited, and liable to fine or punishment." And again, that "persons found guilty of preferring groundless, litigious, or vexatious appeals, shall be punished at the discretion of the Sudder Dewanee Adawlut by an enhancement of the costs, &c., &c."

† *Letter of the Committee of Circuit to Council of Fort William*, *August* 15, 1772.—*Colebrooke's Digest, Supplement.*

granted to the said Company his Royal Charter to constitute Courts of Civil, Criminal, and Ecclesiastical Jurisdiction, and which Charter does not sufficiently provide for the due administration of justice, &c., it is therefore enacted that it shall be lawful for his Majesty to erect a Supreme Court, to consist of a Chief Justice and three other Judges, which said Supreme Court shall have full powers to exercise all civil, criminal, admiralty and ecclesiastical jurisdiction, and appoint such clerks and other ministerial officers, with such salaries as shall be approved of by the said Governor-General and Council, &c., and also, shall be at all times a Court of Record, and a Court of Oyer and Terminer, and a gaol delivery, in and for the said Town of Calcutta, and factory of Fort William in Bengal and the limits thereof, and the factories subordinate thereto."* The old Mayor's Court was superseded by this new tribunal; and English lawyers went out to administer English law after the most approved Westminster model.

Then began the great strife, the history of which has been written in language so attractive, that few are disposed to censure the exaggerations with which it is crusted over. A great and scandalous error was committed by Parliament in not more clearly defining the jurisdiction of the Crown Court; and the new English judges were not disinclined to take advantage of the obscurities of their Charter. They carried with them to India the most inflated ideas of the beauties and benignities of English law. They went out to save, and they destroyed. Instead of maintaining order and preserving peace, they threw the settlement

* The Letters Patent which the King was empowered in the Regulating Act to grant, was dated 26th of March, 1774. It contained a great many clauses intended to define the powers and jurisdiction of the Supreme Court—which had been less clearly stated in the Regulating Act—but it still left them very vague and uncertain.

into confusion, and engendered the most unseemly strife. Instead of a blessing, they conferred a curse upon the people—instead of security, terror. I believe that they were honest and able men—that they believed they were fufilling the intentions of the Legislature, and shielding the people from wrong; but they went out with the most exaggerated ideas of the inefficiency and the turpitude of the Company's Courts, and believed that so long as they were in antagonism with the Company's servants, they were nobly fulfilling their mission as representatives of English law. The whole administration of the country was well-nigh brought to a stand-still.* It is charitable to suppose that these ermined Interlopers, fresh from Westminster Hall and the Inns of Court, did not know what they were doing. They had little acquaintance with the system of internal government, which the Company's servants had built up on the basis of the old Mogul administration. They knew nothing of the language, the institutions, the character and the usages of the people. They scarcely knew a Mahomedan from a Hindoo, or the difference between a Cauzee and a Dewan. But it was ever uppermost in their thoughts that they had come out to administer the English law, as it was administered at Westminster; and they believed that it was their first duty to uphold the dignity and to maintain the integrity of that "perfection of human wisdom," which they inscribed on their banners when they went out to fight the Company and their servants. There were evils,

* "Every class of the population," says Mr. Macaulay, "English and native, with the exception of the ravenous pettifoggers, who fattened on the misery and terror of an immense community, cried out loudly against this fearful oppression. But the judges were immoveable. If a bailiff was resisted, they ordered the soldiers to be called out. If a servant of the Company, in conformity with the orders of his Government, withstand the miserable catchpoles, who, with Impey's writs in their hands, exceeded the insolence and rapacity of gang-robbers, he was flung into prison for contempt. The lapse of sixty years—the virtue and wisdom of many eminent magistrates, who have during that time administered justice in the Supreme Court, have not effaced from the minds of the people of Bengal the recollection of those evil days."

doubtless, to be remedied; but the remedy was far worse than the disease. The man who rides down a field of corn to drive out a hare or pheasant that is nibbling at his crops, is a faint emblem of the Supreme Court during the first years of the Regulating Act. The new Judges went out to India to eradicate certain administrative defects, and they rode down the whole administration of the country without a feeling of remorse. Well might it have been said in the petitions which were presented to Parliament, that unless relief were granted to the Company, they would soon have ports without trade; possessions without revenue; and laws without inhabitants.

The prayers of these petitions were not unheeded.* The excesses of the Supreme Court were taken into due consideration by Parliament, and, in 1781, an Act was passed (21 George III., chap. 70) defining and limiting its powers.† Practically, the evil had somewhat abated before the new Act was brought into operation. The Judges may have seen the error of

* The petition from the British subjects in Bengal, Behar, and Orissa, was drawn up by Mr. Shore, afterwards Lord Teignmouth. It set out by saying that "Whereas your petitioners observed with the deepest concern and affliction, that at the passing of the Act (3 George III.), and previous to it, very erroneous reports had been propagated, and injurious ideas entertained of the principles and practices of the British subjects residing within these provinces, from which it was inferred that they required more vigorous restraints and coercions than have usually been imposed upon Englishmen," &c.

† It was enacted "that the Court should not have, or exercise, any jurisdiction in any matter concerning the revenue, or concerning any act or acts ordered or done in the collection thereof, according to the usage and practice of the country, or the regulations of the Governor-General and Council." It then went on to declare the description of persons to be subject to the jurisdiction of the Court. The old Act had rendered all persons in the employment of the Company amenable to the Crown Court, and the judges had decided that all the Zemindars, and revenue-farmers, and contractors, were servants of the Company, and had issued process against them. The new Act decreed that "no person shall be subject to the jurisdiction of the Supreme Court for or by reason of his being a landowner, landholder, or farmer of land, or of land-rent . . . or those who are his under-tenants in virtue of his farm . . . within the Provinces of Bengal, Behar, and Orissa." It enacted that judicial officers in the Country Courts should not be liable to actions in the Supreme Courts for wrongs done in their judicial offices; and expressly declared the incompetency of the Court to determine any indictment or information against the Governor-General and Council.

their ways, or they may have been subjected to private influences; but the confusion into which the settlement had been thrown was fast subsiding, when the Legislature formally curtailed their power and crushed their licentiousness. From this time, to the present, the Crown Courts have maintained themselves in a state of comparative quiescence, and though, ever and anon, they have come into collision with the Company's servants, there have been none of those open scandals and insolent outrages which in the first years of the Regulating Act convulsed society, and well nigh-overturned the administration.

Meanwhile, the Company's Courts were in process of gradual improvement. From time to time certain changes had been introduced by Warren Hastings and his associates in the Government, but they had not been moulded into " any general and uniform system." But in April, 1780, they took shape in certain Regulations which gave the Company's servants a more clearly defined judicial character then they had been invested with under the Regulations of 1772. Under these Regulations the Collectors had been appointed, *ex officio*, Presidents of the Civil Provincial Courts; but now distinct judicial officers, from among the Company's European servants, were appointed to preside in these Courts, under the title of superintendents of Dewanee Adawlut, with instructions to hold their Courts " three times in every week, and as frequently as occasion may require, but that no cause shall be determined except in open Court, and in the presence of some of the principal officers."* These Courts were to take cognisance of all ordinary civil business; but Revenue suits were to be decided by the Provincial Councils.

* *Regulations passed by the Governor-General and Court, April* 11, 1780.—*Colebrooke's Digest, Supplement.*

In 1781, another change was introduced, which brought the Company's servants into a still closer connexion with the administration of justice in Bengal. The Judges of the Civil Courts were invested with the power, as magistrates, of apprehending Dakoits and persons charged with the commission of any crime or active violence, within their respective jurisdictions—but they had no power to try them. And in this state, the administration of criminal justice being still in the hands of the native officers, Lord Cornwallis found the judicial system of Bengal on his first arrival in the country. As much had been done, as under all circumstances could have been reasonably expected, to bestow upon the natives of India the blessings of a mild and equable dispensation of the law, and imperfect as were these initial efforts, it is still apparent that the system which Warren Hastings introduced, and the practice which he enforced, were great improvements upon those of the Moguls.*

Lord Cornwallis went out to India with definite instructions from the Court of Directors, but with considerable discretionary power. On the subject of the administration of justice, the Court declared that it was their desire "to accommodate their views and interests to the subsisting manners and usages of the people, rather than to any abstract theories drawn from other countries, or applicable to a different state of things."† And, having thus enunciated general principles, the soundness of which is not to be questioned, they proceeded to deliver themselves of specific instructions. They ordered that the Provincial Civil Courts should be again placed under the superintendence of the Collectors,

* See for a very fair statement of the advantages conferred upon the people by our earliest administrative efforts *Mr. Shore's (Lord Teignmouth's) Minute of Feb.* 10, 1790.

† *Letter to the Governor-General in Council, April* 12, 1786.

and that the administration of criminal justice should remain as before, in the hands of the Mahomedan officers. Accordingly a series of Regulations, "revised and adapted to the system established by the orders of the Court of Directors," was passed on the 27th of June, 1787, and translated into Persian and Bengallee, for the information of the people. They revoked all former Regulations, and ordered "that the office of judge of the several Provincial Courts be respectively held by that person who hath, or shall hereafter have, the charge of the revenue in each respective place."* On the same day a series of Regulations for the administration of justice in the Criminal Courts was passed by the Governor-General in Council. The Collectors, as under the Regulations of 1781, were empowered to act as magistrates in their several collectorates; but these powers were now to be extended. Before, the magistrates had been authorised only to apprehend and commit; now they were empowered "to hear and determine, without any reference to the Fouzdarry (or native criminal) Courts, all complaints or prosecutions brought before him for petty offences, such as abusive or calumny, inconsiderable assaults or affrays, and to punish the same, when proved, by corporal punishment, not exceeding fifteen rattans, or imprisonment not exceeding the term of fifteen days; but that in all classes affecting either the life or limbs of the party accused, or subjecting them to a greater punishment than that above specified, the cause be remitted as above prescribed to the hearing of the nearest Criminal Court." We were beginning to nibble at the administration of criminal justice; and it was not long before it passed bodily into our hands.

On the 3rd of December, 1790, a new series of Regulations was issued. The preamble set forth that "the

* Special exceptions were made of Moorshedabad, Patna, and Dacca.

numerous robberies, murders, and other enormities, which have been daily committed throughout the country, evinced that the administration of criminal justice was still in a very defective state," and that therefore the Governor-General in Council had determined "to resume the administration of criminal justice throughout the provinces." Courts of Circuit were accordingly created—four in number; three for the province of Bengal and one for the province of Behar—and over each of these Courts of Circuit were to be superintended by two covenanted civil servants of the Company, to be denominated Judges of the Court of Circuit. The Sudder Nizamut Adawlut, or chief criminal court, which was to be established in Calcutta, was to be presided over by the Governor-General and members of Council, who were to exercise all the powers lately vested in the Naib Nazim, or chief minister of justice.

But although the Mahomedan judges were thus removed from office, the Mahomedan law was still left supreme in the courts. One of the Regulations of the New Code emphatically ordered "that the decisions of the Court be in all cases regulated by the Mahomedan law."* The Mahomedan modes of punishment were, however, to be renounced. It has been seen that the Regulations of 1787 recognised the cruel punishment of mutilation, which was practised in the Fouzdarry Courts a quarter of a century after we became the rulers of the land. But on the 10th of October, 1791, Cornwallis ordained "that the punishment of mutilation shall not be inflicted on any criminal in future." Instead of the loss of two limbs, an offender was to be sentenced to fourteen years' imprisonment; and instead

* One or two exceptions were made, as for example that "the relations of a murdered man be debarred from pardoning the offender." But a subsequent Regulation modified this exception, and decreed that if the heir of the slain should pardon the murderer, sentence should not be passed by the Courts of Circuit, but the case forwarded to the Sudder, or chief court, at Calcutta.

of the loss of one limb, to be imprisoned and kept to hard labor for seven years.

But the time was now approaching when all these shifts and expedients were to give place to one definite and comprehensive system of judicial administration. The benevolent mind of Lord Cornwallis had long been brooding over the defects of the existing Regulations, and the discouraging results of all that had yet been done for the protection of the inhabitants of the British Provinces in Bengal. He believed that the establishment of the Courts of Circuit and the reorganisation of the Police had conferred substantial benefits upon the people. But it was painfully obvious that the Civil Courts, presided over as they then were by the revenue-officers, had been converted into instruments of oppression, and that the inhabitants of the provinces were groaning under the wrongs which had been inflicted upon them by officers in whom the fiscal and judicial authorities had been so unwisely combined, and who consummated in one capacity the injuries which they originated in the other.* There seemed, indeed, to be no remedy, in the existing state of things, for this great evil of unchecked power. The greater part of the people, it was clear, would rather submit to the

* "In these various capacities," said Lord Cornwallis, "there is not an individual in the district whose person or property is not, at some time or other, within the reach of his authority. Such power, vested in an individual, and at a great distance from the seat of supreme control, excites terror in the minds of the people instead of inspiring them with confidence in its protection; and as they can form no judgment of our government but as it is thus shown to them in our representative the collector, there is little encouragement for them when oppressed to rely upon our justice for relief. By the operation of these causes we are to account for whole provinces silently submitting for years to oppression and for the mal-administration of collectors having never reached the ear of Government, until despair getting the better of the terrors of power, the people flock to the Presidency to impeach their oppressor. When the complaint has been brought before the Government, what is the result? If the inquiry into the conduct of the offender is to be made on the spot, there is no court of justice in which it can be made. The offender himself is the sole and chief magistrate of the country. . . . If the inquiry is to be made in Calcutta, by whom is it to be conducted? The time of the supreme Government cannot be given up to a long and intricate investigation."—[*Minute of Lord Cornwallis, written by Mr. Barlow. MS. Records.*]

oppression than undertake the difficult and dangerous work of endeavoring to obtain redress.

With these facts before him—surrounded by wise counsellors—by the recommendation of some of the ablest servants of the Company, and with the encouraging approbation of the judges of the Supreme Court, Cornwallis determined to strike at the very root of the existing system. The first thing to be done was, "to vest the collection of the revenues and the administration of justice in separate officers." With a very different appreciation of the relative importance of the two offices, from that which obtains in the present day, he proposed to appoint the existing collectors judges of the Civil Courts,* whilst their head-assistants were appointed to the different collectorates, for which, said the Government minute, "they will be found sufficiently qualified."† At the cities of Moorshedabad, Dacca, Patna, and in the vicinity of Calcutta, Provincial Courts, each presided over by four judges, were to be established—their jurisdiction over the different collectorates to be co-extensive with that held by them as judges of the Courts of Circuit. A right of appeal to these Courts was to lie from the several district Courts, and from them again, in civil business, to the Sudder Dewanny Adawlut, or Chief Civil Court at Calcutta, and in criminal business to the Sudder Nizamut Adawlut, or Chief Criminal Court. In order

* The judges of these Courts were also to be magistrates in their respective districts.

† I think that some of the joint remarks of Cornwallis and Barlow on the degradation of the judicial office, may be read with advantage at the present time: "The administration of justice was considered as a subordinate duty attached to the office of collector of the revenues. To this day, all Regulations respecting the administration of justice were passed in the revenue-department, although no two departments of Government can be more unconnected than finance and the administration of justice—nor can any reasons be assigned why the name and business of the one should be merged in the other. Consistently with the same principles all salaries and emoluments continue to be annexed to the office of collector of the revenue. The collector receives no salary as judge of the Court of Justice, or as magistrate of the district. These two offices are considered as appendages to that of collector, and the duties of the two former offices stand still whenever they interfere with those of the latter."—[*MS. Records.*]

to expedite the gaol-deliveries, two of the judges were to take one-half of the division, and the two others the other half, and thus, it was said, "the duties of the Circuit would be rendered easy to them, and leave ample time for the discharge of the duties of a Civil Court."* The judgeships, so established, were to be considered appointments "the first in importance in the civil service."—"The persons selected to fill them," it was added, "should be distinguished for their integrity, abilities, and knowledge of the manners, customs, and languages of the natives, and their allowances should be proportionate to the greatness of their trust."† The judges of these Courts were also to be judges of Circuit.

Such was the new constitution of the Company's civil service. But the judicial reforms of Lord Cornwallis were not confined to this redistribution of the different agencies for the internal administration of the country. I have shown how keenly alive he was to the evils of that uncontrolled exercise of power, on the part of the European functionary, which placed the native suitor naked and bleeding at his feet. Eager to remedy this great evil—to give the native inhabitants of the provinces the means of redress against all arbitrary exactions and illegal usurpation of authority, he proposed that "native individuals should be permitted, under certain restrictions, to prosecute the officers of justice in the Courts of justice, for injuries which they may sustain in their persons and properties in opposition to the existing regulations."

Having defined the agency to be employed in the administration of justice, Cornwallis turned his attention to the great subject of Codification. Whether

* *Cornwallis' Minute. MS.*

† It was natural that the elevation of the judicial character should have given great satisfaction to the judges of the Supreme Court. On the margin of that part of the minute, which sketched these Courts of Appeal, and the dignity which was to attach to the office of judge, Sir William J. wrote: "This system is so perfect that I cannot suggest any material addition to it."

they were "laws," or whether they were "regulations,"* which were now to be passed by the supreme authority in India, there was no one point on which Cornwallis and his advisers felt more strongly, than on the necessity of giving them permanent expression and substantial shape, for the guidance alike of those who were to administer and those who were to appeal to them. The Regulations were to be numbered, arranged, printed, and circulated. They were to have a home in every Government office, and to be transmitted to the authorities in England. Hitherto they had existed partly in manuscript, partly in a printed shape, on detached slips of paper, to be lost with the greatest ease and consulted with the greatest difficulty. All this was now to be reformed. And in order that the greatest possible amount of knowledge, experience, and legislative ability might be brought to bear upon the framing of these Regulations, the Company's servants were to be invited to send in their suggestions through the authorised channels, and point out the expediency of making new additions to the code, or modifying and amending any of its existing provisions. Order and regularity were to be substituted for perplexity and confusion, and instead of an exclusive unintelligible system, there was to be one seeking the largest possible publicity, inviting discussion, and coveting the ready comprehension of the people for whose welfare it was designed.

In all honesty and sincerity this was sought. But it was not in all respects attained. Nothing could have been more simple than the original design of this great judicial reformation; but when it came to be moulded into shape, when the great principles for which Cornwallis and Barlow contended came to be shaped and fashioned into Regulations, they lost much

* See *ante*, pages 91-2-3, for the cotemporary discussions on this subject.

of their original simplicity, and were encumbered with perplexing details. An over-anxiety to improve and perfect may have led to the complication of forms of procedure, and what was designed to give full effect to the protective machinery, to some extent, may have embarrassed its action, encumbered its movements, and restricted its utility. But I cannot think otherwise than that it was a great work, and that to admit the existence of some practical defects, is only to admit its humanity.

It is no new thing—it is nothing peculiar to Bengal that justice should defeat its own ends—that the very earnestness and laboriousness of its efforts should recoil upon itself. In two ways now, was this observable. That justice should be cheap and the judgment-seat accessible, are two of the first essentials of a pure judicial system, and Cornwallis endeavored to secure both the accessibility and the cheapness of the Courts. But he did this for the benefit of a people out of measure addicted to litigation; and it soon followed that the number of suitors so blocked up the doors of the Court, that the judge was not accessible to the most clamorous, and justice was not attainable at any cost. It seemed, too, that the new English judges, eager to administer the law strictly and conscientiously according to the Regulations, and to observe all the prescribed formalities, brought so few cases to an issue, that business accumulated fearfully upon their files, and the people wrung their hands in despair to think what a laggard was English justice with the weight of the Regulations on its back. In good truth it could not keep pace with the litigiousness of the native character. And so it happened that the very measures which seemed to entitle our administrators to the gratitude of the people, worked grievously to their hurt.

It then appeared that justice was too cheap, and

that our Courts were too accessible. A supposed remedy lay very close at hand. Its application has been severely condemned. It was proposed to make justice dearer, and, therefore, the Courts less accessible, by taxing litigation and so frightening suitors from their doors. The old system of the deposit-fee on the institution of a suit was revived,* and for a time this measure seemed to have the desired effect. But although the subordinate judicial agency had been greatly increased by the authorisation of the Registers of the Courts to determine suits, and the appointment of duly qualified natives† to decide on disputes of small amount, the accumulation of business was only temporarily kept down; and it was found, at the beginning of the new century, that such was the enormous number of undecided cases on the files, that many of the suitors must wait years for a decision; and in one district it was said that in the ordinary course of events some of them would hardly live to witness the adjudication of their suits.‡ The evil was always admitted—always striven against. The judicial agency was from time to time increased; but still justice was in arrears. The judges despatched a greater amount of business, but still there was an accumulation. The fatal tendency of the people of India to rush into the meshes of the law was not to be repressed.§

* And subsequently by a Regulation requiring that, in all but the lowest courts, law proceedings should only be valid when written on paper bearing the Government stamp.

† Known as "Commissioners," afterwards as Moonsiffs.

‡ It appears that the number of causes depending on the 1st of January, 1802, before the five Courts of Appeal was, 882; before the judges of the twenty-eight City and Zillah Courts 12,262; before the registers of the last-mentioned courts 17,906; and before the native commissioners 131,921. It appears further, that the number of causes which had been decided in the course of the preceding period (from 1793) was, in the Courts of Appeal, 667; by the City and Zillah judges, 8298; by their registers, 14,124; and by the native commissioners, 328,064.

§ In 1810, the Committee of the House of Commons, in their fifth report, said, that up to that time the evil had little abated; but that credit was due to the European functionaries for what they had done; and added that, "in comparison with what is commonly experienced in Europe, the advantage in point of despatch would probably be found to be in favor of the courts of India.

The accumulation of undecided causes was, doubtless, a great evil. But there was evil, too, in the haste with which, at a subsequent period, efforts were made to keep down the accumulation. There was a tendency to estimate the zeal and efficiency of our judicial officers, not by the soundness of their decisions, but by the number of them. Men decided a certain number of suits and the official returns showed that they were not inactive. This foot-rule system, encouraged by the higher authorities, who applied so false a test to the efficiency of their officers, doubtless bore bad fruit in its day. Thus ever whilst endeavoring to avoid one evil we fell into another. Even the stamp system, which was intended to suppress unjust litigation, had a tendency to foster injustice. The stamp gave a sort of respectability and validity to all the proceedings that it covered. It seemed to have the Regulations inscribed on it, and it carried men through a world of chicanery and fraud—often of violence and oppression.* Indeed, this outside show of the Regulations covered a multitude of sins. Men of weak judgments and indolent habits were apt to become mere formalists under their shadow, and never to give a thought to anything beyond the letter of the written law. But I am not sure that this is peculiar to our possessions beyond the seas.

Of the immediate results of our new system of criminal justice something must be said before I pass on to consider the general effect of the Cornwallis system, and the changes which were subsequently introduced. When our European functionaries were first

* "I remember," writes a friend to me, "a case, and I almost blush in my closet to write it down, where a magistrate, being called upon to justify his conduct in having allowed numbers of respectable men to be arrested and brought into the station on charges preferred by a set of men known to be professional Goindahs, or informers, said in his reply, 'What could I do? The complaints were all written on duly stamped 8-anna paper, and the process issued on each was precisely that enjoined by the Regulations, and no more.'"

brought face to face with the crime of the country they were startled by the hideousness of the picture that presented itself, and believed that the inhabitants of India were the most demoralised people in the world. The sketches of national character, which appear in the answers returned to the interrogatories circulated in 1802 to the judges and magistrates, are limned with so harsh a pencil, that we must believe either that they were grossly exaggerated, or that the people have greatly improved.* When asked what had been the effect of our system upon the moral character of the people, they answered that it had been various—partly advantageous, partly disadvantageous; but that the balance was in favor of the former. Sir Henry Strachey, whose authority is usually cited against the Cornwallis Regulations, declared that violence of all kinds, except Dakoitee, had diminished, and that the poor looked up to the law for protection as they had never done before.† To the question whether the number of crimes had diminished since 1793, the most conflicting answers were returned. Some said that they had increased, others that they had diminished; and the causes both of the asserted increase and decrease were almost as various as the respondents. All, however, seemed to agree that Dakoitee had not

* Take, for example, the following, from the evidence of Mr. Paterson, of Dacca:—"Their minds are totally uncultivated; of the duties of morality they have no idea. They possess in a great degree that low cunning which generally accompanies depravity of heart. They are indolent, and grossly sensual. They are cruel and cowardly, insolent and abject. They have superstition without a sense of religion; and, in short, they have all the vices of savage life without any of its virtues."

† "In my opinion," he said, "the system has little direct influence on the morals of the people. They are, probably, somewhat more licentious than formerly. Chicanery, subornation, fraud and perjury, are certainly more common." But he added, "Oppression, cruelty, violence of all sorts, except that of Dakoits, are grown much less frequent. The ill-treatment of women, of servants, of slaves, have nearly ceased. The same may be said of the corporal severities formerly exercised in collecting the revenues. The poor look up to the laws, and not as heretofore, to a patron for protection."

diminished; and many attributed this to the complicity of the police. One gentleman replied that the leniency of the British Government was not at all calculated "to ameliorate the moral character of men so prone to vice, and ready to take advantage of every species of liberty granted to them.*

As represented by figured statements, the results of the new judicial system, during the first ten years of its operation, do not wear a very favourable complexion. But these figured statements scarcely afford a fair test of the results of our administration. It was generally admitted by the Company's judicial officers that the country had improved under our rule†—that popula-

* *Answers to Interrogatories.*—A selection from these was published in the Appendix to the Fifth Report. I quote from a complete set in MS.

† Take a few of the answers to interrogatories. Mr. Webb, of Shahabad, emphatically answered—"The district is in a state of improvement in every particular. I found my opinion on experience. I have no particular facts; the improvement is too notorious to require them." Mr. Paterson, of Dacca, answered—"When I look back to the effect of the famine in 1787, I cannot but conclude that the district is in a state of improvement with respect to cultivation and population." Mr. Paterson added: "There are, however, large tracts of the Zillah which still show the effect of the above-mentioned famine—and which from the vast depopulation occasioned by that scourge are so overrun with jungle and annoyed with elephants and other wild beasts, that they have become almost deserts." Mr. Wordsworth, of Rungpore, answered—"I am of opinion that the population of the district under my jurisdiction has increased considerably of late years, and that cultivation has been greatly extended within these last six years."

Some of the answers to the following question are still more significant:

"Are you of opinion that the inhabitants in general of the city under your jurisdiction, consider their private rights and property secured by the present constitution of the country against infringement, either by the executive officers of Government, or even by the supreme executive authority itself, or by individuals?

Mr. Webb, of Shahabad, briefly answered: "In my opinion they do."—Mr. Paterson, of Dacca, answered: "Those who frequent the Courts of Justice, or who by their connexions with those who do, and are enabled to form a judgment of the principles on which the regulations are framed, acknowledge the security of their private rights and property. Those who have not that intercourse (which is the greater mass of the people) still entertain their old jealousies and prejudices, nor will it be easy to inspire them with confidence in that security, which the institutions of the Government are intended to afford, as they have no idea of power, but what is absolute and arbitrary; and under that notion, consider the regulations of the Government as temporary only—liable to be rescinded and altered at pleasure by the same authority which enacted them. It must require a long experience to change these sentiments. The idea of a supreme executive authority prescribing laws and limits for itself, is not easily conceived by them."—Mr. Wordsworth, of Rungpore, made answer: "I am clearly of opinion that the inhabitants

tion and cultivation had increased, and that there was a greater sense of the security both of life and property under our administration, than under that of the Mogul. Such a system as that introduced by Cornwallis and Barlow was not to be tested by a trial of a few years. Such as it was, it lasted without any material modifications for nearly forty years, and it is not easy to believe that where there has been any departure from its leading principles, the change has contributed to the happiness of the people.*

All through the administrations of Lord Wellesley—of Sir George Barlow—of Lord Minto—of Lord Hastings, and of Lord Amherst, the Cornwallis system of internal administration continued in force, only with such modifications as the mutations of time and circumstance naturally engrafted upon it. But in 1828, Lord William Bentinck arrived in India. Of all the Governors who succeeded Cornwallis, he most resembled that benevolent and upright statesman. As Cornwallis was a reformer, so was Bentinck. He had abundant time to devote himself to measures of domestic improvement, for no miserable war was sitting like a curse upon his arm and paralysing his administrative energies. No honester man ever went out to India; and no man ever addressed himself to the solution of difficult problems of government, and the initiation of dangerous experiments with a larger

in general of the district under my jurisdiction, consider their private rights and property to be secured by the present constitution of the country against infringement, either by the executive officers of Government, or even by the supreme executive authority."

* Not to interrupt the continuity of the narrative, I may state here that the Mayor's Court of Madras was abolished in 1797, when, under 37th George III., chapter 142, a Recorder's Court was established. This, however, was but short-lived; and, under 39th and 40th George III., chapter 79, the Supreme Court of Madras was established three years afterwards. The Supreme Court of Bombay was not erected until 1823, under Act 4th George IV., chapter 71, when the Recorder's Court was abolished. In respect of the Company's courts, the Bengal system has been substantially followed in all places subject to the Regulations. The local variations scarcely call for detailed notice.

amount of moral courage. Of some of the acts, which have most rendered his administration illustrious, as the suppression of Suttee, and the extension of Native Agency I shall speak at another time. I have here only to do with the changes which he introduced into the judicial system of the country. These changes were great and sweeping.

He abolished the Provincial Courts.* These Courts, it must be acknowledged, had, in progress of time, sunk into something very different from what Cornwallis and Barlow had contemplated in their erection. It has been seen how eager they were to raise the dignity of the judicial character—to appoint to these Provincial Courts some of the ablest men in the country. And yet Lord William Bentinck spoke of them "as resting-places for those members of the service who were deemed unfit for higher responsibilities." The fact is that the revenue branch of the service, under successive administrations, had been gradually treading down the judicial. The very evil which Cornwallis and Barlow had sketched so forcibly in their inaugural minute had been asserting itself, with progressive virulence, ever since their removal from the scene of their labors. And now Lord William Bentinck found the Provincial Courts of Appeal and Circuit, which were to have been objects of ambition to the ablest and best men of the Company's civil service, little better than refuges for the destitute and incapable.

I do not doubt that under this degradation of the judicial service, the Provincial Courts had become wofully inefficient. They required picked men to render them efficient, and they had been presided over

* The Provincial Courts of Appeal and Courts of Circuit, in the Madras Presidency, were not abolished till some time afterwards.

by the refuse.* As Courts of Circuit they were especially defective. They held a gaol-delivery twice in every year. The period between commitment and trial was infinitely too long. The prisoner was kept, unjustly, perhaps, for months in confinement, and the prosecutor and his witnesses were carried away from their homes, to eat their hearts out around the walls of the Court-house, whilst all their affairs were being engulfed in ruin. Any measure, the effect of which was to increase the number of gaol-deliveries, could not fail to be a blessing to the people.

This Lord William Bentinck accomplished. But he did much more than this. He struck at the very root of the system which Cornwallis had initiated, not merely at the mode of procedure. It was a great thing to increase the number of gaol-deliveries, but it was not necessary to this end that the functions of the judge and the tax-gatherer should again be combined in the same person. Lord William Bentinck abolished the Provincial Courts, and turned the Revenue Commissioners into Judges of Circuit. They were to superintend both the finance and the criminal justice of their different divisions. They were to look after the Company's coin, and they were to sit in judgment upon gang-robberies—a blending of Somerset House and the Old Bailey.

I need hardly say that this plan was not a successful one. Some of the ablest and most experienced members of the Court of Directors protested against it; and Lord William Bentinck himself soon found that it was a mistake. So he transferred the duties of the Sessions to the civil judges, and decreed that they

* It is probable, also, that the minds of these provincial judges had a tendency to deteriorate, under a system which made them little magnates in their several divisions, perhaps at variance with one another, and each clinging to his own prejudices, without a chance of having them rubbed off by a contact with superior intelligence. I am indebted for this suggestion to an intelligent and experienced friend.

should hold a gaol-delivery every month. There was no objection to this arrangement, provided that the judges had sufficient time for the due discharge of the circuit duties without neglecting their other obligations, and if their new duties were compatible with the old. But this was not the case. The civil judges, under the existing system, were also the magistrates. It was necessary, therefore, to divest them of their magisteral duties. So another class of functionaries was to be found to take up these dropped responsibilities; and, accordingly, they were flung to the collectors. The warmest admirers of Lord William Bentinck and his system admit that this was a mistake. The new arrangement worked as badly as could have been expected, and few reasonable men could have predicated anything but failure as the result. The office of thief-catcher was of course postponed to that of the financier; and the department of Police was the worst regulated of any branch of the administration. The whole system, indeed, was that of the degradation of the office which ought to have been dignified and exalted. But instead of this, by the reversal of the Cornwallis system, the protection of life and property was declared to be a matter of minor importance, and the responsibilities of the criminal judge and the police magistrate were flung about from one class of public functionaries to another, as though it mattered not by whom they were assumed as an appendage to other graver duties.

But there were other reforms instituted by Lord William Bentinck of which too much cannot be said in praise. When Lord Cornwallis projected his scheme of internal administration, he had to look no further than Benares for the limit of its field of operation. Lord William Bentinck found an empire extending nearly to the Sutlej; and yet there was but one Court of final Appeal throughout the whole Presidency of Bengal. Suitors had to travel a thousand miles in search of justice, to brave a new climate and mix with a new race of men. It could not, therefore, be other than a blessing to the people to establish a Court of Appeal in the North-West Provinces of India. Lord William Bentinck erected a Sudder Court at Allahabad, to which appeals lay from all the local judges. And he relieved the pressure upon those judges by an extension of native judicial agency and the enlargement of the authority of the native servants of the State.

The enlargement of the judicial machinery of the country, by means of an extension of Native Agency, had been for some years contemplated by the Court of Directors. As far back as the year 1824, they had written:

> "We are satisfied that to secure a prompt administration of justice to the natives of India in civil cases, native functionaries must be multiplied, so as to enable them to dispose, in the first instance, of all suits of that description, and, as appears to us, without regard to the amount at stake, their decisions being, of course, liable to revision under appeal, where this check may be deemed indispensable; and what, perhaps, is of no less importance, their general conduct being subject to a constant and vigilant supervision on the part of the European functionaries in the districts where they are stationed. It should be the duty of the latter not only to hear appeals, but to inquire into and report to Government periodically, on the efficiency of the native agents employed more immediately under their eyes, and the degree of estimation in which they are held by the community; whilst it should equally be the care of Government to reward the deserving, and to testify, in the most marked manner, its displeasure against persons of an opposite character."

The wishes thus clearly expressed were subsequently many times repeated; but it was not until the year 1831, that, under the administration of Lord William Bentinck, any steps were taken in India to give effect to the recommendations of the Court. Then, for the first time, the claims of the people of the country to a due participation in the duties and emoluments of public employment were publicly recognised. Lord William Bentinck placed in their hands a large share of the judicial duties of the country, and there is no doubt that thereby the effective working of the machinery of justice was greatly improved.

I shall speak of this important subject more generally in another place. I have here only to do with its effects upon public justice. In 1831, a higher grade of native judgeships was established. Previous to that period there had been but two classes of native judges, with very limited powers and very small salaries. The higher class was known as "Sudder Aumeens," the lower as "Moonsiffs." The Moonsiffs, originally denominated "Commissioners," had been appointed by Lord Cornwallis to relieve the pressure on the European judges. In 1793 they were empowered to determine suits relating to accounts not exceeding 50 rupees. In 1803, the office of Sudder Aumeen was instituted, with a jurisdiction extending to suits of 100 rupees. In 1821, after some intermediate enlargement of the powers of both classes, the Moonsiffs had been empowered to try suits extending to 150 rupees, whilst the Sudder Aumeen took cognisance of cases to the amount of 500 rupees. In 1827, the authority in the latter case had been doubled, and the Sudder Aumeen, if so empowered by the Sudder Court, had jurisdiction over cases extending to 1000 rupees.

Lord William Bentinck now established a superior class of judicial officers, known as "Principal Sudder Aumeens," with enlarged powers and higher salaries. They were subsequently authorised to try cases involving property to any amount; and an appeal lay from them to the European judges. The highest salary of these officers was 720*l.* a year—a sum not to be estimated according to our English ideas of income, but to the requirements of the natives of India and the general wages of the country.

The machinery of civil justice having thus been greatly enlarged, the expediency also of a more extensive employment of uncovenanted agency in the criminal branch of the judicial department, forced itself on the minds of our administrators. But it was not until the year 1843, that an act was passed by the Legislative Council, reciting that the exigencies of the public service required that this department should be strengthened by a larger employment of uncovenanted agency, and empowering both the Bengal and Agra Governments to appoint in any Zillah or district one or more uncovenanted deputy-magistrates. Under this act several excellent public officers have been appointed, selected from all classes of society—Europeans, natives, and men of mixed blood. The local Governments are authorised to confer full magisterial powers on these officers, and the authority has sometimes been exercised with good effect.

About this time a further attempt was made to improve the general efficiency of the machinery of criminal justice, by the elevation of the superior native police-officers, known as "Darogahs."* Their

* The duties of the Darogah are thus briefly stated: "On the receipt of information by the Darogah of the occurrence of a heinous offence, he is required to submit a notice thereof to the magistrate, and proceed himself to the spot, to hold a preliminary investigation. On his arrival he sends for the prosecutor or aggrieved party, takes concisely his deposition and the deposition of his witnesses, and makes such inquiries as may appear to him proper, and, if the case be proved, forwards his proceedings, together with the defendant, to take his trial before the magistrate. In cases of simple burglary and theft, the Darogah is forbidden to hold any investigation, unless a petition is presented to him by the injured party, or he be ordered to do so by the magis-

salaries, which had been inexpediently low, were now considerably raised. But they still continued inadequate to the required end; and the department of police still demanded the most vigilant superintendence of the European officer to restrain it from becoming a mighty engine of injustice and oppression. From the very first our administrators had contended in vain against this gigantic evil, the evil of a corrupt police—a police continually in league with the greatest criminals in the country, receiving their pay, sharing their spoils, screening their offences, and probably carrying off innocent men to the magistrate's court in their stead. From the time when, in 1792, Lord Cornwallis, declaring "the establishment of an efficient police throughout the country, whereby offenders may be deprived of all hopes of eluding the pursuit of the officers of justice," to be "as essential towards deterring people from committing crimes, as the speedy and impartial trial of offenders when apprehended," had taken the management of the police immediately into Government hands, we have been endeavouring to secure the services of a well-organised detective force; but continually acknowledging that this very Police is the weakest point of our administration. If the remedy had been as apparent as the disease we should soon have eradicated the latter. But crime in India was so vast, and its organisation so intricate, that it seemed hopeless to construct out of such materials a police force really effective for the protection of the country. We had, indeed, to contend against difficulties unknown in this country. To convey to the untravelled reader some idea of what these difficulties were, and at the same time to show how our officers have endeavoured to overcome them,

trate."—[*Calcutta Review.*] This prohibition, which may appear strange to the European eye, was intended by Lord William Bentinck to check the venality and oppressiveness of the police, who turned these inquiries to purposes of extortion.

I proceed now to the consideration of some of those great crimes, which from generation to generation have rendered both life and property frightfully insecure in India, and of the efforts which, under British administration, have been made for their suppression. I do not know that there is any subject to which, in such a work as this, ampler space should be devoted than to THUGGEE and DAKOITEE.

CHAPTER II.

Thuggee—Increased Knowledge of the Habits of the People—Its Results—Antiquity of Thuggee—Its Progress—Manners and Customs of the Thugs—Thuggee Expeditions—Efforts for the Suppression of Thuggee—The Thuggee Department—Colonel Sleeman and his Associates—Complicity of the Zemindars—Success of our Efforts—Decrease of the Crime.

THERE is nothing more remarkable in our recent connexion with the East than our increased knowledge of the manners and customs, the literature and the religion, the vices and the virtues, of the people. We had been nearly two centuries connected with them, by ties at least of commerce, before we knew very much more about the natives of India than that they were a race of black people, with bare legs, carrying the greater amount of their apparel piled up on the top of their heads. We looked upon them for a great number of years simply as a people to be trafficked with—a people with whom it was our mission to drive hard bargains for muslin or silk. In time we came to look upon them as a people to be subdued; and then, having subdued them, we began to regard our dusky subjects as so many millions of revenue-payers—people from whom it was our duty to extract so much in the shape of rent or taxes in recognition of their subjection. Then, after another lapse of years, we looked upon them as a people to be governed. We invented, as has been seen, new codes of laws for their restraint and correction, and we did our best, whilst keeping them in order, to protect their properties and their lives. But it is only within very recent times that we have thought it worth our while to *know* anything about the natives of India, and to turn our knowledge to profitable account.

The study of books in India preceded the study of men. Learned orientalists, at the close of the last century, took counsel with the Pundits and Moulavees, and wrote elaborate dissertations upon the Hindoo and Mahomedan codes and scriptures, which they diligently translated for the benefit of the Christian world. From these ancient authorities they derived a vast deal of very recondite information, which did not, however, in our commerce with the people, prove to be of much use. That which, perhaps, we most required to know was not set down in these books. It was not, indeed, set down anywhere in written characters; but it was stamped, broadly and deeply—seemingly, indeed, ineffaceably—upon the heart of Indian society. It was not, however, of that kind which he who runs may read. It was not blazoned upon the mosques or inscribed upon the pagodas. An English traveller might make his way from one end of the country to the other and see nothing of the things with which it was so profitable to make permanent acquaintance. He acquired the scantiest possible knowledge of the habits and customs of the people. He passed through them, perhaps lived amongst them, but he only saw the surface of society. Perhaps he did not desire to look beneath the outer shell. Perhaps he beheld feebly some indications of hidden mysteries which he did not care to fathom. Certain it is, that he left much for his successors to drag into the clear light of day. We have much to learn even now. But honor is still due to our cotemporaries for what they have revealed — for what, by stubborn inquiries, by deep probings and subtle anatomisations, they have mastered, and comprehended, and exposed. Little was it that we could do for India until we knew something of the people whom Providence had committed to our care. How could we address ourselves to the remedy of the evils which were preying upon the vitals of Indian society, whilst we had no distinct understanding of what those corrosive evils were?

I do not write this in condemnation or reprehension of our predecessors on Indian soil. It was natural—almost necessary, indeed—that there should have been such short-comings as these. There are truths not to be arrived at except by long and patient induction. There are secrets buried deep beneath the surface which it is a work of time and toil to extricate from the deceptive clay which clings around them. Institutions, purposely veiled in darkness, of a strange, mysterious, almost incredible character, were likely to have escaped the notice of the European eye. It was long before we suspected the systematic war against life and property which had been carried on for years in almost every part of the country from Oude to the Carnatic. It was long before we could bring ourselves to understand that organised bands of professional and hereditary murderers and depredators, recognised, and indeed, to a certain extent tolerated by their fellow-men, were preying upon the uninitiated and unwary sections of society, and committing the most monstrous crimes with as much forethought and ingenuity as though murder were one of the fine arts, and robbery a becoming effort of human skill; nay, indeed, glorying in such achievements, as acts welcome to the deity, and bringing them to perfection with a due observance of all the ceremonial formalities of a cherished religious faith.

But in time we began to understand these things. We obtained a clue and we followed it up, until the hideous mystery was brought out into the clear light of day. There is not an intelligent reader at the present time who does not know what a *Thug* is. The word, indeed, has been adopted into our own language, and has been applied to other depredators than those who worship the Goddess Davee. It is well known that a Thug is a professional murderer. We found the Thugs carrying on their fearful trade, and as soon as we came to understand them we made war upon, and struck them down. The servants of the East India Company have extirpated Thuggee. It is an exploit worthy to be celebrated by every writer who undertakes to chronicle the achievements of the English in the East—one which it is impossible to dwell upon without pleasure and pride.

Of the antiquity of Thuggee there is no doubt. In the creed of its votaries it had, of course, a divine origin. Everything monstrous and abominable in India has the sanction of some puerile or obscene legend to recommend it to the superstitious and the depraved. The legend which declares the divinity of Thuggee is preposterous even for an Oriental tradition. I do not know a more absurd chapter in all that monstrous farrago of absurdities, the Hindoo mythology, than that which sets forth how the Goddess Kalee made war upon a gigantic monster, every drop of whose blood became a destructive demon; how the blood of these demons generated other demons, until the earth was in a fair way to be overrun by the noxious brood; how, at length, the goddess hit upon the notable expedient of creating from the celestial ichor which exuded from her trenchant arm two men, to whom she gave handkerchiefs, or waistbands, with orders to destroy the demons by strangulation without shedding a drop of blood; and how, the demons having been so destroyed, the grateful goddess gave the handkerchiefs to her myrmidons, and told them that thenceforth they and their descendants might carry on a profitable trade by exercising the destroying implements upon the human race. The Thugs, of course, claim to be descended from these unbegotten heroes, and are very proud of the descent. "I am a Thug of the royal records," said one of these professional stranglers; "I and my fathers have been Thugs for twenty generations."*

And what was this royal profession of which the members were so proud? It was simply the cowardly strangling of unsuspecting travellers in remote places, generally committed under circumstances of falsehood and treachery of the deepest dye. These Thugs, leagued together in a great brotherhood of crime, having taken the sacrament with all possible solemnity,† went about the country murdering in their cold bloodless style all the unwary wayfarers whom they could seduce into their toils. There was nothing to distinguish these artists from ordinary travellers. They assumed many different disguises, and played many different parts. They separated on the road, straggled into the towns and villages in little parties of three and four, and met as though they were strangers to each other. Perhaps one of the gang

* Thevenot, who travelled in India in the seventeenth century, has given an account of the Thugs, from which it appears that in those days they employed female decoys:—"Though the road I have been speaking of, from Delhi to Agra, be tolerable, yet hath it many inconveniences. One may meet with tigers, panthers, and lions upon it; and one had best also have a care of robbers, and above all things not to suffer anybody to come near one upon the road. The cunningest robbers in the world are in that country. They use a certain slip, with a running noose, which they can cast with so much sleight about a man's neck, when they are within reach of him, that they never fail, so that they strangle him in a trice. They have another cunning trick also to catch travellers: they send out a handsome woman upon the road, who, with her hair dishevelled, seems to be all in tears, sighing and complaining of some misfortune which she pretends has befallen her. Now, as she takes the same way that the traveller goes, he easily falls into conversation with her, and finding her beautiful, offers her his assistance, which she accepts; but he hath no sooner taken her up behind him on horseback than she throws the snare about his neck and strangles him, or at least stuns him, until the robbers, who lie hid, come running to her assistance, and complete what she hath begun."

† The sacred element was a kind of coarse sugar. According to the Thugs the deity entered largely into it, and there was a kind of transubstantiation, which wrought mightily upon the communicants. At all events, they declared that the sacred sugar changed their whole nature. "It would change the nature of a horse," they said. "Let any one once taste of that sugar and he will be a *Thug*, though he know all the trades and have all the wealth in the world." "My father made me taste of that fatal sugar," said a *Thug* to Colonel Sleeman, "when I was yet a mere boy; and if I were to live a thousand years, I should never be able to follow any other trade."

travelled in some state, as a man of rank, accompanied by numerous attendants, and a few palanquins or doolies, in which were said to be the ladies of his family, though in reality they contained little but the implements of their profession. On the road, so disguised, with nothing about them to awaken suspicion, these traders in death would fall, as though by accident, into the company of other wayfarers, and watching a favorable opportunity on the skirts of some jungle, or in some secluded place bordering upon a convenient watercourse, would throw the murderous waistband or turban-cloth round the neck of their victim, and scientifically do him to death. One man threw the fatal noose, another, seizing the other end of the rope or cloth, drew it tightly round the helpless wretch's neck, the two together pressing his head forward with their disengaged hands, whilst a third seized him by the legs and threw him to the ground. There could be no resistance. The work was quickly done. The body was then stripped, the property secured, and very soon the corpse was buried. The consecrated pickaxe, plied with miraculous silence, soon dug a grave for the body.* If a stranger approached whilst they were thus engaged, they laid a cloth decently and reverently over the carcase of the murdered man, and kneeling down beside it, lifted up their voices and wept, over the death of a beloved comrade.

Various were their artifices—great their cleverness. They were, indeed, consummate actors. If the locality were a dangerous one, the country much frequented,

* The pickaxe, forged with due solemnity, and then consecrated with certain prescribed formalities, was held in especial veneration by the Thugs. It was forbidden to bury the dead with any other instrument; for it was the symbol of their profession, and a legacy left, it was believed, by the goddess herself. "Do we not worship it," said a *Thug* to Colonel Sleeman, "every seventh day? Is it not our standard? Is its sound ever heard, when digging the grave, by any but a *Thug*? And can any man ever swear to a falsehood upon it?" Another asked, "How could we dig with any other instrument? This is the one appointed by Davee and consecrated; and we should never have survived the attempt to use any other."

they would throw up a slight enclosure of canvas, pretending that their women were behind the screens, and bury the body within it. Or, warned of the approach of travellers by one of their scouts, some clever member of the gang would throw himself down by the wayside, and simulate the spasms and convulsions, or the exhaustion and prostration of a dying man; and whilst the sympathising travellers were gathering round him and administering such simple remedies as were within their reach, his companions would conceal the body of their victim, and clear away the traces of their guilt. Sometimes the locality favored a readier and easier mode of disposing of the corpse, which was flung into a neighbouring river, or dropped into a convenient well.

Thus were these murders—systematically, artistically—perpetrated, with an adroit avoidance of detection which seldom or never failed. Human life in India is not of much account. A corpse by the wayside in England fills nearly a whole county with horror and astonishment. In India, even a humane English gentleman passes it by on the other side, and is only so far concerned at the spectacle, that probably his horse has shied at it, as it would at the trunk of a tree. Every one is accustomed to the sight of human bodies drifting down the river—floating islands inhabited by gorging birds of prey; or if you should chance to reside in a villa on the river-side, you are not concerned by the knowledge that the round white balls which dot your lawn like snow-flakes, or with which your little children are playing, are so many human skulls. Still less do the natives of India, by whom the European gentleman is infected, in due time, with this apathy, bestir themselves, body or soul, about these indications of our frail mortality. Death in India comes in many sudden shapes. If a certain Moodoo-sooden, or Rungoo-Lal, is missing from his accustomed place, or does not reach the end of a journey (should any one expect him), his anxious relatives take it for granted that he has been bitten by a serpent—that the cholera has preyed upon his vitals, or a wild beast has eaten him up. No descriptions of the missing one are inserted in the newspapers, and no members of the detective police are employed to discover the cause of his disappearance. Somehow or other he has been absorbed. "*Mur-gya*"—He has gone dead.

And so it happens that hundreds of natives of India disappear;* and their disappearance is either hardly noted, or it creates no astonishment or alarm. A journey in India is an affair of many months; and numerous are the perils which beset the path of the unprotected pedestrian. Hence it is that whole hecatombs were sacrificed to the Goddess Davee, and no one took account of the victims. Travellers likely to be missed were not especial objects of regard with the Thugs. They suffered such noticeable personages to pass on their way unheeded. Or, if tempted by the largeness of the spoil which glittered before them, they were betrayed into a departure from their ordinary cautious mode of procedure, they summoned to their aid something more than the common artifices of their profession, and surpassed themselves in cunning and skill. Sometimes the very envi-

* I ought rather to have written thousands. A correspondent in the Thuggee Department wrote me a few years ago: "In India hundreds of thousands disappear in a year or two, without the most distant clue but Thannadar's reports, to ascertain whether they have not been foully murdered. Villagers have assured me that to their own certain knowledge scores of men murdered by robbers, or in affrays, have been reported dead of cholera, snakebites," &c. It is not easy to arrive at a correct estimate of the number of people murdered annually by the Thugs. A native newspaper (the *Sumachar Durpan*) of great respectability, in 1833 declared that "one hundred *Thugs* slaughter, on an average, *eight hundred persons in a month.* It is not, therefore," added the writer, "going beyond the truth to affirm that, between the Nerbudda and the Sutlej, the number murdered every year is not less than ten thousand." The writer calculates that within these limits a hundred Thugs were always out on their murderous expeditions—probably many more were so employed. And this calculation only relates to a certain tract of country. I am inclined, however, to think that the individual performances of the Thugs is here somewhat overrated.

ronments of the marked man favored the escape of his murderer. The Thugs always knew their men. They never threw the noose without previously acquainting themselves with the circumstances of their victim. If they murdered a Company's Sepoy, on leave to his native village, carrying his savings wrapped up in his waistband, they knew that it would be long before he would be missed, either by his own family, or the adjutant of his regiment ; and that, if missed by the former, his disappearance would be attributed to ordinary death, or if by the latter, to desertion. If they murdered a confidential public or private servant, bearing treasure from one station to another, they knew that the absence of the man, or the party of men at the accustomed place, would be attributed to the dishonesty of the treasure-bearers; and that whilst the police, if set upon the track, were in search of him, they would be far away from the district through which his journey had lain. They took care to leave behind them no living witnesses of their guilt. If they hunted down a man of note, they destroyed all his attendants. They always went *forward ;* they never presented themselves in a town or village through which one of their victims had passed. So that even if they went on, riding the horses or wearing the clothes of the men they had murdered, their appearance excited no mistrust. They had always a ready story at command. They had always a given character to assume. They understood each other thoroughly, and they acted in concert, though often they appeared to be strangers. They had a secret dialect of their own ; but often more serviceable than this were the secret signs by which they silently communicated with each other. They played their parts, indeed, with consummate address ; and they passed on unsuspected to pursue their dreadful trade in the next convenient locality. For such localities they had keen and disciplined eyes, as artists have for the picturesque or sportsmen for good covers; and their faces sparkled and their hearts swelled when they chanced on these good murder-grounds.

It might seem from this account of the depredational excursions of these professional robbers, that they were men without a local habitation or a name, flitting from place to place, and never establishing for themselves such social connexions as were likely to cause their migrations to be matter of observance, or, indeed, to attract any kind of continued notice. But such was not, by any means, the case. They belonged for the most part to particular villages, where they left their wives and children; and they outwardly followed some peaceful calling. They cultivated the fields—rented a few acres of ground—or, perhaps, embarked as agriculturists on a larger scale, and employed laboring men to work under them.* Their occasional absence from the village was necessarily remarked. Sometimes the real cause was not suspected; but often it was a matter of open notoriety. A Thug set out on his dreadful journey, and every one in the village knew the cause of his departure—except, perhaps, his own wife.

It was not, indeed, a matter of much concernment to the villagers that these migratory murderers should set out upon their journeys to remote places, and return richer than they went. They did not murder their neighbours. Indeed, the village directly benefited by the blood-money that was brought home. The Zemindar, or head man, had an immediate interest in the success

* Take from among many instances the following, from the evidence of Colonel Sleeman's approvers:—"I remained in my own house for about a year and a half at Guntoulee, working upon my own fields as a cultivator, for I rented 100 beegahs of land, and employed laborers; the villagers knew that I was a man who went from home occasionally, but they knew not that I was a murderer."—Again: "I remained in my own house for two months after this, cultivating in my fields, for I rented three or four beegahs of land, chiefly, however, as a blind to conceal that I was a Thug, and to make a show that I was a cultivator. I started again on Thuggee."

of the expedition. A certain amount of tribute, or hush-money, was always paid to him; and the police officials, in the same manner, were bribed into silence.* Often, indeed, the brothers, or other near relatives of the village police, were members of the Thug gangs; and Thugs themselves have been known to wear the official brass-plates on their breasts which stamped them as Government employés. The protection of the Zemindars often went the length, especially in the native states, of overt and violent interference, and pitched battles have been fought in defence of the tribute-paying criminals when extermination has threatened the gangs.† The payments made by the Thugs and other depredational leagues, of which I shall speak presently, formed no inconsiderable item of their revenue. They looked to it, indeed, as to a perennial source of income from which they could make good any deficiencies in the amount of the Government claim, and sometimes applied the screw with such freedom that the unhappy Thugs, alarmed by their increasing exactions, migrated altogether from the extortionate village, and sought a resting-place where they might dwell without disgorging so large a share of their murder-gotten wealth. At one time, it may be added, so openly was the traffic carried on, that merchants often came from a distance to purchase the plunder brought home by the migratory gangs; but it would seem that the extension of the Company's judicial machinery, and

* "I always," said one approver, "after my journey, was obliged to give the Zemindar, Ragonauth Sing, of my village, some present, for the whole village knew that I was a Thug, and the Zemindar would have had me put in irons but for these presents. All Thugs thus propitiate their Zemindars."

† "At last," said another approver, "being traced by the Saugor guards, the Gwalior Regent, Bayza Bhaee, was induced, at the suggestion of the British Agent, to send out a detachment of two companies of infantry to secure them. The head man of the village was determined to protect them, in consideration of the share of the booty they had always given him. An action took place, in which several lives were lost, while the camp of the Governor-General of India, Lord William Bentinck, and that of the Bayza Bhaee, were within hearing of the guns. The Thugs all made their escape, in disguise, with the women, but were soon after taken."

the greater vigilance of its officers, soon indicated the necessity of greater caution in the disposal of the spoil.*

It may be doubted whether any class of natives ever followed their peculiar avocations with a keener relish than these Thugs.† They were brought up from early youth to the dreadful trade. Thuggee was to them not merely a profession. It was a religion. They believed that the Goddess Davee smiled down upon their exploits, and communicated with them through the agency of certain recognised sights and sounds. They performed ceremonial rites in propitiation of the deity, and then looked eagerly for the anticipated omens. No augurs, in remote ages of classical antiquity, ever consulted the auspices with more solemn outward observances, or a firmer inward faith in the expected revelations. A larger range of deity-directed signals was, however, embraced in the code of these Eastern soothsayers. Men and women, of different kinds, and in different situations, were pressed into the service as omens, and various animals, wild and tame, were believed to have the same commission from the goddess. There seems to have been no harmony and consistency observed in the inter-

* The following, from a very interesting Report, by the late Captain Lowis, on River Thuggee, contains a very decided opinion on the subject of the complicity of all classes of the village communities:—"To conclude, there seems no doubt that this horrid crime has been fostered by nearly all classes of the community—the landholders, the native officers of our courts, the police, the village authorities—all, I think, have been more or less guilty. My meaning is not, of course, that every member of these classes, but that individuals, varying in number in each class, were concerned. The Foujdaree police gomastahs have, in many instances, been practising Thugs; and the chowkedars, or village watchmen, frequently so. It is much to be feared that men so respectable in position as to make it seem almost incredible that they should give protection to such criminals, have, in fact, done so, for it appears out of the question that the total population of a village should be Thugs engaged in the regular practice of Thuggee, and several of them frequently apprehended on the gravest suspicion of that crime, without the cognisance of the Zemindars."

† I have alighted upon only one statement which militates against this general assertion, and, perhaps "proves the rule." A Thug, named Dhosoo, examined by Captain Paton, at Lucknow, declared "we only thug from necessity, not from pleasure—it is fearful business." But I could pile up proofs of the relish with which they pursued their trade.

preting of these divine manifestations. Thus a lame man and a dancing-master—a potter and an oil-seller, were equally unpropitious. Of the brute creation, the donkey and the jackal were regarded as the most important members, and various were the sights or sounds of encouragement, or warning, eagerly looked for from the unconscious beasts. Certain months of the year, and certain days of the week, were proscribed as of ill omen; and it was necessary that they should regulate both their diet and their toilet in the manner of which Davee was supposed to approve. If they were fortunate, they ascribed all their good fortune to a due regard of these heavenly directions, and if misadventure befel them, they attributed it, with praiseworthy candor, to their own misinterpretations, or neglect of the omens through which the goddess had frequently vouchsafed to make known her wishes to her people. "Even the most sensible approvers," writes Colonel Sleeman, "who have been with me for many years, as well Mussulmans as Hindoos, believe that their good or ill success always depended upon the skill with which their omens were discovered and interpreted, and the strictness with which they were observed and obeyed. One of the old Sindouse stock told me in presence of twelve others, from Hyderabad, Behar, the Dooab, Oude, Rajpootana, and Bundelcund, that had they not attended to these omens they could never have thrived as they did; and that in ordinary cases of murder a man seldom escaped after one of them; while they and their families had for ten generations striven, though they had murdered hundreds of people. 'This,' said he, 'could never have been the case had we not attended to omens, and had not omens been intended for us.' Every Thug present concurred with him from his soul."

When once the omens had shown themselves to be

propitious, and Davee had smiled down upon the enterprise, murder became not only a religious duty, but a pleasant task. No compunctions then visited the enlightened Thug. "And do you never feel sympathy for the persons murdered—never pity or compunction?" asked Colonel Sleeman of a Thug, who had turned approver. "Never," was the answer. "How can you," pursued the English officer, "murder old men and young children, without some emotions of pity—calmly and deliberately as they sit with you, and converse with you—and tell you of their private affairs—of their hopes and fears—and of the wives and children they are going to meet, after years of absence, toil, and suffering?" And the answer returned was: "From the time that the omens have been favorable, we consider them as victims thrown into our hands by the deity to be killed, and that we are the mere instrument in her hands to destroy them; that if we do not kill them, she will never be again propitious to us, and we and our families will be involved in misery and want." "And," questioned Colonel Sleeman, "you can sleep as soundly by the bodies, or over the graves of those you have murdered, and eat your meals with as much appetite as ever?" And still the answer was: "Just the same—we sleep and eat just the same—unless we are afraid of being discovered." These last words do not indicate the fulness of faith which we should have expected to find in such a worshipper of Davee; for it was the professed belief of the Thugs, that if the omens were properly observed and interpreted, they never could be discovered.

Indeed, such was their confidence in the protective power of the goddess, that they believed that she would not only, if religiously served, shield them from harm, but visit with her wrath all who injured them. Nor was this belief confined exclusively to the Thugs Their ravages were regarded with something of superstitious awe even by influential chiefs. At least, such was the statement of the murderers themselves, and there is other evidence to support the supposition. When Colonel Sleeman asked an approver if he knew any instances of influential natives suffering for acts of enmity or opposition to the Thugs, he was answered: "A great many. Was not Nanha, the Rajah of Jhalone, made leprous by Davee for putting to death Bodhoo and his brother Khumoolee, two of the most noted Thugs of their day? He had them trampled under the feet of elephants, but the leprosy broke out upon his body the very next day." "Did he believe," asked Colonel Sleeman, "that this punishment was inflicted by Davee for putting them to death?" "He was quite sensible of it," was the answer. "Did he do anything to appease her?" was then asked. "Everything," replied the approver. "Bodhoo had begun a well in Jhalone; the Rajah built it up in magnificent style; he had a tomb raised to their name, fed Brahmins, and consecrated it; had worship instituted upon it—but all in vain; the disease was incurable, and the Rajah died in a few months a miserable death. The tomb and well are both kept up and visited by hundreds to this day, and no one doubts that the Rajah was punished for putting these two Thugs to death." This was but one of many instances which Colonel Sleeman's approvers were eager to relate. One man, when asked if he knew any other cases of the same kind, replied, "Hundreds! When Madhajee Scindiah caused seventy Thugs to be executed at Multoun, was he not warned in a dream by Davee that he should release them? and did he not the very day after their execution begin to spit blood? and did he not die within three months?" Then other witnesses were ready with other proofs of the omnipotence of Davee, and told how, when certain Rajpoot chiefs arrested eighty Thugs, all their families were afflicted, how they all perished, "not a child left;" and how one who had imposed the certain fines upon the gang, the very day that he took the money lost his only son, "and the best horse in his stable; and was himself taken ill, and died soon after a miserable death." But they all acknowledged that even Davee could not withstand the good fortune of the Company. "The Company's good fortune is such," they said, "that before the sound of your drums, sorcerers, witches, and demons take flight—and how can Thuggee stand?"

Thuggee did not stand—it fell. The great work of rooting out these monstrous depredational leagues was accomplished in a few years by the energies of a few European officers. Up to the year 1829 but little had been done to suppress the abomination. Occasional evidences of the crime had presented themselves some years before, and a few gangs of professional murderers had been arrested. In 1810, General St. Leger, then Commander-in-Chief, issued an order cautioning the troops, especially the Sepoys, about to proceed on leave to their homes, against "a description of murderers denominated Thugs," who infested the districts of the Doab, and other parts of the Upper Provinces. About the same time some of the more active of our magistrates in Upper India had succeeded in securing the persons of a number of these murderers, but although several of them confessed, and the property of the murdered men was found in their houses, the higher judicial authorities did not consider that the evidence was sufficient to convict them. "Mr. Wright apprehended seventy-six, of whom seventeen made confessions which strongly criminated the remaining fifty-nine, who denied. Those who denied, and those who confessed, were alike released by one sweeping order from the Nizamut Adawlut without security or anything else;"* and sent back to carry

* *Letter from G. Stockwell, joint magistrate, Etawah, to T. Wauchope, magistrate, Bundelcund, December*, 1814.

on their old trade, emboldened by impunity and success.

These were but fitful efforts resulting in nothing. The subject excited little general interest, and no organised efforts, on an effective scale, were made to root out the enormous evil. Indeed, its extent was imperfectly known even to the best informed of our officers until about the time which I have indicated, under the government of Lord William Bentinck, operations were formally commenced, and a regular "Department" for the suppression of Thuggee instituted by that enlightened nobleman. And so vigorously was this great work prosecuted—with such remarkable intelligence, and such admirable perseverance were all our measures shaped, and all our projects executed—that, ten years afterwards, Colonel Sleeman, to whose benevolent energies we are, under Providence, mainly indebted for the success of the undertaking, was enabled to write:—"In 1830, Mr. George Swinton, who was then Chief Secretary to the Supreme Government of India, and our best support in the cause which Mr. F. C. Smith and I had undertaken, wrote to him to say that he feared success must be considered as altogether unattainable, for he had been given to understand by those who appeared to be well informed on the subject, that the evil had taken deep root in all parts of India, and extended itself to almost every village community. There were certainly at that time very few districts in India without these resident gangs of Thugs ; and in some, almost every village community was more or less tainted with the system, while there was not one district free from their depredations. No man aware of the fearful extent of the evil could ever have expected to see so much progress made in its suppression within so short a time ; because no man could have calculated on those many extraordinary combinations of circumstances upon which our success has chiefly depended—combinations which it behoves us gratefully to acknowledge, as Providential interpositions for the benefit of the people entrusted to our rule—interpositions which these people themselves firmly believe will never be wanting to rulers whose measures are honestly intended, and wisely designed for the good of their subjects."*

How this great work was accomplished is soon told. These vast criminal leagues had hitherto thriven upon the ignorance of the British authorities. We could do nothing to suppress them, for, indeed, we knew little or nothing about them. They were mighty secrets—hidden mysteries—dimly guessed at, not at all understood. But now Sleeman and his associates, resolved that this trade of Thuggee should no longer be any more a mystery than tailoring or carpentering, began to initiate themselves into all the secrets of the craft, and were soon, in their knowledge of the theory of the profession, little behind the professors themselves.

It need not be said that all this information was derived from frequent intercourse with the Thugs themselves. Our officers having apprehended some of these professional stranglers, selected the likeliest of the party, and by holding out to them promises, not only of pardon, but of employment, soon wormed their secrets out of them. In a little time Sleeman and his associates had learnt from these "approvers" all that was to be learnt from them—all the mysteries of their craft, the whole art of Thuggee—how the murder-gangs set out on their journey, how they propitiated the goddess, how they consulted the omens, how the victim was first beguiled, how the noose was thrown, how the body was buried—how they brought up their children to the trade, how generation after generation of Thugs lived prosperously and securely, and how it happened that the native chiefs

* *Sleeman.* Preface to published Report on the Depredations committed by the Thug gangs of Upper and Central India. Calcutta, 1840.

either protected or stood aloof from them, whilst the English were ignorant of their doings. Everything that these approvers, turning their backs for ever on Davee, and bowing down before the irresistible *ikbal* of the Company, now revealed—and they were tolerably loquacious in their revelations—was carefully noted down, and the statements of one informant collated with those of others. From these men Sleeman and his associates learnt not only the whole theory and practice of Thuggee, but gathered no small amount of knowledge concerning the gangs that were in actual operation, and the men who were connected with them. With such clues as the approvers afforded, it was now easy to hunt down the different gangs which were scattered over the country, and many large captures were made. New approvers were brought upon the lists of the "Department," and new gangs were hunted down. Many criminals were thus brought to trial, convicted, and sentenced either to be hanged, transported, or imprisoned.*

These captures struck terror into the hearts of the whole fraternity of Thugs. And far more terrible than the English officers, environed with the prestige of that irresistible ikbal of the Company, which was acknow-

* One or two extracts from Colonel Sleeman's Reports will suffice to convey an idea of the extent of these captures and their results:—"When they arrived at Dakhola, Captain Borthwick having heard of their proceedings, detached a party of horse to apprehend them. The horsemen came upon the gangs unawares, while encamped outside a village, and accused them of stealing opium; they were glad to have an opportunity of clearing themselves of this unfounded accusation, so accompanied the horsemen to the village for the purpose of being examined; immediately on their arrival they were secured and taken to Captain Borthwick, of whom seventy-nine were made prisoners—viz., five made approvers, seventy-four tried by Colonel Stewart (resident at Hyderabad), thirty-nine condemned to death, twenty-one to imprisonment for life, eleven to limited imprisonment, and three acquitted." Again: "Capt. Borthwick having received intelligence of the residence of these gangs, arranged for their apprehension as soon as a party of them returned from one of their excursions. He proceeded with Capt. Macmahon and about 200 of the Jhowrah cavalry, and came upon their villages before daylight, and so completely surrounded them that the capture of the whole gang was effected without the escape of a single individual—in all fifty-three Thugs; four of whom were made approvers, twenty-two executed, eleven transported, three sentenced to limited imprisonment, and thirteen released for want of evidence."

ledged to be too powerful for Davee to combat, and his well-armed, well-mounted followers, was the knowledge that their own brethren were turning against them, and that ever at the stirrup of the Thug-hunting Englishmen went one or more apostate members of their own murderous Guild. It was plain to them, now that all their secrets were revealed—that there was no safety any longer to be derived from the ignorance of the dominant power—that let them go where they might in the Company's territories, the Thug-led Thug-hunters would be upon their track. Some endeavouring to find in the neighbouring native states a fair field for their operations, or to obtain service under the native chiefs, fled hastily across the boundary-line; but there, too, the Philistines were upon them. English humanity was not brought to a stand at the confines of the country subject to our own regulations, and guarded by our own police. From Northern Oude to Southern Hyderabad our influence at the native Courts, and the labors of our political officers, produced the same results as in our own provinces; and even there some, hopeless of eventual escape, and weary of a life of unceasing anxiety, rushed into the presence of the English officer, flung themselves at his feet, and implored him to receive them as approvers.*

* Indeed the operations of our officers in the Deccan and in Oude do not constitute the least interesting chapter in the great history of Thuggee-suppression. There were greater difficulties to be overcome by those who operated in the native states—difficulties such as are here set forth by Captain Malcolm: "No analogy," he writes, "exists between the proceedings in the Thug Department within the territories of the Honorable Company, or any other well-regulated state, and those which are carried on in the Nizam's dominions, in which no system of police can be said to exist. In the former, the parties charged with this duty are armed with a warrant, before which the gates of every village are thrown open, and the police, if not aiding or furthering the object on which they are employed, dare not openly at any rate throw any obstacles in their way. In the Nizam's territory, however, the case is very different; a few of the principal Talookdars evince the greatest readiness to afford me prompt assistance whenever called on by Government to do so. Their authority, however, does not extend to the villages held on military and other rent-free tenures with which their districts are studded, and the Potails of which affect to attend to no orders but those emanating from their immediate superiors. The consequences frequently are, that when a Thug is traced into a village of this class, the gates are shut in the face of the pursuing party; or should they have been allowed to enter from igno-

But great as was the personal energy and ability brought to bear upon the suppression of the crime of Thuggee, it was hardly probable that our officers should have achieved complete success unless armed with peculiar powers—unless a certain relaxation of the law, warranted by the extraordinary character and the extreme enormity of the crime, had been legalised by the Supreme Government. For some years we had been trying men accused of Thuggee; but they had almost invariably escaped. It had been difficult, to a degree perhaps not readily appreciable by English lawyers or any other residents in this little island of Great Britain, to convict men, upon clear judicial evidence, of specific acts of Thuggee. The migratory character of the murder-gangs —the vast extent of country which they traversed—the number of local screens and fences—the difficulty of personal identification—the craft and subtlety of the offenders themselves—the unlimited amount of false swearing and of false impersonation which, at any time, they could bring into our criminal courts—were obstructions to the course of justice, under a strict interpretation of the existing law, which were seldom or never overcome. A timid or even a cautious—perhaps I ought to write a "conscientious" judge, would be sure to acquit even a notorious Thug for want of satisfactory evidence of the commission of a specific offence. Some of the causes which I have recited contributed largely, also, to the embarrassment of the question of jurisdiction. A murder was committed in one part of the country, and the murderers were apprehended in another, perhaps some hundreds of miles distant from the scene of the

rance of the object of their visit, the Government orders, when produced, are treated with the utmost contempt; and if the party do not quietly take their departure, they are generally forced to do so by the armed men stationed at the place on the part of the Jagheerdars, or by the armed villagers themselves. Serious collisions have in consequence arisen, in which several of my men have at times been severely wounded, and at others treated with the greatest indignity."—[*Captain Malcolm to Captain Reynolds. Preface to Captain Sleeman's Report.*]

atrocity. To limit the jurisdiction in such a case to the particular Zillah in which the crime was committed, was to throw up all sorts of difficulties and delays, and almost to ensure the prisoner's escape. These impediments to the strict and prompt administration of justice were wonderfully protective of Thuggee. The more complicated the machinery, and the more formal the procedure of our courts, the better for these professional stranglers. They throve upon the legal niceties and the judicial reserve of the English tribunals, and laughed our Regulations to scorn.

It was wisely determined, therefore, after due consideration by the supreme Government of India, to make the case of Thuggee an exceptional case, and to sanction a relaxed application of existing laws and regulations to members of the great fraternity of Thugs. Accordingly an Act was passed in 1836, by which a man convicted of belonging, or having belonged, to a gang of Thugs was rendered amenable to imprisonment for life, whilst at the same time, prisoners accused of Thuggee were made liable to the jurisdiction of any of the Company's Courts, without reference to the locality of the alleged offence, and the formality of the Mahomedan *Futwah* was dispensed with as a preliminary to the trial of this class of proscribed offenders.* The

* The act being conveniently short, I may as well give it in a note:

Act XXX., 1836. (1) "It is hereby enacted, that whatever shall be proved to have belonged, either before or after the passing of this Act, to any gang of Thugs, either within or without the territories of the East India Company, shall be punished with imprisonment for life with hard labor. (2) And it is hereby enacted, that every person accused of the offence made punishable by this Act, may be tried by any court, which would have been competent to try him, if his offence had been committed within the Zillah, where that court sits, anything to the contrary, in any Regulation contained, notwithstanding. (3) And it is hereby enacted, that no court shall, on a trial of any person accused of the offence made punishable by this Act, require any Futwah from any law officer."

A supplementary Act (No. XVIII. of 1837) decreed that "any person charged with murder by Thuggee, or with the offence of belonging to a gang of Thugs, made punishable by Act No. XXX. of 1836, may be committed by any magistrate, or joint magistrate, within the territories of the East India Company, for trial before any criminal court competent to try such person on such charge."

good effect of these enactments were soon felt. They were all that the Thuggee officers needed to enable them to carry out the great work which was placed in their hands. The strong defences of the Thug gangs were now struck down. They had no longer our ignorance on the one side, and our judicial over-scrupulousness on the other, to protect them. So the work of suppression went on bravely. The gangs were hunted down; our gaols were filled with Thugs; conviction and condemnation were no longer unattainable ends; and a great institution which had existed for centuries was broken up in a few years.

I do not say that there is no such thing as Thuggee, at the present time, in any part of the Company's dominions. It is probable that still an occasional traveller may, from time to time, be strangled by the wayside. But the cases are few in number, and comparatively insignificant in character. The system is destroyed; the profession is ruined; the Guild is scattered, never again to be associated into a great corporate body. The craft and the mystery of Thuggee will no longer be handed down from father to son. A few English officers, acting under the orders of the supreme administrative authorities, have purged India of this great pollution. If we have done nothing else for the country, we have done this one good thing. It was a great achievement—a great victory. And it is one to be contemplated without any abatement of satisfaction, or any reservation of praise.

It is a greater exploit than the conquest of Sindh or the Punjab, or the annexation of Pegu; and the names of the commander of that little army of Thug-hunters and of his unflinching lieutenants, ought, in every History of India, to have honorable mention, and by every student of that history to be held in grateful remembrance. I cannot conclude this chapter better than by the mention of them. They are Sleeman, Borthwick,* Ramsay, Reynolds, Malcolm, Etwall, Hollings,

* Two examples of gangs captured by Captain, now Colonel, Borthwick, are given in a note at page 372, from Colonel Sleeman's Report. But the first of these is so remarkable, not only for the interesting character of its details, but also from the circumstances of its being an account of the capture of, I believe, the first considerable gang of Dacoits convicted and punished in any part of India, that I am induced to give in this place an amplified version of the story almost in the words that it was related to me :—" Captain Borthwick was at the time Political Agent of the western division of the province of Malwa, in which the principality of Rutlam is comprehended. The chief of this state was then a minor—a circumstance which occasioned a more frequent and minute interference in the administration of its affairs than commonly characterised our political control over the native states of that province. So situated, the Political Officer was necessarily kept constantly informed of all that transpired, both by the Akhbar-Nowese, or news-writer, whom he had stationed in the principality for the purpose, and by the minister himself of the state. In the course of almost daily communications from these individuals, Borthwick received an account stating that five bodies of the Bunnyah or Sudookar class had been discovered in the jungle, a few paces from the high road, ten or twelve miles to the southward of Rutlam, the capital of the state. They were slightly covered with stones, and had the appearance of having been recently murdered. The part of the country where these bodies were stated to have been discovered, was much infested by predatory Bheels, and on reading the report, Borthwick's first impression was that the crime had been committed by them. The unusual atrocity of it, however, determined the British agent immediately to proceed to Rutlam and investigate the case. The inquiry was accordingly commenced; but it had not proceeded far before Borthwick saw that the Bheels were in no way concerned in the murders, but that the perpetrators were evidently Thugs. At the same time it transpired that six or eight days previously, about which time it was supposed that the murders must have been committed, a large body of travellers had passed through that part of the country along the highway towards Hindostan. They had the appearance, and, indeed, gave out that they were pilgrims returning to their homes, after having paid their devotions at a shrine of peculiar sanctity in the western part of Guzerat. All this tended so strongly to excite Borthwick's suspicions that these travellers were the authors of this atrocious deed, that he resolved upon taking immediate measures for arresting them. It was observed that they were travelling very leisurely, but, after the lapse of so many days, they could hardly have proceeded to a distance of less than 100 miles. Resolved, however, upon making the attempt to effect their seizure, and having obtained from different persons, who had well observed and even conversed with some of them, a full description of their appearance, he despatched a party of native horsemen, under the command of a smart and intelligent officer, in pursuit of them, with the strictest orders, when once he came up with them, not to lose sight of them until they were secured and brought in for examination. Furnished with a description of the supposed gang, and with requisitions on the local authorities of the villages and districts through which they would have to pass, calling upon them in the name of the British Government to afford him every assistance in their power to effect this object, the party set out in pursuit. It was only at the village of Dekhola, about 150 miles from Rutlam, whence they were despatched, that they came up with the gang. Having satisfied himself that they were the people of whom he was in pursuit, the officer went to the principal man of the place and presented his requisition for aid; but finding the latter was unable to give him the assistance he required (the village being a small and poor one), he had recourse to a piece of

Lowis, Graham, Paton, Riddell, Ludlow, Birch, Miles, Marsh, Whiteford, and others of good service and good strategy, which is worthy to be held in remembrance for the sake of its own cleverness as well as for its excellent results. The Government of India had established a strict monopoly of opium over Malwa, which had then existed for some time, and these very horsemen formed a portion of the body of troops employed by Captain Borthwick, and posted at the different commanding outlets to prevent the unauthorised export of the drug. So it occurred to the officer, on finding the village could not supply him with means sufficient to use coercion, to take advantage of this circumstance — to denounce the gang as smugglers, and charge them with having contraband opium in their possession. Too glad to find there was not the slightest insinuation thrown out as to their real characters, they were eager with their offers to submit their luggage at once to the officer's inspection. This, however, not suiting his purpose, he pretended that no inspection at so paltry a village, where there were no authorities of sufficient importance to testify to the result, would be satisfactory to the British Agent, and signified his desire to have it made at a place where it could be effected in a more open and authoritative manner. After some hesitation on the part of the gang they agreed to go back with him to Bhulwâra, a stage to the southward of Dekhola, which they had passed a day or two before. At Bhulwâra there was a large body of Sebundies, or police soldiers, which, on arriving there, the authorities, in compliance with the requisition presented by the officer, placed at his disposal. He now considered he had sufficient means to make a capture of the gang, and thinking it no longer necessary to disguise his suspicions and intentions regarding them, openly charged them with being Thugs, and declared his determination to carry them before Captain Borthwick, to be subjected to a strict examination. Boldly and clamorously they attempted to repel the charge. They declared themselves to be innocent and inoffensive people returning from their pilgrimage to shrines in the west of Guzerat. To all this he paid no attention, but was not a little staggered on a paper being presented to him by one of the leaders, which was asserted to be a passport of the English Government, under the protection of which he (the leader) declared they were travelling. This caused doubt and anxiety to the officer, which, however, was in some measure appeased by considering the strictness of his orders, and in feeling assured that if it came to pass that a mistake had been made, every allowance would be shown to him. All his fears, however, were speedily dispelled by one of the gang, in a paroxysm of fear, coming to him and confessing that they were Thugs, and offering, if his life were assured to him, to make a full disclosure of all their proceedings. This was a contingency for which Captain Borthwick had fortunately prepared him, and he accordingly on the instant separated this proffered approver from the gang, and kept him from that moment away from all intercourse with his comrades. In the mean while Captain Borthwick himself, after despatching the officer and party from Rutlam, proceeded to Joura, a small town twenty miles to the north of the former, there to await the result of the measures he had taken. Shortly afterwards he received a report from the officer of the success that had attended him, which was speedily followed by his arrival at Joura with the gang in his custody. Borthwick immediately entered upon the examination of the approver. Of the information which was thereby elicited, that part which contained a full and particular account of the murders committed by the gang, from the time they passed Rutlam until they were overtaken at Dekhola, claimed his immediate attention. The approver gave an account of no less than eighteen different murders committed in that short interval; and in order to confirm this part of his evidence, Capt. Borthwick sent him the following day under a guard, and accompanied by a native writer, to note all that transpired along the line of road upon which the murders were stated by him to have been perpetrated. In every instance stated, the place where the body of the

repute. Many of these were afterwards distinguished as agents for the suppression of professional Dakoitee. But to this important subject I must devote another chapter.

murdered person was deposited was pointed out. The several bodies were disinterred, and each instance was verified by the village authorities nearest to the spots. Thus a complete corroboration of the approver's statements was obtained; and other approvers having come forward, the guilt of the gang, individually and collectively, was fully established by a mass of incontrovertible proof."

CHAPTER III.

Dakoitee—Its Antiquity—Measures of Warren Hastings—Hereditary Robber Castes—Their Customs—Local Dakoitee—Complicity of the Zemindars and Moostajirs—Effects on the Suppression of Dakoitee—Appointment of a Special Commissioner for Lower Bengal—New Act—General Remarks.

THE efforts of these energetic and indefatigable officers at the head of the Thuggee Establishment had hitherto been mainly directed to the suppression of that great crime which gave the name to their Department. But when they had reason to believe that their measures had broken up the greater number of gangs, and suppressed the activity of the evil, if they had not wholly rooted it out, they began to address themselves to the eradication of another foul disease of cognate origin and kindred aspect, which, if not so terrible to contemplate, was more extensively disseminated, and scarcely less fatal in its effects upon the general peace and happiness of the people.

It was no new thing to the comprehension of English residents in India at this time that robberies, attended with violence, often, indeed, with murder, were frequently committed in dwelling-houses by gangs of armed men. For three-quarters of a century had these gang-robbers been known as *Dakoits*, and every one in India, or, indeed, every one with the commonest knowledge of India and her affairs, knew well that *Dakoitee*, or gang-robbery, was a crime of very frequent occurrence in all parts of Hindostan. Ever since we had established police-bands to capture, and law-courts to try, offenders of any kind, we had been capturing and trying Dakoits, and passing laws against them, tinged with more or less of the severity or the leniency of the times. In the days of Warren Hastings, when a sort of unscrupulous vigor, not in effect so injurious to humanity as it seems to be in description, was brought to bear upon the disorders of the country, it was decreed that not only should every convicted Dakoit be executed in his own village, but that the village should be fined "according to the enormity of the crime, each inhabitant according to his substance, and that the family of the criminal should become the slaves of the state, and be disposed of for the general benefit and convenience of the people, according to the discretion of Government."*

* General Regulations for the Administration of Justice, August, 1772. This measure was recommended by the Committee of Circuit at Cossimbazaar. The arguments with which they support it are curious:—"We have judged it necessary to add to the regulations a proposal for the suppression and extirpation of Dakoits, which will appear to be dictated by a spirit of rigor and violence very different from the caution and lenity of our other propositions, as it in some respects involves the innocent with the guilty. We wish a milder expedient could be suggested, but we much fear that this evil has acquired a great degree of its strength from the tenderness and moderation which our Government has exercised towards these banditti, since it has interfered in the internal protection of the provinces. We confess that the means which we propose can in nowise be reconcileable to the spirit of our own constitution; but till that of Bengal shall attain the same perfection, no conclusion can be drawn from the English laws that can properly be applied to the manners or state of this country. * * * We have many instances of their meeting death with the greatest insensibility; it loses, therefore, its effect as an example, but when executed in all the forms and terrors of law in the midst of the neighbours and relations of the criminal; when these are treated as accessories to his guilt, and his family deprived of their liberty, and separated for ever from each other, every passion which before served as an incentive to guilt, now becomes subservient to the purposes of society, by turning them from a vocation in which all they hold dear, besides life, become forfeited by their conviction; at the same time their families, instead of being lost to the community, are made useful members of it, by being adopted into those of the more civilised inhabitants. The ideas of slavery, borrowed from our American colonies, will make every modification of it appear, in the eyes of our own countrymen in England, a horrible evil. But it is far otherwise in this country; here slaves are treated as the children of the families to which they belong, and often acquire a much happier state by their slavery than they could have hoped for by the enjoyment of liberty, so that in effect the apparent rigor thus exercised on the children of convicted robbers, will be no more than a change of condition, by which they will be no sufferers, though it will operate as a warning on others, and is the only means which we can imagine capable of dissipating these desperate and abandoned societies which subsist on the distress of the

But although in those days our early administrators were not without some general knowledge of the habits of this "race of outlaws, living from father to son in a state of warfare against society,"* though it was known that Dakoitee was something more than an accident, a casual blot, a superficial excrescence, it had been but imperfectly ascertained to what extent, and in what perfection, it was an integral institution. But when the same process that had been applied to the exposition of Thuggee, with all its systematised enormities, its creeds, and its rituals, was brought to bear upon the kindred crime of Dakoitee, there was found to be as much system in it, as stern a faith, as engrossing a superstition. It was seen then that Dakoitee was the normal condition of whole tribes born and bred to the profession, that there were robber-castes in India just as there were soldier-castes or writer-castes, and that men went out to prey upon the property of their fellows—and, if need be, on their lives—with strict religious observance of sacrament and sacrifice, strong in the belief that they were only fulfilling their destiny, and doing good service to the deity whom they adored.

I do not mean that there was no such thing as accidental Dakoitee—that men not bred and born to the

general community." The logic of this seems rather to halt in the concluding passages; for if the sale of the families of the Dakoits was calculated to better their condition and enhance their happiness, it could not have operated as a very effectual warning. The Committee of Circuit seem to have recommended the proposed measure as a severe and deterring punishment, and then taken the greatest trouble to demonstrate that it would be no punishment at all.—[*Letter of the Committee of Circuit at Cossimbazaar, August* 15, 1772, *in Colebrooke's Digest. Supplementary Volume.*]

* Warren Hastings (1773). The following description of the Dakoit bands, written eighty years ago, shows that our predecessors in India had a very fair general knowledge of the subject:—"The Dakoits of Bengal are not, like the robbers in England, individuals driven to such desperate courses by sudden want. They are robbers by profession, and even by birth; they are formed into regular communities, and their families subsist by the spoils which they bring home to them; they are all, therefore, alike criminal wretches who have placed themselves in a state of declared war with Government, and are, therefore, wholly excluded from every benefit of its laws."—[*Letter from the Committee of Circuit to the Council of Fort William, dated at Cossimbazaar, August* 15, 1772. *Colebrooke's Digest. Supplementary Volume.*]

profession never, under the force of accidental circumstances, took to Dakoitee for a livelihood—but that it was established upon a broad basis of hereditary caste, and was, for the most part, an organic state of society. "I have always followed the trade of my ancestors—Dakoitee," said Lukha, a noted Dakoit, who subsequently became approver. "My ancestors held this profession before me," said another, "and we train boys in the same manner. In my caste, if there were any honest persons, *i.e.*, not robbers, they would be turned out and not kept with us." The first of these belonged to a robber-tribe known as *Budducks*, one of the largest and most exclusive of the depredational castes; the other was of the tribe of *Hurrees*. Sometimes boys were adopted into these robber-castes. "I was hitherto a Beree by caste," said another approver, "and converted into a *Kheejuck* (another robber-tribe) by one of Jeeteen of that caste, who, seeing me begging and distressed, took me under his protection, and gave me maintenance." Sometimes they married into a robber-caste, and took up the trade with their wives. Sometimes they inherited the profession from the mother's side. "Man Singh, a very noted leader of Budducks," said the same Jukha, whose evidence I have above quoted, "was a Gosaen and not a Dakoit, but he united himself to a Budduck woman, by whom he had Man Singh. This man had been engaged in a hundred enterprises."

Such, read by the light thrown upon this deeply interesting subject by the investigations of our British officers, were the hereditary robber-castes of India; the Budducks, the Kheejucks, the Hurrees, the Dosads, and others. The gangs, composed of these men, were for the most part distinguished by their exclusiveness and uniformity. Dakoitee was conducted by them with all becoming solemnity; it was, like Thuggee, a mysterious institution not to be lightly approached—one into the hallowed precincts of which admission was to be obtained only by formal initiation. But though there were robber-castes, and many gangs of Dakoits composed of these exclusive fraternities, all Dakoitee was not of this constitutional character. There were gangs of a less formal and select kind—gangs composed of men of different tribes,* often strangers to each other; and there were Dakoits not of the hereditary class, lay members, as it were, of the profession, who troubled themselves little about presiding goddesses, and set about their work in a less scientific way. But although in these gangs might be discerned a fusion of many castes, they all seemed to rally round the men of the hereditary robber-castes, without whose agency they believed that they could accomplish little. "A convicted Dakoit in the Purneah gaol," writes an intelligent officer of the Thuggee Department, to whose investigations we are indebted for much of our knowledge of the robber-castes of India, "from whom I sought information, confessed to me his having been with three different gang-leaders, with whom he had been concerned in ten different Dakoitees within the Purneah district. These gangs were promiscuously composed, but the nucleus was composed of the robber-castes, and he laid it down as a rule, well known by the robber fraternity, that no gang could retain its organisation and efficiency without an admixture of the '*janam chors*,' as he styled them, or 'born robbers.' This man was one of the industrial castes which are called by the robber-castes

* "The Budducks," said an approver of one of the local Purneah gangs, "depredate with men of their own caste alone, and no others; and we in this part of the country depredate with people of all castes, and the houses of the different men are not in one place, but various distances remote the one from the other, some 10 or 12 coss (20 or 24 miles), others only 1 or 2 coss (2 or 4 miles), therefore, those who live near them are well known to all, and those who live far off are only known to Moostajirs and Sirdars. The members of the gang, then, do not all know each other, but only the Sirdars and Moostajirs know all."—[*Evidence of Bokhai, Mistry.*]

'*janwars*,' a common term for simplicity and clownishness in India, but by which is here meant the uninitiated. He assured me that his '*oostad*,' or teacher, was a *Dosad* (a notorious robber-caste), and that on one occasion, when he proposed to set up a gang himself, this man told him that without the assistance of the hereditary robber-castes, no gang ever was or ever could be established, for that to them alone had descended, through a long line of ancestors, the '*ilm*,' or secret lore necessary for the purpose."*

This at all events was something to know—but there was much more to be known. The hereditary robber-castes constituted the aristocracy of depredational crime. They were the leaders and instructors of these organised bands of robbers—the pivots upon which the whole machinery turned. Every gang was more or less regulated by them, but every gang was not mainly composed of them. The most noticeable thing of all was the extraordinary extent of these depredational leagues—the thousands of members that they numbered. There seemed, indeed, to be a network of organised plunder spread over the whole face of the country. It was a tremendous suggestion which staggered the credulity, and baffled the comprehension even of men accustomed to the excesses of great criminal leagues. But they set themselves to work vigorously—to learn all they could, and do all they could—believing that as they had stricken down Thuggee, Dakoitee could not stand up much longer before the *ikbal* of the Company.

The first approaches to a full understanding of the subject were made without stumbling on any great difficulties. The greater the segregation of this or that class, the easier is it to trace out and to illustrate its idiosyncrasies. Now the Budducks and Khejucks were not only exclusive, but migratory castes. They carried

* *MS. Notes of Captain Hippisley Marsh.*

on their depredations at a distance from their own homes, and set out in gangs composed entirely of their own fraternity. It was as easy to elicit a full revelation of the practices and observances of the Budducks or Khejucks, as of their fellow-adventurers, the Thugs. Indeed, our previous investigations into the physiology of the one, facilitated our enquiries into the habits of the other, and guided us more directly to the truth. There were many points of analogy between them. They had a secret dialect, and secret signs. They assumed various disguises. They offered up sacrifices. As with the Thugs, so with the Budducks, the goat was the favorite victim. They consulted the auspices. They had the same overflowing faith in the cry of the jackal. They swore oaths of fidelity and secrecy. They were altogether the same sort of comfortable religionists, with the same utter disregard for the happiness of their fellow-men.*

The ordinary practice of these gangs was to set out, after the usual ritual preliminaries, in parties of thirty, or forty, disguised as travellers, or pilgrims, or bird-catchers, or anything else that might promise good chance of concealment. The principal implement of their profession was the spear. The spear-head they carried about with them, concealed on their persons;

* Captain Marsh says that the habits and organisation of the robber-castes of Purneah were analogous with those of the Budducks of Western India. "It is wonderful," he observes, "how perfectly similar are the habits and organisation of the Western Budducks and of the robber-castes of the Purneah district. No Budduck can exist without wine—*i.e.*, fermented liquor—ditto, the robbers of Purneah. No Budduck reaches full manhood without being initiated into the mysteries and dialects of the caste—ditto, the robber castes of Purneah. No Budduck ever heartily consents to till the soil, but will escape it on the first opportunity—ditto, the robber-castes of Purneah. The little land they till is only to make a show, and screen their real profession. No Budduck gang would ever dream of attacking a house without the preliminary rites and *poojah* of Kalee—ditto, the gangs of the robber-castes of Purneah. Every Budduck Dakoit has a peculiar fashion of girding his breast, back, and loins, so as to offer no impediment to his movements, and to protect him from blows, a fashion not used by any description of peaceable men—ditto, the Purneah robber-castes. All this I have learnt from their own lips and their own showing."—[*From an unfinished demi-official Letter from Captain Marsh to Major Sleeman.*]

the handles they either converted into walking-sticks, or buried in a convenient place. One of the party sent on in advance, or some confederate at a distance—a corresponding member of the society—either brought or sent in tidings to the effect that he "had his eye on a rich house." A full description of the locality—of the building itself, of its inhabitants, of the probable means of defence, as far as they could be ascertained, was communicated to the leaders of the gang; and then the night and hour of the attack being determined upon, the gang was duly mustered, and an estimate formed of its adequacy to the intended enterprise. If the party were not considered strong enough to secure success, some "auxiliaries" were called in. These were members of robber-tribes, or local Dakoits, resident in the neighbouring villages. With their party thus augmented they took counsel together, and determined on their plan of operations. It was their policy then to separate for a day or two before the meditated attack, and then to meet at a given hour—an hour after night-fall—and to advance at once to the enterprise. They then collected the handles of their implements, fixed them into the spear-heads and axes, prepared their torches, divested themselves of all their superfluous clothes, and advanced to the attack.

It was always a nocturnal surprise. With flaming torches, and spears glittering in the broad light, they came suddenly on the sleeping inhabitants of the doomed house, and either roused them with their noise, or pricked them up with the points of their weapons. Thus suddenly startled from their sleep, finding themselves surrounded by armed men, whose numbers their fear greatly exaggerated, the unhappy merchants, or bankers, so surprised, could seldom muster either their senses or their courage sufficiently to conduct an effective defence. If by any chance the resistance was obstinate, the Dakoits, who had not always the stoutest hearts to sustain them, were in a fair way to be beaten back. But the chances were greatly in their favor. A party suddenly surprised is always at a disadvantage. So it often happened that the luckless inhabitants, confused, bewildered, panic-struck, like people under the influence of a fearful dream, did all that they were directed to do —pointed out the places where their wealth was hidden, and went like sheep to the slaughter.

Though the ritual formalities of which I have spoken may have been peculiar to particular classes of Dakoits, the mode of procedure here described seems to have been common to all. With the more demonstrative part of the business, indeed, we had been long acquainted. What we now discovered was not only the very curious inner history of the social organisation and religious environments of Dakoitee, but all the secret mechanism of those screens and defences, only dimly known before, which enabled the great crime to run riot over the whole length and breadth of the land. That the location in an Indian village of numbers of professional robbers, ever and anon setting out on depredational journeys, and returning with much spoil in their hands, should be unknown either to the villagers, high or low, or to the rural police, was clearly an impossibility. It was a matter, indeed, of notoriety in the village. It could not be otherwise. In such cases, amongst us, knowledge is exposure and extermination. A gang of robbers could not exist for a day in an English village after their location were once discovered. Every influential man in the neighbourhood would be eager to secure their capture and imprisonment, and the county constabulary would soon beat up their haunts. But in India all this is reversed. The squirearchy and the police are alike interested in the protection and sustentation of Dakoitee. The Zemindar and the Thannadar grow rich upon it. They do not foster the rank weed for nothing. Dakoitee is highly remunerative. The head man of the village shares the spoil with the successful robbers. He has his seigneural rights.* He is a harborer of thieves on a large scale. They come and go freely, uninterruptedly, so long as they are disposed to pay for the privilege; and as their very existence depends upon the payment, they must perforce submit to the exaction. They are, so to speak, the servants or children of the great men, who supply them in time of need with food and clothing, and make moneyed advances to them when they set out upon their expeditions. Indeed, the robber-gangs are often

* From the depositions of a Budduck approver, named Lukha, we gather a full-length picture of a model Zemindar of this kind, whose exactions at last drove a profitable association of Dakoits clean off his estate.

"Five hundred rupees out of this booty," says the approver, after detailing the circumstances of a Dakoitee, "were given to Thakur Dhotal Sing, the great landholder of the village in which we resided."

And again, after another enterprise: "We gave a share of one-fourth of the booty to Thakur Dhotal Sing, the landlord of Sepreea."

The fourth of the spoil, however, did not suffice him. He grew more exorbitant in his demands:

"In five or six days we reached home in safety; but the landlord, Dhotal Sing, exacted from us more than a fourth of this booty as his share. The rest we divided, but the rapacious landlord got us all seized and bound, and taking from us all the gold and bullion, gave us only one hundred rupees each. . . . . . We prepared to leave this man's estate, but he implored us to remain, and swore solemnly never again to behave dishonestly to us."

It seems that they consented to remain; but in a little time the greedy landlord was at his old tricks:

"Dhoulut and I got about a hundred rupees, but we had no sooner got home than Thakur Dhotal Sing came with his son and the other joined proprietors of the estate, seized us all, tied our arms behind our back, and demanded a fourth of our booty. We brought out one of the two hundred rupees, and declared that was all we had gained by the enterprise, but they would not believe us. We protested and remonstrated, and told them that we would leave their estate, as it would never do for us to take all the risk and trouble of Dakoitee, and for them to take all the profit. They were a senseless set of peasants, and all we could say seemed to make no kind of impression upon them—as we committed Dakoitees on others, they committed them on us. They were a short-sighted people, or they would have seen the advantage of observing the same good faith with us that we always observe with our patrons."

This time they acted up to their threats, and betook themselves to another village:

"Dhotal Sing," says the ill-used Dakoit, "the chief of Sepreea, was a rapacious man, and used to extort from us, in some mode or other, a good deal more than the fourth of our booty, which we considered the seigneural, or Zemindaree right; so we went to reside in the village of Bigholee, not far distant."

attended either by one of these landowners in person, or by a delegate from his immediate family. The connexion between them is of the closest kind. Each is necessary to the well-being of the other.

The bare outside fact of this criminal participation of the landlords was no discovery of modern times. It had attracted the attention of Warren Hastings,* who saw at a glance that it was wholly impossible to suppress Dakoitee without proclaiming the responsibility of the Zemindars as accessories to the crime, and in all cases of conviction punishing them with as much severity as the active offenders.† He would have made short work of these nursing mothers of crime, and hung up the fattest Zemindar with as little compunction as the leanest Dakoit. As I have said before, the most vigorous measures are often the most humane; and I have little doubt that if these recommendations had been carried out and persevered in, and a heavy blow thus struck at conniving landlords, we should not now be hearing, after the lapse of three-quarters of a century, that around the immediate seat of the supreme Government—almost under the

* See Proceedings of Governor and Council, April 19, 1774, quoted in "Colebrooke's Digest," supplementary volume.

"At this time I have repeated complaints from all parts of this province of the multitude of Dakoits which have infested it for some years past, and have been guilty of the most daring and alarming excesses. I know not whether the knowledge of these evils has been officially communicated to the members of the Board. To me it has only come through the channel of private information, as I do not recollect to have heard the slightest intimation of them from the Zemindars, farmers, or other officers of the revenue; which may appear extraordinary, but that I am assured that the Zemindars themselves too frequently afford them protection, and that the Ryots, who are the principal sufferers by these ravages, dare not complain, it being an established maxim with the Dakoits to punish with death every information given against them."

† The words of the recommendation are worth quoting: "That such of the Zemindars or farmers as shall be convicted of having neglected to assist the Foujdars in the execution of their trust, shall be made responsible for any loss sustained by such misconduct, or otherwise fined according to the nature of the offence; but that all persons, of whatever degree or profession, who shall be convicted of receiving fees or other pecuniary acknowledgments from robbers, knowing them to be such, or of abetting or conniving in any shape at their practices, shall be adjudged equally criminal with them, and punished with death; and that this be immediately made public throughout the province."—[*Warren Hastings*, 1774, *ut supra.*]

shadow of the vice-regal palace itself—" gang-robberies have increased to such an extent that a feeling of general insecurity has arisen in the minds of the people of these districts." These are the words, not of Warren Hastings, but of Lord Dalhousie. The Governor of 1852 only repeats the complaint of the Governor of 1774. The immunity which the landlords have enjoyed in the interval has been the main cause of the perpetuation of the evil. We have been much too slow in our interference with their vested interests in robbery and murder. Lord Cornwallis, when he re-organised the Police Department, in 1792, proclaimed that landlords, convicted of being accessories to the commission of a robbery, should be "compelled to make good the value of the property, stolen or plundered."* So that, even if the regulations had been put into effect against the Zemindars, it would have been merely a matter of calculation with them—a mere question of profit and loss—the balance being pretty certainly in favor of the former. It is not strange, therefore, that under such regulations the landlords continued to carry on the old trade, and to participate largely in the professional emoluments of the Dakoits.

Warren Hastings complained that the farming system had a tendency to extend and perpetuate this evil. And the same fact is insisted upon and demonstrated on the evidence of the Dakoits themselves, by the present generation of British functionaries. The small Moostajirs, indeed, are the great harborers of Dakoits—the great promoters of Dakoitee. "There could be no Dakoitee without the Moostajirs," was the statement almost in-

* "Landholders and farmers of land are not in future to be considered responsible for robberies committed in their respective estates or farms, unless it shall be proved that they connived at the robbery, received any part of the property stolen or plundered, harbored the offenders, aided, or refused to give effectual assistance to prevent their escape, or omitted to afford every assistance in their power to the officers of Government for their apprehension, in either of which cases they will be compelled to make good the value of the property stolen or plundered."

variably made by the approving Dakoits examined by Captain Marsh and other officers.* Old European residents in the Mofussil confirmed this testimony. "It is my firm opinion," wrote an Indigo planter of long standing in Purneah, "that each and every native Moostajir must of necessity be a Dakoit leader, because, in the first instance, he must know the character of residents in his villages, otherwise he would be constantly subject to have unprofitable tenants; and, secondly, because it is utterly impossible that large gangs could assemble and cross the country in different directions at night without being stopped by the heads of villages, and as the approvers themselves say that no gang will dare to move out without a Moostajir, it appears to me beyond all doubt that one or two Moostajirs are the actual leaders of every Dakoit-gang."†

It would seem, too, if the evidence of the approvers is to be trusted, that if there could be no Dakoitee without the assistance of the Moostajirs, neither could there be Moostajirs without the assistance of the Dakoits. "There is no petty Moostajir," said one man, "free from connexion with Dakoitee; and whoever has a repugnance so

* A few specimens of the evidence on this head, contained in the Official Reports, will suffice:

Question.—If the Moostajir be not in league, cannot the professional robbers practise Dakoitee?

Answer.—It cannot be done without the Moostajir.—[*Evidence of Hazaree Dhurkar.*]

Question.—Can there be no Dakoitee without Moostajirs?

Answer.—There can be no Dakoitee without Moostajirs, for, through their influence, the Thannah people cannot lay hold of us robbers from fear of the Moostajirs; and the use of the Moostajirs is this, that they find the robbers in food and clothes, and lend them money, and give them liquor, and in every way protect our families and ourselves. This is the use of Moostajirs.—[*Evidence of Suroofa Hulwaee.*]

Question.—Since the Moostajir knows he has robbers in his villages, does he make no effort to turn them out?

Answer.—If he gains much by remaining, why should he turn them out? He keeps them for his own benefit.—[*Evidence of Jhubban, approver.*]

Question.—Is this true, that without a Moostajir or Sirdar, no Dakoitee can take place?

Answer.—If the Moostajirs do not join, and there be no Sirdar, how could poor robbers commit *Dakoitee?* without the command of the Moostajir and the Sirdar no *Dakoitee* can be carried on. Under disguise of landholders the Moostajirs set *Dakoitee* on foot.—[*Evidence of Jhubban, Kuraria.*]

† Evidence relating to Dakoitee, printed in Calcutta.

to connect himself, will not take a Moostajiree." "Without being a rogue," said another man, "a Moostajir's profession could not be carried on. No class of rogues come up to the Moostajirs. . . . If there were no robbers in the village, then none would take Moostajiree, and now every class of men become Moostajirs in this hope that they may share in the spoils of Dakoitee." "Moostajiree of villages," said a third, "is taken for purposes of Dakoitee. . . . By becoming a Moostajir he cannot manage without forming a connexion with Dakoits." There is every reason to consider this evidence to be trustworthy, as far as it goes. It relates, however, almost entirely to a particular part of the country;* and the extent to which the evil prevails in other parts may not be safely predicated from it. But the complicity, after one fashion or another, of the landholders, whether Zemindars or Moostajirs, in the depredations of the Dakoits, is not local and accidental, but general and continual. The same system, with slight superficial variations, which prevails in Bengal, prevails also in Oude.† The landholders are the arch-offenders.

Associated with them, in the protection of the more active criminals, are the equally corrupt members of the police. This was no new discovery. Warren Hastings had as clear a perception of the fact as any Superintendent of Police in the present day. But although the Indian constabulary force has been modelled and re-modelled—though first one system has been tried and then another, every description of organisation that has yet been attempted has been found to be equally inefficacious for the

* The Purneah district.

† With certain variations, of course dependent upon the nature of the landed tenures. In the example, which we have quoted from the evidence of a Budduck practising in Oude, the protecting landlord was a powerful Zemindar. In the instances cited by the Khejucks of the Purneah district, the territorial offenders were principally small *Moostajirs*, or Revenue-farmers.

protection of life and property, and the detection and punishment of crime. Instead of protecting life and property, these men, under whatever name they draw a certain amount of salary, whether they belong to the regular police, or are the village watch, only protect rapine and disorder. To such at least point their own unaided instincts; but European superintendence, though powerless hitherto to convert the Indian police into an effective body, has done something to control its excesses. There is still much more to be done. It is the weakest point of our Indian administration. But to break up a gigantic league of this kind, a confederacy between the landlords and the police so contrived, so glossed over—each playing into the hands of the other—as to baffle almost every effort to convict the suspected offenders of actual participation in the delinquencies of the Dakoits, is a work of no very easy accomplishment for a handful of European strangers. The network of this foul conspiracy stretches up to the very doors of the magistrate's cutcherry. It embraces all classes, from the wealthy Zemindar and the influential Amlah to the ill-paid and insignificant village watchman, who, perhaps, is a member of a robber-caste.* The more intricate the machinery

* See the following evidence of a Dakoit approver:

Question.—What class of people become *Chokeedars* (watchmen)?

Answer.—Dosaud, Hurree, Kurraria, &c., &c. (robber-castes); these principally furnish the *Chokeedars.*

Question.—In the course of the month what does such person realise?

Answer.—Two rupees a month for each *Chokeedar* is levied on the Ryots; and they (the *Chokeedars*) realise a great deal from thieves and robbers and *Dakoits*, and this is the real reason why they undertake to be watchmen — to feather their own nests—else no one would willingly undertake so detestable an occupation.

Question.—Do the *Chokeedars* ever go on *Dakoitee?*

Answer.—No: they do not go on Dakoitee, but know all about the *Dakoits.* Whoever leaves his house for *Dakoitee*; he does so with the knowledge of the *Chokeedars*; and they do not go on *Dakoitee* for this reason, that in a village all kinds of people dwell; if any person should be discovered absent by the *Naka-Buskundaz*, he would be reported to the *Thannadar* (native police superintendent), therefore, the watchmen at night do not leave their village, but go on the rounds and set robberies on foot, and take share from robbers and Dakoits.—[*Evidence of Bokai, Mistry, taken by Captain Marsh, July* 19, 1842.]

Again:

Question. — Are the Chokeedars of your caste (Hurree) all thieves?

Answer.—They call themselves Choof our own law-courts, and the more extensive our police establishments, the more subtle become the contrivances by which the conspirators endeavour to cloak the crimes which they are all interested in concealing. Eighty years ago, Warren Hastings regretted that "the regularity and precision which have been introduced into our new courts of justice," should be "among the causes of the increase of robbers." It is not to be doubted, I fear, that in these days the more complicated machinery which we have introduced in furtherance of the improved administration of justice has had a tendency to raise up so many screens or barriers between the eye of the British functionary and the crimes which are committed around him.

Upon this subject, in its general bearings, important as it is, I cannot now afford to enlarge. But this is the proper place in which to speak of the effects of our present system upon the great crime of Dakoitee. It is a distinguishing feature of the practice of these professional depredators that they adapt their ways, with wonderful precision, to the legal machinery which is brought to bear upon them—that they even turn the very engine which is designed for their destruction, into an instrument of defence. They adapt their organisation to our own, and the more intricate it is the greater are their chances of evasion and escape. "The English," writes an officer of great intelligence and experience in the intricacies of these criminal leagues, "having divided the country into districts and Thannas, the robbers have made it a fundamental maxim and *sine quâ non* to attach themselves by divisions to Thannas, in order to bribe every man of real and actual influence over the villagers to enter into a league with their paymasters—their principle being to sacrifice much in order to retain

keedars, and by this deceit engage in robbery and Dakoitee; all the Chokeedars of the Hurree caste are robbers and Dakoits.—[*Evidence of Jhoomuk, Hurree, taken by Captain Marsh, July 20, 1842.*]

a little in certainty and safety. Now the two classes which have supreme actual influence among the village population are the Thannadars (with their myrmidons) and the Revenue-farmers (with theirs). These then are the persons held in the pay of the Dakoits. To ensure regularity in this necessary particular, a robber-division is attached to a Thanna, and a subdivision to a particular form. This robber-division is under a Sirdar (or chief) of robbers; and it is among the first of his duties to pay monthly with his own hand the shares respectively of the Thannadar and the Revenue-farmer."*

Nor does the corruption, as I have already intimated, stop here. "The Sirdars," says another writer, an intelligent and zealous magistrate, "are men who travel in their *palkis* (palanquins), and arrange all these little affairs first with the local police, next with the magistrate's Amlah, and eventually with the Sessions' Amlah and the law officer."† "In short," to use the comprehensive words of another civil officer, the highest authority on such a subject in Bengal, "the whole plan has been got up to meet our rules of evidence, and it is carried on with the help of our ministerial and police Amlah."‡ Whatever we have done, indeed, the Dakoits have turned our doings to their own uses—our revenue system, our police system, our judicial system, have all been impressed into their service. Whatever may have been our administrative organisation, they have adapted to it, with consummate skill, the organisation of their criminal leagues, and out-manœuvred us at all points.

Nor did the triumphs of these astute criminals stop short

* *MS. Correspondence.*—The same writer thus calculates the number of robbers located within one Thanna (or police division):—"I calculate to every Thannadar four Revenue-farmers resident in a Thanna; on every Revenue-farmer's farm four *Sirdars* (or chiefs), with their respective divisions of robbers. To every Sirdar four *Naib-Sirdars* (or captains), and to each *Naib-Sirdar* four burglar gangs, and to every burglar gang five men each. Thus, $1 \times 4 \times 4 \times 4 \times 4 \times 5 = 1280$ members of the depredational league in one Thanna."

† *MS. Correspondence.*

‡ *Ibid.*

even at the doors of the Sessions Court. They reached to the very judgment-seat. So protected by the Amlah, it would have been hard if the Dakoits could not have brought into court any amount of false evidence to secure their acquittal. It never, by any chance, happened that all, or even the most influential, members of a robber-gang were arrested; and they who were at large never failed to exert themselves to obtain the liberation of their more unfortunate comrades who had fallen into the grasp of the law. False witnesses were readily obtainable from among their own people, willing and able to swear him off. The manner in which this evidence was got up was often very clever and interesting. "It is quite out of my power," writes Mr. Wauchope, magistrate of Hooghly (of whose services I shall come to speak presently), to the Superintendent of Police in the Lower Provinces, "to describe on paper the delight with which the Dakoits with me talk about their exploits—of the pleasure parties which Kartich Koura, a famous Sirdar, used to take from Calcutta to his native village, whence they never returned without committing one or more Dakoitees; how on one of these occasions their Sirdar had three of his fingers cut off; how he was arrested and committed to the sessions; or the roars of laughter with which they give the details of the trial before the judge, where he was acquitted on the evidence of a most respectable Brahmin, and a still more respectable Kait—the first being Sirdamund Thakoor, a first-rate leader in the gang, and the second Syud Mytee, now an approver with me, and only lately sentenced to transportation for life."*

A system so complete in its organisation as this was not to be put down by the ordinary judicial machinery applied to accidental offences, and by the ordinary ministers of the law. It was apparent that, as in the

* *MS. Records.*

case of Thuggee, a necessity existed for the adoption of specific measures of a more stringent character, and of a less regular type. Neither the law courts nor the law officers, as then constituted and appointed, were sufficient for the suppression of an evil so complex and so extensive. Something more required to be done.

It was in the month of April, 1837, that the first attempt was made to suppress Dakoitee by means of special measures directed to that one end, and a special machinery employed for their execution. Sir Charles Metcalfe was, at this time, Lieutenant-Governor of the North-Western Provinces. The subject had been for some time pressing urgently upon the consideration of the authorities, and the time had now come for action. A Commission for the suppression of Dakoitee was established; and Mr. Hugh Fraser, a civil servant of good capacity, was appointed Commissioner, with a liberal staff of auxiliary subordinates. Special powers were conferred on him. Throughout the whole of the North-Western Provinces he was invested with magisterial authority. All the magistrates were instructed to co-operate with him, and the police were directed to render every possible assistance to his agents. But the year and a half, during which the Commission was in operation, were distinguished by no important results. There was an attempt rather to strike at accidental symptoms, than to probe down to the seat of the disease. It aimed rather at the conviction of Dakoits than the suppression of Dakoitee. The great subject itself, in all its length and breadth—in all its intricacies and complexities—was not sufficiently studied. But Sleeman had reduced Thuggee to its elements, and he was obviously the proper man to submit to a similar process the kindred crime of Dakoitee. He had already, indeed, acquired much available information regarding the professional robber-castes; and his associates in the

Thuggee Department had approved themselves to be men of the right stamp to co-operate with him. The union of the two offices of the General Superintendent of measures for the suppression of Thuggee and the Commissioner for the suppression of Dakoitee, seemed, indeed, to be recommended by many important considerations, not the least of which was the peculiar fitness of the man who had long held so worthily the former appointment; and now Lord Auckland, at the end of the year 1838, being at Simlah, and holding in his own hands the government of the North-Western Provinces, determined to unite the two offices under the superintendence of Colonel Sleeman. At the commencement of the following year the junction was formally effected, and from that time all the measures for the suppression of Dakoitee under the Bengal Presidency, with the exception of those in the Lower Provinces, which were conducted by the "Superintendent of Police," were under the direction of the man who had done so much to root Thuggee out of the land.

The same system now which had been employed so successfully for the extirpation of Thuggee, was brought into play against the great fraternities of Dakoits. Sleeman's head-quarters were to be in Rohilkund. His assistants were spread out all over Upper India. The plan now to be pursued was simply, as described by Sleeman himself, to hunt down the Dakoits by a simultaneous, vigorous, and well-sustained pursuit throughout all parts of India, and thereby to break up their little communities, and compel them to blend with the rest of mankind in public service or private industry, and by degrees to lose their exclusive feeling, and forget their exclusive language. And this was to be done, firstly by the agency of informers, who were to set our officers on the track, and enable us to detect the offenders; and secondly, by specific legislative enactments, to enable us to punish them.

There was no scarcity of informers. Our gaols were

full of Dakoits. It was astonishing what a mass of serviceable information was locked up within our prison-walls. The whole art and mystery of Dakoitee was there to be had for the asking. Professors proud of their knowledge, and rejoicing in the opportunity of giving free vent, in voluble discourse, to the cherished reminiscences of bygone days, talked without stint to the British officers about their depredational achievements, and openly avowed the eagerness of their desires to be again at the exhilarating work. They could not understand that their profession was not as honorable as it was lucrative and exciting. They had no shame, and they had no remorse. They gloried in their exploits as sportsmen do, and talked over a successful gang-robbery with its attendant murders as our European gentlemen talk over their boar-chases or tiger-hunts. "Whilst talking over their excursions," wrote one of Sleeman's assistants,* "which were to me really very interesting, their eyes gleamed with pleasure, and beating their hands on their foreheads and breasts, and muttering some ejaculations, they bewailed the hardness of their lot, which now ensured their never being able again to participate in such a joyous occupation." It was a pleasant life, and a lucrative employment, beside which the hard labor and slender earnings of honesty cut but a sorry figure in the eyes of the work-eschewing Hindoostanee. When asked, after many years spent in prison, if he would not on regaining his liberty betake himself to honest courses, the gaol-bird would always return the same discouraging answer: "No, no," shaking his head and laughing, "that would never do. Why should I become an honest man—work all day in the sun, rain, and all weathers, and earn what? Some five or six pice a day! We Dakoits lead very agreeable

* Capt. W. M. Ramsay. See Colonel Sleeman's Bhudduck Report. Calcutta, 1849.

and comfortable lives. When from home, which is generally only during the cold season, we march some fourteen or sixteen miles a day, for perhaps a couple of months, or say four at the outside—commit a Dakoitee, and bring home money sufficient to keep us comfortable for a year, or perhaps two. When at home we amuse ourselves by shooting, and visiting our friends, or in any way most agreeable—eat when we please, and sleep when we please—can what you call an honest man do that?"*

But however discouraging all this may have been viewed with regard to any hope that may have been entertained of the reformation of Dakoits, the freedom with which the convicts spoke of their professional achievements promised well for the success of our endeavours to root them out of the land. The Dakoits, indeed, were not to be reformed—they were to be extirpated. It was characteristic of English benevolence that we should have been slow to resort to such a remedy as this—that we should have sought rather to convert these depredational tribes into industrial classes by holding out to them sufficient inducements to honest exertion. But all such projects were seen, upon a closer examination, to be worthy only of an Utopian country, and a Saturnian age. People talked about buying up Dakoitee—about sending out a general invitation to these hereditary robbers to come and settle upon grants of land appropriated to them by Government, and to live a life of peaceful integrity for the remainder of their days. But "the difficulties and risks of such a measure were," as Colonel Sleeman well remarked, "little understood. Our territories did not contain one twentieth part of the great body which we should have had to collect; and we should have found it impossible to collect them by mere invitation, without offering them as little labor, and

* Substance of conversation held with Captain W. M. Ramsay.

as much luxury, as they then enjoyed in their wild state, with all the same hopes of rising to wealth and distinction. We should have had to give a leader of robbers and murderers, with his four or five wives, more pay than we give to a native commissioned officer, who had served our Government faithfully thirty or forty years, who had his breast covered with medals, and his body with honorable scars. Had we at any time increased the labor from absolute idleness, or diminished their subsistence from absolute luxury, they would have been off to their native forests and ravines."*

All this was undeniable. The arguments against so wild a project as the establishment of colonies of reformed Budducks, to be supported at the expense of the industrious inhabitants of the country, were so conclusive, that the scheme was soon reasoned down. Indeed, we had begun to discover by this time that humanity, like ambition, sometimes "overleaps itself, and falls on the other side." Nothing is more remarkable in the history of Dakoitee than the fact of the large number of notorious offenders who have escaped conviction and punishment, partly through the agency of false witnesses and the corruption of the native officers of our law courts, and partly through the unwillingness of the European judicial functionaries to convict and punish, except in cases substantiated by the clearest possible evidence of the commission of a specific offence. The judicial axiom that it is better that twenty guilty men should escape than that one innocent man should be punished, however sound it may be in the abstract, had not certainly, in its application to the case of these great depredational leagues, any tendency to advance the interests of mankind. Such tender mercies as were exhibited, with the best possible intentions, by our enlightened European functionaries, were in effect cruel. Seventy years before, Warren Hastings had clearly

* *Colonel Sleeman's Report. Calcutta*, 1849.

discovered the impossibility of suppressing Dakoitee by judicial proceedings in harmony with our refined English ideas of justice, and a strict observance of rules of evidence as recognised in our English law courts. He saw that such mercy was in effect unmerciful, and that there was no real humanity but vigor. As time advanced, and the machinery of our law courts became more complicated, and our European law officers became more and more the representatives and exponents of the high abstract principles of Western civilisation, it was not likely that the scruples which stood in the way of a larger growth of real justice and humanity should have been less influential upon the decisions of our judicial tribunals. The Dakoits, indeed, from generation to generation, laughed at us and our law courts. "Do you think that we shall succeed in extirpating you?" asked Captain Ramsay. "If you go on in the way the Thugs have been put down," was the answer, "you certainly will; but in the customary way, that is, requiring proof to convict of specific acts of Daiostee, never—it is impossible—we should go on increasing from year to year."

These words, which were spoken in 1839, contain the pith of the whole question of Dakoitee-suppression—the evil laid bare and the remedy suggested. But it was not until 1843 that the remedy was applied. It has been seen that in 1836 an act was passed for the suppression of Thuggee, declaring that any one proved to have belonged at any time to a gang of Thugs should be liable to conviction and punishment on the general charge, and now it was proposed that a similar exemption from the necessity of convicting for specific offences should be applied to the case of professional Dakoitee.* "It is

* The preamble of the Act stated "professional Dakoits, who belonged to certain tribes, systematically employed in carrying on their lawless pursuits in different parts of the country." The reader, bearing these words in mind, will perceive that the specification contained in them subsequently

hereby enacted," said the new Act—No. XXIV. of 1843 —" that whosoever shall be proved to have belonged, either before or after the passing of this Act, to any gang of Dakoits, either within or without the territories of the East India Company, shall be punished with transportation for life, or with imprisonment for any less term with hard labor." The Act at the same time gave general jurisdiction to all magistrates to try offences of this class wheresoever committed, without the formality of "any Futwa from any law officer." It was impossible that such a law as this should not be productive of salutary effects. The difficulty of conviction of a specific offence was great to a degree not readily appreciable in this country. For these gangs of Dakoits, for the most part, depredated at a distance of some hundreds of miles from their homes; and the necessity of bringing witnesses from remote places to give evidence in our law courts was an evil of so intolerable a nature, that, whatsoever might have been the sufferings of men, whatsoever their hopes of justice or their desire after revenge, they shrunk from the long journey to the distant tribunal, and silently submitted to their wrongs.*

Nor were these the only legal measures adopted for the suppression of the great crime. Dakoitee was not an enormity peculiar to the Company's territories. On the contrary, both Thuggee and Dakoitee had thriven with peculiar luxuriance in the native states. Oude, indeed, had long been the hot-bed of both. It often happened that in these native states prisoners had been tried, convicted, and sentenced, as Thugs and Dakoits, but had subsequently contrived to escape; and, having escaped,

embarrassed the Bengal Government, and compelled the passing of another Act, generalising the application of the former one.—See *post*, page 409.

* "To avoid the great loss and inconvenience which the necessity of this attendance involved, it was found that the sufferers did all in their power to conceal their sufferings, and often denied that they had ever been attacked, when the dearest members of their family had been killed or wounded, and all they had in the world been carried off."—[*Sleeman's Budduck Report*, 1849.]

had not only returned to their old trade of robbery and murder, but had fearfully persecuted all who had contributed to their previous detection.* An Act was therefore passed, declaring that all prisoners convicted in native states by a tribunal in which an European covenanted servant was one of the presiding judges, might be received into our gaols to undergo their sentence."† It is a feature, indeed, of our English administration in India, that, in all our humanising measures for the suppression of Suttee, Female Infanticide, Thuggee, Dakoitee, and other kindred abominations, we have not stopped short on the borders of the provinces subject to our own regulations. We have exerted our influence to the utmost to indoctrinate the native courts with our own views, and have seldom failed to elicit their acquiescence and assistance. Grudgingly, perhaps, these may have been given. The zeal with which such measures have been prosecuted by the native princes has fallen greatly short of our own. But we have had British officers at their Durbars to see that their promises are fulfilled, and in reality the measures which they have authorised have been practically our own.‡

* "Either," says Sleeman, "from the negligence or connivance of the guards, or the wish of the officers of such courts to avoid the cost of maintaining them."

† Act XVIII. of 1843.

‡ Since the British Government in India have entered more heartily into the great work of extirpating Thuggee and Dakoitee, and have not only issued specific enactments, but appointed an especial and independent Department to carry out these enactments, the native princes and chiefs have rendered us more assistance than they were wont to do, when the detection and apprehension of Thugs and Dakoits was left to the ordinary civil establishments. Indeed, before the adoption of these special measures, it was often found a work of difficulty to obtain the hearty co-operation of a British Resident at a native Court, who felt that to communicate with the Court respecting the contemplated seizure of a gang of Dakoits was to thwart the undertaking (for if the Court knew, the Aumils knew; and if the Aumils knew, the Dakoits knew what was going on), and yet was unwilling to co-operate without the consent of the Court. An example of this is worth giving. In 1822, the widow of a jemadar of Dakoits went to the judge at Cawnpore, and stating that she had been refused her legitimate of the plunder taken by her late husband's associates, boldly denounced the gang to the British functionary. A certain village in the Oude territory was named as the place in which property captured in several Dakoitees would be found, and the houses of the receivers were indicated by the woman. Immediately afterwards the judge, under cover of a tiger-shooting expedition, visited the village pointed out to him, and the truth of the woman's story was confirmed.

Thus aided by special legislative provisions, Colonel Sleeman and his colleagues set to work as vigorously for the extirpation of the Budduck, and other professional robber-gangs, as they before had done for the extirpation of the Thugs, and, learned in all the mysteries of the craft, and aided by professional approvers, they hunted down large gangs, culled new approvers from the list of detected culprits, and carried on the war with remarkable success. And whilst in the upper provinces of Bengal these energetic officers were thus vigorously employed, in the lower provinces Mr. Dampier, the Superintendent of Police, with one or two of the old assistants in the Thuggee Department, were about the same excellent work. But although the haunts of a large number of robber-gangs were beaten up, and Dakoits were captured and catalogued by hundreds, Dakoitee was not suppressed. I do not underrate the services of Sleeman and his detective police. Those services were very great. An immense deal of good was accomplished. If they did nothing else, they drew away the veil which shrouded the mysteries of Dakoitee. We have advanced a long way towards the cure of a disease when we have learnt thoroughly to understand it. I believe that Dakoitee is now thoroughly understood. But the "Department" did much more than this—they actually captured (as I have said) and either punished or turned into approvers vast numbers of Dakoits.* But, like all men of earnestness and enthusiasm, they were run away with by an idea. The idea was a new and a striking one. It was

On returning to Cawnpore the judge, eager to turn the information he had obtained to good account, wrote to the Resident at Lucknow, suggesting to him to send out a detachment of local troops to aid the agents of the civil officer in the capture of the gang. The Resident consented not without some scruple, and the Nazir was sent with the woman to accompany the party and point out the offenders. But the detachment had not proceeded far, when the Resident's heart failed him, and after a march or two the detachment was recalled.—[*MS. Notes.*]

* The approvers themselves are convicts. Sentence is passed upon them, but not carried into effect. They are indulgently treated, but of real liberty they have none. They are, in fact, prisoners at large, for life.

the great idea of the hereditary robber-tribes of India. It was a very important and a deeply-interesting subject, but they gave themselves too exclusively to it. This matter of the professional robber-castes was a great feature of Dakoitee, but it did not in itself constitute Dakoitee. Sleeman and his associates struck at the robber-castes, and I believe that they were well-nigh extinguished. At all events, as great brotherhoods of crime, they were utterly broken up and dispersed.

Still Dakoitee was not suppressed. Subdued in one form and in one part of the country, it seemed to take a new shape and to break out in another place. The general effect of such measures is to urge the evil, against which they are directed, into more remote demonstrations—to drive the offenders into distant parts of the empire, to carry on their depredations beyond the reach of central supervision. Thus, some little time ago, when there was a great outcry against the practices of the London beggars, and these professional mendicants were, for a time, hunted out of the metropolis, it was observed by all dwellers in the home counties that there was a vast increase of rural mendicity. But in Bengal the effect was directly the reverse of this. Dakoitee, like Government, began to centralise itself, and Calcutta was surrounded by banditti. The men constituting these gangs did not apparently belong to the hereditary robber-tribes of India. They seemed rather to make up an indistinct and heterogeneous *posse comitatus* than a great homogeneous guild or brotherhood. Whether these gangs were partly composed of men who had lost their occupation in the provinces, and, unable any longer to preserve their aristocratic exclusiveness, had fused themselves into the general mass of Dakoitee,* and resigned themselves to the usual conditions of that misfortune

* It would appear from Mr. Wauchope's last report, which I had not seen on writing this, that they were.—See p. 412.

which is said to bring together strange bed-fellows, I do not pretend to know; but I grieve to say that an alarming *increase* of Dakoitee in the lower provinces of Bengal has recently manifested itself, and that only last year gang-robbers were swarming, in a state of intense activity, under the walls of the Supreme Court of Calcutta.

It was at the commencement of the year 1852, that the Superintendent of Police in the lower provinces of Bengal submitted to Government a letter received from Mr. Wauchope, magistrate of Hooghly, "forwarding a list of 287 Dakoits concerned in 83 Dakoitees." In this letter the magistrate reported that the 287 Dakoits mentioned by his approvers were connected with only three gangs; and he added, that he knew at least thirty-five gangs committing similar depredations within fifty miles of Calcutta. Of the Dakoits whom he had catalogued his approvers could give him no detailed account; unlike the Budduck and Khejuck approvers, they seldom knew the parentage or caste of their confederates; but it was ascertained that, for the most part, they had come from some Mofussil village, which they occasionally visited, and located themselves in Calcutta or Chandernagore. To arrest the progress of the evil, it was now suggested by the Superintendent of Police that a Commissioner for the suppression of Dakoitee in Lower Bengal should be appointed, armed with special powers, to operate under the provisions of the Act (XXIV. of 1843) for the suppression of professional Dakoits, belonging to certain tribes systematically employed in carrying on their lawless pursuits. "I feel perfectly convinced," he added, "that unless the Thuggee system is brought into operation against these gangs, we shall fail in putting them down."

Fortunately, it was not difficult to name an officer well qualified for the performance of this important work. The Hooghly magistrate, who had sent in the list of 287

Dakoits, was just the man for such an enterprise. Mr. Wauchope, an officer of rare energy and intelligence, had studied well the habits and practices of the Dakoits, and had a large acquaintance with the personal composition of the principal gangs in the neighbourhood of his court. On one occasion a notorious Dakoit chief was brought up before him under an assumed name. The man loudly declared his innocence—protested he had never been concerned in Dakoitee of any kind, or even suspected of such an offence. Mr. Wauchope heard him out, and then laughingly replied that the story was doubtless a very good one, but that it was not good enough for him—that he knew something more about the matter; that the man, to his certain knowledge, had been arrested under such a name, as concerned in such a Dakoitee, by the magistrate of the twenty-four Pergunnahs, and again in Howrah, under another name, for participation in another Dakoitee; that his real name was so-and-so, but that, to distinguish him from another Dakoit of the same name, he went by a certain nickname in the gang—and by that nickname Mr. Wauchope called him. Astonished and alarmed by this display of knowledge—all his secret history thus laid bare by one whom he had thought to cozen in the old way, by hard lying—the unhappy man felt that he was at the mercy of the English magistrate, and cried out, "Pardon me, my lord; I am ready to tell you all I know."

It was plain that this was the kind of man to deal with the old Bengal Dakoits, of whom it was truly said that "they would never confess unless they saw that they were in the hands of a man from whom there was little or no hope of escape." So Mr. Wauchope was recommended for the office of Special Commissioner for the suppression of Dakoitee, and Government sanctioned the appointment.* But although the man was ready, the

* The appointment was made on the 26th of April, 1852, experimentally for one year, to be reported on at the expiration of that period.

Act was not. A question had arisen, in the course of the preceding year, as to whether Act XXIV. of 1843* could be brought into operation against the Dakoit bands of Lower Bengal; for although the wording of the two first sections was of a general character, and seemed to include in their provisions all kinds of Dakoits practising in the Company's territories, the preamble only specified certain tribes of professional robbers; and to these, therefore, the operation of the Act, strictly interpreted, might be limited. The principal judicial authorities were at variance on the subject, and the supreme Government had expressed its unwillingness to alter the existing law unless it were clearly shown by a judicial decision that its provisions were insufficient. It was proposed, there fore, that the legality of the application of the Act in question to the case of ordinary Dakoits should be tested by certain trials in the Hooghly Court, and the decisions of the Sudder thereupon. This, however, did not go far to solve the ambiguity. One man was tried under the doubtful Act, and the Sudder Court sentenced him to be transported for life. But it was understood that the judges were not all of one opinion on the subject; and it was possible, therefore, that the next case might meet with a different fate.

In the mean while, however, the attention of Government had been called, through another channel, to the alarming increase of crime in the lower provinces of Bengal. A petition had been received from several respectable inhabitants of the districts of Burdwan, Hooghly, and Kishnaghur, setting forth that thefts and gang-robberies had increased to such an extent that there was a general feeling of insecurity throughout the country—an evil mainly to be attributed to the inefficiency of the police, and especially the village watch. This was not an appeal likely to be disregarded. An Act

* See *ante*, page 404.

"for the further repression of Dakoity and other crimes in the lower provinces of Bengal" was drafted, and read for the first time on the 27th of June, 1851. The preamble set forth that, "whereas Dakoitees and other heinous crimes are of frequent occurrence within certain zillahs of the Presidency of Fort William, in Bengal, and whereas it has been doubted whether the laws in force against Dakoits and professional robbers can be put in force, except in the case of those who belong to certain tribes referred to in the preamble to Act XXIV., 1843, and it is expedient that such doubts be removed, and that further provision be made for the more regular and due appointment of the village watchmen;" and the first section decreed that "the provisions of Act XXIV., 1843, shall apply to and be put in force against all persons belonging, or who have at any time belonged to, or robbed in company, with any gang of persons associated for the purpose of practising robbery or extortion, and every such person shall be deemed a Dakoit without reference to the tribe or caste to which he belongs."

The results of Mr. Wauchope's appointment, as far as they are yet apparent, are of the most satisfactory kind. He was appointed provisionally for a year, and ordered to report progress upon the expiration of it. In the mean while the accounts, which he has furnished to his immediate superior, are of the most satisfactory complexion. He reports, within the first six months of his operations, a very large diminution of crime. He has hunted down and broken up some extensive gangs; and the immediate result of his active measures is, that the number of ascertained cases of Dakoitee within his jurisdiction are shown, in 1852, to be only one-half of those which were committed within a corresponding period of the preceding year; and seventy-five per cent. less than those, within a similar space of time, just before his assumption of office in the spring of last year. But there is one great impediment to complete and permanent success, which Mr. Wauchope reports to the Superintendent of Police. Speaking of the detailed results of his labors, he says: "In all, about 1250 men have been denounced as Dakoits—131 have been arrested; 47 of them from Calcutta; almost all of these are well-known Dakoits, driven by the Mofussil Police to take shelter there. The arrest of so many criminals in Calcutta has dispersed the gangs in that city, but unfortunately they have not far to go for a place of refuge. The French settlement of Chandernagore is now swarming with Dakoits driven from Calcutta, or the remnants of Mofussil gangs. From the French territory they sally out and commit depredations in the neighbouring districts. They are perfectly safe, because, having for the most part assumed false names, I cannot call on the French authorities to deliver them up. Neither can my people follow them into the foreign territory to discover their places of concealment."*

Here then the matter rests for the present. The result of all our recent efforts for the suppression of Dakoitee seems to be this—that very much has been done to break up, and indeed to exterminate, the great depredational leagues, consisting of members of robber-castes, often entirely composed of men of one caste, which have been from generation to generation governed by fixed laws and observant of ancient religious usages—that the more regular and complicated machinery of prædatorial crime which the Budducks and Khejucks, and other cognate tribes, had long kept in vigorous action, now either moves languidly, or not at all. And so far, Sleeman and his associates have done great things, and rendered life and property more secure in the provinces of Upper India. But to

* *Mr. Wauchope to Superintendent of Police, Lower Provinces, December* 2, 1852. *MS. Records.*

establish a reign of terror among any class of criminals in one part of a country, is naturally to drive them into another. Many were convicted and punished; many, it is to be hoped, alarmed by the new dangers which surrounded their profession, fell back upon the peaceful calling of the husbandman. But some, it seems, of the scattered fragments of the great leagues which had been broken up in the Mofussil, sought a place of safety under the walls of the Supreme Court of Calcutta. There they were met by a vigorous and experienced Company's officer, who, armed with new powers under a special Act of the Legislature, soon assured them that they had miscalculated their chances of immunity in that part of the world. Another resting-place was, therefore, to be sought; and they found it in the French settlement of Chandernagore. They knew that they were not safe within the Company's territories, and they found a little slip of foreign land whereon to locate themselves out of reach of the Company's officers. Dakoitee seems now to be in a desperate strait, and I doubt whether it will ever be restored to its old vitality and vigor.

Ever since we have had any connexion with the internal administration of India, Dakoitee has been the curse of the country. There is nothing more difficult to ascertain correctly than the statistics of crime. It is almost impossible to discriminate between an increase or decrease of committed offences and an increase or decrease of detected ones. What appears to be the increased criminality of the people may, after all, be only the increased vigilance of the police. I see little room to doubt that throughout the country generally Dakoitee has greatly decreased. Even if there had been no improvement in the police, our improved revenue-systems would by themselves have sufficed to diminish Dakoitee. Although there doubtless were gangs of hereditary robbers, who, delighting in their profession, and proud of their descent, were born and bred to be Dakoits, and followed the hereditary calling irrespectively of all the ordinary inducements to crime and of all accidental circumstances, there were many others who were driven to it, in hard famine times, who took to it when agriculture was precarious and provisions were scarce—the relatives or connexions, perhaps, of members of robber-castes, who were easily persuaded in such seasons to adopt a service which could not fail, so long as there was any property to be plundered. And the members of the robber-castes themselves, who were often agriculturists as well as depredators, were roused into unwonted activity when the crops were failing around them. At all events, it has been ascertained, beyond all question, that, in seasons of scarcity, Dakoitee has always increased. Now, as the tendency of our revenue-systems has been to develop the resources of the country and to prevent the occurrence of these seasons of scarcity, it is reasonable to believe that Dakoitee must have subsided, to some extent, under the healing influence of general prosperity. Whatsoever has a tendency to civilise the people must diminish such an evil as this.

That Dakoitee is far less insolent and violent in its demonstrations—far less sanguinary and unscrupulous, and less openly defiant of authority, than in the early days of our administration, is a fact that admits of no dispute. Dakoitee is now in comparatively few cases attended with murder. At the close of the last century it was no uncommon thing for gangs of Dakoits to kill, with brutal torture, the unhappy wretches whom they had plundered, to hack their bodies to pieces, and to hang the bloody trophies of their successful crime on the neighbouring trees, as they passed on to commit new atrocities, flushed with victory, and carrying everything insolently before them.

It may be said that, after all, what I have written only goes to show that Dakoitee has not been suppressed. It is very true that we found Dakoitee in India, and that if we were to quit the country to-morrow, we should leave it there. All that I have attempted to show is the increased vigor and policy of our measures, and the symptoms of eventual success which have recently been developed. Whatever has been done, earnestly and wisely, for the suppression of this monster evil, has been done within the last twenty years. But it is no easy thing to "abolish crime." Even in the best-governed countries, and with the most elaborate detective establishments, the science of crime is perfected under the very eyes of the police. The greatest evils that can exist under the sun are seen, known, and understood by our detective force, and yet nothing can be done to eradicate the disease with which they are so familiar.*

* Take, for example, the following melancholy fact in the last annual report of Mr. Davis, the Chaplain of Newgate:—"It is a fact much to be regretted that the metropolis contains gangs of men who not only live together for the purposes of stealing, but who educate young persons of profligate habits in the most ready and dexterous methods of stealing. Some are instructed how to pick pockets, others how to use false keys and picklocks; some, not far advanced in crime, are induced to give information and to procure impressions of valuable keys. The law against such persons is not yet strong enough. Youth such as I have referred to are clothed by their employers as well as if they were the children of respectable parents. They are fed extravagantly and indulged in vice. Some are taken to all the large towns and places of fashionable resort in the kingdom, and obtain great plunder by their skill in picking pockets. They are so dressed and so taught that in first-class railway carriages, on the platforms, in the pump-rooms, and at concerts, they disarm suspicion. The detective police will readily point out to the magistrates several establishments for such education in different parts of the metropolis, some of which are visited by them almost daily in consequence of their notorious character. In some of them as many as 20 or 30 boys have been, and probably are now, kept in constant occupation, well fed, handsomely clothed, strictly guarded and taken out by the elder offenders, and by them violently beaten if they give any information to others or umbrage to their thievish masters. These persons are frequently seen by the detective police, who know their names and nicknames, and watch their movements, but have no power until some overt act is committed to put a stop to their iniquity. Men and boys of this dangerous character are seldom convicted of great crimes, which circumstance shows that a distinction should be made between great crimes and great criminals."

There is one great difficulty with which in India, they whose duty it is to endeavour to suppress Dakoitee, have to contend, but of which nothing in these days of a kindred character is known in England —I mean the curse of evil landlords, who harbor and encourage Dakoits, and gorge themselves with a share of the spoil. I cannot help thinking, in this case, of that old mythological simile, which did such good service in my school-boy days—drawn from the story of Hercules and the Hydra. He had no sooner smitten off one head, than another sprung up tauntingly from the bleeding carcase of the monster, and so he might have gone on for ever, if the serviceable Iolas had not cauterised the wound with a hot iron, and burnt out the productiveness of the flesh. It appears to me that if we would thoroughly suppress Dakoitee, so that smitten down in one place it may not spring up in another, we would do well to apply the searing-iron to the productive Zemindars.*

* It must be borne in mind that it has been my design in this chapter to treat of one great series of operations under the Bengal Presidency. What I have written must be regarded rather as an illustration of the subject than as a general treatise on Dakoitee.

CHAPTER IV.

The Company's Civil Service—Its Rise and Progress—the Cornwallis System—Causes of its Exclusiveness—Native Agency—Present State of the Service.

In the early part of this work I have briefly spoken of the rise of the Company's service and its first organisation. I have before me a copy of the first complete list of the Company's civil servants ever sent home to England. It would not occupy half a page of this book. It was compiled in 1615; and it contains thirty-two names. Twenty-one of these were factors, and the rest "attendants on the factory." They were stationed at four different places. The civil servants of the Company are now spread all over the Regulation Provinces of India; and instead of managing the trade of a few petty factories, preside over the internal administration of an immense Empire.

Warren Hastings turned the merchants into revenue-collectors. Lord Cornwallis turned them into judges. The natives of India were thus stripped, little by little, of all the offices they had held under the Moguls. The new men so employed were doubtless better than their predecessors. The system was infinitely better than any which had preceded it. The system, indeed, was better than the men; and it kept the men greatly in check. But, after all, it was only an experiment, and the wonder is that, all things considered, both the men and the system did not turn out much worse than they did.

There was one thing which, more than any other, secured the gradual improvement of the Company's civil servants. In the old times, their recognised pay was little better than a name. In England it would have been the merest pittance. To think that any man would have taken a six months' voyage, and braved an unhealthy climate to earn it, was simply an absurdity, which no man for a moment entertained. The factor had other means of growing rich. Partly, they were recognised means; partly, they were unrecognised. The privileges which were granted to him he generally exceeded, and he made up for what was wanting in his legitimate profits by practices which are only to be palliated by a reference to the temptations which beset his career.

But all this was in time amended. Clive and Hastings had both recognised the expediency of paying substantial salaries to the Company's servants, so that the temptation to grasp at illicit gains might be diminished, if not wholly removed. The civilians, in those days, were slowly rising out of the pure mercantile state, and assuming some administrative importance. But, under Lord Cornwallis, the administrative character became fully developed. All the most important offices of the State, fiscal and judicial, were held by the covenanted servants of the Company; and it was fitting that they should receive fixed salaries in proportion to the dignity of the offices which they held and the responsibilities entailed upon them. Even under the influence of this saving change, men who had been accustomed to sit loosely to their obligations, were not suddenly braced up into a rigid observance of official propriety; but, as the old men made way for a new race, who had not been stalled in the Augæan stable, the character of the service greatly improved. With the morality of the men their intelligence rose also; they began to take a pride in their profession and an interest in the people. They were trained and disciplined, too, for the service. Colleges were established for their instruction alike in the learning of the East and the West; and in time they became not only the best paid service in the world, but one of the most efficient.*

And as the character of the English gentlemen as administrators continued to improve, the debasement of the natives of India became more complete. During the first quarter of the present century they continued in a state of dreary stagnation. There was no awakening of the faculties—no sign of progress within or without. There was nothing surprising in this. The intelligence of the people of India had, for many years, been held in small esteem by their rulers; and they were not likely to rise much above the level which had been practically assigned to them by those who shaped the destinies of the nation. Our system, indeed, had

* Although I think that under the circumstances which had arisen in India, the "Regulations" were much wanted to remedy the prevailing official laxity, I am well inclined to admit that thoroughly good men were likely to get on better without them. I find the following account of the simple style in which old Mr. Forbes, of the Bombay civil service, administered justice in Goozrat about the year 1780, which certainly furnishes a refreshing contrast to one of our Regulation courts:—"I dedicated one day in the week, and more when necessary, to the administration of justice, in which I was assisted by four principal Brahmins; the Cazee and three Mahomedans, conversant in the laws of the Koran; with some respectable merchants, and the heads of other castes. These persons advised me, in doubtful cases, and especially on points relating to the religious ceremonies and customs of the Hindoos. The carpet of justice was spread on the large open hall of the Durbar, where the arbitrators assembled; these I always attended, and, agreeably to ancient custom, referred the decision to a punchayut, or jury of five persons; two were chosen by the plaintiff, two by the defendant, and the fifth by myself, from among these elders. I had by this means the satisfaction of pleasing 100,000 inhabitants, who only made one appeal to the superior Courts at Baroche or Bombay. I was delighted with the simplicity of their mode of proceeding. From having been an alderman and sheriff at Bombay, and for some years worn the black gown as a pleader in the courts of justice at that Presidency, I was not entirely unacquainted with English law; but had I equalled Blackstone in knowledge of British jurisprudence, it would have availed little among a people completely attached to their own customs, and influenced by the prejudices of caste. I was, therefore, happy to accommodate myself to their usages. I believe I may truly say that not a present was ever made to an individual belonging to the Adawlut, nor was a court fee under any description ever exacted."—[*Forbes' Oriental Memoirs*, vol. ii., p. 2.]

been one of depression. Under the administration of Lord Cornwallis, as I have said, all the higher offices of the State had been conferred on European gentlemen—the Covenanted Civil Service of the Company. The practice thus instituted had been followed by subsequent administrators; and the official condition of the natives, in course of time, had rather deteriorated than improved. In fact, it was not only that the highest offices were conferred on the Europeans, but that none but the lowest were bestowed upon the natives. There may have been, in 1790, some wisdom in this. Perhaps it was not so much that Cornwallis and his advisers mistrusted the native, as that they mistrusted the European, functionaries. Cornwallis found his higher European agency, not in the state which had roused the energies of Clive to the great work of "cleansing the Augæan stable," but very far removed from the purity and efficiency which it has attained in the present day. He saw, doubtless, that the native functionary in the hands of his European colleague, or superior, might become a very mischievous tool—a ready-made instrument of extortion — and he determined, therefore, not to mix up the two agencies so perilously together. It is probable that, at that time, many of the higher European judicial functionaries would have exerted themselves to secure the appointment of their own tools to offices immediately beneath them, and by throwing upon the native judges the actual duty of deciding cases in which their patrons were interested, work the mine of corruption beneath the soil, and so cover the worst abuses. The native agent in such a case never betrays his employer; so the European functionary would have been secure. It may not, therefore, I say, have been mistrust of the natives, so much as mistrust of the Europeans, which deterred Cornwallis and his advisers from mixing up the two agencies in the general administration of the country.

But a very different state of things presented itself to the Indian statesman and the British legislator, when, forty years later, the terms of the new Act, under which India was to be thenceforth governed, came to be weighed and considered. The European functionary was then an honest and enlightened English gentleman, who performed a fixed duty for a fixed salary, who had little temptation to yield to besetting influences, and who would not have yielded, if he had been beset. There was no danger then, as far as he was concerned, in bringing him into immediate contact with native functionaries. There was far more likely to be a gulf between the two, than any bond of fellowship between them. It was, at that time, indeed, as expedient as it was just, to give the natives of the country a larger share in its actual administration. The system of exclusiveness had been pushed too far. The tide, indeed, had turned before the Act of 1833, for the better government of India, was hot on the legislative forge. But, in that Act, there was for the first time a specific recognition of the equal claims of all classes of the Anglo-Indian community to employment in the Company's service; and it need not be said how great an impulse such a recognition was calculated to give to the progress of native education.

The 87th clause of the new Act in which this principle was embodied was brief, but emphatic. It went straight to the point:—"And be it enacted," it said, "that no native of the said territories, nor any natural born subject of his Majesty resident therein, shall by reason only of his religion, place of birth, descent, color, or any of them, be disabled from holding any place, office, or employment, under the said Company."

There was nothing in the whole Act, viewed in all

naked significance, more important than this; but it was something which in effect might have a mighty influence upon the future administration of British India, or it might be a mere nullity. It was obvious that the mere removal of legal disabilities, whatever shape they may have taken before, would not open the higher offices of the State to any class of men, so long as there were other barriers to their admission, just as operative as though they were constructed by an Act of Parliament. The primary effect of the clause was, of course, to place in the hands of the Court of Directors a discretionary power to confer writerships and cadetships on young Rajpoots or Parsees. Everything, therefore, depended upon their practical interpretation of the law. But the Act of Parliament, though it opened the services to men of all colors and creeds, did not remove one other great disability. It did not open the doors of office to incompetent candidates for admission. There were, henceforth, to be no external disqualifications. The disqualifications were to be all from within. It was, in any view of the case, a matter of the gravest importance in the eyes of the Court of Directors, and one to which it was incumbent on them to give the profoundest consideration. They did give it this consideration; and having maturely formed them, they placed their opinions on record, and forwarded them to the supreme Government of India. They decided that if, as they believed they were justified in assuming, the people of India were not yet ripe for employment in the highest branch of the public service, it was clearly the duty of their rulers to render them so with the utmost possible despatch. It was desirable, they said, that by the improvement of the native mind the people of India should be qualified to compete at no disadvantage with their European competitors. This is the language of the Court:

By clause 87 of the Act, it is provided that no person, by reason of his birth, creed, or color, shall be disqualified from holding any office in our service.

It is fitting that this important enactment should be understood, in order that its full spirit and intention may be transfused through our whole system of administration.

You will observe that its object is not to ascertain qualification, but to remove disqualification. It does not break down or derange the scheme of our Government as conducted principally through the instrumentality of our regular servants, Civil and Military. To do this would be to abolish, or impair the rules which the Legislature has established for securing the fitness of the functionaries in whose hands the main duties of Indian administration are to be reposed; rules, to which the present Act makes a material addition in the provisions relating to the College at Hayleybury, but the meaning of the enactments we take to be, that there shall be no governing Caste in British India, that whatever other tests of qualification may be adopted, distinctions of race or religion shall not be of the number; that no subject of the King, whether of Indian, or British, or mixed descent, shall be excluded, either from the posts usually conferred on our uncovenanted servants in India, or from the covenanted service itself, provided he be otherwise eligible, consistently with the rules, and agreeably to the conditions, observed and exacted in the one case and in the other.

In the application of this principle, that which will chiefly fall to your share, will be the employment of natives, whether of the whole or the mixed blood, in official situations. So far as respects the former class, we mean natives of the whole blood, it is hardly necessary to say, that the purposes of the Legislature have, in a considerable degree, been anticipated. You will know, and indeed have in some important respects carried into effect, our desire that natives should be admitted to places of trust, as freely and extensively as a regard for the due discharge of the functions attached to such places will permit. Even judicial duties of magnitude and importance are now confided to their hands, partly, no doubt, from considerations of economy, but partly also on the principles of a liberal and comprehensive policy, still, a line of demarcation, to some extent in favor of the natives, to some extent in exclusion of them, has been maintained. Certain offices are appropriated to them; from certain others they are debarred; not because these latter belong to the covenanted service, and the former do not belong to it; but professedly on the ground that the average amount of native qualifications can be presumed only to rise to a certain limit. It is this line of demarcation which the present enactments obliterates, or rather, for which it substitutes another, wholly irrespective of the distinction of races. Fitness is henceforth to be the criterion of eligibility.

To this altered rule it will be necessary that you should, both in your acts and your language, conform. Practically, perhaps, no very marked indifference of results will be occasioned. The distinctions between situations allotted to the covenanted service, and all other situations of an official or public nature, will remain generally as at present.

Into a more particular consideration of the effects that may result from the great principle which the Legislature has now for the first time recognised and established, we do not enter, because we would avoid disquisition of a speculative nature. But there is one practical lesson, which, often as we have on former occasions inculcated it on you, the present subject suggests to us once more to enforce. While, on the one hand, it may be anticipated that the range of public situations accessible to the native and mixed races, will gradually be enlarged, it is, on the other hand, to be recollected that, as settlers from Europe find their way into the country, this class of persons will probably furnish candidates for those very situations to which the natives and mixed race will have admittance. Men of European enterprise and education will appear in the field, and it is by the prospect of this event that we are led particularly to impress the lesson already alluded to, on your attention. In every view it is important that the indigenous people of India, or those among them who by their habits, character, or position, may be induced to aspire to office, should, as far as possible, be qualified to meet their European competitors. Hence there arises a powerful argument for the promotion of every design tending to the improvement of the natives, whether by conferring on them the advantages of education, or by diffusing among them the treasures of science, knowledge, and moral culture. For these desirable results, we are well aware that you, like ourselves, are anxious; and we doubt not that, in order to impel you to increased exertion for the promotion of them, you will need no stimulant beyond a simple reference to the considerations we have here suggested.

While, however, we entertain these wishes and opinions, we must guard against the supposition that it is chiefly by holding out means and opportunities of official distinction, that we expect our Government to benefit the millions subjected to their authority. We have repeatedly expressed to you a very different sentiment. Facilities of official advancement can little affect the bulk of the people under any Government, and perhaps least under a good Government. It is not by holding out incentives to official ambition, but by repressing crime, by securing and guarding property, by creating confidence, by ensuring to industry the fruit of its labor, by protecting men in the undisturbed enjoyment of their rights, and in the unfettered exercise of their faculties, that Governments best minister to the public wealth and happiness. In effect, the free access to office is chiefly valuable when it is a part of general freedom.*

Ever since this admirable letter was written, the natives of India have had a larger and a larger share in the administrative agency of the country, and have been better qualified to maintain their official position. The system, as now established, is this. The lowest grade of judicial officers is that of the "Moonsiff." He is selected from among persons who have passed an examination before a local Committee, and is approved by a Sudder Committee at the Presidency. He is empowered to try suits to the amount of 30*l.* His salary never amounts to more than 200*l.* a year.† From these Moonsiffs the next higher grade of judicial officers—the Sudder Aumeens—are chosen. Their jurisdiction extends to suits of 100*l.* Their salary ranges from 240*l.* to 420*l.* a year. From these Sudder Aumeens the principal Sudder Aumeens are chosen. There is, at present, no limit to the jurisdiction of this latter class.

The administration of civil justice is at present almost entirely in the hands of these native officers. Appeal lies from the lower to the higher grades. But in respect of all suits above 500*l.*, whether tried by

* *The Court of Directors to the Government of India, December*, 1834.

† The salaries of the Moonsiffs, however, are likely ere long to be raised.

the Principal Sudder Aumeen, or by the European Zillah judge,* the appeal is only to the Sudder Court, or chief tribunal. The Principal Sudder Aumeens are thus placed on a level with the highest European functionaries, except the Sudder judges, with this reservation, however, that the European judge has the power of withdrawing any suits from the native courts, and trying them in his own.

In the dispensation of criminal justice the natives of India have less share, but they are not wholly excluded from it. A class of deputy magistrates has been established, the members of which are sometimes vested by the local Governments with the same powers as are possessed by the European magistrates. In this capacity they are competent to pass sentences extending to imprisonment for three years.

Beyond this the power of the European magistrates does not extend. All cases demanding severer punishment are sent to the Sessions judge, who is empowered to sentence to 14 years' imprisonment. If this extent of punishment does not appear to meet the criminality of the case, it is sent, with a written letter from the Sessions judge, stating his opinions, to the chief criminal court, or Sudder Nizamut Adawlut. If the Sudder judges concur in the opinions of the lower court, and the offence is not one demanding the punishment of death, it is sufficient for one judge to try the case. If he dissents from that opinion, or capital punishment seems to be demanded, the case is heard by two judges on the bench.

On the whole, it may be said that the extended em-

* In all such cases, whether original suits or appeals, the European judge is competent to withdraw the case from the court of the principal Sudder Aumeen, and dispose of it himself—but in either case the appeal lies only to the Sudder. Very few original suits, however, are decided by the European judges. It would appear from official statistics, that under the Government of the North-Western Provinces, in 1849, only 20 original suits were so decided, whilst nearly 45,000 were decided by the native judges.

ployment of native agency in the administration of justice has worked as well as there was reason to expect —but not so well as to lead any unprejudiced observer to believe that in not throwing open the doors of office more unreservedly to them any great mistake has been committed.* It appears to me that nothing can be sounder in theory, or more beneficial in practice, than the system by which a people, long deprived of power, are gradually restored to it. The process of restoration can hardly be too gradual. We need look for no better proof that the Court of Directors, when reviewing the famous 87th clause, did not look too disparagingly upon the qualifications, and too grudgingly upon the claims of their native servants, than the fact that the passage I have quoted, though written twenty years ago (and those years have witnessed great improvement in the moral and intellectual character of the class of Government *employés*), is as applicable to the present state of things as if it had been written to-day.

The admission of the natives of India to the highest offices of the State is simply a question of time. "I believe," said a distinguished member of the Company's service,† before the Committee of the House of Commons, "that our mission in India is to qualify them for governing themselves. I say, also," he continued, "that

* Mr. Halliday, who has had the best opportunities of observing the working of this system of native agency, and whose testimony is entitled to great weight, when asked by the Committee of the House of Commons "Is the impression upon the minds of the natives of India generally, that the law as it is, is impartially and honestly administered by the authorities who administer it?" replied, "Speaking of the native courts, that is to say of the courts presided over by natives, without desiring to attribute to them faults, I must say that at present, owing to the long experience of the natives of the corruptibility of their own countrymen, and their great want of confidence in them as compared with the confidence they have acquired in the Europeans, there is not generally in the minds of the natives such a complete reliance upon the impartiality and incorruptibility of the courts under native judges as could be wished; but I believe it will grow up in the course of time, especially as the courts themselves within my observation and knowledge have manifestly improved in regard to integrity and trustworthiness, and as the natives know and see them to improve, their suspicions of course will be lulled, and they will gradually acquire in them the same confidence that they have in the courts presided over by Europeans."

† Mr. Halliday.

the measures of the Government, for a number of years past, have been advisedly directed to so qualifying them, without the slightest reference to any remote consequences upon our administration." Long before it became their duty to review the clauses of the Act of 1833, the Court of Directors had continually exhorted their servants in India to prepare, through the agency of improved systems of education, the natives of the country for higher official positions than they had yet been qualified to hold. And these exhortations had not been thrown away. What the ultimate effect of their great educational measures must be, it is not difficult to conjecture. Our mission will be fulfilled sooner or later. The only question is a question of time.

In the mean while, though the administrative agency to which the internal management of the country is entrusted is not without inherent defects, it seems to be a matter of extremest difficulty to suggest a safe substitute for it. There has been an outcry raised of late against the Company's courts and the Company's judges; but some of the best authorities are of opinion that the natives of the country have unlimited confidence in both.* There may, perhaps, be some local exceptions, and instances of occasional malversation have from time to time been made public. But in almost every case in which a civil servant of the Company has been charged with corrupt practices, a brother civilian has been the accuser. There is no effort to screen the delinquent, but rather an

* Take, for example, the following passage from Mr. Halliday's evidence before the House of Commons:—"Have they (the natives) complete confidence in the administration of justice in those (the Company's) Courts by the English judges? As far as regards the integrity of the judges, their confidence is complete; they have little or no notion of the possibility of corrupting an English judge; it scarcely ever enters into their imagination. They may, perhaps, have sometimes a difference of opinion as to the acuteness and intelligence of some of the judges; and I dare say that, as compared with the acuteness and intelligence of the native judges, those qualities in the English judges are often in the minds of the natives at fault; but in the integrity, and in the honest and earnest desire of the English judges to do justice impartially between man and man, the natives have the highest possible confidence." — [*Mr. Halliday's Evidence.*]

earnest desire, on the part of the general body of the service, to bring his offences to light. As to those judicial inconsistencies and other *bêtises* which have been cited so freely from the records of the Company's Courts in Madras, it appears to me that nothing could be easier than to cite from the records of any courts an equal array of unintelligible decisions. I have a great respect for the English Bench, and the utmost faith in the honesty and ability with which justice is administered in this country; but if incomprehensible decisions, startling sentences, and furious inconsistencies are to be cited as proofs of incapacity and corruption, it would not be difficult to fill a volume with such proofs culled from the Assize Intelligence contained in a six months' file of a London journal.*

It is admitted that there are many defects in the existing system—that justice is administered by men wanting in judicial training, perhaps with no legal habits of mind, and somewhat deficient in ordinary acumen. But there are, probably, even greater wants than these—a want of knowledge of the people—knowledge of their character, of their language, of the habits of their every-day life. There is always, more or less, an imperfect acquaintance with these things. A right knowledge of them is not easy to attain—we only see the outside of the natives, disguised for better or for worse. But this is an evil not peculiar to the condition of the exclusive service of the Company, but inseparable from our position as strangers and aliens in the East. Under the existing system, indeed, it is less felt than it would be under any other. If young men expressly educated for the service, taught perhaps from early boyhood to

* The fact is, that the printed report of a case seldom fairly represents its merits, even when it is given with much amplitude of detail for the amusement of newspaper readers. Every man has read reports of cases which he has heard decided, and admitted that he should never have known the reason of the decision if he had not been himself in court.

look forward to an Indian career, proceeding to India at an early age, perhaps to a home whither his father and brothers have preceded him, cannot sufficiently enlace his interest and his affections with the realities of Indian life, how much less likely is one, coming at a comparatively mature age, fresh from the Inns of Court, to acquire a competent knowledge of the things in which, with all his advantages, the writer is avowedly deficient ?*

It was said by Canning, during the debates on the India Charter of 1813, that there could not be anything radically wrong in the system which had produced all the able Company's servants who had given their evi-

* I think that Sir Edward Ryan's evidence regarding the appointment of English barristers to Indian judgeships is quite conclusive on the subject. "Do you believe that the administration of justice would be improved in India by the selection of barristers from England and from India for that purpose?—I do not think so; barristers from England, I presume, could not go out until perhaps of the age of twenty-five; they would hardly be barristers till that time. I do not know what would tempt many barristers of that age to proceed to India, because it is quite clear that upon their first arrival in that country they would be quite incompetent to fill the offices of judges in the interior. The first thing they have to learn, of course, is the native languages, which would not be so easily acquired at that age as at the earlier age at which civil servants proceed to India; they would have no opportunity of acquiring that species of judicial training to which I have before alluded; namely, becoming familiar with the natives in the transaction of business in the various ways in which civil servants obtain that familiarity in the office of the collector. Not possessing this knowledge of the languages, nor this familiarity with the manners, and usages, and habits of the natives, I do not see how they could become efficient judges in the interior of the country, especially with reference to this; it is not the knowledge of the science of the law which is so much required in the Mofussil Courts, it is the administrative art which is so required, and that can only arise from familiarity with the people, and a knowledge of the people themselves. It is facts that the Court have to deal with; in dealing with facts in a country like that, you are surrounded with infinitely more difficulties than you are here. In the Supreme Court the opportunities and power of dealing with facts are greater than in the Mofussil Courts in one respect; the judge in the Supreme Court, indeed, is unacquainted with the native languages, the greatest part of the witnesses are natives, speaking the native language; but before a witness is produced in that Court he is carried to the office of the attorney, the attorney has under him a principal native manager, that native manager is familiar with the English and the Vernacular languages; he lifts the witness in the office, and he communicates the result of that to the attorney; the attorney communicates it to the barrister. The witness is called in Court after all this preliminary lifting, he is then examined in Court in his own language, by interpreters, who in my time were men of extraordinary ability, he is cross-examined of course in the same way; and after that sifting from the commencement at the attorney's office, and his examination and cross-examination, the judge has very constantly the greatest possible difficulty in coming to a conclusion upon the evidence so sifted. Now what would be the position of an English family in the Mofussil, totally devoid of all those aids, and without the information which the civil servants acquire by the species of training to which I before alluded?"

dence before the Parliamentary Committees. Forty years later the same remark might be made,—with this pungent addition: The system cannot be radically wrong which has produced the able Company's servants whom the Queen's Ministers have selected from time to time, not merely to govern the Crown colonies, but to extricate them from difficulties into which they have been thrown by the intemperance or incapacity of men who have not been trained in the Indian service. When great colonial embarrassments arise—and they do arise sometimes—it is commonly to the talent, to the temper, to the discretion, to the firmness, and to the integrity of some servant of the Company, that the perplexed Minister looks for the saving hand that is to extricate him from his dilemma.

Yet these men are said to be the minions of a corrupt system. The patronage of the East India Company, it is sometimes alleged, is at the bottom of all this vile mess of administrative uncleanliness. Justice is put to the most miserable shifts that the friends of the thirty magnates of Leadenhall-street may draw so many thousands a year from the territorial revenues of India; and the conclusion is, that therefore the doom of the Court ought to be sealed without hesitation or delay. I am told by the Chaplain of Newgate that the reason why, if I send a bank-note, or a ring, or a watch-chain in a letter, it runs no small risk of being stolen by a letter-carrier is, that "the vacancies in the Post-office are filled up by parties recommended to the Postmaster-General by members of Parliament."* To this system Mr. Davis attributes the

* I may as well quote the passage to which I refer, in Mr. Davis's last annual report:—"The watchful care of masters over their servants, to inquire, from time to time, into their habits of life and pursuits in private, should apply to the public establishments of the country. The moral reputation of public servants ought to be taken into consideration, but that branch of the public service where we meet with most failures is the Post-office. Post-office cases, involving, as they do, not merely a serious breach of public trust, but cases of domestic misery that baffle description, have engaged my most earnest attention. In more than one little pamphlet I have addressed the dishonest parties among those employed by the Post-office, in the hope, by some

frequent occurrence of a crime "involving cases of domestic misery that baffle description." From this we may learn the great lesson, that a mischievous administration of the patronage of the State may not only be coexistent with, but be fostered and encouraged by, an institution on which the liberties of the country are mainly dependent. And if letter-carriers' appointments are so jobbed between Ministers and Members of Parliament, how would writerships and cadetships fare in the same immaculate hands?

such appeal to their better feelings, to correct their errors, and if possible prevent the crime. I should like still more to be done in this way, so far as it can, without offence and with hope of success; but I greatly fear that some portion of this unenviable distinction in servants of the Post-office, namely, that a greater number are convicted and transported in that than any other department, arises in some measure from the manner of their appointment. As far as I can learn, but I speak only from rumour, the vacancies in the Post-office are filled up by parties recommended to the Postmaster-General by members of Parliament. It is easy to imagine that for services rendered to these gentlemen they are glad of any opportunity of doing a kindness for great zeal and activity in serving them. Hence there may not be such a rigid inquiry into the past life and habits of the men recommended as seems essential in a duty so important."

PART IV.

CHAPTER I.

The Non-Regulation Provinces—Civil and Military Administrators—Evils of Exclusiveness—Sindh—Defects of the purely Military System—Sir Charles Napier's Government—Arracan—Improvement of the Province—The Punjab—The Board of Administration—The Lawrences—Mr. Mansell—the Subordinate Administrative Machinery—Settlement of the Revenue—Financial and General Results.

I HAVE done with the Regulations. I have said enough of the manner in which the affairs of these provinces, which have long been subject to our fixed Revenue and Judicial systems, are administered by the civil servants of the Company. There are provinces, more recently brought under our rule, which do not bow down to the letter of the Regulations, but are governed after a ruder and simpler fashion—by an executive composed partly of civilians and partly of soldiers, upon a mixed system, into which the spirit of the Regulations is infused in such a manner as to cause it to harmonise and blend itself with all that is good in the spirit of native institutions, and to be respected in the local usages of the country.

The Non-Regulation Provinces are these:—Under the Bengal Presidency are the Saugor and Nerbudda territories; Jaloun and Jhansi; Mairwarra; Assam, Arracan, and the Tenasserim provinces; Goalpara; the districts on the South-Western frontier, as Sumbulpore, Ramgurh, &c.; the Cis-Sutlej states, including Umballah,

Loodhianah, Khytul, Ferozepore, and the territory recently held by the protected Sikh chiefs; and the whole country of the Punjab. These are subject to the controlling authority of the Governor-General, or the Governor of Bengal, and are administered by officers appointed by them. Under the government of the North-Western Provinces are the Dehra Doon; Kumaon and Gurhwal; the Butty territory; Ajmere; Nimaur; Jaunsar and Bawur. Under the Madras government are Ganjam; Vizigapatam; and Kurnool. And under the government of Bombay are Colaba, Sindh, and Sattarah.

The system under which the affairs of these provinces are administered has generally worked well. It has been as successful in the North-West as in the South-East. In Arracan we have tried it for a quarter of a century, and the results have been as advantageous to the governed as they are honorable to the Government. In the Punjab we are only beginning to try it—we are in the first stage of the experiment; but the brightness of the dawn promises a brilliant meridian success.

It must not, however, be assumed that, because this less elaborate and less costly administration has answered every purpose of government in the provinces to which it has been applied, that therefore the more elaborate and expensive machinery which we have set at work in the Regulation provinces has been altogether a mistake. The fact is, that the extension of our empire has brought us closer and closer to the outskirts of civilisation, and that having to do with a ruder people, we have expediently subjected them to a ruder system of government. Bengal had been a quarter of a century in our hands before Cornwallis and Barlow framed their famous Regulations. But imagine what Napier in Sindh, Lawrence in the Punjab, Dixon in Mairwarra, Bogle in Arracan, or any other British officer among a rude people newly brought under our rule, could have made of those Regulations which the ablest lawyers in India pronounced to be worthy of Justinian. What a people suddenly finding themselves under the sovereignty of a new set of rulers most requires, is a government very little in advance of that from which they have been transferred. All abrupt and violent changes are as injurious to the constitution of a nation as they are to the constitution of a man. If you find a creature dying from inanition, and begin to gorge him, you are sure to kill him outright. If you take a drunkard suddenly from his stimulants, the chances are that you cure him of his drunkenness only by sending him to his grave. Changes for the better must be gradual, or they are likely to be changes for the worse. If we find a people groaning under a despotism, we must be despotic ourselves. A little tyranny is absolutely necessary at such times to the welfare of the people, and it is not to be doubted that, on the whole, a military government is best suited to such a state of society. Doubtless the rough ways of Sir Charles Napier were better adapted to the feelings and habits of the Beloochees, after the conquest of Sindh, than the refined tendernesses and the judicial niceties of the gentlest and wisest statesman that ever loved and toiled for a people. "Unsophisticated human nature," it was truly written by the conqueror of Sindh, "and military nature, must both be studied in dealing with barbarians; they would not bear from a civilian arrangements suited to civilisation, but crossing their prejudices; yet to the stern behests of a soldier chief they would bow in submission."*

But we must be careful, in such csses, that we do not rush from one extreme into another equally dangerous. The quick eye of Sir Charles Napier saw at once that too much civilianism would be the ruin of Sindh; but, having seen this, he let down before those quick eyes a

* *Sir W. Napier's "History of Sir Charles Napier's Administration of Scinde."*

shade of strong prejudice, and he did not see, or would not see, that there might be danger in too little civilianism. He took into his hands the whole Revenue and Judicial management of the country, and, with all his energy and all his ability, it was too much for him. In the Judicial department he may not have greatly erred, for he had to deal with men who were little accustomed to technical formalities, and who could better appreciate summary justice than legal delays. Few clear-headed and impartial men will go very wrong, when honestly endeavouring to administer justice among a people not utterly vitiated by the contiguity of venal courts, and taught to rely on falsehood and corruption. But the settlement of the landed revenue of a country is a very difficult matter ; and our new military judges had often to decide upon complicated Revenue cases. It was in the adjudication of these cases that they most frequently erred, for, as they were utterly inexperienced in Revenue matters, they were not likely to be very competent to decide upon them. It was indeed a strange thing to see these "military commissions" sitting in judgment on disputed land-tenures. "I have sat on scores of them," writes one of the Sindh officials, "and have repeatedly been compelled to swear on the Gospel that I would adjudicate and decide on disputed titles to lands 'according to the custom of war in like cases.'"*

Sir Charles Napier did not choose his subordinates unwisely. Such men as Brown and Goldney, for example—I speak of them because I knew and loved them, but there are others, doubtless, well worthy of honorable mention—were suited, no less by their talents than by their energies, to further the efforts of their gallant chief. But neither they, nor their colleagues, were experienced in the work of civil administration. A few covenanted officers of the civil service had been sent down to Sindh,

* *MS. Notes.*

on the first annexation of the province, to assist in the details of its revenue and judicial administration; but Sir Charles Napier, who had an equally low opinion of old and of young civilians,* very soon obtained their dismissal, and the entire management of the country was transferred to the hands of the soldiers. They were zealous and for the most part able men—but they had to transact business that was new to them, and it is no discredit to Sir Charles Napier and his assistants, whose experience as financiers extended little beyond the management, under the tuition of a pay-havildar, of the accounts of a company of Sepoys, that they should have failed in the revenue administration of such a country as Sindh.

It is true that these military administrators, from Sir Charles Napier downwards, being men of no common energy and ability, might have made themselves proficients in the civil duties entrusted to them, but that they had the work of war to do, no less than the work of peace. The restlessness of the predatory hill tribes demanded vigorous coercion, and Sir Charles Napier, pushing aside the portfolio of the civil Governor, mounted his horse, and took the field against the robber clans. He was not a man to delegate such work as this to another. Nor was it likely, when he heard from afar the first mutterings of

* It is hard to say whether Sir Charles Napier thought a young civilian or an old civilian the most dangerous person to meddle with a newly-conquered country. Of the former, he said: "Young, and often very incapable, men are sent to acquire experience and fortunes at the expense of the proprietors' dividends by misgoverning newly-conquered countries. Unknowing how to rule even a settled country, they have to create every branch of administration, and must necessarily manipulate roughly, and, as it were, with horny hands, when the nicest touch is essential—meddling arbitrarily and ignorantly with social and financial affairs, where error may give mortal offence, where parsimony may be folly, and extravagance madness." Of the old civilians, he says: "Length of residence and sensual indulgence weaken body and mind, and give only aptness for official details without enlargement of ideas; and most of these persons generalised as *Old Indians*, because they have worn out originally vigorous appetites and feeble minds whilst enjoying large salaries and the adulation of black clerks, who do all their duties, imagine that they only know the East."—[*Sir C. Napier's Letters in Sir W. Napier's "Administration of Scinde."*] *Utrum horum mavis accipe;* and it is clear that in the estimation of Sir Charles Napier no civilian is fit to take a part in the administration of a new country.

the coming storm on the Sutlej, that he would remain glued to his desk. Where, then, at such times, was the civil Governor? And where were his collectors and deputy-collectors? Sir Charles Napier was at the head of his men, and his military civilians were exerting themselves to collect supplies, and to forward them to the troops moving through the country. Such distractions were not favorable to the progress of civil administration in Sindh. The necessary European superintendence was withdrawn, and the native officials were left, in many places, to carry on the work by themselves. And how it was carried on may be gathered from the statements of a writer, thoroughly acquainted with all the details of British administration in Sindh, who declares that the system in force at this time might not unfaithfully be described as "the retention of all that was oppressive or evil in the old system, the discarding of all that was useful, and adding much evil of our own; whilst experience and honesty were exchanged for inexperience in the superintendence, and fraud and oppression in the subordinate branches."* The fact is, that a slight infusion of civilianism was required, and this Sir Charles Napier had impetuously rejected. All the evil is here traceable to the exclusiveness of the system. The administrators were not merely military men in civil capacities. They were military men distracted from the performance of their civil duties by demands made upon them in their military character. They were not permitted, quietly and uninterruptedly, to accommodate themselves to their new duties; but whilst they ought to have been peacefully settling the country, they were maturing measures for the coercion of refractory tribes.

But although Sir Charles Napier, being like most earnest, energetic men, imbued with strong prejudices,

* *Calcutta Review*, No. xxvii. Art.: "British Administration of Scinde"— a paper which seems to be written with remarkable fairness and impartiality.

fell into this extreme of anti-civilianism, and erred accordingly, I believe that he really had the good of the Sindhians sincerely at heart. He professed himself to be anxious, "whilst fastening on the country a strong military gripe, to apply all softening and healing measures to the vanquished race—all protective and encouraging measures to the liberated population;"* and I do not doubt that he was. Slavery was abolished by a stroke of the pen. It had not existed, among the Sindhians, in any very intolerable shape, but it was well even that the name of such an evil should cease to have legal sanction. Infanticide was very common among the Sindhians. He exerted himself to suppress it. Female life, infant or adult, was held of so little account among them, that men murdered their wives with impunity, and believed that it was as lawful as the killing of sharks. When Sir Charles Napier talked of hanging the murderers, the chiefs asked with astonishment if he would hang a man "for only killing his wife;" but he did hang them, and the gallows in time abated the evil. Then he disarmed the people, and curbed the frequent arbitrement of the sword, and the blood-spillings of private strife. "He also," says Sir William Napier, "put down the practice of Suttee, which, however, was rare in Scinde, by a process extremely characteristic. For judging the real cause of these immolations to be the profits derived by the priests, and hearing of an intended burning, he made it known that he would stop the sacrifice. The priests said it was a

* "To meet the requirements of these different races in the present circumstances my policy must be, whilst fastening on the country a strong military gripe, to apply all softening and healing measures to the vanquished race, all protective and encouraging measures to the liberated population—to make strong even-handed justice be universally felt—to draw forth the abundant natural resources of the country, and repair the terrible evils of the Ameers' misgovernment. The trading Hindoo will then attach himself to a system which protects his calling, and opens a wider scope for its exercise. He will, for his own sake, give timely intelligence of designs to restore the oppressive yoke of the Beloochees, and the rich Banians have a wonderful knowledge of all that is passing."—[*Letter of Sir Charles Napier, quoted in Sir William Napier's "Administration of Scinde."*]

religious rite which must not be meddled with—that all nations had customs which should be respected, and this was a very sacred one. The general, affecting to be struck with the argument, replied, 'Be it so. This burning of widows is your custom. Prepare the funeral pile. But my nation has also a custom. When men *burn* women alive we hang them, and confiscate all their property. My carpenters shall therefore erect gibbets on which to hang all concerned when the widow is consumed. Let us all act according to national customs.'" "No Suttee," adds the historian, "took place then, or afterwards."* It may be questioned, indeed, whether many had taken place before. The population of Sindh is, for the most part, a Mahomedan population, and Suttee is a Hindoo rite.

On the subject of the taxation of the people of Sindh the historian must enter with caution. It has been said, on the one hand, that Sir Charles Napier abolished all the oppressive taxes which he found in operation; and on the other, that he not only greatly increased them, but, moreover, collected them in the most vexatious manner. It has been said, indeed, that the very courtesans of Hyderabad paid a portion of their earnings to the collector. It does not, however, appear impossible to reconcile these conflicting statements. Sir Charles Napier, on his first assumption of the Sindh government, seems to have resorted to all the existing sources of revenue; but at a later period some injurious imposts were abolished which pressed heavily on the industrial energies of the people. These were, firstly, a tax upon shops, which fell with some severity on the Mahomedan artificers; secondly, a tax upon fishermen; and, thirdly, a tax upon Hindoo communities, levied in the aggregate on towns and villages, and divided into individual portions by the tax-payers themselves. By the abolition of these taxes a

* *Sir William Napier's "Administration of Scinde."*

considerable source of revenue was abandoned where revenue was much wanted; but it did much to secure the confidence of the people. It was after Napier's return from his hill campaigns that these imposts were abolished.

To the great subject of artificial irrigation, also, Sir Charles Napier applied the energies of his vigorous mind. He was eager to increase the productiveness of the country by an improved system of water supply. Beyond the tracts of country watered by the Indus itself, this could be effected only by canal-irrigation, and in some parts by the sinking of wells. He had this sincerely at heart, but the results did not keep pace with his desires. There was a scarcity of money, and a scarcity of labor; and such works demanded an abundance of both.* There were adventitious circumstances, too, inseparable from the character of the local government, which rendered it impossible that the benevolent impulses of Sir Charles Napier should ever bear the desired fruit. The element of failure lay in the accident of his position.

It is greatly to be deplored that this question of the Administration of Sindh has been overlaid with such a superincumbent mass of controversy, that the truth is to be seen with difficulty glimmering beneath it, let us dig and scrape as we may. Perhaps, however, if leaving the antagonistic writers on either side, we turn to Sir Charles Napier's own official letters, we may attain to something like an approximation to the fact. "I will now conclude," he wrote to Lord Ripon, "by saying that, though the officers with me and myself might have done more and better, no one will deny that we have had many and

* For the same reasons, perhaps, the work of road-making proceeded slowly, or not at all. It was reserved for Sir Charles Napier's successors to give effect to a scheme for the improvement of the land communications of the province. More has been done within the last year or two than throughout the previous years of our occupation of Sindh. A good road between Sukkur and Shikarpore is now in course of construction; its completion will be attended with excellent results.

great difficulties to struggle with—war and pestilence in its utmost virulence, the destruction of a whole harvest by locusts, and the greatest part of another by a sudden and unprecedented fall of the inundation before the grain was mature, have been amongst the evils afflicting Scinde since 1843. In the midst of an extensive military command, I have had to construct the entire machinery of a civil government, assisted by young officers who had at first starting little or no experience, but whose zeal and abilities have enabled them to serve me well; and by diligence they have overcome the great obstacle of total want of experience, which was at first almost insuperable in the collection of the revenue. How we have succeeded we must leave the world to decide."* The world, doubtless, will decide that in this paragraph Sir Charles Napier has candidly set forth the inherent defects of the system under which he administered the affairs of this important province. When we consider that the civil government was conducted "in the midst of an extensive military command," and that the collection of the revenue was entrusted to young military officers, whose qualifications for such duties consisted in "a total want of experience," the only wonder is, that the experiment should have been half as successful as it was.

The administration of the Arracan provinces has been almost exclusively in the hands of military men; but it has not been an "essentially military" government in the sense that Sindh was to be so regarded under the rule of Sir Charles Napier. The chief magistrate of the province has never been, at the same time, the Commander of the Forces. The civil and military authorities

* *Sir Charles Napier to Lord Ripon, quoted in Sir William Napier's "Administration of Scinde."*—The reader may advantageously compare this passage with one quoted in a note, at page 437, where Sir Charles Napier, speaking of young civilians, complains that "young, and often very incapable, men are sent to acquire experience and fortunes at the expense of the proprietors' dividends by misgoverning a newly-acquired country. Not knowing how to rule a settled country, they have to create every branch of administration, and must necessarily manipulate roughly," &c., &c.

have been distinct from each other, and never have the latter had the least control over the former. It has been all governing and no fighting; and thus far circumstances have favored the development of the system. But if such had not been the case, the necessity of coercing any refractory tribes would not have suspended or impeded, in so far as related to adequate European superintendence, the entire civil administration of the country.

When the pestiferous jungles of Arracan became a component part of the British Empire in the East, the province which it was our new duty to govern was little better than a howling wilderness. Thinly inhabited, scantily cultivated, it presented to the outward eye of the administrator only a discouraging prospect of mortifying failure. It was the very reverse of a land of promise. In 1825, Mr. Robertson was appointed Agent in Arracan, but the Burmese war then entailed upon him pressing duties, from the performance of which he could not turn aside; and all that he could do in the way of internal organisation was to maintain the heads of villages or tribes, known as "Moosoogrees," in their several posts, and to place some portion of the country under the old chiefs, who, after many years of exile spent under our government at Chittagong, now returned to their native land, eager to render good service to the British.* Clearly perceiving the importance at such a time of conciliating the Mug chiefs, Mr. Robertson abstained from anything like a vexatious meddling with details. But upon his departure from Arracan, the superintendence of the province was made over to Captain Paton—a man of gigantic stature, largely acquainted with the native languages—especially the Bengallee—but slenderly endowed with administrative talent and discretion. He had been summoned round from Calcutta,

* They rendered important service to our army, not only by procuring ordinary supplies, but by furnishing us with the means of housing the army.

where he had held the office of police magistate; but he talked better than he ruled, and amidst so much to dispirit and to discourage—for the troops were dying like sheep with the rot, and there was a general impression that the province would be abandoned—it was little likely that the work of internal administration should proceed with any good effect. The treaty of Yandaboo was concluded, and then a Commission, of which Captain Paton and Mr. Richard Hunter of the civil service were the members, was appointed for the civil government of the country. It did not work well. Mr. Hunter was a man of those ordinary business qualifications which make useful public servants in settled offices, the duties of which are clearly defined and well understood. But something more than this was required. Everything went wrong. The Commissioners irritated the chiefs, whom Mr. Robertson had placed in authority, and upon some rumor of disaffection disbanded the Mug levy which he had raised.* But Paton died, and Hunter left the country; and Captain Dickenson, who had commanded the first Mug levy, and was employed, I believe, in its reconstruction, was then appointed Commissioner. He was a man of good parts, but of a quick temper; and an unhappy dispute with a subordinate aggravated his natural irritability, and added nothing to his efficiency as an administrator. Little progress was made during his rule. But better times were beginning to dawn upon the province.

About the year 1835-36, Captain Bogle, who had been in political charge of an extensive district in Assam, was appointed to the Arracan Commissionership. At this time the unhealthiness of the province still continued

* This levy had done good service at a time when both our European and native troops were prostrated by the pestilence. It furnished employment, moreover, to some of the more turbulent natives of the country, who otherwise might have given us some trouble, and who, indeed, on the disbandment of the corps, became regular Dakoits.

to be a proverb. It was no uncommon thing, at certain seasons of the year, to find more than half the European officers attached to the civil and military establishments either prostrate on their beds, or cruising about the Bay of Bengal in a state of doubtful convalescence. I have heard it said, that in one year half the European population died during the rains. The deadly fevers of the country, too, struck down the natives of Hindostan—soldiers and servants, by scores. An order to embark for Arracan was held to be little better than a death-warrant. A few days often did the work. A single ride along the skirts of one of those pestiferous jungles would send a young man, in the full flush of youthful health and vigor, to his grave within a week of his arrival in the province.

But within the space of a very few years Arracan acquired a new reputation. Men who had narrowly escaped with their lives from the influence of the destroying climate, or who remembered how their friends, one after one, had returned, gaunt scarecrows, from that deadly coast, after a few months, or perhaps a few weeks of absence, were startled when they read in the Calcutta papers that English gentlemen and ladies in the vice-regal city were making up pleasure parties to proceed by steam to Arracan, for the sake of the fine sea-breezes. Many went; and all returned strengthened and exhilarated. The province, under Bogle's management, had lived down its bad reputation, and was actually growing into a fashionable sanitarium.

This was only one of the results of the activity and good management of our military administrators. The pestilent jungles in the neighbourhood of our principal stations had been hewn down, and burnt out of the soil; but much more than this had been done. They who had seen the wilderness which passed into our hands in 1825, were delighted on visiting the country some fifteen years afterwards, to find themselves in one of the most prosperous and well-governed provinces under the Presidency of Bengal. Arracan, indeed, was fast earning for itself the name of the "granary of Southern India." A large export trade in rice was established, and the ports, which had before been well-nigh deserted, were soon all alive with shipping. The prosperity of the cultivators continued to increase. Every man's rights were clearly determined; and every man knew precisely the amount which was due by him to the Government. Many carried a memorandum of their liabilities, written on a scrap of palm-leaf, rolled up into a small cylinder, and fastened into a hole through the lobe of their ears.

The vast improvement which has been effected in the internal condition of Arracan is the work entirely of military administrators. No civilian has been officially employed in the province since the time of Mr. Richard Hunter. In Bogle and Phayre the Government of India possessed two officers of strong natural sagacity and unwearied perseverance; and they were not suddenly taken from their regiments to be turned into judges and collectors. The former had served for some years in Assam, under one of the ablest civil administrators in India, and something at least of his efficiency may be attributed to the advantages of that training. His success clearly shows, that under the government of military officers, the civil administration of a province may be so conducted as to confer extensive benefits both on the Government and the governed; but it does not show that it is safe to place untrained men, clever captains and active adjutants, fresh from their troops or companies, in responsible offices, demanding administrative experience such as is not acquired from the study of the order-book, or the Articles of War.

But of all the experiments of government which have recently been made, the greatest is that which has for its seat the country beyond the Sutlej. When that great artillery battle of Goojrat had been fought—when the Sikh Empire lay prostrate at the feet of the Governor-General of India, and an order had gone forth declaring the kingdom of Runjeet Singh then and for ever effaced from the catalogue of Indian principalities, it was no insignificant problem which presented itself for the solution of our Indian statesmen. No tract of country, so vast and so important, had been annexed to our British dominions in the East since, at the dawn of the present century, those "North-Western Provinces," which now form so flourishing a part of our Indian Empire, were first brought under our rule. The Punjab, being conquered, was now to be "settled." We had tried, in other parts, various kinds of "settlement." We had subjected new provinces to different forms of administration, from the purely civil to the purely military, and we had recognised more or less of defectiveness in all the great experiments which had been made, and with an amount of success shedding no faint honor upon the character of our Indian administrators. But the difficulties encountered had been great, and errors had, doubtless, been committed. It was now to be seen how far our Indian statesmen would profit by the lessons of a century of varied experience, and turn to fruitful account the legacies bequeathed to them by their predecessors.

If this were a great work now to be undertaken by Lord Dalhousie, it is certain that he addressed himself to it with unusual advantages on his side. The Punjab was not to us a new country; the Sikhs were not a new people. A considerable tract of country, known as the Jullindur Doab, the lands lying between the Sutlej and Beeas, had been under British administration ever since our first triumphant entry into Lahore. And over the large expanse of territory still left nominally in the hands of the infant son of Runjeet Singh, our British officers had been exercising that kind of influence which every Englishman of the right stamp may derive from his official position at a native Court, and which, in the present instance, far exceeded the ordinary extent to which the dominion of superior intelligence is asserted. A Council of Regency had been established at Lahore, and a British military officer, well versed in diplomacy, had been appointed nominally to assist its deliberations, but substantially to control its acts. This officer was Henry Lawrence, a captain of the Bengal Artillery, who had been for some years graduating in the school of diplomacy, and had, on the death of Major Broadfoot, in the murderous conflict of Ferozshahur, been summoned by Lord Hardinge from Nepaul, where he was then Political Agent, to conduct our negotiations with the Sikhs. I shall come presently to speak more in detail of his character and qualifications. It is enough now to say, that by a British officer, aided by a staff of assistants, young and enterprising men of both services,* from the commencement of the year 1846 up to the time of the final dissolution of the Sikh Empire, the civil affairs of the Punjab had been chiefly administered. Ill supported by a corrupt and selfish Durbar, Lawrence and his associates had been gradually compelled to come forward, far more than they desired, in the character of administrators. Instead of confining themselves to the work of advising and instructing the Sikh officers, and preparing them to take, on the withdrawal of the British, the entire government into their own hands, our English officers had often been necessitated, in spite of their honest endeavours to remain in the background, to assume a more prominent position in the actual direction of affairs. The formality of the Sikh Durbar was there, but the real administration was

* I must not deny myself the pleasure of naming such men as George Lawrence, Herbert Edwardes, James Abbott, Lumsden, Taylor, Nicholson, Pollock, &c., of the military service; and Messrs. Melvill, Cocks, Vans Agnew, Bowring, &c., of the civil.

our own ; and the broad stamp of British beneficence was upon it. After the maintenance of general tranquillity, the development of the resources of a neglected country was the chief thought of the English officer, and he worked as strenuously towards the attainment of this great end as though the country had been actually our own.*

Therefore I say, when the "settlement" of the Punjab became, by our actual possession of the country, a matter of primal concernment to the Governor-General, he addressed himself to the task under such advantages as have been seldom enjoyed by his predecessors. To use a vulgar but expressive phrase, he had "something to go upon." He had not to commit the government of the country to the manipulation of unskilled hands. It was not altogether a vague experiment on which he was about to enter. There were British officers at his disposal, with Lawrence at their head, who knew the country well, and had already initiated a system of internal administration which promised the best results. The men, who had already done so well in connexion with the Sikh Durbar, were obviously those to whom he might, with safety, entrust the further government of the country, openly and independently, as the recognised rulers of the land. The training which they had undergone was of the best kind. They knew the country; and they knew the people. And already, under their

* "The whole country had been surveyed, and the system of taxation laid down on fixed principles; the fiscal and excise systems had been re-adjusted, and oppressive duties and Government monopolies of all sorts abolished. A census had been made, and the population and trades of Lahore determined; and the Durbar had sanctioned the outlay of 30,000*l.* on roads and bridges, to be increased to 60,000*l.* when the state of the country allowed."—[*Buist's Annals of India for the Year* 1848.] To this it may be added, that Colonel Lawrence, anxious to have a very simple code of laws, founded on Sikh customs, reduced to writing and administered by the most respectable men from their own ranks, assembled for the purpose at Lahore some fifty Sikh heads of villages, grey-beards of good local reputation, under the immediate superintendence of Lena Singh; and they had actually prepared the code before ill health compelled Colonel Lawrence to proceed to England.—[*MS. Notes.*]

benign influence, the land was beginning to recover from the exhausting effects of years of continued misrule.

Lord Dalhousie had no prejudices, for or against any particular class of Company's officers. He recognised the merits and the claims of both services. And he believed that the form of administration best suited to the Punjab would be one embracing a judicious intermixture of the civil and military elements—one in which civilians and soldiers might meet on equal terms as executive officers, and the qualification for employment should be simply the individual capacity of the officer seeking to be employed. It was necessary that at the head of such a body of administrators there should be some supreme authority, combining the advantages of local knowledge, military energy, and experience in civil details. But to find such a man was more than difficult. It was impossible. Colonel Lawrence had local knowledge and military energy. He had more civil experience, too, than most soldiers, for he had been long employed in the Revenue Survey, and, as a political officer, had attentively watched the systems of government in the Native States. But something more than this was needed to place so great an experiment beyond the risk of failure. It seemed fit, therefore, to Lord Dalhousie to place the government of the Punjab not under the entire control of a single functionary, but to appoint a Board of Administration, combining in the persons of its several members all the necessary administrative qualifications. At the head of this Board was placed Colonel—then Sir Henry—Lawrence, who knew the Sikh country, the Sikh chiefs, and the Sikh people well; a man of rare energy and ability, sagacious in council, prompt in action, and of so brave a resolution that all difficulties vanished before his unconquerable will. He had almost everything to fit him for his post but physical health; and in the untiring discharge of his duties, in his eager, restless beneficence, of this want he took little account. Often was he moving from place to place, far away from all the appliances of civilised life, at a time when his weakened frame required the comforts and restoratives of a well-ordered home. His friends often trembled for his safety; but he never thought of himself. He had work to do, and he would do it. He knew how much depended on his own personal energies, and whilst there was any need of his activity, he was not one to be still.

But what rendered Lawrence so peculiarly fitted for the post was this. Though largely endowed with that ready vigor—that self-reliant promptitude of action, which is alarmed by the presence of no responsibility, and deterred by the intervention of no false scruples—though he was prepared to strike suddenly and effectively, and was quite the man in an imminent conjuncture for a great and successful *coup*, his desire ever was to evoke, not the fear, but the gratitude of the people, to elevate and encourage them, not to coerce and repress. His benevolence was of the right kind. He knew that a strong Government is in the end a merciful Government—that want of vigor is want of kindness and want of sense—that in such a country as the Punjab a ruler must do something more than study Bentham in an easy-chair. But whilst ever on the alert, ever ready to crush any dangerous manifestations of disaffection, his mind was continually brooding over the means of advancing the happiness of the people. He knew that what the country most needed was repose, and that this could only be secured by a display of vigor at the right time; but it was towards a kindly paternal government that his impulses were ever directing him, and the welfare of a long-oppressed people was the thought dearest to his heart. He disarmed the population of the Punjab; but he opened out to them new fields of peaceful employment, and gave back to them the long alienated right of cultivating their rich lands in security and peace.

Associated in the Board of Administration with this large-minded captain of artillery, were two Bengal civilians. Mr. Mansell had long been favorably known, throughout the Presidency to which he belonged, as one of the ablest financiers in the country. He was a man of a thoughtful nature, and, I am inclined to think, of an original turn of mind; but he was not one to put his ideas, with much promptitude, into action. He was somewhat wanting, indeed, in energy and activity, and his abilities, though of a very high order, found more congenial employment in a settled than in a new country. He was not quick enough and enthusiastic enough for the work that lay before him; and he was, doubtless, glad after a time to be relieved from duties better suited to men of a more sanguine temperament and less abhorrence of responsibility. His colleague, Mr. John Lawrence, had been in charge of the administration of our first territorial acquisition in the Punjab—the Jullindur Doab —and he had acquitted himself, in that capacity, with remarkable address. He was a first-rate civil officer. The extensive experience which he had acquired in the North-Western Provinces of India had been stored up in his mind, as something too precious to lose, and was now ready to be turned to the most profitable account. He understood both the Revenue and the Judicial systems of the country well. He knew the native character; was familiar with native institutions; and thoroughly versed in all those matters of agricultural detail which are the very life itself of a rural population. A "settlement" was to him nothing new or mysterious. He knew how the boundaries of estates were determined; how their productiveness was to be increased; how revenue was to be raised in a manner most advantageous to the State, and least injurious to the people. And with all this extensive knowledge were united energy and activity of the highest order. He had the enthusiasm of youth with the experience of age; and envy and detraction could say nothing worse of him than that he was the brother of Sir Henry Lawrence.

Of such materials were formed, on its first institution, the Lahore Board of Administration. In communication immediately with the Governor-General, and aided by a staff of civil and military assistants, of whom I shall presently speak more in detail, these three members of the Lahore Board conducted the entire internal administration of the great country conquered by our arms. They worked together—separately and collectively. In respect of detail work there was a division of labor; but all official papers were circulated to the three members of the Board, and each member recorded his opinion on every question that came before them. The result was that all matters of importance were well and carefully considered by the entire Board, whilst each individual member brought his own particular experience to bear upon the illustration of administrative details.

The system of administration introduced by Lord Hardinge into the Cis-Sutlej and Trans-Sutlej states in 1846, was followed in 1849, when the entire country was subjected to our rule. The great province was divided into four commissionerships, and each of these commissionerships were divided into four or five districts.* The Deputy-Commissioners, who are placed in charge of these districts, perform all the functions of magistrates and collectors, and are invested with some of the offices of the Judge. To each district, moreover, are attached one or two assistants, chosen from the cove-

* The districts of Hazareh and Peshawur were, until the commencement of 1852, kept directly under the Board; but they have since been created into an independent commissionership under Colonel Mackeson.

nanted services, and also an uncovenanted extra assistant, all of whom are employed in the courts, civil, fiscal, and police. To these last-named appointments natives are eligible; and it has been greatly the desire of the Board to induce the Punjabees to accept employment of this kind, and also to take service as Tehsildars, Thannadars, &c.; but hitherto no great success seems to have crowned our efforts at the employment of native agency in the Punjab. The Punjabees are not very expert in the use of rules and regulations, and though these are pressed into the service, much less in this part of the country than in the provinces of India, it may still be questioned whether they are not too extensively employed.

It may be doubted whether any men in any part of the world ever addressed themselves to the great work of governing a conquered people, so as to make the yoke easy and the burden light, with more singleness of purpose and benevolence of aim than Lawrence and his gifted associates. It was their desire "to make the basis of their rule a light and equable assessment; a strong, vigorous, though uninterfering police; and a quick hearing in all civil and other cases."* And they set to work with an untiring energy, a resolute perseverance, and a disregard of all selfish considerations, with scarcely a parallel in the history of Indian Government. The Revenue Survey was pushed forward with all possible despatch (Henry Lawrence, as I have said, had once been a Revenue-Surveyor), and the revision of the settlement, which few men in India were more competent to superintend than John Lawrence, advanced with rapid strides towards completion. The term of years for which the assessment was settled varied according to the nature of the land. The contracts were principally made with the village communities, which exist in a more perfect state

* *MS. Correspondence.*

in the Punjab than in any other part of our Eastern possessions. In tracts of country already brought into a high state of cultivation, the settlement has been made for thirty years, but where the tract embraces considerable breadth of waste land, and is readily improvable, the assessment has been fixed only for a period of ten years. The amount of the assessment is considerably lower than it was under the old Sikh Government. The reductions, varying from five to fifty per cent., may be set down at an average of about twenty-five per cent. on the whole, or a total amount of thirty lakhs of rupees.

The difficult and delicate question of the resumption of rent-free tenures had to be dealt with by the Board of Administration. They found in the Punjab large tracts of Jagheer land, of the annual value of twenty-five lakhs of rupees. Much of this had been held by the chiefs on the condition of their furnishing certain quotas of troops to the Durbar; and now that this contingency no longer existed, it seemed that the claims of the Jagheerdars to this kind of immunity was gone. But there has been no hasty resumption. These rent-free tenures are inquired into and reported upon, and not until a thorough investigation has been instituted, and the justice of the measure clearly ascertained, is any Jagheerdar deprived of his lands. Even then the resumption is generally so ordered as to press with as little severity as possible on the privileged classes; though, doubtless, whilst the great bulk of the industrial population gain mightily by our innovations, the aristocracy of the Punjab are sufferers by the change. This, however, is inseparable from a system which has for its object the emancipation of the industrial classes from the wretched thraldom to which they had been reduced by the tyranny of the Sirdars. We could not elevate the many without depressing the few.

In the mean while the efforts of the Board for the suppression of crime, and the protection of life and property, have been at least partially successful. A vigorous, well-organised detective police has already done good work in the Punjab. Dakoitee is said to be well-nigh suppressed. We have hunted down these robber gangs, brought them to justice, and made quick work of their punishment. During the first year of our independent administration, nearly a hundred Dakoits were publicly executed, some six or eight at a time. And such terror did these vigorous measures strike into the profession at large, that Dakoitee is now said to be more rare in the Punjab than in any part of the Regulation provinces. In the suppression of minor offences it is admitted that we have been hitherto less successful; and in the dispensing of civil justice the Punjabee Courts have not achieved all that was desired. Earnest endeavours, however, are being made to simplify the law, to expedite its administration, and to render justice accessible to the meanest cultivator in the land. These are stereotyped expressions, often meaning nothing; but in the mouths of such earnest-minded men as the Lawrences there is a real significance in them. The Punjab, as I write, has been less than four years under our rule. I should think less hopefully of the ultimate result if its administrators insisted upon the perfect success of their experiments in every department of the state. But they claim for themselves no such extraordinary merit. They honestly acknowledge that they have not been uniformly successful, and are candid enough even to drop a hint that perhaps they have attempted too much.

Of the external signs of progress in this newly-acquired country, I have already spoken. But the Lawrences are not men to attempt the regeneration of the Punjab only by strivings from without. The great agency of education is being brought to bear upon the inner life of the people. Not that much has yet been done in this direction. These are too early days, indeed, for us reasonably to expect that anything should have been done. But we know that already a good English and vernacular school has been established at Umritsur, and that the Board of Administration are devising measures for the extension of their educational machinery, especially with a view to the practical training of the Punjabees for the public service, and their instruction in those useful sciences which will fit them for employment as engineers and medical practitioners.

Of the financial results of the annexation of the Punjab something should be written in this place. For many years the bare mention of the possible acquisition of the dominions of Runjeet Singh kindled a fever of expectancy in the minds of the English in India. Their imaginations grasped the grand idea of a country of inexhaustible wealth, whose annexation to our own territories would supply a general remedy for all our financial diseases, and strike the word "deficit" for ever out of the vocabulary of Indian Chancellors of the Exchequer. *Omne ignotum pro magnifico.* Much had been related of the exceeding splendor of the Sikh Court—of the almost fabulous value of the gems which shone upon the gorgeous head-dresses of the Sikh chiefs, and of the indescribable splendor of the jewels and gold which glittered upon the trappings of their horses. But we knew little of the natural resources of the country, or brought anything but our grosser senses to bear upon the consideration of its reputed wealth. Otherwise we might have reflected that it was hardly in the nature of things that a country so governed should be a rich country. The dream, however, was one from which the reality of a hostile collision soon awakened us; and when the annexation of the Punjab became something more than an object of vague cupidity, the gorgeous El-Dorado dissolved before our eyes, and a ruder reality looked us in the face. It was then openly doubted whether such an extension of empire would not rather aggravate than relieve our financial embarrassments—whether with a frontier extended to the Indus we should not be poorer than before.

And such, indeed, judged by present results, is actually the case. The Punjab is not yet remunerative. Some little time must elapse before the revenues of the country can be made to exceed the cost of its protective and administrative establishments. The estimated amount of revenue for the years 1851-52 is 130 lakhs of rupees,* with about four lakhs of additional receipts in the shape of proceeds of confiscated Sikh property and refunded charges. The total expenditure is estimated at about 120 lakhs of rupees. This leaves only a surplus of 14 lakhs for the maintenance of the regular troops posted in the Punjab; and, as a large reduction of the army might have been—indeed, would have been, effected but for the annexation of the Sikh states, it cannot be argued that the military expenditure is not fairly chargeable to the province. It is true, of course, that the possession of the Punjab has enabled us to withdraw a considerable body of troops from the line of country which constituted our old frontier, and that a deduction, on this score of frontier defence, must be made from the gross charges of the regular military

* Of this more than a hundred lakhs is derived from the land-revenue. I may as well set down the several items as contained in the Company's last general finance letter:

	Rupees.
Land Revenue	1,03,00,000
Sayer, Abkarree, Salt, Customs	23,00,000
Post Office	1,50,000
Stamps	1,00,000
Judicial fees, &c.	90,000
Sale of Presents	10,000
Miscellaneous Receipts	55,000
Total	130,05,000

establishment employed beyond the Sutlej. Still, the cost of the regular troops fairly chargeable to the Punjab absorbs the estimated surplus, and leaves a balance against the newly-acquired states.

It is necessary, however, to a right understanding of the financial results of the acquisition of the Punjab, that a more minute examination should be made of the last balance-sheet. Although the cost of the regular troops is not set down among the charges, there is a considerable defensive establishment—an establishment of those Local Corps and Military Police which Lawrence so judiciously established—charged against the province. Under the heads of "Civil and Military Police" and "Local Corps," there is an entrance of 40 lakhs of rupees.* To this extent, therefore, it pays for its own defence and protection. This is a charge which I hardly think can be further reduced without burdening the Indian treasury to a larger amount for the maintenance of regular troops.

Under the head of "Political Pensions, &c.," there is an entrance of 18½ lakhs of rupees.† As these pensions are principally, if not entirely *life* pensions, terminable with the present recipients, this item of expenditure will gradually disappear. The charges of revenue collection amount to 17½ lakhs of rupees, and the judicial charges to nearly 14 lakhs. The latter, it is probable, cannot be advantageously reduced. The former, at first sight, appears to be somewhat immoderate, and altogether irreconcileable with our knowledge of the generally simple and uncostly administrative machinery of the Punjab, for the cost of collection

* In the estimate for 1850-51, the amount set down, under these heads, is little short of 47 lakhs. I conclude that this is to be accounted for by a reference to the incidental expenses incurred by the levying and equipment of new corps.

† The estimate for the preceding year had been only 15 lakhs. The increase is probably the result of the Resumption operations of the Board. The absorption of large tracts of Jagheer land has compelled them to grant compensation to the Jagheerdars, in many cases, in the shape of life pensions.

amounts to about one-seventh of the land-revenue, whilst in India generally it is less than one-ninth. But it is to be remembered that hitherto in the Punjab we have had not merely to collect, but to settle the revenue.

But there are other items which, as time advances, will undergo a gradual process of reduction in the ordinary course of events. The "extraordinary charges" will be greatly diminished, for many of them are incidental to the occupation of newly-acquired territory. Sixteen lakhs and a half are set down as the estimated cost of "Buildings and Works" for the last financial year. This is not to be regarded as current expenditure, but as an outlay of capital on reproductive works; and it would be false economy to desist too soon from such profitable expenditure as this. It is to such a wise outlay of the public money that we must look for the permanent blessing of a surplus revenue. But the years of such necessary expenditure are not many, and we may look forward to a not very remote period when the outlay on public works will diminish as the revenue increases. A niggardly policy at such a time would be an erroneous—indeed, an extravagant one. The Punjab has vast capabilities, but it has suffered, and is still suffering, from the effect of long years of misrule, and it demands all the fostering care of a wise and benevolent Government to repair the waste of vital energy resulting from a system which struck in its greed of present gain at the very sources of productiveness, and paralysed the industry of the country.

Returning to the administrative results, I think I am justified in saying that they have hitherto presented a most satisfactory appearance; and that no purely civil administration, like that which obtains in the Regulation provinces—no purely military government like that which Lord Ellenborough established in Sindh—would have accomplished so large an amount of good within so limited a space of time. The success of the experiment is to be attributed partly to the system, and partly to the men. Under no other system could so many rare administrative qualities have been fused into one governing body—could so many excellent parts have been combined into one excellent whole. No system of agency will work well where the agents themselves are deficient in the qualities which contribute to success. Indolence and dulness will render inoperative the best-devised schemes of Government. But there are, on the other hand, modes of administration so faulty in themselves that no amount of energy and ability can wholly overcome their inherent defects. Lord Dalhousie was, doubtless, fortunate in his men; but it was only because he recognised the expediency of establishing a system of administration, to be carried out by a mixed civil and military agency, that he was enabled to associate these men in the Government of the Punjab. He brought the two services into friendly competition with each other—and such men as Henry and John Lawrence—Mansell and Mackeson—Montgomery and Macgregor—Edwardes and Cocks—Lake and Melvill—Abbott and Bowring—all found scope for the exercise of their several qualities, and each, after his kind, contributed to the "full force and joint result" of the entire success.

But we must not, therefore, as I have said, hastily assume, that because this system of administration has worked well in these newly-acquired countries, the more costly and exclusive system which obtains in our old Regulation provinces is altogether a mistake. Two very important considerations are necessary to the right understanding of the matter. The one is that the military administrators, both of the past and present generation, who have distinguished themselves so greatly in all the Presidencies of India, have been and are the *élite* of the service. We should err if we were to regard the Munros and Malcolms, the Sutherlands and the Lawrences, only as average specimens of the class to which they belong. And the other consideration to be kept steadily before us is this : that it is one thing to administer the affairs of a newly-conquered country, where population is meagre, wealth scanty, and rights simple; and another to deal with those more complicated relations to which property in its accumulation and transmission has given birth in the more settled and thickly-peopled districts which have long been under our rule. The Punjabee system is admirably suited to the Punjab, but it would be a dead failure in Bengal.

Moreover, in these settled districts, we have got the "Regulations" for better or for worse, and they are to be handled skilfully only by men who have been trained, from their youth upwards, in the use of them. Whether any other system than that now in force, if adopted a century or half a century ago, would have conferred greater benefits on the country, it is now of little use to inquire. I have my opinion on the subject, and elsewhere I have expressed it. But if I had taken an opposite view of the question, I should still perceive plainly, and admit freely, that it is one thing to apply a tentative system to a new country, where virgin soil presents itself for our experiments, and another to pull down an existing system, and to introduce a new one which might have been adapted to the people as we found them, but certainly is not to the people as we have made them. The idea of turning clever adjutants into Zillah judges, and hoisting dashing majors into the Sudder, is a conception worthy of the man who made a consul of his horse.

CHAPTER II.

Progress of Civilisation—Humanising Efforts of British Officers—Mairwarra—Dixon and the Mairs—Candeish—The Bheels—Outram and the Bheel Corps—Ovans and the Bheel Colonies—Reclamation of Savage Tribes—Augustus Cleveland—General Results.

THEY are good things of which I have spoken in the preceding chapter. I do not think, indeed, that there is any reason to doubt that the transfer of these provinces to the dominion of the British has been attended with substantial benefits to the people. Our English rulers are not now chargeable with obliviousness of their obligations as representatives of Christianity, and agents of Civilisation. Every year they address themselves with greater earnestness to the good work of social regeneration; every year they bring their solemn convictions—solemn convictions of the duty of responsible men, loaded with a weight of obligation, of the due discharge of which, to the utmost tittle, they will have to give strict account—to bear more forcibly and effectually upon the practical consideration of their measures for the government of the nations brought under their rule.

I wish that the necessities of this work did not restrain me from dwelling at a length commensurate with the importance and the attractiveness of the subject upon these civilising measures—upon the successful efforts which have been made, on the acquisition of new tracts of country, to reduce the people thus newly brought under our rule to a state of civilisation unknown to them under their native masters. I am afraid that very little of all this is known in England. I am afraid the general impression is, that in India, when the work of subjugation is done, we think only of the work of taxation—that war and revenue are the only two things earnestly considered by the British officer in the East—and that, so long as we can successfully prosecute the one and make a good show of the other, he is happy and content in himself, and vastly applauded by his masters.

But there can be no greater error than this. The history of India, truly and sufficiently written, would contain many a chapter, full of cheering facts, illustrative of the brighter side of English conquest in the East. The "Victories of Peace" and the "Triumphs of Civilisation" are not the stereotyped promises of florid orators at home, but the substantial performances of men, striving and toiling under the fiery skies of India, and sacrificing often life itself in their efforts to elevate the social condition, and to increase the daily happiness of the people by whom they are surrounded. In such chapters of Indian history would be found many pictures not to be dwelt upon without feelings of national pride and Christian gratitude—pictures of English gentlemen in the deep recesses of a strange country, isolated from their kind, devoting themselves to the noble work of reclaiming the savage people of a newly-acquired province, and making their way, slowly and painfully, through jungles of ignorance and barbarism, folly and superstition, to the great reward of full success. Such success is often the only reward which these good deeds secure to the man of peace and the agent of civilisation. He may win the approbation and the confidence of his employers, but I only utter a threadbare commonplace when I add that a brilliant charge of horse, or an assault on a petty fortress, will secure for him more popular renown, and achieve for him, by the unpremeditated act of a casual half hour, more honorary distinction than can be acquired by years of philanthropic toil. It is the glory of such men as Cleveland and Wilkinson, Dixon, Ovans, and Macpherson, that they have labored on in the cause of humanity, without any of the ordinary encouragements and incentives to exertion, unknown to their brethren at home, almost forgotten by their brethren in India, without the stimulating and sustaining aid of a single note of popular applause.

And yet what great things have been done in India by a few European officers—perhaps by a single European officer, located in the heart of a newly-acquired province, and surrounded by rude barbarians, slaves to the most degraded superstitions, and habitual practisers of almost every vice! Look at the case of Mairwarra.* Thirty years ago we found in that country a race of savage marauders—with little or no regard for human life or liberty—murdering their daughters, selling their mothers, committing every kind of atrocity without shame and without remorse. They were many of them fugitives from other states — men whom society had spued out—the rugged elements of a fearless race of bandits. They were robbers, indeed, by profession and by practice. Everywhere they took what they could, and kept what they could, and lived in continual strife with their neighbours. Their vicinage was always uncomfortable — often dangerous — and when we came into contact with them we swallowed them up. In 1821 we subjugated the country, and brought these freebooters under British rule.

No sooner had the act of absorption been accomplished than the British officers, to whom the "settlement" of the

* The untravelled reader must look for Mairwarra in the map of India, between the Chumbul river and the Arabala hills, which stretch almost from Delhi to Goojrat. It is under the Government of the North-Western Provinces, and contiguous to Ajmere. "It is bounded," says Colonel Dixon, "by Ajmere to the north, and separates Meywar in the east from Marwar on the west; to the south are the hill possessions of Meywar.'

new country had been entrusted, began to address themselves to the work of humanising these wretched people. "The duty to be performed was of no ordinary cast; it was one of considerable anxiety and difficulty. The people had been conquered without calling for the exercise of any extraordinary force or much solicitude. This had proved a matter of comparative ease. We had now to gain their affections, to command their good will in following the path pointed out to them, to win them over to habits of industry, and to habituate them to customs of civilised life. We had to prove to them that, in subduing them, our chief source of solicitude was to improve their social condition, and in all respects to administer to their comfort and welfare." To effect this, it was necessary, in the first instance, to put down the open violence of these marauding clans by an imposing display of force. When we first took charge of the district, authority was openly set at defiance. Armed bands paraded the country, or occupied the passes. The servants of Government were cut off; prisoners were rescued. There was no safety on the public ways. To control these desperate banditti it was necessary to show that on the side of constituted authority there was a power stronger even than their lawless ferocity. And this was speedily done.

It is the rule of the British Government, in these cases, to make the rude barbarians themselves the agents of their own civilisation. We abstain, whenever such forbearance is possible, from a display of foreign force. In Mairwarra, as elsewhere, it was deemed expedient to raise a local battalion, composed of the people of the country, and to employ their energies in the suppression of crime, and the support of the civil authorities. By the establishment of such corps another object is attained. It opens a field for the exercise of a world of restless energy —it reduces to discipline, and holds out objects of honorable competition, to men who have hitherto warred against their neighbours on their own account, and lived in a constant state of predatory strife.

The Mairwarra local battalion was placed under the command of Captain Hall, of the 16th Bengal Native Infantry—an officer who, in the quartermaster's department of the army, had exhibited considerable ability and force of character—and who, now virtually invested with the political charge of the country, brought all his energies to bear upon the reclamation of these savage tribes. The Mairs, disciplined after our European fashion, proved themselves to be good and loyal soldiers, and the criminal combinations, which had thrown the whole district into confusion, were suppressed by the brethren of the men who constituted the robber-gangs. And this primal measure accomplished, Captain Hall took the next great step along the road of civilisation, and addressed himself to the permanent protection of life and property by the introduction of a judicial system in keeping with the character and the requirements of the people.

The Mairs had always had the most primitive ideas of justice. It had been of the wild kind which degenerates into revenge—or else it had ascended only to the scale of trial by ordeal. Either the contending parties, backed by their sympathising kinsmen, resorted to the arbitrement of the sword; and blood-feuds were handed down among them from sire to son. Or the accused was challenged to prove his innocence by thrusting his hand into boiling oil, or grasping a red-hot shot. But under British government a new and better system was introduced. Except in the highest class of offences, resort was had to the *Punchayut*, or arbitration system—a system well adapted to the temper and condition of the people, which worked with the best results; and was one of the most important remedial agents applied to the cure of all these social ills. "It is a strong argument," says Colonel Dixon, "in favor of this system of dispensing justice, that during the last twenty-six years, the period of our rule in Mairwarra, no appeal has been made beyond the superintendent of the district."

But the plough was the chief civiliser. Hitherto the land had been so difficult of cultivation that no one cared to possess it. Mairwarra is a mountainous district, and, without artificial means of retention, the rain that fell was soon lost. The falls of rain, too, were uncertain. Sometimes the water supplies totally failed; and cultivation was at a stand-still. In 1832 there had been a great drought, and the country had been nearly depopulated. The industrial energies of the people were paralysed by this calamity. They lost all faith in agriculture as a means of subsistence, and fell into their old marauding habits. This, indeed, in a greater or a less degree, was the result of every drought, and droughts were of frequent occurrence. To remedy this evil, it plainly appeared would be not only to increase the financial prosperity of the people, but to open out the sources of moral reformation, and to reclaim them from their lawless ways. Nothing could be more readily comprehensible than this, or seemingly more easy of achievement.

Compelled by ill-health to abandon his post, Hall was succeeded in 1835 in the charge of Mairwarra by Captain Dixon, an officer of the Bengal Artillery, whose zeal in the cause of humanity, evinced when in no responsible political employment, had secured for him the good opinion and confidence of Sir Charles Metcalfe, who now selected him for a post in which his benevolence might have free scope for active expression. The trust could not have been confided to better hands. Dixon entered upon his new duties with all the energy and zeal of a man whose heart is in the good work. He saw at once what was the great want of the country. Eager to develop the productiveness of an unyielding soil, and to stimulate the industry of an unsettled people, he addressed himself to this great matter of the water-supply, and left untried no effort to secure it. He appealed to Government. He appealed to the people. Money and labor were both soon at his disposal; and the great want was supplied. By a judicious management of the water-supply, by the digging of tanks and wells, and the construction of embankments, the wasted jungle was soon reclaimed. The plough was in active operation. Every man was encouraged, by small advances of money, to apply himself to agricultural pursuits. The financial results of the experiment were highly favorable. The moral results were more favorable still. A large number of professional robbers were converted into industrious farmers, and peace smiled upon the land.*

Having thus created, by his exertions, a class of peaceful agriculturists, Dixon's next effort was to settle a community of busy traders in this neglected land. Hitherto the Mairs had depended principally upon Ajmere and Nusserabad† for their supplies. Itinerant dealers visited the neighbourhood at times, but their transactions were confined to the Sepoys of the local battalion. With the general population they had no commerce. They seemed to mistrust the Mairs. The object, however, was a great one, and to Dixon it appeared of no very difficult attainment. It seemed to him that if a city were built there would soon be found traders to inhabit it. So a city with a spacious bazaar sprung up at his bidding. It rose with the rapidity of magic. Three months after the laying of the first stone the bazaar was

* "During the last eleven years the sums expended on works of irrigation amounted to 2,41,112 rupees; whilst during that period the excess of revenue beyond the summer of the first year of the present incumbent's superintendence in 1835-36 is 6,41,234 rupees. After reimbursing ourselves for the outlay on public works, there is a surplus given of 4,00,121 rupees. This large amount is our gain in a pecuniary point of view; as far as affects the moral improvement of the people, the advantages are beyond calculation."

† Distant thirty-two and thirty-six miles from Mairwarra.

opened for traffic. At first the Mairs had looked coldly and mistrustfully at the proposal. They thought that the location among them of a party of foreign traders would only have the effect of subjecting them to unaccustomed exactions. But they soon found the advantage of the undertaking, for it supplied them with profitable employment; and they learnt in time that the settlement of capitalists among them, and the centralisation of trade, must be beneficial to indigenous producers. By the Mahajuns, or traders themselves, this want of confidence was reciprocated. As they brought in their merchandise to the new city, they began to tremble for its safety. The very quiescence—the seeming forbearance of a race of men habituated to plunder, roused their suspicions; and they argued among themselves that the Mairs were only holding back until a richer spoil had been accumulated within the circle of the new city. In this conviction, the trading classes asked that a wall should be built around the town for their protection; and what they sought was granted to them. The Government of India had watched, with lively interest, this worthy experiment, had approved and applauded the noble efforts of the superintendent, and were in no case slow to listen to his suggestions. Now, therefore, the present "proposition received the same favorable attention that had characterised the Government in all measures referring to the improvement and happiness of the Mairs." And so the city of Nyanuggar was built, and a wall was built around it, and the Mahajuns brought in their goods, and in a short time it was reported that nearly two thousand families, engaged in various manufacturing and commercial operations, were located within the wall.

In the mean while, the agricultural improvements were going on bravely. Tanks were being dug; wells were being sunk; and a regular supply of water was being secured to the fields. The jungle was being cleared;

the people, many after an absence of years, were returning to their native country, drawn by the report of our ameliorative efforts. To one village ninety families had returned, after the lapse of four generations, to occupy the lands of their progenitors. A general spirit of improvement was possessing these long-degraded Mairs. When money could no longer be advanced by Government, they cast about for the means of raising it for themselves; and by the sale of cattle and the betrothal of their daughters, sometimes acquired the necessary capital for the prosecution of the reproductive works, from which they had been taught to look for such ample returns.

And with all these great commercial and agricultural changes, the moral improvement of the people was advancing with prodigious strides. As early as 1827 Colonel Hall had reported "the complete and voluntary abolition of the two revolting customs—female infanticide, and the sale of women."* The re-marriage of widows was also provided for, and the worst forms of slavery abolished. The predatory habits of the people disappeared. They had once been beyond measure lawless and intractable. They now became docile and obedient, and there was something of child-like confidence in the reliance which these untutored savages began to place in the wisdom and kindliness of the European superintendent.† They had, indeed, an overflowing faith in the man; and he was worthy of their veneration. What

* For a fuller notice of this see the chapter on *Infanticide*.

† "The high degree of prosperity which it (Mairwarra) has now attained, arises, however, from the system introduced by Captain Dixon. He may be said to live amongst the people. He knows minutely the condition of each village, and almost of its habits individually; is ready to redress not only every man's grievances, but to assist them to recover from any pecuniary or other difficulty in which they may be involved. . . . Captain Dixon has no European assistance; but his native establishment is so admirably disciplined and controlled, that whether in the construction of tanks, in the assessment of the revenue, or the administration of justice amongst this simple and primitive people, these establishments conduct all matters to almost as happy an issue as he could do himself."—[*Report of Colonel Sutherland, March 17, 1841.*]

Colonel Dixon did, he did single-handed; he had not one brother-officer to aid him. He worked alone in Mairwarra; and, assuredly, it was no light work that he undertook. The success of the great experiment entirely hinged, in his own words, on the untiring zeal and vigilance of the superintendent. "To carry through his projects, it would be necessary that he disengage himself from all private pursuits and pleasures, and devote his entire undivided energies to the fulfilment of the object. His presence would be essential to inspect every large and small work in each village, and to encourage the people in the undertakings on which they were engaged. He must be constantly in camp, without reference to burning heat or drenching rain; in a word, until all difficulties were overcome, all works of irrigation completed, and permanent prosperity secured, he must be a slave to duty. It remained with him to choose whether he would seek personal comfort and ease in restricting himself to ordinary duties, as is done by some public officers, or whether he would face the difficulties and undergo the toil which must be inseparable from an undertaking of such magnitude, continuing through a long vista of years. Happily, little consideration was required in making his election. He chose usefulness at the expense of personal comfort."* And his name will live as the regenerator of the Mairs. It is no small privilege to the compiler of such a work as this, to chronicle, even in a few imperfect pages, the recent annals of Mairwarra, and to show how a wild and lawless people were reclaimed by a single European officer taken from an Expense Magazine.†

* *Dixon's Mairwarra.* This very interesting quarto volume, with abundant maps, plans, and graphic illustrations, was published at the expense of the East India Company, and has not, I believe, found its way extensively into general circulation.

† It has been hinted to me, from more than one quarter, but always in a friendly spirit, that in a former work I displayed something of a tendency to over-rate the achievements of officers belonging to the Bengal Artillery. Perhaps the same charge may be

In the mean while, in the same western regions, but many miles lower down to the south, in that part of the country with which the English in India first made acquaintance—in the province of Candeish, where one of our earliest settlements was located—another great experiment was going on.* Candeish, in the old days of Mahomedan rule, and during the first half century of British sovereignty in the East, was a great and flourishing province. But in 1802 the Mahrattas had ravaged the country; and in the following year a great famine had desolated the land. What Holkar and God's providence commenced, the mis-rule of the Peishwah's officers completed. The province was reduced to a state of anarchy and desolation not easily to be described. It was, indeed, for some years, almost depopulated; and when the people began slowly to return to their old possessions, a new calamity descended upon them. The Pindarrees ravaged the open country, and certain Arab tribes, establishing themselves in the hill fortresses, laid the neighbouring country under heavy contribution.†

In this province of Candeish were located certain Bheel tribes, constituting in all about an eighth of the population.‡ When the country was in a settled and flourishing state, these people had been principally employed as village-watchmen; and village-watchmen have

brought against me with reference to this work. I confess that I do not record the doings of Colonel Dixon in Mairwarra with less pleasure because he belongs to that distinguished regiment (though he is personally as much a stranger to me as if he had fought under Lord Clive), but the praises which I have bestowed upon him fall short of those which have been lavished upon him by his official superiors, and confirmed by the general voice of all who have ever given a thought to the subject.

* Candeish — an extensive province in Western India, through the northern portion of which the river Tapty runs, will be readily found in the map to the south of the Sauthpooree Hills. It is, however, not to the entire province, but to a district, consisting of various portions of it, acquired in the Mahratta war of 1818, and formed into a collectorate under the Bombay Government, that my remarks, in so far as they relate to our operations for the civilisation of the Bheels, mainly refer.

† *Captain Graham's Historical Sketch of the Bheel tribes, inhabiting the province of Candeish.* See, also, *Reports of Colonel Robertson and Mr. Giberne. MS.*

‡ *Report on the Bheels of Candeish*, by *W. S. Boyd, Esq.*, 1833. *MS.*

in no part of India been celebrated for the regularity of their habits or the honesty of their pursuits. In the best of times it does not seem that these clans were other than a lawless and unscrupulous people. Political disorder and social confusion were, indeed, greatly to their taste. They now rejoiced in the convulsions which rent the province. Their legitimate calling was at an end, and they took readily to the open exercise of a profession, which before they had secretly practised under cover of their recognised pursuits. For many years they existed merely as a group of robber-gangs—either aiding the depredational excesses of more powerful marauders, or working independently for themselves. Heavy retribution often descended upon them. They knew what was the penalty, and they were prepared to pay it. They lived without law, and they often perished without law. It was no uncommon thing, under native rule, for them to be massacred by hundreds. Sometimes, however, a combined effort of the different clans enabled them to beat down constituted authority. On one occasion ten thousand of the Guicowar's troops, sent to coerce them, were driven back defeated and disgraced.*

It was in 1818, at the close of the Pindarree war, that certain parts of this once thriving province of Candeish were brought under British rule. They had been regularly ceded to us by Holkar; but the Arab colonists had occupied a great part of the country, and they could be driven from it only by force. The subjugation of the district, therefore, became necessary. And it was easily subjugated. The Arabs submitted. But the Bheels, who had never been elevated to the dignified position of a recognised enemy, still remained unconquered and unreclaimed. They had suffered too miserably at the hands of other governments to have any faith in the new rulers, who now called upon them to enrol themselves as their

* *Captain Graham's Historical Sketch.*

subjects. They believed that if they came in, they would be massacred without remorse. Native governments would have dealt with them in this way; and they thought that the English troops were only waiting for an opportunity to shoot them down or bayonet them to a man.

So, although the British flag was hoisted in Candeish, and British rule proclaimed, the Bheels held possession of the hill-tracts, defied all authority, and violated all law. It was vain to think of settling the country until these people were coerced. There was little protection for life or property in Candeish beyond the range of our guns. Various measures were attempted without success. Conciliatory proclamations were of no avail, for the Bheels would not believe our promises. Recourse was had to arms; but the country and the climate baffled the gallantry of our troops. The Political Agent, Major Briggs, a man of comprehensive knowledge and enlarged humanity, proposed to pension the marauding Bheels; but the plan was not officially sanctioned.* Liberal landed settlements were offered, but this attempt also failed. The Bheels clung to their old habits. Long oppressing, and long oppressed, they were suspicious and mistrustful; and it seemed that they were neither to be subjected nor reclaimed. The effect of that great civiliser, the gibbet, was tried; some summary executions were ordered; vigorous measures, for a while, took the place of conciliatory schemes—but they were equally unsuccessful.†

* *Captain Graham's Historical Sketch. Reports of Colonel Robertson and Messrs. Giberne and Boyd. MS.*

† The Court of Directors were inclined to think that Major Briggs threw too much severity into his measures; but it does not seem that he betook himself to violence until conciliation had failed. Colonel Robertson, in his Report on the Bheels of Candeish, 1825, nobly vindicates the character of his predecessor. "I will only, on taking leave of the Honorable Court's observations, suggest," he says, "that should a tabular picture be formed from the correspondence regarding the Bheels, of the measures of Major Briggs on the one hand, and of the repeated rejection of all advances, the frequent breaches of engagements, the reiterated aggressions of the Bheels, and the consequent sufferings of the people on the other—

It was time now, after some years of continued ill-success, to look the matter steadfastly in the face. The Court of Directors had earnestly addressed themselves to the consideration of the subject, and, taking a most humane and liberal view of the question, had recommended the continued prosecution of conciliatory measures. They could not bring themselves to believe that these Bheels, who, if they had been much sinning, had also been much sinned against, were altogether irreclaimable; and there were British officers on the spot who entertained the same opinions. It required, it is true, that a large amount of knowledge and sagacity—of patience on the one hand, and energy on the other—should be brought to bear upon the work. It was, indeed, no easy task that lay before them. The Bheels of Candeish might not be wholly irreclaimable; but we knew enough of their character to feel assured that the civilisation of such a people could only be accomplished, under Providence, by such a combination of wisdom and vigor, in planning and achieving, as had seldom been displayed before. They were a wild and predatory people, without laws, without ritualities, almost even without a rude sense of natural religion. Reckless and migratory, they passed from one place to another, throwing up a cluster of rude huts in the course of a few hours, and delighting not in more permanent habitations. Anything like honest industry they abhorred. Indolent and improvident, they lived as they could, from hand to mouth; they hunted down the game in the jungles; collected wild berries and roots; or, by a successful border foray or marauding expedition, secured a sufficiency of plunder to feast them sumptuously for a while.

carefully, in all instances, marking the dates—it would prove that we begun with conciliation, and, though one-half of the crimes of the Bheels are not recorded, continued it longer, it is probable, than was prudent."—[*MS. Records.*] The Court, as the sequel proved, were right in recommending conciliatory measures; but conciliatory measures are never so potential before, as after we have shown our ability to punish.

A few days were spent in dissipated idleness, and then the exhaustion of their stores sent them forth after new pillage. They were the Ishmaelites of that part of the world. Their hands were against every man, and every man's hand was against them. Murder and robbery were habits which sat easily upon them. They streamed down from their mountain-homes, sacked and fired the villages on the plains, drove away the cattle of the villagers, and carried off their head men for the sake of the ransoms they would fetch. Drunkenness, too, was one of their favorite infirmities. They delighted in long debauches. They maddened themselves with burning spirits. It would have been hard to find a more licentious or unscrupulous race, or one with fewer redeeming qualities. It seemed a matter of almost utter hopelessness to reclaim such savages as these.

But there were, fortunately, men in Western India at this time whom the seeming hopelessness of the task only inspired with courage, and roused to vigorous action. It was assuredly a great and worthy experiment that was now to be made. The more irreclaimable these savages, the greater the glory of reclaiming them. The oppressions of the native governments had driven these people to desperation, and made them the reckless criminals they were. The reformatory measures of our benevolent predecessors had consisted chiefly of a number of dreadful massacres. The wells had been choked up with the trunkless heads of the offending Bheels. Whole families had been hewn down and extirpated. They believed that the mark of Cain had been set upon them, and that it was their fate to be hunted and destroyed—hunted and destroyed like the wild beasts of the forest—and therefore, like the wild beasts, they turned and stood at bay before civilised men. To dispel these delusions, and to win their confidence, was therefore the first step towards the great reformation which our English administrators yearned to achieve.

Mountstuart Elphinstone was, at this time, Governor of Bombay. Bringing all his quick intellect, his sound sense, his warm benevolence to bear upon this great matter of the reclamation of the savage Bheels, he soon worked his way to the conclusion that, if a few English gentlemen could be brought into intimate relations with the barbarous tribes—if they could acquaint themselves with the habits, study the feelings, and in time win the confidence of the Bheels, by familiarly associating with them, and proving that the British Government were eager only to do them good, success might be eventually accomplished. It was his desire to turn them from their lawless pursuits by finding other employment, alike pleasant and more profitable. If, for example, we could more convert them into disciplined soldiers and peaceful colonists, not by proclamations and vague offers of reward, but by the immediate influence of English officers living among them, it seemed that we might overcome the barbarism of the tribes in the manner most in accordance with the suggestions of reason and the dictates of humanity.

It seemed to him, in the first place, that if we could induce the Bheels to enter our military service—if we could raise a corps of these savage men, under the command of British officers—we might win the confidence of a few, and through them of many, and, in time, make the Bheels themselves the agents of their own civilisation. He had recommended this course both to Colonel Briggs and his successor, Colonel Robertson; but the political agents, thinking perhaps that the arms which we put in the hands of these lawless men would be turned against ourselves, had not furthered the suggestion. But events soon developed themselves which strengthened

Elphinstone's conviction of the wisdom of the measure, and an order went forth for the formation of a Bheel corps.

This difficult and dangerous duty was entrusted to an officer who has since earned for himself one of the brightest names in the recent history of India. It was entrusted to James Outram, then a lieutenant in the Bombay Native Infantry, who had already foreshadowed those fine soldierly qualities which a quarter of a century of continued action have ripened and refined. He was then a very young man, full of animal spirits, active and courageous; but with all his energies and activities, tempered with strong sense and sound judgment; and he went about his work eagerly, and yet thoughtfully, measuring its difficulties aright, but resolute to overcome them. And he soon had practical proof of their nature and extent. The Bheels were at this time* in the very height of their lawlessness. They were carrying on their depredations up to the very picquets of the British camp, and sweeping off our cattle in triumph. A strange belief held possession of them, that we shrunk from encountering their robber bands, or following them to their mountain homes. And they thought that all this pretence of raising Bheel corps, and offering their people regular pay in the service of the Company, was only a snare to draw them into our camps, and to cut them off in detail. And so the enlistment of the Bheels was, for some time only, a think talked of and desired. The people would not come at our call.

It is characteristic of Outram that he should have desired to show the Bheels at the outset, what our troops were willing and able to do, and to convince them that in no part of the country were they secure from the vengeance of the British Government. He longed to attack them on their own hills; and he soon found fitting opportunity.

* In 1825.

With a handful of his old regiment he beat up their quarters, surprised a strong party just as they were about to start on a marauding expedition, and scattered them like chaff. A cry was raised that the red-coats were upon them, and the Bheels were soon in panic flight. A few were killed; but far more important, a few were captured, and the prisoners, whom Outram had taken in their own mountain homes, enabled him to lay the foundation of his corps.

Releasing some of his captives, and despatching them with friendly messages and offers of employment to their relatives, he contrived to draw the people to his tent, and soon effected an intercourse with some of their leaders. With them he went about, freely and fearlessly, in their jungles. He listened to their stories; he joined in their pastimes; he feasted them when they were well, and doctored them when they were ill; in his own words, he "won their hearts by copious libations of brandy, and their confidence by living unguarded among them;" and it might have been added, their admiration, too, by proving how bold a hunter he was. Keen sportsmen themselves—trusting often to the chase for their daily food—with something of religious faith in the accidents of the field, these wild heathens looked with wonder on the exploits of the Christian Nimrod, and recognised a mighty spirit in him.* It did not seem that he had come among them

* I am no sportsman myself, but I can appreciate all developments of manliness, and I know that the fine sportsman-like qualities of the English have done much to raise them in the estimation of all the hardier Indian tribes. It is not difficult to imagine the effect which such prowess must have had upon the Bheels, especially when we learn that during Outram's connexion with the corps, he and his comrades killed 255 tigers; 18 panthers; 42 bears; 19 wild buffaloes; and numerous hogs, deers, and other smaller game. Among a number of papers relating to Bheel civilisation, I have chanced upon a memorandum by Col. Outram, containing the following curious anecdote relative to the superstitions of the chase, to which I have made allusion in the text. "The Bheels," he says, "have the belief that those who slay a tiger maintain power over that animal in the next world; but that those slain by a tiger are rendered hereafter subservient to the animal. On the occasion when Cundoo Havildar was mortally wounded, he implored me to hasten to kill the tiger, whilst he was yet alive, saying that as

as an enemy, but as a friend and a companion. He was himself, indeed, one of them; and they felt unconstrained in his presence.

And recruits came in at last—slowly at the outset, it is true; but there was no fear of ultimate success when the beginning had once been made. His muster-roll, at first, contained the names only of five men; but the number had soon swollen to twenty-five, and a few months afterwards had risen to a hundred. And in spite of temporary hindrances—in spite of the occasional recurrence of their old fears and suspicions, and the false reports of evil men,* the Bheel corps, once doubted and despaired of, became a substantial fact. Outram brought his wild recruits into familiar contact with high-caste Sepoys of his own regular corps—Brahmins and Rajpoots—and the conciliatory manners of the old soldiers, who conversed freely with them as comrades, and courteously presented them with beetle-nut, went far to rivet the confidence which the bold, frank manner of their young leader had engendered within them. And soon did they settle down into orderly subjects

he had marked the animal down, and left scouts to watch him, its death would be attributable to him, and he might then die in peace. I succeeded in slaying the monster, and hastened to assure Cundoo of the fact. He was just dying when I went to him, but had sense left to understand and express his satisfaction, immediately after which he expired. Several gentlemen witnessed my interviews with the poor Bheel before and after the death of the tiger, and were much affected by the anxiety he expressed at the former time, and the satisfaction and resignation he evinced at the latter. On all occasions of danger the Bheels displayed astonishing presence of mind and *pluck;* and almost invariably when in tracking a tiger they suddenly come upon the animal, they caused him to slink off, from the bold front they maintained. Whether the Bheel singly became opposed to a tiger, or several were together, he never thought of turning or running, but caused the brute to walk off instead, by literally staring him out of countenance. Often in critical moments when hunting on foot has a tiger been turned from me by my faithful Bheels; and one occasion when a panther had got me down, they killed him with their swords, when rolling with me on the ground, with my head in his mouth."—[*MS. Records.*]

* "They were told at one time by the evil-disposed, that the object was to link them in a line like galley slaves, and to extirpate their race; and for a long time there was a fear existing in the minds of most that this assembly or corps were merely drawn together to be destroyed. At the very place where the head-quarters had been fixed, Dhurmgaun, there had been a most cruel and treacherous massacre of those people under the former Government. This strengthened their suspicions."—[*Report on the Bheels of Candeish, by George Giberne, Esq., Collector,* 1828. *MS. Records.*]

and good soldiers—learning the English drill system with diligence and attention, and keeping all their old bad propensities in control. So peaceful was their bearing, that it was soon officially reported that, for many miles around the neighbourhood where they were encamped, no excesses had for some time been committed by the Bheels. Indeed, they not only reformed themselves, but helped to reform the manners of their brethren, and began to exercise very efficiently the duties of a military police. A year after the first attempt to establish the corps, Outram wrote to Mr. Bax, collector of Candeish: "I believe there is no offender at large now within many miles of my head-quarters, and no robbery is ever now heard of within thirty miles of it; and I trust that in the course of a short time the beneficial influence of the corps will extend over the whole province."*

In the mean while our civil officers in Candeish were exerting themselves to bring other remedial measures to bear upon the reformation of the offending Bheels. Several European officers, under the denomination of Bheel Agents, were appointed to aid the Candeish collector in carrying out this good work. They were instructed, by every means in their power, "to preserve the peace of the country; to ameliorate the condition of the Bheels; to keep a watchful eye of superintendence over those in the range committed to their charge; to inspire them with confidence in the Government; to encourage them to turn their attention to industrious pursuits; to be careful that those on whom pensions were conferred were duly paid; to attend to and redress their complaints against each other, as well as against other classes—under certain circumstances pointing out the means of redress against other classes; to act as arbitrators when the parties mutually agreed; to apprehend offenders and commit them for trial, if of a serious nature—if otherwise, to inflict such punishment as might

* *Lieutenant Outram to Mr. Bax, July* 1, 1826. *MS. Records.*

be customary among themselves; and if advisable, a punchayut of their own tribe might be resorted to; and, lastly, to superintend such military operations as might be considered necessary to reduce to order any tribes or bands committing depredations." "To superintend the Bheels," it was added, "the agents should call upon them to give an account of the manner in which they obtain their livelihood; to restrict them from assembling in masses; to prevent them from quitting their regular places of abode without intimation of the same, and to check all assemblage in hutties under any pretence whatever. Security should be taken from all against whom strong suspicions are entertained, and in failure, therefore, the agents are called upon to report all the circumstances of each case to the collector. The agents, to a certain extent, should reward meritorious conduct in aiding the police, or for remarkable industry—such rewards as land, rent-free for a given time, a bullock or plough, or other implements of husbandry or grain, &c., might be given; they should call on the Potails for correct returns of all the Bheels in their range of the mode by which they subsist; and when not adequately provided for, should recommend land and "tuccavee" to be given. The Potails should be encouraged to assist in promoting these objects; and on their distinguishing themselves it should be reported, &c., and marks of approbation should be bestowed."*

Such substantially, stated in official language, were the measures by which it was hoped the reformation of the erring Bheels might now be accomplished. And all this was to be done mainly, as Outram had done his work, by mixing familiarly with the Bheels—by disarming them of their suspicions—by showing that we were really their friends. The great thing was to convert them, if it were possible, into an agricultural population—to convince them that there were better modes of earning a subsistence than

* *Report on the Bheels of Candeish, by George Giberne, Esq., Doolea Collector*, 1828.

by ravaging the country and plundering their neighbours; and to give them every facility for entering advantageously upon their new avocations. Immunity was, therefore, granted for past offences, with written engagements to this effect. At the same time grants of land for cultivation were given to them, under the signature of the Bheel agents, and formally recorded.* And soon a number of peaceful little colonies were established, and a number of ploughs were at work.

The foundation of these Bheel settlements was laid by Mr. Graham, then assistant to the Candeish collector, in whose hands was the charge of the Agency until the autumn of 1825, when it devolved on Major Ovans, whose name has since become especially identified with these measures. The experiment was at first considered a hopeless one; and, doubtless, the difficulties in the way of its success are not easily to be exaggerated. But the might of mildness was everywhere triumphant. One by one the chiefs† were induced to present themselves at the Agency, to receive their grants of land, their written engagements with the Bheel agent, and, perhaps, the advance of money or farm-stock, which was necessary to enable them at once to commence their operations. Many kindly influences were set at work to secure the adhesion of these men to the great reformatory scheme. "The Bheel," wrote Major Ovans, in a very able report of these proceedings, submitted to

* The following is a translation of one of these engagements:

"To —— Bheel, of the village of ——, Pergunnah, ——.

"You have lived in the hills, and plundered the roads and country of the Sirkar, and committed thefts and various crimes; now you are prevented and have petitioned the Sirkar that if pardoned you will not again offend, and that if Tuccavee be given to you you will cultivate and thus earn a subsistence; on this your prayer has been considered, and the Sirkar has shown favor to you, and has this once pardoned your past crimes, and has given you for your support Tuccavee and land to cultivate, and this Kowl is written and presented to you that you may remain in your village and cultivate, and thus gain your livelihood. After this, if you again commit any offence, your former crimes will not be considered as forgiven, but you will have to answer both for them and the new crime.

(Signed) "——, Bheel Agent."

—[*Captain Graham's Historical Sketch.*]

† I use the word most familiar to the English reader. These head-men were known as "Naicks." The Bheels clustered together under the government of these men, and submitted themselves, in all things, to their guidance.

Sir John Malcolm, then Governor of Bombay, "is wonderfully susceptible of being worked upon by kind and liberal treatment. By attention to his little wants and petitions —by a present to his women, and by showing that you take an interest in him and his affairs, anything may be done with him. The true secret, however, of the power we now possess over the minds of this wild people is, that they feel themselves secure in the faith of our 'kowls' (engagements). This they never did before; and it is owing to this implicit reliance on the sanctity of our word that they submitted themselves so readily, and have re-established themselves so generally with their wives and children in the villages on the plains, where upwards of six hundred families are now settled at the plough alone."*

But although much reliance was to be placed on the good feelings of these poor people, it was hardly to be supposed that the erratic desires and habits of a life were to be rooted out in a few months. Ovans wisely determined, therefore, to surround the colonies with a cordon of mild restraint. He established a system of registration, whereby he was enabled to deal with the Bheels of the Agency each in his own individual distinctness. They were required never to leave their village, even for a day, without the permission of the Naicks or Potails; and if this rule was infringed the offence was at once reported at the Agency. A darogah, or police superintendent, was appointed to each talook, or division, whose duty it was to proceed from village to village, and to see that these regulations were enforced, whilst in every colony one of inferior rank was appointed to control and report upon the proceedings of the colonists.

Nor was the establishment of these colonies the only ameliorative measure which took shape under the hands of the Bheel agents. It was a great thing now to re-organise

* *Major Ovans to Sir John Malcolm, August,* 1830. *MS. Records.*

the police of the country, and to call the Bheels back again to their old profession of village watchmen. Indenting upon each village for the materials of this protective body, and providing for them the means of subsistence in such a manner as to warn them against the necessity of ever again resorting to their old predatory ways, he established an effective village police. In conformity with their ancient usages, he placed these men under the supervision of salaried superintendents, residing in their own villages, and entrusted with the preservation of the general peace of the district; and nothing could have worked better than this organisation of Bheel police.

The good effect of these humanising measures was soon apparent. At the very commencement of 1829, the collector reported that the province was in the enjoyment of entire repose. "For upwards of five-and-twenty years," he wrote, "Candeish has been subject to regular organised bodies of Bheels headed by desperate leaders. The enormities committed by them have been so often stated that on the subject no remark is required. But how satisfactory it is to report that the past year is the first after this long period, during which not a single gang or leader of Bheels has existed. The liberality of Government—the anxiety and exertions of its agents towards the reform of this class, is now amply repaid. The same characters exist. Their evil propensities can certainly not be yet eradicated; but the wise measures in force have corrected the one and checked the other."*

From this time the civilisation of the Bheels, under the superintendence of our English officers, a mixed agency of soldiers and civilians, proceeded rapidly to its consummation. Occasional local outbreaks showed that in parts which our influence had not yet reached, the natural character of the Bheels remained unchanged; but even these grew more and more rare, as our operations

* *Mr. Giberne's Police Report, January,* 1829. *MS. Records.*

proceeded, and the country which had once, across its whole length and breadth, been visited by continual fierce spasms of unrest, was soon lapped in general repose. "The districts," to use the comprehensive language of one of the ablest of the Bheel agents, "formerly the scene of every outrage, where neither life nor property were secure, now enjoyed tranquillity; the roads formerly hazardous for the armed party, were traversed at all hours by single passengers, the formidable list of crimes had dwindled down to the report of a few petty thefts, and the Bheels, from outcasts, had become members of the society, daily rising in respectability and appearance, and becoming useful and obedient servants of the State. It was matter of astonishment to behold the rapid change produced by the liberal system of Government, in a race of miserable beings, who without a rag to cover their backs, and hardly a morsel of food to put into their mouths, had so shortly before sued for life and food from the foreigner, and were now fat and sleek and decently clad, living in their own huts, surrounded by swarms of healthy children, ploughing their own lands, and many in the honest possession of flocks and herds. . . . The Bheel now feels a relish for that industry which renders subsistence secure, and life peaceful and comfortable; he unites with the Ryot in the cultivation of those fields which he once ravaged and laid waste, and protects the village, the traveller, and the property of Government, which were formerly the objects of his spoliation; the extensive wilds which heretofore afforded him cover during his bloody expeditions, are now smiling with fruitful crops; and population, industry and opulence, are progressing throughout the land."*

This was written towards the close of 1843. The language of the Bheel agent is not exaggerated. It reflects no more than the truth. Indeed, the whole is not yet

* *Captain Graham's Historical Sketch.*

told. If there were anything to qualify our admiration of the vigorous humanity of Colonel Dixon in the Mairwarra country, it is the fact that this able and benevolent administrator has thought less of educational measures than I should have expected or desired. There is no remedial agent like the schoolmaster. He was not forgotten in the Bheel country. Outram introduced him to his rude levies—and the civil officers soon dotted the province with schools. A new generation of Bheels is now springing up, among whom the lawlessness and violence of their tribes are mere traditions. A quarter of a century has passed since the work of civilisation commenced. The crooked ways have been made straight, and the rough places plain; and now a new race, trained to habits of peace and industry, are gradually replacing the old marauders who had been bred and nurtured in violence and wrong. There can be no fear now of a relapse. The schoolmaster has taken the young Bheel in hand; the life of an outlaw has no charms for him. He has been brought within the pale of civilised life; and he is well contented to abide there.

I need hardly say that such measures as these received the earnest support and warm encouragement of the Company. The Court of Directors had from the first recommended the adoption of kindly, conciliatory measures towards the erring Bheels, believing that they were not irreclaimable; and in April, 1835, they wrote out to the Bombay Government to express their hearty, unqualified approbation of what had been done. "From the period," they wrote, "when measures of severity were abandoned and conciliatory means resorted to, the rapine and disorder which had prevailed for years previously without any sensible diminution, and in spite of the strongest efforts for their suppression, almost immediately ceased, and the admirable conduct of the officers to whom the immediate executive duties were confided, especially of Major Ovans and Lieutenant Outram, has been the means of effecting a complete change in the habits of the Bheel tribes. They have universally abandoned their predatory habits; they are now a prosperous agricultural community; from among them a corps has been formed, which has attained so high a state of discipline and efficiency that to its protection the tranquillity of the country is now in a great degree confided; and by its means a degree of security both of person and of property appears to be maintained, which is scarcely excelled in any part of India.

"This signal instance," continue the Court, "of what we have so often impressed upon you—the superior efficacy of conciliatory means in reducing uncivilised and predatory tribes to order and obedience—is one of the most gratifying events in the recent History of British India; and we trust that the success of your measures will impress upon our Indian Governments the policy, as well as the humanity, of pursuing the same course in all similar cases. This wise and benevolent policy was first adopted by the late Mr. Cleveland in the district of Bhaugulpore, some fifty years ago, and was attended with singular success in reclaiming the Hill people of that district from a state of the utmost barbarism; and the memory of that excellent officer is, we understand, held in reverence, even at the present day, by the rude tribes that inhabit the hills as well as by the inhabitants of the more civilised portion of the district."*

* *MS. Records.*—Although I have incidentally mentioned the name of Cleveland in connexion with this great subject of the civilisation of savage tribes, I cannot help experiencing a feeling of shame and self-reproach as I read this affectionate notice of his labors in the above letter of the Court of Directors. I have been anxious, for the most part, to draw my illustrations from more recent history; but the good deeds of one, which at the early age of twenty-eight had done so much to reclaim the savage people by whom he was surrounded, deserves prominent notice in such a volume as this. Even now I may do something to repair the omission. The history of the civilisation of the Hill people of Bhaugulpore is well sketched in an early volume of the *Asiatic Researches*, from which I may not disadvantageously exhume it:

"Colonel Brown, in his account of these hills, forwarded to Government in 1779, observes that it was about fifteen years since the Hill people had any government among themselves of a general nature, during which period they had become dangerous and troublesome

I trust that these pictures will not be thrown away. They are to be pondered over thoughtfully, and I would

to the Low Country, that their ravages had been the more violent, as they were stimulated by hatred against the Zemindars, for having cut off several of their chiefs by treachery. The colonel might have added, that during that interregnum or dissolution of government, it was a common practice for the Zemindars on the skirts of the hills to invite the chiefs in their vicinity with their adherents to descend and plunder the neighbouring Zemindarees, for which, and for the passage through their lands, the mountaineers divided the booty with them; thus, at one time, from repeated acts of treachery in the Zemindars, the mountaineers were provoked to take ample vengeance on them and their unhappy Ryots; and at other times, from their engaging the chiefs to make predatory incursions, to which they were strongly incited, no less from a desire of plundering their more opulent neighbours, than from the difficulty of obtaining salt and tobacco from the boats, all friendly intercourse was at a stand, the low country bordering on the hills was almost depopulated, and travellers could not pass with safety between Bhaugulpore and Furruckabad, nor could boats, without danger of being plundered, put to for the night on the south side of the Ganges between the before-named places. It was at this period of double treachery on the part of the Zemindars, and predatory hostilities on the part of the mountaineers (from which it may not be a strained inference, that the machinations of the former were in a great measure the cause of that necessity which compelled the latter to such frequent and fatal descents, when these public and private incendiaries were making large strides in ruining these once fertile districts), that Captain Brooke was stationed with a corps of light infantry to avert their utter destruction. On this duty it is well known that he acquitted himself with great credit, from his uncommon exertions and success in pursuing the unfortunate mountaineers into their hills, where numbers must have unavoidably fallen; for it became unquestionably necessary to impress them with a dreadful awe of our prowess; and in this harassing and unpleasant warfare I have been well informed, by officers who were with Captain Brooke, that his gallant conduct could not be too much commended. He made them sensible of the inefficacy of opposing him in the field, and invited the chiefs to wait upon him, and negotiate, when he gave a feast to those who came in, and made them presents of turbans. But before any permanent establishment took place, he was succeeded in the command of the light infantry by Captain Brown, who made further progress in conciliating the minds of the discomfited mountaineers. He placed them on the road from Furruckabad, near Calgong, to protect the Dawks, on which duty they still continue.

"From this and other measures of his, Captain Brooke, and he, it will be allowed, laid the foundation for the most permanent and happy settlement concluded with the Hill Chiefs by the late Mr. Augustus Cleveland, that could possibly be attained: he was sensible from the rapine and decay of these districts, that the peaceable deportment of the mountaineers ought to be purchased; and while he was reconciling them to become subject to the British Government, he bestowed liberal presents, in money and clothes, to the chiefs, and to all the men and women who came down to him. Of his generosity they speak with gratitude; and for the blessings and benefit which they derive from the wise and judicious conditions which he granted, and which were confirmed by Government, I hope they will ever have reason to be thankful: as long as that Government lasts, the comforts and happiness which they derive from them must ever ensure their obedience. To engage their confidence, Mr. Cleveland, in the early part of his intercourse with the mountaineers, entertained all who offered their services as archers, and appointed many of the relations of the chiefs, officers; they were not (nor are they as rangers, though they very seldom now ask their discharges) bound to serve for any limited time; the corps, of course, constantly fluctuated, and was frequently, I understand, above a thousand strong: he clothed them, and in less than two years after they were formed,

hope benignantly, by those who affect to believe that our career in India has been one of continued spoliation and

from the confidence he had in their attachment and fidelity, obtained fire-arms for them, in the use of which, I may venture to observe, that they are expert, and have address; and I can also without hesitation assert, that they are capable of as high a degree of discipline as any native corps in the service; and I trust I shall have the happiness to prove this in due time. Exclusive of having thus employed so many of the mountaineers, Mr. Cleveland fixed the salary of ten rupees per month for each chief of a Tuppah, three rupees ditto for each of his Naibs, and two for the Maungy of each village, from which there shall be a man enrolled in the hill rangers; but from such as supply not a man, the inferior Maungy receives no monthly allowance. In consideration of these establishments, I understand the chiefs are not only responsible for the peaceable deportment of their own adherents, but bound to deliver over all delinquents and disturbers of the public peace within their own limits to the collector, to be tried by an assembly of the chiefs, either at Bhaugulpore or Rajamahall, as already related. It has ever been customary on these occasions to feast the chiefs so assembled; when any report is to be made to the collector, it is the duty of a Naib to wait on him with it, should the chief be indisposed or otherwise prevented.

"From these happy and admirable arrangements, digested by Mr. Cleveland, whose name ought to be dear both to the natives of the hills and lowlands, the ease, comfort, and happiness of the former is ensured (for which they are grateful, and speak of him with reverential sorrow), and peace and safety secured to the latter; and if they have any goodness, they ought not to be less thankful. These solid and essential benefits are attended comparatively with but a trivial expense, and must ultimately be an advantage to Government. I have been led to say more on this subject than I intended; yet it may not be thought foreign to it to add, that the Aumlah and Zemindars erected a monument to the memory of Mr. Cleveland, nearly in the form of a pagoda, and that another was also erected at the expense of Government, by the order of the Honorable the Governor-General and Council; on which is the following inscription:

"'To the memory of AUGUSTUS CLEVELAND, Esq.,
Late collector of the districts of Bhaugulpore and Rajamahall,
Who without bloodshed or the terror of authority,
Employing only the means of conciliation, confidence, and benevolence,
Attempted and accomplished
The entire subjection of the lawless and savage inhabitants of the
Jungleterry of Rajamahall,
Who had long infested the neighbouring lands by their predatory incursions,
Inspired them with a taste for the arts of civilised life,
And attached them to the British Government by a conquest over their minds;
The most permanent, as the most rational, mode of dominion.
The Governor-General and Council of Bengal,
In honor of his character, and for an example to others,
Have ordered this monument to be erected.
He departed this life on the 13th of January, 1784, aged 29.'"

Few of my readers, it is probable, are acquainted with the above, but few are not acquainted with Bishop Heber's delightful "Journal," in which there is a becoming notice of this "excellent young man."

Cleveland was the cousin and beloved friend of John Shore, who was so afflicted by the intelligence of his death, that his health was severely injured by the blow. After a while he gave vent to his sorrow in verse, and an elaborate "monody" was the result. There is so little verse in this volume, that perhaps I shall be forgiven for extracting a few lines from the piece:

"Let History tell the deeds his wisdom plann'd,
His bloodless triumphs o'er a barbarous land.
Bright in his hand the sword of justice gleam'd,
But mercy from her eyes benignant beam'd—

oppression. A philosophical modern historian, in a work which is laid before me whilst I am writing these sheets—it is the first sentence of his book—has truthfully written, "There are many kinds of war and many degrees of heroic renown, but the highest praise is due to those who by their victorious arms have opened new scenes for the civilisation of mankind, and overcome barbarism in some important portion of the world."* This overcoming of barbarism is very pleasant to write about. It seemed a very difficult thing to achieve in Mairwarra and Candeish, but English benevolence and English energy accomplished it at last; and the victory has been complete. The servants of the Company have reclaimed men whose savage propensities had been aggravated and seemingly perpetuated by the cruel discipline, the unscrupulous oppression of their native masters. Instead of endeavouring to extirpate, we endeavoured to civilise them. The good work was done. It was done by the personal energy—the fearless courage—the patience and charity of a very few English gentlemen hoping against hope, and finding possibilities in the impossible.

And mercy won the cause;—the savage band
Forsook their haunts and bowed to his command;
And where the warrior's arm in vain assail'd,
His gentler skill o'er brutal force prevail'd—
As some fond sire mistrusts his darling son,
With fostering care he led wild nature on;
And now, where Rapine mark'd the blood-stained field,
The well-till'd glebes a smiling harvest yield;
Now mended morals check the lust for spoil,
And rising letters prove his generous toil.
The traveller secure pursues his way,
Nor dreads the ruffian ambush'd for his prey;
And gaping savages with ravaged eyes,
See their lord's name in magic symbols rise.
Humanity surveys her rights restored,
And nations yield, subdued without a sword."

I need hardly say that these lines are as applicable to the civilisation of the Mairs and the Bheels, as to the civilisation of the hill-people of Rajmahal.

* *Ranke's Civil Wars and Monarchy of France in the Sixteenth and Seventeenth Centuries. Translated by M. A. Garvey.*

CHAPTER III.

Operations in Goomsur—The Hill Tribes of Orissa—Religion of the Khonds—Prevalence of Human Sacrifice—Efforts for its Suppression—Captain Macpherson—His Measures and Success—Subsequent Efforts—General Results.

I CANNOT dismiss this subject without adducing another noble illustration of the truth with which I prefaced the last chapter. I have taken one example from Bengal, and another from Bombay. I now take a third from Madras.

In the district of Ganjam, which lies on the northern frontier of the Madras Presidency, is the Zemindarry of Goomsur. It was tributary to the British Government; and this relationship might have continued, but that the tribute was not paid, and, after a vain attempt to bring about an amicable arrangement, resort was had to a military force. Early in November, 1835, the British troops occupied Goomsur. The adherents of the Zemindar fired on our camp. Martial law was proclaimed. The forfeiture of the Zemindarry was declared. A reward was offered for the apprehension of the offending chief. And before long it became clear that we were about to be involved in an inglorious but difficult campaign.

The whole country, indeed, was now in a state of open rebellion. Favored by their local knowledge, the insurgents fired from their hills and jungles securely on our advancing troops. We warred against invisible enemies; and one invisible enemy greater than all the rest was striking down our people by scores. The pestilential climate was doing its sure work. Everything, indeed, was against us. We had not a friend in the district. The people abandoned their homes at our approach. Nothing but forsaken fields and deserted huts greeted us as we advanced. No offer of reward—no threat of punishment—brought in adherents to our cause. It seemed altogether a hopeless, profitless adventure. We were being beaten by an enemy whom we could not reach, and perishing in a country which we could not hold.

The Zemindar fled to the hills. The Khond tribes received him with hospitality, and promised him their protection; but he was not suffered to live to see the redemption of their pledge. It seemed that we had hunted him to death; for in the first pause of the chase he laid himself down and died. Twenty years before, the ladies of his Zenana had been dishonored by a British force, and now, with his dying breath, the Goomsur chief, solemnly as in the presence of their gods, bound the tribes not to suffer the *capture* of his family,* in any event, by our advancing troops.

A detachment of British soldiers was sent forward to penetrate the mountain passes, and to secure possession of the family of the deceased. The attempt was, in the first instance, successful. The family of the Goomsur chief were seized; but the tribes, eager to redeem their pledge to the utmost, came down upon a party of our troops, who were escorting some members of the family, overwhelmed them in a difficult defile, and put to death seven ladies of the Zenana, to save them, as they believed, from threatened dishonor. Heavy chastisement descended upon the offending tribes; but they had partially redeemed their pledge.

There was then a lull in our operations. The pestilence which fell upon our troops compelled a season of inactivity. But with the cold weather the war was recommenced. A fresh force of all arms prepared to attack the tribes in their mountain homes. We demanded their unconditional

* *Captain Macpherson's Khond Report. Calcutta,* 1842.

submission. We demanded the surrender of their patriarchal chiefs. We demanded the betrayal of the officers of the Goomsur Zemindar, who had trusted themselves to the protection of the tribes. But they refused to bring either their guests or their patriarchs to the scaffold; and so our troops were let loose upon the land. I need not dwell upon the history of this "little war." I only wish to speak of its results. Here, on this chain of hills skirting the great province of Orissa, our English officers were first brought face to face with a new and a strange people. The tribes of whom I have spoken were the Khonds. Up to this time, the English had known nothing of the Khonds. And the Khonds had known nothing of the English. They had dwelt for nearly a century within a short distance of each other, but there had been no intercourse between them. Now, therefore, when the civilised white men, after the first excitement of war was over, began to inquire into the nature and habits of the heathen barbarians by whom they had been opposed, they found that they had been brought into contact with a people possessing religious creeds and rituals, national usages and social customs, utterly unlike any with which, in all their ethnological experience, they had ever made acquaintance before.

It was at first, to our unaided comprehension, something rather vague and astonishing than clear and intelligible. We only caught glimpses of what we desired to know. We had for a long time, indeed, only a dim perception of the religion of these strange people. Their external usages and ceremonials were speedily revealed to us, but it was only after the patient investigation of years, that we learnt all the articles of faith upon which these usages and ceremonials were based. And then it was mainly, if not wholly, to the laborious researches of one man—researches prompted by the best feelings of humanity, that we were indebted for our knowledge of the inner life of the Khond tribes of the Orissan hills.

The officer of whom I speak, Lieutenant Charters Macpherson, of the Madras Army, during the Goomsur war, in 1836-37, had been employed in the survey of a part of the country at the foot of the hills ; and being naturally a man of a thoughtful and inquiring nature, and of an energetic benevolence of the best kind, he no sooner obtained a little general outside knowledge of the peculiarities of the Khond tribes than he formed the determination of pushing his investigations far beneath the surface, and of mastering the whole subject of the religious and social life of the strange people who had awakened such a kindly interest within him.

Goomsur was subjugated—pacified—and the Khond tribes of that district became British subjects.* There were many other tribes who owed no allegiance to us, and with whom we had no intercourse. But it was enough for Macpherson to prosecute his inquiries among those with whom his official duties brought him into contact, and he spared no pains to acquaint himself intimately with all the peculiarities of this strange variety of mankind. One of the first things which had arrested his attention was the painful fact, that among these people the barbarous rite of human sacrifice was observed—that the tribes were in the habit of offering up to their deities living sacrifices purchased or bred for the purpose.† And it was mainly with the humane desire of rooting out these abominations that Macpherson now labored to render himself familiar with the social institutions of the Khonds, and with all the peculiarities of the dark faith

* Goomsur was exempted from subjection to the Regulations.

† It was not until some time afterwards that he discovered how female infanticide was with other Khond tribes, as with some of the more civilised tribes of Central and Western India, a practice held in no dishonor, but generally observed by the heads of families as a matter of social convenience.

which either ordained or sanctioned such iniquities as these.

What this belief is may be briefly told. The Khonds are divided into two great sects. They have certain common articles of faith. They all believe that the Supreme Being, or God of Light, the source of all good, created for himself a consort, who became the Earth-Goddess, and was the source of all evil. The Supreme Being, the source of good, created the world and loved it; and the Earth-Goddess became jealous of God's people. Then she rebelled against the Supreme Being, and introduced moral and physical evil into the world, and from that time there was strife between the powers of Light and Darkness.

And so far this is the common faith of the Khond tribes. But here begin the divergences of sectarianism. The issue of this great strife between the powers of Light and Darkness is the grand subject of dispute between the two contending sects. The one believes that the God of Light utterly overcame the Earth-Goddess, and has ever since held her in thrall, employing her as the agent of his will—the instrument of his rule. The other holds that the Earth-Goddess is still unconquered; that she holds in her hands the balance of good and evil—that the destinies of man are under her control—and that whatever of happiness is vouchsafed to him is only by her sanction or concession, by the dispensation of blessings in her own gift, or the withdrawal of that antagonism which might prevent their emanation from the God of Light. And thus regarding the supremacy of the Earth-Goddess, they recognise the necessity of a propitiation, and they believe that, only by the worship of the power of Darkness, through the agency of human sacrifice, her favor can be purchased for the tribes.

Therefore, by this one great sect of the Khonds the abomination of human sacrifice is esteemed a sacred rite.

The atoning efficacy of the sacrificial blood is an article of faith among these barbarous people, cherished with as much solemn conviction as it has been by some of the most civilised nations of the world. It is necessarily a very lively, operative faith, one that can never exist in a state of semi-animation ; it must be everything or nothing to a man. If he entertain it at all, it must be a part of his daily life. It must enter largely into all his worldly calculations. The health of his children, the state of his crops, the condition of his flocks and herds, his immunity from the ravages of wild beasts, from the assaults of his enemies, from the storm-blast and the lightning-stroke, all depend upon the observance of this one ceremonial rite. To neglect it is, in the belief of these people, to draw down upon them the anger of the Earth-Goddess, and with it all human ills. Of all superstitions it is the most enslaving; for it is based on fear, abject fear of immediate retribution. The worshipper of Tari Pennu, or the Earth-Goddess, dare not neglect the act of propitiation. All that he has is too immediately under her almighty control.

The Mexicans, before the Spanish invasion, sacrificed human victims by thousands and tens of thousands. The bloody oblations which they offered to their false gods are too stupendous in the recital for human credulity to entertain. And yet their extent is susceptible of proof. No such wholesale sacrifices as these ever defiled the country of the Khonds. The victims were comparatively few.* They were furnished by a regular class of procurers, who either supplied them to order, or raised them on speculation. They were bought, perhaps, from their parents in hard famine-times, or they were kidnapped on

* It was very difficult to ascertain the number of victims offered up every year—especially as many portions of the Khond country were unvisited by our officers. As far as I can arrive at an approximative estimate, it may have been about 500 a year. But even this approximation I venture upon with great diffidence.

the plains; or were perhaps the children of the procurers themselves. Devoted often in their childhood to the Earth-Goddess, they were suffered to grow up as consecrated, privileged beings, to marry wives, to hold lands, and flocks and herds, and other worldly goods—cherished and endowed by the community, for whom they were to die, and in spite of the tremendous curse that overshadowed them, leading happy lives to the last.

It would seem that these human sacrifices were of two kinds. Principally they assumed an associative character; they were the joint offerings of certain tribes or villages on the occasion of their public festivals. But sometimes they were individual—exclusive—intended to avert the wrath of the Earth-Goddess, when there was special reason to believe that it had been awakened against a particular family, and could only be so averted.

"The periodical common sacrifices," says Captain Macpherson, "are generally so arranged by tribes and divisions of tribes, that each head of a family is enabled, at least once a year, to procure a shred of flesh for his fields, and usually about the time when his chief crop is laid down." In the protective virtue of this shred of human flesh the worshipper of the Earth-Goddess had unbounded faith. A representative of each tribe or village was sent to the place of sacrifice to obtain it, whilst his brethren at home, in rigid fast and solemn prayer, awaited his return. Bound to a stake, the victim received the first signal blow from the officiating priest, and then the crowd of attendant deputies rushed forward with their axes, completed the sacrifice, and tore the quivering flesh from the Meriah's bones.* The human shred was then carefully wrapped in leaves, carried home to the village, laid on a cushion of grass in some public place, where the heads of families, attended by the priest, went out to give it solemn recep-

* This was the most generally received ceremonial of sacrifice—but there were other modes of immolation. Sometimes the victim was destroyed by a slow fire.

tion. Then the priest divided the sacred flesh into two parts—one of which he buried in the ground, whilst the other he subdivided into minute particles, and distributed among the attendant heads of families. A scene of wild excitement followed. There was shouting and holloaing—wrestling and fighting—heads were broken, and houses thrown down. This over, the recipient took his apportioned remnant of the sacrifice, and buried it in his favorite field. Then they returned to their homes—ate, drank, and were merry. Three days of ritual observance followed; on the fourth, "the people assembled at the place of sacrifice, slaughtered and feasted on a buffalo, and left its inedible portions as a gratification to the spirit of the Meriah."*

Such is the history of these human sacrifices as ascertained and recorded, after much laborious inquiry, by Captain Macpherson. But, long before we had this amount of knowledge to base our remedial measures upon, our English officers had been endeavouring to root out the horrid custom from the hill districts under our rule. As early as 1836, the broad fact had been announced by Mr. Russel; and it was afterwards ascertained that other Khond tribes were in the habit of murdering their female children, in their infancy, purely as a matter of family convenience. Indeed, among some of the tribes, save in the case when a woman's first child was a girl, no single female infant was spared.† These were lamentable facts, which early arrested the attention of the British authorities, but until the Zemindarry had been formally resumed and the settlement of the country commenced, it was not probable that our consideration of the remedial measures to be adopted should take any definite shape.

* *Macpherson's Account of the Religion of the Khonds in Orissa. Transactions of the Asiatic Society.*—At the place of sacrifice there were three days of feasting, attended with much sensual license.

† "Villages," says Captain Macpherson, "containing a hundred houses, may be seen without a single female child."

But as soon as these objects had been attained, Mr. Russel began fairly to consider the "best mode of effecting the abolishing of this barbarous custom." In an elaborate paper on the subject, he declared that he was "fully impressed with the belief that it can be accomplished only by slow and gradual means." He sincerely believed that "a law denouncing human sacrifices and providing for the punishment of persons engaged therein would, as a general measure, prove abortive, and involve a compromise of character which should not be hazarded." "In my judgment," he added, "our aim should be to improve to the utmost our intercourse with the tribes nearest to us, with the view to civilise and enlighten them, and so reclaim them from the savage practice, using our moral influence rather than our power."* In these views the Madras Government entirely concurred. Time and the contact of civilisation were to be left to do their slow work.

It does not, however, seem that this resolution was persevered in to the entire exclusion of all active efforts for the suppression of the practice. But the measures which from time to time were adopted seemed rather to attack incidental symptoms than to strike at the root of the evil. On one occasion, for example, Captain Campbell, assistant to the collector of Goomsur, ascended the ghauts, with a party of armed peons, just before the periodical season of sacrifice, and rescued a hundred victims. In 1838, Mr. Bannerman, the collector, went himself upon a tour of inspection among the Hill tribes, and determined to surprise a Khond village just as the people were preparing for the ceremony of the sacrifice. "The preparations for the ceremony," he wrote, "appeared to have been completed. The entrance to the hamlet, which was in the form of a square, had been newly fitted up with wickerworks, and in the centre, close to

* *MS. Records, quoted in the Calcutta Review.*

the rude village idol, had been erected a bamboo pole about forty feet high, on the top of which was an effigy in the shape of a bird, with peacock's feathers." This was the stake to which the wretched victim was to have been bound, previous to the sacrifice. "A young woman from the plains" had been prepared for immolation; but she was rescued by the British officer from her cruel fate. And subsequently seven other victims, concealed in different villages, were reluctantly given up to him. He attempted to reason with the chief people; but he found that their perceptions were somewhat clouded and obscured by the strong liquors which they had drunk, in anticipation of the murderous festival, and nothing came of the controversy. No new light broke in upon the mind of the benevolent British functionary; and on his return from this expedition he could only report that, sensible as he was of "the anxiety felt by Government to put a stop to the barbarous custom of sacrificing human victims," he could but "feel difficulty in proposing any practicable measure with the view of carrying its humane wishes into effect."*

There was a suggestion, however, in his report, which seemed worthy of all attention. I have said that the Meriah victims were supplied by a regular class of procurers. It had been decreed that no compassion should be shown to this abominable race of men. They were, therefore, when occasion offered, apprehended, and tried in our criminal courts. But it was not easy to satisfy all the formal requirements of these tribunals, and to substantiate, by a regular chain of recognisable evidence, as evidence is considered by such courts, the actual commission of the offence as set forth in the indictment. This had been the difficulty in the cases of Thuggee and of professional Dakoitee, and it had been found necessary to authorise a certain relaxation of the law for the purpose of checking

* *Report of Mr. Bannerman. MS. Records, quoted in the Calcutta Review.*

the progress of these crimes.* It was now suggested by Mr. Bannerman that a similar relaxation of the law should be authorised in the present instance, and that a regularly appointed officer should have the power of dealing summarily with persons charged with the offence of trafficking in human life. This measure had, I believe, the approbation of the Court of Directors. It seemed a good idea to strike terror into the minds of the procurers, and so to stop the inhuman traffic. But it does not seem that any special enactment emanated from the Legislature.

In fact, for some two or three years after these expeditions to the Hill country, great as was the desire of both the civil and military officers in the Goomsur country to suppress the barbarous practice, and praiseworthy as were their efforts, little or nothing of an effectual character was really done. Lord Elphinstone was at this time Governor of Madras. It must be recorded to his honor, that he was deeply interested in the painful subject, and that he addressed himself, in an earnest and enlightened spirit, to its consideration. In an elaborate minute on the subject, written in 1841, he acknowledged that hitherto our measures for the suppression of Meriah sacrifice had been attended with little success; and he recommended a more systematic and comprehensive scheme than any which had yet been tried—though some of its details had been previously recommended—embracing, *firstly*, the opening of routes and passes through the wild tracts inhabited by the Khond tribes;† *secondly*, the encouraging of commercial intercourse between the hills and the plains by all available means, and the establishment of fairs and marts for that purpose; and *thirdly*, the raising of a semi-military police force from among the Hill men. And the better to carry out these objects, it was proposed that a special agent should be appointed, under the Commissioner

* *See the chapters on Thuggee and Dakoitee—ante*, pp. 354—380.

† I cannot say much for this project. The idea seems to have been that of a road leading from nowhere to nowhere.

of Goomsur, to proceed into the Khond country, to obtain the assistance of a petty Rajah on the other side of the Hills, towards the opening of the communication. This measure was sanctioned by the supreme Government; but when delivering their assent, they thought it necessary to issue a *caveat* to the effect that the Agent "should cautiously approach any inquisition into human sacrifices, and confine himself very closely to the immediate purposes of the Mission."

The officer to whom this Mission was entrusted was Captain Macpherson,* of whose first acquaintance with the Khond tribes I have already spoken. He had sent in an elaborate report upon the social and religious institutions of these strange people—indeed, had brought together a mass of information relating to them, which sufficed at once to indicate that there was no other officer in the service to whom this difficult and delicate work could be more advantageously entrusted. With characteristic earnestness he set about his work; but at every step as he advanced, formidable difficulties met the inquirer. They were very much the same difficulties as, in the Bheel country, had stared Outram and Ovans in the face. There was the extreme unhealthiness of the climate,† and the seemingly insuperable mistrust of the people. But Macpherson determined to brave the one, and to spare no effort to overcome the other. Sickness assailed him; his life was threatened, but he did not turn aside from his purpose. The people fled at his approach. The villages were deserted. But Macpherson did not despair. He halted; he waited; he did everything that could be done to assure the tribes; to prove that he was a man of

* Captain Macpherson, during the first exploring expedition, had suffered so severely in his health, that he was compelled to seek change of air at the Cape of Good Hope. He returned to Madras in the cold weather of 1840-41, when, by the direction of Lord Elphinstone, he wrote the elaborate report which is the basis of our information respecting the manners and customs of the Khonds.

† In the space of twenty-eight days ninety per cent. of the attendants of the Mission were struck down by fever.

peace; and to bring the fugitives back to their homes. And little by little he succeeded. In the neighbourhood of the white man's camp, the villagers who had fled at his approach, soon began to shake off their fears. It was plain that he had not come among them to destroy the people and desolate the country; so they emerged from their protecting forests, and a few of them, doubtfully and mistrustfully at first, came unarmed to the British tents, and were received with encouragement and kindness. Then others, who had been anxiously awaiting the results of the experiment, cautiously crept forward, and were in turn encouraged and assured. And then Macpherson moved forward into the hills; halted again; and again the people come around him; until hostile tribes contended for his favor, and what he sought lay within his reach.* He learnt from the Khonds themselves what were their social institutions, and he learnt—but with greater difficulty, and often longer delay—what was their religious belief.

From any direct interference with the practice of human sacrifice, Macpherson was at this time precluded by the nature of his instructions. But he cautiously felt the ground before him, and spared no pains to ascertain the state of feeling among the Khond patriarchs regarding the wishes and intentions of the British Government. And this much he soon ascertained. "Two general impressions prevailed among them. The first was, that the Government was indifferent to the sacrifice. This view was founded upon the fact, that no decisive and comprehensive measures had been adopted with respect to it, while partial interference had taken place. . . . The second was, that although Government certainly disap-

* The line of Macpherson's advance was between the tracts of country inhabited by the sacrificing and non-sacrificing sects—among the latter of which female infanticide obtained.

proved and desired the abolition of the practice, it was conscious that it had no just right to interfere with it."*

It was plain that no spasmodic efforts for the suppression of the abominable rite could be attended with any general or permanent results. Macpherson did not, therefore, attempt to rescue any particular Khond victims. But he exerted himself to imbue the chiefs with a thorough knowledge of the views and wishes of the British Government; and he especially endeavoured to impress them with the conviction that our "designs were those of paternal benevolence alone." In this he was at least partially successful. He mixed familiarly and conversed freely with them. He made the men presents of cloth and tobacco, and gave them money to purchase liquor. At every station he distributed beads among the women, who received them with expressions of gratitude and delight. It was his object to conciliate them by every means in his power; and he soon made them believe that he had no hostile design in his visit to their mountain homes. He had no lack of argument, either, for their benefit, and perhaps he may have done something to shake their belief in the efficacy of human sacrifice.

As time advanced, it seemed to Macpherson that his prospects of success were beginning to brighten. In the month of June, 1842, "the two tribes of Goomsur, which were best known, most under influence and most accessible, freely and intelligently consented to place themselves in practical subjection to the British Government, on the condition of receiving its protection and justice." They "stipulated that Government should support them with its whole authority in making this diffident and trembling movement."† Nay, indeed, they sought more than this. Still clinging to the old belief in the retri-

* *Captain Macpherson to Mr. Bannerman, April,* 1842. *MS. Records.*

† The same to the same, September, 1843. *MS. Records.*

butory power of the Earth-Goddess, they demanded that they should have full permission to denounce to their gods the British Government in general, and certain of its servants in particular, as the grand authors of their apostacy, and so to render us the vicarious recipients of the divine wrath.

But although even such doubtful concessions had some encouragement in them, it did not seem that, until we could more securely establish our position and our influence as their rightful rulers and protectors, that any permanent advantages would result from such uncertain demonstrations as these. "I conceive," said Captain Macpherson, "the establishment of distinct relations with these tribes as subjects, to be the necessary basis of the authority by which, combined with influences derived from every source within our power, we may hope to effect the suppression of the rite of sacrifice. The relations which I propose to establish are for the nearer tribes—submission to laws directly administered by us. For those more remote the practical acknowledgment of our supremacy."* This matter of the administration of justice among the Khonds was the great pivot upon which all Macpherson's measures subsequently turned. These strange Hill people had a wild unsatisfactory method of settling all disputes among themselves, and they were eager for the establishment of better ordered tribunals to which, in their difficulties, they might betake themselves for substantive justice. They saw at once, indeed, the advantages of this appeal to a power beyond the reach of all sinister influences, and they were glad to divest themselves of the undivided and unsupported responsibility which entailed upon them a world of difficulty and embarrassment, and often involved them in internecine strife.

* *Captain Macpherson to Mr. Bannerman, August,* 1842. *MS. Records.*

Macpherson undertook to preside over their judicial councils, and they hailed the offer with delight.*

It would have been something to see one of those primitive Khond Courts—Macpherson, under a tree, in a Khond village, sitting on a chair, with his chief people, native assistants and others, on their carpets on either side—the Khond chiefs sitting opposite, in tiers, three or four deep, according to their rank—the plaintiff and defendant volubly pleading each his own cause, and bringing in his several witnesses—and the fluctuating crowd of people in the background eagerly watching the proceedings, made up a picture as suggestive to the inner sense as it was striking to the outer. The case was stated. The witnesses were heard. Then the chiefs, one by one, were called upon to pronounce their opinions. And soundly and intelligently for the most part these opinions were pronounced. Then all having been heard, and notes of their several decisions taken, Macpherson proceeded to state what was the collective result. The judgment which he then pronounced was the judgment of the chiefs themselves; and they never doubted that the final decree of the Court was a correct exposition of their wishes.†

This great boon of pure and systematic justice worked mightily among them. "The result," said Macpherson, "surpassed my expectations. A movement began which gradually acquired force and distinctness. The estimate formed by these tribes of the value of the justice dispensed, which relieved society from the accumulation of public and private questions by which it was distracted, was higher than I could have imagined, and the direct

* It was his especial object not to supersede their authority, but to associate himself with, and to support, the chiefs in the administration of justice, after their own fashion.

† The general proceedings of the Court were carried on in the Khond language, but it was interpreted into Oorea, through which dialect Macpherson always communicated with the Khonds.

authority, therefore, derived from its administration was great. But that justice was not less important, regarded as a means of subjecting the people to the influences best calculated to sway them. The adherents and the opponents of the religious change sought it alike. But none could sue for it without full exposure, in some measure, at the discretion of its dispensers, to all the general and personal influences which could be devised to promote the extension and confirmation of the movement."* And under these influences, after a little while, 124 victims were voluntarily given up to the British officer.

Nor was the assistance thus rendered to them in the administration of justice the only benefit which they derived from their close connexion with the British. Increased facilities of traffic with the Low Country were afforded to them. Hitherto they had been much exposed to the chicanery and extortion of the merchants and dealers on the plains. These wild mountaineers were no match for the astute traders of the more civilised districts,†

* *Captain Macpherson to Mr. Bannerman, September*, 1843. *MS. Records.*

The following illustration of the results of this administration of justice, taken from the letters of Macpherson's moonshee, Baba Khan, is worth reading, for more reasons than one:

"My master had not at all an inclination to punish those prisoners as those that steal in the Low Country, for these had thought that in plundering they only obeyed the Rajah's orders and the Deity's will. But if he had not done so, the sacrificing Khonds and those others who carried on thefts would not be in future afraid. The principal ringleader of these thieves could not be apprehended at first; but on hearing the punishment awarded to the prisoners, he came in most submissively of his own accord to my master, and prostrated himself at his feet, at full length, holding a bit of straw in his mouth, which is the general custom in surrendering to a superior, and begged my master's pardon and protection, and declared that 'the Khond country is now the Sircar's (British Government's), and that I cannot hide myself anywhere in its hills, and as the Khonds having given over sacrificing victims, so will I give up robbery from this day, and will never commit thefts; and if there be any others that rob, he would bring them to my master.' Whereupon the poor fellow was pitied and forgiven. He has now reformed, and associates with the best of Khonds very honestly, subsisting himself entirely by work and traffic."

† The Hill people, however, laughed at the superior civilisation of the Low Country, and reasoned about it in a very amusing manner:

"The Khond witnesses who came to give their evidences against the prisoners lived in Lunjapilly, a village of Soondera Singh's, granted to him by Government. One morning on a sunshiny day, while Soondera Singh was coming in his palanquin to see my master with these Khonds, one of them remarked with astonishment and laughter, 'See! that palanquin was made in the Low Country; it is very beautiful, painted with colors, fixed with boards, lined with cloth, and iron fixed to it—how well it looks!' Another said, 'The senses of the Low Country people are not worth a cowry. How many men must

and when they came down from the hills to buy and sell, bringing their turmeric (it is the best that is sold in London) to market, and taking back in exchange scarlet cloths, brass pots, and other commodities in demand among them, they were generally overreached and defrauded. Especial protection was now given to their trade. They were enabled to buy and to sell on better terms than had ever been obtainable from their neighbours. Fairs were established for their especial advantage; and soon they found themselves in the enjoyment of such commercial prosperity as they had never even dreamt of before. This was something readily intelligible to the most obtuse, and appreciable by the most apathetic; and greatly it tended to strengthen and perpetuate British influence among the Khonds.

But these successes, great as they were, had some element of discouragement in them. And for a time, Macpherson was perplexed by new doubts and opposed by new difficulties. In spite of the pledges given, occasional sacrifices, from time to time, were consummated.* His authority was obviously insufficient for the full accomplishment of so great a work. Government had not declared themselves with sufficient distinctness, and there was an enemy in the way. One Sam Bissye,† a Hindoo here-

(it) have taken—how much trouble in making the palanquin! They felled wood, sawed it into planks, placed them together, and formed them into a palanquin—and then it is only comfortable for one individual—and great wastage of money, whilst on account of one person many suffer much labor. If that man were to walk and go, he would save his money and not give trouble to others. Is not this a wise business? If a quarter part of the money expended by Soondera Singh on that palanquin was spent on purchasing good meat and the marrow-bones of buffaloes for himself, and all was so consumed by him, it would give vast strength to his limbs, be palatable to his mouth, and fill his stomach for a long time to his heart's content. The Low Country people have, I think, little sense.'" [*MS. Correspondence of Baba Khan, Moonshee.*]

* These, however, were very few. There was always a small recusant minority, who desired to practise the rite, against the wishes of the general body. But the tribes collectively never wavered, and their anger against the offending exceptions was great.

† It is not easy to describe the exact position of this man. He was a kind of agent or minister to the tribes, managing their internal affairs, and communicating, on their behalf, with foreign Courts. He was rich, clever, and of great personal influence. He had been set over the general body of the tribes by the British Commissioner, on our first settlement of the country.

ditary office-bearer, whose influence with the tribes had been diminished by Macpherson's ascendancy, was striving manfully to neutralise all the efforts of the English officer. He declared that the authorities, to whom Macpherson was subordinate, had sanctioned the continuation of the sacrifices; he promulgated a dangerous report to the effect that the British were about to tax the tribes; and for a time it seemed that the machinations of this man would arrest the onward progress of reform.

In spite of shattered health, the English officer set himself bravely to work to counteract the evil influence of the wily Hindoo. Watching his opportunity, he contrived to blacken the face of Sam Bissye in the eyes of the tribes, and to exercise his own authority in matters very dear to them, so as to increase his own influence over them, and to prove that the higher authorities were with him. In a little while the overthrow of Sam Bissye was complete. He was suspended from office, and seized as a criminal.*

* From the interesting letters written by Captain Macpherson's moonshee, I take a passage or two, illustrative of the evil machinations and the punishment of Sam Bissye. Of the former, the writer says: "Last season the old wolf-faced Sam Bissye summoned the Khonds, on whom he had engrafted nectarious (nefarious?) words, and told them 'Captain Macpherson has agreed with the Government to assess and raise taxes in the Khond country, for his own profit, when you give up the Meriah sacrifices; consequently he is now allowing you all very civilly. Should you, therefore, discontinue from sacrificing, the whole of us will be utterly ruined, and, also, it is very wrong to desist from our ancient rites. If you hearken to the advice of Captain Macpherson, at least perform the sacrifice in secret.' This season Sam Bissye was with Mr. B(annerman), the collector, while we were in the Hill country, and after our return he proceeded to his country and summoned all the Khonds, and told them that 'Mr. B. has given me permission to sacrifice six victims, and my whole body is affected with leprosy, on account of your having discontinued the sacrifice. Come and see; I am going to kill a sacrifice.' He gave them food, and liquor to drink, and asked a Mullick, a chief man in Rissinghur, a friend of his, whether he would kill a sacrifice now or not—that leave was granted by Mr. B. He replied: 'If you give me authority I will do it.' When Sam Bissye gave his consent a victim was sacrificed, and the flesh was taken away by the Khonds. A sacrifice was also executed at Rodunghia, but very secretly, and immediately buried. This is the way Sam Bissye is throwing severe obstacles in our way."

Another instance given in the same letters has double value, as an illustration, partly of Sam Bissye's influence—partly of the domestic history of these Meriah sacrifices. Such a complication of misfortunes as is here described might well have sent a wavering Khond back to his victim-medicine. "My master questioned Jeetoo Mullick. 'Why did you sacrifice?' He answered: 'My family were sick. A barn fell unawares on my wife, and she died; a tiger devoured my buffalo; and another woman died in childbirth; and I also

And for a while the tide of success was turned in his favor. In May, 1844, he was able officially to report to the Madras authorities: "I have the high satisfaction to state that the great season of sacrifice is past, and that there has been no apparent tendency to sacrifice, in any part of the Khond country of Goomsur."

So far as the Goomsur tribes were concerned, Macpherson's success was well-nigh complete. But now arose the great question of the extension to other tribes of these great ameliorative measures. The sacrificing tribes were scattered over a portion of the Hill districts of Orissa partly under the Madras, and partly under the Bengal Presidency.* Macpherson's authority extended only to the former; and in the tracts subordinate to the Bengal Government, though efforts had been made to suppress the inhuman rite, they had not assumed a sustained

was dangerously ill.' Then Gunda Mullick told me, 'What are all these sufferings? Why not sacrifice a victim? I will go and take Sam Bissye's permission to offer one, as I have heard that he has got permission from the Sircar (British Government) to sacrifice victims?' Then I told Gunda M. that 'I have no victims to sacrifice, and am unable to go just now. You had better go for me.' Upon which Gunda M. said: 'You have a piece of land in Hodzogher, and I will procure you a victim for it; then sacrifice and get the better of your sickness.' Then Gunda M. went to Sam Bissye and related of Jetoo's ailment. Sam Bissye stated to him, that although the Sircar prevents you from sacrifice, do not you relinquish it, as that is the most precious medicine, and no other medicine is worth."

The moonshee, in another place, thus graphically relates, after his own fashion, the story of Sam Bissye's seizure:—"While my master sat on a chair, the Zemindarry Sherishtadar of the collector's cutcherry, the principal assistant agent's magistrate's moonshy, with Soondersing and myself of the assistant cutcherry, and several of the Sirdars and principal men of the villages, Ryots, Peons, &c., standing around, Sam Bissye came up with twenty Peon attendants, brought a goat, some oranges and yams, to my master, and one rupee laid at his feet, and stood before him. My master then told Sam Bissye as follows: 'Government has sent orders to suspend you, and you are suspended from this day, and to be placed in confinement.' When Sam Bissye heard this, he stood as a post of wood, not uttering a single word, and all those present at that moment were motionless as a flock of sheep, flocked together in the evening. Awhile, after every one began to disperse, frightened in their minds as the same sheep, when a tiger gets into the flock and devours a large sheep out of it. The large-toothed like a jungle hog, Madara Poricha, who was always Sam Bissye's right arm, was also there; but weapons were taken from him, and he ordered into confinement, with Sam Bissye, because he was accused of robberies. When the Peons went to take them into confinement, Sam Bissye told the twenty Peons who came with him, 'Oh children, come!' But my master told him that he had nothing to do with them, nor they anything with him."—[*MS. Correspondence.*]

* And partly, it might be added, in the Nagpore territory.

character. So the Khonds argued among themselves that it was plain the Government had no very strong impressions on the subject of human sacrifice—that, indeed, their desires and intentions respecting the suppression of the practice were anything but clearly manifested, and that probably, after all, they cared little or nothing about the matter. The two Governments seemed not to be acting in concert with each other, if it were not indeed altogether the crotchet of a single inferior officer, whose acts would not be supported by the authorities above him. This was, indeed, a stumbling-block in the way of the movement; and Macpherson represented the difficulty to the Government. It was plain that if his labours were to be effectual, he should be invested with authority more extensive and more defined. Nor were his representations without avail. Early in 1845 he was appointed Agent to the supreme Government for the suppression of human sacrifice and infanticide in the Hill tracts of Orissa.

Macpherson's course was now comparatively easy. This authoritative manifestation at once convinced the tribes what was the will of the supreme Government. Armed, therefore, with these new powers, and surrounded by the prestige of authority, the Khond Agent stepped at once across the boundary and began to extend his effort to the tribes inhabiting the great district of Boad, under the Bengal Presidency. They had been watching with intense interest the progress of the great experiment that had been going on in Goomsur. Moved by a strong spirit of inquiry, they had crossed the border, attended the Goomsur councils, mixed familiarly with the proselytes, and received from them distinct ideas of the advantages of the relationship subsisting between them and the British Agent. The new light, indeed, had already broken in upon the mind of the Boad tribes. They not only understood the nature of the change, but they clearly saw its advantages. They saw how peaceful and prosperous the country had become, and how happily their neighbours lived under the reformation. There was a great living argument, indeed, better than all theories and speculations, in support of the advocated change. The Goomsur tribes had ceased to defile their hands with the sacrificial blood of their fellow-creatures; and yet there had been two unusually healthy seasons, and two unusually abundant harvests. Providence, in this, had wrought mightily for us. The Boad tribes viewed the result with wondering admiration. They called us Boora Pennu's people—the agents of the God of Light—and believed that superhuman power was in the hands of the people who had done such things. The wrath of the Earth-Goddess, it was clear, could not avail against us.

It was Macpherson's wont, I believe, in all his arguments with these poor people, to deal tenderly with the abomination of human sacrifice, rather as a religious error than as a great practical crime. He did not fail, indeed, to tell them that other nations had, at different periods of time, clung to a belief in the efficacy of human blood as a means of propitiation, but that as those nations had advanced in civilisation, they had abjured the false faith, and abandoned the pernicious practice. And he especially dwelt upon the fact that our own nation, once sunk in darkness and barbarism, had practised the unhallowed rite; but that since we had abandoned and denounced it, we had become the kings of the earth. These arguments were now repeated to the Boad tribes, and listened to with marked respect.*

In the mean while, in the Goomsur country, the crown was set upon the great reformation, and a brilliant incident inaugurated the appointment of the Khond Agent. On a given day, the entire body of the Khond tribes prepared, in their several villages, publicly to perform a simultaneous ceremony of final abjuration of their murder-worship, and their adoption of the religion of the God of

* It is only fair, however, to say that the Khonds were by no means wanting in polemical adroitness, for they contended that it was not impossible that, by reason of their sacrifices, all the world had been saved.

Light. And now the tribes of the non-sacrificing sect really believed that the reformation was complete and permanent, and began to associate with them as brothers. They were no longer polluted by drinking the same water, and using the same fire; and they welcomed the erring ones, fully and unreservedly, into their own fold.

Then the Boad tribes, seeing how matters had progressed in the Goomsur country, prepared to follow the example of their neighbours. They declared, not that all along they had been in error—that their worship had been false—but that a change was now imposed upon them by the triumph of the God of Light. Taking, therefore, solemn farewell of the great distinctive doctrine of their sect, by a stupendous act of immolation, they slaughtered 120 victims, and with this valedictory offering to the Earth-Goddess, declared that they had turned their back upon her for ever.

Knowing that they were in this state of mind, Macpherson prepared to take advantage of it. But a new element of difficulty presented itself, and it needed some address to deal with it aright. The Rajah of Boad, a tributary chief of influence and authority over the tribes, looked askance at his operations. It was Macpherson's desire to ally the Rajah's power with his own, and when he went into the Boad country, the man promised to assist him with all the influence he possessed over the tribes. A meeting was then arranged between the Rajah and the British officer, in the presence of the assembled Khond chiefs. But sinister influences had been at work upon him; and when the time came, he was ready only with vague assurances and delusive protestations. He said that the tribes were opposed to the abandonment of a practice which had been observed by remote generations of their ancestors—that he could only so far overcome their obduracy as to induce them to give up a few victims—and he promised that some twenty Meriahs should be handed over to the British Agent. They were all, he said, of whom he had distinct cognisance. Macpherson held in his hand an authenticated list of some hundreds of Boad victims, but the Rajah still continued to protest that he could do no more with the tribes.

So Macpherson appealed to the assembled Boad chiefs, who had heard the Rajah's declaration. He had brought with him some of the ablest and most zealous of his proselytes, and he now called upon the people of the other district to hear what the men from Goomsur had to say of the great change which had been effected. Well and earnestly the converts bore witness for the truth. Eloquent and striking were their enunciations. But the Boad chiefs declared that they needed not this evidence to convince them. They had crossed the border themselves, and seen with their own eyes the grand results of the reformation. They knew all that the Goomsur men advanced. They admitted, too, that the great oblation of which I have spoken was intended to be a final act of sacrifice, and they declared their willingness to surrender all the victims in their hands. And in the course of a few days a hundred and seventy were in Macpherson's camp.

In the mean while Macpherson had given the Boad tribes a specimen of the manner in which he assisted the Goomsur Khonds to settle their internal disputes. A day was spent in the investigation of a difficult case. And the adjudication was so satisfactory, that one of the staunchest of the opponents of the proposed reform cried, "Now we understand the magic by which the Goomsur Khonds have been gained."

Finding the Boad Khonds were in this satisfactory state of mind, and always desiring to practise as little interference as possible, Macpherson now prepared to withdraw across the border, and to leave the rest to be worked out by the Rajah. But it soon appeared that this man, wrought upon by evil advisers, was bringing all his secret influence to bear upon the counteraction of the Agent's designs. He spread a report that it was Macpherson's intention first to disarm, then to tax them, and to reduce them to a general condition of servility identical with that of the Khonds of the plains. The horror of this loss of liberty was great. It was intended by the insidious circulation of the report, to incite the Khonds to rebellion; and by these, and similar representations, he induced them to demand back the victims they had surrendered. Victims no longer, for their atoning efficacy had been destroyed—their sacred character profaned—they were given up to the Rajah. The responsibility of their safety, and the onus of this retrograde movement, were thrown upon him; but, indeed, without this protection they would have been safe. There was no fear after this pollution of their being sent to the stake.

Fearing that he might be visited by the displeasure of the British Government, the Rajah now declared his willingness to co-operate zealously with Macpherson. But a storm was impending over the country. Rebellion was breaking out on both sides of him. The people were rising both in Ungool and in Goomsur. These movements were unconnected with the question of Meriah sacrifice; but it devolved upon Macpherson to superintend, in his political capacity, the operations which then became necessary. And here the inquirer, who up to this time has been intent on tracing only the beneficent measures of a British officer engaged in an honorable warfare, as the champion of civilisation and humanity, with barbarism, cruelty, and superstition, finds himself plunged at once into a sea of troubled controversy from which he hastens to extricate himself. The disturbances in Ungool and Goomsur brought new actors upon the scene. The political and military authorities came into collision. General Dyce, who commanded the troops, ordered Macpherson out of the country, and sent in a string of charges against him. Sir Herbert Maddock, who was then Deputy-Governor of Bengal, and President of the Council, dismissed Macpherson and all his assistants, down to the lowest native servant of the Mission,* and with that his connexion with the Khonds, for whom he had done so much, was brought precipitately to a close.

I make no comment on these things. It is sufficient to state that one of the ablest of the Company's civil servants† was commissioned to inquire into the charges against Macpherson—the substance of which was that his maladministration had driven the people to rebellion, and was keeping it alive among the tribes—and that the result of the inquiry was a most honorable acquittal upon every charge. "Captain Macpherson," said the Governor-General in Council, "has, with a very little exception, cleared himself and his administration of all General Dyce's accusations;" and he would have taken an opportunity of evincing his undiminished confidence in Macpherson, had he not been compelled, by ill health, to return to Europe. That justice was rendered to the two assistants of the Khond Agency, Dr. Cadenhead‡

* It would seem, however, that Sir Herbert Maddock had resolved on Macpherson's removal before General Dyce's charges had been received.

† Mr. John Peter Grant.

‡ When, in 1844, Capt. Macpherson was driven by sickness from his post, Dr. John Cadenhead, of the Madras army, was appointed to act for him, and carried on the Khond work for above twelve months with entire success. At the close of the inquiry referred to, the supreme Government adopted the following estimate, formed by the Commissioner of Dr. Cadenhead's recent conduct and services:—"During the whole of this period of three months and a half, from the first outbreak in Gullery, he was constantly, in good health or in bad health, scouring these unwholesome jungles and hills, accompanying the troops in all their movements, and present with them in every action; . . . . and my opinion of those proceedings is, that they were conducted with rare spirit and energy, and with great skill, and that they reflect great credit on the conductor of them."

Dr. Cadenhead was afterwards appointed principal assistant in the South-West frontier agency, and on the assumption of the extensive Zemindarry of Sumbhulpore, was selected for the important and delicate task of bringing its rude and turbulent population under the immediate authority of the Government. That duty he executed so as to command the entire approbation of his official superiors, while, by his unceasing devotion to the interests of the people, alike in the lines of public and of private duty, he gained in an extraordinary degree their confidence and affection. Amongst his works of private benevolence may be noticed the institution of a school, which opened in April, 1850, with seven pupils, who soon increased to sixty, including youths of the highest families in the district. The system of tuition was that of Dr. Duff, of Calcutta. On Dr. Cadenhead's death, the inhabitants of Sumbhulpore petitioned the Government to maintain the school. The Commissioner warmly seconded their petition, "not only for the direct good which would accrue from the permanent establishment of the school under Government patronage, but as a monument of the active and characteristic benevolence of the founder." The Government immediately apportioned the sum of 240*l.* per annum for its efficient maintenance.

and Lieutenant Pinkney, by immediately appointing them to offices of equal responsibility.

But although Macpherson had been removed from office, and soon after the conclusion of the investigation into his proceedings he was driven home by the warnings of a constitution shattered by long residence in the Khond country, the good that he had done lived after him. It does not seem that, during the disturbances which rent the country, his proselytes fell back into their old errors, and resorted to their old evil practices. The Khond agency survived, though Macpherson had been recalled ; and Colonel Campbell, who had long been employed in that part of the country, was appointed to fill his place. The good work is going on, under diminished difficulties, towards a prosperous conclusion. It was obviously, indeed, a work of which the beginning may almost be said to be also the middle and the end. The Khonds offered human sacrifices because they believed that in no other way they could propitiate the Earth-Goddess, and that their failure to lay these dreadful offerings at her feet would be visited with the infliction of the most terrible calamities to which humanity is exposed. The *premier pas* was everything in such a case. "The first operations," it is truly said by Colonel Campbell, "among a wild and strange people, always the most difficult and the most hazardous, having been successful, those of succeeding seasons, if the same principles are adhered to, are mere gleanings."* The sacrificing Khonds had made the terrible experiment, and yet the earth had yielded her increase with unwonted prodigality, and the pestilence, which walketh in the darkness, had never been so idle before. And the result was, that in the minds of all the intelligent men in the Khond districts—and the Khonds were by no means wanting in intelligence—the

* *Colonel Campbell to supreme Government, April* 10, 1852.

omnipotence of *Tari Pennu*, the Earth-Goddess, sank down into a delusion and a sham.*

But although the way was smoothed by these initial successes for all subsequent efforts, the later operations in the Khond country ought not to be passed over with this brief incidental notice. Colonel Campbell, as I have said, has been carrying on, with undiminished success, the good work commenced by Macpherson. He has pushed on his inquiries and exerted his authority among tribes unvisited by his predecessor, and the result of each new visit to the hills, in succeeding cold seasons, has been a progressive diminution in the extent of the great crime. Tribe after tribe has yielded to the good influences of the Christian officer.† Victims have been brought in; pledges have been subscribed; and the promises which have been freely made have been faithfully performed. The last report of the Agent for the suppression of the Meriah sacrifice contains the most cheering evidence of the progress of the good work; and it may reasonably be hoped that a few more years of continued activity, animated by the same humanity and intelligence, will see the utter extinction of

* The Court of Directors watched these proceedings with the greatest interest, and wrote out to recommend the same mild, conciliatory measures as Cleveland and Ovans had prosecuted with such good success. "We would recall to your recollection," they said, "the happy effects produced at a former period by the benevolent and judicious arrangements of Mr. Cleveland, the then Collector of Bhaugulpore, to effect the civilisation of the Hill tribes of that district, who bear a strong resemblance in many particulars to the barbarous tribes in the Goomsur country. Similar measures have also been successfully pursued to improve the condition of the various Bheel tribes in different parts of our territory."—[*Court's Letter, June* 16, 1847. *MS. Records.*]

† I must give at least one extract from Colonel Campbell's last report, in illustration of the character of his proceedings and the difficulties which he has overcome. One of the tribes regarding his approach with fear and suspicion, "I used my best endeavours," he says, "for several days to undeceive these wild people, but they either did not comprehend me, or there was some underhand influence at work which I could not detect. After repeated threats and demonstrations, emboldened by the smallness of the force at my disposal and excited by liquor, about three hundred of them attacked my camp, shouting and yelling more like demons than men, supported by as many more, uttering cries of encouragement from the rocks and jungle which surrounded the camp, but a steady and resolute advance soon drove them off, a few shots over their heads, which did no harm, completed the rout, and we pursued them rapidly over the mountains till they

the barbarous rite throughout all the tracts of the Orissan hills.*

were lost in the jungle dells on the other side. The next day delegates arrived from the several villages of the confederation, and the day following, all came, made their submission, delivered up their Meriahs, entered into the usual agreement to forsake the sacrifice of human beings for ever; confidence was established, and my camp was crowded with our late foes, gazing with astonishment at all they saw. The whole population of the neighbouring Mootahs, including those of Chinna Kimedy, were intensely watching the result of the struggle at Lumbragaum, the successful termination of which exercised a most favorable influence on the proceedings which followed in the large Mootah of Sirdapore."

* The following passage from Colonel Campbell's report, touching upon the subject of the colonisation of the rescued Meriah victims, to whom grants of land were made by Government, will be read with considerable interest:—"The several Meriah families settled as cultivators in Goomsur, are doing very well—about a third of the number (those originally established) have this year, for the first time, paid the rent of their land. From a third the full amount was collected; but remitted to support them till next harvest and for seed; and a third or more, recently settled, are maintained at the expense of the state. By the next harvest I anticipate that nearly all will be in a condition to support themselves."—[*Colonel Campbell to the Supreme Government, April 12, 1852. MS. Records.*]

CHAPTER IV.

Suttee—Its Antiquity—Its Origin—General Features of the Practice—Its outward Manifestations—Suttee under the Moguls—Its frequency under British Rule—First idea of its Suppression—Lord Amherst—Lord William Bentinck—Opinions and Instructions of the Court of Directors—Views of the Company's Servants—Suppression of Suttee in the British Provinces—Our Efforts in the Native States.

In the preceding chapters I have endeavoured to show the manner in which the energies and activities of British officers in India have been put forth for the civilisation of savage tribes inhabiting tracts of country brought under our rule, within comparatively recent periods of Indian history, and not subjected to the formal administrative system embraced by the Regulations. In continuation of this interesting inquiry, I propose to devote the two following chapters to the consideration of certain specific measures of the same humanising tendency, not confined to any particular tract of country—measures for the suppression of those abominations of cruelty and unrighteousness, engrafted upon the social institutions of the country, which generation after generation of priest-ridden Hindoos, in their ignorance and credulity, have practised.

Foremost among these abominations is the unholy custom of "Suttee," or widow-burning. Whence it came—what its origin, it is hard to say. Religious sanction it has none.* The great Hindoo lawgiver

* I have come to this conclusion after much consideration and inquiry. Mr. Ward, in his "Account of the Hindoos," quotes no less than eight texts from the Hindoo sacred writings in recommendation of the practice —one of

ordained it not. Constructively he legislated against it. All that can be said positively on the subject is, that it was an ancient custom handed down to the present generation of Hindoos, from remote periods centuries before Christ.

Little more is known about it than this. But many conjectures have been hazarded. It has been suggested by some that the custom was instituted to check an ill habit common among Hindoo wives, who were, it is said, addicted to the vice of poisoning their husbands. Others attribute it, in no small measure, to the selfishness of surviving relatives eager to possess themselves of the widow's share of the inheritance. Then, again, it is said to be only the unhappy result of the degradation to which the Hindoo widow is reduced—a cruel escape from the miseries of a more cruel existence. These are different shapes assumed by the expediency-side of the question. But more tolerant interpretations are not wanting; and charity sometimes assumes that it is an enthusiastic desire to win Heaven for her lord and for herself, that guides the Hindoo widow to the funeral pile of the departed.

Of course it has a traditional origin. Every atrocity and absurdity in Hindooism has some sort of traditional origin. It is said of Suttee, that on the demise of the mortal part of Brahma, his wives, inconsolable in their misery, determined not to survive him, and burnt themselves with his corpse—that the wives of the chief Rajahs and other great personages followed this heroic example—and that the early Brahmins gave currency to

which is from the *Riq-Veda*, and is thus translated—"O Fire, let these women with bodies anointed with clarified butter, eyes colored with stibium and void of tears enter thee, the parent of water, that they may not be separated from their husbands, but may be in union with excellent husbands, be sinless, and jewels among women." Some high authorities, however, as Rammohun Roy, Colebrooke, and Wilson, deny that this is the correct interpretation of the text. The subject is of so much importance, in its practical relations to the question of Suttee-suppression in the native states, that I shall advert to it again in a note at the end of the chapter.

the doctrine, that the spirits of those heroines, then purged of their guilt, ceased from their transmigrations and entered into Paradise without further probation. Others of less note, encouraged by these promises, sought the privilege of dying in the same heroic style, and Suttee became engrafted on the customs of the Gentoos. But for all this, it can hardly be said that widow-burning was ever a national custom. At no time has the practice been so frequent as to constitute more than an exception to the general rule of self-preservation. Still, even in this exceptional state, it was something very horrible and deplorable in Christian eyes, and something to be suppressed, if suppression were possible, by a Christian government established in a heathen land.

But horrible and deplorable as was the practice, even a Christian writer may say, that there was often an unearthly grandeur in the bearing of the deluded woman, which filled the spectator with scarcely less of admiration than of pity. You saw a young woman—one, in our eyes, perhaps, a little more than a child—ascend, with heavenly composure, the funeral pile of her husband, and with an unaltered countenance resign herself to a cruel death. You saw her calmly and gracefully performing the last offices due to the dead, and the last courtesies to the living; serenely decorating her person, as for a bridal, and in an unbroken voice repeating the formulas of prayer dictated by the unpitying priests; then walking with steady tread around the pyre, mounting it without a shudder of fear, and perishing without a murmur. No martyr, in the grand old times of Apostolic Christianity, died with a nobler fortitude, than often did these unhappy women, under the curse of a degrading superstition. But it was not always in this wise. Sometimes the miserable victim went feeble, trembling, in a state of pitiable reluctance, to the funeral pile, was forced upon the sacrificial faggots by the bamboos of the by-standers, and held down among the flames, while the noise of the surrounding drums and the shouts of the spectators drowned the shrieks of the wretched woman, as the flames gathered closely and destroyingly around her.

There are not many of my readers who have not perused, in some volume of travels, or of ethnological research, a touching narrative of the self-immolation of a Hindoo widow. I have a pile of books before me, from any one of which I might take a fitting illustration; but I do not know any better than the following, which is given in old Mr. Holwell's tracts. The incident here narrated occurred more than a century ago, "at the Company's factory in Cossimbazaar, in the time of Sir Francis Russell's chiefship." The author and several other gentlemen of the factory were present, and the details were written down at the time. "At five of the clock on the morning of the 4th of February, 1742-43," thus runs the story, "died Ram Chund Pundit, of the Mahratta tribe, aged twenty-eight years; his widow (for he had but one wife), aged between seventeen and eighteen, as soon as he expired, disdaining to wait the time allowed her for reflection, immediately declared to the Brahmins and witnesses present her resolution to burn. As the family was of no small consideration in Cossimbazaar, and her relations left no argument to dissuade her from it, Lady Russell, with the tenderest humanity, sent her several messages to the same purpose; the infant state of her children (two girls and a boy, the eldest not four years of age), and the terrors and pain of the death she sought, were painted to her in the strongest and most lively coloring. She was deaf to all. She gratefully thanked Lady Russell, and sent her word she had now nothing to live for, but recommended her children to her protection. When the torments of burning were urged *in terrorem* to her, she, with a resolved and calm countenance, put her finger into the fire, and held it there a considerable time; she then with one hand put fire in the palm of the other, sprinkled incense on it, and fumigated the Brahmins. The consideration of her children left destitute was again urged to her. She replied that 'He who made them would take care of them.' She was at last given to understand she should not be permitted to burn; this for a short space seemed to give her deep affliction, but soon recollecting herself, she told them death was in her power, and that if she was not allowed to burn, according to the principles of her caste, she would starve herself. Her friends, finding her thus peremptory and resolved, were obliged at last to assent. The body of the deceased was carried down to the water's side early the following morning. The widow followed about ten o'clock, accompanied by three very principal Brahmins, her children, parents, and relations, and a numerous concourse of people. The order of leave for her burning did not arrive till after one o'clock, and it was then brought down by one of the Soubah's own officers, who had orders to see that she burnt voluntarily. The time they waited for the order was employed in praying with the Brahmins and washing in the Ganges. As soon as it arrived, she retired and stayed for the space of half an hour in the midst of her female relations, amongst whom was her mother. She then divested herself of her bracelets and other ornaments and tied them in a cloth, which hung like an apron before her, and was conducted by her female relations to one corner of the pile. On the pile was an arched arbor, formed of dry sticks, boughs, and leaves, open only at one end to admit her entrance. In this the body of the deceased was deposited, his head at the end opposite the opening. At the corner of the pile to which she had been conducted, the Brahmins had made a small fire, round which she and the three Brahmins sat for some minutes. One of them gave into her hand a leaf of the bale-tree (the wood commonly consecrated to form part of the funeral pile), with sundry things on it, which she threw into the fire; one of the others gave her a second leaf, which she held over the flame, while he dropped three times some ghee on it, which melted and fell into the fire (these two operations were preparatory symbols of her approaching dissolution by fire); and whilst they were performing this, the third Brahmin read to her some portions of the *Aughtorrah Bhade*, and asked her some questions, to which she answered with a steady and serene countenance; but the noise was so great we could not understand what she said, although we were within a yard of her. These over, she was led with great solemnity three times round the pile, the Brahmins reading before her; when she came the third time to the small fire, she stopped, took her rings off her toes and fingers and put them to her other ornaments; here she took a solemn majestic leave of her children, parents, and relations; after which one of the Brahmins dipped a large wick of cotton in some ghee, and gave it ready lighted into her hand, and led her to the open side of the arbor. There all the Brahmins fell at her feet. After she had blessed them, they retired weeping. By two steps she ascended the pile and entered the arbor. On her entrance she made a profound reverence at the feet of the deceased, and advanced and seated herself by his head. She looked, in silent meditation, on his face for the space of a minute, then set fire to the arbor in three places. Observing that she had set fire to leeward, and that the flames blew from her; instantly seeing her error, she rose, set fire to windward, and resumed her station. Ensign Daniel, with his cane, separated the grass and leaves on the windward side, by which means we had a distinct view of her as she sat. With what dignity and undaunted a countenance she set fire to the pile the last time and assumed her seat, can only be conceived, for words cannot convey a just idea of her. The pile being of combustible matters, the supporters of the roof were presently consumed and in tumbled upon her."

Simply and truthfully told, and with an authenticity of detail, abundantly corroborated by other narrators, this story may be taken as a fitting illustration of the unholy practice as it existed under the Mahomedan Governments, and for too many years under our own. But the account is less curious in itself than it is for the comments which accompany it—comments which exhibit the state of feeling among English gentlemen before the conquest of Bengal regarding a practice at once so dreadful and so absurd. "If we view," says Mr. Holwell, "these women in a just light, we shall think more candidly of them, and confess that they act upon heroic as well as upon rational and pious principles ;" and then he proceeds to show how their "ideas are raised to a soothing degree of dignity befitting angelic beings." "Although these principles," he adds, "are in general so diametrically contrary to the prevailing spirit and genius of our fair countrywomen, who (from a happy train of education) in captivating amusements and dissipation find charms sufficient in this world to engage their wishes for a perpetual residence in it, yet we will depend upon their natural goodness of heart, generosity, and candor, that they will, in future, look on these, their Gentoo sisters of the creation, in a more favorable and consistent light than probably they have hitherto done; and not deem that action an infatuation which results from principle. Let them also recollect that their own history affords illustrious examples in both sexes of voluntary sacrifices by fire because they would not subscribe even to a different mode of professing the same faith." There was little hope for the suppression of Suttee, whilst the question was argued in this manner by the most intelligent of the Company's servants. The practice, however, was not always so regarded as one based upon angelic principles to be respected by Christian men. Mr. Holwell himself admits that "there have been instances known when the victim has by Europeans been forcibly rescued from the pile. It is currently said and believed (how truly we will not aver) that the wife of Mr. Job Charnock was by him snatched from this sacrifice."

I have said that this practice of Suttee has never been anything more than an exceptional abomination. It never has been universal throughout India—never in any locality has it been general. "It never," says Elphinstone, "occurs to the south of the river Kishna; and under the Bombay presidency, including the former sovereignty of the Brahmin Peishwas, it amounts to thirty-two in a year. In the rest of the Deckan it is probably more rare."* Mr. Forbes, who lived during the greater part of his life in Western India, and mixed largely with the people, says that he never saw a Suttee. In Bengal and Hindostan Proper, it has been more common—I believe, that in no part of the country has the abomination flourished more than in the immediate neighbourhood of Calcutta.

Under the Mahomedan Governments the practice of Suttee seems at least to have been tolerated. Akbar, it is true, discountenanced it, and by something more effectual than empty words. His abhorrence of the cruel rite was expressed by an act of personal interference. On one occasion when other means had failed to save a doomed widow from the funeral pile, he rode out to the place of cremation and carried her off on his horse. But it does not seem that his successors exhibited any like noble in-

* Mr. Orme in one of the notes of his Historical Fragments, says:—"The Jesuits in Jarrie say that three hundred and seventy-five women burnt with the Naique of Tanjore, who died in 1602—which we suppose to be the honest but enthusiastic credulity of missionaries lamenting the infernal state of the heathens they wished to convert."

stances of humanity. The Hindoos were compelled to obtain the permission of the Mahomedan officers before a widow proceeded to the sacrifice; but this permission was never withheld. It seems, indeed, to have been a source of profit to the local authorities. The Mussulman governors had their pickings before the Brahmins came in for their share. It seems, however, that some compunctions bubbled up in the midst of their cupidity, or that they made a pretence of endeavouring to dissuade the wretched creature from burning herself, for Tavernier says, "The governor, finding that no persuasion will alter the woman's resolution, but more especially perceiving by the signs which his secretary makes him that he has received the coin, in a surly manner gives the woman leave, bidding the devil take her and all her kindred."

And, practically, for a great many years, it must be admitted, this was our own mode of dealing with the evil. We let the women burn according to their pleasure—or according to the pleasure of their friends—or according to the pleasure of the priesthood. Indeed, we officially recognised the right of these poor people to destroy themselves by issuing regulations against the compulsory performance of the ceremony. A circular order of the Nizamut Adawlut* of Bengal set forth the particular circumstances under which the performance of Suttee would be illegal in the British provinces, and so recognised its general legality. The result, as might be expected, was that the abomination steadily increased.†

* April 10, 1810. Mr. Harrington, in a minute, dated Feb. 18, 1827, says that Mr. H. Colebrooke prepared this order—but Mr. Colebrooke denied the charge, alleging that he was at the Cape when the order was issued.

† The Bombay Government, however, claimed credit for having acted with greater wisdom in this matter. "There is a marked difference," wrote Mr. Warden, in a council minute, "in the policy pursued by the two Governments for the purpose of checking Suttee. The supreme Government has promulgated circular orders, containing as well a recognition of the ceremony as a prohibition against its compulsory performance. The Bombay Government has, on the contrary (except in the instance of the form in which the pile was to be constructed, and in respect to which I now regret

It appears by the Bengal returns from 1819, that 650 cases of Suttee were reported, of which 421 were said to have occurred in the Calcutta division alone. The latter number was 43 in excess of the gross amount reported throughout all the Bengal provinces in 1815. The reported increase, it was alleged, might be partly attributable to the greater vigilance of our officers. It might not have been, it was said, so much that more cases had occurred as that more cases had been detected. But making all due allowance for the result of the more energetic inquiries that were instituted, I fear it must still be admitted that the circular orders which had been issued in 1810,* with the humane intention of diminishing the extent of the evil, in reality tended to increase it. Mr. Courtenay Smith, one of the ablest and best judges who ever sat on the Indian bench, officially declared that these orders had "spread and confirmed the execrable usage." It is true that many offenders had been tried and punished for abetting the illegal, or irregular performance of the rite, but it was of little use to strike at accidental symptoms—to prune the offshoots and excrescences, whilst we were laying manure to the very root of the evil itself.

That it was a very grievous and intolerable evil—that the abomination was one to be deplored and execrated by all Christian men, need hardly be asserted in this place; but the Company's servants although, with one consent, they deplored and execrated, were not all of

that we interfered at all), kept the recognitionary principle of the law entirely in the background and prominently brought forward and enforced its prohibitionary provisions. . . . The effects have been equally remarkable. It has gradually declined in the old and new provinces dependent on Bombay, but seems stationary under Bengal." It appears to me, however, that in prescribing a regulation pattern of funeral pile, the Bombay Government recognised the legality of the practice in the clearest and most unmistakeable manner. Would they not have legalised murder if they had issued an order decreeing that the people should thenceforth only kill each other with regulation swords?

* April 10, 1810. See also circular orders of 29th April, 1813, January, 1815, 25th of June and 11th September, 1817. The police were instructed to ascertain that the ceremony was performed in conformity with the rules of the Shustre.

one opinion regarding the duty or the expediency of authoritative interference with a custom hallowed at least by time. Many doubted and wavered — were timid and irresolute—unwilling to take the initiative and recommend the withdrawal of the constructive sanction which had been given to the ceremonial murder of Hindoo women. But the Court of Directors had for some time been brooding over this painful subject— "the killing," as they described it, "the killing (and that in the most horrid mode) of an individual at the desire of the party slain;" a great movement had taken place among them and clearly perceiving their duty, as a Christian Government, they did not hesitate to declare their righteous convictions, and to endeavour to secure their practical enforcement. "It is undeniable," they wrote, "that in tolerating the practice, under any regulations or restrictions whatsoever, you tolerate what you have virtually forbidden in those regulations, and afford the natives grounds for concluding that the practice of Suttee was to be excepted from their operation."

They then proceeded to state the ground on which they believed that the toleration of the practice might be withdrawn. They urged—1stly. That Suttee is not founded on or enjoined by any Hindoo law, and is only recommended, not enjoined, by the Shustres; and as to the law, it is, on the contrary, continually discouraged by their most eminent and venerated lawgiver, Menu, whose decree for the guidance of widows is thus translated by Sir W. Jones. "Let a widow emaciate her body by living voluntarily upon pine-flowers, roots, and fruits, and let her not when her lord is deceased even pronounce the name of another man. Let her continue until death forgetting all injuries, performing harsh duties, avoiding all sensual pleasure, and cheerfully practising the incomparable rules of virtue, which have been followed by such women as were devoted to one only husband," &c.

2ndly. That other barbarous customs and unknown Hindoo practices had been prohibited without dangerous consequences — without even exciting disaffection or murmur. 3rdly. That the British Government having ceased to recognise the impurity of Brahmins without any evil consequences, there could be no ground for supposing that the abolition of Suttee would have an ill effect. 4thly. That there is a great difference of opinion on the subject of Suttee among the Hindoos—that it is discountenanced among the upper and educated classes—that in some districts it is unknown, and in others of rare occurrence. 5thly. That the practice was not permitted by the Foreign States when they held power and territory in India.

And lastly, say the Court, "which we think in itselt conclusive of the practicability of abolishing the practice, or, at least, of the safety with which it might be prohibited, that in many instances it has been actually and effectually prevented from taking place, without exciting even a murmur, by either direct interference on the part of the local authority, or by refusal of permission, or by a procedure similar to that which was adopted by the criminal judge of the Zillah of Masulipatam as we have recently noticed."

This was written in 1824. Lord Amherst was then Governor-General of India. There were some very able men around him, and there were, too, some very able men on the Sudder bench. The question now to be submitted to them, and to all the leading civil and political officers in the three presidencies, was one of the deepest interest and the most pressing importance. Called upon to express freely their opinions, they enunciated their views upon all its religious and legal, its social and political bearings; and never, perhaps before or since, has any question of Indian policy been so thoroughly sifted and so minutely explored. I can only afford to give a few illustrations of the varied opinions which were recorded in response to the inquiries then instituted by the supreme Government.

Foremost among those who recorded a strong opinion in favor of the withdrawal of all authoritative sanction of the cruel rite was Mr. Courtenay Smith, one of the judges of the Sudder. "There would be no discontent," he wrote,* "no disturbance—no general disturbance, certainly, anywhere; and if any local and partial disturbance occurred it might be put down as easily as any breach of the peace. Our native military, were it necessary to call them in, would assist as readily on this as on any other occasion. . . . . I sincerely hope that this foul stain will be removed from the Company's Government before its final expiration, supposed to be near at hand. . . . . So long as having the power we want the will, or having the power and the will, we want the energy to abolish it, it may be fairly doubted whether we are *de jure* rulers of the country."

Mr. Alexander Ross, another judge of the Sudder—a man of a benevolent and thoughtful nature, whose quiet manner and retiring habits were the exterior of moral courage and resolution of a very high order, thus wrote with reference to the report which had been called for from the Nizamut Adawlut—"In the report on Suttee now to be submitted to Government, I think the Court should again urge its total abolition. . . . My opinion is that an enactment prohibiting the sacrifice of Suttee would be regarded by the native army with nearly total indifference, as the civil enactments of the Government generally are."

Another judge of the Sudder, Mr. R. H. Rattray, when called upon for his opinion, boldly declared that he recommended the authoritative suppression of Suttee, and was prepared personally to give effect to his recom-

* Nov. 1, 1826.

mendation. "I would have," he wrote,* "a regulation prepared with a studied perspicuity, explaining in simple but forcible language the religious, the moral, and the legal grounds upon which this rite, abhorrent to God and man, could no longer be tolerated; and by this enactment I would abolish the sacrifice at once and for ever. I would not recommend for execution by others what I should shrink from or evade myself. If this danger be apprehended, and as an executive officer my personal services can aid this consummation so devoutly to be wished, I am as ready to support it as I am to urge the measure; but I maintain that nothing is necessary to its accomplishment but the expressed fiat of the ruling power."

But there were able and conscientious men in the Company's service at this time, who doubted the expediency of any comprehensive measure for the authoritative extinction of Suttee in the Company's domains. At the beginning of 1827, Mr. Butterworth Bayley, one of the most distinguished and experienced administrators in the country, drew up an elaborate minute, in which he recommended that experiments should be made in the first instance in the Non-Regulation Provinces. About the same time Mr. Harrington, who fully concurred in this suggestion, drew up a Regulation, declaring the inhuman practice of burning or burying alive the widows of deceased Hindoos, to be illegal and punishable by our criminal courts. He did not believe that the time had yet come when publicity could be given to such an order, but he submitted it for future consideration. About the same time Mr. C. B. Elliott, after expressing a very strong opinion regarding the iniquity and illegality of the custom, recommended that the experi-

* August 26, 1828.

ment of abolition should be made in the Ceded and Conquered Provinces, because the practice was comparatively rare in that part of the country, whilst it was rife in Bengal.

Upon a review of all the opinions that had been laid before him, Lord Amherst came to the mortifying conclusion that it would not be wise to authorise any direct interference with a hoary custom which the priesthood had an immediate interest in maintaining inviolate. It appeared to him that the wisest course would be to trust to the progress of education, and to leave Suttee to die a natural death. "I am not prepared," he wrote, in March, 1827, "to recommend an enactment prohibiting Suttees altogether. . . . . . I must frankly confess, though at the risk of being considered insensible to the enormity of the evil, that I am inclined to recommend our trusting to the progress now making in the diffusion of knowledge among the natives, for the gradual suppression of this detestable superstition. I cannot believe it possible that the burning or burying alive of widows will long survive the advancement which every fear brings with it in useful and rational learning."

Nor did further consideration and further information induce him to modify this opinion. "The reports of our different officers," he wrote in the following year, "do not appear to me to point out any specific course short of absolute prohibition, by which this barbarous practice could be suddenly checked, or the number of victims very suddenly reduced. But I think there is reason to believe and expect that, except on the occurrence of some very general sickness, such as that which prevailed in the lower parts of Bengal in 1825, the progress of general instruction and the unostentatious exertions of our local officers will produce the happy effect of a gradual diminution, and at no very distant period the final extinction of the barbarous rite of Suttee."*

But the period of Lord Amherst's tenure of office was fast drawing to a close. Before the year in which this minute was written had expired, his successor was occupying the vice-regal chair. The high moral courage of Lord William Bentinck faced the abomination without shrinking. He knew that it was his duty, as a Christian statesman, to incur some risk with so great an object before him as the emancipation of the country from the cruel slavery which an interested priesthood had long riveted upon it. But he did not fling himself hastily and heedlessly into the good work. He advanced with energy, but with caution. He sought the opinions of all qualified to declare themselves with authority on the subject; and having weighed these opinions—many they were and most conflicting—he deliberately formed his own. One thing he knew, which greatly encouraged and sustained him. The Court of Directors had, some time before, spoken out in plain, unmistakeable language, clearly enunciating their views of this great question, and combating all the arguments that could be adduced against the abolition of the rite. The Governor-General, therefore, if he had not before leaving England received the instructions of the Court, or listened to their recommendations, knew that he would be supported by the home authorities if he struck a blow at the abomination. He did not needlessly protract his investigations, or hesitate when once he was in a position to decide. So before the year 1829 had worn to a close, an act was passed in the Council Chamber, prohibiting, under stringent penal enactments, the

* *Minute of Lord Amherst, April* 10, 1828. *Published Papers.*

practice of Suttee throughout the provinces subject to our rule. The importance of the measure induces me to give the Regulation entire:

A Regulation for declaring the practice of Suttee, or of burning or burying alive the widows of Hindoos, illegal, and punishable by the Criminal Courts. Passed by the Governor-General in Council on the 4th December, 1829.

The practice of Suttee, or of burning or burying alive the widows of Hindoos, is revolting to the feelings of human nature. It is nowhere enjoined by the religion of the Hindoos as an imperative duty; on the contrary, a life of piety and retirement on the part of the widow is more especially and preferably inculcated, and by a vast majority of people throughout India the practice is not kept up or observed. In some extensive districts it does not exist; in those in which it has been most frequent, it is notorious that in many instances acts of atrocity have been perpetrated which have been shocking to the Hindoos themselves, and in their eyes unlawful and wicked. The measures hitherto adopted to discourage and prevent such acts have failed of success, and the Governor-General in Council is deeply impressed with the conviction that the abuses in question cannot be effectually put an end to without abolishing the practice altogether. Actuated by these considerations, the Governor-General in Council—without intending to depart from one of the first and most important principles of the system of British government in India, that all classes of the people be secure in the observance of their religious usages, so long as that system can be adhered to without violation of the paramount dictates of justice and humanity—has deemed it right to establish the following rules, which are hereby enacted to be in force from the time of their promulgation throughout the territories immediately subject to the Presidency of Fort William.

I. The practice of Suttee, or of burning or burying alive the widows of Hindoos, is hereby declared illegal, and punishable by the Criminal Court.

II. First. All Zemindars, Talookdars, or other proprietors of land, whether Malguzaree or Lakheraj; all Sudder farmers and under-renters of land of every description; all dependent Talookdars: all Naibs, and other local agents; all native officers employed in the collection of the revenue and rents of lands on the part of the Government or the Courts of Wards; and all Munduls and other head men of villages, are hereby declared especially accountable for the immediate communication to the officers of the nearest police-station of any intended sacrifice of the nature described in the foregoing section, and any Zemindars, or other description of persons above noticed, to whom such responsibility is declared to attach, who may be convicted of wilfully neglecting or delaying to furnish the information above required, shall be liable to be fined by the magistrate in any sum not exceeding two hundred rupees, and in default of payment, to be confined for any period of imprisonment not exceeding six months.

Second. Immediately on receiving intelligence that the sacrifice declared illegal by this Regulation is likely to occur, the police Darogah shall either repair in person to the spot, or depute his Mohurrir or Jemadar, accompanied by one or more Burkundazes of the Hindoo religion ; and it shall be the duty of the police-officers to announce to the persons assembled for the performance of the ceremony, that it is illegal, and to endeavour to prevail on them to disperse, explaining to them that in the event of their persisting in it, they will involve themselves in a crime, and become subject to punishment by the criminal courts. Should the parties assembled proceed, in defiance of these remonstrances, to carry the ceremony into effect, it shall be the duty of the police-officers to use all lawful means in their power to prevent the sacrifice taking place, and to apprehend the principal persons aiding and abetting in the performance of it; and in the event of the peace-officers being unable to apprehend them, they shall endeavour to ascertain their names and places of abode, and shall immediately communicate the whole of the particulars to the magistrate, or the joint magistrates, for his orders.

III. Should intelligence of a sacrifice, declared illegal by this Regulation, not reach the police-officers until after it shall have actually taken place, or should the sacrifice have been carried into effect before their arrival at the spot, they will nevertheless institute a full inquiry into the circumstances of the case, in like manner as on all other occasions of unnatural death, and report them for the information and orders of the magistrate to whom they may be subordinate.

IV. First. On the receipt of the reports required to be made by the police Darogahs, under the provision of the foregoing section, the magistrate, or joint magistrates, of the jurisdiction in which the sacrifice may have taken place, shall inquire into the circumstances of the case, and shall adopt the necessary measures for bringing the parties concerned in promoting it to trial before the Court of Circuit.

Second. It is hereby declared, that after the promulgation of this regulation, all persons convicted of aiding and abetting in the sacrifice of a Hindoo widow, by burning or burying her alive, whether the sacrifice be voluntary on her part or not, shall be deemed guilty of culpable homicide, and shall be liable to punishment by fine or by imprisonment, or by both fine and imprisonment, at the discretion of the Court of Circuit, according to the nature and circumstances of the case, and the degree of guilt established against the offender; nor shall it be held to be any plea of justification that he or she was desired by the party sacrificed to assist in putting her to death.

Third. Persons committed to take their trial before the Court of Circuit for the offence above mentioned, shall be admitted to bail, or not, at the discretion of the magistrate, subject to the general rules in force in regard to the admission of bail.

V. It is further deemed necessary to declare, that nothing contained in this Regulation shall be construed to preclude the Court of Nizamut Adawlut from passing sentence of death on persons convicted of using violence or compulsion, or of having assisted in burning or burying alive a Hindoo widow, while laboring under a state of intoxication or stupefaction, or other cause impeding the exercise of her free will, when, from the aggravated nature of the offence proved against the prisoner, the Court may see no circumstances to render him or her a proper object of mercy.

The event justified the expectations of those who believed that no danger would result from the publication of this prohibitory enactment. It was a great experiment, and a successful one. Its success was fraught with a great lesson. The prime want of human governments is a want of faith. A bold policy is generally a successful one. It is always successful when the boldness is the result of a strong determination to do what is right, and to leave secondary considerations to themselves. We have been continually conjuring up bugbears in the distance only to discover, upon a nearer approach, that they are the merest conceptions of the brain. If we could only believe the great truth, that a righteous policy is sure, in the end, to be a successful one, how much groundless alarm and unnecessary anxiety we should be spared in all our dealings with our fellows.

In our own provinces the work was now complete. The promulgation of the Act gave the death-blow to Suttee throughout the Company's dominions. But it still was a living reality in other parts of India, and had many homes in the native states. The British Government knew well the existence of the evil under the rule of the native princes, but at first they rather desired its suppression than sought to suppress it by any direct exercise of their influence or authority. In these native states we have always a staff of British political or diplomatic officers. In the internal administration of the country, they are expressly prohibited from interfering; but the influence of these representatives of the paramount power at the native Courts, though it may differ according to the personal character of the functionary himself, is in all cases very considerable. It is the influence partly of superior intelligence, partly of the weight of authority derived from the accident of his position. Without any direct interference, any open attempt to dictate or to control, he may, by friendly intercourse with the native officials, and a gentle insinuation of serviceable truths, quietly instil sound opinions, and bring about great reforms. To what extent this influence was exercised, during the few first years after the suppression of Suttee in the British provinces, to induce our native allies to follow our example, I do not pretend to know. I believe, however, that little was done until about the year 1840, when a great movement seems to have been made in Western India and the Guicowar, and several princes of less note, prompted by our British officers, issued proclamations to their subjects prohibitory of Suttee.

But of all the efforts made in the native states, that made in Rajpootana is the most noticeable, both on account of the obstacles to success, and the energy and adroitness with which they were overcome. In that part of India nothing of the kind had ever been attempted before. Colonel Sutherland, Political Agent in Rajpootana, one of the most distinguished Oriental diplomatists, a man of equal courage and humanity, had never conceived the idea of interfering with an ancient custom held in such high esteem by these sensitive people.

It was supposed to be "against the principles of Government" to interfere with such things. But there was one of his assistants, at that time in charge of our political relations with the Jyepore state, who had long been brooding over the great iniquity, and thinking whether something could not be done at least to mitigate the evil. Major Ludlow had achieved great success in an effort to induce the states to co-operate in a measure tending to check the crime of female infanticide; and it occurred to him that, perhaps, his influence might be exerted with the same result to check the kindred abomination of Suttee. But he was obliged to tread warily in such a work—warily but very firmly. First of all, he won over the Finance Minister to his cause—and, through the Finance Minister he contrived to enlist the sympathies and stir the convictions of the High Priest. The arguments of the British officer told upon the sacerdotal mind, and in less than six months he put forth a document, publicly declaring that the right of Suttee had no warrant in the Hindoo Scriptures.* Such a manifesto as this was not without its due effect on the minds of the Jyepore chiefs. The Council of Regency began to waver. Some of the small tributary states actually abjured the rite; then the Jyepore Government, on the 23rd of April, 1846, publicly declared the act illegal; and before the end of the year eleven out of the eighteen Rajpoot states had publicly renounced the rite. Other states subsequently gave in their adhesion. The most important recent adhesion is that of the Rajah of Joudhpore. Of the same clan (Rhatore) are the chiefs of Bekaneer and Kishengurh, who may be expected very soon to follow the example of Joudhpore.

* There is a very interesting record of Colonel Ludlow's measures in Rajpootana, in a recent article in the *Quarterly Review*, which has doubtless rendered them familiar to the public. I give the account of Ludlow's first step: "As an essential condition to success, and on pain of having his operations summarily suspended, Major Ludlow was compelled to work unseen. He determined, if possible, to induce two or three trustworthy and influential natives to undertake the cause; to ply them with the critical objection drawn from the older Scriptures; and by declaring his own resolution to remain neutral till public opinion had declared itself, to excite in them the ambition of taking the lead. He found a person admirably adapted to his purpose in the Financial Minister of the Court at which he was accredited. Seth Manick Chund belonged to a sect whose distaste for destruction in all its forms is singular even in the East. The Oswal tribe do not wilfully slay the meanest animal. . . . One result for this tenderness for life in every form is, that they disapprove of Suttee. To the Financial Minister, therefore, and to his own head Moonshee, Major Ludlow communicated all the arguments he thought likely to be of use; and thus charged, they betook themselves to the High Priest of Jyepore. . . . Warily, and as if on their own account, they pressed this important dignitary with the omission of all mention of Suttee in the Code of Menu; with the inferential prohibition of the rite in the denunciations contained in that work against suicide; and with its promise to widows living chastely of eternal felicity with their husbands—whereas even the writings which countenanced the sacrifice, limited the duration of its recompense to the comparative bagatelle of forty-five millions of years. . . . Major Ludlow wound up these arguments by a shrewd appeal to national pride. Suttee (urged his emissaries), unwarranted by Menu, was the evident invention of some degenerate race, whose women were worthless, and whose widows, if they survived, would bring reproach on the memory of their lords. To such it might be left. The honor of Rajpoot husbands was in safer keeping, and the fair fame of their daughters was aspersed by the mere retention of so disgraceful a security. The High Priest received these representations with surprising candor. In less than six months he was induced to put forth a document, in which he adopted all the theological arguments, and declared authoritatively that the self-immolation of widows was less meritorious than their practising 'the living Suttee of chastity and devotion.'"

With the exception of Oodepore, the Rajpoot states, which are not yet ranged among the abolitionists, are, as regards position and influence, comparatively unimportant.

In distant parts of India, the good example was largely followed; and before the end of 1847, the Governor-General, Lord Hardinge, announced that "Suttee, Infanticide, and Slavery, are prohibited throughout the territory* forming the remotest Hindoo principality of India."†

* Cashmere.

† In a note at the commencement of the chapter I said that I should refer again to the alleged sanction given by the Rig Veda to the practice of Suttee. I had collected some authorities, from the writings of Colebrooke, Ramohun Roy, &c., but the attention of Professor Wilson having recently been drawn to the subject, he examined, I believe, the doubtful texts. At all events, in a lecture delivered in January to the Asiatic Society, he thus settled the question, and I am quite satisfied withthe settlement:—"It was scarcely to be expected that any warrant should be found for the burning of widows, as that practice is not enjoined by the lawgiver Menu, a later authority. One passage in the Rig, cited as authority, has been verified, but with a very unexpected result; for the only passage relating to widowhood inculcates the very reverse of self-immolation. In fact, it seems almost certain that they did not burn but bury their dead."

CHAPTER V.

Infanticide—Varieties of the Crime—Love of Offspring among the Hindoos—Rajpoot Honor—Its Excesses—Causes of the prevalence of the Evil—Our First Remedial Efforts—Jonathan Duncan—Colonel Walker—Failure of our First Endeavours—Disparity of the Sexes—Renewed Attempts—Mr. Willoughby—Major Ludlow—Increased Success—Present State of Infanticide in India.

In this Christian country it is to be feared that the dark crime of infanticide is painfully on the increase. This much at least has been said of late by wise judges on the bench, and by earnest writers in the public journals; and the records of our criminal courts unhappily show that this is no imaginary complaint.* It is a grave fact, wretchedly significant of the state of morals amongst us. Still it is only a crime—incidental, exceptional. In some parts of India it has been, for many generations, a *custom*.

It is curious to contrast the causes of the crime in the two countries. A sagacious Rajpoot arguing the question with us, might, perhaps, point triumphantly to the circumstances which engender the crime in England, in justification of the custom which obtains among his own people. It is, he might say, in anticipation and prevention of those very circumstances that the dreadful practice has been instituted. But to demonstrate the fact is not to prove the justification.

* Mr. Raikes, in his very interesting volume of "Notes on the North-Western Provinces of India," says: "Infanticide is a world-wide crime. Except the land of our own Saxon forefathers, we can scarce name a country unstained by the blood of its infant children." Would to God that we were free from the stain!

In England infant life is secretly destroyed by unmarried females. In an agony of shame and terror a poor girl who has become a mother, but is not a wife, strangles or suffocates her illegitimate babe. In all probability she has been betrayed and deserted, and there is a male offender, of whom the law takes no cognizance, more guilty than the actual murderess. Still, it is the unchastity of the female that is the proximate cause of the crime. The Rajpoot assumes that unchastity is the necessary condition of unmarried life. And to preserve the purity of his daughters, and the honor of his family, he murders his female children a few hours after their birth.

Marriage, in both cases, is the remedy; but the difficulties in the way of its application are diametrically the reverse. In England, marriage is honorable; but celibacy is not disgraceful. In India, celibacy *is* disgraceful. An unmarried daughter is a reproach to her parents, and a reproach to herself.* Indeed, more or less, the birth of a daughter is always a calamity. It is a disappointment in the first instance, because to beget sons is glorious in the estimation of a Hindoo, and there cannot be too many born into his house. And it is a care to him afterwards, because marriage is a necessity, and the circle of suitability is narrowed by the exclusiveness of caste. The higher the social degree of the family, the greater the difficulty. In England infanticide is peculiar to the lower orders; in India it is peculiar to the higher. In England it is the activity of degradation; in India the activity of pride. In England male and female infants are murdered with equal recklessness. In India the destroying hand is laid only on the latter. But in both cases, it is the non-attainment

* "So great a disgrace," says Ward, in his account of the Hindoos, "is incurred by remaining unmarried, that on one occasion a number of old maids were married to an aged Koolin Brahmin, as his friends were carrying him to the river to die."

of honorable marriage in *esse*, or in *posse*, which impels to the commission of the crime.

In a country where polygamy is common, and concubinage not dishonorable—where an unconnected man, indeed, is rarely to be found—it might seem that women would be too much in demand to warrant, at any stage of existence, the destruction of female life. And, in truth, the customs of the country are such that any widely-diffused system of female infanticide must be wholly incompatible with them. Their co-existence would be a physical impossibility. The number of child-murders, committed in the worst of times, has never been sufficiently great to have any general effect upon the population. But confined as it has been to certain localities, and to certain tribes, the sacrifice of life, viewed in connexion with those limits, has been something terrible to contemplate. It has amounted, indeed, to an almost total annihilation of female life in a large number of high-caste families.

The infanticide of which I am now writing is, the systematic female infanticide of Central and Western India. Child-murder among the Hindoos has assumed other forms, but the evil has been less extensive, and more easily repressible when it has been the growth of religious superstition, and has taken a more overt and violent shape. In the latter case, it has been an open sacrifice, with the intent of propitiating one of the bloody deities of the Hindoo mythology. In Southern and Eastern Bengal, children of both sexes have been offered up by their parents sacrifices to Gunga. Here, however, the object that is sought to be attained by the commission of the atrocity, is the very opposite of that which the Rajpoot of Malwah, Jusselmere, or Goojrat sets before him when he commits, or decrees the commission of the crime. In Bengal and Orissa these sacrifices have been consummated in fulfilment of a vow, and are thank-offerings in return for a favorable response to the prayers for offspring with which childless women have wearied their gods, when the curse of barrenness has seemed to press heavily upon them. Slaves to a dreadful superstition, they vow to offer up their firstborn to Gunga if the deity will answer their prayers. In the fulness of time the vow is consummated. The child, doomed from the hour of its birth, is suffered to live long enough to root itself deeply in the affections of its parents, and then, on a given day, is deliberately thrust into the cruel stream.* These, however, are exceptional cases—accidental crimes. The law can reach them, and has reached them; and it may be said that they are now almost blotted out from the catalogue of Pagan atrocities. The love of offspring—the desire to surround themselves with children—has driven these wretched people to offer up these dreadful sacrifices to their false gods. But among the Rajpoots of Central and Western India, it is the desire to lessen the number of their children that impels them to destroy the infant life of their female offspring. There is nothing of a religious sacrifice about it. It is simply a matter of convenience. In very many parts of the world infanticide is a common thing—a rite, a custom. But I believe that in no part of the world is there anything nearly resembling the female infanticide of which I am now writing.

In all parts of India the desire for offspring is very strong. A childless woman is a miserable woman—a

* "The people in some parts of India, particularly the inhabitants of Orissa, and of the eastern parts of Bengal, frequently offer their children to the Goddess Gunga. The following reason is assigned for the practice: When a woman has been long married, and has no children, it is common for the man, or his wife, or both of them, to make a vow to the Goddess Gunga, that if she will bestow the blessing of children upon them, they will devote their firstborn to her. If after this vow they have children, the eldest is nourished till a proper age, which may be three, four, or nine years, according to circumstances, when, on a particular day, appointed for bathing in a holy part of the river, they take the child with them and offer it to this goddess; the child is encouraged to go further and further into the water till it is carried away by the stream, or is pushed off by its inhuman parents."—[*Ward on the Hindoos.*]

hissing, a reproach. She believes that a curse is upon her. She is despised by herself, and scorned by her husband. She thinks—and if she gives birth to children who are taken away from her by death, the same thought comes upon her—that she is thus afflicted for some grievous sin committed in a pre-existent state. The parental instinct is as strong among them as among any people in the world. And even where the parental instinct is not, the tenderness with which strong bearded men devote themselves to the care of young children, is as touching as it is remarkable. It is not indifference, therefore, to infant life, out of which this horrid practice emanates. It is simply the existence among these "chivalrous" Rajpoots of a strong delusion, which some call honor, some pride of birth, and others grossness of ignorance, deadness of conscience — barbarism — devilry— what you will.

It is hard to designate the feeling aright. I shall not attempt to provide the fitting nomenclature. It would be better to illustrate than to define. A score of examples of the strange working of Rajpoot honor readily suggest themselves; but I know not one more striking than the following, which Mr. Forbes, an old Bombay civilian, has set down in his "Oriental Memoirs:"— "About four years before my appointment to Baroche," he writes, of the last quarter of the eighteenth century, "some Mahomedans, walking through a village where a family of Rajpoots resided, approached their house, and accidentally looked into a room where an elderly woman was eating. They intended no insult; they saw her at her meal, and immediately retired. But this accident occasioned a disgrace on the Rajpoot lady for which, on her part, there could be no expiation. She at that time lived with her grandson, a fine young man, who was absent when the Mahomedans committed their trespass;

on his return home she related the circumstance, and her determination not to survive it. She therefore entreated him earnestly to put her to death—a step which she had only deferred that she might fall by his hand. The youth's affection and good sense induced him to remonstrate with his venerable parent, whom he endeavoured to dissuade from her purpose, by alleging that none but her own family knew of the disgrace, the very men who were the innocent cause of it being unconscious of the offence. Persevering, however, in her resolution, but unable to persuade either her grandson or any other person to perform the sacrifice, she calmly waited until he next went from home, and then beat her head against the wall with dreadful violence. On his return he found his venerable parent in this agonising and shocking state. She again entreated he would finish the sacrifice, and release her from misery; he then stabbed her to the heart."*

This is Rajpoot honor—Rajpoot chivalry. It may be called by ennobling names, but, in reality, it is nothing but the densest barbarism. It is easy to understand, and even to admire, the feeling which impels the Tartar warrior, at the approach of a victorious enemy, to slaughter his wives and children. All nations, more or less, comprehend the great aphorism, "Death is better than dishonor." We know what is that dishonor which follows the assault and capture of a hostile town. But the dishonor incurred by an old woman seen, by a

* *Forbes' Oriental Memoirs*, vol. i., p. 490.—The sequel of this story is worth telling, if only as a proof that in those days such atrocities were not sheltered, under any plea of religion or custom, from the just vengeance of the law. "By the English laws," says Mr. Forbes, "he was secured as a murderer, sent to Bombay for trial, and confined in the common prison until the ensuing sessions. The grand jury found a bill for murder; the petty jury, composed half of Europeans and half of natives, found him guilty; and the judges condemned him to death. The Rajpoots in general have a noble mien and dignified character; their high caste is stamped on their countenance; this young man possessed them all. I saw him receive his sentence, not only with composure, but with a mingled look of disdain and delight not easy to de-

passing stranger, in the act of eating her dinner, is not very readily appreciable. The only thing that is very clear about the matter, is that, if a woman is so easily dishonored, it were better that she should eat her dinner in a place where curious travellers cannot see her.

But such being the turgid sense of honor which inflates these chivalrous Rajpoots, it is not strange that the disgrace of unmarried daughters—a disgrace of which all Hindoos are more or less sensible—should be keenly appreciated by them. An overweening idea of the necessities of caste and the suitability of matrimonial alliances renders marriage a matter of difficult achievement. A husband is to be found for the Rajpootnee damsel among the members of her own caste. On no account must she ally herself with one of inferior rank. Within this narrow circle she must find a husband, or the family is disgraced. Nor does the difficulty end with the attainment of the husband. Among the Hindoos there is always a wretched waste of money, varying, of course, according to the rank of the parties, on occasion of marriage ceremonies. Among the people of whom I am speaking, it is a point of honor that these festivals should be celebrated at a cost which must press heavily upon the financial resources of men with whom poverty and pride are too often yoke-fellows. It is not

scribe. Unconscious of the crime laid to his charge, he said that he had nothing to accuse himself of except disobedience to his parent, by permitting humanity and filial affection to supersede his duty and the honor of his caste; that life was no longer desirable; nor, if acquitted by the English laws, would he survive the ignominy of having been confined with European culprits and prisoners of the lowest castes, with whom he had been compelled to eat and associate in a common prison—acts so contrary to everything which he esteemed right and honorable, that the sooner he was transferred to another state of existence the better. However inclined the Government might be to clemency, it would evidently have been fruitless; the noble Rajpoot would not survive the disgrace, and the sentence of the law was executed, in the hope that it might prevent others from following his example."

convenient, therefore, that daughters should grow up in the house. They must be *sarf-kard,* or cleared away.

Such are the causes of female infanticide as it exists in certain parts of Hindostan. There is no religious warrant for it. The Hindoo Shastres are sufficiently clear on the subject of the enormity of child-murder. Indeed, it is almost the one exceptional case of a barbarous custom, that has not the sanction expressed or implied, by precept or example, of the monstrous faith which these people profess. There are, doubtless, some obscure fables, some dim traditions, among them, in which it is pretended that the origin of the enormity is to be found; but even these do not impute to it a divine origin. No god commanded the horrid rite, or set the example of its perpetration. The patron saint of female infanticide is at best no better than "a powerful Rajah."*

It was not likely that on such an iniquity as this the English in India would look with passive unconcern. It was an evil very palpable to the understandings of men, but the proper remedy was not equally apparent. It was, indeed, something very difficult to deal with—an abomination propped up and sustained by feelings deeply implanted in men's hearts, and not to be eradicated without such rendings and revulsions of the whole social and domestic system as might be fraught with the most dangerous results. Still the effort was to be

* Colonel Walker says: "The Jharigahs relate that a powerful Rajah of their caste, who had a daughter of singular beauty and accomplishments, desired his Raj-goor, or family priest, to affiance her to a prince of rank and descent equal to her own. The Raj-goor travelled over many countries without discovering a chief possessed of the requisite qualities. In this dilemma the Rajah consulted the Raj-goor, and he advised him to avoid the disgrace which would attend the princess's remaining unmarried, by having recourse to the desperate expedient of putting his daughter to death. The Rajah was long averse to this expedient. The Raj-goor at length removed his scruples by consenting to load himself with the guilt, and to become in his own person responsible for all the consequence of the sin. Accordingly the princess was put to death, and female infanticide was from that time practised by the Jharigahs."

made—made, wheresoever British influence extended, not merely in districts under our immediate administration, but in parts of the country where the native princes held dominion; and we could only exercise indirect control over the acts of the people through the agency of the British Residents at these foreign Durbars. And it is to the honor of the Company and their officers, that, in spite of all discouragements and denials, all difficulties and all obstacles, they have now for half a century been engaged in this good work, and have achieved an amount of success which, if not full and entire, is at least meet reward and glorious compensation for all the painful labor it has cost.

In the van of those active and benevolent British officers, who have endeavoured to suppress this inhuman practice, stands Jonathan Duncan, many years Resident of Benares, and afterwards Governor of Bombay. He was a simple-minded man, of enlarged benevolence, who, wheresoever his lot was cast in the East, made for himself a place in the affections of the people by whom he was surrounded. Mackintosh said of him that he had been *Brahmanised* by long residence in India; but the word, coined for the purpose by the accomplished Recorder of Bombay, conveys but a half-truth. Inasmuch as that Duncan knew the people of India well, conversed with them as freely as though they had been his own countrymen, and from long intercourse with them, had contracted some Oriental rust, which, in the eyes of one fresh from the literary coteries of the English capital, was something new and strange, he had been *Brahmanised*. But the word unfitly describes the character of one who regarded the people around him, from the highest to the lowest, with deep paternal interest, and whose enlarged toleration and extended sympathies partook not at all of the cruel exclusiveness of the priestly aristocracy of Hindostan. He had been Indianised indeed, but not Brahmanised. He had no toleration of things, which Brahmanism not only tolerates, but encourages; and he set himself against the iniquities which were done in the name of the religion, and sanctioned by the priesthood of the country. And foremost among these iniquities was the female infanticide of Central and Western India. He had first been made acquainted with the existence of the evil in the neighbourhood of Juanpore,* about the year 1789; and had subsequently, on his removal to Western India, clearly traced the extension of the cruel system to the provinces of Cutch and Kattywar. "I am well assured," he wrote, with respect to the former, "and it is, indeed, here generally believed (and being so, it is my duty not to keep such enormities, however sanctioned by usage, from the knowledge of Government), that it is no unfrequent practice among the tribe of Rajkoomar to destroy their daughters, by causing the mothers to refuse them nurture; whence this race of men do often, from necessity, marry into other Rajpoot families. The greatest exception to this melancholy truth that I can find is, that men—and these the more wealthy Rajkoomars—will sometimes spare and bring up their female issue, especially when they happen to have none of the male line. This horrid custom is said to exist also among some other tribes, more especially in the Vizier's dominions, and it is thought to be founded in the extravagant desire of independency enter-

* Sir John Shore, in 1794, speaks of this in a communication to the Asiatic Society:—"That the practice of infanticide," he says, "should ever be so general as to become a custom with any sect or race of people, requires the most unexceptionable evidence to gain belief; and I am sorry to say that the general practice, as far as regards female infants, is fully substantiated with respect to a particular tribe on the frontiers of Juanpur, a district of the province of Benares, adjoining to the country of Oude. A race of Hindoos called Rajkoomars reside here; and it was discovered in 1789 only that the custom of putting to death their female offspring had long subsisted, and did actually then very generally prevail among them. The Resident at Benares (Mr. Duncan, afterwards Governor of Bombay), in a circuit which he made through the country where the Rajkoomars dwell, had an opportunity of authenticating the existence of the custom from their own confessions; he conversed with several; all unequivocally admitted it, though all did not fully admit its atrocity."

tained by this race of men, joined, perhaps, to the supposed necessity of procuring a suitable settlement in marriage for those devoted females were they allowed to grow up, and the disgrace which would ensue from any omission in that respect. Nor is this species of atrocity of recent institution; for a similar prejudice, as existing among the Indians, was known by the ancient Greeks and Romans, as is found in the relations they have left of this quarter of the world."*

This was written in October, 1789, and is remarkable as containing the first official notice of the subject of female infanticide in India. In less than three months from the day on which Jonathan Duncan announced his discovery of the horrid custom, he wrote to Lord Cornwallis that he had taken measures for its suppression. "I have prevailed on those situated within our frontier," he wrote, "to agree to renounce in future this horrid practice, to which effect they have entered into the engagement which will be found translated in the accompanying extract of my proceedings." The words of the covenant are worth quoting:—"Whereas," proceeds this curious document, "it hath become known to the Government of the Honorable East India Company, that we of the tribe of *Rajkumar* do not suffer our female children to live; and whereas, this is a great crime, as mentioned in the *Brehma Bywant Purana*, where it is said that killing even a fœtus is as criminal as killing a Brahman; and that for killing a female or woman, the punishment is to suffer in the Naraka, or Hell called *Kat Shutala*, for as many years as there are hairs on the female's body, and that afterwards such person shall be born again, and successively become a leper and afflicted with the *jakhima;* and whereas, the British Government in India, whose subjects we are, hold in detestation such mur-

* *Jonathan Duncan to Lord Cornwallis, October* 2, 1789. *Moore's Hindoo Infanticide.*

derous practices, and we do ourselves acknowledge that although customary among us, they are highly sinful; we do therefore hereby agree not to commit any longer such detestable acts, and any among us who shall (which God forbid!) be hereafter guilty thereof, or who shall not bring up and get our daughters married to the best of our abilities among those of our own caste, shall be expelled from our tribe, and shall neither eat nor keep society with us, besides suffering hereafter the punishments denounced in the above Purana and Shastra. We have therefore entered into this engagement.—(*Dated 17th December*, 1789.)"

For many years it was believed that this engagement had been observed, and that the Rajkoomars had ceased to murder their female infants. But excellent as was the intention of the covenant, and undeniable as were the truths set forth in its preamble, this great measure had everything in the world to recommend it but practical success.

Meanwhile, happy in the belief of the beneficent issue of his ameliorative efforts in Central India, Jonathan Duncan, now appointed Governor of Bombay, was endeavouring, in like manner, to suppress the barbarous custom as he found it to exist among the Jareejah Rajpoots of Cutch and Kattywar. He was fortunate in the agency he employed. In Major Walker he found an officer combined in whom were the purest philanthropic zeal, sound intelligence, and unfailing perseverance. The difficulties to be encountered were many and formidable. The natives around him declared that the custom would never be suppressed until the Company should take possession of the country in their own name. But, in spite of these discouragements, Walker entered on the great undertaking with sanguine expectations of success. "I conceived," he said, "that reason and feeling would effect the relinquishment of a barbarous custom unconnected with the principles of society, and which all the passions of the human mind, and all the forms and maxims of religion were combined to destroy. As it was evident, also, that the most disinterested humanity had led the Honorable Company to interfere for the abolition of female infanticide, I conceived that this reflection, and the respect due to their mediation, would have disposed the Jareejahs to comply with a request which it was scarcely to be supposed could be at variance with their own sentiments." All this, however, was a mere amiable delusion, and Major Walker was compelled presently to acknowledge that "sentiments of nature and humanity have no influence with the Jareejahs," and reluctantly to abandon his favorable expectations of success.

Undaunted, however, by the discovery that nothing was to be hoped for from the good feelings of the Jareejahs, Walker began now to turn his thoughts towards a new course of action. It was a distasteful—a sickening game that he was called upon to play. The amount of selfishness and bigotry—of falsehood and avarice—of cowardice and chicanery—that he had to encounter, can hardly be over-estimated. But the English officer looked it all steadily in the face. He made this great matter of Female Infanticide the subject of continual discussion, oral and written, with the Jareejah chiefs. He believed that it would be no small thing to familiarise their minds with the idea that the practice of female infanticide, so long unquestioned, was something at least of questionable propriety—something which other nations, and especially that great nation from which springs the paramount power in India, regarded with horror and detestation. And, at all events, from this constant obtrusion of the subject there came this amount of good—that the chiefs seeing how extreme was the eagerness of the British Government to carry this point of the abolition of Female Infanticide, bethought themselves of turning our solicitude to profitable account, and trading upon our humanity. These chivalrous Rajpoots seemed not unwilling to yield, for a consideration, at least an outward assent to the proposals of the British officer. And it seems to have been mainly in expectation of some advantage to themselves that at last they consented, in a cowardly reluctant manner, each endeavouring to push the other forward, to become parties to an engagement similar to that which Mr. Duncan had extracted from the Rajkoomars in the neighbourhood of Juanpore. They *did* sign the covenant at last; and Major Walker saw many good reasons for believing that they would fulfil the promises they had made. And so it came to be considered that, both in Central and in Western India, Infanticide had been suppressed by Duncan and Walker; and learned writers in Encyclopædias, and in brave independent quartos of their own, set forth the gratifying announcement without a doubt of its truth.

But though Duncan and Walker deserved success, it was not in their power to command it. They were the pioneers of humanity and civilisation in that direction, and bravely they labored with axe and hatchet to clear away the dense jungle of barbarism that lay before them; but they did not apply the fire to the root, and the noxious wilderness soon sprung up again above the delusive clearings they had made. For a while it was believed that the horrid custom had been suppressed, alike in the East and the West; little or nothing was heard of the abomination, and no new efforts were made to suppress it. But about the year 1816 it was officially announced that the Rajkoomars were murdering their children after the old fashion. Mr. Shakespear, then acting as Superintendent of Police, reported that though the Regulations of 1795 and 1804 "contain provisions for the prevention and punishment of the inhuman practice prevalent among the tribe of Rajkoomars of causing the female infants to be strangled to death, there is reason to believe that this practice still obtains among them to nearly the same extent as formerly, though a greater degree of caution is preserved to prevent detection;" and the Governor-General in Council expressed his regret that "the measures adopted by Mr. Duncan whilst Resident at Benares, and the provisions of the Regulations, had failed to prevent the inhuman practice." The same lamentable tidings came also from Western India. Major Carnac, Resident at Baroda, officially reported to the Bombay Government, that "the abolition of the inhuman practice in Cutch had not been accomplished." And in the following year Captain Ballantine reported, with reference to the Rajpoots of Goozrat, that "the object of our interference for the suppression of this singular custom has too generally failed to select any individual party for the just vengeance of Government and offended nature." To make the extent of the evil, as then existing, more apparent, this energetic officer drew up a statistical report, containing a register of all the Jareejah families known in Kattywar, with "the age and number of their female offspring saved, or now living, since the introduction of the Infanticide arrangement by Colonel Walker in 1808;" and from this census it appeared that during the space of ten years only sixty-three female Jareejah children had been preserved in the whole of Kattywar; that in none of the large *talooks*, or estates, of the Jareejah chiefs, was there more than one female child to be found, and in some not even one, though containing four hundred families.* Such, in spite of the laudable efforts of Duncan and Walker, was the result of our first humane efforts to suppress this dreadful abomination.

But this mortifying discovery moved the Company's

* Parliamentary Papers, quoted in the *Calcutta Review*, whose admirable summary I have mainly followed.

Government and the Company's servants to order, and to prosecute new efforts for the suppression of the great crime. The Court of Directors wrote out to the Bombay Government, "enjoining them in the most serious and earnest manner to be unremitting in their endeavours to accomplish this humane object in the countries where British influence can be felt and exerted." But it was not very clear, even to the most humane and energetic servants of the Company, how these unremitting endeavours were to be prosecuted, so as to accomplish the great object. The difficulty, indeed, was very great, and, seemingly, insurmountable. Some of the most large-minded men, believing that we could make an impression on the evil only by the adoption of measures so objectionable that it might be questioned whether the remedy were not worse than the disease, seemed, in spite of the strong instincts of humanity which urged them forward, almost inclined to counsel an adherence for the future to the old measures of moral discouragement, which had proved so abortive in the past. The great standing difficulty was this. The general prevalence of the crime was acknowledged. Its results were sufficiently apparent in the fact, that the number of female children to be found among the Jareejahs was only *one-sixth* of the number of males. But it was difficult—indeed, impossible—to bring to light specific acts of infanticide without such an intrusion into the domestic privacy of high-caste Rajpoot families as would be regarded with horror, and resented with indignation. This systematic child-murder, indeed, was altogether an affair of the Zenana. The mother was herself the executioner. She rubbed the nipples of her breasts with opium, and the babe sucked in poison with its first milk.* Every-

* A significant hint from the fathers, not conveyed in words, generally sealed the fate of the child. "Simtook Ram, minister of Amjherra," writes Sir John Malcolm in his *Central India*, "told me he was sitting with Predum Singh, the present Thakoor, when he heard the birth of a female child whispered in his ear. He saw him preparing between his fingers the

thing was done so secretly behind the *purdah;* even the very birth of the child was so little noised abroad, that the disappearance of whole families of female children, one after another, in individual succession, could not be clearly traced. Public notoriety pointed vaguely to the general fact. But the lips of all who were competent to speak to individual offences were closed. No man willingly bore witness against his neighbour. How, then, were we to penetrate the obscurity, and break down the exclusiveness of domestic life — an exclusiveness so jealously guarded, so religiously maintained, that it almost seemed as though dishonor would enter the female apartments with the sunbeams or the west wind? It was proposed that hired informers should be employed; but the proposal did not find favor in the eyes of authority. Mount-Stuart Elphinstone—a statesman of equal wisdom and humanity—set his face steadfastly against it. "No effectual check," he wrote, "can be imposed on this atrocious practice, so long as it is so completely congenial to the general feelings of the people, unless by employing hired agents, as proposed by Major Ballantine, whose duty it should be to detect offenders of this description; and such a measure would lead to so much intrusion into the most private and domestic proceedings of the superior castes (among whom alone infanticide prevails), and would be open to so many abuses on the part of the informers, that I do not think the chance of success would compensate for the disaffection which it would create. It may also be doubted how far we have a right to interfere to such an extraordinary pitch with the private life of a people, with whose civil government and internal policy we do not pretend to have any concern. We must therefore be content to follow the foot-

fatal pill of opium (the usual signal), but he implored that the child might live: his request was granted, and this little girl (added Simtook Ram), now eight years of age, is always called my daughter."

steps of our predecessors (without attempting to go beyond them) in their most meritorious endeavours to discountenance this enormity; and we may safely flatter ourselves, that as the manners of the people become softened by a continuance of tranquillity and good order, they will gradually discontinue a practice which is not more inconsistent with reason than repugnant to natural instinct."

This was written in 1821. There was, seemingly, nothing very hopeful in it. The *laisser-faire* system was to be tried again. Moral discouragements were to be left to work out their slow results. "In speaking to those natives," writes Sir John Malcolm, with reference to the Rajpoots of Central India, "who enjoyed superior rank and station under the authority or control of the British Government, I have always expressed my horror at self-immolation (Suttee), and my hope that through their influence in society, and their desire not to outrage the feelings of their European superiors, it would in time be abolished. But with regard to infanticide I have ever, when it was mentioned, stated my abhorrence of the murders that were committed under the plea of this usage, and refused to see those who practiced it. Such sentiments," he added, "were never known to give offence." In Western India the same discouragements were at work; and they were not wholly without success. Many good and able European officers, among whom may be especially named Colonel Miles, Major Barnewell, and Mr. Blaine; and, subsequently, in the regions of Cutch, Henry Pottinger and Alexander Burnes exerted themselves to put down the abomination by such gentle, moral force as they conceived themselves justified in applying, and the result was not wholly a blank. It is officially reported, that whilst the number of female children belonging to the murderous tribes in Kattywar, preserved from destruction in 1808, only amounted to 32, it had risen, in 1817, to 63; and in 1824, to 266. In Cutch, the numbers had increased from 93, in 1823, to 143 in 1826; and, a few years later, Captain Burnes reported that the number had risen to 211. This last calculation was made from a census of more than a hundred villages, in which it was ascertained that there were, at the same time, 1167 male children; the girls being thus shown, in proportion to the boys, to be little more than as one to six. These returns, however, must be received with some caution. It is difficult to obtain a correct census of the people in these Rajpoot villages; and the returns, therefore, must be regarded rather as approximations, than as accurately ascertained results.

In the interval, however, of which I am now writing, between the years 1820 and 1830, there is one successful episode in the history of this great war against infanticide, which is worthy of especial recital. Among the rude people of Mairwarra, Colonel Hall had exerted himself to some purpose; for in a report dated July 31st, 1827, he reported "the complete and voluntary abolition of the two revolting customs—female infanticide and the sale of women." "Both crimes," he wrote, "were closely connected, having had their origin in the heavy expense attending marriage contracts. The sums were payable by the male side, were unalterable, equal for the rich and the poor, without any abatement whatever in favor of the latter. What first established the payment is unknown; but it was so sacred and inviolable, and even a partial deviation so disgraceful, that the more necessitous of the tribe would not incur the imputation. . . . Hence arose Infanticide. The sums payable were beyond the means of so many, that daughters necessarily remained on hand after maturity, entailed immortal disgrace, and thus imposed a necessity for all female progeny becoming victims to their family honor. On the establishment of

British rule, both evils gradually diminished. . . . . Female Infanticide was at once prohibited, and though many, no doubt, still fell secret sacrifices from the great facility of undetected destruction, yet the danger, aided by improved feeling, increased the survivors so considerably, as to force upon the Mairs a due sense of the root of the evil, and a general wish for its removal by a reduction of the regulated sum of contract; but they were averse—indeed, declared their inability—to alter their long-established sacred custom themselves, and earnestly entreated that it might be done by an order of authority, binding all to obedience by heavy penalties. This was promised in a general way in case of necessity; but as there were many points to be settled, and it was advisable to ascertain the general feeling with accuracy, as well as to avoid interference, if possible, a general *punchayut* was strongly urged either to decide the matter, or, at all events, aid in the framing of appropriate regulations. After the lapse of a few months allowed for consideration, the whole was settled in public punchayut, and its resolutions were confirmed without the slightest alteration; so that the proceeding originated with, and has been carried through by, the inhabitants themselves; nor has there been a single petition against it, either pending or subsequent to adjustment. They have lowered the sum payable on marriage contracts, abolished all right of subsequent sale, and fixed a year's imprisonment, or 200 rupees fine, with exclusion from caste, as the punishment for deviation."* The result seems to have justified the sanguine expectations of Colonel Hall. Writing more than twenty years afterwards, his successor, Colonel Dixon, says: "Thus Infanticide received its death-blow through the diminution of the expenses attending on marriage, which was now brought within the reach of all sections of society. For many years

* *Report of Colonel Hall, July*, 1827, *quoted in Dixon's Mairwarra.*

past no female children have been put to death. The practice has fallen altogether into desuetude. Indeed, so greatly have the ideas of the people changed on this and other usages since the introduction of our rule, that the commission of such an act would now be viewed as a most heinous crime."*

Thus the first unequivocal success resulted from the establishment of sumptuary regulations. But it was easier to deal with these rugged Mairs, just rescued from a state of extreme barbarism, than with the "chivalrous" Rajpoots of Central and Western India. It is not improbable that if the British, or any other Government, had undertaken to portion the Jharijah girls, the dreadful custom would have been annihilated. The plan was, indeed, proposed, and negatived by the higher authorities. And the extreme alternative of putting down the abomination by force was rejected upon the ground that the Rajpoots of Western India were not our subjects, but our allies, and that such a mode of procedure would be inconsistent with the terms of our treaties. In 1831 Sir John Malcolm, then Governor of Bombay, went down to Booj and addressed the assembled Jharijah chiefs on the enormity of the crime so prevalent among them. He told them that so strong in England was the feeling against such abominations, that the nation would call upon the East India Company to sever their connexion with a people so polluted. The chiefs, seemingly abashed, falsely denied their participation in the prevailing guilt—and promises and pledges were not wanting. Indeed, the "chivalrous" Rajpoots were at no time chary of their promises and pledges—and now, as our English officers became more and more energetic in their efforts to put down the abomination, these promises and pledges became more and more plentiful.

In Central India, promises were as readily made and

* *Dixon's Mairwarra.*

as readily broken as in the West. Many earnest-minded men were exerting themselves, about this time, in Rajpootana, to push forward the good work. Distinguished among these was Mr. Wilkinson, whose name is ever to be held in remembrance by those who would record the good deeds of the Company's servants. He was a man of the kindliest and the most catholic sympathies, of large intelligence, and unwearying perseverance. He lived and toiled for the people, and he died, at his post, amongst them, warmly loved and deeply deplored. All that earnest desire and energetic action could do to wean the Rajpoots of Central India from the accursed practice of Infanticide, was now done by this full-hearted civilian. He assembled the chiefs; he addressed them; he reasoned with them; he expostulated with them; and at last he persuaded them to adopt certain resolutions, by an adherence to which it seemed probable that the iniquity might be suppressed. And many of the petty sovereigns of Rajpootana not only undertook to prohibit the practice, but issued proclamations declaring it illegal. Other officers in Central India, as Colonel Sutherland, Captain Richards, Captain Ludlow, and others, had been exerting themselves in the same good cause, and there were many encouraging promises and seemingly genuine renunciations to reward their labors.

The Rana of Oudipore, the chief of the independent sovereigns of Rajpootana, was forward to set the example —a potential one—of prohibition; and in January, 1834, Lord William Bentinck wrote to express the "pure and unmixed satisfaction" which he felt, and to utter words of further encouragement; but all these promises and renunciations were mere unmeaning words. The princes and chiefs had not been convinced, or they feared to reduce their convictions to practice. At all events, Wilkinson, who had labored so long and so diligently, and whose heart was so thoroughly in his work, was forced back upon the mortifying conclusion that no real impression had been made upon the minds of the magnates of the land. Only two months after he had explained to the chief people the enormity of the crime of infanticide and received their assurances of renunciation, he ascertained that two of their number had since put their daughters to death. The promised proclamations might have been issued; but no pains were taken to circulate them. He found, in the course of his circuits, that some of the states had not even heard of the prohibitory edict; and, under the government of that very Rana of Oudipore whom Lord William Bentinck had so commended, some of the people told Mr. Wilkinson that it was true they had heard it whispered "that female infanticide had been prohibited some time before along with the killing of peacocks."

All this was very discouraging—but still Mr. Wilkinson did not despair of the effect of moral influence. He secured the services of some learned Brahmins to write pamphlets condemnatory of the crime, which he circulated among the people. He bethought himself, too, of the effect upon their minds of pictorial representations; but all this was of no avail. "It has been my object," he wrote, "to excite such a genuine and general feeling of execration as should lead to a voluntary abandonment of the practice. Still, when we reflect on the inveteracy of habit, and the extreme tardiness with which new ideas are spread in the world, it would be idle to hope that the abandonment of the practice will be effected by the measures already taken."

In the mean while a great experiment was being initiated in Western India. In 1831, Mr. J. P. Willoughby, of the Bombay Civil Service, was appointed Political Agent in Kattywar. He soon began to give his thoughts to the painful subject of Female Infanticide, and collected all the information he could acquire regarding the dreadful practice and all that had been done towards its suppression. Reviewing the labors of his predecessors, and deriving wisdom from the past, he sent in an elaborate report to Government, in which he took a retrospective view of the results of our bygone efforts, and then sketched out a plan of future proceedings.

The measures suggested by Mr. Willoughby were these. *First*, that steps should be taken to obtain a complete census of the Jharijah population, as without it no data could exist for computing the number of female infants who were born, and thence deducing an approximation to the number actually destroyed. *Second*, that every Jharijah chief should be called upon to furnish a half-yearly register of all the marriages, betrothals, births, and deaths occurring among his tribe residing in his district; and that, if he failed in this obligation, or furnished a false return, he should be severely punished.* *Third*, that the Political Agent should furnish an annual report on the subject of Infanticide, together with a register of all marriages, betrothals, births, and deaths that have occurred among the tribe within the year reported on. *Fourth*, that a proclamation should be issued by the British Government throughout Kattywar, requiring the Jharijah chiefs to enforce the observance of their Infanticide engagements, and noticing in terms of approbation or condemnation their adherence to or departure from these engagements, and guaranteeing to all able or willing to supply information relating to the commission of the crime, a reward in proportion to the rank of the

* Mr. Willoughby, in the admirable Report which contains these suggestions, shows that this important matter had not escaped the attention of the Court of Directors. "This is no new suggestion," he says, "on my part, for in the correspondence on my records I find allusion made to instructions issued many years ago to the Honorable Court of Directors, that in addition to such intermediate reports as might become necessary, one general statement should be submitted at the end of each year, showing how far the amended system had been acted on and observed, what deviations are known or suspected to have been made from its rules, and what measures pursued for their enforcement, with an estimate of the number of lives saved."

party convicted, and the protection of the British Government. *Fifth*, that every Rajpoot in Kattywar should be enjoined to make it an express stipulation in every marriage contract on giving his daughter to a Jharijah chief that the issue of the union should be preserved. *Sixth*, that presents of cloth, money, &c., should be made, out of the *Infanticide Fund*, to the chiefs and inferior members of the Jharijah tribes who preserved their female children.*

These measures, approved and sanctioned by the higher authorities, were pushed forward with promptitude and energy. The vigilance of the British officers was not without its results. In the course of eighteen months, it was reported that seventy-three female infants were preserved by the Jharijah tribes; of these, forty, it was said, would have perished but for our humane intervention. Still, in spite of all our efforts, there remained the lamentable fact, that at least one-half of the female infants born were murdered by their remorseless parents. It was, however, no small thing to convict certain offenders of specific acts of infanticide; and charges were now brought and fully established against the chief of Rajkote. "The barbarous insensibility evinced by him on the occasion, proved him to have little claim to forgiveness." He was fined 12,000 rupees, to be paid to the Infanticide Fund; and his estate was attached as security for its payment. This conviction produced the most salutary effect throughout Kattywar, and was soon followed by other cases. Another petty chief, convicted on the clearest evidence of

* "The Infanticide Fund was established in 1825. It is composed of all fines, under 20,000 rupees, imposed upon the tributaries for breaches of the peace or other misconduct, and of realisation under the head of Mohsullee. The British Government set the example. His Highness the Guicowar, being subsequently induced to consent that all fines imposed upon his tributaries should be similarly appropriated. From this source occasional remissions of tribute, presents to the chiefs, and pecuniary assistance on the marriage of their daughters, have been granted to those who have practically renounced the custom; and another mode of testifying approbation to those who have preserved their daughters, is by postponing the payment of the tribute to suit their convenience." — [*Mr. Willoughby's Report.*]

the same offence, was sentenced to suffer twelve months' imprisonment, and to pay a fine of 3000 rupees. These were followed by other cases of detection and punishment. But though the evil sensibly diminished under these influences, it was not entirely suppressed. Here and there a case was brought struggling into light, but scores of cases of cruel child-murder, behind the sanctity of the purdah, escaped detection and exposure.

Perhaps, it would have been unreasonable to expect in such a case anything more than progressive improvement. It was, indeed, the hardest task that we had ever set ourselves—the hardest we have ever set ourselves since. I believe that in this country, where we all of us live comparatively out of doors — *coram populo* — an extensive system of Female Infanticide might be carried on without detection. I believe that married women in England might murder their sucklings by hundreds without suspicion. A little seemingly accidental neglect—a little want of active care at particular periods, will snap the thread of infant life, and give no sign of premeditated crime. But the nursery of the Hindoo woman, even of the poorest, is surrounded by social screens and fences which, however flimsy may be their material structure, are morally so impassable, so impenetrable, that the vigilance and activity of authority is utterly baffled and repelled by them. It was this that rendered the task so difficult—that rendered success, even under the best and most encouraging circumstances, so vague and uncertain. With such formidable obstructions before us it was a great thing to make any progress. It was a great thing that the Bombay Government should be enabled to write: "The complete suspension of the crime, originating in ignorance, prejudice, and false pride, must doubtless be the work of time; yet, looking back to the past, and seeing how much had been accomplished within the last few years, they were encouraged strongly to hope that a steady and constant perseverance in the measures in operation would, in the end, be rewarded by full and complete success."

Mr. Willoughby, promoted to higher office, quitted Kattywar in 1835, and was succeeded in the Political Agency by Mr. Erskine, who continued the good work which had been pushed forward so energetically by his predecessor. But it was plain still that there was much to be done. In 1837, upon a census of twenty-seven districts, it appeared that there were 1422 boys, and only 409 girls. In 1841, Captain Jacob, who was associated with Mr. Erskine on this great field of humanising labor, reported that the number of males under the age of twenty was 2923, whilst the females reached the encouraging amount of 1209, little less than one-half of the entire juvenile population. The result, indeed, led Captain Jacob to observe: "It must be highly gratifying to those benevolent men who had labored for the suppression of Infanticide, to see the progressive return to the order of nature, in the relative proportion of sexes, that must be attributed to their labor alone;" and called forth the commendatory remark of the Bombay Government, which I have quoted above.

Nor were these anticipations of the gradual suppression of the horrid practice unjustified by the result. I cannot afford to trace, year by year, the progressive improvement in the appearance of the census of the male and female population of Kattywar. But, perhaps, the good effects of our humanising measures may be best illustrated by passing on at once to the cheering details contained in the two last Infanticide Reports which have made their way into official record. In the Infanticide Report for the year 1849, from Kattywar, of which Major Lang, who has long been zealously employed in that province, is now Political Agent, there is this cheering announcement: "The proportion of female children to males in all the tribes is now so nearly equal, and the progressive increase of the female population so regular, that if the returns can be depended upon in other respects, there would appear to be every ground for believing that the practice of Infanticide must have become almost entirely extinct in this province." And then he goes on to report these encouraging statistical facts. "When the census for 1845 was forwarded with my Report of the 25th of August, 1846, there were two Jharijahs with five daughters each, 19 with four, 105 with three, and 387 with two. . . . . By the returns now submitted there are one Jharijah with six daughters, 11 with five, 49 with four, 159 with three, and 522 with two."* The Report of the following year, though less detailed, is equally satisfactory. It shows that the female Jharijah population has increased to a greater extent than the male. The former had increased, during the year 1850, by 186; the latter only by 149. "The only accusation of Infanticide," writes Major Lang, "which was brought forward during the year under review, was that reported in my letter of the 25th of September, 1850, which was found on investigation by my assistant, Captain Barr, to be entirely groundless."† But to make the progressive results of these great measures fully apparent, it would be well to give a brief tabular statement of the male and female Jharijah population of Kattywar, extending over the six years from 1845 to 1850, inclusive:‡

* *Major Lang to Bombay Government. MS. Records, December* 31, 1850. I have omitted the details of the smaller tribes, which are no less gratifying.

† *Major Lang to Bombay Government, December* 26, 1851. *MS. Records.*

‡ Well might Mr. Willoughby, when a seat in the Bombay Council gave him an opportunity of commenting on such results as these, congratulate himself on the success of his measures.

"I trust I shall be pardoned the expression," he wrote, "of the high gratification I have derived from the perusal of this and other similar Reports, establishing that the success which has attended our measures for the extirpation of the crime of Female Infanticide from Kattywar and Cutch has been far greater and much more rapid than the most sanguine could have anticipated. It was my good fortune to have been the originator of these measures, the success of which is mainly to be attributed to the vigorous manner in which I dealt with several proved cases of Infanticide before I left the province. I recollect that, by some whose opinion I valued, I was thought to have invaded too strictly the sanctity of Rajpoot domestic privacy, and that the measures I had

	1845.	1846.	1847.	1848.	1849.	1850.
Males	6617	6600	6844	7356	7353	7502
Females	2334	2429	2779	3090	3273	3423

It must necessarily take many years to restore the balance of the sexes, fearfully disturbed as it has been from generation to generation; but with such results as these before me, remembering that the time was when the number of female children to be found among the Jharijahs was only *one-sixth* of the number of males, and that on some large estates containing as many as 400 families not one female child was to be found,* I think I am justified in saying that what has been done is most honorable to the British nation, and that the rest is but "a work of time."

Whilst these measures were being thus energetically pursued in Western India, another group of British officers were carrying out the same good work in the Central Rajpoot states, with the approval and co-operation of the princes and chiefs themselves. The process, however, by which they hoped to attain the same great result, differed from that which Mr. Willoughby had introduced into Kattywar. It was based upon the admitted fact, that in those states the one great sustaining cause of the unholy practice was the extreme costliness of marriage ceremonials. To marry his daughter was often to ruin a man. There was a wretched brood of men known as "Charans" and "Bhats," who turned to vile uses two of the noblest functions of humanity, and degraded the priestly and the bardic office into a sort of

recourse to were too harsh, and likely to outrage the feelings of the whole Rajpoot community. But I argued that those philanthropic men, Governor Duncan and Colonel Walker, never intended that the engagements which they induced the Jharijahs to enter into should be waste paper; and although I was aware that I was touching on delicate ground, I felt assured that I should find a powerful ally in those feelings of parental affection which exist in the human breast in every stage and degree of civilisation. The result has certainly proved I was not mistaken."—[*Minute, March* 28, 1851. *Bombay Consultations. MS. Records.*]

* See *ante*, pages 559, 560.

tyrannous mendicancy, which the Rajpoots feared to resist. The exorbitant fees claimed by these men,* who would have cursed the grudging giver, or, worse still in the estimation of the proud and sensitive Rajpoot, pilloried him with ridicule, constituted the heaviest tax levied upon the luckless father. It was admitted that these large sums of money were reluctantly paid—that the thraldom of this aristocratic custom sat heavily upon the tribes.† They would have escaped from it if they could, but they feared to take the responsibility of such an innovation upon themselves. The Durbars, timid and hesitating, though not unwilling to co-operate for the suppression of what they knew and acknowledged to be an abomination, shrunk from an authoritative demonstration without the open support and encouragement of the paramount power. They were fearful, indeed, of taking the initiative in such a procedure ; but if they could push forward the British Government as the instigators of the needed reform, they might venture to co-operate with us and set their seal upon the sumptuary enactments which our officers were eager to suggest.

The right men were in Rajpootana. Colonel Sutherland, Major Thoresby, and Major Ludlow, all gave their hearts to the work. The two great objects were these: firstly to limit the influx of these bards on the occasion of nuptial ceremonies—to keep out the incursion of foreigners,‡ who swelled the chorus of hungry appli-

* It is said that the Rana of Odeypore, though in an impoverished state at the time, gave a lakh of rupees to the chief bard. The profession, being a lucrative and not a laborious one, is considerably over-stocked. The Joudpore Vakeel stated that there were 20,000 Charans in Marwar, and sometimes 4000 or 5000 graced the nuptials of an important chief.

† This is very clearly stated by one of our political officers in Rajpootana, who has been forward in the good work of Infanticide-suppression. "Far from having prejudices to combat (as we should unquestionably have as regards the rite of Suttee, and to a certain extent in the question of Surna), we shall in the course proposed carry with us the sense of the whole of the Rajpoot tribes, who have hitherto been forced reluctantly by the tyranny of custom to destroy their female offspring."—[*Major Ludlow to Major Thoresby. MS. Records.*]

‡ That is, of Charans and Bhats not

cants ; and secondly, to fix a ratable amount to be paid to the domestic bards who were suffered to have a legitimate right to enrich themselves on these occasions. It was not difficult to persuade the princes of Rajpootana to enter into engagements for the enforcement of these measures, and to issue edicts enunciating them. Thus, instigated by Major Ludlow, the Jyepore Durbar, which was then the organ of an infant prince, sent forth "a proclamation of the Raj of Jyepore made by Major Ludlow and the Council of Regency," containing a forcible denunciation of the crime of Infanticide* and a clear specification of the suggested remedies. The lawful tax thenceforth to be paid was not to exceed a tithe of the annual income of the father of the bride. This was to be the maximum sum payable by the Jagheedars, but people with a less settled income were allowed only to disburse a smaller amount. The Jyepore authorities enforced these regulations with good effect; and Ludlow was soon able to report that an incursion of foreign bards had been successfully resisted, and had withdrawn, ungorged, unsatisfied, without a breach of the peace.

Nor was this all that was done. The other states, through Ludlow's instrumentality, were induced to follow the example of Jyepore. They responded, indeed, with acclamation to the appeal, and followed the letter of the Jyepore proclamation. Not one of the states, after these edicts were issued, admitted the foreign bards to their nuptial ceremonies. Indeed, so glad were the

belonging to the particular part of the country in which the marriage was celebrated, but who scented a far-off wedding as a jackal scents carrion, and hurried in flocks to their prey.

* "It is notorious that many Rajpoots kill their female daughters at the birth, and the cause would appear to exist in the distress and annoyance arising from the demand of Tyag (nuptial presents) on marriage occasions made by Charans, Bhats, &c., and from the abuse and revilings showered by these persons upon those who are not in circumstances to satisfy them to the extent of their demands. The act of Infanticide is a grievous tyranny and a great sin, which attaches alike to those who perpetrate it, and the sovereign in whose territory it occurs, and therefore the amounts receivable in future by Bhats, Charans, &c., are represented in this proclamation, &c., &c." —[*MS. Records.*] Cause and effect are here very plainly indicated. *Sublatâ causâ tollitur effectus.*

Thakoors to rid themselves entirely of the intolerable tyranny under which they had groaned so long, that they made the proclamations an excuse for not listening to the claims of their own "Bhats," and "Charans," whom they now learnt to send away empty-handed, under the pretext that the order of the Durbar for their payment must be first obtained. These people were the terror of Rajpootana. Their influence is now thoroughly broken down ; and they dare not even enforce the payment of the tithe permitted by the Sumptuary Regulations.

The effect of these measures on the great crime itself in Central India does not so distinctly appear as in the case of the Jharijah and other tribes of Kattywar, inasmuch as the results are not represented by a detailed census of the population. But it is not to be doubted that at least one great thing had been done. A change had been wrought in public opinion. It was clearly the interest of all classes of Rajpoots to resist a tax which often involved them in frightful pecuniary embarrassments. Nor was this all that was done. There was something more than an appeal to their purses. In Jyepore, Ludlow, seeing clearly where lay the only real remedy, exerted himself to appeal to their intelligence. He did everything that he could to encourage the diffusion of education in the states. And neither Suttee, nor Infanticide, nor Thuggee, nor human sacrifice, nor any other kindred abomination, can long stand up against so mighty a conqueror as that.

These measures for the suppression of Female Infanticide in Kattywar and in the Rajpoot states of Central India, it must be understood by the European reader, were carried on not within the dominions of the East India Company, but in the territories of the native princes over which we exercise only a moral control through the agency of our British Residents. But it may be asked whether, all this time, in our own provinces, there was no such thing as Female Infanticide. And I am afraid it must be answered that there *was*. The extent to which the crime was perpetrated, under our own immediate rule, was very limited; and it was confined to one or two collectorates. But still under the very eyes of British authority child-murder was going on, for some time, unchecked. The Purdah screened it from our sight. It was long before we ascertained the fact. And when we did ascertain its existence, both in Western and Central India, the evil appeared to be one not easily to be held in subjection. It may be thought that nothing could be easier than to drag the offenders into our criminal courts, and to convict them of the capital offence. And so it would have been if a woman had beaten out the brains of her child against the walls of the cutcherry or the magistrate's house. But perpetrated as the crime was in secret, nothing was more easy than accusation—nothing more difficult than conviction. The Regulations, powerful as they were, could not deal with this abstruse abomination.

The districts in Western and Central India, under which it was discovered that the crime of Infanticide was practised by certain tribes, were Ahmedabad, in the Bombay Presidency, and Mynpooree, under the government of the North-Western Provinces. In Ahmedabad the existence of the crime was first brought to the notice of Government by Mr. Fawcett, at the end of 1847. The disparity of the sexes had been pointed out to him by a native functionary, and he knew the meaning of that terrible sign. The native officer was instructed to exert himself to bring the chief people into an arrangement tending to annihilate the dreadful practice. They were not unwilling to discuss the subject. They assembled and set forth the facts of the case. Admitting the truth of the charge, they said it was simply the extreme costliness of marriage ceremonials which compelled the people of the child-murdering tribes to suppress the growth of female life. They knew that it was a great evil; and they entered into an agreement to reduce the sums paid, on these nuptial occasions, to less than an eighth of the old amount.* But, I fear that those compacts were not observed; and that the great evil was unsubdued. "Past experience," wrote Mr. Willoughby, in a Council-minute, "has unhappily elsewhere proved, that written agreements are insufficient to extirpate the offence, unless unceasing vigilance is exercised to secure adherence to them." And he then, in 1848, recommended that an annual census of the castes, in which the offence was supposed to be committed, should be forwarded to Government; and that the Sudder Judges should be requested to issue a circular to all magistrates, directing them to institute inquiries as to whether the crime was perpetrated in any part of the country within their jurisdiction. The result of that investigation was, that only among the marked tribes in the Ahmedabad and the Kaira collectorates were there any indubitable traces of the existence of the atrocity. Broach was suspected, but upon closer examination the suspicion was shown to be unfounded.†

* The compact was entered into by fifty-eight villages, inhabited by the Lewa Koombee tribe. The chief people promised to reduce the expenses paid them from 3800 to 480 rupees. The Lewa Koombees of the city of Ahmedabad afterwards came into the arrangement, and undertook to reduce their expenses to one-third of the whole amount.—[*Minute of Mr. Willoughby, Sept.* 9, 1848—1851. *MS. Records.*]

† In one of the answers returned, a circumstance is mentioned which illustrates the benefits derived from the publication of those summaries of facts which make up the staple-contents of "review articles :"

"Opposed to the conclusions thus derived," wrote one of the magistrates, "I confess to having approached the subject with no knowledge of my own, nor did the records of this magistracy in any way assist me; they were absolutely silent on the subject. Neither should I up to the present time have improved my stock of information, but for accidentally meeting with an able article in the *Calcutta Review* for August, 1844, from which, it appears, that Parliamentary Papers have been published giving the results of all the inquiries set on foot into the practice of female infanticide in Central and Western India; and I must here be permitted to suggest respectfully that a copy of this record would be of material importance in every Zillah, not only as conveying the most authentic information hitherto collected upon a most interesting topic, but as leading the uninformed into approved channels of further inquiry."—[*MS. Records.*]

Turning now to another part of the country, I would show what has recently been done in the neighbourhood of Mynpoorie. A statement on this subject was recently drawn up by Mr. Charles Raikes, magistrate and collector of that district. Originally published in a local periodical,* it was subsequently printed in a detached shape, and, in accordance with that system of diffusiveness of which I have spoken in another part of this work, widely circulated by order of the Government of the North-Western Provinces.† I cannot do better than quote from this paper the following statement of encouraging facts:

"Many of our readers will recollect the famine of 1838 (none, indeed, who were then in the N. W. Provinces will ever forget it), when mothers sold their children for a morsel of bread, when the rage of hunger obliterated even the distinctions of caste, and the Brahmin might be seen devouring the leavings of the Dhom. Nowhere did hunger and disease press heavier than in the plains of the mid Doab. Whole villages were depopulated, and every effort of public or private benevolence failed to meet the wants of a starving population. The Government did much to relieve the sufferers at the time, but a merely temporary assistance was not sufficient, and it became necessary to lower the revenue demand in many villages. Mr. Unwin, then collector of Mynpoorie, was in 1842 engaged in fixing the amount of this revision, and his camp was pitched in the midst of the villages of the Chohan Rajpoots. In the course of his proceedings it was found desirable to ascertain how far the population had been affected by the famine, and with this object Mr. Unwin determined to take ten villages in each pergunnah, and selecting one house in each of these villages, to count in person every head in it. 'In so doing,' we use his own words, 'I observed what previous information led me to expect, that no single Chohanee (female Chohan), young or old, was forthcoming. I remarked this to the Zemindars and people themselves, who, of course, were in numbers all about me on these occasions, and told them I knew the cause, and should look after them in future.'

* The *Benares Magazine.*

† It was subsequently embodied in Mr. Raikes' pleasant and instructive volume of "Notes on the North-Western Provinces of India," from which I now quote.

"Mr. Unwin acted with zeal and discretion, and above all things (in India) with *promptitude*. At once and on his own responsibility he established a system of watchful inspection, which was thus described by the officiating magistrate of Mynpoorie (in 1848), in reply to a call for information from the Court of Directors:

"'In Chohan villages the watchmen are ordered to give information of the birth of a female child forthwith at the police-station. A burkundauze goes to the house and sees the child, the thanadar informs the magistrate, upon which an order is passed, that after one month the health of the new-born child should be reported. The watchmen are further bound to give information if any illness attack the child, when a superior police-officer (either thanadar, jemadar, or mohurrir) at once goes to the village, sees the child, and sends a report to the magistrate. In suspicious cases the body of the child is sent for and submitted to the civil surgeon.'

"The effect of Mr. Unwin's measures was soon felt in the district. Amongst other incidents we may quote the following, as partaking of that almost grotesque character which in these matter-of-fact days seems peculiar to India. The Government had watched Mr. Unwin's proceedings with approbation, and took an early opportunity to notify in a public manner the interest which was felt in the success of his measures.

"There is at Mynpoorie an old fortress, which looks far over the valley of the Esun river. This has been for centuries the stronghold of the Rajahs of Mynpoorie, Chohans whose ancient blood, descending from the great Pirthee Raj and the regal stem of Neem-rana, represents *la crême de la crême* of Rajpoot aristocracy. Here, when a son, a nephew, a grandson, was born to the reigning chief, the event was announced to the neighbouring city by the loud discharge of wall-pieces and matchlocks; but centuries had passed away, and no infant daughter had been known to smile within those walls.

"In 1845, however, thanks to the vigilance of Mr. Unwin, a little grand-daughter was preserved by the Rajah of that day. The fact was duly notified to the Government, and a letter of congratulation and a dress of honor were at once despatched from head-quarters to the Rajah.

"We have called this incident, the giving a robe of honor to a man because he did not destroy his grand-daughter, a *grotesque* one ; but it is very far from being a ridiculous incident. When the people see that the highest authorities in the land take an interest in their social or domestic reforms, those reforms receive an impetus which no lesser influences can give them. The very next year after the investiture of the Rajah, the number of female infants preserved in the district was *trebled!* Fifty-seven had been saved in 1845 ; in 1846, one hundred and eighty were preserved ; and the number has gone on steadily increasing ever since. This is the best answer to those who would sneer at the *paternal* style of government, and who would advocate mere red-tape, law, and bayonets for the people of India.

" Influence is everything in Hindostan. Indeed in all countries good government, like true religion, depends upon influences and motives quite as much as upon mere rules and restrictions. In England, influence does *much ;* in India, we repeat, it does *all.* To go against the *law* is nothing to the native of India, but he rarely consents to go against the *magistrate.* When a government of mere law comes in, when *codes* instead of *men* are to rule India, the sooner the English are off to their ships the better. Let us see what local influence, supported by the influence of the Government, but scarcely assisted by legal sanction, has done for the suppression of female infanticide in Mynpoorie. In 1843, not a single female Chohan infant was to be found in the district; at the present moment there are fourteen hundred girls living, between the ages of one and six. We subjoin an extract from the official Registers, from 1844 to 1850, inclusive. The girls born during the year, and still alive at the end of the year, are only entered.

Name of Thannah.	1844.	1845.	1846.	1847.	1848.	1849.	1850.	Total.	Girls of 6 years and under, living in May, 1851.
Koorowlie ...	7	2	19	1	15	15	24	83	119
Shekoabad ...	9	8	2	6	13	15	22	75	80
Bhowgong ...	5	4	3	8	8	7	10	45	60
Koosmurra	11	3	3	2	5	3	17	44	55
Kurhul	1	7	5	4	9	7	10	43	33
Sumao	58	8	35	44	53	46	43	287	145
Mynpoorie ...	28	10	57	57	77	97	108	434	353
Ghurour	15	9	21	41	36	61	57	240	234
Sirsa-gunge	0	2	2	2	1	0	1	8	8
Kyleyee	0	4	25	43	29	38	43	182	140
Phurrah	0	0	8	1	15	13	13	50	38
Total	134	57	180	209	261	302	348	1491	1265

"To check these results, a census of the entire Chohan population of the district, of six years old and under, has been made in the present year. The plan adopted was, first to call upon the village accountants to report the number of boys and girls, up to the age of six, living in their respective villages. These returns were then tested as closely as possible by other independent officials, and, as the result of that examination, the number of females was reduced eleven per cent. The return thus corrected is as follows, and is given for pergunnahs, not for the thannahs, noted in the former table.

Names of Pergunnahs.	Boys 6 years and under.	Girls 6 years and under.
Ghurour	297	194
Souj	376	219
Kurhul	52	33
Koorowlie...	33	17
Mustúfabad and Shekoabad ...	474	299
Kishnee Nubbee Gunge... ...	261	102
Munchuna	364	246
Bhowgong...	283	150
Aleepoor Puttee	21	3
Total ...	2161	1263"

I will only add to this that Mr. Raikes himself has been active in this good work, and that he is now, I believe, pushing forward, with unabated energy and undiminished success, the good work of which he is here the exponent.

One more illustration of the good results of British interference must be adduced before I bring this chapter to a close. The practice of female infanticide was very prevalent on those Orissan hill-tracts, where Macpherson and Campbell achieved such great things for the suppression of the rite of human sacrifice. In some of the tribes it prevailed to such an extent, that no female infant was spared except when a woman's first child was a female. Villages containing a hundred houses were to be seen without a single female child. The practice had its origin in the social customs of the people, very different from those which obtain among the Rajpoots, of whom I have heretofore spoken. "So far," says Captain Macpherson, "is constancy to her husband from being required in a wife, that her pretensions do not, at least, suffer diminution in the eyes of either sex when fines are levied on her convicted lovers; while, on the other hand, infidelity on the part of a married man is held to be highly dishonorable, and is often punished by the deprivation of many social privileges. A wife, moreover, may quit her husband at any time, except within a year of her marriage, or when she expects offspring, or within a year after the birth of a child; and she may then return to her father's house, or contract a new marriage; while no man who is without a wife may, without entailing disgrace on himself and his tribe, refuse to receive any woman who may choose to enter his house and establish herself as its mistress. Now, a bridegroom gives for a wife of these tribes in which so few women are brought up, a large consideration in cattle and money. The sum is chiefly subscribed by his near relatives and his branch of his tribe, and is paid to his wife's father, who, again, distributes it amongst the heads of families of his own branch. But, when a wife quits her husband, he has a right to reclaim immediately from her father the whole sum paid for her; while the father, at the same time, becomes entitled to levy a like sum from any new husband to whom she may attach herself. And, it being observed that every man's tribe is at once answerable for all his debts, and bound in honor to enforce his claims, it will be understood that these restitutions and exactions, whether to be made betwixt persons belonging to different tribes or to different branches of the same tribe, must be, even in the simplest cases, productive of infinite difficulty and vexation; while they have given rise to three-fourths of the sanguinary quarrels and hereditary feuds which distract the Khond country. Thence, say the Khonds —'To any man but a rich and powerful chief, who desires to form connexions, and is able to make large and sudden restitutions, and to his tribe—a married daughter is a curse. By the death of our female infants before they see the light, the lives of men without number are saved, and we live in comparative peace.' "

I cannot afford to trace in detail the efforts which were made by Macpherson to root out this dreadful custom from among the Khonds. His exertions were characterised by the same energy and the same success as had attended his great crusade against human sacrifice. To use his own words: "The practice of female infanticide was suppressed in the greatest portion of the Khond country of Souradah, including Coradah, before the middle of 1844, and early in the present year throughout those Zemindaries—that the measures by which that change was accomplished materially affected the system of life and the chief interests of the Khond tribes, their aim being to establish an ascendancy over the Khond population founded upon a sense of benefits derived from their connexion with the Government—such as the benefit of justice, and that of protection in their intercourse with the low countries, and to remove the principal causes of infanticide, by preventing or settling disputes connected with property involved in marriage contracts, &c."* To this must be added, at least, an allusion to the interesting fact that the female victims, whom Macpherson had rescued, were given from time to time, when of ripe age, in marriage to men of the Khond tribes, and that these women put forth their influence most suc-

* *Capt. Macpherson to Mr. Halliday, Nov.* 11, 1846. *MS. Records.*

cessfully to wean the people from the hoary custom which had dwelt so cruelly among them.

I have every reason to believe that in this part of the country the efforts of our British officers have been attended with complete success, and that the good results of their humane efforts are likely to be abiding. The last report from the Khond agency contains these encouraging words:—"The lateness of the season," says Captain Campbell, "and the difficulty of procuring a sufficiency of water for my camp, prevented my visiting the infanticidal tribes, but many of the chiefs and a great number of the Meriah females, who had been married to Khonds of these tracts, visited me at Sooradah with their children, and from them I learnt with satisfaction that female children were now generally preserved; and in cases where they were destroyed it was done with great secrecy, and not openly as in former times. An officer of the Sebundies, well acquainted with the infanticidal tribes, and employed in superintending them, confirms this report."*

These good deeds require no gloss—I leave such statements to make their own way. It would be difficult to supply a fitting commentary, and impertinent to comment upon them in language not rising to the height of so great an argument. There are works which the English will leave behind them, mightier than any material fabrics which human skill can fashion and human labor construct. Let us rear what great substantial structures we may—and even in such works we are far surpassing the Moguls—History will be able to record nothing better of British rule in the East than that under the Government of the East India Company the widow ceased to burn herself on the funeral pile of her husband—the mother ceased habitually to destroy the

* *Colonel Campbell to the Government of India, April* 10, 1852. *MS. Records.*

infant life of her daughters—men ceased to purchase and to rear children for sacrifice to a cruel goddess—murder ceased to be a science and its practice an honorable profession—and that many wild tribes, by the conciliatory efforts of the servants of the Company, were weaned from a life of rapine, and raised from a state of barbarism, to become peaceful agriculturists and civilised rational men.*

* I have said nothing in this chapter about the suppression of Female Infanticide in Cutch, not because I was unmindful of the subject, but because I could not afford any further to extend the dimensions of this chapter. I believe that very gratifying progress has been made in that part of the world. My friend, Dr. Duff, when in Western India, was assured by the Rao (how interesting must have been a conversation on such a subject between two such men) that there had been, for some years, a gradual diminution of the great crime; and the assertion was satisfactorily proved by detailed statistics.

PART V.

CHAPTER I.

Native Education—Parliamentary Enactments—Encouragement of Oriental Literature—Rise and Progress of the Hindoo College—Substitution of the English System—Lord William Bentinck's Measures—Native Agency—Education in the North-Western Provinces—In Bombay—The Jubbulpore School of Industry—The Roorkhee College—Missionary Efforts—Statistics of Education.

In the two preceding books, I have treated largely of what may be called the institutional crimes of India. I have shown how human wickedness, on a gigantic scale, has been fostered by error and superstition; and how the servants of the Company have brought all their humanity, all their intelligence, and all their energy, to the great work of rooting out the enormities, which from generation to generation have grievously afflicted the land. I have shown how they have toiled and striven, and with what great success, to win the benighted savage to the paths of civilisation, and to purge the land of those cruel rites which their false gods were believed to sanction. There is nothing in all history more honorable to the British nation than the record of these humanising labors. It is impossible to write of them without a glow of pleasure and of pride.

But noble as have been these endeavours, and great as has been the success, which up to a certain point has attended them, there is something incredibly painful in the thought that, after all, they are fixed upon an insecure basis; that hitherto the action has been rather from without than from within; that we have not generally made an abiding impression upon the native mind; and that, therefore, there is always danger of relapse. In many of the cases which I have selected to illustrate the great victories of European civilisation, it will have been seen that it was the weight of external authority and personal influence which, more than anything else, enabled our countrymen to push forward their civilising measures to anything like a successful termination. The grand obstacle to complete and permanent success, was the gross ignorance of the people—that twofold ignorance which includes the darkness of the intelligence and the deadness of the moral sense. It was hard to awaken the heathens to a living belief in the absurdity of the superstitions to which they bowed themselves, and the wickedness of the practices which they observed.

In most cases, I say, the people yielded to the influences of authority, or were moved by self-interest, to conform outwardly to the wishes of their masters—but they were seldom convinced. It was a great thing to bring about even a diminution of these great crimes, which had inflicted so much misery upon countless thousands of our fellow-creatures. But having achieved this amount of success, our officers by no means thought that the work was complete. They felt it might often happen that the people, withdrawn from the immediate sphere of these good influences, would subside into their old evil ways—that, indeed, we might be only casting out devils, to return again to find their old habitations swept and cleansed for their reception, and to wanton there more riotously than before: and they one and all said that the only certain remedy, to which they could look for an abiding cure, was that great remedial agent—EDUCATION.

In many cases, the men of whose benevolent labors I have spoken, did their best, with the slender means at their disposal, to employ this great remedy in furtherance of their more substantial outward measures; but such educational efforts were necessarily local and accidental, and of limited application. Thus Sleeman had established Schools of Industry, at Jubbulpore, for the children of the Thugs; Outram had put to school in Candeish, the little Bheels, whose fathers he had reclaimed; and Macpherson had turned to similar account his opportunities in favor of the victims whom he had rescued from the hands of the sacrificing Khonds. And, doubtless, these benign endeavours will bear good fruit in their season. But the disease, at which we have to strike, is eating into the very life of the whole country; and it is only by a great and comprehensive effort that we can hope to eradicate it.

It is only within a comparatively recent period that the education of the people has taken any substantial shape in the administration of the British Government in the East. There was a sort of dim recognition, in some of the early charters, of the Christian duty of instructing the Gentoos; but it was not until the year 1813 that there was anything like a decided manifestation of the will of the Government in connexion with this great subject. The Charter Act, passed in that year, contained a clause, enacting that "a sum of not less than a lakh of rupees in each year shall be set apart and applied to the revival and improvement of literature, and the encouragement of the learned natives of India, and for the introduction and promotion of a knowledge of the sciences among the inhabitants of the British territories in India."* What

* *Act 53rd George III., chap.* 155, *clause* 43.

this might precisely mean was not very clear; but it seemed to point rather to the encouragement of Oriental than of European learning, and those were days in which the former was held to be of prodigious account. Nothing, however, for some years, of a practical character emanated from this decree of the Legislature. The money thus appropriated, was left to accumulate, and not until ten years after the Act had passed did the local Government take any steps to carry out its intentions. Then a Committee of Public Instruction was established in Calcutta, and the arrears of the Parliamentary grant were placed at their disposal.

Such, in a few words, are all the noticeable officialities of native education up to the year 1823. But there was a movement going on of which no record is to be found in official papers. All that the Government even at this time thought of doing for the education of the people, was through the agency of Pundits and Gooroos; but there were men then in Bengal who held Oriental learning at its true worth, as an instrument of civilisation, and thought that better things were to be found in the writings of the great masters of the English language. First in time, and foremost in enthusiasm among these, was Mr. David Hare. He was a man of a rude exterior and an uncultivated mind—by trade, I believe, a watchmaker. He lacked the power of expression both in oral and written discourse. But for these wants a large infusion of earnestness and perseverance in his character did much to atone; and he achieved what learned and eloquent men might have striven to accomplish in vain. He originated the Hindoo College of Calcutta. He stirred up others to carry out his designs. The seed which he scattered fell on good ground. Sir Hyde East, then Chief Justice of Bengal, took up the project with hearty good will;

and on the 14th of May, 1816, a public meeting was held in his house for the furtherance of this great object. The scheme was fully discussed by European and native gentlemen—and a few days afterwards, at an adjourned meeting, it was resolved that an institution should be founded to bear the name of the "Hindoo College of Calcutta." A committee and certain office-bearers were then appointed to give effect to the resolution.

It is generally the fate of great undertakings to be assailed by difficulties at the outset, and to struggle slowly into full success. The Hindoo College of Calcutta, in its infancy, put forth nothing but indications of a complete and humiliating failure. In January, 1817, the school was formally opened in the presence of Sir Hyde East, Mr. Harrington, and other influential gentlemen. Upwards of 6000*l*. had been raised by private contributions to give effect to the benevolent views of the projectors. But for some time there were thirty members on the committee, and only twenty pupils in the school. After the lapse of a few months the number on the books rose to seventy, and there for six years it remained. Every effort was made to render the institution acceptable to the natives of Calcutta. All sorts of compromises were attempted. The Bengallee and Persian languages were taught in the school—but still the people hung back, awed by the efforts to make their children familiar with the dangerous literature of the Feringhees. The college, indeed, was almost at its last gasp. European and native supporters were alike deserting it, when Mr. Hare came to the rescue. He sought the sustaining hand of Government; and he obtained what he sought.

This was in the year 1823, when, as I have said, the local Government first turned their serious attention to the subject of native education. They acceded to the request that was made in behalf of the Hindoo College; and stretched out their hands in time to save the institution from the premature extinction that menaced it. They had money then at their command for educational purposes, and although the encouragement of Oriental learning was uppermost in their thoughts, they consented to contribute towards the funds of the new institution, and undertook to erect a building for its use.* But having granted this material support, they naturally desired to exercise some authoritative control over the proceedings of the managers. It was proposed therefore to appoint, on the part of Government, a Visitor ostensibly to see that the money-grant was properly appropriated, but really to watch over and direct the management of the institution. This at first the Baboos resented; but there were some among them who were ready candidly to acknowledge, that after seven years' operation the college had produced nothing better than a few "krannees,"† and that little in the way of enlightened education was to be expected, except from a larger infusion of European energy and talent into the agency employed to carry out the designs of its founders.

The native managers yielded; and a medical officer in the service of the Company was appointed in the capacity of Visitor to give effect to the wishes of the Government. The Indian medical service, from that remote period when Joseph Hume called himself an assistant-surgeon, down to the present time, when the science of William O'Shaughnessy is about to annihilate space between the Indus and the Cauvery, has been bright with the names of distinguished men. But

* That is, it was resolved to construct a building which would answer the purposes both of a Sanskrit and a Hindoo college.

† A *krannee* is a clerk, in a Government or other office—but the word is hardly translatable into our language, as it by no means represents the high intelligence of the clerks in our own public establishments, or in our banking and mercantile firms.

I do not know that there is one member of that profession who has earned for himself a wider European reputation than Horace Hayman Wilson. He it was who, a quarter of a century ago, was appointed by authority to bring into good working order the fast-failing institution. A man of very varied accomplishments,* but with a predominant taste for Oriental literature, he was not likely to push to an excess the great educational reform which was now beginning to take shape in Bengal. But he threw no common amount of energy into all his proceedings. Under his hands paralysis became activity; exhaustion, strength; decadence, stability. The institution was soon in a state of vigorous energetic action. The Hindoo College became the fashion. Even the old bigoted Hindoo Baboos sent their children there without reluctance; and in the course of a few years, under Wilson's auspices, the class-lists contained the names of four hundred young Bengallees, many of them of good family and position, and all eager for the new knowledge which was opening out its fascinations before them.

But still there was nothing like a decided movement in favor of European learning. The Orientalists were paramount alike in the Vice-Regal city and the Provincial towns,† and Wilson himself was among the

* The following sketch of Professor Wilson's varied accomplishments is really not overcharged. It is written by one who differs widely from him on many essential points, and is uninfluenced by personal friendship :—"Perhaps no man since the days of the 'admirable Crichton,' has united in himself such varied, accurate, and apparently opposite talents and accomplishments. A profound Sanskrit scholar, a grammarian, a philosopher, and a poet, he was at the same time the life of society and a practical clear-headed man of business. On the stage as an amateur, or in the professor's chair as the first Orientalist of our time, he seemed always to be in his place. He has written on the antiquities, the numismatology, on the history, literature, chronology, and ethnology of Hindostan; and on all these subjects not even Colebrooke himself has written so much and so well. His works show all the erudition of the German school, without its heaviness, pedantry, and conceit; and his style is the best of all styles, the style of an accomplished English gentleman."—[*Calcutta Review.*]

† The oldest educational institution in India supported by Government, is the Mahomedan Madressa, established in 1781, under the auspices of Warren Hastings. About ten years afterwards the Sanskrit College, at Benares, was founded by Jonathan Dunn.

chief of them. "Previous to 1835," says Mr. Kerr, the present principal of the Hindoo College, in his Review of Public Instruction in Bengal, "all the larger educational establishments, supported by Government, with the exception of the Hindoo College of Calcutta, were decidedly Oriental in character. The medium of instruction was Oriental. The mode of instruction was Oriental. The whole scope of the instruction was Oriental, designed to conciliate old prejudices, and to propagate old ideas." Professors and teachers of the Oriental languages were liberally paid. Stipends were given to the students in the Oriental Colleges. Large sums of money were spent on the printing and the translation of books. But under the influence of such a system, little progress was made in the enlightenment of the natives of India. Such efforts did not rouse them from the sleep of apathy, or stimulate their appetite for knowledge. The whole thing, indeed, was a dreary failure, consummated at a large expense.

Nothing was clearer than this fact. It was as clear in Leadenhall-street as it was in Calcutta. The Court of Directors, before the close of 1830, had openly recognised the expediency of a vigorous movement in favor of European education, and had written out simultaneously to the Government of all the three Presidencies, clearly enunciating their views on the subject.* The letters which were then despatched to

* See, for example, the following passage of the letter of the 18th of February, 1829, to the Bombay Government:—"It is our anxious desire to afford to the higher classes of the natives of India the means of instruction in European science, and of access to the literature of civilised Europe. The character which may be given to the classes possessed of leisure and natural influence, ultimately determine that of the whole people. We are sensible, moreover, that it is our duty to afford the best equivalent in our power to these classes for the advantages of which the introduction of our Government has deprived them; and for this and other reasons, of which you are well aware, we are extremely desirous that their education should be such as to qualify them for higher situations in the civil government of India, than any to which natives have hitherto been eligible." The letters to the Bengal and Madras Governments are in the same strain.

India were conceived in a liberal and enlightened spirit. There was no reservation of the truth in them. They admitted that our assumption of the administration of the country had so far been injurious to the higher classes of the people of India as that it had deprived them of official employment; and urged that it was, therefore, the duty of the State to afford them "the best equivalent in their power." Nothing better could be offered than that sound European instruction which would gradually qualify them for restoration to much of the official employment of which they had been deprived. Lord William Bentinck was at this time at the head of the Government of India. His own unaided judgment had led him to similar conclusions; and he was well prepared to lay the axe to the trunk of the great tree of Oriental learning, with all its privileges and patronages, its monopolies and endowments. But it was not until 1835 that, thinking that as the old Charter of 1813 had been buried, the errors to which it had given birth might die with it, gave the death-blow to the Oriental system, and in a famous minute, dated March 7, thus declared his opinions:—

"His Lordship in Council is of opinion that the great object of the British Government ought to be the promotion of European literature and science among the nations of India, and that all the funds appropriated for the purposes of education would be best employed on English education alone.

"It is not the intention of his Lordship to abolish any college or school of native learning, while the population shall appear to be inclined to avail themselves of the advantages it affords.

"His Lordship in Council decidedly objects to the practice which has hitherto prevailed, of supporting the students during the period of their education. He conceives that the only effect of such a system can be to give artificial encouragement to branches of learning, which, in the natural course of things, would be superseded by more useful studies; and he directs that no stipend shall be given to any student, who may hereafter enter at any of these institutions; and that when any professor of Oriental learning shall vacate his situation, the Committee shall report to the Government the number and state of the class, in order that the Government may be able to decide upon the expediency of appointing a successor.

"It has come to the knowledge of his Lordship in Council, that a large sum has been expended by the Committee in the printing of Oriental works. His Lordship in Council directs that no portion of the funds shall hereafter be so employed.

"His Lordship in Council directs that all the funds, which these reforms will leave at the disposal of the Committee, be henceforth employed in imparting to the native population a knowledge of English literature and science through the medium of the English language."

Never was any reformation more complete and irresistible than this. The Orientalists stood aghast before it, for there lay their idol broken at their feet. The President of the Educational Committee, Mr. Shakespear, had thrown up his office in anticipatory disgust. But there were men of higher intelligence on the other side —men who had prompted Lord William Bentinck, and were now eager to support him. Foremost among these were Macaulay and Trevelyan.* The former

* I had written this before the appearance of Mr. Cameron's "Address to Parliament on the Duties of Great Britain to India in respect of the Education of the Natives," made me acquainted with the language of Mr. Macaulay's minute of the 2nd of February, 1835, in which he reviews, in a masterly manner, the whole question of Government patronage of education. I cannot refrain from quoting the conclusion of this paper:

"I would strictly respect all existing interests. I would deal even generously with all individuals who have had fair reason to expect a pecuniary provision. But I would strike at the root of the bad system which has hitherto been fostered by us. I would at once stop the printing of Arabic and Sanscrit books. I would abolish the Madrassa and the Sanscrit College at Calcutta. Benares is the great seat of Brahmanical learning; Delhi, of Arabic learning. If we retain the Sanscrit College at Benares and the Mahometan College at Delhi, we do enough, and much more than enough in my opinion, for the Eastern languages. If the Benares and Delhi Colleges should be retained, I would at least recommend that no stipends shall be given to any students who may hereafter repair thither, but that the people shall be left to make their own choice between the rival systems of education without being bribed by us to learn what they have no desire to know. The funds which would thus be placed at our disposal would enable us to give larger encouragement to the Hindoo College at Calcutta, and to establish in the principal cities throughout the Presidencies of Fort William and Agra schools in

seated himself in the vacant President's chair; and from that time English education has been as dominant in the chief Government schools throughout India, as before it was languid and depressed.

But by the reader ignorant of all the bearings of the great educational controversy which twenty years ago agitated the learned world of Bengal, and was echoed in the other presidencies of India, it must not be supposed that Lord William Bentinck and his supporters ever contemplated the degradation of the vernacular. The blow which they struck was aimed not at the living but at the dead languages of the country—at the Sanscrit and the Arabic—at languages which were not employed as vehicles of intercommunication, and which contained little in their books to elevate the mind, to invigorate the understanding, or to facilitate the business of life. The importance of the vernacular language as a medium of instruction was admitted; perhaps, with no great heartiness and sincerity. The Court of Directors, however, had consistently urged upon the local Governments the expediency of promoting the extension of indigenous education.* And now the

which the English language might be well *and thoroughly taught*.

"If the decision of his Lordship in Council should be such as I anticipate, I shall enter on the performance of my duties with the greatest zeal and alacrity. If, on the other hand, it be the opinion of the Government that the present system ought to remain unchanged, I beg that I may be permitted to retire from the chair of the Committee. I feel that I could not be of the smallest use there. I feel, also, that I should be lending my countenance to what I firmly believe to be a mere delusion. I believe that the present system tends, not to accelerate the progress of truth, but to delay the natural death of expiring errors. I conceive that we have at present no right to the respectable name of a Board of Public Instruction. We are a board for wasting public money, for printing books which are of less value than the paper on which they are printed was while it was blank; for giving artificial encouragement to absurd history, absurd metaphysics, absurd physics, absurd theology; for raising up a breed of scholars who find their scholarship an encumbrance and a blemish, who live on the public while they are receiving their education, and whose education is so utterly useless to them that, when they have received it, they must either starve or live on the public all the rest of their lives. Entertaining these opinions, I am naturally desirous to decline all share in the responsibility of a body which, unless it alters its whole mode of proceeding, I must consider not merely as useless, but as positively noxious.

"T. B. MACAULAY."

* See the Court's letter to Bengal, written in September, 1829: "We must put you on your guard against a disposition of which we perceive some traces

educational authorities declared themselves in nowise willing to deprive the people of the most obvious means of acquiring information through the spoken languages of the country; and directed that in all the Government colleges and schools the cultivation of the vernacular should go hand in hand with that of the English language.*

It was in furtherance of this great object of encouraging the study of the spoken languages of the country, that in the beginning of 1835, Mr. William Adam, a gentleman of considerable local experience, and of a thoughtful inquiring mind, who had originally gone out to India as a Baptist missionary, but who had lapsed into Socianism, and become the editor of a Calcutta journal, was despatched by Lord William Bentinck on a special commission, to inquire into the state of indigenous education in Bengal and Behar. He prosecuted his inquiries with great earnestness, and amassed an immense store of information relating to the state of the vernacular schools, and, indeed, the general condition of native society in those pro-

in the general Committee, and still more in the local Committee of Delhi, to underrate the importance of what may be done to spread useful knowledge among the natives, through the medium of books and instruction in their own languages. That more complete education, which is to commence by a thorough study of the English language, can be placed within the reach of a very small proportion cf the natives of India; but intelligent natives, who have been thus educated, may, as teachers in colleges and schools, or as the writers and translators of useful books, contribute in an eminent degree to the more general extension among their countrymen of a portion of the acquirements which they have themselves gained, and may communicate in some degree to the native literature, and to the minds of the native community, that improved spirit which it is to be hoped, they will themselves have imbibed from the influence of European ideas and sentiments." — [*The Court of Directors to the Government of Bengal, September* 28, 1830, *quoted in Mr. Willoughby's Minute.*]

* See the following manifesto on the subject put forth by the Committee of Public Instruction:

"The general committee are deeply sensible of the importance of encouraging the cultivation of the vernacular languages. That they do not consider that the order of the 7th of March precludes this, and they have constantly acted on this construction. In the discussions which preceded that order, the claims of the vernacular languages were broadly and prominently admitted by all parties; and the questions submitted for the decision of Government only concerned the relative advantage of teaching English on the one side, and the learned Eastern languages on the other."

vinces. The reports which he furnished to Government are as interesting as they are instructive. The great fact which they set forth, clearly and unmistakeably, was, that there was very little education of any kind in Bengal and Behar, and that that little was lamentably bad. In some thannas, or police divisions, the per centage of educated youth—taking the period of education to lie between the fifth and the fourteenth years—was as low as two-and-a-half. In others it was much higher. But it was shown, at the same time, with equal clearness, that the per centage of adult education was considerably lower. And Mr. Adam arrived at the conclusion, "that within a comparatively recent period, certain classes of the native population, hitherto excluded by usage from vernacular instruction, have begun to aspire to its advantages, and that this hitherto unobserved movement in native society has taken place to a greater extent in Bengal than in Behar. Such a movement apparently will have the effect which has been found actually to exist—that of increasing the proportion of juvenile instruction as compared with that of adult instruction, and of increasing it in a higher ration in Bengal than in Behar." This mission did something for vernacular education; but, doubtless, it was not much.

The system established by Lord William Bentinck has been maintained with little variation by his successors. The Committee of Public Instruction, now known as the Council of Education, has numbered among its members some of the ablest and most enlightened men who have ever braved the damp heats of Bengal.* Under their superintendence, encouraged alike by the local and the home Governments, they have given due effect to this system, and the result has

* The Council of Education is an honorary Board with a salaried secretary. It is composed partly of European gentlemen (some of them not in the Company's service) and partly of natives.

been, that with the aid of a highly-cultivated staff of educational officers, they have rendered a large number of Hindoo and Mahomedan youths familiar with the amenities of European literature. The proficiency attained in the principal scholastic institutions is such as is very rarely acquired by boys of the same age in any other country in the world. I do not believe that there are half a dozen boys at Eton or Harrow who could explain an obscure passage in Milton or Shakspeare, or answer a series of historical questions, extending from the days of Alexander to the days of Napoleon, with as much critical acuteness and accuracy of information, as the white-muslined students who, with so much ease, master the difficult examination-papers which it has taxed all the learning and all the ingenuity of highly-educated English gentlemen of ripe experience to prepare, would in any such trial of skill put our young aristocrats to confusion.

All this is past dispute—the proficiency is admitted. But there has seldom been much more than the proficiency of the clever boy. A very few exceptional cases, just sufficient to prove the rule on the other side, might be adduced to show that European education *has* struck deep root in the native mind; but the good seed commonly fell by the way-side, and the birds of the air devoured it. All the enervating and enfeebling environments of Indian life, at the critical period of adolescence, closed around the native youth, to stupify and to deaden both the intellectual faculties and the moral sense. The Hookah and the Zenana did their sure work. And in a year or two there was little left of the bright-faced, quick-witted boy who could put the Penseroso into good English prose, tell you who were Pepin and Charles Martel, and explain the character of the "self-denying ordinance" as accurately as Hallam or Macaulay.

The children of India were, perhaps, the most impressionable—the most teachable children in the world. But, left to itself, the impression was soon effaced; the teaching soon became profitless. The mere mechanical power of reading and writing remained. The native students became expert penmen, and remained expert penmen to the last. Much of the copying work in the Government offices had long been done by them. But it was impossible to read any number of documents so copied without the conviction that the copyist had brought the smallest possible amount of intelligence to bear upon his work. The eye seemed to communicate directly with the hand; there was no intervention of the brain. The process was merely that of the machine. The member was instructed—but the mind was not cultivated. The intelligence of the well-tutored boy was seldom carried into the practicalities of actual life.

It was mainly to remedy this evil—to check the retrograde tendency of which I speak—that under the administration of Lord Auckland, certain scholarships were founded in the principal Government institutions. It was obvious that any system which would have the effect of riveting the knowledge, which we imparted, on the minds of the students, and preserving their literary ardor from early extinction, would confer great benefits on the people. Of infinite moment was it that the native student should not glide away from beneath the eye of his preceptor, just at that most important stage of life when the boy passes over the bridge to manhood. The scholarship system was designed to render the effects of all this good Government teaching rather an abiding influence than a transitory impression. And as far as its advantages have extended, I believe that there is a solid reality in them. In all the Presidencies of India scholarships have been founded, both in connexion with the English and the Vernacular schools. And this alone is sufficient to associate the administration of Lord Auckland honorably with the cause of native education.

But the good effect of this encouragement was necessarily limited. Something more was required to give a general impulse to native education, even among the more influential classes of society. The Court of Directors, it has been seen, had always associated native education with official employment, and the local governments had, partially at least, given effect to the wishes of the Court. But it seemed that a more authoritative declaration of the views of Government should now be put forth, with respect to this important matter of public employment—that something, indeed, in the shape of a pledge, should be given to the educated natives, that their claims would be duly regarded. Lord Hardinge, before he was compelled to push aside the portfolio and take the sword into his hand, had given his mind earnestly to the subject of native education. Regarding it both in connexion with its general effects upon the elevation of the national character, and upon the qualification of the people for employment in the public service, he came to the conclusion that conformably both with the decrees of the Legislature, and the expressed desire of the Court of Directors, those objects would be best attained by a more authoritative enunciation of the views of Government—by a specific declaration that it was their intention, thenceforth, to recognise a certain educational test of qualification for the public service, and by so doing, both to encourage the diffusion of knowledge, and to raise the character of the native agency employed in the service of the State. Whether education were to be promoted that this agency might be improved, or whether these inducements were to be offered that education might be promoted, was in reality of little consequence, so long as the reciprocal action of the two was secured. Lord Hardinge believed that both ends could be attained by an authoritative enunciation of his views and intentions; and he prepared a minute, which has since become very famous in the later history of native education, wherein, under date, October 10, 1844, he thus declares the intentions of the Government:—

"The Governor-General, having taken into his consideration the existing state of education in Bengal, and being of opinion that it is highly desirable to afford it every reasonable encouragement, by holding out to those who have taken advantage of the opportunity of instruction afforded to them, a fair prospect of employment in the public service; and thereby not only to reward individual merit, but to enable the State to profit as largely and as early as possible, by the result of the measures adopted of late years for the instruction of the people, as well by the Government as by private individuals and societies, has resolved, that in every possible case, a preference shall be given, in the selection of candidates for public employment, to those who have been educated in the institutions thus established, and especially to those who have distinguished themselves therein by a more than ordinary degree of merit and attainment."

To the Council of Education, as the general educational executive, it was left to carry out the details of a scheme at once liberal and wise; but it often happens that the wise liberality of an original project, passed through the filtre of mechanical detail, is purged of all its heartiness and sincerity, and weakened and reduced to something narrow and exclusive, and most unlike the first design. Lord Hardinge's minute was subjected to this process of filtration; and all its catholicity was left behind in the machine. The Council of Education prescribed a test, based entirely on the educational system of the Government colleges,* so that the pupils of those institutions which had been established "by private individuals and societies" were practically excluded from the competition.

The Court of Directors entirely disapproved of this decision. "It appears to us," they wrote, "that the standard can only be attained by the students in the Government colleges, and that therefore it virtually gives to them a monopoly of public patronage." "We are also of opinion," they added, "that this high test, instead of promoting, will in effect discourage the general acquisition of the English language. Those who cannot hope to pass this test will not think it worth their while to bestow any time upon learning the English language, at least with a view to employment in the public service." And they argued that men might be well qualified by their general character and attainments for public employment, although they were but imperfectly acquainted with the writings of Shakspeare and Ben Jonson, or, indeed, with the English language at all. "Where from local circumstances," they said, "the persons whom it would be most desirable to employ are found deficient in that knowledge, we would not, on that account, peremptorily exclude them from employment, though other qualifications being equal, or nearly so, we would allow a knowledge of the English language to give a claim to preference."

Nothing could have been heartier than the wish of the Court to have ever "at their disposal a body of natives qualified by their habits and acquirements to take a larger share, and occupy higher situations in

* The examination was to be similar to that to which candidates for the senior scholarships at the Calcutta and Hooghly colleges were subjected.

civil administrations than had hitherto been the practice." But this liberal desire soon overleapt itself. For the native students, encouraged by the known wishes of the Court, and the declarations of the local Government, so strove to qualify themselves for office, and so eagerly sought Government employ, that many were necessarily disappointed. Employment could not readily be found for them. And this discouraging, though inevitable fact, was emphatically pointed out by some of the heads of colleges to the superintending authorities. Thus, in the report of the Delhi College for 1850, it is stated, that " several of the more advanced students had, during the past year, been attending the civil courts, with the view of familiarising themselves with the forms of official business. The officiating principal, in noticing this, remarked, that from the press of competition, it not unfrequently happened that youths, whose qualifications were undoubted, remained long after quitting the college without any provision. He therefore proposed that any *élève* of the college who could procure a certificate of his fitness for official employment from the officer whose court he had been attending, should at once be appointed a supernumerary, on a small salary, till such time as a vacancy might occur. " The principal of the Benares College also observed, that much difficulty was experienced even by his best pupils in their search for employment after quitting the college. He therefore proposed that the passing of an examination of some fixed and high standard should entitle the successful student to immediate employment under Government, on a salary of 30 rupees (per mensem) or thereabouts : should no vacancy exist at the moment, the passed candidate might be directed to prosecute his studies at the college, and to employ himself under the direction of the committee in the preparation of translations and treatises in the vernacular."—"A class," it was added, "like that of the fellows of our English colleges would thus be formed, the members of which might be drafted off as their services were required, into the educational or other departments."

But these proposals did not altogether meet the approbation of the authorities. It was declared that there was no reluctance on the part of heads of departments to employ the passed students of the Government colleges and schools—that on the other hand every practicable effort would be made to afford them the encouragement which they sought; but that it was clearly impossible to find employment in the Government service for all candidates urging the claims of a collegiate education; and that it was inexpedient that a general impression should obtain among them that such education conferred upon them any *right* to official employment. No Government in the world could afford systematically to recognise such claims. It is one thing to hold out an inducement to exertion by showing that successful efforts will strengthen the chances of obtaining official employment; another, to admit that such efforts constitute a prescriptive right to office. All that Government could possibly do was to hold out encouragements of the former class. It was clearly impossible to pledge themselves to the latter.

It would appear from these statements that considerable difficulty has attended the efforts which have been made to give practical effect to the wise and benevolent intentions of the Court of Directors. The design was one of a reciprocal beneficial action—the hope of public employment giving an impulse to education, and education mightily improving the character of the public service. But there was a defect in the national character which did much to embarrass the practical working of this admirable design. The natives of India, when once their expectations are raised, lean with child-like helplessness on the strong arm of Government, and, instead of exerting themselves, believe that everything will be done for them. Instead of something conditional, they thought that they saw something absolute in the promises of Government, and believed that they had only to conform to a certain test to secure official employment. The tendency of this was to give them narrow and exclusive views of the advantages of education, and greatly to limit private enterprise.

It was clearly mischievous that the natives should look upon official employment as the one great aim and end of education. Mr. Cameron, therefore, did wisely when he cautioned the native students of Bengal against this dangerous delusion. "Do not imagine," he said, "that the sole or the main use of a liberal education is to fit yourselves for the public service; or rather do not imagine that the public can only be served by the performance of duties in the offices of Government . . . Besides the public service and the pursuits of literature and science, there are open to you the learned professions, law, medicine, the highly honorable profession of a teacher, and that which has but lately become a profession, civil engineering."* It was a great thing that the natives should be encouraged to cultivate their minds by the promise of the high reward of official employment; but it was a still greater thing that they should learn to rely on themselves—to look to education as the means of independent advancement in life. So often is it that in the very best of human designs, there is some germ of failure at the bottom.

In the mean while a great experiment was going

* Address of the President (Mr. Cameron) of the Council of Education to the students under its superintendence.—[*Cameron's Address to Parliament, &c.*]

on in the North-West. In 1845 circular letters were addressed to all the revenue-collectors, calling their especial attention to the subject of education. These letters are a model of sound practical sense combined with the purest benevolence. They set forth a general admission that "the standard of education amongst the people is very low;" and then they proceed to show that "causes are at work, which tend rapidly to raise the standard and improve the intellectual state of the whole population." These causes were mainly to be found in the operation of the new settlement. "The people of Hindostan," continues the secretary of the North-Western Government, "are essentially an agricultural people. Anything "which concerns their land immediately rivets their "attention and excites their interest. During the late "settlement a measurement has been made, and a map "drawn of every field in these provinces, and a record "formed of every right attaching to the field. The "'Putwaree's' papers, based upon this settlement, con-"stitute an annual registry of these rights, and are re-"gularly filed in the collector's office. They are com-"piled on an uniform system, and are the acknowledged "groundwork of all judicial orders regarding rights in "land." The case thus stated, as between the Government and the agriculturist, the former proceeded to show the direct interest which every man had, under such a system, in the education of himself and his children. "It is important," they wrote, "for his own "protection that every one possessing any interest in "the land should be so far acquainted with the prin-"ciples on which these papers are compiled as to be "able to satisfy himself that the entries affecting "himself are correct. There is thus a direct and "powerful inducement to the mind of almost every "individual to acquire so much of reading, writing, "arithmetic, and mensuration, as may suffice for the "protection of his rights; until this knowledge be "universal, it is vain to hope that any great degree "of accuracy can be attained in the preparation of "the papers."*

Thus, for the first time, was it plainly manifested to the people, that the maintenance of their individual rights was dependent upon their own power of ascertaining them—that without the rudiments of education they were liable to be wrongfully dealt with—that, in short, the power of reading and writing was essential to the very life of an agricultural population. An appeal was thus directly made to the self-interest of the people. It was something that every one could understand; and was far more likely to be responded to by the rude peasants of Upper India than any abstract propositions regarding the value of learning and the duty of improving the mind. But although this was to be the beginning, it was not to be the end. It was believed that if self-interest were to lead them a little way along the paths of learning, they would be induced by higher motives to advance further in the march of mind. "When the mind of the whole people," it was said, "has thus been raised to a sense of the importance of knowledge, it is natural to suppose that many from the mass will advance further, and cultivate literature for the higher rewards it offers, or even for the pleasure which its acquisition occasions."†

* Three years afterwards it was declared that the progress of time had tended to confirm these views of the connexion between the revenue-system and the education of the country:—"Subsequent experience has confirmed the lieutenant-governor in his opinion that those features of our present revenue-system, which affect the registration of all landed property, afford the proper means by which the mass of the people may be roused to a sense of the importance of sound elementary instruction. If the people at large continue as ignorant as they now are, the system cannot work out for them all the advantages it is calculated to produce. These advantages are so palpable to their minds, that when rightly apprehended they form the strongest incentive to any exertion which will secure their attainment."—[*Government of North-Western Provinces to Government of India, April* 19, 1848.]

† *Ibid.*

For the furtherance of these ends the collectors were exhorted, above all things, to endeavour to carry the people with them—not to think of introducing novel and barely intelligible systems among them—but to accommodate themselves, as far as possible, to existing institutions. "Judicious encouragement," it was said, "would promote the formation of village schools, and enlist in the work of education the persons whom the people themselves might select as their teachers and support for that purpose." The preparation of a series of village school-books was commenced for circulation among the people. Detailed instructions were given to the Tehsildars, or native revenue-officers, who were to be employed as the immediate agency for the persecution of this scheme; and the utmost endeavour was made to collect, from all parts of the provinces, detailed educational statistics wherefrom to construct the groundwork of their operations. It was not the design of the Government to establish schools of its own, but to encourage the maintenance of old institutions, and to stimulate the people to extend the benefits of the existing system.

The statistical inquiries, thus directed, were pushed forward with hearty good-will. To the majority of those concerned in the new settlement it was a congenial task. A valuable series of reports was thus prepared, and a vast mass of information was collected. The aggregate result was a deplorable picture of the state of education in Upper India. It was ascertained that "on an average less than 5 per cent. of the youth who are of an age to attend schools obtain any instruction, and that instruction which they do receive is of a very imperfect kind."*

* *Government of the North-Western Provinces to Government of India, November* 18, 1846.

In the preface to the "Memoir on the Statistics of Indigenous Education within the North-Western Provinces of the Bengal Presidency," to which I am indebted for the information contained

To supply this grievous want, Mr. Thomason now proposed the endowment of a school in every considerable village. The plan which he desired to carry out he believed to be in accordance with the feelings of the people and the character of their institutions. He suggested that the endowment should be secured by small grants of land—that jagheers of from five to ten acres each, yielding a rental varying from twenty to forty rupees per annum, should be granted to the village communities for the purpose of maintaining their schoolmasters. But this proposal* did not meet the approbation of the Court of Directors. They acknowledged, in the most unqualified manner, "the necessity for giving some powerful impulse to elementary education in the North-Western Provinces." They declared themselves "prepared to sanction the adoption of some more comprehensive plan of extending and improving the means of popular instruction throughout the country;" but they doubted the expediency of sanctioning the proposed plan of landed endowments.

in this and some of the following pages, Mr. R. Thornton, the compiler, says:—"Out of a population, which numbered in 1848, 23,200,000 souls, and in which were consequently included more than 1,900,000 males of a school-going age, we can trace but 68,200 as in the receipt of any education whatever. In Prussia nine-tenths of this portion of the population is stated to be under instruction. In Russia, the most barbarous of the European monarchies, the proportion is as one to nine. In India, even with a large allowance for those receiving domestic and private education, it is as one to twenty-five. Low, however, as this proportion is, it is only when considered in connexion with the degree of information imparted, that it conveys any idea of the extent of the deficiency to be supplied." But it was not only that the per centage was very low in comparison with that exhibited by the educational statistics of Europe, but that as compared with the state of the Lower Provinces of Bengal—the darkness of the Upper seemed to be very apparent. "Assuming," said the Agra Government, "boys from the commencement of their fifth to the end of their fourteenth year to be of an age best adapted for receiving instruction, it is calculated that, in the Lower Provinces, the per centage of such boys now receiving instruction varies from 32 in Bengal to a little more than 5 in Behar. In Bombay it appears to vary from 7 to 13. In Agra, one of the most favored districts in these provinces, it is only 5½."

* The proposal was supported by an argument of a general kind, worthy of notice. "It is the standing reproach of the British Government," wrote the Agra secretary, "that whilst it continually resumes the endowments of former sovereigns, it abstains from making any, even for those purchases which it considers most laudable. The present measure will in some degree remove this reproach, and that in a manner most acceptable to the feelings of the people at large."

"It has, no doubt," they wrote, "the advantages "ascribed to it, and is apparently the most economical "arrangement for effecting the object proposed. En-"dowments of land are, however, open to obvious "objection. They have an inherent tendency to assume "the character of permanent and hereditary property, "independent of any reference to the tenure by which "they were originally held. An actual occupant, even "should he prove inefficient, would think himself de-"prived of a right if he was removed, and a son would "claim to succeed to his father whether he were com-"petent or not. The evil would be aggravated by the "extreme difficulty of exercising a vigilant control "over such numerous establishments, and in one or "two generations it might happen that the alienation "of revenue would be of little avail in securing the "education of the people."*

Moved by these considerations, the soundness of which is not to be denied, the Court declared themselves in favor of the expediency of moneyed payments. They were ready, they said, to give their attention to any plan inviting the payment of monthly stipends to the village schoolmasters, or a direct expenditure of money in any other manner most likely to secure the great end of the diffusion of knowledge among the people. "Too thankful for the liberality of these concessions to lay any stress on the rejection of his particular scheme," Mr. Thomason now set himself with earnestness to devise a plan which should meet the wishes of the Court. He frequently discussed the best mode of accomplishing this object with all the officers of Government with whom he came into communication in the course of his annual tour. And the result of this discussion was a strong convic-

* *Despatch of Court of Directors, August* 25, 1847.

tion that the system of moneyed payments to village schoolmasters was open to very grave objections. He proposed, therefore, that the ordinary village schools should remain as before, self-supporting institutions; but that in every tehseldarree, or revenue-district, a model school should be established at the general expense, "to provide a powerful agency for visiting all the indigenous schools, for furnishing the people and the teachers with advice, assistance, and encouragement, and for rewarding those schoolmasters who may be found the most deserving."* To each district was to be attached a Zillah visitor and three Pergunnah visitors—the system being one of visitation and superintendence—and these officers were to be emphatically enjoined "to conduct themselves with the greatest courtesy both to the people at large and to the village teachers." They were carefully to avoid anything that might offend the prejudices or be unnecessarily distasteful to the feeling of those with whom they have communication. "Their duty," it was added, "will be to persuade, encourage, assist, and reward, and to that duty they will confine themselves."

It was calculated that this scheme, when carried out in all its completeness, would necessitate an expenditure of about 20,000*l.* per annum. A partial experiment was proposed in the first instance; and it was suggested at the same time that a visitor-general should be selected from among the civil servants of the Company to communicate with the subordinate agency, to direct and control their operations, and secure the efficient working of the entire scheme. The Court of Directors sanctioned the arrangement; and a Resolution of the Government of the North-Western Pro-

* *Government of the North-Western Provinces to Government of India, April* 19, 1848.

vinces, dated 9th of February, 1850, formally inaugurated the plan.

Turning now to the general statistics of education, it would appear from the most recent statements that there are in the Lower Provinces of the Bengal Presidency 30 Government colleges and schools in which English is taught—that these schools are conducted by 283 masters, and that the number of pupils receiving instruction in them is 5465 ; and that among these 291 scholarships, of the annual value of 5000*l.* in all, are held up for competition. In the same part of the country there are 33 Government Vernacular schools, with 104 pupils, and 4685 scholars. The entire annual expenditure upon English and benevolent schools in Lower Bengal is about 38,000*l.**

In the North-Western Provinces there are 7 colleges and schools, supported by Government, in which English is taught. In these there are 112 masters, 1582 pupils, and 232 scholarships, of the value of about 2300*l.* Besides these are 8 model schools, of the origin and intent of which I have spoken. The total expenditure in the North-Western Provinces amounts to 13,350*l.*

It appears from the same official record that, under the Madras Presidency, there is only one school in which English is taught—the Madras University High School—with 13 masters and 180 pupils. The number of Vernacular schools seems to be uncertain. The gross expenditure is 4350*l.* Education is in a more depressed condition in Madras than in any other part of the Company's territories.

From Bombay the reports are more encouraging. It

* In the last Report of Public Instruction in Lower Bengal (1853), prepared since these statistics were made out, it is stated that, "during the past year (1852), there were in the Government institutions of Bengal, including the Vernacular schools, upwards of 11,000 pupils, of whom 103 were Christians, 791 Mahomedans, 189 Arricanese, Thugs, Bhaugulpore Hill boys, and Coles—and the rest Hindoos."

appears that there are 14 Government colleges and schools in which English is taught, with 62 masters and 2066 scholars, amongst whom 84 scholarships of the aggregate annual value of 588*l.* are divided. Besides these there are 233 Vernacular schools, with the same number of masters and 11,394 students. The total expenditure, on account of education in this Presidency, is 15,000*l.*

It would appear from these statements that the annual expenditure on account of education in the three Presidencies is about 70,000*l.* The Madras returns being imperfect, the actual number of pupils under instruction in the Government schools cannot be given. Perhaps it may be estimated at about 30,000.

The number of scholars in the Government schools has, with a few exceptions, steadily increased. Thus, in the Hindoo College of Calcutta, in 1833, there were 318 pupils; the last returns (1851) exhibit a total of 471. In the medical college of Calcutta the advance has been rapid and striking. In 1835 there were 67 students on the books; the last returns show that the number had risen to 228. In the Dacca College the number has risen from 144, in 1835, to 383 in 1851. In the Midnapore School the number was 45 in 1836, and 125 in 1851. In the Chitagong School there has been an advance from 61 in 1837, to 125 in 1851. In Sylhet, from 62, in 1843, to 114 in 1851. These cases are all taken from the returns of the Lower Provinces of Bengal.* There are no comparative tables to the same extent in the reports from other parts of the country. The last Bombay reports give the returns of Vernacular education for the last two years, from which it would appear that in 1851 there were 10,965 pupils, and in 1852, 11,088. I can only gather the progress in the North-Western Provinces from scattered fragments in the different detailed reports. Thus, from

* In the last Report of the Committee of Public Instruction.

Saugor, it is reported that "the applications for admittance to the English class had exceeded in number those of any previous year, and the desire for English knowledge was evidently on the increase, whilst the institution generally appeared to be appreciated by the inhabitants of Saugor, and was resorted to by the children of all classes." From Jubbulpore it is reported that "the constituency of the school had increased during the past year by 94 pupils, a result which the head master attributed to the increased favor with which the institution was regarded by the inhabitants of Saugor and its vicinity." From the Delhi College it is reported, that in 1848 the number of pupils in the English departments was 218; and in the following year 234. From the last report of the Madras University, it would appear that the number of pupils had risen in the last year to 180 from 173, the number in the preceding year.

It is clearly beyond the scope of a mere chapter on Native Education to treat in detail of the different institutions established and supported by the East India Company. But there are two or three, of an exceptional and so interesting a character, that I must devote a few pages to them before the chapter is brought to a close. I think that the foundation of the Medical College of Calcutta is one of the greatest facts in the recent history of Indian Administration. Half a century ago, a project for the establishment of an institution, intended to convey to the natives of India instruction in European medical and surgical science, would have been scouted as the chimera of a madman. Even a quarter of a century ago, when Lord William Bentinck first arrived in India, men of sound judgment and long experience shook their heads and said that the natives of India, to whom the touch of a corpse is the deadliest contamination, could never be brought to face the science of anatomy as European students face it in the dissecting-room. But the experiment, under his auspices, was tried. It was tried and it succeeded. The Medical College of Calcutta was founded; and Hindoos of the highest caste learnt their lessons in anatomy, not from models of wax or wood, but from the human subject. The beginning was small; but the progressive advancement was striking. In 1837—the first year of which a record was kept—sixty bodies were dissected before the students. In the next year it was precisely doubled. In 1844 the number had risen to upwards of 500. The college was highly popular. There was evidently a strong desire on the part of the native youths for medical and surgical knowledge, and their prejudices gave way beneath it. But a greater victory, even than that which was to be seen in the dissecting-room, was now soon about to be achieved. In 1844, that liberal and enlightened native gentleman, Dwarkanath Tagore, offered to take to England and to educate at his own expense two students of the Medical College.

The proposal was communicated to Dr. Mouat, the secretary of the college—a gentleman of a large and liberal mind, to whose energy and intelligence the cause of native education is greatly indebted. In the assembled school he made the announcement, pointed out the advantages the proposal offered, and asked whether any were inclined to profit by the liberality of their distinguished countryman. On this, three native students volunteered unconditionally to cross the black water. They were all, with a fourth fellow-student, enabled to proceed to England,* and in our English colleges, competing with the best scientific scholarship of the West, they earned great distinction and carried off high rewards.

* Dr. Goodeve, one of the professors of the college, offered to take a third pupil at his own expense, and raised an additional sum, by private subscription, which enabled him to take a fourth. "The four pupils who accompanied the professor, and started in the steamer Bentinck on the 8th of March, were

Of an equally practical, but of a different kind, is the Engineering College of Roorkhee, in the North-Western Provinces. It was suggested by the progress of the great public works in the Doab, of which I have spoken in detail. Its object is to afford a good education in practical science both to Europeans and natives —to train up a new race of public servants, by whose aid these great works may be successfully prosecuted to their completion. For many years past there has existed a large demand for skill in every branch of practical engineering. Efforts were made for some time to find the means of special scientific training in existing institutions, but they were found to be inadequate to such a purpose; and on the 25th of November, 1847, Mr. Thomason published a "Prospectus of a College for Civil Engineering," which is now established at Roorkhee, and on the first day of the following year the first pupils were formally enrolled. By the middle of 1848 the establishment was completed, the buildings erected, and the classes opened.

An institution of this kind is calculated to be of immense advantage, both to the Government and the people. It is estimated that the expenditure on public works,* in the North-Western Provinces, including those the cost of which is defrayed from the road

Bholonath Bose, a pupil of Lord Auckland's school at Barrackpore, who was supported at the medical college by his lordship for five years, and was considered by the late Mr. Griffith, the most promising botanical pupil in the school—Gopaul Chunder Seal—Dwarkanath Bose, a native Christian, educated in the General Assembly's Institution, and employed for some time as assistant in the Museum—together with Surprice Comar Chuckerbutty, a Brahmin, native of Comillah, a junior pupil, and a lad of much spirit and promise."—[*Report of the Medical College for* 1844.]

* "The problem, then, for the Government to solve is, how they can most economically manage this large expenditure. Many civil engineers, artificers, and laborers must be employed in the disbursement. Whatever will increase the science, skill, and character of these agents, will cause a material saving in the expenditure. Whatever tends to multiply the number of well-qualified agents will facilitate the operations and cheapen the supply. It cannot be an unthrifty course which appropriates less than one and a half per cent. of the whole estimated minimum expenditure to training up an efficient agency, and sending them forth with all the appliances which may make them intelligent and trustworthy servants of the State."—[*Report on Roorkhee College, printed by order of Government of North-Western Provinces in* 1851.]

and ferry funds, is not less than 580,000*l*. It is of the first importance to secure an efficient and economical agency for the execution of these works. In no way can this great end be so well secured as by raising a class of engineers on the spot under the eyes of British officers. A great impulse will thus be given to native education. Few things are so much wanted as honorable professions attractive to the youth of the country; nor are the only advantages those which immediately occur to the employers and the employed. "It is evidently impossible," to use the words of the official exposition of the scheme, "that an agency, such as it is designed to connect with Roorkhee College, should be brought into exercise in the midst of the dense population of the Northern Doab, without materially improving the social condition of the inhabitants. The certain discoveries of modern science would be substituted for the crude and mistaken notions which now prevail on all subjects connected with natural philosophy. The people would have daily before their eyes some of the greatest achievements of scientific skill, and they would be taught the steps by which that skill is acquired, and the means by which it is brought into operation. A stimulus will be given to the native mind, which cannot fail to be highly beneficial. This is in itself an object worthy of the aim of a great Government. It is a purpose for which the State has appropriated large sums of money in all parts of the country."*

Of one other institution I must briefly speak. It is one of peculiar interest. When Sleeman and his associates had stricken down Thuggee, it seemed to them that it would be a great thing, and, as it were, set the crown upon their work, if a school were to be esta-

* *Report on Roorkhee College, printed by order of Government of North-Western Provinces in* 1851.

blished, not only for the education of the children of these convicted murderers, but also for the instruction of such of the criminals themselves as had been induced to become approvers. With this object, a school of industry was established at Jubbulpore. I believe that the idea first took shape in the mind of Lieutenant Brown, and that he was the originator of the institution. It had, like other great works, a small beginning; but it has now become an important establishment, viewed with regard both to its material and moral results. Within a factory, enclosing a space of 350 feet by 224, are to be seen continually at work, blacksmiths, dyers, spinners, tape-makers, chintz-printers, carpenters, carpet-makers, tent-makers, and other artisans. "None of them knew any trade but that of robbery and murder when the school was established in 1837."* "All now work with the greatest cheerfulness, and even rivalry; manufactures of great variety and excellent quality are produced in abundance. . . The whole exhibits a scene of industrious activity which is highly refreshing, and cannot but exercise a most beneficial influence on its inhabitants."† During a part of the day the children are instructed in reading and writing, and instead of becoming habituated to murder from their boyhood, there is every likelihood of their growing up to be not only peaceful and well-conducted men, but skilled artisans, able to gain a livelihood for themselves, far in advance of that which is procured by the common labor of the country.‡

I am writing of the administrative efforts of the Company and their servants; and in this chapter it only comes within my original design to give some account of the educational system and institutions of

* *Colonel Sleeman to Government, July 23, 1846. MS. Records.*

† *Police of Mr. Macleod. MS.*

‡ See for some further information relative to these schools, Appendix.

the Government. But I cannot refrain from turning aside in this place to bestow a few words on the great and successful exertions of private bodies to diffuse, principally through missionary agency, the light of knowledge among the people. It would be pleasant to write in detail of what has been done by different religious communities to disseminate European learning in the large towns, and to promote Vernacular education in outlying districts, but I cannot do more than illustrate and exemplify the good that has been done by the private efforts of these Christian men. It is not difficult to select the illustrative example of the many Protestant communities who are now earnestly and diligently laboring in the great cause of native education; there is, perhaps, not one that would not cheerfully acknowledge that the foremost place amongst these educational benefactors of India is due to Alexander Duff and his associates—to that little party of Presbyterian ministers who now for more than twenty years have been toiling for the people of India with such unwearying zeal, and with such wonderful success.

It was in the month of May, 1830, that Alexander Duff, a minister of the Church of Scotland, arrived at Calcutta. He was then a very young man, but his wisdom was far in advance of his years. Never was purer zeal—never sturdier energy devoted to a high and holy calling. He went out to India charged by the General Assembly of the Church of Scotland with the duty of establishing an educational institution for the purpose of conferring on native youths all the advantages of social and comprehensive European education—an education, indeed, of the highest order, "in inseparable conjunction with the principles of the Christian faith." It was a great experiment—a few years before it would have been a dangerous one. But Duff never so regarded it. He began his work;

and he waited. He opened his school with seven pupils; and ere long he had 1200. There was never any reservation on the part of Duff and his associates.* It was openly and generally avowed that the Holy Scriptures were taught in the schools. But the native children came freely to the Christian institution, and regarded their Christian teachers with affection.† There are missionary schools scattered over all parts of India, and freely the children come to be taught, but there is not one which, either for the magnitude or for the success of the experiment, can be compared with those presided over by Duff and his associates. Bombay and Madras share worthily in these honors; and the educational achievements of their Scotch divines deserve to be held in lasting remembrance.

There are some, perhaps, who, reading this, may feel disposed to ask, why cannot the Government do likewise—why, if the natives of India flock to the Bible-schools, is the Bible so rigorously excluded from the Government institutions? My individual opinion is, that the Bible might be safely and profitably admitted into the Government school-rooms, like any other class-book. But there are very many able and right-minded men who think differently on this most important subject, and there are some who say that it would be unworthy of our Government to submit to such a compromise, and that the Gospel ought not to be taught like algebra in the schools. I know that there is a vast difference between the use of the Bible in a private school and in one under the immediate superintendence of the servants of the Government, and that what in one case would be regarded with in-

* The Rev. W. S. Mackay, T. Smith, Ewart, and Macdonald—who died at his post—all men of great piety and intelligence.

† For further information regarding these institutions, and for many other matters of the deepest interest, see Dr. Duff's interesting and eloquent work, "India and India Missions."

difference, in the other might create irritation and alarm in the native mind. I shall touch briefly on the general subject of Government interference in the next chapter. But it is not the object of this work to deal with controversial matters, or to attempt to settle vexed questions of so delicate a character as this.

It will have been gathered from this rapid sketch of Native Education, especially as it has progressed under the Bengal Presidency, that public instruction is as yet only in its infancy. I cannot doubt, however, that very much has already been done by means of this great regenerative agent to advance the progress of civilisation among the people. It is true that when the entire number of pupils under education in the Government schools is compared with the population of the British provinces, it will be seen that our educational schemes are making very little direct impression upon the minds of the great mass of the people. But this is very far from the view which any reasonable man would take of this great question. We can only hope to work upon the uninstructed many through the agency of the instructed few.* We must trust, as it were, to the contagion of education. It is hard to say how many are indirectly benefited by the blessings conferred directly upon one pupil educated at the public expense. There is a reproductiveness in knowledge—a diffusiveness in truth—which renders it impossible for us to calculate the results of such instruction as is being conferred upon the

* Colonel Sykes, in a very valuable paper on the "Statistics of Government Education," published in 1845, gives a table showing "The employment of the students who have left the Government schools and colleges (in Bengal) up to 1839-40;" from which it appears that the largest number, except that embraced by the comprehensive term "Miscellaneous," went out into the world to teach: 83 became English teachers; 33, Arabic teachers; 133, Persian teachers; 50, Sanscrit teachers; 20, Bengallee teachers; 4, Hindoo teachers; and 5, Urdu teachers.

people of India by the Government and the Missionary schools.*

* I should be glad to see a little more attention given to Vernacular Education, and the Normal School principle well carried out. It appears from an admirable Minute on Native Education, drawn up by Mr. Willoughby shortly before leaving Bombay, that in the principal institutions there the Vernacular languages are held of less account even than they are in the Bengal colleges. The writer says : "But to revert to the subject of Vernacular education, I would now inquire why, when a boy is admitted into the English college or school, should instruction in this mother tongue cease? Why, in fact, should not the study of English and Vernacular be combined?—a system which, I understand, has been successfully introduced into the plan of education pursued in the Hindoo College at Calcutta. By compelling the student to give his undivided attention to the new language, there must be a great risk of his losing the knowledge, at the best but superficial, he had previously acquired of his own language. I see no reason for this, but, on the contrary, think the study of both languages, being proceeded with *pari passu*, would in several respects be exceedingly advantageous to the student. Indeed, I am happy to observe that the system of combined instruction has recently been introduced here, though not to the extent which appears to me advisable."

CHAPTER II.

The Past and the Present—The First Indian Chaplains—Rise and Progress of the Church Establishment—Charles Grant—The Charter of 1813—the First Indian Bishop—Increase of the Church Establishment—Missionary Efforts—Progress of Christianity.

Of all the great controversial questions, which have arisen out of British connexion with the East, not one has been discussed with so much earnestness and so much acrimony as that which relates to the introduction of Christianity into India. Happily the controversy is now at an end, and the acrimony has died with it. It is well, always, that we should be tolerant of exploded errors, and remember that the demonstrated of the present may not have been the demonstrable of the past. There is no subject on which I entertain a stronger opinion than this—none, perhaps, on which I have thought and written so much. But I do not know what I might have thought or written if I had lived in India half a century ago. Many very good and able men have advocated a system of non-interference, under a rooted conviction that any attempt to convert the natives of India to the Christian faith would be attended with the most calamitous results. After events have shown the groundlessness of their alarms; but candor admits that there may have been reason, half a century ago, in what now appears unreasonable and absurd.

In the reign of William and Mary the conversion of

the Gentoos was decreed by Act of Parliament. The Charter granted to the second East India Company in 1698 contained a clause, enacting that the said Company should constantly maintain "one minister in every garrison and superior factory," that they should in such "garrison or factories provide or set apart a decent and convenient place for divine service only;" and furthermore, that "all such ministers as shall be sent to reside in India shall be obliged to learn, within one year after their arrival, the Portuguese language, and shall apply themselves to learn the native language of the country where they shall reside, the better to enable them to instruct the Gentoos, that shall be the servants or slaves of the said Company, or of their agents, in the Protestant religion."

Though the Company previous to this may never have cherished this great Parliamentary idea of the conversion of the Gentoos, by the agency of their own chaplains, they had not from the very first been unmindful of the spiritual interests of their own people. Some at least of their early ships took out chaplains, and it had been the custom for all to receive a sort of ecclesiastical benediction before braving the perils of the deep. A farewell sermon was preached on board by some learned divine, often in the presence of the governor and committees of the Company.* The prin-

* Mr. Anderson, in his very valuable "History of the Colonial Church," quotes one of these farewell sermons, by John Wood, Doctor in Divinitie, which was published in 1618. The discourse was delivered on board the *Royal James*, and is dedicated to Sir Thomas Smith, Governor of the Company, and his colleagues. It appears that Dr. Wood had several times before preached to the crews of vessels about to depart for India. A passage in the epistle dedicatory, quoted by Mr. Anderson, leaves a very favorable impression on the mind of the general character of the managers of the Company. "I must needs set down," says the old divine, "that as God hath greatly encreased your store, so ye have not been backward to impart much and more than any societie (that ever I could heare of) to the supply of the wants of his poore members; your daily reliefe of poore ministers of the Gospell; your charitie to prisoners, to widowes, to orphans, and to all well-minded poore people that you finde to stand in neede of your helpe, cannot but plead for you in the eyes of God and all good men. Goe on therefore (in God's name) in your noble designs, and rest ye still upon his blessing, who (I doubt not) hath many

cipal part, indeed, of the Company's establishments were on board the ships, and it would seem that the factors ashore relied mainly on the vessels both for spiritual and corporeal consolation. The surgeons and chaplains were not, it would appear, attached to the factories, but were part of the staff of the generals and captains who came out in the Company's ships. But there were godly men at that time among the factors who longed for something more than this. Old Joseph Stalbank, whose letters I have quoted in the early part of this work, wrote urgently to the Company for zealous and able divines to teach the heathens, and counteract the subtle influence of the Jesuits. "Pray censure it not as a part of boldness in me," he said, "to advertise you of one matter, which may seem to be much fitter to be spoken of or written by another man than myself, even of your preachers and ministers, that you send hither to reside amongst us, and to break unto us the blessed manna of the Heavenly Gospel—very convenient it will be for you to provide such as are not only sufficient and solid divines, that may be able to encounter with the arch-enemies of our religion, if occasion should so require, those main supporters of the hierarchy of the Church of Rome, I mean the Jesuits, or rather (as I may truly term them) Jebusites, whereof some are mingled here in several places in the King's dominions amongst us—but also godly, zealous, and devout persons, such as may, by their piety and purity of life give good example to those with whom they live, whereby they will no less instruct and feed their little flock committed unto

more in store for you; and so long as you conscionably seek to honour his name among the heathen, and (under him) to advance the state wherein ye live, will (no doubt) affoord you many comfortable assurances of his love and favour, both to your bodies and soules here in this life, and crowne you with eternall glorie with himself in the life to come." Mr. Copeland, who afterwards did good service to the interests of Christianity in the West Indies, sailed as chaplain in the *Royal James*.

them, no less by the sincerity of the doctrine they teach them."*

The earliest mention of a Company's chaplain that I have been able to find is in a letter dated Ajmere, April 27, 1616. It is written by Sir Thomas Roe to "Mr. Lescke, chaplain at Surat." There was about this same time at Surat a Mr. Copeland, chaplain on board the *Royal James*, whose name subsequently became associated with the early history of the West Indian Church.† A curious letter, dated "Swally, March 4, 1617," relating to the conversion of a Mogul Atheist, is among the early records of the Company. On the first establishment of our factory at Madras, it would seem that in the absence of a Protestant ministry the settlers were fain to avail themselves of the ecclesiastical assistance of a Capuchin friar, who paid the penalty of his toleration by enduring imprisonment for five years in the dungeons of the Inquisition at Goa.‡ In 1655, a Protestant chaplain was ministering at that settlement.§ In 1667, Mr. Walter Hooke, and in

* *Joseph Salbank to the Company, Agra, November* 22, 1617. *India House Records.*—There is some obscurity in this passage as there often is in the phraseology of these old factors. Whether the writer meant to say that the matter whereof he advertised the Company was "even your preachers and ministers that (whom) you send hither (or are in the habit of sending hither) to reside amongst us"—or "even your preachers and ministers that you (should) send (some) hither to reside amongst us"—is not very apparent. He may either have meant that the Company should send ministers, as there were none then among them; or that they should send better ones than those appointed before.

† *Anderson's History of the Colonial Church.*

‡ See Orme's "Historical Fragments." The historian states that in 1661 the Presidency of Surat blamed the Madras agency for persisting in giving protection to two or three Capuchin friars, although one of them had suffered an imprisonment of five years in the Inquisition at Goa, for accommodating his ministry to the convenience of the settlement.

§ There may have been one before him, but this is the earliest mention of a Madras chaplain that I have been able to find. The passage in which it is contained is curious on other accounts. It is part of a report of a consultation held at Metchlapatam (Masulapatam) December 4, 1655. "Next was had into consideration what proportion of means was thought needful to be allowed to such of the Company's servants as are to reside at Madraspatam and Metchlapatam, and the subordinate factories, for their necessary expenses, charges, garrison, &c., excepted, it was agreed that 30 old pagodas should be allowed to Mr. Edward Winter to uphold the Company's houses at Metchlapatam, Verasheeroon, Pettepollee, Daleepadee, and 60 new pagodas for the president

1668, Mr. William Thomson, were elected chaplains for Madras.* But it was not until 1680 that the first stone of the first English church in India was laid at Madras by Streynsham Master, chief of the factory, who carried on the pious work at his own charge, and never halted till he had brought it to an end.

At the beginning of the eighteenth century this church was finished, furnished, and, to a certain extent, endowed. Two ministers were attached to it, each on a salary of 100*l.* a year. Prayers were read in it twice a day. On Sundays, the whole settlement, headed by the President, proceeded thither in great state, through a street of soldiers, and reverently joined in the service, according to the forms of the Anglican Church.†

In 1716, an English Protestant church was erected in Calcutta, and two years later one was completed at Bombay. From that time there was necessarily more

and two factors, *the minister and his wife*, and chirurgeon, at Fort St. George."—[*India House Records. MS.*]

* From a list of "Chaplains in India prior to the union of the two Companies," given by Mr. Anderson in his "History of the Colonial Church," as obtained by him at the India House. Mr. Hooke's is the first name on the list, but it is certain that there were chaplains before him. I find mention of a Mr. Thomson and his wife at Madras in the year 1655. "It was propounded touching Mr. Thomson and his wife, that if they cannot find this year convenient passage for their own country, and if they remain at Fort St. George, they shall have diet at the Company's table—but Mr. Thomson himself is to be referred to the Company's pleasure what salary he shall have for his pains." I believe this to be the same Mr. Thomson as is referred to in the text, and that he and Mrs. Thomson are the "minister and his wife" alluded to in the preceding note.

† See a curious account by Charles Lockyer, who visited Madras about the year 1703: "The church is a large pile of arched building, adorned with curious carved work, a stately altar, organs, a white copper candlestick, very large windows, &c., which render it inferior to the churches of London in nothing but bells—there being one only to mind sinners of devotion, tho' I've heard a contribution for a set was formerly remitted the Company. . . . Prayers are read twice a day; but on Sundays religious worship is most strictly observed. Betwixt eight and nine, the bell tells us the hour of devotion draws near; a whole company of above 200 soldiers is drawn out from the inner fort to the church-door, for a guard to the passing President. Ladies throng to their pews, and gentlemen take a serious walk in the yard, if not too hot. On the Governor's approach, the organs strike up and continue a welcome till he is seated; when the minister discharges the duty of his function, according to the forms appointed by our prudent ancestors for the Church of England."—[*An Account of the Trade in India, &c., &c., by Charles Lockyer*, 1711.]

outward recognition of the duties of religion, but, except in such exceptional cases as it is to be hoped will ever be presented by communities of Christian men, however limited their numbers, there was little genuine piety and little morality of life. Throughout the remainder of the century, the Company's ecclesiastical establishment, like its civil and military services, continued to grow in numerical strength; and even then there were earnest-minded men at home, as Dean Prideaux and others, who were eager to see that church-establishment placed under episcopal superintendence, and who would have sent out bishops and archdeacons, even an archbishop, to take spiritual command of the small bodies of Christians who were then located in the settlements of India. Perhaps such superintendence might have had an improving effect upon the lives of the Company's chaplains. It would seem that at the close of the last century they were a money-making race of men. There is a curious entry in the Journal of Mr. Kiernander, the old Danish missionary, running in these words: "The Rev. Mr. Blanshard is preparing to go to England upon an American ship in about a fortnight, worth five lakhs (of rupees). Mr. Owen two and a half lakhs. Mr. Johnson three and a half lakhs."* This was at the commencement of 1797. The first had been twenty-three years attached to the Indian ministry; the second, ten years; and the third, thirteen years. An average annual saving, if Kiernander is to be trusted, of 2500*l.*! It is needless to say that these fortunes could not have been realised out of the Company's allowances, even with the addition of the ministerial fees, which in India are liberally bestowed.† These churchmen must have devoted themselves to

* See Kiernander's Journal, in the *Calcutta Review.*

† In those days there may have been no lack of burials—but Christian marriages and baptisms were few.

something more lucrative than the cure of souls and the burial of the dead. What it was may be readily conjectured.

But with the new century came a new race of men to preside over the English Church in Bengal. In the rooms of a Fellow of King's College, Cambridge, a little group of young men might have been seen assembled when the studies of the day were at an end. They went thither to hear such truths as did not fall very readily from the lips of their ordinary preceptors; and what they then learnt was seldom forgotten. It seemed to be the peculiar privilege of Charles Simeon to prepare young men of large intellectual capacity and strong religious convictions for the active work of the Anglo-Indian ministry. It was, happily, too, in his power to do more than teach. Held in the highest esteem and veneration by such men as Henry Thornton and Charles Grant, he had little difficulty in furthering the views of his disciples, and Indian chaplaincies were readily procurable from Directors of the Company, who, not unmindful of the responsibilities of ecclesiastical patronage, joyfully availed themselves of every such occasion of turning their opportunities to profitable account. What Halle and Franke, years before, had been to the Danish mission, Cambridge and Simeon became to the English Protestant Church. David Brown, Claudius Buchanan, Henry Martyn, Daniel Corrie, and Thomas Thomason, were all of them chaplains on the Company's establishment in Bengal. They obeyed the orders of a Governor-General, and received every month from the public treasury a heavy bag of rupees. They were not missionaries, but the missionary spirit was strong within them, and in one, at least, it glowed with as burning and as chaste a zeal as in the breast of a Xavier or a Ziegenbalg. They were all of them single-hearted, pure-minded men; men, too, of more than common intellectual capacity, and of industry which shrunk from no accumulation of labor in a cause so dear to their hearts. Of this little band of Christian athletes David Brown was the father and the chief. One after one, as the younger men followed him to the scene of his ministrations, he opened his doors to receive them, and send them on their way with a message of encouragement and advice.

And as they were speeding on their godly journey other words of encouragement came to them from high places far off across the seas. It was no small thing for them to know that they had not gone abroad to be forgotten—that good men and great men were thinking of them, and praying for them at home, and strenuously supporting their efforts. Charles Grant had not been long in the Direction before his influence became little less than that of the Company itself. It is slight exaggeration to say that for many years he was not a Director, but the Direction. He was a man of a solid understanding, of large experience, and of a resolute industry which took no account of mental or bodily fatigue. The exhausting climate of Bengal had not impaired his energies or unstrung his nerves. He was always ready braced for work; the claims of the country in which he had built up his fortune, of the people among whom he had spent all the best years of his life, pressed heavily upon his mind. He had attained less of worldly distinction in India than his friend and neighbour, John Shore, Lord Teignmouth, but he brought home to England a larger zeal, a more active benevolence, and far greater strength to measure himself with his cotemporaries at home and take his proper place among them. It was no small thing at such a time for a retired Governor-General of India to write pamphlets in behalf of Christian missions, and to preside over a society having for its object the circulation of the Holy Scriptures throughout all the dark places of the earth. But what Lord Teignmouth did for India, after his withdrawal from the scene of his vice-regal labors, was in comparison with the busy stirring practicalities of Charles Grant's new career, very much the work of a recluse. The head-piece of the Company in Leadenhall-street, the mouth-piece of the Company in St. Stephen's, the oracle, on all subjects of Indian import, of that little knot of warm-hearted, earnest-minded men who discussed great measures of humanity on Clapham-common, Charles Grant, whether writing elaborate despatches to the Governor-General, or addressing the House of Commons, or imparting his ample stores of Indian experience to William Wilberforce or Henry Thornton, so tempered the earnestness of his spiritual zeal with sound knowledge and strong practical sense, that whatever he said carried a weighty significance with it. Such a man was much needed at that time. He was needed to exercise a double influence—an influence alike over the minds of men of different classes in India, and of his colleagues and compatriots at home. So, whilst he was writing out elaborate despatches to the Governor-General of India—such despatches as had never before been received by an Indian viceroy—and to more than one of the Company's chaplains in India, letters of affectionate encouragement and parental advice, he was brushing away the cobwebs of error with which men's minds were fouled and clouded at home, and uttering sound practical truths with the stamp of authority upon them, such as no one ever ventured to designate as the amiable enthusiasm of a dreamer of dreams and seer of visions.

Conspicuous among his Indian correspondents was Claudius Buchanan. This able and excellent man had been one of the recipients of Henry Thornton's bounty, and had by him, and I believe also by Isaac Milner, been recommended for an Indian chaplaincy to Charles Grant. The Director was not slow to recognise the merits of the young Scotchman, and Buchanan was sent to Bengal. He had less of the missionary spirit than Henry Martyn. He was altogether less earnest, less enthusiastic, less self-denying. The expansive Christianity of the son of the Cornish miner wandered out into illimitable space, far beyond the narrow sphere of archdeaconries and episcopal sees. But Buchanan, with a more worldy judgment and intellectual qualities of a more serviceable kind, believed in his heart that the regeneration of India was to be accomplished mainly by a Church Establishment. And, full of this idea, he drew up elaborate schemes of ecclesiastical extension, and wrote letter after letter to Charles Grant, and to many of the highest dignitaries of the English Church, setting forth the expediency of a large augmentation of the number of Indian chaplains, and the subjection of the whole body to the authority of a bishop, or rather a group of bishops, with a primate at their head. "An archbishop," he wrote, "is wanted for India; a sacred and exalted character, surrounded by his bishops, of ample revenues and extensive sway; a venerable personage, whose name shall be greater than that of the transitory governors of the land; and whose fame for piety, and for the will and power to do good, may pass throughout every region." His ideas upon this subject, indeed, were somewhat exuberant; and even now, after the lapse of nearly half a century, can scarcely be read without a smile. "It is certain," he said, "that nothing would more alarm the portentous invader of nations (Napoleon) than our taking a religious possession of Hindostan. Five hundred respectable clergy of the English Church, established in our

Gentoo cities, would more perplex his views of conquest than an army of fifty thousand British soldiers. The army of fifty thousand would melt away in seven years; but the influence of an upright clergyman among the natives of the district, would be permanent. He would be to them in time their mouth and mind, and speak for them peace or war."* Buchanan did not write this to Charles Grant, but to the Archbishop of Canterbury. The sagacious, large-browed Director would probably have smiled at the idea of the overthrow of Napoleon's invading legions by an army of five hundred Company's chaplains, with an archbishop at their head. But this great political heresy was, after all, not much more absurd than the orthodox belief which was, at that time, accepted by a large proportion of the most intelligent European gentlemen in the East. The current faith was not that the Bible would beat Napoleon's artillery, but that it would expedite our overthrow more surely and more rapidly. How curious and instructive is it to contrast such a passage as that which I have just quoted from the correspondence of Claudius Buchanan, with the following, taken from a letter now before me, written in 1808, by one of the most intelligent officers in the Company's service —a Resident at a native Court—to a high civil functionary in Calcutta. The reference, also, in this case is to the rumoured invasion of Napoleon:

"I most cordially assent to all the sentiments you express of the impolicy, or rather madness, of attempting the conversion of the natives of this country, or of giving them any more learning, or any other description of learning, than they at present possess. With respect to the Hindoos, they appear to me to have as good a system of faith and of morals as most people; and with regard to the Moossulmans, it is quite sufficient if we endeavour to con-

* The writer adds: "Friendly, admonitory, social intercourse is what is wanting to enchain the hearts of the people of Hindostan, and to make them *our* people." Nothing can be more true.

ciliate their confidence, and to mitigate their vindictive spirit. Sir Willlam Jones has in a very few words given us a correct outline of the only system of government adapted to this country—'To give them (the Hindoos) protection for their persons and places of abode; justice in their temporal concerns; indulgence to the prejudices of their religion; and the benefit of those laws, which they have been taught to believe sacred, and which alone they can possibly comprehend'—I can assure you that I do not feel so much anxiety and apprehension from the menaced designs of Buonaparte, as from the plans which have become so fashionable amongst the Puritans of the India House. This alarm has been chiefly excited by the perusal of some pamphlets, which have been lately published in London, and have been issued from your Bible Societies, your Christian Societies, and other corporations of bigotry. You have a Mr. or Dr. Buchanan—an officer of your College, who appears to me to have done a great deal of harm. For the prizes, which he presumed to offer for certain Exercises at the University of Cambridge, I am convinced that he is a man of wretched and most unchristianlike vanity. I do not even approve of your zeal in the translation of the Bible and New Testament into I know not how many languages. The Scriptures may appear very admirable to us, who are prepared to venerate them as the instrument of revelation. But I do not think they are calculated to excite respect and admiration in the garb of translations, in the minds of men who are prepared to deny their truth."*

It would be difficult to find a more remarkable contrast than is displayed in these two passages, and equally difficult to decide whether the one or the other is more preposterous in its exaggerations. A battalion of Company's chaplains was not less likely to defend India against the encroachments of Napoleon, than the Puritans of the India House were to facilitate his aggressive designs.

It was about this time that the great controversy was at its height. Never at any period was the one

* *MS. Correspondence.*

party more strenuous in its efforts to demonstrate the danger of making a show of Christianity in India, and never was the other more zealous in its endeavours to prove the fallacy of these tremendous expectations. That well-known historical event — the massacre at Vellore—came, at an inopportune moment, to stimulate and exasperate the controversy. There were not wanting, either in England or in India,* writers and speakers to attribute this calamity to the alarm excited in the breasts of the people by the movements of the very few missionaries who were then suffered to pursue their peaceful calling in the Company's territories. The people of India, it was said, believing that their ancestral faith was threatened by the European usurpers, had risen up against their conquerors, and murdered them in their beds. This was but a foretaste, it was prophesied, of greater horrors to come. If the Bible were not shelved, and the missionaries recalled, the cantonments of the white men, from one end of India to the other, would be deluged with Christian blood. Reason and candor could not but pronounce all this a monstrous fable. But to many prejudiced minds, it was too acceptable not to be readily taken on trust, and the fiction found favor in London, no less than in Calcutta and Madras.

The currency which the fiction acquired for itself disquieted the "Puritans of the India House." It could not stand the touch of reason, it is true, but fictions that cannot stand the touch of reason are often very long-lived and robust, for there are thousands and tens of thousands of people who never reason at all. It was easy for such a man as Charles Grant to explode the error in a few argumentative sentences, but he was too sagacious not clearly to perceive the mischief of its dissemination:—

* *MS. Correspondence.*

"I most of all suffer," he wrote, "from the absurd, malevolent, and wicked stories, which the weak, the prejudiced, the enemies of Christianity, have poured forth on this occasion to discredit, to bring into suspicion, to blacken as dangerous and mischievous, the few poor and assuredly harmless efforts, which have been made under the British Governments, to introduce the light of the Gospel into India. Greater efforts were made by other nations, centuries anterior to our ascendancy there. The natives have seen converts made to Christianity, though in small numbers, from age to age. No influence to disturb the public peace has ever followed. In our time, what perfect indifference have the generality of the Europeans shown to the religion they call theirs—what complacence in the superstitions of the country—how utterly abhorrent of everything that looked like compulsion. What have the few missionaries labouring there done but proposed a message of peace in the language and temper of peace, reason, and affection? Was there a missionary, or a chaplain, or any ostensible advocate for Christianity anywhere near Vellore? But I am hurrying into a subject which requires to be treated with deliberation and seriousness. All the disaffected to the propagation of the Gospel, among our own people both in India and here, take this opportunity to speak of the danger of allowing missionaries to exercise their functions in India. Doubtless prudence and discretion are always necessary in that work—they are particularly so now; but if from unworthy fears we should disavow our religion, or even be led to silence all attempts to communicate it to our subjects in a mild rational way, I should fear that the Great Author of that religion would be provoked to withdraw his protection there from us."*

And again he wrote, with how much sound sense, and with what a clear perception of the real weakness and the real strength of all human governments:

"They predict dreadful consequences from the preaching, writing, and itinerating of a few missionaries. These men, as far as I can judge, are remarkably peaceable, humble, pious, and affectionate in their whole demeanour, and pretending to no influence but what the truth, fairly exhibited, is calculated to produce. I

* *MS. Correspondence.*

know that the idea of converting the natives to Christianity has always been offensive to many of our countrymen in India, but chiefly to those who were no friends of Christianity in their own persons. And from such men the cry now comes that the activity of those missionaries will excite the jealousy and resentment of the natives; although no one instance of any expression of such suspicion or dissatisfaction on the part of the natives against the Government is given, or I believe can be given. I fear that these reports, taken up and re-echoed here, will lead to some precipitate measure, offensive to God, and all the more serious part of the community of this country, as well as injurious to the real interests of the Company abroad and at home. They have already various enemies who will oppose the renewal of the Charter, and if they act upon any principle which, however, disguised amounts in effect to an exclusion of the Gospel from the natives of India, a weight will be thrown into the opposing scale likely to bear them down.

"I have for many years considered the question of introducing Christianity among our Indian subjects. . . . . Caution and prudence are at all times necessary in proposing the truths of Christianity to heathens; there may be particular conjunctures when these, and perhaps a degree of forbearance are specially required—but for a Christian nation to say deliberately that they will prohibit the communication of that religion which comes from God to fifty millions of men, sunk in idolatry, superstition, and vice, is a proposition so monstrous and shocking, so contrary to the most rational and probable cause to be assigned for the conduct of Providence in committing so vast an empire to our care, that I tremble at the thought of it and the consequences it would be likely to produce. . . . . Minor questions are agitated about the irregular entrance of some missionaries into India, and the imprudence of continuing their labors, after the natives have shown so much alarm (in the reports chiefly I believe of Europeans), but the real question depending is whether the door shall be shut to the entrance of missionaries into British India? It would require much time and space to advance all that is to be said upon the question, but if ever it is deliberately settled in the negative, I shall consider the warrant is signed for the transition of our empire there, and I hold this opinion with men of greater authority and name than mine."*

* *MS. Correspondence.*

As the period for which the old Charter of 1793 had been granted wore to a close, men began to bestir themselves in England about this great matter of Christianity in India. The question which then agitated the mind of the religious community was twofold. There was a comparatively small, but most respectable, party, who believed that the great end to be gained was an extension of the Church establishment—who looked up to the lawn sleeves of the bishop as the great agent of evangelisation, and scarcely shrunk from the avowal of an opinion that the stability of British rule in the East much depended on the foundation of archdeaconries and episcopal sees. There was another, and much larger party, who took but little account of dignities and dignitaries—who, remembering what had been done by fishermen and tent-makers, sought only that earnest-minded Christian men, no matter of what worldly estate, should be suffered, on their own responsibility, as men without any official stamp upon them, to visit and teach the Gentiles. These questions, much brooded over in private before, were now publicly discussed. Many and various the opinions expressed—many and various the exponents of those opinions and the outward shape of the exposition. Some betook themselves to the printing-press, and a war of pamphlets commenced. Others embodied their views in public petitions, and a heavy rain of memorials then began to descend upon the Legislature. Others, again, declared their sentiments before Parliamentary Committees, and set forth the experiences of their lives in such a manner as to make the uninitiated wonder how any two men of similar antecedents should deduce from their connexion with the past such dissimilar conclusions.* And

* Compare the evidence given by Warren Hastings and by Lord Teignmouth. It is instructive on more than one account to read the examination of the latter in the present day. The Committee seemed to know the kind of man they had to deal with, and assailed him at starting by putting an extreme

finally, members of Parliament, in both Houses, spoke out with much antagonistic earnestness, and brought both questions to an issue.

On the 22nd of March, 1813, the House of Commons went into committee on the India Bill. Lord Castle-

case: "Would it be consistent with the security of the British empire in India, that missionaries should preach publicly, with a view to the conversion of the native Indians, that Mahomet is an impostor, or should speak in opprobrious terms of the Brahmins, or their religious rites?" To this, of course, Lord Teignmouth replied, that there might be danger in such indiscretion; but that no one contemplated the conversion of the natives of India by such means; and when, soon afterwards, the question was put, "Is your lordship aware that an opinion prevails in India, that it is the intention of the British Government to take means to convert the natives of the country to the Christian religion?" he answered, without a moment's hesitation, "*I never heard it, or suspected it.*" One would have thought that there was little need after this to put the case hypothetically; but the witness was presently asked whether, allowing such an opinion to exist among the natives, the appearance of a bishop on the stage would not increase the danger. "I should think," said Lord Teignmouth, "it would be viewed with perfect indifference." Determined to work the hypothesis a little more, the Committee asked him whether, "*were* the Hindoos possessed with an idea that we had an intention of changing their religion and converting them into Christians, it would be attended with any bad consequences at all?" "I will expatiate a little in my answer to that question," said Lord Teignmouth; and he then delivered himself of the following explanation, the admirable good sense of which is not to be surpassed by anything to be found in the entire mass of evidence, elicited throughout the inquiry, upon all points of the Company's charter:

"Both the Hindoos and Mahomedans, subject to the British Government in India, have had the experience of some years, that, in all the public acts of that Government, every attention has been paid to their prejudices, civil and religious, and that the freest toleration is allowed to them; that there are many regulations of Government which prove the disposition of Government to leave them perfectly free and unmolested in their religious ordinances; and that any attempt at an infringement upon their religion or superstitions would be punished by the Government of India. With that conviction, which arises from experience, I do not apprehend that they would be brought to believe that the Government ever meant to impose upon them the religion of this country."

But the Committee had not yet done with their hypothesis, and were determined not to let the witness, whatever might be his opinion of its absurdity, escape without giving a direct answer; so they assailed him again, by asking, "*Should the state of things be altered, and we not observe the conduct we have hitherto observed, but introduce new modes, and enact new laws, for the carrying into effect the conversion of the natives to Christianity*, would not that be attended with disagreeable consequences?" To this, of course, but one answer could be given; and Lord Teignmouth gave that answer, leaving the Committee to make what use of it they could. "If a law were to be enacted," he said, "for converting the natives of India to Christianity, in such a manner as to have the appearance of a compulsory law upon their consciences, I have no hesitation in saying that, in that case, it would be attended with very great danger." Surely this is not the way to elicit the truth. I cannot help thinking that the licence given to this kind of wild questioning, which still obtains in committee-rooms, rather calculated to embarrass and obscure the truth than to develop it. Wilberforce, writing to Lord Wellesley at the time of the last charter discussions, said, "Your lordship can scarcely conceive, if I may judge of the House of Lords from the general condition of the members of the House of Commons, how ignorant in general their lordships are likely to be regarding India, and therefore how little they are qualified to ask questions in committee."

2 T

reagh was then Foreign Secretary and Leader of the House of Commons. It devolved on him to state the intentions of Government, which had been embodied in a series of resolutions. When he came to what were irreverently called the "pious clauses," he seemed to think that it was necessary to speak apologetically of the proposed measure, and expedient to hurry over the ground with all possible despatch.

"Another resolution," he said, "which he should "propose to the House, would be on the subject of Re-"ligion. He was aware that it was unwise to encroach "on the subject of religion generally, and that this, "under the circumstances of our Government in India, "was a most delicate question. But there was one "regulation on the subject necessary, even for the sake "of decency. The Company entrusted with the supreme "Government, in this as in other matters, had per-"mitted the free exercise of religion at their settle-"ments; but there was no sort of religious control, and "the members of the Church of England could not re-"ceive the benefits of those parts of their religion, to "which the Episcopalian functions were necessary,—for "example, the ceremony of Confirmation. He hoped "that the House did not think he was coming out with "a great ecclesiastical establishment, for it would only "amount to one bishop and three archdeacons, to su-"perintend the chaplains of the different settlements. "The Company, he hoped, would not think it an en-"croachment on their rights, that while British subjects "in India were governed by British laws, they should "be permitted to exercise their national religion."

The Resolutions, as I have said, were stated to the House on the 22nd of March, but it was not until the 17th of June* that the twelfth clause, "That it is the

* There had been some intermediate discussions, in which the two Charles Grants, father and son, had taken leading parts. The younger, on the 31st of March, had made a brilliant speech in favour of the "pious clauses." It must have been a fine thing to see the two fighting side by side on the floor of the House of Commons.

"opinion of this Committee, that it is expedient that "the Church establishment in the British territories "should be placed under the superintendence of a "bishop and three archdeacons, and that adequate "provision should be made, from the territorial revenues of India, for their maintenance," came formally under discussion. It passed without a division. The Missionary clause came next. That was the field on which the great battle was to be fought between the Christian and the Philo-Hindoo parties. The resolution, cautiously worded, so as to contain no direct mention of missionaries and Christianity, was: "That it is the "opinion of this Committee, that it is the duty of this "country to promote the interest and happiness of the "native inhabitants of the British dominions in India, "and that such measures ought to be adopted as may "tend to the introduction among them of useful know"ledge, and of religious and moral improvement. That "in the furtherance of the above objects, sufficient "facilities shall be afforded by law, to persons desirous "of going to, and remaining in, India, for the pur"pose of accomplishing those benevolent designs." A special day, the 22nd of June, was fixed for the discussion. Wilberforce, who twenty years before had fought the battle of Christianity almost single-handed, and who now took intense interest in the great struggle, had girded himself for the conflict, and gone down to the House with quite an encyclopædia of authorities in support of his favorite opinions. His whole heart was in the encounter. He spoke long and well, tossing about the testimonies of the learned with a prodigality that was quite overwhelming. He quoted the opinions of all the Governors-General, one after the other, to show that the people of India were the most abandoned people on the face of the earth. He quoted the historians; he quoted the missionaries; he quoted the civil servants of the Company. He quoted Orme, Verelst, Scrafton, Bolts, Malcolm, Grant, Mackintosh, Colebrooke, Kerr, Marshman, Carey, Ward, and an infinite number of official reports. He piled up authority upon authority to demonstrate the claims of this unhappy and most benighted people, upon the Christian sympathies of the British nation. It was a noble piece of special pleading, not exempt from exaggeration—that exaggeration, which is perhaps seldom absent from the addresses of a man very full of his subject, very earnest and energetic, thoroughly convinced in his own mind, and intensely eager to bring conviction to the minds of others. The grandeur of its aims, the high character and pure sincerity of the speaker, imparted a dignity and a purity to the address which it was impossible not to venerate. It made an impression upon the House; it made an impression out of the House; it made an impression throughout the country. Carefully corrected by the speaker, the speech was published by Hatchard, and found its way into extensive circulation. Its course was one of not unobstructed success. The Resolution was carried that night by a majority of 89 to 36; but, after a day or two, the question was re-opened in another stage of the business. On the 28th, the elder Grant made a long and able speech in defence of the Company. Mr. Lushington followed, with a reply to Mr. Wilberforce, and a defence of the Hindoos, to be answered by stout William Smith, who, with Mr. Stephen, in more than one good battle on the side of Christianity, had fought as the lieutenants of Mr. Wilberforce. On the 1st of July, the discussion was again resumed, and a very remarkable speech, on the wrong side of the question, was delivered by Mr. Charles Marsh, a gentleman who had formerly been a member of the legal profession at Madras. It created a strong sensation in the House, but not an abiding one. His hearers admired the eloquence of the speaker, but were not convinced by his arguments. The address, which he delivered on the 1st of July, 1813—an elaborate protest against Christian liberty in India—even now that a second Charter has nearly expired since it was reported, cannot be read without the strongest feelings of regret, that such fine talents were turned to such bad account.*

This speech called forth a rejoinder from Wilberforce, distinguished by no common ability. Southey had ransacked his marvellous common-place book to supply illustrations, drawn from Portuguese history, of the little danger, that attends interference with the customs of the people of India. And now the speaker, thus fortified by the erudition of the newly-appointed laureate, cited Albuquerque with good effect; entered into an elaborate explanation of the causes of the massacre of Vellore (an event which Mr. Marsh had of course emphatically dwelt upon, for it was the stock in trade of his party); spoke of the suppression of female infanticide by Jonathan Duncan and Colonel Walker, and of the Saugor sacrifices by Lord Wellesley; rebuked Mr. Marsh for speaking of the Missionaries as Anabaptists and fanatics; and compared the present contest with the great struggle, in which he and his friends had so long been engaged, for the suppression of the slave-trade. He was followed by Mr.

* "There was little or nothing in this address that had not been said before; but Mr. Marsh assuredly said it better than it had been said before. He said, indeed, everything that could be said upon the subject; and he said it extremely well. A dexterous allusion to the murder at Blackheath of Mr. and Mrs. Bonar by their footman, Nicholson, which was to the year 1813, what the Manning murder was to 1849; and to the still mysterious affair of the alleged attack upon the Duke of Cumberland by his valet, Sellis—two incidents which were then exciting the public mind—told with something of novel effect on the House, and must be regarded as an original illustration of the superior virtue of the native servants, who sleep at the doors of Anglo-Indian residents."—[*Author in the Calcutta Review.*]

Forbes, Mr. William Smith, and other speakers, among whom was Whitbread, who spoke out manfully in favor of the Resolution. "I am charmed with Whitbread," wrote Buchanan to a friend, a few days afterwards, "when he sounds the right note." The House divided; and there were fifty-four votes for the clause, and thirty-two against it. A hundred members could not be induced to sit out this important debate. Five hundred had divided a few weeks before on the Roman Catholic Relief Bill. In the House of Lords the Resolution passed without a division.

And so the victory was gained. I must briefly speak of its results. On the 28th of November, 1814, the first Indian bishop ascended the steps of one of the ghâts of Calcutta. His landing, in his own words, "was without any *éclat*, for fear of alarming the prejudices of the natives." On Christmas-day he preached his first sermon, before a congregation of 1300 persons, and administered the sacrament to 160 communicants, including the judges and the members of council. "The day," he wrote to his friends in England, "will long be remembered in Calcutta."

And so commenced the episcopal period of Christianity in India. There was no commotion—no excitement at its dawn. Offended Hindooism did not start up in arms; nor indignant Mahomedanism raise a war-cry of death to the infidel. English gentlemen asked each other, on the course, or at the dinner-table, if they had seen the bishop; and officious native sircars pressed their services upon the "Lord Padre Sahib." But the heart of Hindoo society beat calmly as was its wont. Brahmanism stood not aghast at the sight of the lawn sleeves of the bishop; he preached in the Christian temple on the Christian's *bara din;* and that night the Europeans in Calcutta slept securely in their beds—securely next morning they went forth to their accustomed work. There was not a massacre; there was not a rebellion. Chowringhee was not in a blaze; the waters of the "Lall Diggy" did not run crimson with Christian blood. The merchant took his place at his desk; the public servant entered his office; and the native underlings salamed meekly and reverentially as ever. In the Fort, the English captain faced his native company; and the sepoy, whatever his caste, responded to the well-known word of command, with the ready discipline he had learned under the old charter. Everything went on according to wonted custom, in spite of the bishop, and his lawn sleeves, and his sermon on Christmas-day. No one looked differently; no one felt differently; and it really seemed probable, after all, that British dominion in the East would survive the episcopal blow.

The truth is, that such of the natives—the better educated and more intelligent few—as really thought anything about the matter, thought the better of us for evincing this outward respect for our religion, and have thought the better of us and our faith ever since. All that was written and spoken, of old, about alarming the Hindoos, and weakening our hold of India; all the ominous allusions to the Vellore massacre, and anticipations of new catastrophes of the same class, now appeared in their true light, and were valued at their proper worth. Mr. Buchanan's "sanguinary doctrines," as Mr. Twining ludicrously called them, in one of his pamphlets, had now been fully reduced to practice; and yet not a drop of blood had been shed—not a blow struck—not a menace uttered—not a symptom of disquiet had evinced itself. Our empire in India was then "not worth a year's purchase;" and yet now for forty years has it survived that first awful episcopal sermon on Christmas-day.*

Bengal had become accustomed to the great episcopal

* Author in the *Calcutta Review.*

danger when the bishop prepared to set out on a visitation tour, and threw Madras into a paroxysm of alarm. The Coast authorities had not forgotten the Vellore massacre. Visions of blood were still floating before their eyes. It seemed to them that the visit of the bishop to the south would be the signal for another rising, more grievous than the last, as Hindoos and Mahomedans might for once be banded together. But the further he proceeded the more apparent it became that the natives regarded his approach without a feeling of alarm, and his presence without a sentiment of aversion. Native princes received the Christian bishop with reverence, and embraced him with affection. Native priests came out from their temples to welcome him, and implored his assistance in their behalf. He visited the great pagodas of Chillumbrum; where the Brahmins pressed forward to gaze at the chief-priest of the Feringhees. They showed him all the noticeable things of their temple, and, instead of anticipating that he had come to demolish it, asked for a little money for its repair. Elsewhere the same feeling prevailed. A deputation of Brahmins from the Tinnivelly Pagodas visited the bishop at Palamcottah. They came respectfully to the Lord Padre to seek his sympathy and assistance as a brother hierarch. They were, they said, in a miserable state of depression. Their church-lands, after paying the Government demands, yielded so little that the priests were in danger of starving. Could not the head of the Christian Church, they meekly suggested, intercede in their behalf, and induce Government to better their position?

From that time it became apparent that any amount of Church establishment that the British Legislature could be induced to sanction would never alarm or irritate the natives. The establishment in Middleton's time was miserably small. "The total number of clergy, both civil and military," says Mr. Le Bas, in his life of Bishop Middleton, "did not, there is reason to believe, in 1814, exceed thirty-two in the proportion of fifteen for Bengal, twelve for Madras, and five for Bombay. This number, small as it was, was subject to continual reduction, by illness, death, necessary absence, or return to England; such, for instance, was the amount of these casualties at Bombay, on the arrival of Archdeacon Barnes, in 1814, that he found at that Presidency only one efficient clergyman." A more recent writer on the state of the Anglican Church in India, Mr. Whitehead, says that this computation is too high, and makes a corrected statement on the authority of Mr. Abbott, the Ecclesiastical Register:—"On the arrival of Bishop Middleton, in 1814, he found effective resident chaplains in Bengal, eight; in Madras, five or six; and in Bombay, one. Missionaries under episcopal jurisdiction, or licensed by the bishop, there were none. India then possessed fifteen parochial clergy." From that period, however, the Anglican Church has progressively increased in extent and importance. Under the Act of 1833, the bishop and the three archdeacons, whom Lord Castlereagh had apologetically introduced to the notice of the House, grew into three bishops and three archdeacons.

Madras and Bombay were raised to the dignity of episcopal sees; and with this increase of ecclesiastical supervision there was also an increase of ordinary ecclesiastical agency. The establishment had gradually grown under the Charter of 1813; but there has been greater growth since its close. In 1832-33 there were on the establishment of the Bengal Presidency *thirty-seven* chaplains; in 1850-51 there were *sixty-one*. Under the Madras Government there were, in 1832-33, *twenty-three* chaplains; in 1850-51 there were *twenty-nine*. Attached to Bombay, in 1832-33, there were *fifteen* chaplains; in 1850-51 there were *twenty-three*. The total cost of these establishments was, in 1832-33, 96,000*l.*; in 1850-51 it had risen to 112,000*l.*

But far more important than this extension of the Church establishment, was the removal of the great barrier which had hitherto restrained the tide of missionary labor from flowing freely into India—almost, it may be said, from flowing there at all. It is curious in these days, when Christian missionaries cover the country by hundreds, to think of the dismay which the efforts of missionary units excited in the minds of the members of Lord Minto's Government, and the efforts which were made to control these dangerous excesses. Materials are not wanting for a vivid picture of the alarm which the mild efforts of the Serampore missionaries excited in the Council Chamber of Calcutta; but it hardly comes within the scope of this work to enter into such details. I would merely speak of the ascertained results of the labors of Wilberforce, Charles Grant, and their Christian comrades, which emancipated the Gospel throughout our British possessions in the East. A vast impulse was necessarily given to Christian missions by the "pious clauses" of the Charter Act of 1813, and all through the twenty years of its operation the magnitude of our missionary works steadily increased, and the results of missionary labor were more apparent. But in this, as in every other great field of operation, it is since the passing of the Act under which India is now governed that the greatest strides forward have been made. In 1830 there were 10 missionary societies at work in India; in 1850 there were 22. In 1830 there were 106 missionary stations; in 1850 there were 260. In 1830 there were 147 missionaries in the field; in 1850 there were 403. Such has been the progress made in the twenty years between 1830 and 1850.*

* These missionary statistics are taken from an elaborate paper, entitled "Results of Missionary Labors in India," originally contributed by the Rev. Mr. Mullins, in the *Calcutta Review*, and subsequently published in a sepa-

The effect of this increased agency may, in some measure, be gathered from the following statistical paper, laid before the Missionary Conference in Calcutta a few years ago. It showed, that in Lower Bengal, exclusive of Kishnaghur, the accessions of native converts to the Christian Church had been made thus:

From 1793 to 1802	27
„ 1803 to 1812	161
„ 1813 to 1822	403
„ 1823 to 1832	675
„ 1833 to 1842	1045
„ 1843 and 1844 (two years) . .	485*

I have no doubt that there are many readers who will be glad to see, in one comprehensive view, the statistics of Protestant mission in India, as existing at the present time:

——	Missionaries.	Native Preachers.	Churches.	Members.	Christians.
In Bengal, Orissa, and Assam . . .	101	135	71	3,416	14,401
In the N. W. Provinces	58	39	21	608	1,828
In the Madras Presidency . . .	164	308	162	10,464	74,512
In the Bombay Presidency . . .	37	11	12	223	554
In Ceylon . . .	43	58	43	2,645	11,859
Total . .	403	551	309	17,356	103,154

It will be gathered from this statement, that under the Presidency of Madras, which does not in respect of secular affairs exhibit very encouraging signs of progress, missionary labor has hitherto made the greatest impression.† But it is probable that the progressive results are more satisfactory in Bengal.

rate form. I am told that these statistics have been most rigorously tested, and that their accuracy has been abundantly demonstrated.

* Mullins.

† The causes of this are well explained by Mr. Mullins in the paper which I quoted above: "By far the greatest progress has been made in South India, in the provinces of Tinnevelley and Travancore. Missionary work has long been carried on in these districts, and the people are far more open to the Gospel than other Hindoos. In Travancore there is a native Government, and the Brahmins are both numerous and powerful. But the majority of the people, both there and in Tinnevelly, are not Hindoos like those in Northern India. They are Shanars, a large body devoted especially to the cultivation of the palm-tree: and, whether immigrants, or a portion of the aborigines of the land, who have been enslaved by Brahmin conquerors, they still retain their original customs. They

The number of missionaries, mission stations, churches, and converts, entered under the Bombay head, is comparatively small—comparatively with the agency at work under the other presidencies—but comparatively with the past, how great. In 1847, on his departure from Western India, Mr. Fyvie, an American missionary at Surat, spoke thus of the changes which he had lived to witness in Bombay:

"Persons arriving at Bombay now visit it under different circumstances from what it was twenty-five or thirty years ago. When I landed on your shores, there was only one church in Bombay, and one service on the Lord's Day, very thinly attended indeed. There are now six places of public worship on this island for divine service in English, and a seventh is now building. Thirty or thirty-five years ago, evangelical preaching was, I fear, but little known on this island; but now the case is happily very

are all devil-worshippers, and worship the objects of their fear with horrible ceremonies and disgusting dances. They continually add to the number of their devils: and singularly enough in one district, *an Englishman was worshipped as such*, for many years. The offerings presented on his tomb, were *spirits and cigars!* The Shanars are said to be 'the least intellectual people found in India.' Their long servitude and oppression have debased them to a very low level: and, though a few are found to possess considerable ability, the majority are marked by apathy, indifference, ignorance, and vice, and are unable to carry out a process of thought for any length of time. Their social bonds, such as those of parents to children, are feeble; and their social amusements few. But withal they are a docile and pliant people, and decidedly willing to improve. The causes, which led to such a rapid progress of Christianity among them, are readily discernible. Their religion sat very lightly on them; their caste is low; the religion of Europeans, was, of course, looked upon with favor. In Travancore a special reason existed. Many years ago, General Munro procured an order from the Rani, that Christians should be exempted from work on their sabbath, and from employment in the Hindoo festivals. These circumstances have contributed much towards the easy passage of so many converts from Heathenism to Christianity. The whole number, now under instruction, we reckon to be 52,000. It must not, however, be supposed that they are all true Christians. None know this better, or have spoken it more plainly, than the missionaries, who instruct them. Yet had they only given up their abominable devil-worship, a great thing would have been accomplished. But they have done more. They have placed themselves under an evangelical ministry; they regularly attend public worship: more than 17,000 children and young people are daily instructed in Christian schools, some of whom are being educated as teachers, and others as preachers to their countrymen. Best of all, a goodly number have exhibited in their lives the fruits of conversion to God. A great improvement has taken place in this numerous body of Christian natives; a great desire is evinced for increased instruction; family prayer is not uncommon; the public services are well attended; and a large sum in the aggregate is annually contributed for Christian books and for the poor. The whole Shanar population, 120,000 in number, is open to missionaries; and, if societies are faithful, and missionaries faithful, we may hope, in two or three generations, to see the whole of the southern provinces of India entirely Christianised."

different, and has long been so. Less than thirty-five years ago, there were no Educational, Bible, Tract, or Missionary Societies here. Is not the case now very different? Then one hardly knew where to look for a decidedly pious person, for the worship of God in families, and prayer-meetings in public. In how many pious families, in this place and at other stations, is the voice of prayer and praise presented to God, morning and evening, at the family altar: while weekly prayer-meetings are also numerous. In viewing all that has been done among our countrymen, have we no cause to say, 'What hath God wrought!'

"Thirty years ago, if any native had wished to become acquainted with Christianity, there was then no Bible, Tract, or Christian book in Mahrathi or Gujuratt, to put into his hand. During the last twenty-five years, however, the Bible has been translated and printed in both these languages, so that the people can now read in their own tongues the wonderful works of God. Tracts, discourses, prayers, and catechisms, have been prepared and widely circulated, and are read by thousands throughout the length and breadth of the land. Some of the heathen at the different missionary stations have believed the Gospel report; others, an increasing number, are convinced of the truth of Christianity, but have not yet sufficient moral courage to put on Christ, and to forsake all for his name: some of the converts have become preachers of the Gospel. When I arrived in India, the American brethren, Messrs. Hall and Newell, were laboring amidst many discouragements to establish their first native school. Now there are numerous schools at all the different missionary stations; and they might be greatly increased. When I arrived, with the exception of the two American brethren mentioned, there were no missionaries in the whole of Western India. Since that time, the great Lord of the harvest has thrust forth many laborers from Great Britain and Ireland, America, and the Continent of Europe. Let us bless God for this: and pray that they may be upheld, directed, comforted, and sanctified, and their labors greatly blessed. No doubt, but in due time, they or their successors shall reap largely, if they faint not."

In the whole history of Indian progress there is nothing that cheers the heart more than the progress of morality and religion among our own people. It was said of old that we must begin there—that we must first convert ourselves, and then think of converting the people of India. It is certain that the English, in our Eastern settlement, are not now open to the old reproach, "Christian-man—Devil-man." As to the conversion of the heathen, it is equally certain that our people have labored diligently for it—that they have done much, and suffered much, in the good cause—and that the results, as far as the human eye can discern them, have well repaid all this toil. What the amount of real conversion may be, humanity cannot determine; it can only speak of the palpable results. I have now before me, from the pen of one who speaks of what he has seen,* some account of the encouraging indications of a change coming, or come:

"Temples are being allowed, to a great extent, to fall into decay, while the number of new ones erected is by no means large. In those parts where missions have been carried on most extensively, a considerable falling off in the attendance at the great festivals is distinctly observable. The swinging festival, for instance, in Lower Bengal is very different from what it used to be. The number of idols sold at festivals is greatly diminished, and the offerings at the great temples are of far less value than they once were. A great change has taken place in the views and in the spirit of the people at large. Formerly they knew nothing of what true religion really is; but they have been enlightened on the nature of moral obligation, the duty of love to God, of love to men, and the nature and evil of sin. Missions have gone far, during the last fifty years, in developing a conscience amongst the natives, in whom it was in a deadly sleep. Is not this alone a great result? The Hindoos, too, have begun to lay aside some of their old notions. The Brahmins are no longer so highly honored; the clever Sudras thrust them aside from place and power without scruple; by far the greater increase of wealth and wisdom has been diffused among the latter. Thousands now approve of female education; and, in the great cities, the ladies of numerous families are being privately taught. Even the remarriage of widows is discussed by the native papers, and its

* Mr. Mullins.

advantages fully acknowledged. A numerous body is coming forward in society, possessing far more enlightened notions than their fathers did; a body of men, who put little faith in the Shastras, and look upon the old pandits and teachers as ignorant bigots. The great contrast between these two parties shows how great a step has been made in the process of public enlightenment. The spirit, in which Bible truth is heard, has also greatly improved. Formerly, when a missionary preached, he was compelled to enter into disagreeable and apparently useless controversies; the same objections were brought forward again and again; and the discussion was frequently closed, with the practical application of broken pots, sand, dirt, and cries of 'Hari bol!' But now, in all the older missionary stations and even beyond them, discussions seldom occur. The people come to the chapels, and often listen to the end: frequently acknowledging aloud the truth of what is said. What is even more singular is, that small companies have been found in various parts of the country, who have gathered a little collection of Christian books, and meet together to read and study them. These facts are full of encouragement from the proofs they furnish, that the word of God, though hidden, is not lost; but that, like good seed, it *will* spring up and put forth, first the blade, then the ear, after that the full corn in the ear. Only let this word, so extensively known, be applied with power 'by the Holy Ghost sent down from heaven,' and, at once, 'the little one will become a thousand, and the small one a great nation.'"

I think that these signs are most cheering. God only knows what they indicate. But this I know, and may say, that the missionaries have proved themselves worthy of the confidence reposed in them, and that they have seldom or never done anything to embarrass the Government, under which, without molestation from the State, and with much encouragement generally from the servants of the State, they have conducted their peaceful operations. The improved relations, indeed, between the missionaries and the Government are in themselves no small evidence of the better temper of the latter.

I know that it may be said, as it often has been said, that the Indian Government still countenances much that it knows to be wrong—much error, much superstition, much that every Christian man must desire to see rooted out of the land. I am anxious to state the case with all fairness. It is not to be denied that the question, when it presented itself for the solution of Christian administrators, was a very difficult one. The question was not whether Christianity was to be supported in India, and heathenism discouraged; but how far, consistently with outstanding pledges and existing obligations, Christianity could be supported and heathenism discouraged. Whether those pledges were wisely given—those obligations wisely contracted—might have been another question; but it is of little use now to discuss it. There they were in legible black and white, in substantive regulations, and there was now no ignoring them. It remained only for us to put upon them the right practical construction, and it was only in respect of this construction that any difference of opinion could have arisen among reasonable and well-informed men.

The practical observation of a solemn pledge, deliberately given and distinctly enunciated to the natives of India, was plainly and unmistakeably incumbent upon us, and we should err if we neglected it by going in search of any more remote and speculative, perhaps unattainable, good. But it is our duty, at the same time, to be cautious of going beyond the pledge—of giving too literal a construction to the words of the obligations which we have taken upon ourselves. I think that there was a tendency at one time to run into this extreme. At all events, the British-Indian Government, from year's end to year's end, has been growing less and less tenacious on the score of the over-strict observance of these old pledges, and has been gradually loosening its connexion with idolatry in the manner least calculated to excite alarm, or to occasion offence. There is a great difference between active participation in evil, and simple toleration of it. The Regulations of 1793 had promised the natives of India "to preserve to them the laws of the Shaster and the Koran," and to "protect them in the free exercise of their religion." But they had not pledged our Government to interfere in the internal management of their temples, the decoration of their idols, and the ordering of their religious processions. Little by little these errors were swept out of our administrative system. From the time when, in 1809, Government decreed that "the superintendence of the idol of Juggernauth and its interior economy" should be thenceforth vested in the Rajah of Koordah, the chains which have bound us to the externalities of the false creeds of the country have gradually been loosened; and now there is little left of a system which, in these days, few Christians are prepared to commend. It was partly, in a spirit of tenderness and compassion for the poor people whom we had trodden down with the iron heel of conquest, partly from considerations of policy, that, at the outset of our career, as rulers, we had been more regardful for the honor of the Hindoo religion than for our own. But the error, founded as it was on what we then believed to be a sense of justice, has given way to the increased regard which the rulers of India entertain for the obligations of the religion they profess; and, whilst on the one side they have learned to treat with courtesy and respect the bringers of glad tidings, whom of old they cast out with reproach, they have ceased to cherish the abominations against which the good men whom they discarded were not suffered to do battle by themselves.

It is fitting that a sketch of Indian Progress should be closed with a brief mention of these things. Never at any time has the Government of India evinced, by acts of practical beneficence, so kindly an interest in the welfare of the people, as within the last few years of its rule.

It has bethought itself of better means of securing the allegiance of the people than by pampering their priests and decorating their idols. It has not only, in these latter days, loosened the chains which bound the rulers of the country to the idolatry, which from remote ages has been the curse of the people, but has loosened the chains which bound to it the Gentile worshipper himself. It has been well said that, "as soon as a little fellow could be made to understand that the earth was 25,000 miles round there was an end of the Shastre."

My labors draw on to a close. In looking back at what I have written, I find that I have left unsaid much that I had comprehended in the original scheme of my work. But I think I have written enough to show that the East India Company and their servants have not been unmindful of the great trust that has been reposed in them, and that their administration has been one of progressive improvement—improvement which is now advancing with strides such as have never been made before. Never were the rulers of India so mindful as now of the duties and responsibilities which have devolved upon them, as guardians of the happiness of that immense section of the great human family, which Providence has so mysteriously committed to their care. The last twenty years have witnessed more great changes tending to increase the prosperity, the happiness, the civilisation of the people of India, than the antecedent two centuries of British connexion with the East. But the changes which have been consummated, and of which we are now witnessing the results, are small in proportion to those which we have originated, and of which the next cycle of twenty years will witness the completion. If the great administrative system, under which our Empire in India has been built up, remains fundamentally unchanged, those will be bright chapters of Indian progress which will grow beneath the pen of the historian of 1873. I believe that under no other system would that Empire have risen to its present height—under no other system would it have survived the assaults of time and the shocks of circumstance. If India had been grievously misgoverned, we should not have been masters of it now.

An acute author of the present day has observed: "The historian knows the end of many of the transactions he narrates. If he did not, how differently often he would narrate them. It would be a most instructive thing to give a man the materials for the account of a great transaction, stopping short at the end, and then see how different would be his account from the ordinary ones."* I have often thought, when consulting the early records of the Company, how different would be my forecast of the issue of all these rude struggles of our English adventurers in the time of the Stuarts, if I had addressed myself to the task of research in utter ignorance of more recent events—if, indeed, I had groped my way along paths of virgin inquiry, making discoveries at every step, as in the pages of a new romance. But I think that the essayist has stopped short at a point where his reflection was susceptible of a much more important application than that to which he has directed it. It is from the difference between our own rough-hewing and the shaping of our ends by a higher power† that the great lesson is to be learnt. The inequality of the means to the end — the seemingly irreconcileable difference between the magnitude of the effect and the pettiness of the cause—the utter unlikelihood, prospectively, of such a sequence of events as, retrospectively, we know to have arisen—the entire confusion, indeed, of all the calculations of human wisdom,

* *Friends in Council.*

† There's a Divinity that shapes our ends
Rough-hew them as we may.

which we so plainly discern when we look at such an event as the establishment of our Indian Empire in its inchoate fragmentary state, as with the eyes of a cotemporary of Bacon or Clarendon—are so many finger-prints of the "hand of God in history," which he who would read the annals of the Company aright, should dwell upon with reverence and humility.

In the inscrutable manner in which, whilst the nationalities of the East and the West, were breaking up around us, Providence preserved that little party of London merchants to work out its great designs, is to be found the key-note of Anglo-Indian history. It was not for any petty ends that this great miracle was wrought in our behalf. It was not for any petty ends that principality after principality was surrendered into our hands, and the will of the Company became law from the banks of the Indus to the banks of Irrawaddy. It was that the great Christian nation, thus mysteriously selected, should achieve great things in the East, and finally work out the scheme of India's emancipation. How we are now fulfilling our mission, I have in some sort endeavoured to show. Physically* and morally —materially and intellectually, we are impressing ourselves abidingly on the country and on the people. I hope that I have shown that the English in India have not sat down idly under the weight of their responsibilities and fallen asleep in the shade, whilst they ought to have been bearing the burden and heat of the day in strenous efforts for the elevation of a long-oppressed fallen race.

* I feel that I ought, as, indeed, I intended, in this work, to have said something of the efforts that have been made in India to improve the *physique* of the people, by means of great sanatory measures. It is hard to say to what extent the intellectual and moral character of the natives of India is influenced by these causes. The diffusion of the medical science of the West will, doubtless, do much to invigorate the people; but, perhaps, the sanatory measures, initiated by Mr. J. R. Martin in the capital, and radiating thence into all parts of the country, will still more extensively affect the character of the people. In the regeneration of the people of India, this will not be one of the least effective agents.

I believe that our Indian Empire is the admiration and the envy of the European world. There is not a foreign state that does not wonder at the marvellous success which has attended, not only the progress of our arms, but the progress of our administration. France, under the burden and the trouble of a new Empire in Algeria, seeks counsel from the East India Company as to the true mode of governing Mahomedan subjects.* Austria looks on with respectful wonder, gravely confessing a right understanding of all the elements of our national grandeur, except our marvellous Empire in the East.† Prussia sends forth her princes to see the great marvel for themselves, and to tell on their return how we conquer kingdoms and how we retain them. Russia, with ill-disguised chagrin, tries to believe the falsehoods of our enemies, and yet knows in her inmost heart what is the wisdom and beneficence of our rule.‡ The marvel and the mystery are more patent to stranger eyes than to our own.§ We think too little of the

* This, I believe, was in 1847.

† The Duke of Newcastle stated, in a speech delivered at Haileybury in the summer of 1852, that travelling, in the Austrian Tyrol, he fell in with a very intelligent Austrian general, who, in the course of a conversation on our national resources, said that he could understand all the elements of our greatness, except our Anglo-Indian Empire, and *that* he could not understand. The vast amount of administrative wisdom, which the good government of such an Empire demanded, baffled his comprehension.

‡ I am told that De Warren's *L'Inde Anglaise* is a text-book with the Russian officers on the Eastern frontier. What are their real ideas of the duties of Christian states may, perhaps, be gathered from the fact that Prince Saltikoff told an English officer, who had been exerting himself to bring about the suppression of Suttee in Rajpootana, that he thought it a pity to suppress anything so romantic, for that in proportion as such customs as these were abolished the people of India would cease to be interesting.

§ Hear the evidence of another nation. Italy, through Sismondi, says:—"Such as they are, however, the English are still the best masters that India has ever had. Wherever in this vast continent their dominion is direct, it is a real benefit. They have re-established security and justice; they have given the people a feeling of duration, and of something to look forward to; and exactly because they keep themselves apart, because they do not wish to direct everything, to change everything, they have permitted Indian civilisation under them to resume its natural progress. Agriculture is flourishing; the arts are cultivated with ease; population and riches begin to increase; intelligence makes some progress; and European opinions engraft themselves naturally and gently on the old ideas of India; in short, the conquered people have learnt to defend the foreign rule; the native army is formidable, and there is little probability that if the road to India were opened to the Russians, they could sustain a struggle against the English."

mighty Providence which out of a petty mercantile adventure has evolved the grandest fact recorded in the History of the World.

We should never close our eyes against the great truth of this mysterious interference. It should enter largely into all our thoughts of the practicalities of Indian administration. The face of God has never yet been turned away from us save when we have done manifestly wrong. Often, in the weakness of our faith, we have doubted and hesitated; we have given ourselves up to petty shifts and temporary expedients, only to find that the very essence of political wisdom is to dare to do right. When that large-minded director of the Company, Charles Grant, declared that "if from unworthy fears we should disavow our religion, he should fear that the Great Author of that religion would be provoked to withdraw his protection there from us,"* he uttered sentiments which, forty years ago, were declared to be those only of an amiable fanatic. But what was once believed to be the wild mouthing of enthusiasm, is now looked upon as the language of calm and authoritative reason. Since our Indian statesmen and soldiers began to take more solemn views of their duties as Christian men, and the Directors of the Company have recognised more clearly and more gratefully the wonderful interposition of Providence in their behalf, they have achieved an amount of practical success such as never attended their efforts, when they suffered manifold idle fears and vain vaticinations to arrest the stream of Indian Progress.

* *Ante*, p. 638.

APPENDIX.

APPENDIX.

(A)

THE SALT DUTIES.

[*From the Statistical Papers relating to India, prepared at the India House.*]

BENGAL.

THE supply of salt in Bengal is provided partly by manufacture, conducted on account of the Government,* partly by importation, and in one instance† by private manufacture, under a system of excise. The duty‡ on all imported salt is two and a half rupees per maund of 82lbs., or about three farthings per lb. The same rate of duty is levied as excise on salt manufactured by private individuals; and the Government salt may be purchased at all times in quantities of not less than 50 maunds, at a fixed price, which is composed of the cost price, with the addition of two and a half rupees per maund, or three farthings per lb. The average cost price of production§ is about 80 rupees per 100 maunds, or a trifle below one farthing per lb., thus making the Government selling price under a penny per lb. The supply of salt is no longer a monopoly; its manufacture and sale have not been relinquished by Government, but individuals participate in its provision, both by importation and manufacture, under a combined system of customs and excise.

The system of *fixed prices* and *open warehouses* commenced in

* The manufacture is carried on, not by hired labour on the part of the Government, but by a system of pecuniary advances; the parties receiving them being bound to deliver, at a fixed price, all the salt manufactured. Probably 100,000 laborers (called Molunghees) are engaged in the manufacture in the Sunderbunds.

† Mr. Prinsep's salt-works at Narrainpore.

‡ The duty is levied at the time of the clearance of the salt from the bonded warehouses.

§ The salt agencies are located along the head of the Bay of Bengal, viz. at Hidgelee, Tumlook, Chittagong, Arracan, Cuttack, Balasore, Khoredah.

1836-37, when the previous system of *fixed qualities* and *periodical sales* was abolished.*

	Maunds of 82 lbs.
During the seven years commencing with 1837-38 and ending with 1843-44, the duty on salt was 3rs. 4a. per maund. The annual average† quantity of salt sold and imported during that period was	4,627,030
In November, 1844, the duty was reduced to 3rs. per maund, and the annual average sale increased to	4,966,917
In April, 1847, the duty was further reduced to 2rs. 12a. per maund, and the annual sale increased to........	5,452,909
In April, 1849, the duty was again subjected to reduction, when it was fixed for five years at its present rate of 2rs. 8a. per maund.	

It will thus be seen that in the five years above adverted to, the reduction effected in the salt-tax amounted to nearly 25 per cent.; but it would appear that no further reduction can, for the present, be expected consistently with the maintenance of the revenue, the last reduction in 1849 having led to no further increase of consumption.

NORTH-WESTERN PROVINCES.

The supply of salt to the North-Western Provinces is furnished partly from the lower provinces of Bengal, and partly from the Sambhur Salt Lake,‡ in Rajpootana, and other localities on the western side of India. The salt of Bengal having paid the excise or import duty of 2 rupees 8 a. per maund, passes free into the North-Westen Provinces. The Sambhur and other salt, on crossing the north-western frontier customs line, is subjected to a duty of 2 rupees per maund, and to a further duty of half a rupee§ per maund on transmission to the eastward of Allahabad, thus coming into competition with the salt of Bengal under an equal duty of 2 rupees 8 a. per maund.

MADRAS.

At Madras salt is manufactured on account of Government, and

* As recommended by the Select Committee of the House of Commons in 1836. All the recommendations of that Committee have now been fully and fairly carried out, viz.—

1st. Open warehouses and fixed prices.

2nd. Imported salt to be subjected to the same rate of duty as native manufactured salt.

3rd. The rate of duty to be fixed below the average of net profits for a series of ten years (such average having been calculated at 3 rupees per maund).

† These averages are exclusive of the quantities disposed of by retail sales, which cannot be given with perfect accuracy.

‡ The Sambhur Lake belongs to the native States of Joudpore and Jyepore.

§ The Allahabad special duty was fixed by Act 14 of 1843 at one rupee per maund; but in 1847, and again in 1849, when reduction of duty on Bengal salt was effected, corresponding reductions were made in the Allahabad duty.

sold for internal consumption at one rupee per maund, or under one farthing per lb.* The duty on imported foreign salt was 3 rupees per maund, but it has been recommended by the home authorities that the import duty should (as in Bengal) be equal only to the difference between the selling price and the cost of manufacture; the difference between the cost price and the price at which the salt is given out for consumption being the duty to be realised.

BOMBAY.

In Bombay the manufacture of salt is carried on by individuals, but subject to an excise duty of twelve annas (1*s.* 6*d.*) per maund,† a similar duty being imposed on imported salt. Salt exported from this presidency to Calcutta is subject to the above excise duty, but credit for that amount is given at Calcutta in the adjustment of the local duty. Facilities are also afforded for the export of salt to Malabar, Travancore, Cochin, and other places.

PUNJAB.

The excise duty on salt at the Punjab salt mines has been fixed at 2 rupees per maund.

English salt, it is said, may be laid down at Calcutta at 44s. per ton, or about 80 rs. per 100 maunds.‡

According to another authority,§ 65 rs. per 100 maunds is the lowest possible rate at which the transaction could be effected. But salt from the Persian Gulf and other Arab States is laid down at Calcutta at 40 rs. per 100 maunds. It is therefore the high cost of producing Bengal salt (80 rs. per 100 maunds) which alone enables English salt to keep a footing in the Calcutta market.

In Bengal salt is obtained by boiling the sea-water.

In Bombay and Madras the process is that of solar evaporation.

In the Punjab it is extracted in a pure state from the salt mines.

The Sambhur Salt Lake, in Rajpootana, overflows during the rains, and when the waters subside, a deep incrustation of salt is deposited on its shores for several miles round.

* By Act 6 of 1844, sect. 43, the selling price of the Government salt was fixed at one and a half rupees per maund. It has subsequently been reduced to one rupee, by order of the Court.

† The duty on salt on delivery from salt-works was fixed, by Act 27 of 1837, at half a rupee per maund. It was subsequently increased to one rupee per maund by Act 16 of 1844, and reduced to twelve annas, its present price, by order of the Court in the same year.

‡ *Aylwyn on Salt Trade.*

§ *Calcutta Review.*

Salt purchased at Calcutta at 1d. per lb., the Government price, is sold at Benares (400 miles from Calcutta, where it comes into competition with the salt from Rajpootana) at 12 lbs. the rupee, or 2d. per lb.; and, moreover, it is stated to be then considerably adulterated. The consumption of salt in India has been usually estimated* at 12 lbs. per head per annum; and assuming the wages of agricultural labor† at 3 rupees per mensem (the rate now paid on the Calcutta and Bombay mail-road, and also to village watchmen), it would, at Calcutta, absorb the income of five days' labor to provide the quantity required for a year. The salt duty thus operates as a tax of about 1½ per cent. upon the laborer's wages, if he have none but himself to provide for. If he have a wife or children, the per-centage will of course be increased by the amount of their consumption. It is to be observed, however, on the other side, that the wife and children would generally contribute something to the common fund by the earnings of their labor, and thus again reduce the per-centage.

At Benares the purchase of the same quantity of salt (12 lbs.) would absorb ten days' earnings, thus constituting a charge of 3 per cent. on the laborer's income. But for this additional charge the Government duty is in nowise accountable. The difference in price is occasioned by the cost of conveyance, profits of trade, wastage, &c., the ordinary charges of commerce.‡

The pressure of the salt-tax on the laborer cannot be regarded as severe, inasmuch as it is the only way in which he contributes to the pecuniary necessities of the State; in all other respects he is not necessarily subject to taxation.

The preceding remarks apply to the Upper and Lower Provinces of Bengal. In the territories of Madras and Bombay the duty on salt is only about one-third of that which prevails in Bengal; but from other causes the mass of the people are believed to be in inferior circumstances to those of Bengal. In Madras they are still subject to various taxes (moturpha tax, duty on tobacco, &c.), which have been abolished elsewhere.

A comparison of the amount of salt produced with the numbers of the population consuming it, will show that the estimate which assigns 12 lbs. as the ordinary annual consumption of an individual, is nearly in correspondence with fact. The quantity of

* *Report of Board of Customs, Salt and Opium: Calcutta*, 1819. Also *Calcutta Review*, 1847.

† In 1846, 2000 laborers were engaged for employment on the Calcutta and Bombay mail-road, at 3 rupees per head per mensem.—See also *Regulation XXII. of* 1816, *sect.* 4.

‡ Of these the principal item is cost of carriages, but on the completion of the railway now in progress this will be greatly reduced in the districts which it traverses. It is computed that the expense of conveying a ton of merchandise will not exceed 2¾d. per mile; consequently salt may be carried from Calcutta to Benares for one halfpenny per lb.

salt sold wholesale and retail or imported was, in 1846-47, as under:

	Maunds of 82lbs.
Bengal	6,166,258
North-Western Provinces	2,670,943
Madras	4,587,720
Bombay	2,573,625
	15,998,546
	82
	31,997,092
	127,988,368
	1,311,880,772lbs.

If the entire population of *British* India be assumed at ninety-nine millions, which from the latest official information may be considered as about its actual extent, the above-mentioned quantity of salt would afford to each individual about 13 lbs., the facts collected by statistical research thus corroborating an estimate founded on observation of the habits of the people.

The following table exhibits the quantity of salt imported into Calcutta from all countries, and also from England, for the last seven years:*

—	Imported from all Countries.	From England.
	Maunds.	Maunds.
1844-45	970,595	791
1845-46	1,581,968	502,616
1846-47	1,466,744	352,835
1847-48	1,615,084	752,998
1848-49	1,626,706	459,803
1849-50	2,126,848	624,673
1850-51 (the first six months of)	1,455,007	672,092

* *Board of Customs, Salt and Opium.*

STATEMENT exhibiting the Net Revenue derived from Salt from all sources—viz., Government Sales, Excise on Private Manufacture, and Customs Duty, from the year 1839-40.

Year.	Bengal.	N.-W. Prov.	Madras.	Bombay.	TOTAL.
	Rupees.	Rupees.	Rupees.	Rupees.	Rupees.
1839-40 ...	1,61,94,188	26,90,511	33,82,422	12,72,209	2,35,39,330
1840-41 ...	1,63,80,084	24,43,614	30,21,805	14,58,218	2,33,03,721
1841-42 ...	1,57,50,967	26,81,822	33,61,806	13,42,601	2,31,37,196
1842-43 ...	1,64,33,412	25,06,731	32,10,959	16,25,339	2,36,76,441
1843-44 ...	1,55,78,010	35,86,467	37,35,644	16,99,579	2,45,99,700
1844-45 ...	1,60,42,730	47,82,645	37,81,369	18,47,502	2,64,54,246
1845-46 ...	1,49,09,021	37,75,196	40,34,020	21,01,109	2,48,19,346
1846-47 ...	1,62,79,725	52,47,071	39,84,188	17,77,565	2,72,88,549
1847-48 ...	1,65,83,668	48,26,209	41,94,855	23,45,006	2,79,49,738
1848-49 ...	1,41,44,321	45,65,642	37,69,440	21,06,855	2,45,86,258
1849-50 ...	1,61,07,384	53,79,810	38,33,312	21,57,591	2,74,78,097*

[Having given above the Statistics of the Salt Duties, I append some remarks, written by a friend in India, on the social and moral aspects of the question. They appear to me to be as just as they are able.]

Of all the great sources of Indian revenue not one has been so much assailed as the "monopoly" of Salt. It is here that the philanthropist will find his most palpable object of censure, the partisan of free-trade his most vulnerable point of attack, and the advocate of the Company his least defensible position. Now it is conceded at once, that salt is as necessary a daily condiment to the Indian cultivator as it is to the English peasant: that in a country where sudden and mysterious attacks of disease are common, it has been thought essential to a healthy condition of the physical system: that in some parts of Bengal it may be manufactured at a trifling cost and with the slightest amount of labor by any one who will scrape together a few handfuls of earth, and yet that in those very localities, where it is most readily made, the transport of salt is only permitted under the most rigid observance of certain forms, and under the safeguard of authenticated passes, whilst the adulteration, the import, the manufacture or even connivance at

	Rupees.
* Government Sales and Excise Duty	1,75,98,287
Customs Duty on importation by sea............	45,00,000
On passing North-West Frontier customs line	53,79,810
	2,74,78,097

the manufacture thereof, are punishable by severe fines and by imprisonment. For a clear understanding of the subject I must state first that the salt eaten by the inhabitants of the whole of the Agra and the Bengal Presidencies including the Punjab, is supplied from four different great sources. 1. The salt manufactured by the Bengal Government. 2. Sea-imported salt which pays duty at Calcutta. 3. Salt imported into the Agra Presidency from native states. 4. Rock salt brought from the salt range in the Punjab. From all four sources the Government derives some revenue, but as the idea of monopoly is generally associated with the direct manufacture of the article by the Government, I will proceed first to describe the state of things in the salt producing localities of Lower Bengal, where the laws against illegal transport, store or manufacture, are by means of a preventive establishment maintained in all their severity. The reader who may choose to consult the map of Bengal, will see along and above the tract known as the Sunderbunds, a number of tidal creeks and rivers of all sizes, by which the waters of the Gangetic Delta and of the whole of Bengal find their way to the sea. From the hills which border the Eastern frontier to the province of Cuttack in the West, and from the very shores of the Bay northward as far as the spring tide reaches in the dry season, the soil impregnated with saline particles is singularly well fitted for the manufacture of salt. For a great part of this tract, which may be four hundred miles in length and one hundred and twenty in depth, there is a dense and increasing population who subsist principally on rice and fish. Any landholder in these parts, were it not for the Salt Laws, would have only to lay out a moderate amount of capital in order to establish a successful and lucrative salt manufactory. Any Ryot without capital, with the help of a stew-pan, a few sticks and a few handsful of earth, would extract day by day, or week by week, salt sufficient for the consumption of himself and his family. But I will take a somewhat parallel case in England, though it does not apparently equal the present one in hardship. In a well-wooded, well-watered, and rich country in England there is a large estate, of ten thousand acres, the proprietor of which is a strict preserver of game. His tenants, who pay a high rent, are not permitted to shoot one single head of the hundreds of pheasants and scores of hares which devastate their finest crops. Poaching is visited with unrelenting severity by magistrates, who have a fellow-feeling with the game-preserving landlord. The law creates offences, and punishes with rigor the offences it creates. Still, in defence of this system it may be said that winged and four-footed game, in such plenty, is not the spontaneous production of the climate and the soil; on the breeding, rearing, and multiplying of pheasants, much care, time, and money have been expended by the proprietor. His love of field sports helps to bind him to the estate. It is not essential to the health and prosperity of his tenants that they should dine off pheasants and partridges, or to the punctual payment of rents, that they should despatch bags of game to the poulterers in town. Harsh as the system may appear to a philanthropist, it has some redeeming points, and it is associated with much that is attractive in the character of an English gentleman, his delight in active exercises, his healthful recreation, his love of a rural life. It is looked on by farmers, the sportsman will say, sometimes with positive indifference, rarely with hatred. It does not on the whole press heavily on the poor man who earns a few shillings a week. But in the salt-producing localities of Bengal, a small proprietor and a poor cultivator, placed within arms' length, as it were, of this condiment, are, by a code of laws cunningly devised, carefully guarded, and enforced to the letter, forbidden, except through the intervention of Government, to procure one single handful thereof for their simplest meal.

I believe that the most avowed opponent of the Company must allow that the above are the most damaging accusations which could, with any just foundation, be brought against the Salt-tax. As to the statements relative to the bad quality and excessive price of the Company's salt, I trust to show that they are without good foundation. I return to the locality in which the salt of Bengal is produced, for, as it is there that the salt code is rigorously enforced, it is the inhabitants of those parts, and those only, who have any right to cry out against it as a hardship. The reasoning which I ventured to adopt in the case of the opium monopoly, I may venture, *mutatis mutandis*, to apply to this case also. The law is a dead letter where no temptation to break or evade it exists, even though that law be in theory harsh, oppressive, and unjust. It is no more a hardship to tell the inhabitant of Patna or Ghazepore that he shall not manufacture salt, or the rice eater of the Sunderbunds that he shall on no account cultivate the poppy, than it is to tell an elderly gentleman that he must not rob an orchard, or an Oxford undergraduate that he is not to play at marbles in the High-street. I will, however, proceed to describe briefly the mode followed by the Indian Government in making salt. At and near the spots best suited to the purpose are situated the salt agencies, which are six in number. The land most capable of producing salt is retained in the hands of Government, and the proprietors thereof are indemnified for the loss of revenue otherwise attainable from its cultivation. The salt is manufactured yearly, to the amount fixed by the Board of Revenue, by a class of men who gain their livelihood in this manner, and who receive every year advances in hard cash for the purposes of manufacture. These men, molunghees, as they are termed in Indian parlance, agree to deliver the salt at so much a maund at the various store-houses of Government. A great portion of the salt so manufactured and stored is transported to large store-houses at the Presidency, where it is sold to the native dealers in this article, who retail it all over the country. A certain duty added to the cost of transport and to that of manufacture is what Government pretends to levy. At the present time salt is manufactured at the different agencies, at an average rather under one shilling a maund, and is sold at that price, plus a fixed duty of five shillings for the same quantity. Add to this the cost of transport to the Presidency, and you will have the sum total at which salt is purchased by the native dealer from Government. In round numbers it is rather more than six shillings a maund, and a maund is equal to eighty-two English pounds.

The salt stored in the repositories of Government is a sound, pure, and healthy edible. Any doubt on the subject may be instantaneously removed by an inspection of the great storehouses at the Presidency, near the terminus of the railway, when it will at once be acknowledged that the stories of the Indian Government making, by means of an unjust monopoly, a dear and unwholesome article, are so many idle tales. If the salt of Government is adulterated, it is adulterated by the retail dealer, and what system, whether confined to Government or open to all speculators, could guarantee the prevention of this evil? I repeat, too, that the Salt Laws operate differently in other parts of the empire to what they do in the salt-producing localities. In the tract mentioned as stretching along the Bay of Bengal within the influence of the tides, their operation is certainly severe and uniform. It is a misdemeanor, within this tract, for any private individual to manufacture salt, to store the article, or to transport it from one place to another without passes specifying its destination, owner, date of sale, and other minute particulars. Within this tract, too, preventive officers may stop and search any boats whatever, adapted to sea navigation, on mere suspicion of their containing salt: and they are permitted, in the presence of regular police-officers, to make a forcible entry into any house or warehouse in which they may have received information that salt, exceeding one maund in quantity, is actually stored. The limits of the tides are the limits of the preventive establishments, armed with these apparently terrible powers—the limits, in short, within which the salt code is vigorously upheld: but now comes the other side of the picture. The practical result of the code in increasing the number of inmates of gaols and reducing poor men to beggary is nil; the means taken to mitigate its severity and to supply salt to the cultivator are judicious. Men who have the welfare of the Indian population at heart will be glad to learn that in this large tract of country the number of cases instituted against individuals for the illegal manufacture of salt were in the year considerably within two hundred, and the number of men imprisoned for offences against the Salt Laws of all kinds did not at the close thereof exceed *one dozen*. That is to say, in a tract of country comprising at least three millions of inhabitants, who have every apparent temptation to violate the law, a mere fraction of the population had been found to engage in the illicit manufacture. Let this result be compared with the results of the operation of the Game Laws in any three counties in England! The reason for the fewness of convictions is neither a want of diligence on the part of the preventive officer, nor a want of spirit on that of the desponding cultivator. The reason is partly, that Government, anxious to mitigate the harshness of the monopoly, has directed that, in the salt-producing tract, where there is most temptation to manufacture or smuggle, salt shall be retailed by its own officers, at its own shops, at a price sufficiently low to take away from the poorest cultivator the temptation of violating the law; and partly because hundreds of Ryots, too lazy to go as far as the retail shops, do occasionally scrape together a few handsful of earth within the precincts of their huts, and manufacture each a pound or so of salt without the cognisance of the preventive officer. Cases in which individuals have been arraigned for transporting salt without any protective documents, or with documents of an informal character, or for transporting more salt than the quantity specified in their passes, are naturally more numerous than those of mere illicit manufacture. But the penalties enforced in these cases fall on individuals of a very different class from the mere tiller of the earth. They fall on habitual and determined smugglers, on merchants who cannot be content with their reasonable gains, on men, in short, who, under any Government or system in the world, would be the first to speculate on the best mode of baffling authority or resisting the payment of any lawful dues. They fall, too, in many cases, on the very men who derive a direct benefit from the monopoly, as it centres the traffic of salt in their hands. It is not in behalf of men like these that philanthropy should be anxious or sympathy be awakened.

Still, some objector may say, that if the salt monopoly were abandoned, and every man in the salt-producing localities were permitted to turn salt-manufacturer, the condition of the peasantry would be bettered, and the sources of wealth would be enlarged. It is impossible to argue on a supposition like this except from the known character of landlords, and tenants, and speculators, in the East. There is little doubt but that an individual or company might, with a little capital, manufacture salt for the Indian market at a cheaper rate than it is now made by Government, and thus consumers in the Bengal and Behar provinces might be benefited, but whether the inhabitants of the salt tract would be the better for it, is another question. Abandon the monopoly, and salt would be manufactured by every native landholder who could command money and energy enough for the purpose, or by every foreign adventurer who could obtain a lease of land from the apathetic or heedless Zemindar. It is not likely that such men would quietly permit every tenant on their estates to boil salt in his own salt pans, and enjoy a new luxury without interruption. The localities in which the salt of Bengal is manufactured are those in all India where rapacious landlords and their unscrupulous agents are most adept in practising extortion on a peasantry feeble by nature, enervated by climate, timorous by example, and vilified by the domination of centuries. Every person conversant with Lower Bengal will know the amount of dread which a wealthy Zemindar can strike into his tenantry by his rank and position, by his armed retainers, by the influence of superstition, by a control more strict than could be ever exercised by any preventive force of Government, by the unlimited command of evidence to suit every unforeseen occurrence in a long course of litigation, and by working on that unconquerable feeling which still pervades the masses in the East, and whispers to them that such men are set above the law. The testimony of hundreds of witnesses and the records of litigation for half a century present us with one dreary picture of landlords enhancing rents, forcing cultivators to purchase the necessaries of life only at their own markets; deciding disputes in the village on the principle that both disputants are to pay something into the judge's privy purse, levying every sort of illegal cess on the most frivolous pretences, and making of Eastern society only two great divisions, those who suffer, and those who inflict. It is idle to talk to a Bengali peasant about defending his rights and acting with a manly spirit. It is idle to say that there are courts open, European functionaries accessible, and prompt justice at hand, which neither money can purchase nor power defy. If, in our own England, it is well known that tenants have been ruined and driven forth houseless, because at some election they would not vote with the Lord of the Manor, it may easily be conceived what sort of remedy would be possessed in law by that Eastern tenant who should dare to lessen, by one penny, the profits of his landlord, or cross the most trivial of his cherished aims.

The abandonment of the salt monopoly in the rich alluvial and saline districts of Bengal, would in all probability, have the effect of enriching a few individuals, of supplying some of the up-country markets with a somewhat cheaper article, of depriving the Government of about a million of revenue, of preventing the free import of Liverpool and Manchester salt by sea, and of leaving the peasantry of the salt-producing localities in the condition in which they have always been.

Before quitting this part of the subject it is impossible not to notice a singularly erroneous statement which has lately appeared on the salt monopoly, and which has been read probably by some thousands of readers in a periodical, captivating from its variety, usually accurate in its statements, and just in its conclusions. In the number of the "Household Words," for July, 1851, the following are gravely set down as "Facts about Salt." I enumerate them in due succession, and as far as possible in the author's own words. "The salt manufactories are situated in dreary marshes. The workers, following their occupation in pestiferous regions, annually fall victims, by hundreds, to the plague or the floods. The price of salt to the Indian consumer is about eightpence a pound. In addition to the vast powers vested in the hands of the preventive officers, fines may be inflicted on a person who erects a distilling apparatus in his own house, without any proof of the same, and at the discretion of the judge. The monopoly gives the East India Company a revenue of three millions sterling, and besides acting as an incubus on the energies, the mental resources, and social advancement of the immense population of India, it in a great measure engenders and facilitates the ravages of the cholera."

I confess, sir, that I read the above "Facts about Salt," with mingled amusement, regret, and surprise. In a periodical originating with genius and fostered by talent, appears an account so entirely at variance with the truth, and yet so plausible in its appearance, as to be calculated to deceive many a "Household," whose knowledge of the subject may be confined to "words" so written for their instruction. Either from wilful malevolence or astounding credulity, or "*crassa ignorantia*," some points are mistaken, and others are introduced where they have no meaning or connexion, in order that the Salt Monopoly of India may appear in the eyes of grievance-mongers, real philanthropists, and the English public in general, a monopoly of so "odious and oppressive a nature as only to be worthy of the old Spanish Inquisition." I proceed, however, in due order emphatically to deny, and to refute from personal observation, as well as from other sources, every one of the assertions selected above. The "dreary marshes" are not peculiar to the salt-producing localities. They exist in eight or ten districts, out of reach of the tides. They are to be found, more or less, wherever the rice crop is sown and grown: they are the result of the tremendous down-pourings of the rainy season, which falling on a rich, tenacious, and alluvial soil, convert the whole country for four, five, or six months in the year, into one enormous marsh, not dreary, nor unproductive, nor invariably inimical to life, but prolific in vegetation, teeming in resources and tenanted by thousands, or even millions of inhabitants. That Bengal Proper is remarkable for a moist and humid and not a dry climate: that tropical showers which the clayey soil refuses to drink up, and the brilliant sun can only exhale by degrees, are favorable to the spread of vegetation: that vegetation unchecked is apt to produce miasma: that over miles of country in districts, where not one ounce of salt is ever manufactured, or one clause of the Salt Laws enforced, the communication is carried on in boats from July to November as it has been carried on for centuries: that an Indian cultivator may step from his house into his light shallop and on his way to the bi-weekly market pass over an extent of plain converted into a "marsh," but covered everywhere with a magnificent rice-crop growing, in water five and six feet deep—are all facts which are undeniable. But they only prove that those who choose or are compelled to live in Bengal at all during the rainy season must often be content to live on the borders of a "dreary marsh," whether their occupation be to manufacture salt, or to cultivate indigo, or as a servant of Government to do justice between one man and another. The factories are not selected on account of the "dreary marshes," but the marshes will persist in locating themselves in proximity to the factories. Moreover, out of the six salt agencies where the monopoly is carried on, only two, that of Hidgellee and that of Tumlook, are situated in localities at all remarkable for unhealthiness: and as the manufacture of the article can only be carried on during the dry season from December to May, when there are no rains, no inundations, and in consequence no miasma, the assertion that the workers of salt fall victims to the floods, is quite contrary to fact. In making mention of the "plague" as the destroyer of victims, it is difficult to believe that the writer in the "Household Words" can have had any other wish than to see how far he could impose with impunity on the credulity of Englishmen. The non-occurrence and non-existence of the plague in India is a fact as well established in science as is the non-existence of tropical vegetation on the summit of Mount Hecla, or of an eternal glacier on the chalk hills of Kent. The next "fact" stated is, that the price of salt to the consumer is about eightpence a pound, and that thirty millions of public, whose average earnings are three shillings a week, are compelled to expend one fourth of that pittance in the purchase of salt. Now, in no part of the Bengal or Agra Provinces does salt cost the consumer more than one fourth of the above price; and in many places it only costs him one eighth. In the case of the higher price, the increase arises from the carriage of the article, and to convey salt some four hundred miles from the place of manufacture, not unnaturally raises the price thereof on arrival at its destination. This must be the case whether salt still continue to be manufactured by the Indian Government, or whether all the superfluous capital and indignant philanthropy of Manchester be suddenly let loose to improve the tracts bordering on the Sunderbunds. The Government takes no part in the transport of Bengal salt, nor is it bound to provide that the article shall be sold in the districts of Behar for the same price as it is sold at the retail shops within the tidal limits: and it must not be forgotten, that beyond those limits and their preventive establishments, the transport and the retail of salt is open equally to the native dealer, the foreign adventurer, and the champion of suffering humanity.

The next startling " fact" is, that any person who erects a distilling apparatus is liable to a ruinous fine, without proof, at the discretion of the judge. The writer has here applied to the case of a supposed distiller, a penalty which may be incurred by landholders, who permit the illicit manufacture of salt on their estates. It is part of the system of the Indian Government to make landholders, in consideration of their position and influence, to assist in the administration of justice by giving early information of all offences against the law, and such a provision as that adverted to and misapplied by the writer in the "Household Words," does exist in the salt code. But it is rarely put in force. In the space of a year it is enforced perhaps on one occasion. The last "fact" is, that the monopoly so described raises a revenue of three millions. It raises a revenue of one million. The tax on imported salt and that levied in the Punjab, which of course are exclusive of this, have nothing to do with the manufactures as carried on by Government. So much for the "Facts about Salt," which when circulated in India were variously ridiculed and refuted by the local press, never slow to comment severely on the policy and to arraign the general administration of affairs in the East.

I have done with the sphere in which salt is largely manufactured, and I turn now to other localities out of reach of the tides which comprise the remainder of the provinces under the Governments of Bengal and Agra. It is a misdemeanor to manufacture salt in any part of the above localities, but as the facilities for manufacture there are neither frequent nor enticing, as there is no special preventive establishment for the prevention of smuggling or illicit traffic, as salt merchants convey their cargoes of salt to the various marts therein without let or hindrance, or inspection by any person, as houses there are never searched, nor boats detained, nor "poor Indians" punished, it is clear that over a very large surface of the empire the monopoly does not press with severity on mental resources or social advancement.

There is, however, one additional impost laid on the transport of certain salt at the junction of the Bengal and Agra provinces, and this brings us to another species of salt, supplied by native states, and consumed in the North-West Provinces. This duty is levied on salt which finds its way into those provinces from the independent native states south of the river Jumna, from the Sambhur Lake near Ajmere, and from the salt range in the Punjab. The duty has at various times ranged from two to four shillings a maund. In the case of salt manufactured in independent states, this duty is an extra duty, the first duty having been levied when the salt crossed the line which separates the British from the native states. In the case of rock salt from the Punjab, it is the only duty levied in transit, a line of preventive stations on the banks of the Sutlej and the frontiers of the Punjab, having lately been abolished. The custom-houses then, extend in a line from Allahabad to Juanpore, and guard the frontier of the respective Governments of Bengal and Agra. But they are only intended to levy duty on the salt which enters Bengal from Agra, and not on that which enters Agra from Bengal. This latter salt, whether it be that of the monopoly of manufacture, or that imported by sea, once clear of Calcutta and the tidal limits, may travel in any direction without paying a farthing. Salt descending into Bengal from the Upper Provinces pays a moderate duty of one shilling where it enters the Lower division of the presidency. The policy is to protect Bengal from being invaded by salt from the Upper Provinces, and to let Bengal and Manchester salt overrun those provinces, if it can. But in any case the consumer, whether he eats the salt of the Bengal Government, or that of native states, or the rock-salt of the Punjab, or that of Liverpool, pays for his condiment, where cheapest a penny a pound, where dearest twopence, and in some rare instances, twopence three farthings. The practical result of the salt system may briefly be summed up as follows: The monopoly or manufacture by the Bengal Government gives a net revenue of about a million*—not three millions as stated by the writer in the "Household Words"—and this salt supplies the cultivators of Bengal Proper and of Behar, where it meets the salt from native states and from the Punjab, and unable to compete with the cheaper article, retires from the field. The salt of native independent states, which yearly pays to the exchequer about five hundred thousand pounds in the shape of frontier duty, supplies the country between the Ganges and the Jumna, and generally the other districts of the Agra Government. From the salt of the Punjab range is derived a revenue of one hundred and fifty thousand pounds, and the condiment of the stalwark Sikh, the agricultural Jat, and the other dwellers by the five rivers. The salt imported by sea adds to the revenue about four hundred and eighty thousand pounds, displaces a proportionate quantity of Sunderbund or Government salt, and manfully competes with the salt descending from the Upper Provinces even beyond the junction of the two divisions of the Presidency. The result is to place salt within reach of the poorest peasant in India,

* It will be understood that the writer here only speaks of the produce of what is called the "monopoly." Estimating the amount of the Salt-Revenues, in the text, I have included the Customs duty.—K.

at a fair price, and to secure to the Government, in the least vexatious manner, an addition to its revenue, which it positively cannot spare. In any case the sale of all four kinds of salt is naturally affected and regulated by distance and by the expenses of transport.

To reiterate the most prominent and remarkable of the facts concerning salt it may be said that in the whole of that part of the Indian Empire which extends from Peshawar beyond the Indus downwards to the tidal limits of the Bay of Bengal, the manufacture of salt is not susceptible of the employment of a large amount of capital: that the salt which supplies the greater part of Upper India, is either the natural produce of the great salt range of the Punjab, and as such is the property of the paramount power, or is manufactured in independent or tributary states: that the duty levied on this latter salt on its entrance on the frontier or during its transit within the British territories is neither exorbitant, nor in principle contrary to a sound administration, which must provide money to support its armies, and maintain its establishments: that besides the salt manufactured by Government under a code of stringency in one corner of the empire, there is a further abundant and increasing supply of this article imported by sea, on payment at Calcutta of a duty of five shillings a maund: that it is certain that no extreme penalties are imposed by the salt tribunals on men who break or evade the law, while reasonable precautions are taken to deprive cultivators of inducement to illicit traffic: that it is an open question whether the abandonment of the monopoly would ameliorate the condition of those agriculturists who are said to suffer by it, while, to judge from experience, that abandonment would cause increased litigation, and loss of revenue: and that a net revenue of one million of our money is now raised by the most willing of manufacturers, the native Molunghees, amongst a population, to whose substantial social evils or moral degradation that monopoly does not certainly contribute.

(B)

THE OPIUM DUTIES.

[*From the Statistics relating to India, prepared at the India House.*]

BENGAL.

In Bengal, the revenue from opium is realised by means of a Government monopoly. No person within the Bengal territories is allowed to grow the poppy except on account of the Government.* Annual engagements are entered into by the cultivators, under a system of pecuniary advances, to sow a certain quantity of land with the poppy, and the whole produce in the form of opium is delivered to the Government at a fixed rate.† The engagements‡ on the part of the cultivators are optional.

The ordinary consequences of monopoly, increase of price to the consumer, and restriction on the employment of capital and industry, are not wanting in the working of the opium revenue system. The free cultivation of the poppy would doubtless lead to the larger outlay of capital, and to greater economy in production. But the poppy requires the richest description of land, and its extended cultivation must therefore displace other products. The price, too, is almost wholly paid by foreign consumers, viz., Chinese, Malays, &c.,§ and in obtaining the largest returns with the smallest outlay, the best interests of India would appear to be consulted.

* The cultivation of the poppy was prohibited in Bengal by Regulation VI. of 1799, sect. 3; and in the North-Western Provinces by Regulation XLI. of 1803, sect. 2.

The importation of opium into Bengal is virtually prohibited, the duty being fixed at 24 rupees per seer, of 2lbs., or about double the amount of its present selling price at the Calcutta Government sales.

† Three and a half rupees per seer, or about 3s. 6d. per lb.

‡ In the month of August contracts are entered into with the Ryots, and an advance without interest of 4 rupees per beega (nearly two-thirds of an acre) granted by the Government. The sowings commence in November, when another advance is made of 3 rupees per beega. Again, in January and February, when the crop arrives at maturity, a third advance of about 3 rupees per beega takes place, to assist the cultivator in gathering the produce, The crop is collected by the end of March.

§ Under the Convention of 1815, the French Government of Pondicherry are supplied with 300 chests of opium annually, at the average price obtained at the Calcutta sales.

BOMBAY.

Opium grown and manufactured within the territories of Bombay is held to be subject to the duty of 12 rupees per Surat seer,* imposed by Bombay Regulation XXI. of 1827, upon opium "imported or brought into any harbour, or roads, or port, or place, either by land or sea, within the Presidency of Bombay, or territories subordinate thereto;" and this duty must be paid before its removal. The object of this heavy duty is to discourage its production. The cultivation of the poppy is stated to have ceased in the district of Ahmedabad in 1839, and nearly so in those of Kaira and Candeish. In Scinde the production of opium has been prohibited. The Government purchase all that is produced in Bombay, and supply, through the licensed retailers, the quantity required for home consumption.

CENTRAL INDIA.

A large revenue is derived from the transit of the opium of Malwa through the British territories to Bombay for exportation to China. Previous to the year 1831 the British Government reserved to itself a monopoly† of the article, which was purchased by the British resident at Indore, and sold by auction, either at Bombay or at Calcutta. But in that year it was deemed advisable, chiefly on account of the large quantity of opium smuggled to the Portuguese settlements of Demaun, &c., on the coast, to relinquish the monopoly, to open the trade to the operations of private enterprise, and to substitute, as a source of revenue, in place of the abandoned system, the grant, at a specified rate, of passes to cover the transit of opium through the Company's territories to Bombay. In determining the amount of transit duty, it was proposed to be guided by a comparison of the cost of transit direct to Bombay, with that of the transmission of the drug to the coast by the cheapest of the more circuitous routes through the territories of native states; and on the basis of such a comparison it was fixed at 175 rupees per chest of 140 lbs. each. In 1835, the results of the preceding official year being unfavourable, the shipments of opium from Bombay having largely declined, while those from Demaun had greatly increased, the rate was reduced to 125 rupees per chest.

The subjugation of Scinde afforded opportunity for the levy of

* The Surat seer consists only of 35 tolahs; the duty on opium is, therefore, somewhat heavier than in Bengal.

† By separate treaties with the native princes of Central India, and which were subsequently cancelled.

a higher rate. Down to the period of that event, a large portion of the opium of Malwa had been conveyed through Scinde to Kurrachee, and thence onwards to the Portuguese ports of Diu and Demaun. That route was now closed, and it was reasonably expected that an advance might be made in the charge of passes, without risk of loss to the revenue from a diminished demand for them. The rate was accordingly increased, in October, 1843, from 125 rupees to 200 rupees per chest. Upon the principle that it was desirable to fix the price at the highest amount which could be levied, without forcing the trade into other channels, a further increase was made in 1845, when it was determined that the charge should be 300 rupees per chest. Under the like views it was, in 1847, raised to 400 per chest.

Poppy seed is sown in Malwa in November; the plants are in flower in the early part of March, and from that time till the end of April the extraction of the juice proceeds. During the hot weather in May, the extracted juice is allowed to settle, and in June, and early in July, the cakes are manufactured.

STATEMENT showing the Receipts from the Opium Revenue, from the Year 1834-35.

Years.	Net Receipts from Bengal.	Net Receipts from Bombay.	Total Company's Rupees.	Total £ Sterling at 2s. the Sicca Rupee.
1834-35 ...	63,26,894	14,41,711	77,68,605	728,517
1835-36 ...	1,32,01,613	17,18,455	1,49,20,068	1,399,009
1836-37 ...	1,33,40,968	20,08,710	1,53,49,678	1,439,031
1837-38 ...	1,43,67,238	14,97,202	1,58,64,440	1,487,291
1838-39 ...	69,87,990	25,43,318	95,31,308	893,560
1839-40 ...	32,60,761	1,17,014	33,77,775	316,666
1840-41 ...	64,96,324	22,46,452	87,42,776	819,635
1841-42 ...	80,38,669	21,48,989	1,01,87,658	955,093
1842-43 ...	1,32,23,436	25,42,382	1,57,65,818	1,478,046
1843-44 ...	1,67,59,482	34,88,780	2,02,48,262	1,898,274
1844-45 ...	1,80,83,454	37,29,431	2,18,12,885	2,044,958
1845-46 ...	2,20,79,262	59,56,243	2,80,35,505	2,628,140
1846-47 ...	2,27,93,387	60,68,628	2,88,62,015	2,705,813
1847-48 ...	1,29,15,296	37,18,549	1,66,33,845	1,559,423
1848-49 ...	1,95,82,562	88,75,066	2,84,57,628	2,667,902
1849-50 ...	2,80,07,968	72,94,835	3,53,02,803	3,309,637

Note.—A chest of Bengal opium, containing 164 lbs., or 80 seers, would cost the Government, at 3rs. 8a. per seer, 280rs., and sell at Calcutta for upwards of 900rs., yielding a profit of about 7s. 6d. per lb.

A chest of Malwa opium, containing 140 lbs., upon which the transit duty of 400rs. had been paid, would afford a revenue to Government of about 5s. 8d. per lb.

[The following observations on the opium monopoly are by the friend, to whom I am indebted for the previous commentary on the salt duties. They have been published in the *Morning Chronicle.*]

The opium monopoly, which I shall now briefly discuss, is a subject which presents, comparatively, few salient points, and suggests no very intricate questions. Its history embraces a consideration of the precautions by which the cultivation of the poppy is reserved to the State alone, of the locality where the poppy can be cultivated, of its effects on agriculture, and of its financial results. First, then, I will enumerate the precautions taken to prevent the unlimited or the indiscriminate cultivation of the plant. It is an offence against the law of the Bengal Code for individuals to cultivate the poppy, just as much as it is an offence in England to sell beer without a licence, to sell spirits within certain hours on Sundays, to harness dogs to a little cart, to collect a mob in Regent-street or the Strand. In both cases a simple act is created an offence by the law, though it will naturally be said that the principle of the Eastern Code is capricious and arbitrary, and does not lead to the protection of morality. Not only are Indian cultivators prohibited from cultivating the poppy, without a licence, and then only for the good of the State, not only are they liable, for an infringement of the law, to see their illicit crops attached and to incur imprisonment or fine; but police officers, village watchmen, and Government officials of every description, are required on pain of fine, and liability to dismissal, to assist in the suppression of the illegal cultivation, of the manufacture of the raw material, and of the sale of the produce. Even landholders are not exempt from liability, and as on the one hand they are liable to be fined if they do not give the earliest information to the police of illicit cultivation, so, on the other, they are at liberty, in virtue of their position as lords of the manor, at once and without any order or decree to that effect, to attach a crop of the poppy not grown by the permission of Government. The whole aim and scope of the law is in fact to reserve to the Government the right of determining where, in what quantity, and by whom, the poppy shall be cultivated. So much for the law. The second point for consideration is the tract of country suited to this kind of produce. Now, the poppy is cultivated with success only in the large central Gangetic tract which extends from the borders of the kingdom of Oude to Agra on the west, and to the district of Dinagepore on the south. This stretch of country is about five hundred miles in length and two hundred in depth or breadth. It follows, consequently, that whatever harshness may be imputed to the opium laws, their effects must be confined to the limits of the above tract. Where there is no temptation to break the law, there can be no occasion to enforce its penalties. In a locality where the poppy will not grow, or will not be productive, it is superfluous to tell the Ryot that he must not there manufacture opium. In the principal plains of Eastern Bengal, on the banks of the Lower Ganges, in the whole province of Orissa, in the northern part of the Agra division and in the Punjab, the whole of the laws for the protection of the opium monopoly are a dead letter. It remains then to be considered with what force the monopoly presses on the agricultural population in the great poppy districts, which brings us naturally to the third point under review. The opium manufacture from the plant grown within the limits above described, is carried on at two separate agencies, that of Benares, of which the head station is at Ghazipore, and that of Behar, of which the head station is at Patna, the ancient capital of that province. The system agriculturally is, then, as follows: It is no part of the plan to mark out and reserve a portion of the best lands of a district for the poppy, or to cultivate it on a Government or home farm, through the agency of hired laborers. The system proceeds on far broader principles—those of making advances to any Ryot who may choose to enter into an agreement to cultivate the poppy for Government. The Ryot takes the money, sows the field, watches over the growth of the plant, presses the juice, and conveys it to the Government factory. It is a fundamental principle to leave it entirely optional with every one to enter into such an agreement or not. Recruits are not inveigled by the distant prospect of remuneration, fictitious statements are not cooked to entrap the unwary, the weight of authority is never brought to influence the wavering, the refractory, or the weak. If, however, a Ryot does become a party to a contract, it becomes necessary to provide for its due performance. There are, consequently, stipulations made, in order that the number of acres, for which an agreement is signed, shall be duly cultivated, that an amount of produce, calculated from what may appear to be the probable out-turn of the field of poppy when in full growth, shall be delivered to the officers of Government, that the juice in its primitive state shall not be adulterated, and that the advances made shall either be repaid by an equivalent in produce, or be recovered by legal means. Thereis then no compulsion, and no disclosure of unforeseen contingencies. The cultivator, moreover, enjoys an advantage which no other kind of cultivation could possibly bring him. He gets at the commencement of every season, advances in hard cash equal to one-half of the estimated out-turn, for which he is subjected to no interest or commission, while he has the chance of making his profit by bringing to the factory, produce exceeding the advances, or remarkable for purity and weight. No outstanding balances are suffered to remain at the close of one season, or held, *in terrorem*, over the unhappy cultivator in the next. Accounts are squared after the drug is manufactured, and the return is either set off against the advances, or if any part of the advance remains unrepaid, it is recovered by legal process, or it is written off to profit and loss. In this way lacs of rupees are yearly advanced and yearly repaid within a few rupees. That Government has acquired the character of a fair and indulgent landlord is easily seen by the readiness with which Ryots flock to take advances, and is proved by the fact that it has occasionally been found necessary to discourage the cultivation of the poppy and restrain it within moderate bounds. In the year 1849-50, in the smallest of the two agencies, the amount of land under poppy cultivation was in round numbers, 35,000 acres. Over so many miles of country there circulates yearly a constant and steady amount of capital. But to prove the advantages which may result from a monopoly wisely administered, there is nothing like a comparison between a system as carried on by Government, and a system as carried on by individuals. Such a comparison I find at hand between the manufacture of opium by Government and that of indigo by individuals. Both kinds of cultivation require command of money, constant supervision, favorable seasons, and agricultural skill: both the articles manufactured form a large and lucrative branch of trade. The one is manufactured solely on account of Government, which in this retains some of the old trading habits by which an empire was won. The other, not restricted, not confined to any particular class, and rarely noticed in the Indian code, is manufactured from a plant largely cultivated in the rich plains of Bengal, and the more sandy districts of the Upper Provinces. Under both there is the same selection of suitable localities, the same system of advances at the commencement of the season repayable by the produce at its close: the same healthy circulation of capital: some of the same benefits exhibited in progressive intercourse and extended agriculture. But here the parallel must cease. Under the Government monopoly, there is no intimidation, no violence or deceit: accounts are opened and adjusted yearly: if the master is satisfied with the produce, so is the man with his honest gains. In the cultivation of indigo carried on by European speculators of all nations, Hindoo and Mahomedan landholders, and commercial firms, there is on the part of the capitalist a free recourse to the influence of position, to the awe produced by authority, and to downright force, on the part of the Ryot there is unwillingness, subterfuge, and discontent. In addition to this, the disputes between cultivator and capitalist, or between two capitalists with their respective tenantry, have been the cause, especially in former years, of an endless amount of litigation, and a vast increase of agrarian crime. It is fair to state that matters are now better managed, and the cultivation of indigo is at present carried on without burdening the calender or filling the gaols. But the Ryot is not more contented, nor richer than before. On the other hand, by the retention of the poppy cultivation in the hands of the state, benefits fall directly on the cultivator, and indirectly on the landlord to whom he may pay rent. Advantage results directly to the tenant, because the agent of Government deals with him alone. He signs the agreement: he receives the advances: he looks after the standing crop: he weeds and manures: he pierces the ripe capsules of the poppy: he conveys the drug in its first elementary condition to the Government factory: the liability and the benefits alike fall on him. The Zemindar, who is not only forbidden to cultivate on his own account but is held responsible for any illicit cultivation carried on by his tenants, derives merely that advantage from the system which may be expected from the presence of an active and willing peasantry, engaged in a pursuit which fills their pockets with hard cash. But beyond the advantages of a substantial peasantry, ready to pay their rents, the landlord gains no advantage. He is distinctly forbidden to enhance the rents of those lands on which tenants are raising a crop for Government. No doubt if the opium monopoly were abandoned to-morrow, many natives and Europeans would immediately set up their factories, clear their vats, give out their advances, and at the close of a successful season, freight a whole fleet of country boats, or load one of the numerous steamers plying up and down the Ganges, with chests of this valuable export, for transmission to Calcutta. But under such a system it would be unlikely that the drug fashioned in half a dozen different modes, would retain the consistency and purity which gives it a high value in the China market. At present the greatest care and attention are lavished on the manufacture, the drying process, the examination, the packing, and the transport of the drug. Some of the chests on arrival at Calcutta are inspected by an examiner appointed by Government, and exposed to view for the satisfaction of members of the mercantile community. No doubt the same precautions which are taken by Government to make produce saleable and to ensure a lucrative branch of the public revenue against loss, would be taken by British capitalists wielding the usual amount of energy, skill, and resources, and stimulated by the prospect of a considerable return. But it is very doubtful whether Ryots could derive more benefit from any conceivable system, other than the present. The appearance of whole districts as highly cultivated as Kent or Middlesex, the spontaneous testimony of thousands of cultivators, the unfrequency of recourse to legal process to adjust claims arising out of the system, and the small number of persons ever punished for infringement of the law by which that system is preserved, tend to prove this. A monopoly, which deprives rich individuals of some contingent advantages to secure positive blessings and solid fruits to the tenant, which gives employment to a host of natives, and places many situations of emolument within the reach of clever and energetic Europeans, not members of any of the covenanted services, which is least felt where most strictly maintained, is surely deprived of the objectionable features which in the minds of most Englishmen are supposed to belong to that title.

The last point to be considered in the opium question is its financial result. There are twelve sales of the drug during the year. They are held at Calcutta, and the clear gain to Government after deducting expenses of all kinds, advances, manufacture, transport, salaries of large establishments and incidental or contingent charges, is in round numbers, two millions of our money. But this addition to the revenue is obtained not from the Indian cultivator or his landlord, nor from suffering provinces, but from Chinese merchants, and from the consumers of the drug in the Celestial Empire. The opium manufacture may, if men choose, be termed a monopoly of the productive resources of a large tract of country, but no inquiry will ever prove that, as a tax, it weighs on a single individual in any one district: nor will it be easy to persuade any man who knows anything of the condition of the Ryot, that an abandonment of the monopoly would be followed by an increase of wealth or competence in the agricultural classes. The morality of the traffic is an entirely different question: and on that ground alone were it thought incumbent to prohibit the manufacture and the export of opium, the prohibition should equally apply to the drug when manufactured by individuals. A trade productive of nothing but demoralisation ought to be stopped while it originated with a private house, or with a chartered company, or with the rulers of a great empire. But the truth is that, men who have been in China, while they describe in striking terms the fearful effects of the drug on the confirmed and habitual opium-eater, just as a man who had been in England might, from a few instances of delirium tremens, descant on the fearful effects of intemperance, allow that a moderate use of this stimulant is attended with beneficial effects. Moreover it has been ascertained from the same trustworthy source that the poppy cultivation is gradually increasing and is now countenanced by the authorities in the Chinese Empire. The delicate question of monopolising a cultivation, which ends in the surreptitious introduction of a compound into a large kingdom, may consequently find its own solution in a very few years.

(C)

COTTON CULTIVATION IN INDIA.

[The following comprehensive history of the efforts which have been made for the development of the cotton resources of India, is taken from the India House Statistics, already quoted.]

THERE are two principal descriptions of cotton-plant now cultivated in India, the indigenous and the American.

The indigenous plant of India is an annual, and succeeds best in the rich black soil found in various parts of the country. The American plant, though a perennial, is practically an annual in India.* In some parts of India it is grown successfully† on the black soil, but it thrives better on the light red lands. Each of these productions is possessed of some advantages not inherent in the other. The Indian cotton is capable of being manufactured into fabrics of extraordinary durability, and no less extraordinary fineness; its color is superior, and on this account is it frequently used in this country in combination with American cotton, to improve the color of the latter; but its staple is short. In addition to the greater length of staple, American cotton has further advantages over the indigenous production of India; the plant produces more flowers, and each flower a larger pod; while the quantity of seed contained in the pod is smaller and more readily separated from the fibre.

For a period of upwards of sixty years, attempts have been made by the East India Company to extend the cultivation of cotton and to improve its staple, as well as the modes of cleaning and packing. Seeds from different cotton-growing countries have been procured; rewards offered to stimulate exertion; and instruments, both agricultural and mechanical, superior to those in native use, have been extensively introduced. The distribution of seed of superior quality commenced as early as 1788. In 1813 the services of an American were obtained, with a view of furthering the desired improvement in cultivation and cleaning, and American gins were then imported. In 1818, and again in 1831, renewed efforts were made. At the latter period, experimental farms were

* Neither American nor Indian cotton is cultivated on the same ground in India more than once in three years, their properties being found to exhaust the productive powers of the soil.—[*Evidence before Cotton Committee in* 1848, *Question* 2110, &c.]

† Dr. Royle, in evidence before Commons Committee on growth of Cotton in India, 1848, Question 481.

established in the southern Mahratta country,* and in Guzerat;† but these, after a considerable expenditure, having failed, were, in 1836, abolished by the local Government. In the despatch in which the approval and confirmation of this step were conveyed, the Court expressed anxiety "that no means should be left untried which might be likely to assist the desirable object of improving and extending the cotton cultivation on the Bombay side of India." And, in the same despatch, a qualified assent was given to a proposal made in general terms by the local Government, for authorising collectors to grant farms of land on favorable terms to respectable persons desirous of cultivating cotton, and when necessary to make to such persons pecuniary advances, on security. But previously to the receipt of this permission, the Bombay Government had determined upon giving a very large measure of encouragement to this cultivation by exempting from land-revenue, for five years, all lands sown with cotton in the Poona and Ahmednuggur collectorates. This proceeding was greatly disapproved by the Government of India, and on the discussion which ensued coming before the Court, their decision was given in favor of the supreme Government. The Government of India had desired that the effect of the notice to grant the proposed exemption should be limited as much as possible; but the Court directed its immediate formal revocation, respect being had to the rights of those who might previously have taken advantage of it.

In 1839 it was determined to seek information in the cotton-producing districts of the United States, and, if practicable, to engage *there* duly qualified persons to proceed to India for the purpose of instructing the natives in improved modes of culture and a better system of cleaning. The design was carried into effect. Ten Americans, experienced in the management of cotton plantations, were engaged, despatched to India, and their services distributed in the different presidencies. Government farms were again established in Broach, Dharwar, and Candeish, as were also experimental cotton gardens in Rutnagherry. In the last-named collectorate the cultivation of cotton was not generally practised, and after a short unsuccessful trial the experiment terminated. In Broach, the culture of the New Orleans cotton was stated to have proved a complete failure, and, notwithstanding a large expenditure, no good effects were produced on the staple of the country, beyond the limits of the farm. At a subsequent period the farms in Dharwar were abolished, and the contract system‡ of cotton

* The tract of country comprehending the British districts of Dharwar and Belgaum, and various native jaghires in their vicinity, is thus denominated.

† Guzerat comprises an addition to the territory of the Guicowar, the four British districts of Broach, Surat, Kaira, and Ahmedabad.

‡ That is, where cotton of a certain description is grown by the natives, without any interference on the part of

culture introduced both there and in Candeish, in which collectorate the soil and climate are said to be well adapted to the culture of Bourbon, Egyptian, New Orleans, and other foreign varieties of cotton.

The results of American management in the Presidency of Bombay up to the year 1844, are exhibited in the report* from Mr. W. R. Mercer, one of the American cultivators, dated Dharwar, 12th October of that year. The writer of this paper, which is marked by great clearness, fairness, and intelligence, affirms that Indian cotton has long been known to possess two very remarkable qualities: it "mills" or swells in bleaching, thereby yielding a more substantial fabric; it takes and retains color better than American cotton; and it would command a good market, provided it were sent in regular supply and of uniform cleanness. Mr. Mercer further expresses his opinion, that the capability of furnishing an article suited to the manufactures of Great Britain, is not limited to Broach and Surat, but extends to the whole of Candeish, the southern Mahratta country, and other parts of Western India; the capabilities of the North-Western Provinces, and large portions of the eastern and southern parts of the Madras territory being inferior. The difference of price between the cotton of Broach and Surat, being *sea-board* districts, and that of other more inland districts, he attributes to "difference of handling and the distance and badness of the routes over which the latter travels. After discussing the comparative effects of soil, climate, and culture (to the second of which he attributes great importance), Mr. Mercer comes to the conclusion that the natives of large tracts already employ a mode of cultivating the cotton plant in principle nearly the same as the American, but better suited in some respects to locality, &c. The great inferiority of much of the Indian article, he says, is the result of what befalls it subsequent to its production in the fields, that is, in the way in which it is gathered and stored, and chiefly the way in which it is separated from the seed and prepared for market, as well as in its transmission to market. At the gathering, in his opinion, the effort for improvement should commence.

Various improvements having been made in the cotton saw-gin, with a view to render it more suitable to Indian use, the Court, in 1846, desirous of arriving at a just conclusion in regard to the results, as exemplified in Bombay saw-ginned cotton, directed consignments to be made annually of 6000 bales, to be continued for a period of three years; and in the following year, with a view of testing the capabilities of the different districts, directions were given that the annual consignment should consist

the Government beyond an engagement to receive the produce at a fixed price.

* *East India Company's Manuscript Documents.*

of equal quantities of New Orleans and indigenous cotton, and should be drawn from the four collectorates in which measures for the improvement of the article were in progress—viz., Dharwar, Belgaum, Broach, and Candeish. It may here be mentioned, that in forwarding to Bombay the account sales of this cotton, the results were stated to be highly satisfactory. Very favorable opinions were pronounced on the article by spinners and other competent judges, and the prices realised were good, for some samples high. In fact, the question as to the capability of India to produce cotton suitable for the use of British manufactures might thenceforth be considered settled.

In 1848, in adverting to the promised supply from the four collectorates, the Court intimated their desire that Government should abstain from entering the market as large purchasers of cotton from American seed, if it found a ready sale among local dealers. The superiority of that cotton being generally recognised in the south Mahratta country, they were of opinion that Government might confine their operations to the supply of seed, and the introduction of improved methods of cleaning by saw-gins, &c.

In the Madras territories, cotton farms were established in the districts of Coimbatore, Tinnevelly, and other localities. These farms have been recently discontinued, the object for which they were formed having been fully attained, by demonstrating that soil and climate are capable of producing cotton suitable to the British market.

It thus appears that within the two subordinate presidencies there is a considerable extent of country, the soil and climate of which are well adapted to the growth, not only of the indigenous cotton plant, but also of the American plant. The experiments have moreover brought to light a fact, which might have admitted of some doubt, viz., that for the most part the natives are well acquainted with the proper modes of cultivation, and that little or no advantage is likely to be gained from further interference with the ordinary course of agriculture and trade. An ample provision of seed of the superior kinds of cotton for the use of the cultivators (till such time as, by its general diffusion, all interference, even in this way, on the part of the Government shall become unnecessary) seems all, as far as cultivation is concerned, that can now be beneficial.

The cleaning and packing of the cotton seem, however, still to be very far from perfect, and the introduction of improved methods continues to engage the attention of the home authorities.*

The duty on the export of cotton, and the inland transit-duty

* The services of some of the American planters, Mr. Blount, Mr. Frost, and others, have been re-engaged for the purpose of preparing machinery, superintending cotton experiments, &c. —*Vide* Court's Correspondence, 1852.

having been abolished, all the encouragement that can properly be afforded by fiscal regulations has been extended to this production. There remains another mode in which Government can promote the extension of the growth of cotton and the improvement of its quality, viz., by facilitating the construction of tramways and railroads, where the anticipated amount of traffic would justify the outlay. In some districts the expenses of cultivation and assessment are not so heavy as the expense of carriage to market.

In competition with America for the British trade, India will always have to encounter the disadvantage of distance. But it is not too much to hope that this may be greatly moderated, especially as the cotton manufactures of Great Britian appear to require new and increased sources of supply. Indian cotton is adapted to varieties of goods amounting in weight to about 75* per cent. of the total cotton manufacture of Great Britain. The cultivation has to contend with sundry disadvantages,† but these are compensated by the cheapness‡ of the cost of production this, in many parts of India, being only 1½d. per lb., while in America it is from fifty to one hundred per cent. more,§ ranging from 2¼d. to 3d.

The power of contributing to the required supply is, however, limited by circumstances, some of which only would appear to be under control. The cotton of the lower provinces of Bengal is said to be unsuitable to the British market. In the north-west the experimental culture was tried to a certain extent without success, but discouraging incidents appear to have led, in some degree at least, to its somewhat premature abandonment. At Madras, improvement in quality has been simultaneous with extended cultivation; but from the latest official information it would appear that even if the whole of the lands in that presidency, adapted for the production of cotton, were so appropriated, the supply, after deducting the quantity required for local consumption and export to China, would bear a very small proportion to the wants of the British market. Looking to existing circumstances, it will be seen that, if instead of a part only, the present entire export of cotton from Madras found its way to Great Britain, it would not

* Chapman on Cotton and Commerce of India, page 4.

† The inferior productiveness of the Indian soil and inferior yield of the cotton plant, the combined operation of the *two* causes, restrict the average outturn to 100 lbs. of clean cotton per acre, while in America the same area gives at least double the quantity.

‡ Evidence before Cotton Committee, 1848. Manufactures of coarse goods in Manchester have a table, by which they see at a glance the respective prices at which American and Indian cotton are equivalent to each other.

Evidence before Cotton Committee, 1848, Questions 632, 1206.

§ *Vide* Bazley's Evidence, Question 769 ; also Memo. from Mr. Turner, Chairman of Manchester Commercial Association, page 67, note.

furnish 2 per cent, of the supply required by the British manufacturers.

For many years past the chief supply of *Indian* cotton, both to Great Britain and the world at large, has been furnished from the port of Bombay, the greater part being raised in Guzerat;* but a just view of the extent and capabilities of the whole of the cotton land lying along the Gulf of Cambay, would lead to the conclusion, that the present growth of Guzerat cotton cannot be materially increased.

Taking the last four years of the tabular statement, at the end of this paper, the export of cotton from India may be regarded as having attained an amount of between 160,000,000 lbs. and 170,000,000 lbs. per annum;† and it would not appear that in the present condition of India this supply can be greatly exceeded; for though the export of cotton from India to Great Britain fluctuates from year to year (sometimes to the extent of 60 or 70 per cent.),‡ yet it will be seen, on reference to the tabular statement, that the increased or diminished amount is invariably attended by a corresponding diminution or increase in the supplies

* The total export of cotton from India in 1849-50 was 165,655,220 lbs. The Bombay contributions to this total amounted to 150,754,963 lbs., of which 94,226,779 lbs. was the growth of Guzerat. (Report on internal and external Commerce.)

† EXPORTS TO ALL COUNTRIES.

	lbs.
1846-47	169,080,831
1847-48	160,317,295
1848-49	168,631,466
1849-50	165,665,220

The Exports of 1849-50 are made up as follows:—

—	To England.	To all other Places.	Total.
	lbs.	lbs.	lbs.
From Bengal ...	27,306	1,817,971	1,845,277
„ Madras ...	502,6,023	8,038,957	13,064,980
„ Bombay ...	105,637,028	45,117,935	150,754,963
	110,690,357	54,974,863	165,665,220

‡ EXPORTS OF COTTON.

—	To Great Britain.	China and other Ports.	Total.
	lbs.	lbs.	lbs.
1848-49	67,203,519	101,427,947	168,631,466
1849-50	110,690,357	54,974,863	165,665,220

to other countries, and that the aggregate annual export from India remains without variation. It may, therefore, be fairly inferred, that the quantity of cotton which under current prices India can export at a profit, does not greatly exceed 170,000,000 lbs. per annum.

The average yield of clean cotton in India being not more than 100 lbs. per acre, and cotton being cultivated on the same ground once only in three years, it follows, that to produce the quantity now exported annually, an area equal to upwards of five millions of acres, or nearly eight thousand square miles, must be appropriated to the purpose.

But if by means of railroads the great cotton* field of Berar, situate within the dominions of the Nizam or ruler of Hyderabad, were placed nearly on an equality in point of facility of transport with the maritime cotton districts, then a breadth of land sufficient for the growth of a quantity equal to the full demand of Great Britain might at once be made available. It is, however, only by means of a railroad that the territory of Berar can be placed in a position to become a cotton-exporting country.†

* Evidence before Commons Committee on growth of Cotton in India, Questions 1822—4850.

† That cotton cannot be conveyed at a profit from Berar, except by railway, may be proved by the analogous case of salt.

Salt, having paid duty at 2½ rupees per maund, is sold at Benares (400 miles from Calcutta), according to the Government *Gazette*, at 12 lbs. the rupee, or 2d. per lb.

At Calcutta, the price of salt is 1d. per lb., which is thus made up:

Duty at 2½ rupees per maund of 82 lbs. .	0¾d.
Cost of manufacture .	0¼d.
	1d. per lb.

The cost of conveyance of salt for 400 miles, and other necessary charges, therefore enhance the price 1d. per lb., exclusive of the gain made by adulteration, which, it is said, takes place extensively. The cost of conveying cotton could not be less,*a* but by railway it might be carried for 2¾d. per ton per mile. Cotton might, therefore, be conveyed from Oomrawuttee, and other cotton marts in Berar, to Bombay (400 miles), for ½d. per lb.; and thus brought to market at a price from 15 to 20 per cent. cheaper than at present, it would be enabled to compete with cotton from America:

1 Ton=2240 lbs, 400 miles, at 2¾d. per mile = 1100d. or . . .	0½ per lb.
Price of cotton, Berar .	1½
Conveyance to Bombay per rail	0½
Freight to England at 3*l.* per ton of 1375 measurement . . .	0½
	2½

a The wastage on cotton in transit appears to be equal to that on salt. In the revenue letter from Madras, dated 19th September, 1848, the rate of loss on cotton in transit to the place of export is stated at from 2 to 8¼ per cent.

(D)

THE REVENUE-SURVEY SYSTEM.

[*From the Calcutta Review.—Condensed from the "Manual of Surveying," by Captains R. Smith and Thuillier, of the Artillery.*]

FIRST of all the settlement-officer, or revenue-collector, is charged with the duty of marking out the boundaries of the Parganahs on the ground, and furnishing to the surveyor a rough sketch called a *Thak-bust*, or demarcation map. With this sketch in his hand a man goes round the boundary of the Parganah, fixing stations at its various points, and clearing the ground for the measurement of lines and the observation of angles from station to station. Another man, or set of men, are set to perambulate the boundaries of each village within the Parganah. All this is preliminary to the survey, properly so called. The revenue-collector ought to be a year in advance of the surveyors, and the "line-cutters" must at least keep well ahead of them, so that no delay may occur. The surveyor's duty is then to run a line from station to station, and to ascertain the length and direction of every part of it. As this line cannot follow the windings of the boundary exactly, it is carried as near to the boundary as possible within or without; and offsets are measured to the boundary itself. Every measurement, whether of length or direction, is entered in a field book. When the surveyor has gone quite round the Parganah, and returned to the point whence he set out, it is evident that on transferring all his lines to paper, in proportionate lengths and in the right directions, the plan ought exactly to "close," or the last line ought to end where the first began. This it will never do exactly, but it must do so within certain limits of error, and if these limits be exceeded, every effort must be made to discover where the error has occurred; and, if these efforts fail, the work must be done over again. If the amount of error be within the limits, it must be apportioned amongst the several lines and angles.

While the Parganah-boundary-surveyor has been going on with this process, several parties of village-boundary-surveyors have been performing precisely the same process with respect to the several villages within the circuit. It is evident that the work of each one of these surveyors also must "close" with itself; and not only so, but the aggregate of the villages must just fill up the Parganah.

If the fields belonging to a village be tolerably large, and with moderately straight and well-defined boundaries, it seems to be the duty of the village surveyor to measure and define them, and to fill up all the topographical information necessary to give a complete view of the face of the country, its trees, its buildings, and its crops. This is done both by entry in the field book, and by the construction of what are called " chudder maps," which present a general idea of the character of the country. But if the fields be very small, and their boundaries very irregular, the survey of them is handed over to a native official, who conducts it in a much ruder way than that adopted in the main survey. This is called the *khusrah* measurement; and, as it is always checked by the general survey, since the whole ground measured must always fill its boundary, it is sufficiently accurate for all practical purposes.

Such is the whole of the work performed in the field. Sufficient data are obtained for the construction of accurate maps of the district surveyed; and the preparation of these maps is the duty of a portion of the establishment during the period when field operations are suspended by the weather. The survey department is required to furnish in duplicate a village map, on the scale of one mile to an inch, and a Parganah map, on the scale of four miles to an inch, for every village and Parganah surveyed. These are constructed from the *chudder* maps and field-books of the surveyors and *khusrah* measurers. These Parganah maps are again built up into Zillah maps on the scale of sixteen miles to an inch. It is also required of the department to construct for Government all the maps that they may require for any purpose, civil or military, such as the records stored up in the Surveyor-General's Office enable them to construct.

All this seems very short and simple in the description; but it is necessarily a tedious, and in many cases, a difficult process. The village boundaries are so irregular, and the limits of error allowed are so small, that the surveyor requires to have all his eyes about him. As moreover a great part of the details of the work is done by natives who do not understand English, it may be conceived that the process of constructing a map from their field-books is not a very attractive amusement. " With such an extent of native agency (say Captains Smith and Thuillier) as is employed on all the surveys in India, it is a great object to plot all work in the field. It saves an immensity of labor, and the chances of accuracy are greatly increased. By the aid of the drawing board much can be sketched in, and the first impression of a locality is not lost, but at once represented on the plan. Field-books kept by natives ignorant of English may better be imagined than described.

It is always difficult for any surveyor to understand fully a field-book kept by another person; but where novices on 10 or 15 rupees per mensem attempt to keep such records, and hurry on at the railroad pace of a revenue-survey in the present age, we do not envy the person who has to protract from them. The native surveyor, who brings in his board well filled, displays at once what amount of work he has done; and a superintending officer is able to see at a glance what confidence is to be placed on the topography so defined."

We have omitted to mention that another thing is necessary in order to make any of these maps complete, that is, the determination of the meridian line. For all that we have said hitherto, a map might lie in any direction ; but whenever the direction of any one line upon it is fixed, then the direction of the whole of the lines, and the proper bearings of every point, are ascertained. It is therefore necessary to ascertain the direction of the meridian line at some place within the district surveyed, or rather at several places, in order that one ascertainment may be a check upon the others. This is done in each Parganah survey by astronomical observations. For the village surveys, it is sufficient to ascertain it by the compass, allowing for variation.

We should also have stated that it is the duty of the survey department to calculate the area of each field, village, and Parganah in the North-West Provinces, these computations are the basis of the revenue-settlement. In the Lower Provinces, where the permanent settlement obtains, this is not necessary ; but the survey is not the less useful in these provinces, as in its absence much of the land is apt to be lost sight of altogether, small estates being swallowed up by large ones. Then when the Jumma or revenue on these estates is not paid, and the estates are put up for sale, it is found impossible to put the purchaser in possession.

To give an idea of the extent to which the revenue-survey in this presidency has proceeded, we cannot do better than present the following extract, which exhibits clearly both what has been done, and what remains to be accomplished:

" From the year 1822, when the revenue surveys first commenced, up to the year 1830, the rate of progress at which the operations proceeded was extremely limited. Only 3020 square miles, a little more than half a square degree, had then been performed in seven years, with ten officers employed in the department —the annual rate of progress of each surveyor ranging from fifty square miles to 338 as a maximum: and at this rate it was estimated that, the area of Bengal and the North-Western Provinces being 310,000 square miles or 77 square degrees, would require 481 years to accomplish. The officers employed in those days, however, had little or no assistance; and the duties performed then by the revenue-surveyor himself, are now entrusted to competent asssistants and sub-assistants, with large native establishments under them, whilst the surveyor acts as a superintendent over the whole as described in a former chapter ; the result of which has been, that during the last twenty years, or since 1830, the whole of the North-Western Province Districts, all Behar and Orissa, and a considerable portion of Bengal Proper, have been completed. No less than 46 districts of unsettled estates, amounting to 101,519 square miles, and 13 districts of Bengal and Behar, perpetually settled estates, yielding an area of 53,295 square miles, have thus been surveyed in detail and mapped, leaving twenty districts of Bengal, comprising 57,990 square miles, to be taken up, five of which are now in hand.

"In addition to this, the newly acquired territory of the Punjab and Cis and Trans Sutledge have come under the revenue operations, and afford a fine field of employment for the department.

"The total area of the British possessions in India, including Scinde, Punjab, Jullundhur Dooab and Tenasserim, has been carefully estimated at 800,758 square miles, and the Native States at 508,422 square miles, making a grand total of 1,309,200 square miles as the area of British India. This vast superficial extent of territory is confined within a length of 11,260 miles of external boundary. The *inland* frontier from Tenasserim round by the Himalayan range of mountains to Cape Monze in Scinde is 4680 miles, whilst the *coast* line from Singapore round the Bay of Bengal, up the Malabar Coast to Kurrachee, is 6580 miles Of the Native States about 200,000 square miles are already surveyed, leaving about 308,442, almost all wild hilly jungle, and of little value, to be taken up."

To this we shall only add that about fifteen and a half lakhs of rupees have been already expended, and that the work still to be done may be expected to cost about eleven and a half lakhs—a very moderate sum, certainly, for the survey of such an immense empire, and better expended than many of the sums that go into the disbursement side in the financial accounts of many governments.

(E)

MEMORANDUM OF THE BAREE DOAB CANAL.

INDEPENDENTLY of survey, 2157 miles of levelling, with traverse work, were executed for the Baree Doab Canal project up to August, 1850. The trial levelling was commenced on the 8th March, 1850, and its project sent in complete on the 14th December of the same year. Said project consists of upwards of 200 pages of closely-written foolscap, one-half being devoted to the report (which is illustrated with sketches), and the other to calculations and estimates, with 33 sheets (double elephant) of maps and plans. A copy of all being, of course, retained in the Canal-office, and and another (third) of the greater portion forwarded to the civil engineer for his own use. The proposed canal takes out of a branch of the river Ravee at Madhopoor, about 7 miles N.N.W. from Pulhamkot. It is to be 466 miles long. The main line being 247 miles, the Kussoor branch 84, the Sobraon branch 61, and the Lahore branch 74. There are besides, 22 miles of escape, making in all 488 miles of channel to be excavated. The capacity of canal channel, from its head to the head of irrigation (at mile 30), is calculated for 3000 cubic feet of water per second—a little above the minimum discharge of the river Ravee—that of the main line at the head of the Kussoor branch for 2000; of the same at the head of Lahore branch, 1200; of the Kussoor branch at its head (mile 30 of main line), 1100; of the same at the head of Sobraon branch, 500; of the Sobraon branch at its head (mile 7 of Kussoor branch), 500; and of the Lahore branch at its head (mile 55 of main line), 600 cubic feet per second. These four lines of canal irrigate almost the entire of the "Bangur" of the Doab, which, above Kussoor, is divided into four minor Doabs, as it were, by three drainage lines—the Pussee and Kussoor Nullas flowing to the Sutlej, and the Cadyara Nulla towards the Ravee. A line of canal takes possession of each minor Doab. The main line tails into the Ravee at Turrindka-kow, a small village about 58 miles above Mooltan, to which place, however, it will hereafter be extended, if possible. The Kussoor branch tails into the Kussoor Nulla a little above Kussoor. The Sobraon branch tails into the Putter Nulla below Putter, and near Sobraon; and the Lahore branch into the Ravee river at Manga, a large town about 26 miles below Lahore. The slope of the canal bed for the first ten miles of its course has been set down at 6 feet per mile, being through boulders the whole way; and even this slope will probably be exceeded in actual execution. After the 10th mile, the slope of main line, as the 100th mile, is 2 feet per mile; thence it is 1.4 foot, the minimum slope anywhere given. The Kussoor and Sobraon branches have a slope of 2 feet per mile throughout. The Lahore branch has the same slope to mile 45, whence it is reduced to 1.5 foot. It is proposed that a still-water canal of navigation shall connect the Sutlej at Hurreekee, the junction of the river Sutlej and Beas with the Ravee at Lahore, crossing and being connected with each of the four lines of irrigation canal, which is navigable throughout. A depôt to be established at Hurreekee. It was hoped that a further supply of water (the Ravee being the smallest of the five rivers) might be obtained from the Beas. On taking the requisite levels and surveys, the possibility of doing so was placed beyond a doubt; but the expense was found to be so great, that the design has been abandoned, at least for the present. The heavy works and difficulties on the canal are—1st. The head works, consisting of a masonry drain of 500 feet long across the branch of the Ravee from which the canal is taken, with a regulation attached. The slope of the bed of branch is 27¾ feet per mile, and floods arise 4 feet above the cold weather level. 2nd. The deep digging through the high bank of the Ravee, the maximum depth being 60 feet, and the soil full of boulders. The digging works out in two miles. 3rd. The passage of the Jennah torrent by a masonry dam of 300 feet, with regulating bridge attached. This torrent has a slope of 22½ feet per mile, and rises six feet in floods. 4th. The passage of the Ravee branch of the Chakky torrent by a masonry drain 1200 feet long, with regulating bridge attached. The torrent rises 4½ feet in floods, and has a slope of 16 feet per mile. The Chakky is a most extraordinary torrent, and very ticklish to deal with. A little above the point of crossing at Goolpoor, it separates into two branches, one flowing to the Ravee, and the other to the Beas. Extensive works are now being constructed, by which it is hoped the main body of the torrent may, during the coming rains, be diverted to the Beas branch, leaving the Ravee branch comparatively dry. These works comprise about a mile of boulder binds and spurs, strengthened by brush and crib work, with nearly an equal length of excavated channel, and of cuts through bars, &c., &c. If they succeed even partially, the immense masonry drain estimated for will be saved, as an escape merely will then prove sufficient. 5th. The rapids and falls required for the purpose of overcoming the excessive slope of the country. On the main line 82 feet have to be overcome by artificial rapids of boulder work, and an equal number by masonry falls; on the Sobraon branch the same, and on the Lahore branch 19 feet in the same manner, making a total of 239 feet to be overcome by artificial means. The extent of water-power, however, thus placed at the disposal of the inhabitants of different parts of the country may be imagined. It will soon pay off the cost of the works required, particularly as the Punjabees seem to take to machinery much more kindly than the inhabitants of the North-Western Provinces. 6th. The carrying such a large body of water (120 feet wide and 5½ deep) for about 3 miles along the top of a narrow ridge, which is tortuous, that curves of only a mile radius have to be given to the line, and down the sides of which numerous drainages run, requiring constant attention to prevent them cutting back into the canal. 7th. The passage of the same body of water across an extraordinary hollow about a mile wide and 15 feet deep: heavy embankment is required here. The probable cost of the canal is estimated as follows:

MAIN LINE.		
Boulder and Shingle Bunds, Works for protection of line experiments, &c., &c.	81,760	
Excavation of Channel	1,635,283	
Ditto of Escapes	185,869	
Masonry Works	997,682	
Contingencies	145,029	
		3,045,623
KUSSOOR BRANCH.		
Excavation of Channel	275,704	
Masonry Works	158,388	
Contingencies	21,704	
		455,796
SOBRAON BRANCH.		
Excavation of Channel	198,267	
Masonry Works	129,205	
Contingencies	16,374	
		343,846
LAHORE BRANCH.		
Excavation of Channel	296,424	
Masonry Works	129,930	
Contingencies	21,318	
		447,672
Total Cost of Works, Co.'s Rs.		4,292,937
Add Establishment for five years		744,000
Grand Total Cost of Baree Doab Canal		5,036,937

The probable returns are thus estimated.

It has been ascertained (from the canals already in existence) that a constant supply of a cubic foot of water per second, is sufficient to irrigate throughout the year 218 acres.

The average annual water sent also is a rupee an acre. Hence:—

In water sent we have 3000 × 218 = Co.'s Rs.	654,000
Set down Mill sent at	50,000
Transit duties, &c., at	20,000
And Canal produce, Sundries, &c., at	11,000
This gives a Total of	735,000
And suppose the amount annually in repairs, Establishments, &c., to be	200,000
And we shall have a direct annual return of	535,000

Giving on the original outlay of 50 lakhs a return of 10.7 per cent. per annum.

Now for the indirect return, solely due to the canal, by the increase of the land revenue:—

In the Meerut district (the least irrigated in North-Western Provinces) the increase of revenue, due to the Eastern Jumna canal, averages 8 annas per acre. And in the irrigated portion of that district, one-third of the village are actually watered. Hence:—

We have 654,000 × 3 = 1,962,000 acres, at 8 annas ...		981,000
D.D. for increased expenses in the Civil Departments ...	42,425	
And for Canal ground-rent at the very highest rate, though one-third of it will occupy is now dense jungle —12,540 acres, at 188 rupees per 100 acres	23,575	
		66,000
And we shall have an Annual Return of		915,000

Giving on the original outlay a return of 18.3 per cent. per annum. Hence the total return from the Baree Doab canal will be 29 per cent. per annum.

The returns will probably be much more as the inirrigative portion of the Meerut district pays on an average 138 rupees per 100 acres, while half the land through which the Baree Doab canal will run, pays at present little or nothing. The Western Jumna canal returns 36 per cent. per annum on the original outlay, and the Eastern Jumna canal 24 per cent. per annum. In conclusion, I may add that there are practical difficulties in the way of this work, which do not exist in the construction of the Ganges canal, or indeed of any work in the North-Western Provinces. 1st. Sal timbers (or any hard wood, in sufficient quantity), is not to be had, the only timber available being Dryar Koll, and Chul, all soft woods, and these at very high prices. 2nd. The carpenters of the Punjab are very indifferent workmen, yet they, as well as all other laborers, Coolies not excepted, demand one-third more wages than better workmen receive in the North-Western Provinces. There are no jungles at the head of the Doab (where all the heaviest works are situated) as there are at the foot of the Sewalik hills near Hurdwar. The villagers also, and civil authorities do not seem inclined to give Koorah (the dry rubbish of dungheaps, sweepings of the village, &c.) gratis, as they do on the Ganges canal. Hence, fuel for burning bricks and lime is most expensive. 4th. The limestone procurable at the head of the Doab, is not of good quality, nothing like the stone of the Dhoon. 5th. There is not a single hackery in the upper part of the Doab, and if there was there is but one, the main road on which it could travel. The cross country roads are about 4 feet wide, and between high fences, and are impracticable for any carriage but camels, bullocks, and donkeys. 6th The people seem most unwilling to take contracts for the supply of materials of any description, and are utterly devoid of the spirit of speculation or competition. All steadily combined to raise the price of articles, some of which were a short time ago tolerably cheap. 7th. There is no building stone sufficiently hard and durable for waterworks, within a moderate distance of the line. 8th. The Kunkur does not appear to be of good quality for lime, until about half-way between Bettala and Umritser. 9th. For the last 147 miles of the main line, there are so few villages, that it will be difficult to procure workmen in sufficient numbers, and for the same reason wells must be dug all along the line before any building can be erected, channel excavated, or bricks made. The water is 60 feet below the surface of the country. These are all serious impediments to cheap and expeditious work, and must have considerable effect in delaying the opening of the canal.

April, **1851.**

(F)

PROPOSED SUTLEJ CANAL.

[*From the Calcutta Review.*]

THE practicability of turning the waters of the Sutlej to use for purposes of irrigation early attracted the attention of our Mahomedan predecessors, and several traces of ancient canals from that river still exist. Such historical records as are available attribute most of them to the period of Feroze so fruitful in works of irrigation; but it must be confessed, that the allusion to his Sutlej canals are so indistinct, and in some cases so irreconcilable with the topographical features of the country, that it is almost impossible to make anything satisfactory out of them. We need not, therefore, do more than allude to these old works; and we now proceed to detail what has been done by the British Government.

To Major W. E. Baker, of the Bengal Engineers, belongs the merit of having first clearly and satisfactorily established the perfect practicability of a canal of irrigation from the Sutlej, and of having supplied such data as admit of a fair approximate estimate of the probable expense and returns from such a work being made.

Major Baker's project does not affect to be the best that could be framed. The brief period allowed for his survey made it impossible for him to examine the country in that degree of detail, which is a necessary preliminary to the actual execution of a great canal. But he has proved in the clearest manner the following most important facts; that an immense tract of British territory, now a desert, is admirably suited, both by the nature of its soil, and the profile of its surface, to take the fullest advantage of any means of irrigation that may be placed within its reach; that the introduction into this tract of a stream of water from the Sutlej is physically practicable; and that the probable benefit is so great, as to warrant Government in undertaking the work, when means are available.

The tract of country, whose improvement is contemplated by the Sutlej canal, consists of part of the district of Hissar, and nearly the whole of Bhuttiana, called commonly the "Hard Desert." It is a bleak, wretched, and (without water) most sterile land. The wells are so deep that artificial irrigation is impossible: the water is so brackish and impure, that none, save natives of the tract, can drink it with impunity; rains are scanty, and precarious vegetation is represented by a few stunted thorn bushes, or a temporary crop of grass over the great parched plains. Under circumstances so ungenial, the population is necessarily scanty and lawless, deriving their subsistence chiefly from herds of cattle, and addicted to the marauding habits common to pastoral tribes.

The question here is, therefore, not to improve agriculture, but to create it; not to provide, as in the Doab, for the casual occurrence of an unfavorable season, but to supply by the resources of science a substitute for that deficiency of rain, which is the rule, and not the exception; and finally, to enable an extensive and capable province to become, by its increased resources, and the progressive improvement of its inhabitants, a source of strength and revenue to the state, instead of being, as now, a burden and weakness.

These are noble aims, worthy of an enlightened and Christian Government, and we shall now briefly detail the measures by which it is proposed to attain them.

The river Sutlej, after flowing for between 300 and 400 miles within the Himalayan range, breaks through the low hills on the southern face of these mountains at the town of Roopur. For twelve or fourteen miles above this point, the stream flows through a valley, varying from 1 to 4 miles in width, bounded by low ranges of hills, consisting generally of unconsolidated strata of clay and sand, intermixed with kunkur. The discharge is estimated at 5400 cubic feet per second; the fall is about 4 feet per mile; and the bed is generally sandy, with occasional layers of shingle.

On judicious and satisfactory grounds, the head of the proposed canal is fixed at a place called Bunga, thirteen miles above Roopur.

At this point traces of an ancient canal, said to have been excavated by Mirza Kundi, the Governor of Sirhind under Mahommed Shah (probably IV.), were found, and with occasional interruptions were observed as far to the southward as Sirhind.

To restore this old line, connecting it with the Sirhind Nala, whereby the stream would be carried in one main channel to Sungrur, a total distance from the head of nearly ninety miles, appeared to Major Baker to be the most economical plan of delivering the water at a point from which it might be favorably distributed, by two branch canals, to northern Hissar, and the Bhutti states.* The Hissar branch would be forty miles, the Bhuttiana branch 100 miles in length.

The chief, indeed the only, difficulties occur in the first forty miles from the head. These are three in number. The first is the want of permanence in the bed of the Sutlej, giving cause to anticipate some difficulty in maintaining the canal supply. This it is proposed to remedy by building a masonry dam across the bed of the stream, whereby considerable security against alteration would be obtained. The second, is the deficiency of fall in the country from Bunga to Sirhind. This fall is only 40 feet in forty-one miles; and, as the depth of digging at the canal head is

* That the plan proposed by Major Baker would be the cheapest available may be true, but that it would be the best is, we think, open to question. Nothing is more certain than that the occupation of old lines, and the employment of existing river beds, have proved fruitful sources of evil on canals now in operation, and we believe that it would be true economy to avoid them. The levels are almost universally low, and the channels tortuous, both objections of serious importance in canals of irrigation; and we therefore trust the Sutlej canal, if ever undertaken, will be constructed independently of former lines, or nalas, even although this should entail some additional expense.

6 feet, the effective fall available for the canal channel is only 34 feet in forty-one miles, or 9.9 inches, say 10 inches, per mile. This is a small slope certainly for an Indian canal; but it might be increased to 12 inches, by adopting planks, or gates, to the piers of the masonry dam, so as to obtain during the season of irrigation 5 or 6 feet of additional head water. With even the lower regimen of slope, however, we believe the canal would be found efficient; and we hold the difficulty to be of no great importance. The third, is the very deep excavation, ranging in the first fifteen miles south of the Sissuwala Nala from 32 to 20 feet. It is considered probable that farther examination might lead to a better line being found, south of Roopur—a very likely result; but, even if unattained, the deep digging is not without its advantages, inasmuch as it admits of the hill drainage being all passed *over* the canal instead of through it, as is the case on the Jumna canals, where it is the source of so much evil and expense. On the whole, therefore, the difficulties of the project are not of serious consequence at their worst; and we doubt not but that the resources of the officers who may be employed on the works will prove adequate to vanquish them all.

The estimated expense of the Sutlej canal, with works on such a scale as to make it competent to a discharge of 2500 cubic feet per second, is 25,00,000 rupees, or 250,000*l.* This estimate is a liberal and sufficient one, and would probably be found to exceed considerably the actual cost.

The probable returns, so far as the Government is concerned, will consist of water rent, and such increase of land rent as irrigated tracts under similar circumstances have been found to yield. As regards the first item, it is calculated that 2000 cubic feet of water will reach the irrigating districts; and, assuming the low average rate of the Western Jumna canals as the standard, this discharge is competent to the irrigation of 312,000 acres. The average water rent, west of the Jumna, is exactly one rupee per acre; consequently the return to Government from this source would amount to 3,12,000 rupees per annum.

To form an approximate estimate of the increase of land-revenue which Government may anticipate, we avail ourselves of the statistical table of the Western Jumna canals formerly given; and we assume that the influence of these canals on the district of Hissar may be taken as a guide in forming an opinion as to the influence of the Sutlej canal on the same district, and the adjoining one of Bhuttiana.

From the table we accordingly find that, while the rate of land-revenue per square mile of unirrigated localities in the district of Hissar is 156 rupees, that for irrigated tracts is 485 rupees, giving a difference in favor of the latter of 329 rupees per square mile. Again, we find that the area on which the increased land rent is calculated, bears to the area actually watered the proportion of 2 to 1; hence, as the Sutlej canal actually waters 312,000 acres, the increased land-revenue must be calculated on twice this area, or 624,000 acres, being 737 square miles. The increase of land-revenue may therefore at once be shown as below: 737 square miles of irrigated land at 329 rupees per square mile = 2,42,473 rupees.

The total direct pecuniary return to Government from both the preceding sources would accordingly be 5,54,473 rupees per annum, on an invested capital of 25,00,000 rupees, or nearly 22 per cent.

We must not, however, restrict our views to the benefits Government will derive from the project. We must consider also the gain to the community, by bringing so large a surface of country, now a desert, under cultivation to the same extent as we find it on the Western Jumna canals. The benefit to the community will be represented by the gross value of the agricultural produce, which the Sutlej canal will admit of being obtained from land which now yields none. Taking the results on the Western Jumna canals again as our guides, we estimate the value of the produce alluded to as below:

					Rupees.
KHURIF CROPS.					
13,000	Acres	of Sugar Cane,	at Rs.	80	= 10,40,000
52,000	,,	of Cotton	at ,,	48	= 24,96,000
52,000	,,	of Rice, Jowar, &c.,	at ,,	38-4	= 19,89,000
RUBI CROPS.					
195,000	,,	of Wheat, Barley, &c.,	at Rs.	48	= 93,60,000
Total Gross value of Crops on Sutlej Canal					1,48,85,000

Time will, of course, be required to create this property of the value of nearly one and a half millions sterling per annum; but it is only necessary to compare the state of the Hissar district, before the Western Jumna canals were restored, with its condition in its irrigating villages for the last ten years, to be satisfied that, with the supply of water, the first necessity of agriculture in North-Western India, there will come a population able and willing to use it.

The benefits of the proposed canal now mentioned are such as admit of being approximately estimated in money; but there are others which are measurable by no such standard. Among these are the moral benefits to be derived from introducing agricultural habits among a lawless and semi-barbarous people, converting them from wandering shepherds into settled, contented, and prosperous cultivators; and the physical benefits to be anticipated from restoring fertility to a large tract of country, the increased moisture of which may probably so re-act, as to secure more constant and more abundant supplies of rain over the adjoining districts, and thus improve the condition of those who cannot directly benefit by the canal. The numerous traces of former rivers unconnected with any mountain ranges and the ruins of towns along their banks, show that these desert regions once enjoyed a far more generous supply of rain than they now do. We may hope again to re-establish this happier state of things, and thus to check that deluge of sand, which threatens to submerge so large a portion of their surface.

The secretary to Government (North-Western Provinces), in the correspondence before us, justly characterises the Sutlej canal as "a splendid undertaking." When the time arrives at which Government can carry the project into effect, we trust it will be made even more "splendid," by such an extension of its dimensions, as will admit of its bringing into use the entire supply of the Sutlej at Roopur. The sole objection to this is, that for three or four months of the year, the navigation between Ferozepur and Ludiana would be impeded; but the extent of this navigation must be trifling indeed, in comparison with the advantage to the state and the community from doubling the effective discharge of the canal. Major Baker's estimate for the original project is so liberal, that we believe the proposed extension would be effected for about one half more than the sum he mentions, while all returns would be doubled. We are, therefore, disposed to hope, that as the Grand Ganges canal will render memorable in these provinces the civil administration of Lord Auckland, so the Grand Sutlej canal may illustrate that of Lord Dalhousie.

(G)

THE JUBBULPORE SCHOOLS OF INDUSTRY.

[*From Colonel Sleeman's Report, July* 23, 1846.]

THE factory is inclosed in a space of 350 feet by 224 feet, forming a parallelogram, with a high Kutchea brick wall all round, with a gateway at each end. There are two centre work slopes each 136 feet long, by 68 feet broad, and all round inside the walls are sheds, 12 feet deep, supported on brick pillars. The sheds are occupied by blacksmiths, dyers, spinners, tape-makers, chintz-printers, and carpenters, while the large buildings accommodate the carpet, cloth, and tent-makers; the outer walls of the workshop are all of picked bricks. The roofs are all tiled. The cost of these buildings, over and above the labor of the prisoners, was 4000 rupees, which has been defrayed out of the funds.

In this factory 324 Thug and Dakoit approvers and 150 prisoners, of both classes, work daily from six A.M. to five P.M., having one hour allowed at noon for rest and food. The approvers are all paid by piece-work to encourage them, and the best of them receive from the factory about two rupees a month over and above their diet, at the rate of about one rupee four annas, which they get from Government. There are about 100 boys, the sons of Thugs, at work in the factory, earning from one rupee eight annas to two rupees eight annas a month by piecework. The wages of the paid agency employed in the factory to teach trades, blacksmiths, carpenters, tent-makers, carpet and papermakers, &c., at first amounted to 180 rupees a month. It has been gradually reduced to one-half, and will soon be dispensed with altogether, as the approvers are becoming masters of the trades which they were employed to teach. None of them knew any trade but that of robbery and murder when the factory was first established in 1837.

The ranges of buildings for the accommodation of the approvers' families form a village near the factory, surrounded by a high mud wall. Each approver has a separate house in these ranges for his family; and those who have done good service, and have proved themselves deserving of confidence and indulgence by a long course of steady conduct, are permitted to reside in this village with their families, subject to surveillance, being regularly called over when the gates are closed of an evening, and again when opened in the morning. Those who have no family ties at Jubbulpore, or whose conduct gives them no particular claim to confidence or indulgence, are confined at night in the lock-ups. None of the approvers are ironed, excepting as a punishment for misconduct or breach of discipline, and this, with temporary exclusion from the village and fine, are the only punishments had recourse to, and for these the necessity is now very rare.

[To this I may add the following passage from a Police Report, by an able member of the Civil Service, Mr. Macleod.]

I would avail myself, however, of this opportunity of bringing to notice the remarkable success which has attended the "School of Industry" established at Jubbulpore by Major Sleeman, General Superintendent for the suppression of Thuggee and Dakoitee, and superintended by his assistant, Captain Brown. As it is impossible for one connected with the suppression of crime and the employment of condemned persons to regard an institution of this kind otherwise than with feelings of great interest, an increasing class of persons, who, as "king's evidence," considered themselves pardoned, and at first evinced a strong disinclination to work, have had their scruples entirely overcome by mild and judicious treatment. All now work with the greatest cheerfulness, and even rivalry; manufactures of great variety and of excellent quality are produced in abundance, and I believe with very fair profit. Even novel productions have been turned out by the ingenuity of Captain Brown, aided by the gentry of the station, who almost all evince a lively interest in the establishment, and by the great diligence and good sense of Mr. Williams, the superintendent. The whole exhibits a scene of industrious activity which is highly refreshing, and cannot but exercise a most beneficial influence upon its inmates. So great a contrast does it afford to the wrangling idleness of a convict gang working on the roads, that I have been forcibly impressed with the desirableness of entrusting the greater part, at all events, of the prisoners of this and perhaps of all the districts to the same management.

From the profitable character of the institution, it has been found practicable, without loss, to furnish employment to the children of the inmates, and a school has recently been opened within it by Captain Brown for their instruction, during a part of the day, in reading and writing. This is, perhaps, the most admirable and important feature in the whole institution; for it is well known that in this as in every other country, the mass of crime is by no means the result of chance, or the spontaneous influence of the passions, but is brought about by systematic, and for the most part hereditary, education. Hence, it is manifest that if the children of old offenders can be withdrawn from the practice and the necessity for such a course, the labors of the police will be immensely contracted. It may, no doubt, be argued that this advantage cannot be generally calculated on, as it is only the peculiarity of the system followed for the suppression of Thuggee which has brought their families within our control. But if the question be examined to the bottom, I believe it will be found that the same control may with every facility, and the greatest advantage, be extended to every class of persons matured in crime. The same question, under another form, has been recently canvassed in England. Here it has been practically carried into effect with a particular section, in a manner unlooked for and without pretension.

Further, the institution promises to be productive of benefit in another important point of view. In America, where the system of producing manufactures in the jail has been extensively carried into effect, it is complained that injury results to the honest tradesman. But here, in consequence of the arts being in their infancy, an establishment of this kind, conducted, as it certainly is by Captain Brown in an eminent degree, with combined skill and prudent moderation, is calculated, by the introduction of improved methods and new manufactures, to give them an immense stimulus. Already has this been the case in a very perceptible degree; and I have not the least doubt that if carried on with its present spirit, and not deprived of the services of Captain Brown, it will beget results in this respect which will extend their influence far beyond the confines of the commissionership. It promises literally to become a "school of arts and manufactures," not only to its inmates, but the country around it.

THE END.

C. WHITING, BEAUFORT HOUSE, STRAND.